THE
AMERICAN
HEALTH
FOOD·BOOK

THE
AMERICAN
HEALTH
FOOD·BOOK

MORE THAN 250 FABULOUS RECIPES—
PLUS UP-TO-THE-MINUTE NUTRITION NEWS

ROBERT A. BARNETT, EDITOR
NAO HAUSER, FOOD EDITOR
WITH THE STAFF OF *AMERICAN HEALTH*

A DUTTON BOOK

DUTTON
Published by the Penguin Group
Penguin Books USA Inc., 375 Hudson Street, New York, New York 10014, U.S.A.
Penguin Books Ltd, 27 Wrights Lane, London W8 5TZ, England
Penguin Books Australia Ltd, Ringwood, Victoria, Australia
Penguin Books Canada Ltd, 10 Alcorn Avenue, Toronto, Ontario, Canada M4V 3B2
Penguin Books (N.Z.) Ltd, 182–190 Wairau Road, Auckland 10, New Zealand

Penguin Books Ltd, Registered Offices: Harmondsworth, Middlesex, England

First published by Dutton, an imprint of New American Library,
a division of Penguin Books USA Inc.
Distributed in Canada by McClelland & Stewart Inc.

First Printing, December, 1991

1   3   5   7   9   10   8   6   4   2

Copyright © RD Publications, Inc., 1991
All rights reserved

REGISTERED TRADEMARK—MARCA REGISTRADA

Library of Congress Cataloging-in-Publication Data:
The American health food book : more than 250 fabulous recipes—plus up-to-
the-minute nutrition news / edited by Robert A. Barnett and food editor,
Nao Hauser, and the staff of American health.
p.   cm.
ISBN 0-525-24908-7
1. Cookery. 2. Nutrition. I. Barnett, Robert A. II. Hauser, Nao.
III. American Health (New York, N.Y.)
TX714.A46   1991
641.5—dc20   90-24938
                                                            CIP

Printed in the United States of America
Set in Cheltenham Book
Designed by Eve L. Kirch

To my mother, in memoriam

◇ CONTENTS ◇

THE AMERICAN HEALTH PANTRY

◊ PREFACE ◊

You can taste the rich emotions in this book, the pungent aroma of honest research, the spicy scent of ideas still cooking.

Forgive me for sensuous sentences, but great foods ought not to get watered down by senseless words. Nor can I turn through this book without realizing that it comes out of a unique moment in the history of food and eating, one that flashed upon us like a meteor and left us changed forever. One central idea can be found on every page: What's good for you has to be good to eat, and what tastes good must be made so it's good for you.

When *American Health* magazine was founded in the early nineteen-eighties, serious cooking was dominated by classical French cuisine, with its rich cream sauces, fat-laden meats, and sweet desserts prepared with still more cream. Standard American cuisine was worse—mainly fried everything.

In exact contrast, health food was brown and tasted bad—as if to prove it was good for you. And scientific nutrition was just beginning to use the subtle new tools of biochemistry to measure exactly what foods do which bad things to the body, which do good, and how. Gourmet cooks of any sort considered nutrition scientists to be their worst enemies, and vice versa.

In just one decade, all that has changed. What's nutritious has been made delicious, mainly by going back to whole grains and fish and lean meat that is more like real game, plus a cornucopia of fruits and vegetables and nuts still rich in natural flavors and rich nutrients. The salt, sugar, and fat in sauces have given way to a spicy variety of peppers, herbs, and other seasonings. This book is a one-of-a-kind look at that transformation, a story told in part in the metaphor of the great new recipes it features.

The book grew directly out of the work of one unusual group of editors, researchers, and writers gathered around one audacious new magazine, *American Health.* At *American Health,* we would stop at nothing to dig a new research finding out of a lab, and then to find out how to use the new learnings to make a particular dish both healthier and tastier. Month after month, we raced against bigger, better-known magazines to put together the most advanced reports—and recipes—that chronicled the growing love affair between nutritionists and the great cooks, those former enemies who now found that each desperately needed the other to make the delicious nutritious and the nutritious delicious.

In the five years that showed us Americans how to rejoice in foods that are nature's most wholesome, former *American Health* Senior Editor Robert Barnett worked on this book with the robust energy that drove his monthly food features and nutrition research reports. He used the magazine to find the best material for the book, and the book to help him locate the best stories for the magazine.

Bob is a natural reporter who casts a suspicious eye on anything that might harm a reader/eater. His mission has been much like Ralph Nader's: ever optimistic, he is proud to locate and expose wrongdoers, especially food producers who produce bum food. Thus, in *The American Health Food Book*, you'll find cautions aplenty about things that are not good for your innards. But Bob also dug deep into the research to discover a more mysterious matter that many food writers did not know how to report—the friendly tricks that nature plays on us. Despite scary headlines, the huge advances in nutrition research were mainly bringing us good news—of the hidden benefits in foods we had long since been taking for granted.

The American Health Food Book is, in fact, both a work of love and a unique document. The next decade will produce many surprises in nutrition research, but nothing to touch the first-time encounter between traditional cooking and nutrition science that is captured in these passionate pages.

The book's main message—about the friendly conjunction between good nutrition and good food—became clear very early, then became a driving vision. We were discovering in the most ordinary of food—such as garlic and squash and beans—healthy benefits that make us wonder how Providence had been able to put it all together.

The implications of the nutritional discoveries are quite astonishing, often ironic, and sometimes downright poetic. In fact, I began to think of Mother Nature as a witty lady who loves to play jokes on us children.

The 19th-century poets who used to find in the beauties of the skies evidence of God's kind hand, would go crazy with recent discoveries on beta carotene. Each summer, just as the hot sun blasts our naked skin and depletes its protective levels of carotenoids, a new crop of carotenoid-rich yellow and red and dark-green fresh fruits and vegetables arrive at the market. Plants produced such handy protective goodies, even as our evolution-

ary forebears climbed out of the water onto the oxygen-rich land, where we needed such antioxidants to keep the toxicity of oxygen from doing us in.

Then there are beans. Bob Barnett was one of the first food specialists in our trade to realize the importance of the new discoveries about soluble fibers, which, among other tasks, can lower blood cholesterol. The lowly bean, treated like a country cousin since Bible days, would find itself in the upper class in a hurry. My friend Andy Miller soon put pork and beans on his fancy Spa Menu at the Four Seasons, one of New York's great restaurants; he may serve the only $40 plate of pork and beans in America.

It turns out that dishes featuring hot peppers, which seem anything but gentle, are astonishingly healthy, especially for people with cause to worry about their hearts. Chili peppers are full of antioxidant vitamins A and C and thus act to protect the heart against the oxidation of cholesterol that can become plaque and block arteries. Peppers even contain an anticoagulant to help prevent the formation of blood clots. They are high in potassium and low in sodium, ideal for heart patients on both counts. Better yet, a hot-pepper diet has long been the way people everywhere get taste excitement—*without* the heavy supply of fats that bond with subtle aromas to add flavor to both French and American traditional cuisines.

Going from scientific research into historical evidence, I discovered that ever since Christopher Columbus came and discovered American hot peppers, people all over the world had been using the delight of pepper as a replacement for costly fats. As I have a partial blockage in one heart artery, I am even more enthusiastic than ever about eating hot peppers. My enthusiasm led me to discover another advantage: prepared correctly, hot peppers provide a satisfying substitute for salt in dishes with lean meat.

And we've discovered that red meat, long considered a he-man's dish, is rich in the very micronutrients a busy young *woman* is apt to need most urgently. So I contend that lean meat should be packaged to be more attractive to today's women—the able, strong young women who need to have plenty of iron.

To turn to another discovery: lettuce is a love food, rich in folic acid, the micronutrient pregnant women need to protect against genetic disorders such as Fragile X Syndrome. But while nutritional protection is essential during pregnancy, there's evidence that it's as important beforehand. One of my nutritionist friends believes that a future mother and father should eat food containing folic acid even before the sperm penetrates the egg. So I now urge young couples going away for a sensuous weekend to be sure and eat lots of salad, the true love food.

There were tough times aplenty in the years that built this book, and many a health traditionalist charged that we were taking the fun out of eating. We tended to publish stories on the leading edge of nutrition, and old-fashioned chefs thought of us as troublemakers. We were accused of starting the "calcium craze," offering evidence that most women fail to get enough calcium. I started collecting bran muffin recipes very early, after one of our editors discovered that many cancer doctors make a point of eating bran—all this before there was scientific evidence clear enough to make the case. And when I told a television audience that dieting makes you fat, I was accused by one television critic of irresponsible journalism.

The most persistent worry came from people who felt, as many still do, that thinking about nutrition keeps people from the innocent pleasures of simply enjoying good food. Some argue that the public gets so confused about what is okay that they no longer eat anything without worry. A sort of know-nothing resentment often arises—don't tell me too much—from the natural food side as much as from the traditionalists.

This is a book for people who want to know. Herein you'll discover the delights of bountiful nature, as treated with the artistry of good cooks. Both your mind and your palate will be appreciative.

My hope is that, through this book, you begin to find a bit of the extra pleasure that comes to me now at every meal. Knowing the subtle ways that great foods work to make my innards happy adds a new dimension of delight to the many pleasures already built into a good, hearty meal.

—T George Harris,
Founding Editor,
American Health

◇ ACKNOWLEDGMENTS ◇

In its way, this book is a conversation, born of thousands of smaller conversations, among a remarkable group of people who both care about health and love good food. We are, variously, journalists, food writers, nutritionists, scientists, chefs. Like visitors to each other's countries, we have learned to speak each other's language. And like true immigrants, we learned over food.

For too long, the health community and the food world have mistrusted and misunderstood each other. That is changing. One reason is mutual respect, born of mutual need: Food professionals realize the public wants healthy food, and health professionals realize that what motivates most eaters isn't just principle, but also pleasure.

Along with this come subtle conceptual shifts. The idea that diet is the basis of well-being, and that cuisine is one of the practical arts of health—a view perhaps more common in China than France—is now accepted by more and more American culinary and health leaders. Nutrition science is moving toward an appreciation of the unique role individual foods may play in supporting health, as part of a growing appreciation of the ecological integrity of a varied, whole-foods diet—even, perhaps, of entire cuisines rooted in history and place. Meanwhile, culinary leaders are deepening their conviction that the basis of a new American way of cooking lies in a primacy of quality ingredients—locally grown, appropriately seasonal, and, often, indigenous. Along the way, the public began to view some foods, such as beef

and eggs and cheese and sugar, as the focus of fear, while others, such as garlic and oat bran and fish and cabbage, came to be seen as agents of hope. Clearly, we needed to communicate.

Where we met was the kitchen—not to mention the library, the data-base, the nutritional analysis program, the word processor, the food processor, the microwave oven, the conference table, and, most of all, the telephone.

As often as anyone, the person on the other end of the phone was Nao Hauser, the book's Food Editor. Her experience, patience, common sense, and most of all, humor, has been essential in preserving the intrinsic values of taste throughout the project. This book is truly a partnership.

Indeed, if I had to pinpoint its origin, I might start in Seville, Spain, in late 1985, when Nao, a new acquaintance on a press trip, asked me if I had ever considered cruciferous vegetables. I had, but not as a cook. When I conceived of a series of articles for the magazine, centered on food "families" such as cruciferous vegetables, beans, and fish, combining the latest science with the culinary arts, Nao was one of the first people I called. As we expanded that series into this book, she has become a truly remarkable conversational partner, guiding my sometimes theoretical nutritional enthusiasms, calmly and wisely, into culinary practice. Together, we explored ways to remain true to both health and taste.

What was intriguing—and challenging and often frustrating—about this project, is that no one had fully mapped the territory before. To whatever degree we have extended the chartings in this new world, I am indebted to a group of scientists, nutritionists, journalists, and food writers who labored tirelessly and often passionately to that end.

First among equals is Kathy Johnson-Schlichting, M.S., R.D., Associate Editor at *American Health* magazine, and this project's nutritionist. Coming to an already established project, she brought intelligence, dedication, and professionalism to the often painstaking task of reviewing dozens of calculations for each recipe, raising questions and keeping us honest. Her good cheer and careful regard to the material helped make this book work.

But she was not alone. This project was nourished by four interns from New York University's Nutrition Department—and I am grateful, not only to the individuals, but to the university. Many of them continued working on the project on a freelance basis after their internships ended.

In the early stages of the endeavor, Cathy Campfield Bonnot, R.D., analyzed recipes, suggesting modest changes (or more rarely, wholesale reconstruction) in recipes to bring them into line with our nutritional principles. Diligent work it was, and we benefited from her knowledge of food as well as of nutrition. My only regret is that we didn't get to include that fish soup recipe she sent us on a postcard from her home in Provence. Kathy Field Berkowitz, M.S., R.D., who also started as an intern and was hired as a free-lancer, worked tirelessly to collect the nutritional data that is now incorporated in the food profiles at the back of the book; she analyzed recipes, did research, and was a pleasure to work with. Marci Barbour Fiacci, R.D., checked plenty of numbers, and went on to write an excellent chapter on squash. Corey Wu, R.D., provided some useful research on beverages. Toward the end of the project, Janet Majewski Jemmott, M.S., spent an intense summer updating the nutritional data in the food profiles in the back of the book, checking facts and teaching us a few things about yogurt to boot.

Jeanine Barone, M.S., was this project's investigative ace. Whether it was tracking down scientists in China or Montana, researching the bibliography, finding out the amount of niacin in amaranth, or other arcane essentials, she was a stalwart ally—sharp, funny and determined. Lisa Chobanian, M.S., R.D., provided research and fact-checking for a number of the chapters, wrote a complete early draft of the food profiles, and infused our work with her enthusiasm. Mona Sue Boyd, R.D., helped us with some fact-checking, before I appropriated her for magazine writing.

From the outside, a few seasoned professionals helped keep us on track. Evette M. Hackman, R.D., Ph.D., oversaw the first few drafts of the nutritional analysis, helped us with diabetic exchanges, provided continuous counsel, and contributed an excellent cobbler recipe. Joyce Nettleton, R.D., Ph.D., gave us a careful, annotated reading of the introduction and the fish chapter, helped us secure some elusive nutritional data, and provided the backbone of the scientific bibliography. Wayne Calloway, M.D., was also quite helpful on the bibliography, as were all the scientists and colleagues who gave me their best citations on telephone, and Barbara Kafka and Nach Waxman, who helped with the reading list.

Then there is the case of James A. Duke, Ph.D., who not only wrote a number of the chapters on the spices and seasonings that define the margin of food and medicine, but provided a seemingly endless supply of scientific abstracts, papers, musings and some very bad poetry, self-admitted. His generosity with time and knowledge, and his extraordinary ability to pair pharmacological data with folklore, helped to ground the project, even as he challenged us to widen its reach.

Proof is fine, however, but it doesn't mean much without the pudding. The food writers who contributed recipes to this book took stringent nutritional standards merely as a spur to creativity, and were consistently patient in testing, and in some cases, rethinking, recipes so as to satisfy the dictates of both health and taste. Nao Hauser, besides being an editor, is a major contributor to the book, and her recipes are practical and stylish, innovative yet rooted in cultural context. Ceri Hadda's recipes, hearty, homey, and elegant all at once, are well represented here: Her chayote lattkes, in the Squash chapter, to single out but one recipe, are to me a perfect example of unpretentious culinary wit. Marie Simmons graced us with her manifest joy and understanding of fish and shellfish, as well as beverages, in recipes that are sophisticated and warm, yet simple in execution. Debby Maugans gave us bright tastes and a very American kind of food charm in her well-conceived recipes. Mary Estella, with her experience in natural foods, helped navigate us around the clichés of "health food" in recipes with foods such as tempeh, kombu, and quinoa, which are practical, elegant, and fun. Although we didn't have the pleasure of including any recipes by Rebecca Wood in this edition, she was generous in guiding us through the uses of quinoa, amaranth, and Job's tears.

Back at home plate, catching and pitching and batting all this marvelous information were the remarkable spirits of Gina Chalkley and Mickey Stellevato, the only actual full-time employees of this project. Mickey and Gina taught me the true meaning of a labor of love. Mickey could organize chaos, and is indispensable, probably to the universe. Gina's natural talent, enjoyment, and ease with food made her invaluable in coordinating and testing recipes. Enlisting their friends—Billy, Barbara, and Elizabeth—to test recipes, put a veritable community behind us. (Cindy Smyser also tested a number of recipes, as did Diane Kochilas, before her own rich explorations of Greece.) I remember one moment in particular, when we discovered a statistical error and were under deadline. Gina and Mickey barricaded themselves in their office, calculators whizzing for three days running, until, yet again, everything was running smoothly. They gave the project legs.

Although this list is already long, I feel as if I've only scratched the surface. Chapter by chapter, and recipe by recipe, you will see contributors bylined, and, needless to say, I am grateful to each of them. I am particularly thankful to Amy Barr, M.S., R.D., and Carol Wapner of the Good Housekeeping Institute, who contributed ideas, recipes, and comments, and tested some recipes. Betty Bianconi was thoroughly cheerful and professional in adapting the entire recipe manuscript for microwave, wherever appropriate; the instructions are hers. Gail A. Levey, M.S., R.D., helped with early, excellent chapters on beans and cruciferous vegetables, and provided nutritional guidance, cheerfully.

As much as anything, this project owes its existence to the rich, creative, often chaotic but always stimulating atmosphere at *American Health* magazine, founded by T George Harris. Owen Lipstein deserves some credit for that creative environment. The early support of Will Hopkins, Kate Stuart, Judie Groch, and Joel Gurin, and the later support of Claudia Valentino, as I struggled month by month with magazine deadlines and book responsibilities, was crucial. Madonna Behen wrote the roots chapter; Cathy Sears contributed much of the research in the nuts chapter. Indeed, the entire staff of the magazine, editorial assistants, copy editors, fact checkers, and art researchers fostered an environment where this work could take place. I am deeply thankful for the opportunity to have worked with such a talented group of people. I'd also like to thank Alice Martell for her legal advice, and the Reader's Digest corporation for fulfilling obligations reached before their stewardship of *American Health* magazine began.

Each of the scientists, cooks and writers we touched up for information, from David and Nikki Goldbeck to Harold McGee, to Elizabeth Schneider, to Marion Nestle, Ph.D., M.P.H., to Mary Abbott Hess, Ph.D., R.D., to Terry Leighton, Ph.D., to William E. Connor, M.D., to Walter Mertz, M.D., some quoted, others invisible, were almost invariably generous. For all our problems, we are still a remarkably open society, where the presumption remains that information belongs to the people. I am thankful for them, and for all the people, who, over the years, provided tips, articles, phone numbers, suggestions and were otherwise helpful in this project.

And, in the end, every editor needs an editor, and I am very fortunate to have drawn Alexia Dorszynski for mine. Over the years, in a project that threatened to daunt us both, she remained nevertheless dauntless, providing both deft advice and persistence in turning this manuscript into the book you have before you.

Finally, I would like to thank my family and friends for their support, and especially my mother, who saw this project begun but not finished. From my mother, I learned a little of the inseparability of love and intelligence—the possibility of a moral beauty. As she would have said, pass it on.

This is my attempt. Of course it is flawed. The full responsibility for that is mine alone. But then, although my colleagues and I have made every attempt at thoroughness and completion, this book isn't really finished.

It needs you, the reader, to complete it. Perhaps you will grace us with your comments, suggestions, observations, even corrections; an address is provided at the end of the bibliography. After all, what is conversation for, if it doesn't lead on to richer conversation?

Robert Barnett, Editor

◇ INTRODUCTION ◇

by Robert Barnett

"Health results from a harmony between food and exercise," wrote Hippocrates, the founder of Western medicine, in the fourth century A.D. Of food, he wrote that "whole meal bread cleans out the gut."

Variety, moderation, and balance, the central principles of modern nutrition, are as old as civilization. Older. Animals practice them. Wild predators such as wolves often favor certain species of prey, but wolves that surfeit on favored prey, even when it's abundant, often turn to less favored food sources. Nutritional behaviorists such as Professor Barbara Rolls of Johns Hopkins University in Baltimore speculate that humans have inherited this instinct for variety, which conveys an evolutionary advantage by ensuring a nutritionally balanced diet.

That was before the invention of bubble gum ice cream, however. Today's challenges are a little different. Yet the knowledge of the core of a healthy diet has never been clearer. A scientific consensus, unique in modern history, has emerged that a proper diet can improve the quality of our health and the span of our longevity. As the Surgeon General's *Report on Nutrition and Health* (U.S. Department of Health and Human Services, 1988) puts it, "For two out of three adult Americans who do not smoke and do not drink excessively, one personal choice seems to influence long-term health prospects more than any other: What we eat. . . . what we eat may affect our risk for several of the leading causes of death

for Americans, notably, coronary heart disease, stroke, atherosclerosis, diabetes, and some types of cancer."

Modern words, but not necessarily new. In his notes to *Queen Mab*, the English poet Percy Bysshe Shelley wrote, "There is no disease, bodily or mental, which adoption of vegetable diet and pure water has not infallibly mitigated, wherever the experiment has been fairly tried."

A radical proposition. Yet the poet held some truth in his words. A good first rule of nutrition, as good as any, might well be, *Eat more plant foods, fewer animal products.*

Politics may preclude public documents from making such bald statements, but that is clearly their import. Consider a current federal consensus on diet, the National Research Council's *Diet and Health: Implications for Reducing Chronic Disease Risk* (National Academy Press, 1989). The main points advocated there:

♦ Balance food intake and physical activity to maintain appropriate body weight.

♦ Reduce total fat to 30 percent of calories or less. Cut saturated fat to under 10 percent. Cholesterol should be less than 300 milligrams daily.

♦ Eat five or more daily servings of fruits and vegetables, especially green and yellow vegetables and citrus fruits.

♦ Eat six or more daily servings of bread, cereals, and legumes to increase complex carbohydrate intake.

♦ Maintain protein at moderate levels. "This committee does not recommend against eating meat; rather, it recommends consuming lean meat in smaller and fewer portions than is customary in the United States."

♦ Maintain adequate calcium intake, an especially important concern for women and adolescents.

To achieve such goals, the report advises we eat less red meat and poultry, more fish and shellfish, and low-fat rather than whole dairy products. Yet the greatest shift would be away from animal foods to grains, vegetables, and fruits. That is, more plant foods, fewer animal. "By using plant products (e.g., cereals and legumes) instead of animal products as sources of protein, one can also reduce the amount of saturated fatty acids and cholesterol in the diet," it states.

For most people, cutting fat and moderating protein "implies an increase in calories from carbohydrates . . . from whole-grain cereals and breads." Of vegetables, "the committee's recommendations would lead to a substantial increase in consumption frequency and portion sizes for the average person."

So now we have a core diet: complex carbohydrates. That's grains, vegetables, and fruits. If you're a vegan, that's your menu already; if you're a lacto-ovo vegetarian, you'll supplement the core with cheese, yogurt, milk, eggs; if you're an omnivore, red meat, poultry, and fish will round out the table.

This is the way humans have been eating for millennia: a core diet of complex carbohydrates sauced with vegetables or meat. This is in fact the nutritional basis for settled civilization. "Most great (and many minor) sedentary civilizations have been built on the cultivation of a particular complex carbohydrate, such as maize or potatoes or rice or millet or wheat," writes Johns Hopkins University anthropologist Sidney Mintz in *Sweetness and Power* (Penguin, 1985). "Other plant foods, oils, flesh, fowl, fish, fruits, nuts, and seasonings—many of the ingredients of which are nutritively essential—will also be consumed, but the users themselves usually view them as secondary, even if necessary, additions to the major starch."

* * *

How do you eat? How do you plan dinner? If you're like most Americans, you start with a protein-rich animal flesh main dish: a juicy steak, a fillet of salmon, scallops, liver and onions, a broiler chicken. If you're a gourmet, squab. We are a rich people and can afford something that's historically scarce: We eat animal foods rich in protein and fat as our staple, plant foods rich in carbohydrates as our side dishes. We're used to it, but it's a far cry from the predominant human diet of a staple starch rich in complex carbohydrates and fiber complemented by side dishes of meats, dairy foods, vegetables and fruits, fermented foods, spices, and herbs.

Mintz quotes anthropologist Audrey Richards on the Bemba people of southern Bantu: "To the Bemba each meal, to be satisfactory, must be composed of two constituents: a thick porridge *(ubwali)* made of millet and the relish *(umunani)* of vegetables, meat or fish, which is eaten with it."

Whether it's Bemban ubwali spiked with umunani, or Mexican tortillas turned into food by chili peppers, or Irish potatoes seasoned into dinner with carrots and lamb, it begins with a core carbohydrate. Zydeco, the Cajun accordion music, gets its name from a 1920s song lament about eating "verts san sel"—being so poor you couldn't afford salt pork for your greens and rice. A common East European combination, Mintz tells us, was "black bread, chicken fat, raw garlic, and salt." Pasta is eaten with a sauce, couscous with stew, Ethiopian injera bread with lamb. Culinary cultures have been based on cornmeal, couscous, bulgur, millet, yams, and many more.

Does that mean you can't have hamburgers for dinner? Of course you can. But instead of having an 8-ounce burger on a skimpy white bread bun, you might try preparing a lean 4-ounce patty on a big, thick whole-grain baguette stuffed with plenty of romaine lettuce and tomato. The latter leans more on the core carbohydrates, less on fat and protein from animal foods. As we'll see, it's all a question of balance. And that balance can often be attained without a big change in your diet habits.

Paul Lachance, a professor of nutrition at Rutgers University in New Brunswick, New Jersey, puts the issue simply and graphically: Think of the Basic Four—meat, dairy, grains, and fruits and vegetables. As we'll see a little later, it may be an outdated way of thinking, but it's the way we all grew up.

Now think of a peace sign symbol. It's got two big sections near the top, two smaller ones on the bottom. That peace sign is your dinner plate. For most Americans, that plate looks like this:

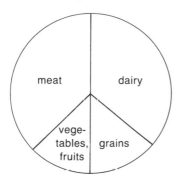

What it really should look like is the opposite:

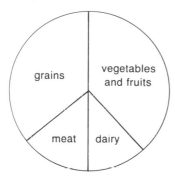

That's the advice of the federal government's primary nutrition document for consumers: the USDA's Dietary Guidelines for Americans (Third Edition, 1990). The main goals are simple: *Eat a variety of foods; maintain healthy weight; choose a diet low in fat, saturated fat, and cholesterol; choose a diet with plenty of vegetables, fruits, and grain products; use sugars only in moderation; use salt and sodium only in moderation; and if you drink alcoholic beverages, do so in moderation.* The new edition recommends that every day we eat:

♦ Three to five servings of vegetables, including dark-green leafy and deep-yellow vegetables, dry beans and peas, and starchy vegetables such as potatoes and corn.

♦ Two to four servings of fruits, including citrus fruits or juices, melons, and berries. Choose fruits as desserts, juices as beverages.

♦ Six to eleven servings of grain products, including a variety of grains, such as wheat, rice, oats, and corn; several servings of whole-grain breads and cereals.

♦ Two to three servings of milk, yogurt, and cheese. A serving is one cup of milk or yogurt, 1½ ounces of cheese. Choose skim or low-fat products.

♦ Two to three servings of meats, poultry, fish, dry beans and peas, eggs, and nuts, for a daily total of about six ounces. Trim fat from meat; take skin off poultry. Have cooked dry beans and peas occasionally instead of meat.

♦ Use fats and oils sparingly in cooking.

It's not a question of good foods or bad; it's a question of balance. Years ago, mainstream nutritionists would have considered such advice quite odd. In the 1930s and 1940s, scientists reached consensus on the minimum amounts of newly discovered vitamins and minerals we need each day. We need minute amounts of these substances, yet they are absolutely essential. To this day, when many people think of nutrition, what comes to mind are vitamins and minerals.

Yet mainstream nutrition has moved decisively away from micronutrient orientation in the last 15 years. The emphasis is now on the bigger picture, on "macronutrients": total calories, fat, saturated fat, cholesterol, sodium, fiber, complex carbohydrates, simple sugars.

This new approach to nutrition comes from a public health perspective. Harvard nutritionist Mark Hegsted, who conducted pioneering, now-classic research into vitamins and minerals in the 1930s and 1940s and turned to public heath issues in the 1950s, poses the new challenge as a paradox. Though RDA vitamin and mineral requirements run into the dozens, he notes that actual nutrient deficiency is quite rare in this country. At the same time, however, more than half of all Americans die of nutrition-related diseases such as heart disease, diabetes, and stroke. Clearly, there is more to nourishing the human body than getting enough vitamins and minerals.

When it comes to preventing major chronic diseases, the issues that matter are weight control and exercise, total calories, total fat, saturated fat, cholesterol, soldium intake, and, on the positive side, complex carbohydrates and fiber.

If you focus on old-fashioned nutrition, the new federal guidelines make little sense. Animal foods are often nutrient-dense; few better sources of iron and zinc exist than red meat. Yet red meat and dairy products contribute more than half of the saturated fat that Americans consume. The Surgeon General tells us that cutting total fat and saturated fat should be our number one nutritional goal. In that context, a large steak seems less of a nutritional bargain.

Vegetarianism illustrates the differences between a micronutrient and macronutrient approach. Becoming a vegetarian may seem risky because you're arbitrarily avoiding many nutrient-dense foods. Vegans, who eat no animal products at all, run a risk of consuming diets low in iron and other minerals, in calcium, and in vitamin B-12. There have been some cases of American vegan children who failed to thrive. Yet vegans tend to eat more complex carbohydrates, more grains and fruits and vegetables, more fiber, less protein, and less fat than meat eaters. For an adult, going on a vegan diet will tend to lower blood pressure, lower blood levels of cholesterol and other fats, promote weight loss and stabilization at a lower weight, and, by virtue of the fiber in plant foods, speed food through the digestion system and improve elimination. Vegan children tend to have lower cholesterol than omnivore children.

So the choice seems to be between a nutritionally adequate diet and one that helps prevent major chronic diseases. Or is it? Nutritionists have been studying vegetarians with renewed vigor lately. What they find is surprising: American vegetarians are generally well nourished. An executive summary of a special issue of the *American Journal of Clinical Nutrition* (Supplement, Vol. 48, no. 3) devoted to vegetarianism concludes: "With the exception of magnesium and manganese balance among American vegetarians, the intake and balance of all other minerals examined was higher than or equal to that of non-vegetarians."

Perhaps that means that vegetarianism is the ideal. Yet few cultures in history have eschewed animal foods, which provide taste, vital nutrients, and variety. Classic nutritional concerns have value: the phenomenon of nutrition-conscious women who sup on white-meat chicken and tuna and so invite anemia is a real one. Perhaps the trick is to eat our animal foods, hoping our cholesterol levels don't rise.

That notion would come as a surprise to USDA nutritionist Rita Dougherty. She put 40 men on a low-fat diet, but this was no brown rice and tofu experience. The men ate red meat, poultry, fish, dairy foods, and eggs. They just followed standard nutritional advice. Fats were trimmed from all meat. Skin was removed from fowl. Margarine took the place of butter, skim milk replaced whole, vegetable oil was used instead of animal cooking fats. When the study began, the men were getting 40 to 44 percent of their calories from fat, as well as 600 milligrams of cholesterol daily. Average blood cholesterol: 218; blood pressure: 135/85. The new diet was only 25 percent fat calories, 300 milligrams of cholesterol, and average blood cholesterol dropped to 185, blood pressure to 124/79.

For the study to work right, however, the actual number of calories needed to stay the same. But fats are highly caloric. To replace fat calories, the men actually had to eat more food. They were fed more grains, more vegetables, more fruits. A funny thing happened. Not only did the macronutrient profile of their meals improve—more complex carbohydrates, less fat—but the micronutrients took to the sky. Vitamin C, thiamin, riboflavin, niacin, B-6, B-12, folic acid, potassium, iron, calcium, magnesium, phosphorus, and zinc all went up.

So the conflict between clinical and public health nutritionists dissolves. You *can* consume more vitamins and minerals while you lower your blood pressure and cholesterol level. The issue gets resolved where it should, at the table, in the kitchen, over food.

Balanced meals are low in fat, low in saturated fat, low in salt, moderate in protein, rich in complex carbohydrates and fiber, high in micronutrients including iron, calcium, potassium, magnesium, beta-carotene, vitamin C, B vitamins—the works. Just take a peek at some of our recipes, how they balance large carbohydrate portions with smaller protein servings. Then look at the nutritional information to see how low-fat high-carbohydrate dishes can be extraordinarily nutritious.

Get the core right, and the rest will fall into place. Eat more grains and fresh fruits and vegetables and fish, and you'll automatically be taking in many newly discovered substances such as isothiocyanates in cabbage family vegetables (page 165) that may protect against cancer, and Omega 3 fatty acids in fish (page 212) that may protect against heart disease. Overwhelming evidence supports the claim that eating more fruits and vegetables, especially raw, protects against a number of cancers. Every year, scientists discover new reasons to eat our peas and carrots.

Marrying complex carbohydrates with vegetables, dairy foods, red meat, poultry, and seafood is a universal culinary experience. That's why a healthful cookbook such as this one can be extraordinarily delicious. We're not just cutting back on favorite foods, although our nutritional standards are quite strict. Rather, we're exploring a vast international culinary resource: the many ways traditional foods have balanced small portions of protein foods over a large base of complex carbohydrates.

So we meet at the table. What is a balanced diet? The key is in the balance. *That* brings us to the kitchen, for this is above all a practical book. Each chapter explores the role a category of food— root vegetables, or shellfish, or pasta—plays in a healthy diet. Our goal is to encourage you to become more familiar with the foods in your market and perhaps a little more adventurous. Variety is the spice, moderation the governing principle.

In each chapter you'll find a discussion of nutrition, cooking basics, and, of course, kitchen-tested recipes, adapted where appropriate for the microwave, with full nutritional information and food exchanges after each dish. The Food Guide in back is a resource: Buy nearly any unprocessed food in the marketplace—a rutabaga, sesame seeds, a rabbit—and you'll find out a little about storage and nutrition.

Nobody needs to eat all the foods in this book, but once you learn a few simple rules of nutrition and how to apply them, you'll develop an intuitive sense of how to balance your diet. It's not a question of numbers and charts, although they can help point the way. It's common sense. A nutritious meal can be as simple as toast and apple butter, as fancy as venison with chanterelles. The recipes themselves range from simple and hearty to elegant for entertaining, with a fair measure of international ethnic tricks thrown into the pot.

Science has reached consensus on the optimal diet for healthy people. This book assumes you are in general good health, and you want to stay that way. But diet can also help treat obesity, lower blood pressure, lower levels of blood sugar and cholesterol, reduce constipation, and alleviate diverticulitis. A healthy diet is often the first step toward controlling medical risk factors for heart disease, diabetes, stroke, and certain cancers. If those concern you, consult your physician. Find a life-style plan: exercise, stress control, nutrition. Use this book as an information source. The foods in this book are family foods, and many of the recipes ideal for young children, but much of the nutritional information is geared for adults. If you're pregnant or breastfeeding or have an infant under two, purchase a good book about childhood nutrition and then use this book to put those principles into practice.

Many people, sick or well, who want to learn how to fit better eating into their lives, find the services of a registered dietitian (R.D.) very helpful. The more you know about your own specific nutritional needs, the more valuable this book will be.

How you put it together in your own life, with your own schedule and relationships, is your discovery.

Although it covers nutrition and abounds in recipes, this is a *food* book. That's because the marriage of nutrition and cuisine is an affair of food. Nutrition is science. Cuisine is taste and technique. They meet in the supermarket and the kitchen. Bring more healthful foods home, learn a few new ways to prepare and cook them, and odds are you'll start to eat healthier, more delicious, and more economical meals. Home cooks don't need to blanket all dishes in a taste "safety net" of fat, or prepare vegetables hours in advance so they lose vitamins at the steam table. When you do eat out, the food skills you've gained will make it easier to order more healthfully in restaurants.

Explore fresh whole foods and you'll gain an appreciation of the farm, the seas, the lakes, and the woods that supply our needs. In this age of a threatened food supply, such knowledge, and relationships between suppliers and consumers, may be life-saving. Vegetables grown without synthetic pesticides, beef and poultry raised on organic grain without hormones, and other pure foods are increasingly available at our supermarkets and farmers' markets. Perhaps more important, bringing food home and cooking it is a simple way to take charge of your own life.

Food is fun. It's sensual, biological, creative, social, essential, pleasurable, delicious. Food nourishes. But it can also overnourish. It can fatten, overwork your system, weaken. This book is about food that gives both pleasure and strength.

THE
AMERICAN HEALTH
FOOD BOOK

THE CORE DIET:
◇ MEALS AND MENUS ◇

by Robert Barnett

Food is composed of both macronutrients and micronutrients. Macronutrients include carbohydrates, protein, fat, and fiber. These comprise large amounts of the food we eat, occurring in grams (abbreviated g), a visible measure. One hundred grams, a standard nutritional serving size for many foods, is about 3½ ounces—just under a quarter of a pound.

Carbohydrates are generally classed as either complex or simple. Wheat is composed primarily of complex carbohydrates; table sugar is a simple carbohydrate. Protein is composed of amino acids.

Fat itself can be characterized as saturated, monounsaturated, or polyunsaturated. Thus, a meal might contain 21 grams of fat, of which a third (7 grams) is saturated, a third (7 grams) monounsaturated, and a third (7 grams) polyunsaturated.

Micronutrients are substances that occur in tiny amounts, yet are essential: vitamins such as vitamin C, minerals such as iron, electrolytes such as potassium and sodium, trace elements such as selenium. They occur in much smaller amounts, usually in milligrams (abbreviated mg)—one thousandth of a gram. A woman's daily need for iron, for example, is only 15 milligrams, a man's 10 milligrams. Some nutrients we need in such small quantities that they are measured in micro-

grams—one thousandth of a milligram. The daily average need for folic acid, or folacin, for example, is 400 micrograms (0.4 milligrams).

Most Americans consume an imbalance of macronutrients and a shortage of certain micronutrients. The standard American diet is too high in fat, saturated fat, protein, simple sugars, cholesterol, and sodium, and too low in complex carbohydrates and fiber. Yet, typically, it's also low in certain micronutrients, such as iron, calcium, folic acid, and vitamin B-6.

A balanced diet is rich in complex carbohydrates and fiber, low in fat and saturated fat, moderate in protein and low in sodium, yet provides adequate amounts of iron, calcium, potassium, vitamin B-6, manganese, and the entire cast of essential nutrients.

Carbohydrates are life's best fuel. When we eat carbohydrates, complex or simple, we use them to fuel our muscles. Eat complex carbohydrates—bread or rice or oats or beans—and blood sugar forms in a slow, steady, gentle way. You'll produce only a small amount of insulin. Consume mostly simple sugars, however, and your body will convert them to blood sugar quickly, boosting insulin quickly. That insulin will overcompensate, so blood sugar may drop suddenly. Complex carbohydrates are high in fiber and give us the steady-as-she-goes energy we need to lead busy lives. *We should get at least 55 percent and as much as 75 or 80 percent of our calories from carbohydrates, primarily complex carbohydrates.*

Complex carbohydrate foods tend to be rich in fiber, an important macronutrient. Fiber was once considered a non-nutrient, but the weight of evidence convinces us we need it every day. Fiber is most simply defined as that part of food we can't digest. Yet scientists now find that we can digest many fibers, not in the stomach, but throughout the lower intestines. Fiber is essential for moving food through the digestive system efficiently; when fiber is broken down, bacteria produce chemicals with a generally salutary effect on the lower intestines and colon. Fiber is classed as either insoluble or soluble. Insoluble fibers improve digestion and elimination. Soluble fibers—such as those found in oats (page 91), barley (page 92), beans and legumes (page 119), carrots (page 105), and onions (page 194)—tend to lower blood levels of cholesterol in ways not yet fully understood. Food fiber is found only in plant foods. *A healthy diet contains between 20 and 35 grams of dietary fiber daily from sources both soluble and insoluble.*

Protein is an essential macronutrient. It provides the raw chemical material—amino acids—for an astounding range of physiological processes. When we eat just the right amount of protein, our bodies convert the protein to amino acids which in turn become the building blocks of peptides, neurotransmitters, and many other substances. We don't need much protein to serve the purpose, however. *A healthy diet provides between 12 and 15 percent of its calories from protein, with an upper limit of about 20 percent.* Consume more—and some Americans take in 30 percent or more protein calories—and your body will convert excess protein to simple blood sugars. That's a wasteful process. It stresses the kidneys and causes us to excrete increased amounts of calcium, which may eventually contribute to osteoporosis, the brittle-bone disease.

Protein comes from both animal and plant foods. Animal protein—red meat, poultry, fish, eggs, cheese, and milk—contain a good balance of amino acids. Most plant foods need to comple-

ment each other to create a good amino acid balance. When grains, such as bread or rice or barley, mix with beans and legumes or seeds or nuts or even mushrooms, the resulting protein is well balanced. Animal sources of protein tend to be diluted with fat, whereas plant sources are accompanied by complex carbohydrates and fiber. *At least half of our protein sources should come from plant foods.*

Cholesterol is a waxy substance that is strictly speaking neither a macro- nor a micronutrient; we don't need to ingest it because our bodies manufacture it. Found only in animal foods, cholesterol also tends to raise blood levels of cholesterol, though not as dramatically as saturated fat does. *Cholesterol intake should not exceed 300 milligrams a day.*

The sodium found in table salt is an essential element. Most of us eat much more salt than we need, however. Too much salt can cause water retention. It can also raise blood pressure in between a third and a half of all people who are susceptible to high blood pressure. Some authorities argue that salt restriction is less important than was once thought, but over a certain small amount salt does us no good and may do harm. It masks the true taste of food, it makes us thirsty, and it may lead us to eat too much fat: Dietary surveys find a strong link between salt intake and fat intake. Just think of potato chips. *Dietary goals advise us to consume no more than 3,000 milligrams of sodium a day. Some advise a limit of 2,400 milligrams.* (That's about what's in a teaspoon of salt.)

Fats are the stored form of energy. As animals, we evolved in conditions of scarcity with occasional surpluses, so our bodies are adept at storing dietary fat. We're saving it to survive the next famine. When we eat dietary fat, we tend to store it as body fat. In other words, fat makes you fatter. If you want to lose weight, or maintain your normal weight, cutting fat is the most effective dietary action you can take. (Exercise is the most effective nondietary action.) Too much dietary fat also tends to raise blood cholesterol, predispose to gallstones, and increase the risk of heart disease and certain kinds of cancer. *Dietary fat should be less than 30 percent of total calories.* Cutting dietary fat down to 25 percent or even 20 percent may even confer additional health benefits.

Learn a little math for your health. It's the only math we'll ask you to learn in this book. To calculate the percentage of calories from fat in any food, from a package of cheese to a frozen dinner, count the grams of fat. Multiply that number by 9 (each gram of fat has 9 calories), then divide that number by the total number of calories in the food. Thus if a frozen dinner has 360 calories and 20 grams of fat, you'd multiply 20 by 9, yielding 180 calories from fat. Then you'd divide 180 by 360, yielding 0.5, or 50 percent. That means 50 percent of the calories from that dinner comes from fat. A lot!

Balance your fat over days and weeks, not hours, and balance it over meals rather than individual foods. Even lean meat is 40 percent fat calories, but many grains are under 10 percent, vegetables under 5 percent. So mix meat and lean dairy with vegetables and grains and you'll likely have a low-fat meal. The percentage of fat begins to be more important as the picture widens. If the dish is a main dish, the percentage of calories from fat means more. If it's an entire meal, it means even more. The overall goal is to reduce the fat calories in your weekly diet to 30 percent or less of the total.

And keep track of total grams as well as the percentage. Fresh greens are so low in calories (and rich in nutrients) that even a few teaspoons of oil can produce a salad that's 35 percent fat calories or more. But if your salad has only a gram of fat, you're in fine shape no matter what the percentage.

If you need 2,000 calories a day, that means you should get no more than 600 calories from fat; that's 30 percent, about 67 grams of fat. If your lunch yogurt has 10 grams of fat, you've already used up a good chunk of your daily limit; if it's lowfat, with 3 or 4 grams, you'll be able to have more fat at dinner. Perhaps you like ice cream; it's perhaps 80 percent fat calories. If you eat two scoops a day, it will be well nigh impossible to balance out a week's diet at under 30 percent fat calories. But if you eat one scoop twice a week, it'll be easier to eat a healthy diet.

The quality of the fats we eat is very important, too. As mentioned earlier, fats are classed as saturated, monunsaturated, or polyunsaturated. Cooking oils and food fats actually cover a spectrum of saturation. Palm oil is more saturated than butter, which in turn is more saturated than olive oil. Saturated fats tend to raise blood cholesterol and increase the risk of heart disease. Our bodies have no need for them whatsoever.

As you cut total fat and saturated fat, you'll be consuming a greater proportion of monounsaturated or polyunsaturated fats. Which is better? According to current research, monounsaturates. Each type can help lower blood cholesterol, although there is some evidence that monounsaturated fats may be less likely to lower the beneficial HDL type of cholesterol. Furthermore, monounsaturated fats may be safer.

Polyunsaturated fats, with many double bonds in their chemical structure, are inherently less stable—as much as 20 times more reactive with oxygen—than monounsaturated fats. Oxidizing readily, they form free radicals, which can damage cells and tissues, and, ultimately, may predispose to chronic diseases such as arthritis, cataracts, and cancer. Many, though not all, animal studies in which a carcinogen is introduced and then diet is studied find that there are fewer tumors on a high-mono diet, compared with a high-poly or high-saturated fat diet. Furthermore, polyunsaturated fats may impair various cells of the immune system, which doesn't occur with monounsaturated. This isn't to say that polyunsaturated fats cause cancer. That's far from established. But it's a concern—one that makes monounsaturated fats look better. *A healthy diet contains fat that's less than one-third saturated (the less, the better), less than one-third polyunsaturated, and the rest in monounsaturates.* Total fat needs to stay low—some animal studies have shown that when total fat is low enough, the negative effects of polyunsaturated fats don't occur.

Olive oil, a primarily monounsaturated fat, may be the healthiest cooking oil in the world. But a healthy diet can include such cooking oils as canola oil, soybean oil, sesame oil, walnut oil, hazelnut oil, sunflower oil, corn oil, and safflower oil. It can also include margarine, especially the less saturated soft margarines, and diet margarines, which have more water and less fat. Recent evidence that trans fatty acids—formed when polyunsaturated and monounsaturated fats are artificially hydrogenated to make them more solid—can raise blood cholesterol makes softer margarines even more attractive. It can even use butter, with its irreplaceable flavor, in reasonably small amounts. It can use a nonstick vegetable cooking spray. The key is taking in as little fat as is needed and making sure the fat you take in is as low in saturated fat as is practical. Add a teaspoon of butter to three tablespoons of olive oil and you'll increase the saturation a little, but not much.

In the recipes in this book, we've cut fat wherever we could do so without cutting flavor. The variety of foods in this book calls for flexibility where the choice of oils and fats is concerned. We've kept our eyes on the bottom line: How saturated is it? That's why each recipe includes the total *amount* of fat; the percentage of calories from fat, protein, and carbohydrates; and the balance of saturated, monunsaturated, and polyunsaturated in that fat. Each recipe lists dietary cholesterol (in milligrams), dietary fiber (in grams), and sodium (in milligrams) as well as its essential counterpart potassium (in milligrams), which may help prevent strokes.

We all need vitamins and minerals in our diet. Federal guidelines for vitamins and minerals are generally expressed as RDAs—recommended dietary allowances. These are adjusted for age, gender, and status, such as pregnancy. In this book, we use the more universal measure, the USRDA. There is only one USRDA for each particular nutrient; it's usually set about the level of the highest RDA, to help ensure that everyone's needs are met. Thus, if your day's meals provide 100 percent of the USRDAs, you're probably getting more than enough for your actual, individual needs. It's a safety net.

Food labels are expressed as percentages of the USRDAs. But though you can read the label on a box of breakfast cereal, there's no such label on an apple, or an apple cobbler. Each recipe includes the percentage of the USRDA for nutrients that are 10 percent or greater. Thus, if a squash muffin contains 37 percent of the USRDA for vitamin A, we'll list it; if it fills 7 percent of daily zinc needs, we won't list it.

Good menus and meals are rich in complex carbohydrates, moderate in protein, low in fat and saturated fats, low in sodium, low in cholesterol, and high in fiber. They provide adequate amounts of iron; calcium; magnesium; potassium; vitamins A, C, D, E, B-1, B-2, B-3, B-6, B-12; zinc; copper; chromium; manganese; selenium; boron; and other elements.

This goal is easier to achieve than you might imagine. As proof, we've created a week's worth of menus that showcase the recipes in this book and demonstrate how they can be combined in healthy, delicious ways. Whenever a dish is a recipe, we've included the chapter it comes from in brackets, e.g., Poached Huevos Rancheros [Eggs, p. 269].

THE SEVEN-DAY BALANCED DIET
by Robert Barnett, Kathy Johnson-Schlichting, R.D., and Nao Hauser

Day One

BREAKFAST

Let's start the day off with a high-fiber, complex carbohydrate—Brown Rice Cereal with Apricots, from the chapter on Rice. Cereal is an excellent way to start the day. Studies show that people who eat cereal for breakfast tend to eat less fat and more nutrients during the day and are also likely to be fitter.

Which comes first, the fitness or the cereal, is an open question, but from the food profiles in the back of this book, we can see that a half cup of brown rice, which cooks up to about a cup and a half, is nutrient-rich:

½ Cup of Brown Rice, Raw

Cal: 340   Pro: 7g/9%   Carb: 71g/84%   Fat: 3g/7%
Sodium: 7mg   Potassium: 205mg   Fiber: 7.2g   B1: 25%

B3: 23% B6: 23% Panto: 14% P: 31% Mg: 33%
Zn: 12% Cu: 13% Mn: 98%

Brown rice has lots of carbohydrates and plenty of fiber. It's a good source of B vitamins, as well as some trace elements. But it's not entirely balanced. First of all, we're looking at a lot of rice; you'd probably eat less. And it's low in a number of vitamins primarily found in fresh fruits and vegetables, such as vitamin C and folic acid. Adding orange juice to the meal will help:

An 8-Ounce Glass of Orange Juice

Cal: 112 Pro: 2g/6% Carb: 26g/90% Fat: .6g/4% Chol: 0mg Sodium: 2mg Potassium: 596mg Fiber: 2g C: 206% Folic: 34%

Now we've got our folic acid and vitamin C, plus some potassium. But let's get back to the rice. To turn it into a good-tasting cereal, we prepare it with dried apricots and skim milk and serve it in smaller portions. Here's what the Brown Rice Cereal with Apricots [Rice, p. 80] looks like:

One Serving of Brown Rice Cereal
with Apricots

Cal: 277 Pro: 12g/17% Carb: 51g/70% Fat: 4g/13% Chol: 4mg Sodium: 134mg Potassium: 899mg Fiber: 5g A: 45% D: 26% E: 12% B1: 11% B2: 26% B3: 11% B12: 15% Panto: 10% Ca: 34% P: 37% Fe: 12% Mg: 15% Cu: 15% Mn: 27% Se: 25%

That gives more protein (from the milk), more potassium (apricots), more calcium (milk), even a little iron (apricots). Complete the breakfast menu with an English muffin:

BREAKFAST

Brown Rice Cereal with Apricots
1/2 whole wheat English muffin
with 1 teaspoon margarine
8 ounces orange juice
Tea or coffee

By balancing a complex carbohydrate, a dairy food, and a few fruits, we're on our way to a well-nourished day. Here's lunch:

LUNCH

Tuna, Red Cabbage, and Caper Salad
[Fish, p. 212] on a Kaiser roll
1 cup fruited yogurt
2 plums

The salad itself provides a nice balance. Tuna gives us low-fat protein, not to mention Omega 3 fatty acids for our hearts, and the cabbage, as well as the onions and garlic in the recipe, gives us a storehouse of vitamins. Yogurt provides protein and calcium. And the plums give us a little vitamin C. The roll is carbohydrate, to keep our day from becoming too protein-heavy.

Let's look at the nutritional profile of the salad:

Cal: 147 Pro: 17g/44% Carb: 7g/18% Fat: 6g/37% (S:16% M:70% P:14%) Chol: 37mg Sodium: 241mg Potassium: 407mg Fiber: 2g Omega-3: 1.3g C: 64% E: 20% B3: 35% B6: 18% B12: 43% P: 15% Cu: 22% Se: 89%

We've added a good amount of protein, a little fat, some fiber, plenty of vitamin C, more B vitamins, and some trace minerals (seafood is good for minerals). Here's dinner:

DINNER

Spinach Salad with Lemon
[Salad and Greens, p. 174]
Meat and Potato Loaf
[Red Meat and Game, p. 242]
Bulgur Pilaf [Wheat, p. 43]
Whole wheat roll with 1 teaspoon margarine
3/4 cup sliced steamed carrots
Banana Pops [Fruit, p. 296]

The salad is a simple dish of greens, which will give us more folic acid, beta-carotene (vitamin A), and vitamin C. The meat and potato loaf is a clever combination of lean red meat, rich in iron and other minerals, and potatoes, to keep our carbohydrate consumption on course. Bulgur pilaf adds more complex carbohydrates as does the roll. Carrots give us more vitamins. And a banana pop, rich in potassium, is a delicious, cool dessert.

Here's the nutritional profile for the entire day's 1800 calories:

Cal: 1822   Pro: 88g/19%   Carb: 304g/64%
Fat: 35/17%   (S:28%   M:50%   P:22%)   Chol:
103mg   Sodium: 1691mg   Potassium: 4380mg
Fiber: 30g   A: 729%   C: 425%   E: 77%   B1: 106%
B2: 112%   B3: 127%   B6: 105%   B12: 106%
Folic: 93%   Ca: 101%   P: 152%   Fe: 73%
Mg: 76%   Zn: 51%   Cu: 63%   Mn: 50%   Se: 209%
Cr: 70%

How does the first day stack up? Carbohydrates provide 64 percent of the calories, almost all of them complex (there are few sugars in this meal), which is excellent. Fat is only 17 percent of total calories. Protein is 19 percent—reasonably low. Cholesterol is low, as is sodium, and potassium is high. Fiber is as high as the National Cancer Institute would recommend.

Now let's look at the vitamins. A and C are off the roof, and most of the rest are above 70 percent. Is that all right? Is it okay that manganese (Mn) is only 50 percent, that iron (Fe) is only 73 percent? Yes, for a number of important reasons. First, because nutrient data are still inadequate, there is probably more iron or manganese or whatever in our actual menu than in our estimates; some foods have minerals but haven't been well tested for them. Second, the USRDA is set higher than actual need, so it can be used for labeling purposes and to protect populations. So getting 70 percent or 80 percent of the USRDA for a nutrient may mean you are getting enough RDA for you. But the third reason is the most important: Nobody said you should balance your diet at every meal or even every day. It's the balance over days and weeks that matters. That's why we've provided a week's worth of menus. If one day is a little high in fat, to take one example, you can balance it out by eating lean meals the next day.

The next question you may be asking is, Why 1800 calories? We picked that because it's a reasonable amount to expect a physically active adult woman to consume. An active man might need an additional 600 calories, so we've provided a 2400 calorie menu, too. Here's how to turn Day One into a 2400-calorie day:

BREAKFAST

Add another ½ whole wheat muffin with 1 teaspoon margarine, and a banana

SNACK

Lemon-Zucchini Muffin [Squash, p. 154]

DINNER

Add another ½ serving of Meat and Potato Loaf and Bulgur Pilaf.

Here's how these additions stack up:

Cal: 2397   Pro: 111g/18%   Carb: 398/64%   Fat:
49g/18%   (S:28%   M:44%   P:28%)   Chol: 142mg
Sodium: 2191mg   Potassium: 5397mg   Fiber: 40g
A: 739%   C: 455%   E: 115%   B1: 134%   B2: 136%
B3: 159%   B6: 153%   B12: 123%   Folic: 112%
Ca: 111%   P: 189%   Fe: 97%   Mg: 102%   Zn: 70%
Cu: 85%   Mn: 55%   Se: 245%   Cr: 74%

You'll notice that a number of nutrients go up. That's not surprising; you're eating more foods. There's more fiber, more iron, more zinc, etc. This illustrates a simple but often overlooked point: Exercise is essential to good nutrition. When you exercise, you not only do immediate direct good to your circulation and other physiological functions, you also allow for more calories. And if you pick the right ones, that improves your nutrition. On the other hand, it's when you diet and don't exercise that you're likely to undernourish yourself, even as you fail, on a long-term basis, to lose weight. That's why some people call exercise "nutrient E."

Let's move on to the second day:

_____ *Day Two* _____

BREAKFAST

1 cup diced fresh pineapple
1 cup nonfat yogurt
with Sesame-Maple Oat Crunch
[The New Grains, p. 91]
1 slice whole wheat toast
with 1 teaspoon margarine

LUNCH

Marie's Mushroom-Leek Soup [Soyfoods, p. 129]
Herbed Egg Salad [Eggs, p. 269] on a bed of
fresh spinach leaves and cherry tomatoes
Toasted whole wheat bagel
Tangerine

SNACK

Apricot-Oat Bread
[Sugars and Sweeteners, p. 306]
with 1 teaspoon margarine

DINNER

Mixed Green Salad with Feta Cheese
[Cheese, p. 289]
Skewered Swordfish and Orange
with Thyme [Fish, p. 212]
1 cup brown rice
Garlicky Spinach [Garlic and Onions, p. 194]
Strawberry or Raspberry Ice Milk
[Milk and Yogurt, p. 278]

Here's the profile for this day:

Cal: 1839 Pro: 85g/18% Carb: 270g/56%
Fat: 56g/26% (S:24% M:43% P:33%) Chol: 166mg
Sodium: 1751mg Potassium: 4414mg Fiber: 37g
A: 692% C: 367% E: 137% B1: 134% B2: 134%
B3: 141% B6: 90% B12: 67% Folic: 144% Panto:
69% Ca: 124% P: 162% Fe: 116% Mg: 115% Zn:
63% Cu: 98% Mn: 193% Se: 169% Cr: 112%

You'll notice that iron is particularly high, while
yesterday it was low. These things even out, if
you eat a well-balanced diet.
  For 2400 calories:

Breakfast: Add 1 slice whole wheat toast
with 1 teaspoon margarine
Lunch: Add another serving of Herbed Egg
Salad [Eggs, p. 269] and 1 more tangerine
Snack: Add 8 ounces skim milk
Dinner: Add ½ skewer more swordfish
and a whole wheat roll
with 1 teaspoon margarine

Cal: 2407 Pro: 118g/19% Carb: 344g/55%
Fat: 74g/26% (S:24% M:38% P:38%)
Chol: 274mg Sodium: 2475mg Potassium:
5749mg Fiber: 43g A: 903% C: 490% E: 168%
B1: 173% B2: 175% B3: 188% B6: 119% B12:
103% Folic: 162% Panto: 101% Ca: 170% P:
225% Fe: 137% Mg: 152% Zn: 76% Cu: 118%
Mn: 204% Se: 228% Cr: 144%

_____ *Day Three* _____

Today, try something a little different first thing
in the morning:

BREAKFAST

Banana Health Shake [Beverages, p. 314]
1 cup Raisin Bran with 4 ounces skim milk

Nor does lunch have to be quotidian:

LUNCH

Warm Potato Salad with Sardines
and Mustard Dressing [Fish, p. 212]
Sliced red and green pepper rings
2 whole wheat bread sticks
Orange

You've already had some good carbohydrates
by midday. For dinner, a delicate steamed Oriental chicken dish will provide some protein, and
rice will continue to give us our complex carbohydrates. The low-fat milk in the corn chowder
recipe gives calcium.

DINNER

Corn Chowder [Corn, p. 70]
4 oz. Steamed Chicken
with Shimeji Mushrooms [Mushrooms, p. 146]
1 cup brown rice
¾ cup steamed asparagus
Fruit Crisp [Sugars and Sweeteners, p. 306]

Cal: 1823 Pro: 89g/19% Carb: 322g/67%
Fat: 30g/15% (S:36% M:41% P:23%)

Chol: 147mg Sodium: 2493mg   Potassium:
4108mg Fiber: 34g A: 122% C: 594% E: 69%
B1: 141% B2: 139% B3: 182% B6: 148%
B12: 119% Folic: 131% Panto: 53% Ca: 99% P:
155% Fe: 97% Mg: 93% Zn: 51% Cu: 64% Mn:
58% Se: 147% Cr: 96

For 2400 calories:

Breakfast: Add 1 slice whole wheat toast
with 1 teaspoon margarine
Lunch: Add ½ serving more
warm potato salad
Snack: 2 Apple-Wheat Bars [Wheat, p. 43] and
Real Cranberry Juice [Beverages, p. 314]
Dinner: Add 1 ounce more steamed chicken,
and an 8-ounce glass of skim milk

Cal: 2430 Pro: 114g/18% Carb: 414g/66%
Fat: 46g/16% (S:30% M:41% P:27%)
Chol: 202mg Sodium: 3562mg Potassium:
5140mg Fiber: 35g A: 140% C: 652% E: 105%
B1: 164% B2: 175% B3: 219% B6: 175%
B12: 162% Folic: 142% Panto: 71% Ca: 140%
P: 211% Fe: 114% Mg: 117% Zn: 66%
Mn: 62% Cu: 82% Se: 174% Cr: 121%

_____ Day Four _____

Try something really unusual for breakfast today:

BREAKFAST

8-ounce glass orange juice
Breakfast Potato Treat [Cheese, p. 289]
1 cup sliced strawberries and kiwis
with a dollop of vanilla yogurt

A hearty soup can become lunch. If variety is
the spice of life, as well as a touchstone for
healthy eating, this dish has it: onions, garlic,
zucchini, carrot, celery, fennel, olives, tomato,
chicken broth, and cheese tortellini. By eating a
wide variety of whole foods, we safeguard our
health.

LUNCH

Carrot and celery sticks
Italian Vegetable Soup with
Tortellini and Olives [Pasta, p. 59]
1 slice Italian bread with 1 teaspoon margarine

SNACK

2 Bran-Oatmeal Cookies [Wheat, p. 43], and
an 8-ounce glass of skim milk

The potato treat, made with low-fat cheese,
provided a little protein this morning, but it's been
a fairly low protein day. That's okay, as most of
us eat too much protein all the time. But there's
room in our day for a little more. We don't want
to be eating red meat more than three or four
times a week, but today might be just the day to
get some Matambre, made with lean flank steak,
with its cargo of iron, for dinner:

DINNER

Matambre [Red Meat and Game, p. 242]
Herbed Couscous [Wheat, p. 43]
¾ cup steamed broccoli
1 slice whole wheat bread
with 1 teaspoon margarine
Poached Pears [Fruit, p. 296]

The couscous and the bread keep us on the side
of the carbohydrate angels. The steamed broccoli
gives us plenty of vitamins. And the pears are
sweet, with very few calories. Here's how the day
shapes up:

Cal: 1764 Pro: 94g/21% Carb: 254g/57%
Fat: 43g/22% (S:35% M:37% P:28%) Chol: 144g
Sodium: 1889mg Potassium: 4533mg Fiber: 35g
A: 1349% C: 667% E: 94% B1: 93% B2: 134%
B3: 98% B6: 98% B12: 92% Folic: 116%
Panto: 52% Ca: 107% P: 159% Fe: 102%
Mg: 101% Zn: 89% Cu: 168% Mn: 77%
Se: 154% Cr: 133%

For 2400 calories:

Breakfast: Increase yogurt to 1 cup
Lunch: Add ½ more serving
of tortellini soup and 1 more
slice of Italian bread with margarine
Snack: Add 2 more Bran-Oatmeal Cookies
Dinner: Add another serving
of Herbed Couscous

Cal: 2460 Pro: 118g/19% Carb: 366g/59%
Fat: 60g/22% (S:33% M:40% P:27%)
Chol: 169mg Sodium: 2469mg   Potassium:
5629mg Fiber: 40g A: 1436% C: 716% E: 115%
B1: 130% B2: 179% B3: 134% B6: 114%
B12: 113% Folic: 135% Panto: 67% Ca: 156%
P: 216% Fe: 121% Mg: 124% Zn: 123%
Cu: 103% Mn: 87% Se: 194% Cr: 169%

Day Five

Time for a simple grain-based breakfast again:

BREAKFAST

1 cup bran flakes with 1 tablespoon each
sliced almonds and raisins
4 ounces skim milk
Honey Corn Muffin [Corn, p. 72]
Banana

Lunch gives us plenty of protein, iron, calcium:

LUNCH

Beef and Cellophane Noodle Salad [Pasta, p. 59]
Warm pita bread
Peach Tapioca [Milk and Yogurt, p. 278]

With all this red meat, though, even in small
portions as part of salads, it feels like time for a
vegetarian dinner:

DINNER

Garlic Whole Wheat Focaccia
[Wheat, p. 54]

Spaghetti Squash with Pepper Sauce
[Squash, p. 158]
Stella's Greek Barley Salad
[The New Grains, p. 91]
¾ cup steamed green beans
1 cup honeydew melon chunks

Cal: 1807 Pro: 67g/14% Carb: 309g/64%
Fat: 47g/22% (S:27% M:47% P:26%) Chol:
87mg Sodium: 1638mg Potassium: 4468mg Fiber:
43g A: 448% C: 494% E: 98% B1: 139% B2:
151% B3: 137% B6: 151% B12: 86% Folic:
152% Panto: 48% Ca: 105% P: 155% Fe: 140%
Mg: 131% Zn: 81% Cu: 102% Mn: 99% Se: 67%
Cr: 111%

For 2400 calories:
Breakfast: Add an 8-ounce glass of orange juice
and 1 teaspoon margarine for the muffin
Snack: Whole Wheat Oatmeal Raisin Bread
[Wheat, p. 43] with 1 teaspoon margarine and
8 ounces skim milk
Dinner: Add another slice of Garlic
Whole Wheat Focaccia

Cal: 2464 Pro: 85/14% Carb: 396g/64%
Fat: 60g/22% (S:25% M:46% P:29%) Chol:
91mg Sodium: 2197mg Potassium: 5578mg Fiber:
50g A: 475% C: 705% E: 132% B1: 187% B2:
189% B3: 159% B6: 166% B12: 101% Folic:
206% Panto: 66% Ca: 141% P: 203% Fe: 161%
Mg: 158% Zn: 94% Cu: 119% Mn: 100%
Se: 72% Cr: 116%

Day Six

We haven't had eggs for breakfast yet. Sure,
they've got cholesterol. But eat in moderation,
and these things balance out:

BREAKFAST

½ pink grapefruit
Poached Huevos Rancheros [Eggs, p. 269]
An 8-ounce glass of skim milk

On spring days, a couple of salads make lunch.
Legumes, especially with a grain such as a whole

wheat roll, give us a nearly perfect, low-fat, low-saturated fat, mineral-rich source of protein:

LUNCH

Lentil Salad with Peanuts [Nuts and Seeds, p. 137]
Moroccan Carrot Salad [Roots, p. 104]
Whole wheat roll
Apple

For dinner, it feels like time for fish. But the wild rice salad, in generous proportions, and the snowpeas and summer squash help keep our diets centered on carbohydrates. And the cheesecake, rich in calcium, is mostly noteworthy for its taste and the fat and calories it eschews:

DINNER

Poached Salmon with Cucumber, Yogurt,
Mint, and Dill Sauce [Fish, p. 212]
Wild Rice Salad [Rice, p. 80]
1 cup steamed snowpeas and
yellow summer squash
1 slice Lemon Cheesecake [Cheese, p. 289]

Cal: 1786 Pro: 105g/23% Carb: 224g/50%
Fat: 54g/27% (S:28% M:44% P:28%)
Chol: 281mg Sodium: 1381mg Potassium:
4500mg Fiber: 37g A: 971% C: 402% E: 128%
B1: 103% B2: 115% B3: 114% B6: 130%
B12: 116% Folic: 77% Panto: 70% Ca: 115%
P: 164% Fe: 96% Mg: 87% Zn: 60% Cu: 85%
Mn: 105% Se: 60% Cr: 118%

For 2400 calories:

Breakfast: Add 2 warm corn tortillas
Lunch: Add another wheat roll and
2 teaspoons margarine
Snack: Savory Corn Bread [Corn, p. 70], fresh
pear, and an 8-ounce glass of skim milk

Cal: 2389 Pro: 124/20% 324g/54% Fat: 69g/
26% (S:26% M:42% P:32%) Chol: 285mg
Sodium: 2065mg Potassium: 5391mg Fiber: 45g A:
988% C: 417% E: 165% B1: 125% B2: 146% B3:
118% B6: 139% B12: 181% Folic: 86% Panto:
80% Ca: 158% Fe: 109% P: 212% Mg: 116% Zn:
74% Cu: 108% Mn: 105% Se: 111% Cr: 118%

_____ Day Seven _____

When the weather's cold, try some hot fruit and toast:

BREAKFAST

Mulled Fresh Fruit with Hazelnuts
[Nuts and Seeds, p. 137]
2 slices whole wheat toast with
2 teaspoons margarine
An 8-ounce glass of orange juice

Soup, salad, and milk can be a nearly perfect nutritional combination:

LUNCH

Mixed green salad with 1 tablespoon
Tangy Cucumber Dressing
[Salad and Greens, p. 174]
Three-Bean Goulash Soup [Legumes, p. 118]
2 breadsticks
1 cup grapes
An 8-ounce glass of skim milk

When you bake garlic, it becomes as soft as butter:

Snack

Café Venezia's Baked Garlic [Garlic and
Onions, p. 194] on Italian bread

This evening meal will keep the chill off:

DINNER

Parsley, Sage, Rosemary, and Lamb
[Red Meat and Game, p. 242]
Comfort Potatoes [Roots, p. 104]
3/4 cup steamed brussels sprouts
Baked Apples Plus [Fruit, p. 296]

Cal: 1818 Pro: 92g/20% Carb: 266g/57%
Fat: 49g/23% (S:34% M:48% P:18%) Chol:
144mg Sodium: 2304mg Potassium: 4268mg
Fiber: 35g A: 209% C: 501% E: 83% B1: 115%
B2: 91% B3: 92% B6: 91% B12: 65% Folic: 117%
Panto: 44% Ca: 85% Fe: 93% P: 139% Mg: 91%
Zn: 75% Cu: 85% Mn: 62% Se: 79% Cr: 77%

For 2400 calories:

Breakfast: Add ¼ cup more Mulled
Fresh Fruit with Hazelnuts
Lunch: Add 2 more breadsticks
Snack: Add 1 more slice Café Venezia's
Baked Garlic on Italian bread and
an 8-ounce glass of skim milk

Cal: 2437 Pro: 113g/18% Carb: 356g/59%
Fat: 61g/23% (S:33% M:50% P:16%) Chol:
156mg Sodium: 3753mg Potassium: 5074mg
Fiber: 45g A: 229% C: 540% E: 88% B1: 140%
B2: 127% B3: 106% B6: 101% B12: 83% Folic:
127% Panto: 57% Ca: 130% P: 184% Fe: 105%
Mg: 100% Zn: 79% Cu: 93% Mn: 72% Se: 90%
Cr: 89%

That's our week. Some menus are more appropriate for April, some for November, but the basic principle remains the same: base the day on whole grains, with plenty of fresh fruits and vegetables, low-fat dairy foods, legumes, and small portions of fish, chicken, and lean red meats. If you average out the entire week, here's what it comes to on a daily basis:

Cal: 1808 Pro: 89g/19% Carb: 278g/59%
Fat: 45g/22% (S:30% M:43% P:27%) Chol:
153mg Sodium: 1829mg Potassium: 4382mg
Fiber: 36g A: 646% C: 493% E: 98 B1: 119%
B2: 124% B3: 126% B6: 115% B12: 100% Folic:
119% Panto: 55% Ca: 105% P: 154% Fe: 101%
Mg: 99% Zn: 67% Cu: 83% Se: 126% Mn: 92%
Cr: 102%

The entire week's menu gets only 22 percent of its calories from fat, well under the 30 percent limit. Saturated fat is only 30 percent of that, or about 6 percent of total calories—well under the 10 percent limit. Carbohydrates are 59 percent, a healthy amount, and protein a reasonable 19 percent. Cholesterol, at 153 milligrams, is well under the 300 milligrams limit. Sodium is about two-thirds of the upper limit. Potassium is high. Fiber is quite high. Levels of vitamins A and C are sky-high, which is natural when we eat more fruits and vegetables—and that, along with the fiber and the lack of fat, makes this an ideal candidate for a cancer-prevention diet. Meanwhile, just about

every other vitamin, mineral, and trace element is at or above 100 percent of the USRDA. Here's how it looks for 2400 calories:

Cal: 2426 Pro: 112g/18% Carb: 371g/60%
Fat: 60g/22% (S:28% M:43% P:29%) Chol:
188mg Sodium: 2673mg Potassium: 5422mg
Fiber: 43g A: 701% C: 568% E: 127%
B1: 150% B2: 161% B3: 155% B6: 138%
B12: 124% Folic: 139% Panto: 71% Ca: 144%
P: 206% Fe: 121% Mg: 124% Zn: 83% Cu: 101%
Se: 159% Cr: 119% Mn: 98%

That's even better. When it comes right down to it, there's no conflict between being well-nourished and avoiding those nutritional excesses that can lead to disease. The proof is in the eating!

Some More Balanced Menu Suggestions

BREAKFASTS AND BRUNCH

CONTINENTAL BREAKFAST

8-ounce glass grapefruit juice
Rice and Spice Muffins [Rice, p. 80]
2 tablespoons Yogurt Cream Cheese [Milk and
Yogurt, p. 278]
1 tablespoon No-Sugar Apple Grape Jam [Sugar
and Sweeteners, p. 309]

SUMMER BREAKFAST

½ sliced mango and 1 sliced kiwi
Two-Berry Yogurt Cooler [Beverages, p. 306]
1 toasted bagel with 2 teaspoons butter

SUNDAY BRUNCH

8-ounce glass orange juice
Fresh Fruit Omelet [Eggs, p. 269]
Cracked Wheat and Bran Bread [Wheat, p. 43]
Café au lait

COUNTRY BRUNCH

½ cup canteloupe and ½ cup strawberries
Corn and Banana Pancakes [Corn, p. 70] with
½ cup yogurt and 1 tablespoon maple syrup
Fresh Pork Sausage [Red Meat and Game, p. 242]

LUNCHES

ORIENTAL LUNCH BOX

Enoki and Cucumber Salad [Mushrooms, p. 146]
California Nori Rolls [Sea Vegetables, p. 184]
Pineapple in Gingered Plum Wine
[Ginger, p. 188]

SUMMERY ITALIAN TASTES

Cold Tomato, Buttermilk, and Basil Bisque
[Milk and Yogurt, p. 278]
Antipasto Green Salad with Artichoke Dressing
[Salad and Greens, p. 174]
Whole wheat Italian bread

KEEP COOL LUNCH

Iced Ginger Lemon Tea [Beverages, p. 314]
Chicken Salad with Fruits and Curry [Fruit, p. 296]
½ sliced tomato and ¼ sliced cucumber
Pita Bread

DOWNHOME LUNCH

Chili Con Carne [Legumes, p. 118]
½ cup rice or 4 soda crackers
Susan's Calico Coleslaw
[Cruciferous Vegetables, p. 164]
1 cup applesauce

SOUP AND SALAD LUNCH

Watercress-Mushroom Salad
[Cruciferous Vegetables, p. 164]
Gingered Squash and Millet Soup
[The "New" Grains, p. 91]
Whole wheat bread
1 cup grapes

FAMILY DINNERS

NOT FOR KIDS ONLY I

1 cup carrot, 1 cup celery, and
½ cup green bell pepper sticks
with Tofu-Spinach Dip [Soyfoods, p. 129]
1 slice Whole Wheat Pizza [Wheat, p. 43]
Chocolati [Milk and Yogurt, p. 278]

NOT FOR KIDS ONLY II

1 cup carrot, ½ cup celery, and
½ cup green bell pepper sticks
Spaghetti with Meat Sauce
[Red Meat and Game, p. 242]
Peach Tapioca [Milk and Yogurt, p. 278]

NOT FOR KIDS ONLY III

Mixed green salad
Autumn Beef Stew [Squash, p. 154]
1 slice whole wheat bread
Poached pears with raspberry yogurt

SUPPERS AND DINNERS

BISTRO-STYLE SUPPER

Kohlrabi-Beet Salad with Port and Walnuts
[Cruciferous Vegetables, p. 164]
Cassoulet-Style Beans [Legumes, p. 118]
Light Crème Brulée
[Sugars and Sweeteners, p. 306]

TRATTORIA-STYLE SUPPER

Steamed asparagus (or artichokes) with fresh
lemon juice and 1 tsp. olive oil
Italian Risotto with Shrimp [Rice, p. 80]
Espresso-Flavored Frozen Yogurt [Milk and
Yogurt, p. 278]

HIT-THE-SPOT CHINESE SUPPER

Shiitake Mushroom Soup with Tofu
[Mushrooms, p. 146]
Chinese Fried Rice [Rice, p. 80]
1 cup pineapple, melon, or grapes

SOUP FOR SUPPER

Minestrone [Legumes, p. 118] or Turnip-Corn
Soup [Cruciferous Vegetables, p. 164]
1 slice whole wheat bread
Baked Apple Plus [Fruit, p. 296]
or 1 cup fresh fruit

EASY FAMILY BARBECUE

Summer Garden Salad [Peppers, p. 204]
Barbecued Chicken [Fowl, p. 257]
1 medium corn on the cob
1 whole wheat roll
Watermelon

A WINTER SUPPER
OF OLD-FASHIONED FLAVORS

Hungarian Noodle Kugel [Pasta, p. 59]
Pot-Roasted Carrots and Parsnips [Roots, p. 104]
Pear-Applesauce [Fruit, p. 296]

MIDDLE EASTERN TASTES

Grilled Chicken with Yogurt Topping
[Fowl, p. 257]
Bulgur Pilaf [Wheat, p. 43]
Moroccan Carrot Salad [Roots, p. 104] (served
hot)
1 orange or 1 cup melon

VERY FAST VEGETARIAN MEAL

Pan-Fried Tofu and Noodle Dinner
[Soyfoods, p. 129]
1½ cups steamed broccoli
1 slice whole wheat bread

DINNER'S IN THE OVEN

Crudités and breadsticks
Baked Marinated Chicken [Fowl, p. 257]
Tian of Zucchini and Tomatoes [Squash, p. 154]
Rice
Apple-Wheat Bars [Wheat, p. 43]

◇ THE HEALTHY KITCHEN ◇

by Nao Hauser

The habits of healthy cooking are easy to acquire. They don't differ much from other modes of food preparation, nor do they take more time. They require only that cooks learn to trust that food can taste delicious without excess fat or salt.

There's no secret to building that trust. You need only slice open a ripe tomato, mince a green onion, bake a sweet potato, or poach a salmon steak to sniff the truth: The flavors within ingredients are wonderful and enticing all by themselves. They don't need a "safety net" of added fat and salt; indeed, too much of these obscures what's good.

Discovering the intrinsic tastes of foods is an age-old odyssey. Yet each cook who repeats it feels anew the triumph and joy. And nowadays, though most of us do not live on farms, there's much to celebrate, for the harvests of all regions are available in our markets. The result is that you can appreciate not just rice but ten kinds of rice, not just carrots but carrots nurtured in dozens of different soils.

So the first step to healthy cooking is becoming a food connoisseur. All the rest stems from that. The basic techniques are those that highlight intrinsic flavors. The most useful utensils are those that help you to both exploit and protect flavor elements. There are many nuances of seasoning to learn and many ways to organize meals to save time. But that's true of all cooking. The main difference in healthy cooking is that you aim to consume less fat and salt.

The Cooking Context

The major difference you can make in fat consumption comes from what you eat rather than how you cook it. Grains and produce should provide at least half the calories of most meals, so a cook's priorities lie in making the most of these. It can be as simple a matter as serving a big baked potato and a little piece of steak, or making a sandwich with one ounce of cheese rather than two, or treating stir-fried seafood as the topping for a bowl of rice. All this is just the arithmetic of good nutrition, and it's more a question of custom than method.

The techniques of healthy cooking address the same issue but from the opposite direction: How do you prepare low-fat foods without adding so much fat that you upset the mealtime balance? It's one thing to eat more bread and broccoli, and quite another to leave off the butter. Well, you don't have to omit the butter—at least, not entirely.

The first and most obvious way to minimize fat is to use minimal amounts of it. Measure it out and you'll find that a teaspoon of butter provides a lot of flavor. Keep measuring and you'll also discover that a teaspoon or two of oil in a skillet is almost always enough to prevent sticking or scorching, especially if used with a non-stick pan or vegetable-oil cooking spray. Less should suffice when it comes to salt, too; if you are accustomed to waving the shaker, measure out ⅛ to

¼ teaspoon for every four servings until you can judge just by looking. What experience will teach you is that if you need more fat or salt for flavor it's because something else is missing from the dish.

Intrinsic Flavors and Basic Techniques

Low-fat cooking uses certain flavor-enhancing techniques, none of them new. You can find them detailed in standard cookbooks; indeed, some of them restore to prominence the frugal—and thus low-fat—customs of peasant cooks. For example, you're more apt to steam fish than fry it, and more likely to sauce the catch with fresh vegetables than with hollandaise. The only aspect that is truly modern is our access to certain appliances that can make low-fat preparations as fast and easy as those that rely on the use of fat. What follows are the basic cooking methods and, when applicable, the equipment that can prove helpful.

RELEASING JUICES

Cutting is perhaps the most important technique in low-fat cooking. Just by cutting up fresh vegetables, fruits, and herbs, you release juices that tantalize—and thus compensate for the flavoring power of butter, oil, or salt. Press a clove of garlic, chop an onion, or mince a bunch of parsley, and the fragrance fills the air; leave these ingredients uncut, and their presence is much subtler. The power of cutting can also be seen when you choose to mince an onion rather than slice it thick, or purée a tomato instead of chopping it; the more you cut the more juices you release, and the stronger the fragrance and taste will be. Compare, for example, two salads made of the same ingredients. For the low-fat version, combine very, very thinly sliced purple or green onion, diced tomato and cucumber, lettuce torn into bite-size pieces, and lots of minced parsley in a salad bowl. Contrast this mixture with an arrangement of whole lettuce leaves, tomato wedges, thick slices of onion and cucumber, and parsley sprigs. The first salad will have a strong, fresh "bouquet" and enough moisture to minimize the need for a dressing; the second will be less fragrant and much drier.

How much you cut will depend, of course, on how much juice you want to release. You can always control the balance of flavors and textures within a dish by cutting smaller those ingredients that you want to play a more aromatic role and leaving larger the ingredients that will contribute unique texture. In the context of the salad example above, this might mean mincing the green onion and parsley and sprinkling them over thick slices of tomato and cucumber for a combination that would feature the pungency of the onion and herb but also the meatiness of the tomato and the cucumber's crunch. The seasoning principle remains constant, but the opportunities to vary proportions guarantee infinite possible tastes.

The importance of cutting underscores the need for good hand tools: chef's and paring knives (not just well wrought but comfortable for you to handle); graters in various sizes, whether individual or combined in the "box grater" style; a sturdy garlic press; and implements designed for citrus, specifically a small juicer and a zester. For many cooks, an electric food chopper or a mini–food processor can prove invaluable as an everyday alternative to a knife for mincing a small bunch of herbs or a couple of onions. You can use a standard-size food processor for these tasks too, but the smaller choppers are generally easier to clean and thus more conducive to routine use with small quantities of food. A standard-size food processor makes fast work of other essential cutting tasks, chopping large quantities of produce as well as meats, poultry, and fish, and puréeing raw and cooked produce and quickly shredding big batches of vegetables. A strong blender can produce a smoother purée than a food processor but it won't work without sufficient liquid; so a blender might be the better appliance to use for a soup, salad dressing, or beverage based on a purée of fresh produce, but it won't do the job with plain cooked carrots or fresh pineapple, for example, unless you can add some liquid without thinning the purée too much.

SWEATING ONIONS

As the term suggests, sweating is another way to get vegetables to release juices. It means cooking the ingredients slowly until they are wilted but not browned. The low-fat version of the method differs from that of classic French cooking in that little or no fat is used; so you have to cover the pan to prevent sticking, and the process becomes a form of steaming. It can be applied to any firm vegetable that will taste sweeter when gently heated, such as chopped celery or carrots, but its primary use is with onions, which become so sweet when wilted that they can substitute for the mellowing effect of butter or oil. It takes about 30 minutes of slow cooking to elicit this sweetness from two chopped onions, and you'll often find that you have to add some liquid—water, stock, wine, or fruit juice will work fine, depending on compatibility with the rest of the dish— after about 15 minutes to prevent sticking. Technically, the method approaches braising once you add the liquid, but that's just a matter of semantics. What's important is that the onions cook over low to medium heat until thoroughly wilted. Stir as needed to prevent sticking. The test of doneness is fragrance—the onions should smell not pungent but sweet.

Any covered pot or pan can be used to sweat onions, but one that's thick-bottomed will hold heat more evenly. If your pan is thin, you'll probably have to stir more often or use more liquid to prevent sticking. To sweat a pound of onions in the microwave oven, cook them covered with plastic wrap at medium-high, stirring occasionally, until they meet the fragrance test—about 15 minutes, or less if you use full power and stir more often.

PAN-STEAMING

Used less often than sweating, but worth mentioning as its next of kin, pan-steaming is an easy way to prepare foods that will cook quickly in their own moisture. It yields fine results with spinach, for example: Just put the spinach and any water that clings from washing in a covered pot; cook over medium heat until wilted but still bright green. Shellfish and thin pieces of fish offer an-

other application: Arrange them on a layer of chopped tomatoes or other very moist (and preferably herb-seasoned) vegetable and cook tightly covered until done. No fat is needed, and all the tempting juices are retained. The technique translates especially well to microwave cooking: Cover the dish with plastic wrap and microwave at full power until done. The speed and moist heat of microwave cooking broaden the range of dishes that can be prepared this way; boneless chicken breast and fish, with or without vegetables and herbs, come out quite delicious.

STEAMING

Conventional steaming—cooking food in the steam that rises from a simmering liquid— protects the juices of all lean foods. It works beautifully with green vegetables, chicken, and fish, because steam conducts heat so uniformly in an enclosed space that it minimizes the danger of overcooking parts of these delicate foods before the rest is done. For maximum control over timing, bring the water to a simmer before you place food over it and be sure the pot lid fits tightly.

Pots designed for steaming come with basket inserts to hold the food. These are valuable for large quantities, and the more so because the pot without the insert can be used for stocks, soups, and boiling pasta. But a Chinese bamboo steamer that fits into a wok, or a collapsible steamer basket, will do the same job in a covered pot. When you want to steam an item that won't fit into any steamer you have, you can always improvise an arrangement by balancing a baking rack over the water on emptied flat cans (with top and bottom removed) or even small custard cups. The domed lids of electric fry pans make them excellent for steaming when fitted with a basket or rack. The fastest and easiest way to steam foods is to microwave them in a plastic microwave steamer; there's no need to presimmer the water and the steam ensures even cooking without frequent stirring.

BRAISING

The rich flavors of braised foods come from the mingling of the natural juices of ingredients with a robust cooking liquid—usually a stock or broth. The food, partially submerged in liquid, cooks slowly. This technique, unlike steaming, is not meant for delicate ingredients such as broccoli or chicken breast, which cook best when they cook fast, but for those, such as pot roasts and some of the sturdier vegetables, that benefit from a process slow enough to break down fibers and allow some of the cooking liquid to be absorbed. Conventional braising often begins with searing the ingredients in fat to enhance flavor. You can always omit this step and count on the flavoring power of a bed of sweated onions and/or a good stock or broth instead.

Potatoes, carrots, cabbage, brussels sprouts, and other vegetables that take well to braising can be cooked on top of the stove in a pan with a tight-fitting lid: Bring the vegetables and stock to a simmer, cover, reduce heat, and cook over medium-low to medium heat until done. Start with enough stock to submerge the vegetables about halfway; then remove the vegetables to a serving dish with a slotted spoon and boil the stock until it is reduced to a syrupy, saucelike consistency. Sprinkle the vegetable with chopped parsley, dill, or other seasoning and toss with the reduced stock.

Meats braise better in a slow to moderate oven in a very heavy dutch oven; the heat of the pot will brown the meat and caramelize juices, making pre-searing unnecessary. A cast-iron pot with a lid is worth owning just for this, because it will retain the juices and hold the heat best. Clay pots do a fine job of steam-braising, especially with chicken and meat stews, in both conventional and microwave ovens.

To braise vegetables you must have a good stock or broth, but with stews and pot-roasted meats you can hedge a little, using red wine with beef or orange juice with pork, for example, because the meat cooks to a large extent in its own juices. Since this is the case, it's worth seasoning the meat well by tossing small pieces with a spice mixture, or rubbing a roast with a paste of mustard or horseradish and herbs, and/or marinating it. Braised meats, more than any other food, benefit from being cooked ahead and reheated, because they will absorb more of the pot liquid as they stand.

POACHING

Like braising, poaching involves simmering food in a liquid. Technically, the methods differ in how much liquid is used and its temperature when the food is added; also, poaching doesn't require the bed of sweated vegetables often called for with braised meats and poultry. But the practical distinction is this: Poaching is used much more often than braising to ensure moist results with lean fish and poultry. Shallow poaching is like braising in that the food is not completely submerged in liquid, but it differs in that the liquid is heated before the food is added; the heat seals in the juices of thin pieces of fish and chicken, the foods most often prepared this way. Deep poaching, where the food is completely submerged, is commonly reserved for whole fish, though some connoisseurs swear by the results with whole chicken and turkey and even red meat. As with braising, the liquid plays a seasoning role, and therefore its quality counts.

For shallow poaching, use fish or chicken stock, either straight or diluted with wine or water; it can be reduced, after the food has been removed, to serve as a complementary sauce. Court-bouillon, a seasoned mixture of wine and water, is often favored for whole fish, because it is simple to prepare in whatever quantity you need and helps to firm the fish with its acidity. (For the basics of making a court-bouillon, see the recipe for poached salmon, page 227.) Strain and freeze court-bouillon for re-use and it will feature the flavor bonus of juices from the fish it poached previously; for safety's sake, be sure to heat it to boiling after defrosting.

Whenever you're using wine for poaching, whether alone—and it can work well if it's a good wine—or in combination, be sure to pre-simmer the liquid long enough to cook off most of the alcohol, which can overwhelm the tastes of delicate fish and chicken. The logistics of submerging and retrieving a whole fish call for a fish poacher, which is long, deep, and fitted with a rack. All other poaching can be done in any covered pot or pan wide and deep enough to hold the food; tie a whole chicken or turkey in several places with kitchen twine to facilitate lowering it into the liquid and lifting it out with cooking forks.

At dessert time, poaching takes preeminence with pears, which hold their shape despite the simmering and are flattered by the seasoned liquid (you'll find several recipes detailing methods in this book), but it can also yield luscious figs, plums, apples, and peaches.

SIMMERING

Steaming, braising, and poaching are low-fat alternatives to other modes of cooking. Simmering, by contrast, is an established way to cook some old-fashioned staples that never did and never will require much fat. Ranging from stocks and soups to beans and spaghetti sauce, these are the economical foods that depend largely on a liquid being maintained at a temperature lower than boiling until it has done its work—which may be extracting flavor from ingredients, softening them, or both. Because all foods prepared this way can be refrigerated and reheated with no loss of flavor, you can wait for the fat from meats and bones to solidify on the surface for easy removal.

With simmered foods, the pot—and it can be any pot—does all the work after it's been filled. You can put a lid on to prevent or slow evaporation, but the rest is just a matter of letting time pass. A heat diffuser—a metal plate designed to fit over a stove burner, and often labeled a "Flame Tamer"—can be very helpful; it will ensure that the liquid doesn't get so hot that it boils even in a lightweight pot. If you want to make the time pass a lot faster, use a pressure cooker, which works exceptionally well to extract flavor from meat bones for stocks and soups. Either a pressure cooker or a microwave oven will considerably reduce bean cooking time without diminishing results.

BOILING

A few foods—notably green beans, beets, and pasta—seem to be flattered by fast cooking in a lot of water. All that's required is a pot large enough to ensure that there is plenty of water circulating around the food. There may be no point in watching the pot, as the old saying goes, but there's every reason to watch the food, because the intense heat means that only a minute or two need elapse between perfectly cooked and overdone. Because retained heat will cause the food to continue to cook, green beans, pasta, and other delicate items should be drained and served immediately.

SEARING

Healthy cooking tends to emphasize moist-heat methods because these prevent naturally lean foods from drying out. But there's no need to eschew fattier, tender cuts of beef, pork, and lamb. Small amounts of these can add flavor out of proportion to their size, as well as concentrated nutrients, to grain and vegetable dishes. Cut the meat into thin strips; small pieces will go much farther tastewise than large ones. Then turn to the classic technique called searing to cook the meat very fast without adding fat. To sear, heat a heavy skillet over high heat; add the meat, one-fourth to one-third pound at a time, and cook until browned on both sides—about 1 to 2 minutes per side, depending on whether you want it cooked through. The meat is properly seared at the point when the fat has melted and the meat no longer sticks to the pan, but hasn't begun to throw off juices, which indicates that the fibers are shrinking and toughening. After the meat has been seared and removed, pour about 1/3 cup of wine, broth, or juice into the pan and scrape the bottom to deglaze any little bits that stick; stir this savory liquid with the meat into whatever dish you're making.

A cast-iron skillet makes it easy to sear meat without scorching or sticking. The reason lies primarily in the metal, which holds intense heat evenly, but also in the fact that the seasoning (or very fine coating of oil) that cast iron acquires with use helps to prevent sticking, just as it helps prevent rusting.

STIR-FRYING

Strips or cubes of boneless chicken, shellfish, and chopped or thin-sliced vegetables need to be treated more gently than red meats. Searing would toughen or scorch them at once. But if you use a slightly lower temperature—about medium-high—and just a bit of oil, you can cook them very fast without much fat. Frequent stirring is essential to prevent overheating the fragile ingredients; thus the term "stir-frying." Be aware, however, that to avoid using the quantities of cooking oil called for in traditional Chinese stir-frying, it is often necessary to add some liquid at the end and to cover the pan, so that the partially stir-fried food actually finishes cooking in steam.

You can stir-fry in any skillet or wok. If you coat the pan with cooking spray, you'll rarely need more than two teaspoons of oil to stir-fry a pound of cut-up ingredients.

BROILING AND GRILLING

The key to broiling and grilling in low-fat cooking lies in protecting the food from the direct heat, so that it doesn't dry out and require unwanted fat. There are many ways to do this, and perhaps the most important is to follow the rule of all broiling and grilling: keep the food far enough from the broiler's heating element, and be sure that a grill fire is tame enough, to prevent the outside from burning before the inside is done. The proper distance will depend on the thickness of the food—generally, the thicker the piece the farther it should be. All lean foods will still need some insulation. The skin can play this role with chicken and whole fish; remove it after cooking to reduce fat intake. Brush fish steaks and fillets and vegetables with a very thin coating of oil (about ⅛ teaspoon per fish steak) or a low-fat basting sauce or marinade. Vinaigrette salad dressings work well for both marinating and basting, but so do mixtures based on nonfat yogurt and fruit and vegetable juices. Indeed, marinating can be doubly recommended for all low-fat dry-heat cooking, since it not only protects lean foods by adding moisture but also more than compensates for the flavoring attributes of butter and oils.

ROASTING/BAKING

Foods that come with some natural protection can be roasted (or baked—the process is the same; the difference is that the different words are commonly used with different foods) without added fat. These include fatty meats, poultry, and fish—such as beef rib roast, duck, and whole mackerel—and vegetables and fruits with sturdy skins or rinds—such as Idaho potatoes, winter squash, eggplant, and apples. In conventional cooking, foods with less natural protection are brushed and basted with fat to seal the surfaces and prevent juices from evaporating. The way to get around this in low-fat cooking is to add some liquid to the pan.

Technically, the use of liquid violates the aim of roasting, which relies on dry heat to keep food surfaces firm and even crisp. But in truth, the hybrid technique of roasting with some liquid, which might be called steam-roasting, well suits the hybrid nature of many foods. Chicken and turkey, for example, have enough fat in the skin to come out of the oven looking browned and tempting, but the lean breast meat is not best served by the prolonged exposure to dry heat. A similar situation arises with large roasts of pork, veal, and sometimes leg of lamb, depending on desired degree of doneness; there is enough fat on the meat to make the roasted surface irresistible, but the meat can become dry if roasted throughout. A compromise that produces excellent results with chicken is to pour about ¼ cup of chicken stock or broth over the bird before you put it in the oven; then baste it with an additional ¼ cup of stock and the resulting pan juices every 10 to 15 minutes. The chicken will have a nicely browned skin and the pan juices can be skimmed of fat and served as is or further reduced with seasonings on top of the stove to make a delicious sauce. Turkeys and other large roasts benefit from being "oven steamed" with about an inch of liquid in a covered pan for the first half of the cooking time. Remove the lid, pour off the liquid into a saucepan to reduce and season on top of the stove, and elevate the meat on a rack, if you wish, to finish roasting.

The bonus of pan juices recommends these procedures as much as the moistness of the meat. The better the liquid you start with, the better the juices will be. If you don't have chicken stock or broth to use with poultry, put a layer of thinly sliced onions in the bottom of the pan and use water or a combination of water and wine, sherry, or juice; the juice from the onions will season the water. Red meats always benefit from being rubbed with a seasoning paste, and leg of lamb takes well to several days of marinating in wine. The stronger the flavor of the meat, the more varied the roasting liquid options. Stick to veal stock and/or a good white wine with loin and leg cuts of veal, for example, but feel free, with pork, to try citrus juice, beer, or port wine with water. After you have poured off the pan juices, spoon off as much fat as you can (or use a handy fat separator), simmer until reduced to desired flavor strength, and season with a splash of sherry (good with poultry) or brandy and chopped fresh herbs. The resulting low-fat meat moistener will compare well with any fancier sauce. If you end up with more pan juice than you need for serving with the meat, refrigerate it, remove the fat, freeze if desired, and use it to cook grains, vegetables, or another roast.

DOUGH-MAKING

Yeast breads and pasta are prepared exactly the same way in low-fat cooking as they are conventionally, so there's no need for any technical discussion here. But the cooking context warrants a reminder that not a few connoisseurs cherish a loaf of bread fresh from the oven more than a rich pastry, and that a plate of homemade pasta is a special treat at any table. So you might want to prepare these foods often. Some cooks wouldn't miss the tactile satisfaction of mixing and kneading doughs by hand; others would gladly trade it for the speed and ease of using a food processor or an electric mixer fitted with a dough hook. If you want to bake a lot of bread, it's worth owning a large-capacity machine, because extra loaves freeze well. Although pasta-makers will bicker endlessly over the relative merits of hand-rolled versus hand-cranked versus machine-extruded noodles, the fact is that any freshly made noodle tastes delicious. So when you're comparing methods and costs, you might want to opt simply for the equipment you can afford that will make things most convenient. You can always vary the fare by hand-rolling one night and pushing a button the next.

GARNISHING

Vegetable garnishes are an intrinsic part of the classic French repertoire, which advises not only which embellishments to use but also how to cut them—julienne, batons, dice, or whatever—to best complement the main ingredient. Low-fat and low-sodium cooking takes the approach further, relying on garnishes not only for color and textural contrast but also for juices that will moisten and season the food. In principle, this brings the discussion right back to the importance of cutting to release juices. In practice, low-fat cooking provokes the imagination, bringing into play another critical dimension of, say, the chopped tomato or red pepper you might use to brighten a portion of chicken. Both vegetables are red, but the tomato will add a tangy note, the pepper a sweet one. You can choose either one—or use both the sweet and sour garnishes with some chopped fresh parsley or basil, for a touch of bitterness, and translate the garnish into a satisfying "sauce." The infinite taste possibilities are the joy of healthy cooking; you'll find more ways to exploit them in the section on Seasonings, page 34.

A Perspective on Ingredients

The quality of the ingredients is integral to the success of low-fat cooking. The same could be said of all cooking, except that fat is a potent flavor enhancer. Without it, it's somewhat harder to make an out-of-season vegetable or a piece of less-than-perfectly-moist fish taste palatable.

We are fortunate to have year-round access to excellent fresh ingredients, but a cook must be versatile. You have to be ready to prepare the root vegetables of autumn no less than the leafy greens of spring, winter's long-simmered soups and stews as well as summer's fast barbecues. You should get to know your local fish, whether it's Great Lakes walleye, farm-raised catfish, the varieties of Gulf snapper, or the family of Atlantic cod; the closer the catch, the fresher and cheaper it's likely to be. If at all possible—and it usually is—find a farmer's market or butcher shop that sells locally raised poultry. Take advantage of a sunny window to stretch the harvest season for a pot of basil and other herbs that grow easily.

Yet be assured that the staples of low-fat cooking fill supermarket shelves. These include not only grains, dried beans, flours, and pasta, but also the foods well-preserved by freezing, such as turkey, some seafood, and vegetables that retain significant percentages of nutrients despite processing—notably vitamin A–rich squash and leafy greens, and starchy peas, lima beans, and corn. When time is of the essence, there's no reason not to trade freshest taste for the convenience of using prechopped garlic or garlic paste, frozen onions, frozen bread dough, frozen carrots, or any of the other readily available low-fat, low-sodium products. You may forfeit some flavor but you almost always gain nutritionally by cooking at home instead of turning to restaurant fast food.

HEALTHY SUBSTITUTIONS

In the vast majority of cooking situations you can substitute reduced-fat and low-sodium products for their commercial kin without damaging flavor or texture. So the routine use of skim milk, nonfat yogurt, and items processed without salt simply adds up to cooking wisdom. The exceptions to this rule are usually self-evident: low-fat milk, instead of skim, will provide more attractive color in white foods, such as mashed potatoes; a couple of tablespoons of whole-milk yogurt can provide the creaminess one might crave in a potato salad. It would be silly to impose austerity in such situations, when the truer goal is lifetime habits of reduced fat consumption.

Another direct way to reduce fat is to substitute two egg whites for a whole egg whenever the eggs serve to bind or leaven rather than enrich. But here again the emphasis is on reduction rather than elimination, since eggs also provide desirable flavor in some recipes; for more precise guidelines, see the Eggs chapter. Less direct, but quite easy to master, is the routine substitution of cooking spray for part or all of the oil needed to lubricate a skillet or baking pans. If you object to the spray, you can effect a similar economy of fat

by rubbing oil lightly over the pan surface with a paper towel or waxed paper instead of pouring it in. Non-stick pans work well too, although they almost always require a small amount of fat to prevent all but high-moisture and high-fat foods from toughening and batters and starches from sticking.

FLAVOR ENHANCERS

The most often used flavoring agents of healthy cooking differ not in kind but only in quantity from those of conventional cooking. However, the amounts used—much less of some ingredients and more of others—do call for certain choices in the buying and preparation of these staples.

Fats

When you avoid using large quantities of fat, the fat itself becomes all the more precious for the flavor it can impart. If you're only going to use a teaspoon of fat to sauté a chicken breast, for example, it makes sense to choose butter or a fruity olive oil or whatever tastes best to you. Neither the cholesterol in the butter nor the nutritional benefits of the olive oil will add up to much in this context, but the intense flavor of either will go a long way. Apply this principle when you're shopping by choosing French walnut and hazelnut oil and Chinese-style sesame oil, rather than the American versions, which tend to be too bland to offer much taste. Olive oils vary greatly in flavor according to both region of origin and brand; it's worth sampling the exquisite (and expensive) extra virgin oils of Tuscany, the more robust oils of southern Italy and France, and the diverse products of Spain and Greece just to see what's available (and at what price). You may want to keep at least two kinds of olive oil on hand: one distinctly fruity for salads and Mediterranean-style dishes, and another, more neutral-tasting, for general cooking purposes. Refrigerate nut and olive oils to keep them from turning rancid before you use them up; olive oil will solidify in the refrigerator but melt again at room temperature.

When you are using fat just to lubricate a pan and you don't want any flavor interference, or when you want to subdue some of the intensity of a nut or olive oil, choose a vegetable oil high in monounsaturated fat, such as canola (rapeseed) or soybean. These oils are of uniformly good quality and keep well at room temperature.

Acids

Because the acidic elements in foods cook off quickly, their absence is often noticeable—but not always identified as such. When you learn to make the connection between a bland, flat-tasting food and the need to add some acid you can save yourself from a lot of salt. Try adding some fresh lemon or lime juice to a soup or stew—the foods most likely to "need something," because they cook longest—and you'll taste the difference between a dish that begs for a lot of salt and one flattered by a little or none.

Moreover, the variety of acidic ingredients yields a vast territory for flavor exploration. Here's an abbreviated sampler, with just a few of the foods each complements:

♦ lemon juice and/or zest (the colored part of the rind): green vegetables, rice, cracked wheat, chicken, shellfish, veal, lamb

♦ lime juice: fish, turkey, avocados, melon, sweet potatoes, black beans, corn, pork

♦ orange juice and/or zest: brown rice, buckwheat, sweet potatoes, tomato sauce, pork, duck

♦ chopped tomatoes: salads, fish, shellfish, chicken, white beans, lima beans, eggplant, zucchini, pasta, egg dishes

♦ red and white wine vinegars: soups, stews, chicken, fatty fish

♦ balsamic vinegar (rich flavor, slightly sweet): salads, roasted peppers, fruits, grilled foods

♦ sherry vinegar: salads, pork, soups

♦ rice wine vinegar (milder than most other vinegars): marinated salads, stir-fried dishes, brown rice, fatty fish

♦ malt vinegar (rich, mild): beans, meats, potatoes, barley

♦ cider vinegar: salads, chicken, pork, corn, onions, cabbage

♦ fruit-flavored vinegars: chicken, salads

♦ yogurt (plain and citrus flavors): white and sweet potatoes, brown rice, winter squash, chicken, pasta

♦ prepared mustard (made with vinegar or white wine): chicken, meats, beans, soups, stews

In addition, many of the acids provide especially nice flavors when combined. You can mix orange, lemon, and lime juices, for example, to create a spectrum of subtly sweet and sour tastes for marinating and basting fish and shellfish. Sherry vinegar and mustard have an affinity that shows up well in soups of beans and greens. Tomatoes and orange juice and zest, mildly acidic and also somewhat sweet, tend to underscore one another, as do fruit vinegars and citrus juice.

Some tips on using acids: The taste of citrus zest is not only stronger than that of the juice but also cooks off more slowly, so use the zest judiciously. The finest vinegars—balsamic, Spanish sherry, malt, and fruit especially—add more than just an acid note, so it's often worth adding some at the beginning of the cooking time for fundamental flavor and then a bit more toward the finish. But generally speaking, acids are used to fine-tune flavor toward the end of cooking time. Add them to taste, and if you add a little too much, be assured that the excess will cook off fast. Do add additional acid when you reheat soups, grains, and anything else that reheats well—it will make all the difference between fresh and "leftover" flavor.

Bittering Agents

When a dish "needs something," the element other than acid it's most likely to need is a bittering agent. Herbs and spices are the most important of these, and you'll find extended discussion of their uses in the Seasonings section. Other good sources, easy to keep on hand, are fortified wines, such as sherry, vermouth, Marsala, and Port, and brandies of all sorts. Use these sparingly and cook them long enough to burn off most of the alcohol; they will contribute ineffable depth of flavor—a little bitter, a little sweet, and "a little something" that comes of their careful formulation. (Some alcohol remains in most dishes; see Cooking with Alcohol in the Beverages chapter, p. 319.)

Sweeteners

The use of sweeteners in desserts is discussed in Sugars and Sweeteners, but it's worth remembering that the sensation of sweetness also enhances savory dishes. In conventional cooking, the sweetness comes routinely from butter, cream or olive oil. When you're not using much of these, you may have to think about other sources that will balance the flavors of a dish. Sweated onions, orange juice, and fortified wines all contribute some sweetness along with other elements of taste. When seasonings need a quick adjustment toward the end of cooking time, a little bit of Port wine, apricot or pear nectar, apple or raspberry juice, or Worcestershire sauce, depending on the other ingredients, can be just what the taste buds desire.

Salt

And when all else is balanced—sweet, sour, and bitter—there may still be a need for salt. Foods that have some natural sodium, such as fish, meats, and many vegetables, shouldn't require much; low-sodium grains often need more. Add a little just before serving or at the table, because the food will taste saltier if the salt is on the surface. Another way to make a little salt go a long way is to add it in the form of grated Parmesan cheese or chopped olives—ingredients that have enough fat to hold the salt sensation in the mouth. Or use reduced-sodium soy sauce, which also tastes more intense than straight salt.

COOKING LIQUIDS

The emphasis on moist-heat methods in low-fat cooking eventually turns a cook's attention to the flavoring potential of liquids. In braising, poaching, and simmering, the liquid can serve as seasoning and sauce, as well as mere heat conductor. These are some of the alternatives to plain water:

Wine

If you like a wine in the glass, you'll like it in the pot as well. The major difference is that the alcohol will prove too harsh in large quantities; so be sure to evaporate it by pre-simmering the wine or cooking it a long time with the food. Wine, diluted with water or fish stock, is especially effective for poaching fish, not only because the tastes combine well but also because the acidity helps to keep the fish firm; use white wine for low-fat, delicate species, but do try light red wines with moderately fat and more assertively flavored fish, such as salmon. Acidity and alcohol also make wine a wonderful marinade for meats; refrigerate smaller pieces overnight, large roasts up to several days, turning daily. Use the marinade to braise the meat or in the bottom of the roasting pan, or pour it into a saucepan on top of the stove and boil it to cook off the alcohol and concentrate flavor. Wine is too austere to serve as a sauce by itself, but given a chance to mingle with meat juices, stock, or fruit juice, sweated onions, or fresh or dried fruit, it becomes suitably enriched.

Fruit and Vegetable Juices

There is a fascinating range of flavors in the cans and jars of supermarket juice shelves, and they couldn't be more convenient to use. Old-fashioned applications that deserve to remain in style include apple juice or cider to braise pork, tomato juice with beef pot roast or baked rice, and orange juice with steamed rice or simmered sweet potatoes. New-fashioned uses have turned many a chef's attention to juice extractors and other means of obtaining such flavorings as carrot, onion, and even asparagus juice to accent meats, poultry, and fish. But you don't have to be that daring. It's enough to see what apricot nectar, diluted with water or wine, can do for spiced beef or baked chicken, or how vegetable juice seems to perk up meat loaf or bean soup.

Quick Extractions

Every really good cook is a food conservator, tossing out nothing that might provide an extra fillip of flavor. This means that the water used to soak dried mushrooms, for example, gets strained and tossed into the pot. The juices collected from roasted peppers may become the seasoning for a sauce or salad dressing (if they're not too bitter).

And, perhaps most important, every spare meat bone and scrap becomes the source of a savory liquid—and not necessarily a long-simmered stock. There are several ways to make the most of stray pieces. One is to brown scraps and small bones in a cast-iron or other heavy skillet and then add wine or water to deglaze the pan; strain the liquid and use for a braise or soup. Another is to brown the scraps and bones trimmed from a roast prior to cooking in a roasting pan and then add about an inch of wine or water to the pan; set the roast on a rack over the scraps and liquid, strain the pan liquid at the end of roasting time, skim, and reduce it to make a sauce. A third way is simply to bury the scraps and bones, browned or not, in a long-simmering pot of beans or soup. None of these procedures will yield a liquid as rich as a stock, but you will reap a flavor—and often a nutritional—bonus with little time investment.

Stocks and Broths

Simmer bones in water long enough to extract their treasury of protein and minerals, and the resulting liquid is a stock. Simmer meat, poultry, fish, or vegetables in either water or a previously made stock, and the extraction is called a broth. A fish stock made with some wine and some sweated vegetables is usually called a fumet, indicating a liquid more fragrant than plain fish stock. There are many arguments regarding the nomenclature and best procedures for all of these, but the fact remains that any slow extraction of flavor yields an extremely useful liquid. Moreover, a good stock needs no salt, and a concentrated meat, poultry, or fish stock will thicken to sauce consistency and taste luxurious without added fat. Stocks and broth are also convenience foods; they can be frozen for months and pulled out on short notice to give soups and stews a big headstart or turn roasts, sautés, and broiled foods into elegantly sauced fare. And not least important in healthy cooking, the substitution of a stock or broth for water makes grains and braised or baked vegetables irresistibly delicious.

There are commercially made salt-free stocks and broths, but they are not always available and they rarely provide the flavor and body of home-made products. If you are using a regular commercial broth, dilute it with water by about half to reduce the saltiness. But a better compromise is to make your own without worrying about whether it's the best possible stock. It simply doesn't take much effort to throw some purchased soup bones or carcasses from roast chickens into a pot with water to cover and simmer until the water has taken on some flavor; it will have more flavor if you brown meat bones first and add onions, carrots, celery, and parsley, but there's no need to turn stock-making into a ritual. You need a rich stock to make a classic French sauce, but a weaker stock will work fine with grains, beans, and thick soups. Homemade stocks are also much cheaper than high-quality canned products—no small consideration when you're routinely preparing rice, kasha, and other foods that soak up liquid. For some basic stock and broth recipes, see page 27.

Vegetable broth is the easiest to keep on hand, since the ingredients are readily available and they don't have to be simmered nearly as long as meat or chicken bones to extract fullest flavor; moreover this broth is all-purpose—excellent with grains and in vegetable soups but also good for braising meats or mixing one to one with commercial chicken broth to baste a bird. Fish stock or fumet is necessarily cooked quickly because the flavor becomes too strong if the bones are simmered too long. With poultry and meat stocks, the timing depends on the aim of the cook and the specific ingredients: If you simmer bones a long, long time, you'll get a very gelatinous stock that will taste "salty" from the dissolved minerals. If you use more meat than bones you'll get a very flavorful liquid faster. The smaller the pieces of meat or bones, the faster the extraction; thus, you can make a very fast broth from lean ground beef. A stock pot needn't be watched; a layer of curly parsley laid over the top will act as a mesh to trap impurities, so that you don't have to skim, and a heat diffuser will ensure that a very slow simmer is maintained. The recipes provided here outline various options, including one fast and one slow chicken stock. Choose according to your own criteria of economy in the use of time and ingredients, and don't be afraid to effect your own compromises with more or less meat and appropriate adjustments in timing.

Time Economies

All the talk of such techniques as simmering, braising, and stock-making can easily frighten time-pressed cooks, but it shouldn't. Just remember that anything that cooks in liquid a long time will reheat well if made in advance—and this category includes not only soups and stews but also beans and grains. A microwave oven is especially useful for reheating because almost no moisture is lost in the process; if you are reheating on top of the stove, add more liquid—and proportionate seasonings, including an acid—as needed.

Other groups of foods that can almost always be prepared at your scheduling convenience are low-fat salad dressings, desserts, and breads. It's well worth keeping the first two on hand, so that you don't reach for high-fat commercial products instead. With low-fat yeast breads, it doesn't matter nutritionally whether the product is purchased or homemade; either way, an extra loaf or two in the freezer can be called on to balance a meal when there's no time to prepare a grain in another form.

The wisdom of serving smaller meat portions implies another way to save time. Roast or braise a large piece of meat or poultry one day; then use the leftovers in casseroles and stir-fries on other occasions. The cooked meat enables you to skip a step in many recipes, and there will be little, if any, flavor loss, especially if you can save some of the pan juices to reheat with the meat. The extra meat can be cut up and frozen in convenient-size packets, so that it needn't be served on consecutive days.

The emphasis on increased carbohydrates and reduced fat consumption suggests also a more radical way of streamlining preparations, and that is to simplify meals. If you have only enough time to prepare two dishes for dinner—as is commonly the case with busy cooks—then plan to serve rice and steamed vegetables, or a salad, poached fish, and bread, or yesterday's lentils with today's baked potato and some chopped raw vegetables. Remember that you don't have to ingest every nutrient at every meal or even every day. Sometimes the easiest way to deal with a hurried dinner hour is to recognize what you've already eaten for breakfast and lunch, and cut back the cooking accordingly. Planned leftovers can help a great deal in this context, since they provide a cook with flexibility in tailoring meals according to family members' varying needs.

But much healthy food is intrinsically "fast food." Green vegetables, seafood, and chicken shouldn't be cooked too long. Fruits and dairy products needn't be cooked at all. Warm-weather harvests of such treats as garden tomatoes, fresh herbs, and corn anticipate a summer cook's longing for leisure, just as winter-harvest soups and stews feed needs for both warmth and nutrition.

Whatever time you spend cooking represents an investment in nutrition. The aim of healthy cooking is not to spend more time or less, but to safeguard the investment, so that it serves good health as well as good appetite.

Basic Recipes for Stocks and Broths

Because the ingredients in stocks and broths are strained out, it's difficult to estimate actual nutritional information short of analyzing samples in a lab. The following is an *average* for no-salt-added stocks and broths (for one cup):

Cal: 28 Pro: 4g Carb: .5g Fat: 1 g Sod: 85mg Pot: 170 mg

Vegetable Broth
by Nao Hauser

This is an excellent base for vegetable soups and a flavorful substitute for water when cooking rice, barley, kasha, bulgur, or couscous. It can be used instead of chicken or beef broth in most recipes, the exceptions being those in which you are making a sauce to go with poultry or meat.

> 3 large onions, very thinly sliced
> 1½ pounds carrots, sliced
> 10 ounces parsnips, sliced
> 6 ribs celery with leaves, sliced
> 1 small bunch fresh parsley, torn into pieces
> 1 small bunch fresh dill, torn into pieces
> ½ to 1 ounce dried sliced mushrooms
> 6 to 8 cloves garlic, peeled and sliced
> 2 teaspoons dried thyme
> 4 bay leaves

PREPARATION TIME: 30 minutes
COOKING TIME: 2 hours, 45 minutes
YIELD: about 2 quarts

Place the onions and 2 cups of water in a large pot; cook covered over medium heat, stirring occasionally, 1 hour. Add the remaining ingredients and 3 quarts of water; heat to boiling. Reduce heat; simmer uncovered 1½ hours. Strain the broth; discard the solids. Refrigerate in a covered container up to 5 days or freeze up to 6 months.

Chicken Stock

by Nao Hauser

> 1¼ pounds onions, unpeeled, ends trimmed, cut into chunks
> 1 pound carrots, cut into chunks
> 1 small bunch celery with leaves, cut into chunks
> 1 large bunch fresh parsley, or combined parsley and carrot tops, torn into pieces
> 1 small bunch fresh dill, torn into pieces
> 2 whole chickens (3 to 3½ pounds each), giblets and sac at end of tail bone removed

PREPARATION TIME: 30 minutes
COOKING TIME: 12 hours plus
YIELD: 3 to 4 quarts

Place the onions, carrots, and celery in an 8-quart or larger pot. Add 3 quarts of water.

Arrange the parsley and dill in a layer on the surface. Heat to boiling, reduce heat, and simmer 1 hour.

Place the chickens over the greens, breast-side up. (Only the bottoms of the chickens should be submerged; if pot is too narrow to wedge in both chickens, cook them one at a time.) Cook covered over low heat until the juices run clear when the thigh joint is pierced, 40 to 50 minutes. *Be careful not to overcook;* the meat should be firm. Remove the chickens; let stand until cool enough to handle. Remove and discard the skin. Cut off the wings, legs, and thighs. Remove the meat from all the chicken pieces and reserve for another use.

Return the chicken bones to the pot, burying them under the greens. Pour in 3 more quarts of water. Cook over very low heat until the water is reduced by at least one third, 10 hours or longer. Strain the stock through a strainer lined with a coffee filter or several layers of cheesecloth. Discard the solids. Refrigerate the stock until chilled; remove the fat from the top with the edge of a spoon. Refrigerate the stock in a covered container up to 3 days. Freeze for longer storage, up to 3 months. Be sure to heat stock to boiling before eating.

Microwave Chicken Broth

by Nao Hauser

The microwave method produces a rich broth in a relatively short time, but it is not appropriate for large quantities and the cost per cup of broth is higher because it requires more chicken to season less liquid.

> 2 pounds chicken thighs, skin removed
> 1 medium onion, ends trimmed, unpeeled, sliced
> 1 carrot, sliced
> 1 rib celery with leaves, sliced
> 1 cup snipped parsley or carrot tops, or a combination
> 1 tablespoon minced fresh dill, or 1 teaspoon dried (optional)

PREPARATION TIME: 10 minutes
COOKING TIME: 45 minutes
YIELD: about 3 cups

Place all the ingredients in a 4-quart microwave-safe bowl with 4 cups of water; cover tightly with plastic wrap. Microwave on High (100% power) 45 minutes. Let stand until cool enough to handle. Strain the broth; discard the solids. Refrigerate until cold; remove fat with the edge of a spoon. Refrigerate in a covered container up to 3 days or freeze up to 3 months.

Brown Veal Stock

by Nao Hauser

    5 pounds veal bones, including at least
      1 knuckle
1 1/4 pounds carrots, cut into chunks
    3 onions, unpeeled, ends trimmed, cut into
      chunks
    5 ribs celery with leaves, cut into chunks
    4 cloves garlic, peeled and split
    5 bay leaves, broken
    1 large bunch fresh parsley (about 6 ounces),
      torn, or a combination of parsley and
      carrot tops

PREPARATION TIME: 20 minutes
COOKING TIME: 16 hours plus
YIELD: 3 quarts

Preheat the oven to 450° F.
Place the bones in a jelly roll pan or a shallow roasting pan and roast, turning over once, until browned, 35 to 40 minutes.
Place the bones in an 8-quart or larger pot. Add 6 quarts of water and heat just to a very slow simmer over medium-low heat. (It should take at least an hour for the water to reach a slow simmer.) Continue cooking at a slow simmer, skimming scum from surface as needed, for 4 hours. Add the carrots, onions, celery, garlic, and bay leaves. Arrange the parsley in a layer on the surface. Simmer slowly until the liquid is reduced by about half, at least 10 hours and preferably much longer.

Let the stock stand until cool enough to handle. Strain through a strainer lined with a coffee filter or several layers of cheesecloth. Discard the solids. Refrigerate the stock until chilled; remove the fat with the edge of a spoon. Refrigerate in a covered container up to 4 days. Freeze for longer storage, up to 6 months.

Fish Fumet

by Nao Hauser

    2 pounds fish frames from lean, white fish,
      with heads and some meat but no skin (for
      lean fish, see page 219)
    1 small onion, chopped
    1 small carrot, grated
    1 cup dry white wine
    4 slices lemon
    1 ounce parsley sprigs, torn into pieces
    1 bay leaf, broken
 1/2 teaspoon dried thyme leaves

PREPARATION TIME: 25 minutes
COOKING TIME: 1 hour 10 minutes
YIELD: 3 cups

Break up the fish frames so they lie flat in a 4-quart pot. Arrange the onion and carrot around the bones. Pour in the wine. Cook covered over medium-low heat 20 minutes. Add 3 1/2 cups water, the lemon, parsley, and bay leaf. Heat to simmering over medium heat. As the liquid comes to a simmer, skim the foam from the top. After the liquid is simmering and most of the foam has been skimmed, add the thyme. Simmer uncovered, skimming occasionally, 35 minutes.
Let the stock stand 5 minutes; then strain through a strainer lined with a coffee filter or several layers of cheesecloth. Discard the solids. Refrigerate the stock until chilled; remove any fat with the edge of a spoon. Refrigerate in a covered container up to 2 days. Freeze for longer storage, up to 1 month.

◇ Spice Medicine ◇

by James A. Duke, Ph.D.

Variety may be the spice of life, but what's more surprising is that the spices and herbs you use may be medicines. There's garlic for high blood pressure, ginger for seasickness, cinnamon for nervous stomach, basil for flatulence, clove for toothache, and red pepper for frostbite. Some lower blood pressure, others sooth a cough.

Many herbs and spices are potent antioxidants; spices are often antibacterial and antiviral. Cumin, in the carrot family, and probably in your chili powder, is antioxidant, antibacterial, and insecticidal. In the days before refrigeration, the antiseptic qualities helped slow food spoilage, while the antioxidant effect slowed rancidity. Perhaps they will help protect us from oxidation as well. (Even so, improperly processed spices can support mold, even the carcinogen aflatoxin. Don't keep spices more than a year or so.)

Several members of the mint and carrot families, which yield more than a third of our culinary herbs, are digestives: They dispel intestinal gas, relieve cramps, and settle an unquiet stomach. The list includes caraway, dill, savory, peppermint, marjoram, anise. Marjoram (mint family) is a potent antispasmodic and folk remedy for abdominal cramps. Caraway (carrot family) relieves gas and cramps through its antispasmodic, carvacrol.

For colic I think that I will
Never find an herb better than dill

Still I'll bet a nickle
You know the dill pickle,
But never took a dill pill.

In animal experiments, dill oil reduces cramps of the smooth muscles—the type of muscles involved in the intestines. It also lowers blood pressure, dilates blood vessels, stimulates respiration and slows heart rate. In humans, scientific experiments have validated the use of dill water (made from diluted dill oil) for colic in infants and dyspepsia in older children. Similar uses prevail for fennel.

The myrtle family gives us cloves and allspice, both of which contain cineole, an antiseptic that has been shown to suppress coughs in animal studies. Mother used cloves in her apple pie, and if I had a toothache afterward, we would topically apply oil of clove, rich in eugenol, which is both antiseptic, killing off some of the cavity-causing bacteria, and anesthetic, killing the pain.

The new flower of a tree,
That's what the clove turns out to be.
In potpourris and sachets,
Used in infinite ways,
The clove's cured a toothache for me.

One of my favorite activities is matching folk medicines with scientific rationales. Here are a few of my favorites:

ALLSPICE

FAMILY: MYRTLE

Cloves and allspice, like a number of herbs and spices (especially rosemary and sage), have antioxidant properties. Eugenol, the major aromatic component of clove, is a dental anesthetic. If I had a toothache, I wouldn't hesitate to plug a dab of allspice into the cavity.

BASIL

FAMILY: MINT

Herbalists recommend a tea made from the leaves for nausea, gas pains, and dysentery. Roman naturalist Pliny wrote that basil relieves flatulence; modern pharmacology supports the claim.

Spotlight: Herbs Instead of Salt

These herbs often show up in salt substitutes, alone or in combination: anise seed, basil, celery seed, clove, coriander, cumin, garlic, lemon peel, lemon thyme, marjoram, oregano, pepper, rosemary, sage, sassafras, savory, and tarragon.

BAY

FAMILY: LAUREL

The bay in some strange way
Keeps the cool cockroach at bay.
Yet the leaves are often seen
In the best of French cuisine.
The chef rides his laurels, you might say.

Bay leaves contains cineole (up to 45 percent of the oil), a major ingredient in cough drops, so I add them to herb teas when I have a cold. The oil also contains small amounts (4 percent) of a natural tranquilizer methyl eugenol (not to be confused with eugenol, also a sedative). Bay leaves that are not removed from a dish can stick in the throat, so, for safety, try using them in bou-

quet garni bags, removed like tea bags before serving a dish. *Sassafras,* also in the laurel family, contains the mild carcinogen safrol in the roots, but the leaves—the *filé* of filé gumbo—are innocent and tasty.

CELERY

FAMILY: CARROT

Both celery, a vegetable, and celery seeds, a culinary herb, contain sedatives known as phthalides. It's no wonder my mother gave me a relaxing, antibiotic soup made of celery and onions when I had a fretful cold as a kid.

CINNAMON

FAMILY: LAUREL

A clever young woman in Proverbs
Resorted to spices and herbs.
Cinnamon and myrrh
Lured her lover to her,
More effectively than pronouns and verbs.

Both my mother and my wife recommend cinnamon toast for an upset stomach. Others recommend cinnamon for hangovers. Both cinnamon and cassia are chemically dominated by the aromatic compound cinnamaldehyde, whose reputation, folk and real, is for fever and insomnia. Eugenol, also present, has painkilling properties. The oil is antioxidant and antibiotic. According to studies at the USDA Human Nutrition Research Center in Beltsville, MD, cinnamon (along with cloves, turmeric and bay leaves) may boost the activity of insulin, a potential boon to diabetics.

Spotlight: Tummy Herbs

The following herbs have some scientifically validated reputation for relieving intestinal gas: anise, basil, caraway, coriander, dill, fennel, lavender, lovage, parsley, peppermint, rosemary, sage, and thyme.

FENNEL

FAMILY: CARROT

Fennel is a mildly sweet bulb that tastes a little like anise; the seeds are culinary herbs. To fish, fish soup, sausage, salads or antipasto, fennel adds a subtle and delightful Mediterranean flavor. It may also help you digest dinner. Fennel *seeds* are widely used as carminatives—that is, they clear the stomach of gas. Fennel is rich in anethole, which, like dill, reduces gas. Mothers can pour hot water over a teaspoon or two of crushed fennel seeds, let the mixture steep for a few minutes and strain the liquid, then dilute with water and serve to colicky babies. Fennel seeds, and to a lesser extent fennel bulbs (which have some anethole, too), may soothe adult tummies even as they delight adult palates. Anethole may even augment a mother's flow of milk.

LOVAGE

FAMILY: CARROT

Lovage extracts are strongly diuretic in experimental animals, and might be tried along with chervil by humans looking for a natural diuretic mix. Remember, though, that "He who self-medicates has a fool for a doctor." Seek an M.D. with natural inclinations.

Spotlight: Herbs That Lower Blood Pressure

The following herbs have some scientifically validated reputation for lowering blood pressure: celery, garlic, onion, turmeric, fenugreek, parsley, tarragon, valerian. (Licorice *raises* blood pressure; ginseng contains substances that both raise and lower pressure.) Three ounces of celery juice lowered blood pressure in fourteen of sixteen patients in one Chinese study. Why not try making a little carrot/celery juice in your juicer or blender? Or try a soup made with onions, garlic, celery, and turmeric.

OREGANO

FAMILY: MINT

More a smell than a plant. The aroma of oregano comes from the biologically active compound, carvacrol, found in many plants. It has antiseptic, antispasmodic, and throat-relaxing properties.

ROSEMARY

FAMILY: MINT

Some have the notion
That rosemary lotion
Can purify air
And stimulate hair
And secure a lover's devotion.

Rosemary is reputed in folklore to improve memory, a reputation Shakespeare's Ophelia alluded to in her famous soliloquy to Hamlet. If rosemary does boost the memory, it might be because of the strong antioxidants it contains. Many scientists now blame aspects of the aging process, such as memory loss, on oxidation of the body's tissues—and suggest that antioxidants could help prevent these symptoms. In the last decade, scientists have discovered many new antioxidants in the herb. Some of these, e.g. epirosmanol and isorosmanol, are about four times more active than the synthetic antioxidants BHA and BHT. But there's still no science behind this bit of folklore: a sprig of rosemary under the bed was believed to induce sound sleep, devoid of nightmares.

SAGE

FAMILY: MINT

Sage contains strong antioxidants, with a deserved folklore reputation as a gargle for bleeding gums, sore throat, and tonsilitis. Certainly it is antiseptic. Salvin, a compound found in sage, is effective in the test tube against *Staphylococcus* bacteria. Sage contains several antibiotic compounds and the astringent tannin.

Spotlight: Antioxidant Herbs

You'll hear a lot about antioxidants in this book. They preserve food, and people, too. Eating more antioxidant-rich foods, such as dark-green and dark-yellow vegetables, as well as certain herbs and spices, is a very healthy habit.

Antioxidants protect body cells, and even genetic material such as DNA, from damage caused by destructive forms of oxygen—free radicals—that are created by normal physiological functions of living but are accelerated by smoking, air pollution, and dietary toxins. Evidence continues to mount that a diet rich in antioxidants may slow or prevent chronic diseases, from cancer to cataracts to heart disease. These antioxidants include standard vitamins, especially vitamins C and E and the plant form of vitamin A, beta-carotene; and the minerals zinc and selenium.

As we go to press, the case for antioxidants against heart disease, for example, is getting stronger: A report out of the Physicians' Health Study finds that of 333 men with signs of heart disease, those who took beta-carotene supplements over six years suffered only half as many major cardiovascular events, such as heart disease and stroke, as those taking placebo pills. The antioxidants prevent a form of blood cholesterol, LDL, from oxidizing into a form that damages artery wall cells and building up plaque, once called "hardening of the arteries." For more on beta-carotene and its carotenoid cousins, see Squash, page 154.

Many fresh herbs and spices, as well as fresh fruits and vegetables, contain beta-carotene, but they also contain many, many antioxidants not classified as vitamins—at least not yet. The following herbs, most of which haven't been studied in terms of human health, nevertheless have scientifically validated antioxidant activity: alfalfa, allspice, celery seed, clove, cumin, ginger, lemon balm (melissa), lemon grass, mace, marjoram, mint, nutmeg, pepper, rosemary, sage, slippery elm, stinging nettle, and tomato seeds. Even as they add variety to your culinary palette, they may be keeping you young.

—Robert Barnett and James Duke

THYME

FAMILY: MINT

Thyme's a bit strong for cuisine
And, to my taste, too strong for tisane
The best of thyme tea
Tastes like mouthwash to me,
But it's antiseptic and clean!

Thymol, an active ingredient in the oil, is a proven antiseptic. It gives one famous "antiseptic mouthwash" its unpleasant, though cleansing, flavor. Thyme also has antispasmodic properties—that is, it may relieve cramps. (Personally, I drink thyme—that is, tea—when my lower back flares up; though appropriate back exercises seem better as prevention than thyme tea as cure.) Thymol is also throat-relaxing as well as antispasmodic, so thyme tea should be good for coughing spasms. The herb is safe, but the essential oil, like the essential oils of many herbs, is so concentrated it can be dangerous, even fatal, so don't self-medicate with any herb oils.

◇ SEASONINGS ◇

by Nao Hauser

You need only look at supermarket spice shelves to appreciate how wealthy we are. Those little jars that account for but a tiny fraction of the average American food budget were once exclusively the perquisite of the rich. Columbus and Da Gama risked their lives on the high seas for seasoning treasures. Today, the harvests of the Far East are as commonplace to our markets as local farmers' milk. So are herbs from hillsides in Europe, North Africa, South America, Mexico, and California.

These seasonings are the great solace of cooks who cut back on fat and salt. They restore one's sense of affluence without threatening either health or pocketbook. And they flavor the imagination, the spur to all great cooking. About two dozen kinds of dried herbs and spices, in addition to steady supplies of parsley, garlic, and ginger root, will meet most cooking needs. (See seasonings list, page 34.) Add about a dozen more unusual seasonings, and fresh herbs when available, and you can match the tastes of any historical king.

There are all kinds of caveats about buying and storing seasonings, and they are all valid. But cooks don't keep on cooking unless they learn to simplify matters. So here are the guidelines, both ways:

♦ Buy only as much of a dried herb as you can use within six months to a year—less time for ground, more for dried leaves—and only a year's

worth of ground spices. If an old, infrequently used spice smells musty and dull, throw it out. But if it simply smells weak, use more to compensate for the inevitable loss of fragrance over time.

Whole spices, such as cinnamon sticks and cloves, keep indefinitely in a cool, dark place. Grind your own in an electric spice or coffee grinder. Keep a nutmeg grater handy and at least one peppermill.

♦ Store herbs and spices in a cool, dark place. The refrigerator is ideal, but it's easier for most of us to use cabinet shelves—just be sure they're far from the stove or oven. A cabinet or closet is better than an open rack where light can penetrate.

♦ Freshness varies in the dried herbs we buy. If you dry your own fresh herbs, you can appreciate how much more fragrant they are than purchased products—as well as how much pungency they lose from one summer's harvest to the next.

♦ You can keep fresh herbs in the refrigerator at least a week and sometimes longer, depending on the herb. Parsley and some of the smaller leafed herbs, such as tarragon and rosemary, can be kept in sealed plastic bags in the vegetable bin for over a week if they are thoroughly dry; don't wash them prior to storage. Stand bunches of more fragile herbs, such as basil and coriander, in containers of water and cover them with plastic bags. Freeze herbs on baking sheets and then store in plastic bags; they can be used in cooking mixtures but not in salads or garnishes.

MAXIMIZING THE ASSETS

Here are some general techniques for making the most of herbs and spices in various forms:

♦ Strip leaves from herbs with woody stems, such as rosemary and oregano, by running your thumb and index finger down the length of the stem; discard the stems. Remove leaves from more fragile herbs, such as dill, by laying sprigs on a cutting board and cutting leafy parts from the stem; use stems to season soups and sauces, if desired.

♦ Use a food processor or mini-chopper to mince large quantities of parsley and other herbs. But you can lose valuable juices in the food processor, and the heat of the processing will dissipate the fragrance. So you'll get more flavor out of small amounts of herbs if you snip the leaves with kitchen shears, make a fine julienne on a board with a knife, or just tear the leaves.

♦ Crush dried herbs between your fingers to release fragrance quickly—an important consideration with fast-cooking foods and salads.

♦ Whenever appropriate, mince dried herbs with parsley before adding them to a dish. The liquid released from the parsley, as well as the act of mincing, goes far to revive the dried leaves.

♦ When using dried herbs in salad dressings and sauces that contain an acid, such as citrus juice or vinegar, steep the herbs in the acid for 5 to 10 minutes before mixing both with the other ingredients.

♦ Toast seeds and other dried whole spices before using them. Spread them in a heavy pan over medium heat and cook, stirring often, for a minute or two—just until they smell quite fragrant (and not until they burn and smell acrid). If you will be using the spices in a dish that requires sautéing in vegetable oil, toast the spices in some of the oil, so that as the oils in the spices come to the surface (the whole point of toasting), they will dissolve into the cooking oil.

♦ Add spices and herbs in increments to season dishes that cook a long time. Their potency will diminish the longer they are heated, and they will dissolve into the liquid given off by many long-simmered foods. So when making a stew, for example, you might season the meat first, add more herbs and spices with the vegetables, and supplement the seasonings again just before serving.

♦ Add fresh herbs, or additional fresh herbs, near the end of cooking time, as these lose fragrance very fast when heated. The corollary offers cooks a safety net: If you have added too much of a fresh herb, you often can undo some of the damage with longer cooking.

FINDING THE HAPPY BALANCE

There is no way to predict precisely how much of an herb or spice will suit a dish. When you are following a written recipe, be ready to adjust quantities according to taste, since the potency of herbs and spices varies as do the intrinsic flavors of other ingredients. Part of the joy of cooking is the wonderment: No two tomatoes taste exactly alike, nor do any chickens—nor, of course, do cooks' tastes conform! Part of the value of seasonings is their effectiveness in countering bland and unbalanced flavors in the other ingredients of a dish. When you are improvising with herbs and spices, you can, however, anticipate the general effects of these factors:

♦ Dried herbs are generally 2 to 3 times stronger than fresh herbs. But the intensification of flavor from drying varies greatly among herbs, and storage diminishes strength. So be prepared to adjust to taste. Some herbs, it should be added, retain so little flavor when dried that they are hardly worth using. These include chervil, coriander leaves (cilantro), lemon balm, and summer savory.

♦ Heat dissipates flavor, so use more seasonings in long-simmered foods, less in quick and uncooked dishes. One major factor, however, complicates this rule: Various herbs and spices react to being heated at different rates. So rosemary, for example, will hold up for hours, while saffron seems to diminish in a wink. Oregano is sturdy and true; basil takes quick leave of the scene. There are no formal timetables, but you can protect yourself simply by starting with smaller amounts of seasonings that smell strongest initially and adding a little bit more of everything near the end if necessary.

♦ Liquid dilutes the impact. Obviously, you can

use more seasonings if you add a quart of water to a dish than if you add only a cup. But not so obviously, you can use more seasonings with foods that give off a lot of water in the cooking, such as spinach and tomatoes, than with foods that remain firm and dry.

♦ Sugar balances herbs and spices, which is why sweet foods such as applesauce, sweet potatoes, and pineapple juice take so well to strong doses of cinnamon, nutmeg, and mint, respectively.

♦ Bland, starchy foods highlight herbs and spices by virtue of the contrast. Nutmeg will have a more distinctive taste when sprinkled on a baked white potato than it will on a sweet potato, for example, because the white potato won't counter the taste with its own sweetness. (For this reason, pieces of a baked white potato are a good, neutral palette for tasting seasonings you are unfamiliar with. Just sprinkle a little bit on and give it a try.)

♦ Time diminishes seasonings and cold temperatures dull taste buds. So if you're cooking something that will then be chilled before serving, such as a cold soup, it should taste slightly overseasoned (although not oversalted!) when hot.

AGE-OLD FORMULAS

As any lover of curries, chili, or even mulled cider knows, herbs and spices are never as interesting individually as when combined. The potential harmonies are infinite, and a good cook never stops seeking them. Fortunately for novices, some particularly pleasing combinations have been codified in various cuisines, and many are marketed commercially. So take these as a starting point: taste, amend with varied proportions, add other ingredients, if you wish, and you will be well embarked on the odyssey of seasonings. If you are new to the art, be aware that with a little practice you'll learn to anticipate tastes by smelling herb and spice blends—no small matter of convenience when you're improvising at the stove.

Bouquet Garni
This French term refers not to specific combinations of herbs but simply to a little bundle of herbs tied with string or wrapped in cheesecloth for easy retrieval from a sauce, soup, or stew. However, the basic bouquet garni is made up of parsley, thyme, and bay leaf, with at least twice as much parsley as thyme and rarely more than one bay leaf. These are the requisites for seasoning stocks and stock-based stews and sauces. You can add any other herb to the bouquet, such as basil for tomato sauces or a sprig of celery for vegetable soup.

Fines Herbes

Parsley, chervil, tarragon, and chives are the elements of this French formula. When you can obtain all four fresh, mince equal parts and stir into pan juices to spoon over chicken, veal, fish, and other delicate foods. Don't heat this group too long or their perfume will be lost. Remember that dried herbs will be at least twice as strong as fresh and adjust proportions accordingly; mince the dried with the fresh to revive them.

Fines Épices

There are many classic French recipes for spice mixes, and all are complex. The principle behind them is the pleasing effects you can achieve with a mixture roughly composed of one-fourth to one-third peppercorns and the remainder divided about equally between sweet spices, such as nutmeg, cloves, allspice, cinnamon, and mace, and strongly flavored herbs, such as bay leaves, thyme, sage, marjoram, and rosemary. Whichever elements you choose to grind together, the result will be an assertive seasoning—good to spread over pork or game before roasting or braising.

Quatre Épices

The commercial descendant of French spice mixes is composed of cinnamon, cloves, nutmeg, and pepper, and sometimes ginger. Use small amounts to spice and gently perfume pork, game, and all dark-meat turkey. Round out the bouquet with thyme, sage, rosemary, and garlic.

Peppercorns and Allspice

The everyday shortcut to mixed spices is the practice of filling a peppergrinder with equal parts of black peppercorns, white peppercorns, and whole allspice. Use this instead of straight pepper for a little sweeter zing in almost anything.

Five-Spice Powder

Star anise makes this Chinese blend startling to the American palate—and uniquely beloved in pork and chicken dishes. The powder's other ingredients are cinnamon, cloves, fennel seeds, and Szechuan peppercorns. Because the star anise doesn't cook off quickly, a little of the powder goes a long way. But its uses need not conform to the Chinese repertoire; it is as delicious on garlic-studded pork roast as in a delicate steamed dumpling.

Pumpkin Pie Spice

This is America's version of mixed spices—cinnamon, nutmeg, cloves, and ginger gently balanced to match the sweetness of winter squashes and sweet potatoes. Because nutmeg, cloves, and ginger can be quite sharp, it's interesting to see how the commercial proportion of sweet cinnamon subdues them. Add pepper and you underscore all the tastes. Add more of any one of the elements and the blend becomes a back-up quartet to the star.

Chili Powder

Commercial versions are probably harsher and perhaps mustier than ground chilies should be, and they usually contain salt. However, they are also extremely convenient, because they deliver the combined warmth of chilies and cumin, the combined sharpness of peppers and garlic powder, and the strong herbal scent of oregano—all in a simple shake of the container. You might not want to jeopardize the subtlety of a carefully prepared Mexican dish or a long-simmered chili with this powder, but small pinches work wonders with quickly sautéed meats, bean dishes, soups, and stews that seem otherwise to beg for salt. Mix the powder with more cumin and oregano and freshly minced garlic to counter its harshness. Or take the commercial recipe as a cue for grinding your own heavenly mix of dried chilies, cumin seeds, dried whole oregano, and garlic cloves—a true elixir for pork roasts and pork and turkey stews as well as Tex-Mex chili.

Curry Powder

Although it's even further in taste from its origins than chili powder, commercial curry powder is also very convenient for time-pressed cooks. Brands differ considerably; so it is worth sniffing and selecting among them. But the basic powder is yellow from turmeric and also includes ground coriander and fenugreek seeds, cumin, ginger, red and black peppers, and often nutmeg, cloves, bay leaves, and celery seed. All of this can scent a dish sufficiently to obviate the need for salt. The powder's mix of hot, bitter, and sweet spices makes it a pleasing counterpoint, in small amounts, to the sour tastes of dill and green onions, the blandness of cucumbers and cauliflower, and the sweetness of carrots and winter squash. Sprinkle a very modest amount on chicken breasts or white ocean fish fillets to underscore their delicacy.

Garam Masala

In Indian cooking, garam masala is a mixture of "warm" spices, including those we associate with sweet foods, such as cinnamon and cardamom, and those we use for heat, such as chilies and black pepper. Indian cooks toast and grind varying mixtures according to personal taste, local customs, and the specific foods they are preparing.

Like curry powder, purchased garam masala is a great convenience, and quite cosmopolitan; indeed, the two can be used to complement each other in a quick seasoning strategy, since the curry has bitter overtones and the garam masala sweet ones. You can enhance the harmony of packaged garam masal by adding more of any of its ingredients, such as cinnamon or cumin, to suit your taste. You'll find a choice of brands in Indian grocery stores; all of them lose fragrance within four or five months after the container has been opened.

Using spices and herbs creatively is a healthy cook's secret weapon. The potential pairings are vast. For specific answers to the age-old question, What goes with what?, turn to the cooking essays in individual chapters.

KEY TO
◇ NUTRITIONAL INFORMATION ◇

Each recipe contains nutritional information. This is an explanation of the abbreviations and terms used.

Calories = Cal

Protein = Pro Protein is listed both by weight in grams (abbreviated as g) and by percentage of calories. Thus, 5g/10% means the food has five grams of protein, which contributes 10 percent of its calories.

Carbohydrate = Carb Carbohydrates are listed by weight and grams, the same as protein.

Fat Fat is listed by weight and grams. In recipes where the total fat is greater than 15 percent of calories, we've also listed the "fat breakdown"—what percentage of fat is saturated (S), monounsaturated (M), and polyunsaturated (P). Thus, you may see the fat content of a recipe listed as Fat: 10g/23% (S:33% M:33% P:34%). That means that the entire recipe has 10 grams of fat, which makes up about 23 percent of the calories, and that the fat is evenly divided between saturated, monounsaturated, and polyunsaturated.

Alcohol = Alc Alcohol is listed as a percentage of calories.

Cholesterol = Chol Cholesterol is listed in milligrams (mg).

Sodium Sodium is listed in milligrams.

Potassium Potassium is listed in milligrams.

Fiber All fiber data refers to dietary fiber. The part of total fiber that is soluble is listed separately when it exceeds 1.5 mg.

Omega 3 Omega 3 is listed in grams, in recipes with fish or seafood.

Vitamins, Minerals, and Trace Elements These are listed as a percentage of the USRDA, when that percentage is 10 percent or greater.

Some nutrients, such as chromium, are not well enough studied to yield a USRDA. Instead, they have a "safe and adequate range" established by the RDA committee. In those cases, we've used the midpoint of that range and listed the nutrient when it's 10 percent or more than that number. For selenium, which has been given an RDA but not yet a USRDA, we used the second highest current RDA for adults who are not breastfeeding.

Remember: Macronutrients are listed as percentages *of calories,* whereas vitamins and minerals (so-called micronutrients) are listed as percentages *of USRDAs.* In general, the greater the percentage of vitamins and minerals in a food, the better. Thus, A: 87% means the food provides 87 percent of the USRDA for vitamin A, or nearly a day's supply. Fat: 30%, on the other hand, means the food gets 30 percent of its calories from fat. You wouldn't want more!

Vitamins, minerals and trace elements are listed this way:

Vitamin A	= A	*Calcium*	= Ca
Vitamin C	= C	*Phosphorus*	= P
Vitamin D	= D	*Iron*	= Fe
Vitamin E	= E	*Iodine*	= Io
Vitamin B1	= B1	*Magnesium*	= Mg
Vitamin B2	= B2	*Zinc*	= Zn
Vitamin B3	= B3	*Copper*	= Cu
Vitamin B6	= B6	*Manganese*	= Mn
Vitamin B12	= B12	*Selenium*	= Se
Folic Acid	= Folic	*Chromium*	= Cr
Pantothenic		*Molybdenum*	= Mo
Acid	= Panto		

Diabetic Exchanges: Each recipe provides diabetic exchanges, a simple system used by nutritionists to plan menus for diabetics. A similar system is used by consumers in popular weight loss programs such as Weight Watchers and by many nutritionists in helping clients plan diets. The exchanges are:

Meat: Lean Meat, Medium (Med.) Meat, or High-Fat Meat. (Note: our lean meats are in general lower in fat than standard lean meats used in exchanges.)
Milk: Skim, Lowfat, or Whole
Bread
Vegetable = Veg
Fruit
Fat (When a recipe includes a significant amount of alcohol, the calories from alcohol are listed as fat exchanges.)

A note of caution, however: Although the same low-fat high-carbohydrate principles of good nutrition underlie a diabetic diet, these recipes were not designed specifically for diabetics. Some contain sugar, for example. Please consult your registered dietician before incorporating these recipes and exchanges in your meal plan. For more information on diabetic exchanges, contact the local office of the American Diabetes Association.

Analysis Method: The recipes were analyzed using the Nutritionist III computer program, augmented by additional data from the USDA. Because of gaps in that data, some recipes may appear to be lower in nutrients than they actually are; shellfish, for example, is a good source of many trace minerals, but not all that information is available, so shellfish recipes may appear falsely to be low in zinc or copper, to take two examples. Wherever possible, we have noted that missing information is "N.A.," or not available. When one ingredient is not available in the analysis program, we used a similar ingredient, e.g., raisins for currants.

Optional ingredients are not included in the recipe analysis, unless specifically noted. Because as much as 75 percent of the alcohol in some cooked dishes may remain (see Beverages, p. 314), we have included the full amount of alcohol in our analyses, when that exceeds 20 calories per serving. Thus, most cooked dishes made with wine or spirits actually have less alcohol, and slightly fewer calories, than indicated. (If you are a recovering alcoholic and wish to abstain from all alcohol, it may behoove you to avoid even dishes with cooked spirits.)

When a recipe calls for unsalted chicken (or other) stock (many do), we used the Nutritionist III stock, with the sodium adjusted. When canned foods such as beans are rinsed, sodium is reduced, but there is so little data available that we did not reduce soldium in analyses. So, some recipes may be lower in sodium than they appear.

Recipes are analyzed per serving. When a dish yields a range of servings, e.g., 6 to 8, we analyzed for the smaller portion size (the larger number of servings), unless otherwise noted. When an *ingredient* is given in a range, i.e., $1/4$ to $1/2$ teaspoon salt, we analyzed for the mean amount, e.g., $3/8$ teaspoon.

A final note on salt: We have used as little as reasonable for good taste. Many recipes contain no added salt. If you'd like to add some, remember that $1/8$ of a teaspoon has 267 mg sodium.

All nutrient data in the food profiles come from USDA Handbook 8 unless otherwise noted.

Microwave Directions: All methods were developed and tested in 650- to 700-watt microwave ovens; if you are using a lower watt oven, you may need to add more cooking time.

NUTRITION NEWS
AND RECIPES

◇ WHEAT ◇

The Main Grain: Wheat

by Susan Lang

Wheat is the world's main grain. It can thrive nearly anywhere on earth, from Antarctica to the Equator, from the edge of the sea to the Andes.

No wonder. It can rise into bread, the world's first convenience food. Corn and rice can't do that. Gluten, the elastic matrix of proteins in wheat, expands to contain the gases created by yeast as it grows.

It's our favorite complex carbohydrate, and a good source of dietary fiber. We should be doubling our complex carbohydrate intake, many health experts say, getting at least half our calories from them. More carbohydrate-rich foods—breads, cereals, beans, pasta, fruits, and vegetables—could displace some of the high-fat and cholesterol-laden foods that may invite heart disease, hypertension, and cancer. A recent study at New York Hospital Cornell Medical Center found that men and women at high risk of colon cancer who ate a diet enriched with fiber-rich wheat bran had fewer potentially cancerous colon polyps. Combine wheat with beans, nuts and seeds, or any animal protein food such as cheese or eggs for a nutritionally complete protein.

Complex carbohydrates can also help us control our weight. They contain very little fat, are full of fiber that bulks our food in the GI tract, fill us up, and can displace fattier foods. In the 1970s, Michigan State University nutrition professor Olaf

Mickelsen gave healthy volunteers 9 to 12 pieces of bread a day for 8 to 10 weeks—as part of a low-fat diet. They lost more than a dozen pounds per person on average; the more fiber in the bread, the greater the weight loss. A 1986 study at Hunter College, for example, found that volunteers lost an average of 9 pounds over 10 weeks when they ate 8 slices of bread a day. With whole wheat bread they lost 13 pounds. "Bread is so maligned," says nutritionist Tom Watkins, director of the Hunter College study. "Many people claim it's fattening but that's such a myth. It's an excellent aid in appetite control and it's completely safe." Bread, says Mickelsen, "is an innocent vehicle for the fattening foods many people heap on top of it."

Traditional unprocessed wheat foods, such as whole wheat bread and the whole grain berries in pumpernickel bread, bulgur, and cracked wheat, can actually lower fat and triglyceride levels in the blood, finds David Jenkins, professor of nutrition and medicine at the University of Toronto. The body digests these foods very slowly, so they cause blood sugar (glucose) to rise quite slowly, which could help regulate our energy and appetite. Simple and refined carbohydrates, such as sweets, instant rice, and white bread, are digested so quickly they pour into the system, with the result that glucose levels in the blood rise. Triglycerides are then formed to store the excess glucose; both factors are associated with cardiovascular disease. Diabetics, of course, also have trouble coping with large amounts of glucose.

Even the particle size of the bran makes a difference. In one study, Jenkins' group found that "wholegrain" breads are beneficial, whereas "wholemeal" breads, in which the grain has been milled into a fine flour, are metabolized much like white flour. That's a good argument for stone-ground whole wheat flour—the bran is usually coarser than in other whole wheat flours.

Wheat's a cornucopia of nutrients, too. Whole wheat offers 37 of the 44 known essential nutrients naturally obtained from foods. Increasing our wheat consumption would also benefit those who are marginally deficient in the B vitamins. Although not a major health issue, many Americans, particularly the elderly, dieters, heavy drinkers, and strenuous exercisers, may be marginally deficient in thiamin, riboflavin, and niacin, says John Pinto, a nutritional biochemist at Cornell University Medical College. Symptoms range from feelings of lethargy and general malaise to, in extreme cases, neurological dysfunction.

One B vitamin is of particular concern. About half of all Americans don't get their RDA for vitamin B-6. Women on oral contraceptives, the elderly, and adolescents are particularly likely to lack it. If low intakes lead to a full-blown deficiency, symptoms can include stomach problems and depression. In one study, many women on birth control who complained of depression turned out to be B-6 deficient; supplementing their diet with the vitamin helped them lose the blues. A diet rich in whole wheat would have helped, too: A quarter cup of wheat berries (whole wheat kernels), which cooks up to three-quarters of a cup, for example, provides 20 percent of the US-RDA for B-6. In addition, infants breast-fed on milk rich in B-6 tend to cry less often than those fed on low-B-6 milk, a Purdue University study finds.

A slice of bread or a bowl of pasta isn't dramatically rich in nutrients. But wheat is such a large part of our diet that its overall contribution is large. It gives us about a fifth of our calories, more than a fifth of our daily intake of thiamin, riboflavin, niacin, and iron.

Whole wheat gives us much more. Wheat germ, which is milled out to make white flour, consists of a mere 2½ percent of the whole kernel by weight. Yet it contains 67 percent of the thiamin and 25 percent of the riboflavin and vitamin B-6 in wheat. If everyone in America ate whole wheat every time they ate a wheat product, calculates University of Texas at Austin nutrition researcher Donald Davis, we'd get on average 33 percent of the 25 essential nutrients. If it all came from enriched white flour, we'd only get 14 percent.

Wheat germ is a particularly good source of vitamin E. One quarter of a cup, with 108 calories, provides about 20 percent of the USRDA. An antioxidant, vitamin E inactivates free radicals that damage tissues and may contribute to heart disease and cancer. It may prevent blood cholesterol from converting to an oxidized form that can damage blood vessels and lead to arterial plaque, according to research at the University of Australia. In Finland, one study finds that individuals with higher blood levels of vitamin E had lower risk of pancreatic and stomach cancers. Vitamin E may also slow progression of Parkinson's disease and prevent the clouding in the lens referred to as cataracts. It also bolsters the immune system, especially in the elderly.

Removing the germ has an advantage for flour's shelf life, though. Wheat germ has oil and so can turn rancid. Some whole wheat flours are milled with the germ oil; others are milled without the oil, and so can last indefinitely.

The bran, with most of the fiber, is also lost in refining. Though only 14 percent of the kernel by weight, the bran contains three-quarters of the B-6, half the pantothenic acid and riboflavin, one-third the thiamin and one-fifth the protein. The bran also contains phytic acid, which can bind with excess iron in the colon before it oxidizes (e.g., rusts), and thus may help prevent colon cancer, notes University of Minnesota professor John Eaton, Ph.D.

The endosperm, the starchy midkernel source of white flour, has about a third of the riboflavin and three-quarters of the protein. So when the kernel is separated by modern milling techniques to provide us with a light, snowy white flour, about 80 percent of the original nutrients and almost all the fiber are discarded with the bran and germ. About 80 percent of the wheat we consume is refined.

Enrichment helps restore some of what's lost.

Thiamin, riboflavin, niacin, and iron are added back to their original levels. Still, 18 vitamins and minerals remain significantly diminished in enriched white flour.

Although we eat twice as much whole wheat bread now as we did in 1967, eating more could make a nutritional difference, according to Davis. More than half of our wheat intake is in the form of bread, and white bread is chosen over whole wheat bread more than two to one.

"Some people think, though, that white bread is poison, and that's wrong," says nutritionist Christina Stark of Cornell University in Ithaca, New York. She recommends emphasizing whole wheat bread whenever possible but stresses that it's not an all-or-nothing proposition. When white wheat products are chosen, though, make sure they are enriched.

Bleaching white flour is usually done with chlorine dioxide to whiten otherwise yellowish flour. The process partially destroys vitamin B-6 and folic acid and almost completely destroys vitamin E. According to Davis, this is a moot point if the bran and germ have already been removed. "It's like locking the door after the horse has escaped," he says.

In addition to bleaching, flour is aged or bromated, either with chlorine dioxide, potassium bromate, or iodate. Aged flour makes better bread, and although flour can age naturally in two months or so, chemicals are used to accelerate and control the aging. Even unbleached flour is aged.

Although wheat is the "staff of life," it can be hazardous to the health of 1 in about 2,500 Americans. They suffer from celiac sprue, an inherited intolerance to the gluten in whole wheat as well as rye, barley, and sometimes oats that can be a serious problem if untreated. Symptoms may include weight loss, anemia, diarrhea, brittle bones, and intestinal problems, explains Steve Taylor, a food scientist at the University of Nebraska at Lincoln. Celiac sprue sufferers must avoid all wheat, rye, barley, and oat products and foods that contain gluten. That includes some salad dressings, ice creams, hot dogs, and processed meats, and all soy sauces, wheat starches, and hydrolyzed vegetable proteins.

For those with an allergy to wheat—a much less common condition—the golden grain can occasionally be life threatening, though it's usually just an annoyance. Reactions can range from hives, breathing difficulties, skin rash, or gastrointestinal problems. Like those with celiac sprue, people allergic to wheat must stick to rice and corn for grains or eat specially formulated breads made from potatoes (page 106) or rice starch with soy or egg proteins. Some people find that kamut and spelt, two ancient grains in the wheat family, are less allergenic than modern hybrids. Health food stores carry these "new" varieties. If you think you have either celiac sprue or wheat allergy, see an allergist or a gastroenterologist to get an accurate diagnosis.

For most of us, though, whole wheat's our staple of choice. As former Surgeon General C. Everett Koop said, "Wheat-based foods can be an individual's best one-stop source of carbohydrates, fiber, protein, B vitamins and important trace minerals. Wheat foods are abundant and inexpensive, yet they are not fattening."

Cooking with Wheat_____
by Ceri Hadda

Wheat can be folded, literally, into our diets in many ways, from the wheat germ we sprinkle on our cereal, to chewy wheat berries (whole wheat kernels) in our casseroles to the wheat flakes with texture and culinary use similar to oats. In this essay, we'll talk about all kinds of wheats from the least processed (wheat berries, bran and germ), to the minimally processed (cracked wheat, wheat flakes, bulgur, and couscous), to the flours we use to bake our daily bread. Not to mention muffins!

Wheat Berries

The whole kernel of wheat with only the inedible hull removed, the wheat berry is nutty in flavor and chewy in texture, sort of a cross between wild rice and brown rice. Like these other grains, wheat berries can be used as a side dish, a salad or meatloaf ingredient, as stuffing for poultry, fish, and vegetables such as peppers, tomatoes, and zucchini. The cooked berries also impart a pleasing moist, chewy characteristic to breads. (Be sure to cool the berries completely before kneading them into any dough.)

Because they are mild, wheat berries combine well with most herbs and spices. They should be parboiled for 15 minutes before the flavorings are added, so that their softened exterior will be better able to absorb them.

As with rice and wild rice, a tangy vinaigrette balances the somewhat bland flavor of wheat berries. For stuffed tomatoes, add chopped fresh basil to the vinaigrette before tossing it with the wheat berries. For a fish or poultry stuffing, combine the fully cooked wheat berries with a mixture of sauteed onion, celery, and/or fennel.

Wheat Germ

Wheat germ imparts both nutty flavor and subtle sweetness to whatever it's added to. It can be used in many of the same ways as cornmeal, in pancake and waffle batters, pastry doughs and breads. It can also be added wherever you would add bran, although its flavor is, in my opinion, more delectable than that of bran.

Be sure to buy plain or toasted wheat germ, rather than the presweetened variety. The wheat germ has quite a bit of natural sweetness on its own, and its use is limited if it's already sweetened.

In his book *The Grains Cookbook*, the late Bert Greene recommends using wheat germ to replace up to $1/2$ of the ground nuts or bread crumbs a recipe calls for, but no more. Add about $1/4$ cup wheat germ to meat loaf mixtures, cookie doughs and crumb toppings for fruit crisps and pies.

Wheat Bran

Raw, unprocessed bran is a curious substance. Because eating it straight is akin to chewing on sawdust, it is often mixed with other ingredients to mask its presence. At other times—for instance, in bran muffins and breads—it is featured proudly and prominently.

In general, where bran is used raw, it's best to give it a low profile: Mix a tablespoon or two into applesauce or creamed spinach, for example, and

it will hardly be noticed. Or add bran to the dry ingredients for pie crusts, cookies, muffins, and breads. Even a tablespoon per cup of flour will modestly boost the fiber content of whatever you are baking. For bran muffins, a ratio of 1:1 flour to bran produces good results.

To bring out bran's toasty taste, dry-roast it in a heavy skillet over moderate heat, stirring constantly, until it deepens in color and smells nutty. Cool completely before storing. For a finer texture, pulverize the bran in the food processor, to flour-like consistency. This finer bran, alone or in combination with whole wheat bread crumbs, is great for coating chicken and fish before "oven-frying" it.

Mix bran into hamburger and meatloaf mixtures, stuffings for vegetables such as tomatoes, zucchini, and peppers, toppings for fruit crumbles, and other foods where you would normally use bread crumbs.

Cracked Wheat

Cracked wheat differs in that it is cracked after drying, rather than after steaming and drying, as is bulgur. Unlike bulgur, which can be merely presoaked or minimally cooked before using, cracked wheat must be cooked before it can be eaten or used as an ingredient.

Prepare cracked wheat as you would rice, using a 2 to 1 ratio of liquid to wheat and simmering the wheat about 20 minutes. Serve the wheat as a pilaf-like side dish. Or cool it and add it to whole wheat bread dough for an incomparably moist, chewy bread.

Wheat Flakes

Wheat berries are cooked, then rolled into flakes similar to rolled oats. Prepare like rolled oats, adding flakes to boiling water (using a 2 to 1 ratio), returning the water to boiling and simmering 1 minute. Serve the cereal with milk, chopped nuts, and a dusting of ground cinnamon. Or cool the cereal and sauté patties that have been dredged in flour in a nonstick skillet.

Add the flakes as you would oat flakes, to muffins and cookies and as an attractive garnish for the tops of breads and rolls. Like oat flakes, wheat flakes also make a delicious alternative to crumb crusts for frozen yogurt and fruit fillings: Mix

1⅓ cups with ¼ cup tightly packed brown sugar and 3 tablespoons melted butter; press into a pie dish and bake at 350°F for 10 to 15 minutes, until golden. Cool completely before using.

Bulgur

Bulgur is wheat that has been steamed, then dried, before being cracked into coarse, medium, or fine grains. Although there are no hard and fast rules as to which grind of bulgur to use when, the coarse grind is usually used in pilafs and stuffings, the medium grind for salads such as tabouli, and the fine grind in baking and dessert making.

Bulgur can be prepared in one of the following ways:

♦ Boil and serve it like rice, using 1 cup bulgur to 2 cups liquid; cover and simmer until all of the liquid has been absorbed, about 15 to 20 minutes; remove from the heat, then let stand, covered, for 10 minutes longer before fluffing with a fork and serving. The bulgur is delicious blended with sautéed mushrooms and onions, served as a side dish.

♦ Pour boiling, lightly salted water over the bulgur in a heatproof bowl, using about 3 cups of water for each cup of bulgur; let stand 40 minutes, until the bulgur is soft. Drain in a colander, squeezing out any excess water. The bulgur can now be used in tabouli or other cold salads. Dress with a tangy lemon vinaigrette and toss in plenty of chopped fresh mint and parsley. Serve in tomato cups for a colorful presentation.

♦ Use the same procedure as in previous method, but double the soaking time; more water will be absorbed. Some people claim this method results in a chewier grain.

Couscous

Prepared from semolina, couscous is available in regular and instant forms. Either can be served as a side dish—plain, or mixed with sautéed onions and other vegetables—or as a base for stews and casseroles.

Though many cooking experts shun the instant variety, it takes a mere 15 minutes to prepare and is easy to embellish for a quick main dish or accompaniment.

When using the non-instant variety of couscous, plan on an hour of cooking time. Each time the grain is removed from the heat, it should be gently stirred with a fork to remove the lumps that inevitably develop. Toss the couscous with oil (about 1 tablespoon per cup of uncooked couscous), then steam it in the steam pan of a couscousière (dish specially made for preparing couscous), a sieve, or a cheesecloth-lined colander set over hot water for 20 minutes. Remove from the heat, stir in ½ cup of cold water, and continue steaming for 20 minutes. After this, a third steaming will be necessary: Stir in ½ cup hot water, then place the couscous over a simmering stew or back over the simmering water.

To add flavor to instant couscous, replace all or part of the water called for with chicken stock; add a cardamom pod or two to the stock as it comes to a simmer. When the liquid boils, add the couscous, cover the pan, and remove from the heat. Let stand 10 minutes, then fluff with a fork and serve.

Cooked couscous can be used as a warm or room temperature salad ingredient; use it in combinations similar to rice salad, bound with a vinaigrette or creamy dressing. For a quick dessert, prepare couscous with part water, part apple juice; add a cinnamon stick, if desired. When the couscous is cooked, fold in yogurt, raisins, and a few chopped nuts. Or heat the couscous in milk, sweeten lightly, and serve as you would rice pudding.

Flours

The designations hard and soft refer to the type of wheat used to make flour. Hard flours are high in gluten, that stretchy substance produced by proteins in flour when the flour is moistened. It is gluten that gives dough elasticity—highly desirable when you're making bread, not so hot when you want a delicate-to-the-tooth cake or pastry. Hard (bread) flour requires hard treatment, while soft (cake or pastry) flour should be handled softly. All-purpose flours from different parts of the country and different companies vary; all are a blend of hard and soft wheats, making them good for general cooking and baking uses.

When using all-purpose flour instead of cake

flour, measure 1 cup of all-purpose flour, then si-phon off 2 tablespoons for each cup of cake flour required in a recipe. When using cake flour, be careful to distinguish between the plain and self-rising varieties. Avoid the latter; it's high in sodium.

Before substituting whole wheat flour for all-purpose flour in a recipe, decide on how impor-tant texture is to the final outcome. Muffins, cakes, and cookies, for example, will be nutty yet not leaden if you use 1/2 all-purpose flour, 1/2 whole wheat flour. Bread, however, can be made with up to 100 percent whole wheat flour. When you want a more delicate texture use whole wheat pastry flour. However, I've found that mix-ing whole wheat and all-purpose flours works just as well.

Yeast Breads

Today's baker can choose from fresh yeast, ac-tive dry yeast, or the new quick yeast, which is a special type of yeast that reduces rising time by 50 percent. Fresh yeast comes in 0.6-ounce cakes. Dry yeast is available in strips of three 1-tablespoon envelopes and in jars of loose gran-ules. Both the fresh and dry forms must be kept refrigerated to preserve their potency; fresh yeast can also be frozen, but it should be defrosted at room temperature, and then used at once. Bread bakers test the temperature of liquid used to dis-solve yeast on the inside of their wrists, much as doting parents check the milk for a baby. That's because yeast is a living organism; when dis-solved on its own—along with a little sugar to feed it—it must be gently treated. If the liquid feels comfortably warm to you (105° to 115°F), it's right for the yeast, too. Recipes that combine the dry yeast with other dry ingredients before liquid is added don't need quite such gentle care, since the yeast granules are somewhat insulated. Quick yeast, on the other hand, not only takes the heat, it requires it to dissolve properly. Check the package for temperatures. Pasteurized milk does not require scalding when used in breads, since the enzymes that make loaves soggy (and that required the scalding in times gone by) are destroyed during pasteurization.

Thorough kneading is essential to a well-formed loaf with a good texture (and it's a workout for the upper arms, too!). Kneading develops the elastic gluten that allows the dough to rise and hold its height during baking; it also eliminates any lumps that may lurk. Turn out the dough onto a flour-sprinkled surface and begin pushing the dough away from you, turning it 45 degrees, pushing it away, and so on. An occasional throw from a height of a few inches doesn't hurt, either, and allows for a total workout of the dough. Con-tinue adding a little flour at a time, until the dough no longer sticks to the surface. Continue knead-ing, usually 8 to 10 minutes, until the dough is "smooth and elastic": supple, stretchy, and free of lumps. You'll see and feel the difference! If a little more time is necessary, take it.

Once mixed and properly kneaded, yeast dough needs a warm spot, one free of drafts, to rise to glory. Place it in a greased bowl, turn the dough over to expose the greased side (this prevents the dough from forming a hard skin), and loosely cover the dough with a damp cloth. If you need to promote warmth, place the bowl of dough near the warmth of a radiator (but not on it), in an unlit oven, or set in a deeper bowl of lukewarm water.

In general, slow rising promotes a more flavor-ful bread. That's why, in my opinion, the fast-acting yeasts just don't produce the same results as the regular-strength yeasts do. On the other hand, most bread bakers agree that there is no discernible difference between dry and fresh yeasts in the final taste and appearance of the bread. Whichever yeast you use, allow the dough to rise until it is doubled in bulk: Not only will the dough double in volume, it will also hold the depressions of two fingers if they are pressed into it. To give the dough a hard, glossy crust, brush it with beaten egg whites. An ovenproof bowl of hot water placed on the bottom shelf of the oven will create steam as the bread bakes, resulting in a desirably crusty bread. Most bread bakes at 400°F, although those with a high sugar, fat and/or dried fruit content usually benefit from slower temperature, 350° to 375°F.

Quick Breads

Quick breads and muffins are leavened with bak-ing soda and/or baking powder rather than yeast.

They are fast to assemble and quick to bake. Most quick breads bake at 350°F; muffins and biscuits are baked even more quickly, at 400° to 450°F.

The high gluten needed in yeast baking is not desirable with quick-leavened mixtures. For this reason, all-purpose flour, or whole-wheat pastry flour, is preferable to bread flour. Also, the mixing of the batter should be thorough but gentle and quick. It's better to have a few unincorporated lumps of flour in the batter than to overwork the mixture and wind up with a tough loaf, muffin, or biscuit. (If you cut into a baked muffin or loaf and see holes and tunnels, the mixture was overbeaten.) It's important to work as quickly as possible between finishing the dough, filling the pan and placing the pan in the oven. In other words, quick breads should be prepared quickly!

Mushroom-Wheat Soup
by Ceri Hadda

1 ounce dried cèpes (also called porcini) or
* other dried mushrooms*
1/3 cup chopped celery
1 large onion, chopped
1 tablespoon vegetable oil
1/2 pound fresh mushrooms, sliced thin
1/2 cup wheat berries
4 cups unsalted chicken or vegetable broth or
* stock (see page 27)*

PREPARATION TIME: 30 minutes
COOKING TIME: 1 hour 15 minutes
YIELD: 4 servings

Soak the cèpes in warm water to cover in a small bowl for 30 minutes. Lift the mushrooms from the soaking liquid and strain the liquid through fine cheesecloth or a coffee filter set over a cup; reserve liquid and mushrooms. Sauté the celery and onion in oil in a medium saucepan until evenly coated with oil. Cover and steam-cook the vegetables about 5 minutes. Uncover and add the fresh mushrooms. Sauté 2 minutes, stirring constantly. Add the wheat berries; sauté 1 minute longer, stirring. Add the broth and the cèpes and their strained liquid to the pan. Bring to boiling; lower heat. Cover and simmer soup about 1 hour, or until the wheat berries are cooked and the broth is richly flavored.

NOTE: For a slightly thicker soup, puree part of the mixture in a blender or food processor, then return the purée to the remaining soup.

NUTRITION INFORMATION: Cal: 184 Pro: 9g/ 19% Carb: 26g/54% Fat: 6g/27% (S:19% M:30% P:51%) Chol: 1mg Sod: 96mg Potassium: 662mg Fiber: 2g C: 12% E: 18% B1: 12% B2: 24% B3: 40% Panto: 19% P: 23% Fe: 17% Cu: 22% Cr: 25%
EXCHANGE: Bread: 1¼ Veg: 1½ Fat: ¾

MICROWAVE METHOD: Soak the cèpes in liquid as described above. In a 3-quart microwave-safe casserole or bowl, cook the celery and onion in only 2 teaspoons oil on High (100% power) until tender, about 2 to 3 minutes. Add the fresh mushrooms and wheat berries. Cook covered on High 2 minutes. Add the broth, cèpes, and 1 cup of the reserved liquid. Cook on High to boiling, about 7 to 9 minutes. Reduce power to Medium (50% power); cook until the berries are tender, about 35 to 40 minutes; stir twice.

Wheat Berry Salad with Lemon Dressing
by Ceri Hadda

1 cup wheat berries
1/2 teaspoon salt (optional)
1/4 cup minced shallot or onion
2 tablespoons olive oil
1 tablespoon tomato juice or chicken broth or
* stock*
2 tablespoons fresh lemon juice
1/4 teaspoon dried thyme, crumbled
* Pinch cayenne*
* Salt*
* Freshly ground black pepper*

PREPARATION TIME: 15 minutes
COOKING TIME: 1 hour 15 minutes
YIELD: 4 appetizers or side dish servings

Combine the wheat berries, 3 cups water, and salt if desired, in a medium saucepan over moderate heat. Bring to a boil; boil 5 minutes. Lower the heat, cover, and simmer about 1 hour, or until the wheat berries are tender but still chewy and the liquid is absorbed. (Check the pan once or twice to make sure the berries are not burning; add additional water if necessary.) Meanwhile, sauté shallot or onion in 1 tablespoon of the olive oil in a small sauté pan until tender but not brown, about 5 minutes. Remove from heat; stir in the remaining olive oil and the tomato juice, lemon juice, thyme, cayenne, and salt and pepper to taste.

In a serving bowl, toss the warm wheat berries with the lemon dressing. Serve warm or at room temperature, on its own or with romaine leaves or scooped into hollowed-out tomato cups.

NUTRITION INFORMATION: Cal: 226 Pro: 4g/ 7% Carb: 37g/64% Fat: 7g/29% (S:13% M:75% P:12%) Chol: 1 mg Sodium: 14mg Potassium: 161mg Fiber: 4g B3: 10% P: 15% Fe: 13% EXCHANGE: Bread: 2¼ Veg: ¼ Fat: 1½

MICROWAVE METHOD: In a 1½- to 2-quart microwave-safe casserole or bowl, cook the wheat berries and 3 cups water on High (100% power) to boiling, about 6 to 7 minutes. Reduce to Medium (50% power); cook until berries are tender, about 35 to 40 minutes. Let stand. In a 2-cup microwave-safe measuring cup, cook the shallot and only 1 tablespoon olive oil on High until tender, about 1½ to 2 minutes. Into the drained wheat berries, stir the remaining ingredients and continue as above.

Herbed Couscous

by Ceri Hadda

2 cups unsalted chicken or vegetable broth or
  stock (see page 27)
¾ cup chopped scallions (use both white and
  green parts)
1 small ripe tomato, chopped
1 tablespoon olive oil
1 cup quick-cooking couscous
⅓ cup chopped fresh basil
⅓ cup chopped fresh parsley

PREPARATION TIME: 15 minutes
COOKING TIME: 5 minutes
YIELD: 6 servings

Combine the chicken stock, scallions, tomato, and olive oil in a small saucepan over moderate heat; bring to a boil. Stir in the couscous slowly with a fork; stir in half of the basil and parsley; cover. Let stand 10 minutes, or until the liquid is absorbed. Fluff with a fork, transfer to a serving dish, and sprinkle with the remaining herbs.

NUTRITION INFORMATION: Cal: 149 Pro: 5g/13% Carb: 26g/68% Fat: 3g/19% (S:14% M:68% P:14%) Chol: 1 mg Sodium: 36mg Potassium: 280mg Fiber: 1g A: 23% C: 22% B3: 12% P: 13%. Fe: 14% EXCHANGE: Bread: 1½ Veg: ¼ Fat: ½

MICROWAVE METHOD: In a 1½- to 2-quart microwave-safe casserole or bowl, cook the stock, scallions, tomato, and oil, covered, on High (100% power) to boiling, about 3½ to 4½ minutes. Stir in the couscous and continue as directed above.

Orange-Mint Tabouli

by Ceri Hadda

Delicious with lamb!

3 cups boiling water
1 cup bulgur wheat
2 navel oranges
⅓ cup fresh lemon juice, or more to taste
2 tablespoons light olive oil
¼ cup chopped fresh mint (see Note)
¼ cup chopped fresh parsley
1 small red onion, chopped fine

PREPARATION TIME: 30 minutes plus standing time
YIELD: 4 servings

Pour the boiling water over the bulgur in a medium bowl; cover; let stand at least 1 hour, or until most of the water is absorbed and the wheat is expanded and fluffy.

Meanwhile, grate enough rind from one of the oranges to yield ½ teaspoon. Squeeze enough juice from the orange to yield ¹/₃ cup. In a small bowl, combine the grated orange rind, orange juice, lemon juice, olive oil, and half of each herb.

Peel the remaining orange, quarter lengthwise, then cut into crosswise slices; reserve. Drain the bulgur and remove excess water by placing the bulgur in a sieve and pressing hard to extract liquid. Toss the bulgur in a serving bowl with the orange dressing. Add the red onion and mix well. Taste, and add additional lemon juice if desired. Sprinkle with the remaining fresh herbs, and garnish with reserved orange slices.

NOTE: If fresh mint is not available, substitute minced fresh coriander or 3 tablespoons dried mint plus 3 tablespoons additional minced fresh parsley.

NUTRITION INFORMATION: Cal: 258 Pro: 5g/ 7% Carb: 45g/68% Fat: 8g/25% (S:15% M:76% P:9%) Chol: 0mg Sodium: 3mg Potassium: 308mg Fiber: 4g C: 72% B1: 14% B3: 11% P: 16% Fe: 14%
EXCHANGE: Bread: 2 Veg: ¹/₂ Fruit: ¹/₂ Fat: 1¹/₂

Bulgur Pilaf
by Ceri Hadda

¹/₂ cup chopped onion
 2 teaspoons unsalted butter or margarine
 1 cup bulgur wheat
 1 tablespoon pignoli (pine nuts)
 2 cups unsalted chicken or vegetable broth or
    stock (see page 27)
¹/₈ teaspoon ground saffron (optional)

PREPARATION TIME: 20 minutes
COOKING TIME: 20 minutes
YIELD: 4 servings

Sauté the onion in the butter or margarine in a medium saucepan for 3 minutes or until golden. Add the bulgur and pignoli; sauté 1 minute longer, stirring constantly, or until nuts are golden. Add the broth, and the saffron if desired. Bring to a boil, lower the heat, and cover. Simmer 15 minutes, or until the broth is absorbed. Let stand 5 minutes. Fluff with a fork.

VARIATIONS: This pilaf can be varied with the addition of other vegetables such as celery and carrot, other herbs such as marjoram or oregano, and other liquids such as tomato juice or part wine/part broth.

NUTRITION INFORMATION: Cal: 221 Pro: 8g/14% Carb: 37g/66% Fat: 5g/20% (S:50% M:37% P:13%) Chol: 6mg Sodium: 43mg Potassium: 279mg Fiber: 4g B1: 11% B3: 18% P: 20% Fe: 14%
EXCHANGE: Bread: 2¹/₄ Veg: ¹/₄ Fat: 1

MICROWAVE METHOD: In a 2-quart microwave-safe casserole or bowl, cook the pignoli in the butter or margarine on High (100% power) until lightly browned, about 1¹/₂ to 2 minutes. Add the onion. Cook on High until tender, about 2 to 3 minutes. Add the bulgur, broth, and saffron. Cook tightly covered on High until the liquid is absorbed, about 12 to 14 minutes. Let stand 5 minutes. Fluff with a fork.

Spinach and Wheat Pilaf
by Ceri Hadda

This is an ideal side dish with veal, chicken, or fish. It can also be used as a stuffing for them.

¹/₂ cup chopped onion
¹/₂ cup chopped scallions
 1 tablespoon olive oil
 1 cup bulgur wheat
 2 cups unsalted chicken or vegetable broth or
    stock (see page 27)
¹/₄ cup fresh lemon juice
    Salt (optional)
    Freshly ground black pepper
 2 10-ounce packages frozen chopped spinach

PREPARATION TIME: 20 minutes
COOKING TIME: 30 minutes
YIELD: 8 servings

Sauté the onion and scallions in the oil in a medium saucepan for 4 to 5 minutes, or until tender. Add the bulgur; sauté 1 minute longer, stirring constantly. Add the broth, lemon juice, salt, if desired, and pepper to taste. Bring to a boil over moderate heat. Lower heat, cover, and simmer 5 minutes. Add the frozen spinach, burying the frozen blocks in simmering broth. Cover and simmer 15 minutes longer, stirring occasionally with a fork to break up spinach, or until spinach is cooked and most of the liquid is absorbed. Let stand, covered, 5 minutes. Fluff with a fork.

NUTRITION INFORMATION: Cal: 131 Pro: 6g/17% Carb: 24g/69% Fat: 2g/14% (S:18% M:68% P:14%) Chol: 1mg Sodium: 69mg Potassium: 395mg Fiber: 4g A: 126% C: 34% E: 13% B2: 11% Folic: 20% Ca: 13% P: 13% Fe: 14% Mg: 14% Mn: 21%

EXCHANGE: Bread: 1¼ Veg: 1¼ Fat: ¼

MICROWAVE METHOD: Remove the outer wrapper from the packages of frozen spinach. Place in a microwave-safe casserole or dish; cook on Defrost (30% power) until soft, about 5 to 6 minutes. Drain; let stand. In a 2-quart microwave-safe casserole or bowl, cook the onions and only 1 teaspoon oil on High (100% power) until tender, about 2 to 3 minutes. Add the bulgur, broth, lemon juice, and salt and pepper to taste. Cook tightly covered on High until the liquid is almost all absorbed, about 10 to 12 minutes. Stir the spinach to break up; then stir into the bulgur. Cook tightly covered on High until all the liquid is absorbed and the spinach is hot, about 3 to 5 minutes. Let stand 3 minutes. Fluff with a fork.

Curried Bulgur-Stuffed Peppers

by Ceri Hadda

A fresh tomato sauce or sautéed chopped tomatoes would go perfectly with these peppers. If you're preparing this recipe in the microwave, you might want to substitute tomato juice for the water and spoon some of it over the cooked peppers.

1 large onion, chopped
2 teaspoons olive oil
2 large cloves garlic, peeled and minced
1 carrot, shredded
½ cup bulgur wheat
½ teaspoon ground cumin, or more to taste
½ teaspoon ground coriander, or more to taste
½ teaspoon ground turmeric, or more to taste
⅛ teaspoon cayenne, or more to taste
  Dash ground cinnamon
3 tablespoons white wine
3 tablespoons fresh lemon juice
  Salt (optional)
¾ pound extra-lean ground beef (see page 247)
6 medium green and/or red bell peppers
  Plain nonfat yogurt for garnish (optional)

PREPARATION TIME: 30 minutes
COOKING TIME: 45 minutes
YIELD: 6 servings

Sauté the onion in the oil in a large skillet over moderate heat 5 minutes, or until golden. Add the garlic; sauté 1 minute. Add the carrot, bulgur, cumin, coriander, turmeric, cayenne, and cinnamon. Sauté, stirring constantly, 1 to 2 minutes, or until the wheat is slightly toasted. Remove from heat; add the wine, lemon juice, and salt, if desired. Let cool.

In a skillet, cook the ground beef over medium-high heat until browned, stirring occasionally; spoon off any excess fat. Combine the bulgur mixture with the beef just until blended (do not overmix). Slice off the tops of the peppers and remove the seeds. Slice off a tiny piece from the bottom of each pepper so they will stand straight without wobbling. Stuff the peppers with the meat mixture; replace the tops. Place the peppers on a steamer rack or bamboo steamer over simmering water in a wok or large saucepan; cover the pan. Steam 30 minutes, or until the filling is cooked and the peppers are tender. Serve hot or at room temperature, garnished with dollops of plain yogurt if desired.

NUTRITION INFORMATION: Cal: 249 Pro: 17g/ 27% Carb: 21g/33% Fat: 11g/40% (S:40% M:53% P:7%) Chol: 48mg Sodium: 62mg Potassium:

442mg Fiber: 2g A: 134% C: 146% B1: 10% B2: 13% B3: 19% B6: 18% B12: 20% P: 17% Fe: 17% Zn: 22% Se: 21% Cr: 18%
EXCHANGE: Med. Meat: 2¼ Bread: ¾ Veg: 1½ Fat: ¼

MICROWAVE METHOD: In a 1½-quart microwave-safe casserole, cook the onion, oil, and garlic on High (100% power) until tender, about 2 to 3 minutes. Add the carrot, bulgur, cumin, coriander, turmeric, cayenne, and cinnamon. Cook on High 2 minutes. Stir in the wine, lemon juice, and salt, if desired. Let stand covered. In a microwave-safe colander over a microwave-safe bowl or casserole, cook the beef on High until cooked, about 4 to 6 minutes. Stir into the bulgur mixture. Prepare the peppers and stuff as above. In 2½- to 3-quart shallow microwave-safe casserole, place the peppers. Add ½ cup water and cook, covered with plastic wrap, on High until the peppers are tender, about 18 minutes; rotate the dish halfway through. Let stand 5 minutes. Serve as above.

Chicken Couscous
by Ceri Hadda

This adaptation of a traditional Moroccan dish is a cross between a stew and a soup. It can be prepared in the minimum time indicated, but it improves in flavor if simmered an additional 40 minutes or so. If you like zucchini crisp-tender and you are simmering the couscous for the additional time, add it during the last 15 minutes.

        1 3-pound broiler-fryer chicken, cut in 8
           pieces, skin and visible fat removed
     ½ teaspoon ground cinnamon
        2 cardamom pods
        1 teaspoon ground ginger
        2 large yellow onions, quartered and
           sliced
        1 cup canned crushed tomatoes, no salt
           added
        1 small butternut or acorn squash (about
           2 pounds), quartered, pared, seeded,
           and cut into 1 × 2-inch pieces
        3 large carrots, cut into 1-inch pieces

        1 20-ounce can chick-peas, rinsed and
           drained
     ¼ cup raisins
        8 dried apricots, quartered
¼ to ½ teaspoon cayenne
        2 large zucchini, cut into 1-inch pieces
           Salt (optional)
           Fresh lemon juice
           Chopped fresh parsley
        6 cups hot cooked couscous

PREPARATION TIME: 40 minutes
COOKING TIME: 1½ to 2¼ hours (additional 45 minutes for simmering optional)
YIELD: 8 servings

Combine the chicken pieces, 2 quarts water, cinnamon, cardamom, ginger, onions, and crushed tomatoes in a large Dutch oven or stock pot. Bring to a boil over moderate heat, lower the heat, and cover. Simmer the mixture 15 minutes, skimming the surface once or twice. Add the squash, cover, and simmer 10 minutes. Add the carrots, cover, and simmer 30 minutes. Add the chick-peas, raisins, apricots, and cayenne, cover, and simmer 15 minutes to 1 hour longer. Add the zucchini for the last 15 minutes of cooking time. Taste, and add salt, if desired, and lemon juice to taste. Sprinkle with parsley. Divide the couscous among 8 deep soup bowls and spoon the chicken, vegetables, and broth over it. If desired, bone the chicken before serving.

NUTRITION INFORMATION: Cal: 536 Pro: 32g/23% Carb: 88g/64% Fat: 8g/13% Chol: 63mg Sodium: 425mg Potassium: 770mg Fiber: 11g A: 213% C: 59% E: 18% B1: 38% B2: 20% B3: 60% B6: 45% Folic: 16% Panto: 20% Ca: 17% P: 52% Fe: 42% Mag: 36% Zn: 20% Cu: 29% Mn: 18% Se: 37% Cr: 21%
EXCHANGE: Lean Meat: 3 Bread: 4½ Fruit: ¼ Veg: 1¾

Whole Wheat Pizza

by *American Health*

2½ cups whole wheat flour
    About 3 cups all-purpose flour
1½ teaspoons sugar
1½ teaspoons salt
  1 package active dry yeast
  2 cups hot water (120° to 130°F)
  2 tablespoons olive oil
    Vegetable oil
  1 6-ounce can tomato paste, no salt added
  1 small garlic clove, peeled and minced
½ teaspoon dried oregano, or more to taste
½ teaspoon dried basil, or more to taste
¼ teaspoon freshly ground black pepper
  1 16-ounce package part-skim mozzarella
    cheese, shredded

PREPARATION TIME: 1 hour plus rising time
COOKING TIME: 40 minutes
YIELD: 24 servings

In a large bowl, combine the whole wheat flour with 2½ cups all-purpose flour. In another large bowl, combine the sugar, 1 teaspoon salt, yeast, and 2 cups of the flour mixture. With an electric mixer at low speed, gradually pour the hot water and olive oil into the dry ingredients. Increase speed to medium; beat 2 minutes, occasionally scraping the bowl with a rubber spatula. Beat in 1½ cups more flour mixture, or enough to make a thick batter; continue beating 2 minutes, occasionally scraping the bowl. With a wooden spoon, stir in the remaining flour to make a soft dough.

Turn the dough onto a lightly floured surface and knead until smooth and elastic, about 10 minutes, adding more all-purpose flour while kneading. Shape the dough into a ball and place in a large bowl lightly oiled with vegetable oil, turning the dough over so that the top is greased. Cover with a towel and let rise in a warm place (80° to 85°F), away from drafts, until doubled, about 1 hour.

Preheat the oven to 450°F. Punch the dough down and turn onto a lightly floured surface; cover with the bowl and let rest 15 minutes. Use vegetable oil to lightly grease two 17¼- by 11½-

inch shallow roasting pans or two 15- by 10-inch jelly roll pans (pizza will be thicker).

Meanwhile, prepare the sauce: In a 2-quart saucepan over medium heat, bring the tomato paste, the remaining ½ teaspoon salt, 1 cup water and the next four ingredients to a boil: reduce the heat and simmer about 10 minutes.

Divide the dough in half; with wet or floured hands, pat each half into the bottom and halfway up the sides of the roasting pans. Spread the sauce over the dough; top with mozzarella. Place the pans on two oven racks. Bake in the preheated oven 15 minutes. Switch the pans between upper and lower oven racks and bake about 10 minutes longer, or until hot and bubbly.

NOTE: If you wish to freeze the pizza prior to baking, line the pan with aluminum foil and cover the foil with plastic wrap, allowing sufficient overhang to wrap the pizza. Shape the pizza in the pan, wrap, and freeze. Unwrap but do not thaw before baking; allow additional baking time, about 10 to 15 minutes.

NUTRITION INFORMATION: Cal: 161   Pro: 8g/ 20% Carb: 22g/55% Fat: 5g/25% (S:53% M:42% P:5%) Chol: 11mg Sodium: 228mg Potassium: 150mg Fiber: 2g B1: 12% Ca: 14% P: 16% Io: 15%
EXCHANGE: Med. Meat: ¾ Bread: 1¼ Veg: ¼ Fat: ¼

Garlic Whole Wheat Focaccia

by Ceri Hadda

Focaccia makes a delicious base for pizza and grilled sandwiches.

  1 package active dry yeast
  1 cup warm water (105° to 115°F)
  1 tablespoon sugar
  1 teaspoon salt
1½ cups whole wheat flour
½ to 1 cup unbleached all-purpose flour
    Vegetable oil

1½ tablespoons olive oil
2 cloves garlic, peeled and minced
¾ teaspoon dried oregano, crushed
½ teaspoon crushed red pepper flakes

PREPARATION TIME: 40 minutes plus rising time
COOKING TIME: 30 minutes
YIELD: 12 servings

Sprinkle the yeast over the warm water in a large mixing bowl; stir to dissolve. Add the sugar, salt, whole wheat flour, and ½ cup all-purpose flour. Beat with a wooden spoon until well blended. Add enough remaining all-purpose flour to form a stiff dough. Turn the dough onto a floured surface; knead 5 minutes, or until smooth and elastic. Use vegetable oil to lightly grease a large bowl. Place the dough in the greased bowl; turn the dough so that the top is greased. Cover with a towel and let rise in a warm place, away from drafts, 30 minutes, or until doubled in bulk. Knead in 1 tablespoon olive oil. Cover the bowl and let dough rise again, about 30 minutes more.

Preheat the oven to 400°F. Use ½ teaspoon olive oil to lightly grease a rectangular baking sheet or two round 8-inch baking pans. Press the dough into the greased pan, flattening it with your fingertips. Turn the dough over. Make ½-inch-long incisions 1 inch apart all over the dough. Sprinkle the garlic, oregano, and pepper flakes over the dough, pressing them in with your fingertips. Drizzle the bread with 1 teaspoon olive oil. Bake in the preheated oven 20 to 30 minutes, or until the bread is golden brown on the underside. Cut into 12 squares or wedges to serve.

VARIATIONS: Other toppings that may be sprinkled on top of the bread include fennel, caraway, poppy, and sesame seeds, and rosemary and thyme.

NUTRITION INFORMATION: Cal: 107 Pro: 3g/ 12% Carb: 19g/71% Fat: 2g/17% (S:18% M:74% P:8%) Chol: 0mg Sodium: 163mg Potassium: 81mg Fiber: 2g
EXCHANGE: Bread: 1 Fat: ½

Raisin Wheat Berry Bread

by *American Health*

¾ cup wheat berries
  Vegetable cooking spray
1 cup whole wheat flour
1 cup dark seedless raisins
¾ cup unbleached all-purpose flour
¼ cup sugar
1 teaspoon baking soda
½ teaspoon salt
1 egg
1 cup buttermilk
2 tablespoons vegetable oil

PREPARATION TIME: 30 minutes
COOKING TIME: 2½ hours
YIELD: 1 loaf (16 slices per loaf)

In a 4-quart saucepan over high heat, heat 2¼ cups of water and the wheat berries to boiling; cook 3 minutes. Remove from heat; cover, let stand 1 hour. Over high heat, bring to a boil. Reduce heat to low; simmer 1¼ hours; drain, if necessary; set aside.

Preheat the oven to 350°F. Spray an 8½- by 4½-inch loaf pan with cooking spray. In a large bowl, mix the whole wheat flour and the next five ingredients. In a small bowl with a fork, beat the egg slightly; stir in the buttermilk and vegetable oil. Stir the egg mixture and the wheat berries into flour mixture just until all the flour is moistened. Spoon the batter evenly into the loaf pan and bake in the preheated oven 1 hour. Cool in the pan on a wire rack 10 minutes; remove from pan.

NUTRITION INFORMATION (per slice): Cal: 140 Pro: 4g/10% Carb: 27g/74% Fat: 3g/16% (S:20% M:30% P:50%) Chol: 14mg Sodium: 140mg Potassium: 150mg Fiber: 2g E: 10%
EXCHANGE: Bread: 1¼ Fruit: ½ Fat: ½

MICROWAVE TIP: In a 3-quart microwave-safe casserole, cook the water and wheat berries tightly covered on High (100% power) to boiling, about 6 to 7 minutes. Stir. Cook tightly covered on Medium (50% power) 2 minutes. Let stand 1 hour. Cook tightly covered on High to boiling, 5 to 6 minutes. Reduce to Medium; cook until berries are tender, about 35 to 40 minutes. Continue as directed above.

Cracked Wheat and Bran Bread
by Ceri Hadda

1 cup boiling water
3/4 cup cracked wheat
   About 4 1/2 cups whole wheat flour
2 packages active dry yeast
3 tablespoons sugar
2 teaspoons salt
1/2 cup skim milk
1/4 cup vegetable oil
1/2 cup bran
   Vegetable oil
1 egg white, lightly beaten
   All-Bran Cereal (optional)

PREPARATION TIME: 35 minutes plus standing and rising time
COOKING TIME: 35 minutes
YIELD: 2 loaves (12 slices per loaf)

Pour the boiling water over the cracked wheat in a small bowl; let stand until most of the liquid is absorbed, about 30 minutes. (This can be done up to one day ahead; cover and refrigerate until ready to proceed with recipe.)

Combine 2 cups of the flour with the yeast, sugar, and salt in a large bowl. Heat 1 cup water, milk, and oil in a small saucepan over moderate heat until the mixture is very warm (120° to 130°F). Gradually pour the hot liquid over the dry ingredients. Beat with an electric mixer at medium speed 2 minutes, or until smooth. Add the soaked cracked wheat and any liquid that has not been absorbed plus the bran. Beat with electric mixer at high speed 2 minutes, or until smooth. With a wooden spoon, add enough of the remaining flour to make a soft dough. Turn the dough out onto a lightly floured board and knead until smooth and elastic, about 6 to 8 minutes, adding additional flour to the board to prevent the dough from sticking.

Use vegetable oil to lightly grease a bowl. Place the dough in the bowl; turn over so the top is greased. Cover the bowl with a damp cloth and let rise in a warm place, free of drafts, 45 minutes to 1 hour, or until doubled in bulk. Punch the dough down; knead lightly; divide in half. Shape each half into a loaf shape; place in two 8 1/2- by 4 1/2- by 2 1/2-inch loaf pans lightly greased with vegetable oil. Cover the pans with a damp cloth and let rise in a warm place, free of drafts, about 45 minutes, or until doubled in bulk.

Meanwhile, preheat the oven to 400°F. Brush the tops of the loaves lightly with beaten egg white; sprinkle with cereal flakes, if desired. Bake in the preheated oven 30 minutes, or until the tops are golden brown and the loaves make a hollow sound when lightly tapped with knuckles. Remove from pans to wire racks to cool. Slice thinly.

NOTE: The dough can also be baked in two free-form loaves on a lightly greased baking sheet. The loaves will be wider and flatter than if baked in pans.

NUTRITION INFORMATION (per slice): Cal: 136 Pro: 5g/13% Carb: 25g/69% Fat: 3g/18% (S:17% M:26% P:57%) Chol: 1mg Sodium: 169mg Potassium: 144mg Fiber: 4g E: 15% B1: 15% P: 14% Se: 39%
EXCHANGE: Bread: 1 1/2 Fat: 1/2

Whole Wheat Oatmeal Raisin Bread
by Ceri Hadda

A sweet loaf you'll be tempted to eat for dessert!

1 1/2 cups rolled oats
1/3 cup sugar
2 teaspoons salt
1/2 cup raisins

3 cups boiling water
2 packages active dry yeast
1/2 cup warm water (105° to 115°F)
3 tablespoons vegetable oil
1 tablespoon ground cinnamon
4 cups unbleached all-purpose flour
1 1/2 cups whole wheat flour
1 cup oat bran
   Vegetable oil
3 tablespoons sugar mixed with 1 teaspoon
   ground cinnamon
1 egg white, lightly beaten (optional)

PREPARATION TIME: 1 hour plus rising time
COOKING TIME: 45 minutes
YIELD: 2 loaves (12 slices per loaf)

Combine the oats, sugar, salt, and raisins in a large bowl; stir in the boiling water. Let stand until mixture is lukewarm. Dissolve the yeast in the warm water in a small bowl. Stir the yeast mixture into the oat mixture with 3 tablespoons oil, cinnamon, 2 cups of the all-purpose flour, the whole wheat flour, and oat bran. Add enough remaining all-purpose flour to make a fairly stiff dough. Turn the dough onto a lightly floured surface. Knead 10 to 15 minutes, or until the dough is smooth and elastic. Use vegetable oil to lightly grease a large bowl. Place the dough in the bowl; turn the dough so that the top is greased. Cover with a towel and let rise in a warm place, away from drafts, 45 to 60 minutes, or until doubled in bulk. Punch the dough down; divide in half. Let the dough rest, covered, 10 minutes. Roll each half of dough into a rectangle, 10 by 8 inches, on a floured surface. Sprinkle each rectangle with half of the cinnamon sugar. Roll up tightly from a long side, jelly-roll style; pinch the seams to keep the roll tight. Place each roll, seam side down, in a 9- by 5-inch loaf pan lightly greased with vegetable oil. Let rise, covered, 30 minutes, or until almost doubled in bulk.

Meanwhile, preheat the oven to 400°F. If desired, gently brush surface of the risen loaves with beaten egg white and sprinkle with additional rolled oats. Bake in the preheated oven 35 to 45 minutes, or until the loaves are golden and make a hollow sound when lightly tapped on the bottom. Remove from pans and cool on wire racks.

NUTRITION INFORMATION (per slice): Cal: 162 Pro: 5g/12% Carb: 30g/73% Fat: 3g/15% (S:17% M:23% P:60%) Chol: 0mg Sodium: 166mg Potassium: 123mg Fiber: 3g B1: 17% EXCHANGE: Bread: 2 Fat: 1/2

Triple Wheat Banana Muffins
by Ceri Hadda

   Vegetable cooking spray
1/4 cup toasted wheat germ, plus additional for
   sprinkling pan
1 cup whole wheat pastry flour
3/4 cup bran
1 tablespoon baking powder
1/4 teaspoon baking soda
1/2 teaspoon salt
3 ripe bananas, mashed (about 1 cup)
1/4 cup plain low-fat yogurt
1 egg, lightly beaten
1/3 cup honey

PREPARATION TIME: 25 minutes
COOKING TIME: 15 minutes
YIELD: 12 muffins

Lightly spray twelve nonstick muffin pan cups with cooking spray and sprinkle with some wheat germ.

Preheat the oven to 425°F. Stir together the flour, bran, 1/4 cup wheat germ, baking powder, baking soda, and salt in a medium bowl until well blended. Combine the bananas, yogurt, egg, and honey in a small bowl; add the mixture all at once to the dry ingredients, stirring just until moistened. (Do not overbeat or the muffins will be tough.) Spoon the batter into the prepared muffin pan cups, dividing evenly. Bake in the preheated oven 15 minutes, or until the tops are golden. Remove from pan to wire racks to cool. Muffins may be frozen and reheated.

NUTRITION INFORMATION: Cal: 120 Pro: 4g/12% Carb: 27g/79% Fat: 1g/9% Chol: 18mg Sodium: 194mg Potassium: 260mg Fiber: 5g B3: 11% B6: 16% Mg: 14% Mn: 15% Se: 83% EXCHANGE: Bread: 1 Fruit: 1

Bran-Oatmeal Cookies

by *American Health*

1 cup 100% bran cereal (such as All-Bran)
1/2 cup unbleached all-purpose flour
1/2 cup quick-cooking oats, uncooked
1/2 cup packed light brown sugar
1/3 cup margarine
1/2 teaspoon salt
1/2 teaspoon baking soda
1/2 teaspoon ground ginger
1/2 teaspoon ground cinnamon
1/2 teaspoon ground cloves
1/2 teaspoon grated lemon peel
1/2 teaspoon vanilla extract
1 egg

PREPARATION TIME: 25 minutes
COOKING TIME: 25 minutes
YIELD: about 4 dozen cookies

Preheat the oven to 375°F. Measure all the ingredients into a large bowl. With an electric mixer at low speed, beat until well blended, scraping the bowl down with a rubber spatula. Drop the dough by level half tablespoonfuls, about 2 inches apart, onto ungreased cookie sheets. Bake 12 minutes or until golden.

NUTRITION INFORMATION (per 2-cookie serving): Cal: 67 Pro: 1g/7% Carb: 10g/56% Fat: 3g/37% (S:19% M:38% P:43%) Chol: 8mg Sodium: 140mg Potassium: 73mg Fiber: 1g
EXCHANGE: Bread: 1/2 Fat: 1/2

Apple-Wheat Bars

by Ceri Hadda

These moist, spicy bars are similar to gingerbread. And like gingerbread, they taste even better after standing overnight.

1 stick corn-oil margarine or unsalted butter
  (4 ounces)
1/2 cup honey
1 egg
1/4 cup skim milk
1 cup unbleached all-purpose flour
1 cup whole wheat pastry flour
2 tablespoons bran
1 teaspoon ground cinnamon
1 teaspoon baking soda
1/2 teaspoon salt (optional)
1 cup finely chopped, peeled tart apple
1/2 cup raisins
1/4 cup finely chopped walnuts or pecans

PREPARATION TIME: 30 minutes
COOKING TIME: 25 to 30 minutes
YIELD: 40 bars

Grease a 9- by 13-inch baking pan with 2 teaspoons of the margarine. Preheat the oven to 350°F. Beat the remaining margarine with the honey with an electric mixer at high speed in a large bowl until creamy and well blended. Add the egg and beat until blended, then beat in the milk.

In a small bowl stir together the flours, bran, cinnamon, baking soda, and salt (if desired). Add the dry ingredients to the honey mixture; beat at low speed until blended (if mixture is too thick for mixer, finish blending with a wooden spoon). Stir in the apple, raisins, and nuts with a wooden spoon. Spread the batter into the prepared pan, smoothing the top. Bake in the preheated oven for 25 to 30 minutes, or until the top is golden. Cool in pan on a wire rack. Cut lengthwise into ten strips, widthwise into quarters. Store in an airtight container, or wrap and freeze.

NUTRITION INFORMATION: Cal: 69 Pro: 1g/7% Carb: 10g/57% Fat: 3g/36% (S:19% M:43% P:37%) Chol: 5mg Sodium: 50mg Potassium: 45mg Fiber: .8g E: 10%
EXCHANGE: Bread: 1/2 Fat: 1/2

◇ PASTA ◇

Pasta Perfect

by Eileen Behan

"Everything you see, I owe to spaghetti,"
—Sophia Loren

Pasta, the wheat with a thousand faces, is fit food for the fit. Think of running and carboloading, and you'll likely be thinking pasta. But it's got the stuff to keep all of us lean and well-fueled. A complex carbohydrate that's low in calories and nearly fat free—210 calories per cooked cup, but only 9 of those calories from fat—pasta's ideal for dieters who want a heart-healthy, high-carbo, low-fat diet to help get lean and stay lean.

Any carbohydrate will do. Pasta, though, is also chock-full of vitamins such as niacin, thiamin, and riboflavin, with some protein and iron (if enriched), and very little sodium.

The New Carbo-Loading

In a typical year, the New York Road Runners Club invites about 20,000 New York City Marathon entrants to dinner. Not all show up, but those that do sup on over 3,000 pounds of pasta, squeezing as much glycogen into their muscles and livers as possible, to provide energy at the twentieth mile and beyond.

What endurance athletes need is a diet that's at least 55 percent complex carbohydrates while they train, explains Boston-based sports nutritionist Nancy Clark, R.D. Then, two or three days before the race, athletes should cut down training workouts and boost their carbohydrate intake to 70 to 80 percent of their calorie intake. If you're running a 10 k or shorter race, just make sure you eat a "high carbohydrate meal the day before," she advises.

A high-carbohydrate diet may even help an athlete's spirit. A study at Auburn University in Alabama finds that athletes on high-carb diets had less anxiety, depression, hostility, fatigue, and confusion than athletes on a high-protein, low-carb diet.

Pasta is energy food for ordinary mortals as well, but only if you cook it lightly and combine it well with other foods. As is true for beans and most other complex carbohydrates, the body digests pasta slowly, releasing sugar slowly into the bloodstream, which is why pasta is recommended for diabetics. A slow release of sugar causes a gentle rise in insulin, gentle enough to sustain body energy and curb hunger.

Just make sure you cook it *al dente*—tender but still chewy.

Overcook any pasta and its sugars will get into the bloodstream faster, sparking insulin to over-react and bring blood sugar too low, notes diet/diabetes expert Phyllis Crapo of the University of California, San Diego. Result: fatigue and hunger.

Nobody eats pasta by itself, of course; what you add makes a big difference. Sprinkle in a bit of olive oil and a handful of cooked mussels or clams and it's one thing. But smother your fettuccine with heavy cream and you're eating mostly fat.

That can hurt not only your arteries and your weight, but also your alertness. Fat is hard to digest, so blood floods to your stomach for hours, instead of going to your brain. Eating carbohydrates without protein may not benefit your alertness either—some studies at MIT and elsewhere suggest that you may feel sluggish an hour or two later. So, while pasta *sans* protein might be nice for a calming supper, make sure pasta lunches include lean protein. Eat a bite of protein first, too, as an appetizer.

If you're allergic to wheat, pasta could be a problem, but it needn't be. Many pastas are now made without wheat. Sunchokes (Jerusalem artichokes) are made into a delicious pasta. Some Asian pastas are made from mung beans; some are made from rice. In this country, sweet lupin, a legume, is made into a high-protein pasta.

Cooking Pasta

by Nao Hauser

Although homemade pasta is the finest you'll ever taste (and is not all that hard to make—see recipe for Lidia's Papardelle, page 65), purchased pasta is to be cherished for its convenience. All that's required to cook it is a big pot of boiling water—and some types don't even need that.

The few caveats for consuming wheat pasta are these: Use fresh pasta, which is almost always made with eggs and usually sold refrigerated, within a day or two of purchase; freeze it for longer storage. Look for packages labeled "durum whole wheat" or "durum semolina" when you're buying dried pasta; the high protein content of durum wheat makes the pasta very elastic, so that its cooked texture is chewy rather than mushy. Cook fresh or dried pasta in at least 4 (and preferably 6) quarts of boiling water just until tender; the color of the noodles will lighten when they're done. Timing will depend on how dry the pasta is, how large the pieces are, and the quality of the flour. Fresh pasta may be done as soon as the water returns to a boil. Poor quality dried pasta may begin to fall apart after 5 minutes of boiling; a sturdy durum whole wheat pasta may need to boil as long as 10 minutes. So watch the pot, because timing is not predictable and overcooking diminishes flavor. Stir the noodles several times during cooking to keep them separated.

It is not necessary to add salt or oil to the cooking water, but you can do so in good conscience, because most of it will be poured off when you drain the pasta. As little as a half teaspoon of salt per 4 quarts of boiling water will perk up the taste of the noodles, and a tablespoon of oil helps ensure that they won't stick together. Drain pasta well (it's worth owning a jumbo-size colander just for this) to prevent sogginess and sauce dilution. Serve immediately; rinse with cold water only if you want to chill the pasta for a salad.

Pasta's potential pitfall is its blandness. The same neutrality that turns wheat noodles into a cook's canvas for everything from meat sauce to truffles can also invite an unhealthy dosage of fat and salt. One way to get around this is to anticipate the blandness and treat it as a marvelous foil for garlic, ginger, fresh parsley or basil, minced green chili and cilantro, and other assertive seasonings. You'll need some sauce vehicle for the seasoning, such as olive oil with the garlic, sesame oil with the ginger, or mashed ripe avocado with the chili and cilantro, but you can stretch small quantities of these to cover a lot of pasta by whisking them with such low-fat liquid ingredients as chicken broth, citrus juice, or chopped fresh tomatoes. Indeed, another way to minimize fat is to serve pasta in a well-seasoned liquid, such as a ginger- and soy-spiked chicken broth, or basil-scented tomato soup.

The world of pasta is considerably enlarged by Oriental noodles. Chinese egg noodles (sold fresh and dried) and Japanese wheat and wheat/buckwheat noodles (soba) can be cooked like any other wheat pasta, or with the add-water method given in "How to Cook Japanese Noodles" (page 61). The non-wheat noodles need less cooking. For example, fresh rice noodles, a wonderful chewy staple found in Thai grocery stores, need only be left to soften briefly in very hot water; they can then be served in broth or stir-fried in a wok (but only briefly, because rice noodles, lacking the gluten of wheat, fall apart fast). Dried rice noodles need to be softened in hot water and then simmered a few minutes. Bean thread, or cellophane, noodles, made from mung bean starch,

Spotlight: How to Cook Japanese Noodles

Japanese cooks have an unusual way of boiling noodles. After the noodles are added to boiling water and brought to a full boil again, cold water is added to slow the process. This is repeated two or three times. The result is tender, but not mushy, noodles. The process takes about 30 minutes.

To cook one 8-ounce package of udon (whole wheat noodles) or soba noodles (buckwheat), bring approximately 2 quarts water to a boil in a good-sized pot. The water should remain boiling while you add the noodles. Add about a quarter of the package at a time. Stir occasionally to prevent the noodles from sticking to each other and the bottom of the pot.

When the simmering noodles come to a full boil again, add 1 cup cold water. The water should stop the boiling. When the water boils for a second time, add another cup of cold water. Repeat a third time. On the third boil, test one of the noodles by rinsing under cold water and taking a bite. They should be more tender than Italian-style *"al dente,"* and cooked through the center.

Drain the noodles in a colander. Serve, or, if you wish to store, rinse carefully under running water to remove the starch and stop the cooking process. The noodles should be completely drained before storing in a sealed container.

To reheat the noodles, place them in a colander and suspend the colander in a pot of boiling water. Shake (or gently stir) the noodles and separate the strands so they heat completely. Drain again before serving with a dipping sauce or in a savory broth. Recipes for Japanese noodles in broth and in sesame tahini sauce follow.

—Mary Estella

usually need to be cut into manageable lengths with kitchen shears either before or after soaking; after they have been soaked long enough to turn pliable, they can be simmered in a broth or gravy for up to 20 minutes to absorb the liquid's flavor. A good guide to using these and other non-wheat noodles is *Asian Pasta* (Aris Books, 1985, $12.95).

Japanese Noodles in Broth

by Mary Estella

Ever wonder how to make the clear, flavorful broth served in Japanese restaurants? The recipe is surprisingly simple—once you purchase the few unusual ingredients in an Asian or natural foods store.

> *1 8-ounce package udon or soba noodles (see Note)*
> *1 or 2 6- to 8-inch strips kombu (giant kelp; see Note)*
> *1 cup dried bonito flakes (hana-katsuo; about 1 ounce; see Note)*
> *2 to 3 tablespoons reduced-sodium soy sauce*
> *2 to 3 tablespoons mirin (sweet rice wine; see Note)*
> *1/2 to 1 teaspoon fresh ginger juice (from grating a small piece of fresh ginger on the small holes of a hand grater)*
> *Sea vegetable "shake" or seasoning (nori or dulse flakes; see Note)*

PREPARATION TIME: 10 minutes
COOKING TIME: 30 minutes
YIELD: 4 servings

Boil the udon or soba according to the directions on page 61 and set aside. Wipe off the kombu with a paper towel and place in the bottom of a small soup pot. Add 1 quart cold water and slowly bring to a boil, uncovered, over medium-low heat. When the water comes to a boil, after 10 or 12 minutes, remove the kombu; it should be soft. (For a stronger flavor, simmer a few more minutes.) Bring the clear kombu broth to a boil again. Add the bonito flakes, but don't stir. Once the broth has come to a boil again, remove from heat. Allow the bonito flakes to sink to the bottom of the pot. After a few minutes, pour the broth through a cheesecloth-lined sieve over a bowl. (Broth may be cooled at this point and refrigerated covered up to 4 days.)

Heat the broth and add the soy sauce, mirin, and ginger juice. Simmer for 10 minutes and keep hot. Reheat noodles as directed on page 61 and drain. Arrange the hot noodles in a deep dish or serving bowl. Pour the hot broth over the noodles and garnish with sea vegetable flakes.

NOTE: Udon and soba noodles, kombu, hana-katsuo, mirin, and nori or dulse flakes are available at Asian food stores.

NUTRITION INFORMATION: Cal: 214 Pro: 8g/14% Carb: 43g/81% Fat: 1g/5% Chol: 0mg Sodium: 447mg Potassium: 39mg Fiber: 2g Fe: 17% Mg: 17%
EXCHANGE: Bread: 2½ Veg: ½

Soba Noodles in Sesame Tahini Sauce
by Mary Estella

A cool noodle salad is a quick satisfying meal on a hot day. This creamy sauce whips together quickly—with no cooking. Serve the noodles either simply garnished with scallions or with a crunchy watercress and radish salad. It's an easy recipe to enhance with your own favorite ingredients.

    3 tablespoons fresh lime juice
    3 tablespoons water
    2 tablespoons white or rice miso
    2 tablespoons sesame tahini
    1 8-ounce package soba noodles, cooked
        according to directions on page 61,
        drained, and refrigerated
  3 to 4 scallions, sliced, for garnish

PREPARATION TIME: 10 minutes
COOKING TIME: 15 minutes
YIELD: 3 servings

Combine all the ingredients except the noodles and scallions in a mixing bowl large enough to hold the cooked noodles. Using a wire whisk, beat until smooth. (Don't worry if the sauce looks curdled; just keep mixing.) Toss the drained noodles with the sauce to coat evenly. Garnish with scallions.

VARIATIONS:
♦ Use your favorite Italian pasta or rice in place of soba noodles.
♦ Try lemon juice in place of lime.
♦ Mirin (sweet rice wine) can replace the water; reduced-sodium soy sauce can replace the miso.
♦ Add garlic, fresh ginger juice (obtained by grating a piece of whole fresh ginger on the small holes of a hand grater), or a pinch of cayenne for extra flavor.
♦ Serve with sautéed broccoli, mushrooms, and garlic. Or garnish the noodles with a cup of steamed snow peas and sliced red bell pepper, and sprinkle with black sesame seeds.

NUTRITION INFORMATION: Cal: 359 Pro: 14g/15% Carb: 61g/66% Fat: 8g/19% (S:16% M:24% P:60%) Chol: 0mg Sodium: 422mg Potassium: 50mg Fiber: 3g C: 12% E: 11% Fe: 19% Mg: 17% Cr: 41%
EXCHANGE: Bread: 3½ Veg: ¾ Fat: 1½

Pasta e Fagioli
by Ceri Hadda

A traditional Italian bean and pasta soup that's hearty enough to serve as a main dish.

½ pound lean ground beef (see page 247)
  1 tablespoon olive oil
  1 medium onion, chopped
  1 medium carrot, halved and sliced
  1 large celery stalk, sliced
  1 14-ounce can peeled tomatoes, no salt
      added, chopped (reserve juice)

1 16-ounce can cannellini (white kidney beans)
    or small white beans, rinsed and drained
1 quart unsalted beef broth
1 teaspoon leaf marjoram, crumbled
    Freshly ground black pepper
3/4 cup dry elbow macaroni
2 tablespoons chopped fresh parsley
1/2 cup fresh lemon juice
2 teaspoons liquid red pepper seasoning (like
    Tabasco)

PREPARATION TIME: 30 minutes
COOKING TIME: 45 minutes
YIELD: 6 servings

Sauté the beef in olive oil in a large saucepan over moderately high heat; remove the beef with a slotted spoon and reserve. Sauté the onion, carrot, and celery in the drippings. Add the tomatoes and their liquid, cover, and simmer 10 minutes. Return the beef to the pan, add the beans, broth, marjoram, and pepper to taste. Cover and simmer 15 minutes. Bring the mixture to a boil; add the macaroni. Boil 6 to 7 minutes, or until the macaroni is barely tender. Stir in the parsley, lemon juice, and red pepper seasoning.

NUTRITION INFORMATION: Cal: 253 Pro: 18g/27% Carb: 28g/41% Fat: 8g/29% (S:34% M:57% P:9%) Chol: 24mg Sodium: 123mg Potassium: 543mg Fiber: 6g A: 106% C: 39% B2: 12% B3: 24% B6: 13% B12: 13% P: 14% Fe: 12% Zn: 14% Cu: 11% Se: 30% Cr: 13%
EXCHANGE: Lean Meat: 1½ Bread: 1½ Veg: 1 Fat: ½

MICROWAVE METHOD: In a 3-quart microwave-safe casserole or bowl, cook the crumbled ground beef on High (100% power) until it loses its pink color, about 3 to 4 minutes. Drain and reserve. In the same casserole, cook only 1 teaspoon oil and the onion, carrot, and celery on High until tender, about 4 to 5 minutes. Add the tomatoes and their liquid, beef, beans, broth, marjoram, and ground pepper. Cook covered on High to boiling, about 8 to 10 minutes. Add the macaroni. Cook covered on High until the macaroni is barely tender, about 5 to 6 minutes. Let stand covered 5 minutes. Stir in the parsley, pepper seasoning, and only ¼ cup lemon juice.

Chicken and Rice-Noodle Soup
by Ceri Hadda

This gingery, lemon-lime soup is filling enough to be a meal if you team it with a salad.

Half 6-ounce package rice noodles (py mai
    fun; see Note)
1 whole chicken breast (about 12 ounces),
    boned, skin and all visible fat removed
1½ quarts unsalted chicken stock or broth
    (may be part water) (see page 28)
2 scallions, sliced
4 slices fresh ginger, peeled and shredded
    (about ¼ cup; see Note)
1 cup frozen peas
¼ cup fresh lemon and/or lime juice (see
    note)
¼ cup snipped chives

PREPARATION TIME: 25 minutes
COOKING TIME: 15 minutes
YIELD: 4 servings

Cook the noodles in 4 cups of boiling water 3 minutes, or until soft. Drain, rinse with cold water, and drain again. Cut the noodles in half (this makes them easier to serve and eat). Reserve. Cut the chicken breast into ⅓- by 2-inch strips. Reserve. Bring the chicken stock, scallions, and ginger to a boil over moderate heat. Lower the heat, add the chicken, and simmer 2 minutes. Add the peas; simmer 1 minute longer.

Stir in the lemon and/or lime juice, chives, and noodles. Serve immediately.

NOTE: Py mai fun are available in Asian food stores. The ginger and lemon/lime flavors in this soup are quite strong and tangy. You can reduce the amount of both or either for a milder flavor. Also, if you don't like the taste of ginger pieces, they may be tied in cheesecloth and removed before the soup is served.

NUTRITION INFORMATION: Cal: 280 Pro: 32g/47% Carb: 25g/37% Fat: 5g/16% (S:32% M:44% P:24%) Chol: 56mg Sodium: 211mg Potassium:

603mg Fiber: 2g A: 12% C: 25% B1: 12%
B2: 14% B3: 72% B6: 24% B12: 10% P: 30%
Fe: 17% Mg: 14% Cu: 14% Mn: 16% Se: 41%
Cr: 26%
EXCHANGE: Lean Meat: 3¼ Bread: 1½ Veg: ¼

MICROWAVE METHOD: In a 2-quart microwave-safe casserole or bowl, cook 4 cups water on High (100% power) to boiling, about 6 to 8 minutes. Add the noodles and cook, covered, on High until soft, about 1½ to 2 minutes. Drain, and prepare noodles as directed above. Cut the chicken. In the same 2-quart casserole, cook the stock, scallions, and ginger, covered, on High to boiling, about 10 to 12 minutes. Add the chicken. Cook covered on High 2 minutes. Add the peas. Let stand, covered, 5 minutes. Stir in the remaining ingredients and the noodles. Serve immediately.

Beef and Cellophane Noodle Salad

by Ceri Hadda

This is a satisfying main-course salad.

10 dried Chinese mushrooms
½ pound boneless sirloin steak (trimmed
    weight), all visible fat removed
1 tablespoon sesame seeds, toasted (see Note)
1 scallion, trimmed and chopped
4 cloves garlic
1 tablespoon honey
5 fresh mint leaves, or 1 teaspoon dried mint
    soaked in 1 tablespoon water
1 tablespoon reduced-sodium dark soy sauce
1 tablespoon red wine vinegar
    Juice of 1 lime
1 small jalapeño pepper, halved and seeded
1 tablespoon sesame oil
1 tablespoon corn oil
1 3⅞-ounce package cellophane noodles
2 scallions, sliced into ⅓-inch pieces
½ pound fresh spinach, well washed and
    trimmed
1 cup julienne-cut carrot
¼ cup unsalted beef broth or water
    Julienne-cut scallion for garnish
    Spinach leaves for garnish

PREPARATION TIME: 35 minutes plus standing time
COOKING TIME: 10 minutes
YIELD: 4 servings

Soak the mushrooms in 1½ cups hot water in a small bowl 30 minutes, or until soft; drain. Cut off the stems and cut the caps into thin slices. Reserve. Meanwhile, freeze the steak for 10 minutes to facilitate slicing; then make the marinade. Combine the toasted sesame seeds, scallion, garlic, honey, mint, soy sauce, vinegar, lime juice, jalapeño pepper, and sesame and corn oils in a blender or mini food processor and process until the mixture is smooth.

Slice the chilled meat into very thin pieces using a sharp chef's knife. Place in a small bowl. Pour the marinade over the meat, tossing to combine, and let stand 30 minutes. Pour boiling water over the noodles in a large bowl; let stand 5 to 10 minutes, or until soft. Drain; rinse with cold water; drain again. Place in a large bowl and set aside.

Sauté the beef and marinade in a nonstick skillet over moderately high heat 3 minutes, stirring all the time. Add the mushrooms and scallions. Sauté 3 minutes longer. Add to noodles. Add the spinach, carrot julienne, and beef broth to the skillet. Cover and cook 2 to 3 minutes, or until spinach wilts and the carrot julienne are tender-crisp. Add to the noodles and beef. Toss to combine. Serve warm or at room temperature, garnished with additional scallion and sliced spinach leaves if desired.

NOTE: To toast sesame seeds, place them in a small skillet over moderately low heat. Cook, stirring constantly, just until the sesame seeds turn golden. Remove from heat. The sesame seeds will continue to cook a few minutes longer.

NUTRITION INFORMATION: Cal: 344 Pro: 18g/20% Carb: 40g/45% Fat: 14g/35% (S:26% M:39% P:35%) Chol: 38mg Sodium: 313mg Potassium: 1017mg Fiber: 5g A: 294% C: 66% E: 39% B1: 16% B2: 26% B3: 23% B6: 24% B12: 20% Folic: 52% Panto: 10% Ca: 16% P: 24% Fe: 34% Mg: 28% Zn: 26% Cu: 22% Se: 29% Mn: 30% Cr: 26% Mo: 19%
EXCHANGE: Med. Meat: 1½ Bread: 1½ Veg: 2 Fat: 1½

Lidia's Papardelle

by Lidia Bastianich

This fresh pasta is long and flat, like fettucine but wider.

3¹/₂ cups unbleached all-purpose flour
2 eggs
¹/₄ teaspoon salt
1 teaspoon olive oil

PREPARATION TIME: 45 minutes plus standing time
COOKING TIME: 10 minutes
YIELD: 6 servings (1 pound fresh pasta)

Place 3 cups flour on a dry work surface. Make a well in the center. Beat the eggs and salt together; pour into the well. Stir the eggs with your fingertips; gradually incorporate the flour. When about half the flour is incorporated, drizzle the oil over the mixture. Use a little oil to rub sticky bits from your fingers. Continue to add unincorporated flour alternately with ³/₄ cup warm water until you have worked in all the flour and just enough water to form a mass that is supple, not sticky. Knead the dough on a lightly floured board until very smooth and silky, about 10 minutes. Add water if too firm, flour if too sticky. Cover and let rest 30 minutes.

Cut the dough into three pieces. Roll out each piece on a lightly floured board to about a ¹/₁₆-inch thickness. Starting from the end nearest you, roll the dough around the rolling pin until all is rolled up. Cut the dough down the length of the rolling pin, then cut into 1- by 5-inch strips. Separate the strips and arrange on a tray lined with a floured cloth, dredging strips lightly in the flour to prevent them from sticking together. Let dry at least 10 minutes and up to several hours, uncovered, in the refrigerator. Add gradually to 5 quarts of boiling water, stir with a wooden spoon, and boil uncovered until just tender, 2 to 4 minutes. Drain well. Serve immediately.

NUTRITION INFORMATION: Cal: 278 Pro: 9g/ 13% Carb: 52g/76% Fat: 3g/11% Chol: 71mg Sodium: 113mg Potassium: 85mg Fiber: 2g

B1: 30% B2: 19% B3: 18% Fe: 13% Se: 10% Cr: 16%
EXCHANGE: Med. Meat: ¹/₄ Bread: 3¹/₄

Pasutice Istriana

by Lidia Bastianich

Delicate fresh pasta with a light, Mediterranean-style seafood sauce. The wide, short cut of the noodles goes well with the pieces of seafood, but a long pasta, such as fettucine, will work fine, too.

Pasutice (1 recipe Lidia's Papardelle, see
recipe, above; see Note, below)
3 cloves garlic, crushed
4 teaspoons olive oil
¹/₂ pound small shelled and deveined shrimp
(see page 233)
¹/₂ pound bay scallops, rinsed and cut into
quarters
10 littleneck clams, cleaned (see page 233),
shucked, and chopped, with juice from
chopping
1¹/₂ cups canned peeled tomatoes, no salt
added, coarsely chopped, drained
2 tablespoons chopped fresh flat-leaf parsley
Dash liquid red pepper seasoning (like
Tabasco)

PREPARATION TIME: 30 minutes plus pasta-making time
COOKING TIME: 15 minutes
YIELD: 6 servings

Follow the preparation and cooking instructions for Lidia's Papardelle (see recipe, above), but cut strips at 1¹/₂-inch intervals to form 1- by 1¹/₂-inch rectangles.

Lightly brown the garlic in oil. Add the shrimp and scallops; sauté 1 minute. Add the remaining ingredients and let simmer for 7 to 10 minutes. Cook the pasutice and drain well. Stir half of the sauce into the pasta. Arrange on a serving plate and top with the remaining seafood and sauce.

NOTE: You can use 1 pound of any other fresh pasta, such as fettucine, instead. The clams can be steamed just to open, conventionally or in microwave, then shucked, chopped, and added to the shrimp; simmer 7 minutes or just until the scallops are opaque.

NUTRITION INFORMATION: Cal: 363 Pro: 24g/26% Carb: 57g/61% Fat: 5g/13% (S:16% M:70% P:14%) Chol: 73mg Sodium: 152mg Potassium: 519mg Fiber: 2g A: 18% C: 24% E: 14% B1: 24% B2: 14% B3: 19% B12: 76% P: 28% Fe: 29% Mg: 13% Zn: 11% Se: 174% Cr: 15%

EXCHANGE: Lean Meat: 1½ Bread: 3½ Veg: ¾ Fat: ½

Penne with Crab and Asparagus
by Ceri Hadda

Cut ziti or half a recipe of Lidia's Papardelle (page 65) may be substituted for the penne.

¼ teaspoon dried oregano
2 tablespoons dry sherry
1 cup part-skim ricotta cheese
2 scallions, cut into 1-inch pieces
2 tablespoons fresh lemon juice
    Few drops liquid red pepper seasoning (like Tabasco)
½ pound fresh asparagus spears, cut into 1- to 2½-inch pieces
½ pound dried penne
½ pound fresh crab meat, picked over for shells and cartilage, or a 6-ounce package frozen crab meat, thawed
2 tablespoons snipped fresh or dried chives
2 tablespoons freshly grated Parmesan cheese
    Freshly ground black pepper

PREPARATION TIME: 25 minutes
COOKING TIME: 15 minutes
YIELD: 3 servings

Soak the oregano in the sherry for 5 minutes. In a food processor or blender, combine the sherry mixture, ricotta cheese, scallions, lemon juice, and red pepper seasoning. Cover and blend well at high speed.

Place the asparagus in a metal strainer and immerse in a large pot of boiling water; simmer 2 to 3 minutes or until crisply tender. Remove in strainer, rinse under cold running water, and drain well. Cook the pasta in the same pot of water until *al dente*, generally 8 to 10 minutes; drain, reserving about ½ cup of the cooking water. Return the pasta to the pot. Add the ricotta sauce, asparagus, and crab meat. Toss gently over low heat, adding reserved cooking water as needed to produce a creamy sauce. Divide among three plates; sprinkle each portion with 2 teaspoons chives and Parmesan cheese, and freshly ground black pepper to taste.

NUTRITION INFORMATION: Cal: 464 Pro: 34g/29% Carb: 61g/50% Fat: 10g/20% (S:62% M:8% P:30%) Chol: 60mg Sodium: 829mg Potassium: 630mg Fiber: 2g A: 25% C: 35% E: 13% B1: 29% B2: 27% B3: 20% B6: 12% Folic: 22% Ca: 36% P: 51% Fe: 19% Mg: 21% Zn: 47% Cu: 41% Se: 100% Cr: 37%

EXCHANGE: Lean Meat: 3¼ Bread: 3½ Veg: ¾

Linguine with Lobster and Saffron Sauce
by Four Seasons Hotels Alternative Cuisine

5 tablespoons minced shallots
½ teaspoon corn-oil margarine
1 cup dry white wine
½ teaspoon ground saffron
3 cups fish stock or fumet (see page 29)
1 tablespoon cornstarch dissolved in 1 tablespoon dry white wine
½ cup low-fat milk
    Salt
    Freshly ground black pepper
8 ounces dry linguine
2 cups cut-up cooked lobster
¼ cup dry vermouth
4 scallions, green part only, finely chopped, for garnish

PREPARATION TIME: 35 minutes
COOKING TIME: 25 minutes
YIELD: 4 servings

In a saucepan, sauté 1 tablespoon of the shallots in margarine until golden, about 5 minutes. Stir in the white wine and saffron; boil, uncovered, until the liquid is reduced to about $\frac{1}{4}$ cup, about 5 minutes. Add the fish stock and simmer 5 minutes. Add the dissolved cornstarch; continue cooking until slightly thickened, stirring constantly. Stir in the milk and heat through. Strain the sauce through a fine sieve, discarding all solids. Add salt and pepper to taste. Cook the linguine according to package directions; drain. Return to saucepot; keep warm.

In another saucepan, combine the remaining shallots with the lobster and vermouth; simmer, covered, about 5 minutes, or until liquid evaporates. Toss the linguine with the sauce and lobster mixture and garnish with scallions.

VARIATION: 6 ounces lump crab meat or $\frac{1}{2}$ pound cubed cooked monkfish can be substituted for the lobster.

NUTRITION INFORMATION: Cal: 382 Pro: 27g/28% Carb: 47g/49% Fat: 3g/8% Alc: 15% Chol: 54mg Sodium: 403mg Potassium: 699mg Fiber: 1g B1: 18% B2: 17% B3: 26% B12: 42% Ca: 12% P: 32% Fe: 14% Mg: 16% Zn: 21% Cu: 77% Mn: 16% Se: 56% Cr: 28%
EXCHANGE: Lean Meat: $2\frac{1}{2}$ Bread: $2\frac{3}{4}$ Veg: $\frac{1}{2}$ Fat: $\frac{1}{2}$

Pasta with Summer Vegetables
by Ceri Hadda

The mushrooms and zucchini in this recipe can be replaced with an equal weight of other vegetables, such as green beans, blanched chopped broccoli or cauliflower, or diced green and red pepper.

4 cloves garlic, peeled
1 large onion, quartered
2 medium carrots, quartered
6 radishes, trimmed
3 tablespoons olive oil
4 large tomatoes (about $1\frac{1}{2}$ pounds), cored
1 cup canned crushed tomatoes, no salt added
$\frac{1}{2}$ cup dry white wine
1 pound dry fusilli or penne
$\frac{1}{2}$ pound mushrooms, trimmed and sliced
1 large zucchini, halved lengthwise and sliced
$\frac{1}{2}$ cup tightly packed fresh basil leaves, chopped
2 tablespoons freshly grated Parmesan cheese (optional)

PREPARATION TIME: 30 minutes
COOKING TIME: 35 minutes
YIELD: 4 servings

Place the garlic, onion, carrots, and radishes in a food processor fitted with the metal blade. Cover and process with on and off turns until the vegetables are coarsely chopped.

Heat the oil in a large saucepan over moderate heat and sauté the chopped vegetables until soft, about 5 minutes, stirring often. Meanwhile, coarsely chop the tomatoes in the processor. Add the tomatoes to the vegetables and sauté 5 minutes longer, or until the tomatoes have released some of their juice. Add the crushed tomatoes and wine to the saucepan. Bring to a boil, cover, lower the heat, and simmer 10 minutes. Cook the pasta according to package directions; drain. Return to saucepot to keep warm.

Add the mushroom and zucchini slices to sauce; cover. Simmer 10 minutes longer, or until vegetables are tender but not overcooked. Toss the pasta with the basil and vegetable sauce. Top each portion with $1\frac{1}{2}$ teaspoons grated Parmesan, if desired.

NUTRITION INFORMATION: Cal: 627 Pro: 19g/12% Carb: 105g/64% Fat: 13g/18% (S:15% M:73% P:12%) Alc: 6% Chol: 0mg Sodium: 83mg Potassium: 1456mg Fiber: 7g A: 269% C: 102% E: 18% B1: 51% B2: 40% B3: 40% B6: 25% Folic: 22% Panto: 20% Ca: 12% P: 36% Fe: 33% Mag: 31% Zn: 16% Cu: 22% Mn: 24% Se: 100% Cr: 121%
EXCHANGE: Bread: $5\frac{1}{4}$ Veg: $4\frac{1}{2}$ Fat: $2\frac{1}{2}$

MICROWAVE METHOD: Cook the pasta according to package directions; drain; keep warm. Prepare the vegetables and process as above. In a 2-quart microwave-safe casserole or bowl, cook the chopped vegetables including all the tomatoes and only ¼ cup wine, covered, on High (100% power) to boiling, about 8 to 10 minutes. Add the zucchini and mushrooms. Cook covered on High until the vegetables are tender-crisp, about 2 to 3 minutes. Toss with the pasta and basil; serve as above.

Spaghetti with Herb Sauce

by *American Health*

¼ cup olive or vegetable oil
¼ cup chopped fresh parsley
¼ cup chopped fresh basil, or 2 tablespoons
   dried
 2 tablespoons freshly grated Parmesan cheese
 2 tablespoons ground walnuts
½ teaspoon ground nutmeg
 1 clove garlic, peeled and minced
½ cup unsalted chicken broth or stock (see
   page 28)
 1 pound dry spaghetti

PREPARATION TIME: 15 minutes
COOKING TIME: 15 to 20 minutes
YIELD: 5 to 6 servings

In a blender at medium speed, blend all the ingredients except the spaghetti until smooth.
   Cook the spaghetti according to package directions; drain.
   Toss the sauce with the hot spaghetti.

NUTRITION INFORMATION: Cal: 368 Pro: 12g/ 12% Carb: 54g/58% Fat: 13g/30% (S:17% M:67% P:16%) Chol: 2mg Sodium: 49mg Potassium: 236mg Fiber: 2g E: 19% B1: 21% B2: 12% B3: 14% P: 16% Fe: 16% Mg: 12% Se: 152%
   EXCHANGE: Bread: 3½ Fat: 2

Hungarian Noodle Kugel

by Ceri Hadda

This delicious pudding needs nothing more than a steamed vegetable to make a complete meal.

 2 cups chopped onion
 1 tablespoon unsalted margarine or butter
 3 tablespoons poppy seeds
 2 teaspoons sweet paprika
 4 eggs
 8 ounces 1%-fat cottage cheese
½ cup skim milk
½ cup plain low-fat yogurt
¼ teaspoon ground white pepper
½ pound dry broad egg noodles
   Vegetable cooking spray
 2 tablespoons wheat germ

PREPARATION TIME: 30 minutes
COOKING TIME: 50 minutes
YIELD: 6 servings

Slowly sauté the onion in the margarine or butter in a nonstick skillet over moderate heat 10 minutes, or until translucent. Add the poppy seeds and paprika; sauté 1 minute longer, stirring often. Cool. Combine the eggs, cottage cheese, skim milk, yogurt, and white pepper in a food processor; cover and blend well. Preheat the oven to 350°F.
   Parboil the noodles 4 or 5 minutes, or until barely tender. Drain and run under cold water; drain well. In a large bowl, toss together the noodles, onion mixture, and cheese mixture until well blended. Spray a 9-inch-square baking pan with cooking spray; sprinkle with wheat germ. Spoon the noodle mixture into the pan and smooth the top until even. Bake in the preheated oven 30 to 40 minutes, or until set and golden on top. Cut into squares to serve.

NUTRITION INFORMATION: Cal: 301 Pro: 17g/ 23% Carb: 35g/47% Fat: 10g/30% (S:28% M:38% P:34%) Chol: 176mg Sodium: 229mg Potassium: 353mg Fiber: 2g A: 16% E: 11% B1: 21% B2: 21% B6: 15% B12: 16% Folic: 15% Ca: 19% P: 30% Fe: 15% Io: 21% Mg: 17% Zn:

12% Cu: 15% Mn: 16% Se: 114% Cr: 10% Mo: 38%

EXCHANGE: Med. Meat: 1¼ Skim Milk: ¼ Bread: 1¾ Veg: ¾ Fat: ½

Italian Vegetable Soup with Tortellini and Olives

by Joanna Bergman

2 tablespoons olive oil
2 medium onions, coarsely chopped
1 clove garlic, peeled and minced
1 medium zucchini, coarsely chopped
1 medium carrot, chopped
1 celery rib and leaves, chopped
1 small fennel bulb, chopped
8 Greek or other oil-cured black olives, pitted and chopped
1 medium tomato, seeded and chopped
6 cups unsalted chicken broth or stock (see page 28)
¼ cup dry white wine
¾ pound cheese tortellini
  Freshly ground black pepper
1 teaspoon chopped fresh basil
1 teaspoon chopped fresh parsley

PREPARATION TIME: 40 minutes
COOKING TIME: 50 to 55 minutes
YIELD: 8 servings

In a large stockpot, heat the oil over medium heat. Add the onions and garlic and lower heat. Sauté gently until they are tender, about 20 minutes.

Add the zucchini, carrot, celery, fennel, olives, and tomato to the pot with onions and garlic. Continue to cook over low heat, stirring, until vegetables are tender but not brown, about 20 minutes.

Add the chicken broth, white wine, and tortellini to stockpot; heat to boiling. Boil broth mixture until the tortellini test done, 3 to 5 minutes.

Add pepper to taste. Ladle into bowls, evenly dividing vegetables and tortellini. Garnish with the chopped basil and parsley.

NUTRITION INFORMATION: Cal: 263 Pro: 13g/19% Carb: 35g/52% Fat: 9g/29% (S:35% M:55% P:10%) Chol: 9mg Sodium: 240mg Potassium: 596mg Fiber: 3g A: 108% C: 22% B1: 15% B2: 13% B3: 21% B6: 12% Ca: 15% P: 21% Fe: 12% Mg: 11% Cu: 12% Mn: 15% Se: 44% Cr: 35%

EXCHANGE: Med. Meat: ½ Bread: 1¾ Veg: 1½ Fat: 1

MICROWAVE METHOD: In a 3-quart microwave-safe casserole place oil, onions, and garlic and cook on High (100% power) until onion is tender, about 3 minutes. Add the broth and wine. Cook, covered, on High just to boiling, about 10 to 12 minutes. Add the zucchini, carrot, celery, fennel, olives, and tomato. Cook, covered, on High until vegetables are tender, about 10 minutes, stirring once. Add the tortellini. Cook, covered, on High until tortellini are tender, about 3 to 4 minutes. Let stand 5 minutes. Serve as directed above.

◊ CORN ◊

As American As Corn

by Susan Lang

From sea to shining sea, corn reigns supreme as king of America's farmland. Our native son covers more acreage and turns sunshine into sustenance more efficiently than most crops.

We don't eat most of what we grow, though—at least not directly. As with soybeans, the lion's share goes to feed the hogs and other livestock. A good portion of the rest is processed into corn oil and the commercial sweetener high-fructose corn syrup. Corn by-products also find their way into foods such as gum, gravy, pickles, peanut butter, and sausage, even dog biscuits. Not to mention crayons, drugs, dice, sandpaper, straws, and surgical gloves.

We prefer it fresh! Indeed, how many experiences can rival a barefoot summer's first taste of steaming sweet corn on the cob?

But we also like cornmeal, ground from dent, or field corn, which contributes an unmistakable corny taste to corn breads and muffins, Southern fritters and grits, New England Indian pudding, Hopi blue corn bread (pikis), and Mexican tortillas.

Whole fresh corn is a good complex carbohydrate, offering moderate amounts of the B vitamins, vitamin C, folic acid, and potassium. It's also rich in fiber: A cup of cooked corn has over 7 grams of dietary fiber. Yellow corn is a good source of vitamin A; white corn, not so good. A cup of cooked yellow corn gives you about 10 percent of the USRDA for vitamin A; white corn, less than half a percent. Similarly, 3½ ounces of dry yellow cornmeal, just under a cup, provides about 10 percent, while white cornmeal yields essentially no vitamin A at all.

Other than the vitamin A content, the scores of varieties of corn vary little nutritionally, says USDA nutritionist Dennis Drake. The sugar content may vary, but that's largely a function of how old the corn is. Although when fresh it is served as a vegetable, corn is actually a grain. It is fairly low in protein, compared with wheat or rice, but becomes a complete protein when complemented with legumes (dried beans, peas, and lentils), dairy products, fish, poultry, or meat. Thus succotash, which combines corn and lima beans, provides complete protein. Even a morning corn muffin has complete protein: The eggs and milk in the muffin complement the cornmeal. Each Honey Corn Muffin on page 78 has 3.5 grams of protein, 6 percent of the daily needs of a 150-pound adult. If even a muffin yields a little protein, consider how misplaced are our protein fears, even among vegetarians. In the American diet, protein is everywhere.

Cornmeal

Cornmeal, as well as its more finely ground cousin corn flour, is a fine staple. But much depends on how we treat it. As with wheat, most cornmeal has been stripped of its mineral-, oil-, and protein-rich germ and high-fiber bran (hull), and then enriched with thiamin, riboflavin, niacin, and iron to the levels found in whole wheat.

A better bet is stoneground whole cornmeal, often found in health food stores. It has significantly more calcium, potassium, phosphorus, magnesium, and dietary fiber than its degerminated, enriched counterpart. The latter, though, does have one advantage: Without the oil-rich germ, cornmeal may be stored indefinitely; whole grain cornmeal must be refrigerated or frozen or it will go rancid in a few days.

Better yet: We can go native. Cornmeal grown, processed, and prepared with traditional native American methods—including those that have become central to Mexican cooking—is often much more nourishing than even our modern stoneground variety.

If it weren't for an Indian stash of plain old field corn, the Pilgrims might have perished their first winter here. Native Americans had been reaping and revering the sunny grass for centuries. The Indians used nearly every part of the corn plant; even the fungal parasites that attack the ripening grain were considered a delicacy. Corn silks—those golden strands we chuck when husking—were brewed for a tea (see Spotlight).

It was the kernels, though, that provided the staple for North American Indians. A nutritious staple it was, too. Hopi cornmeal, for example, provides four times more zinc and magnesium and twice as much potassium, manganese, calcium, phosphorus, copper, and iron as our degermed, iron-enriched cornmeal.

How the plant is bred, grown, and processed all contribute to the native food's superiority, researchers believe.

Take processing. The Hopi custom—shared by the Navajos, Pueblos, and others—of adding ash from cooking fires (often derived from burned juniper branches) to blue cornmeal ensures a mush the color of slate blue; when mixed with a liquid, the color is lavender. Before processing, blue cornmeal is a little higher in protein, iron, magnesium, and zinc than whole ground yellowcorn, but it has less phosphorus and calcium, and twice as much fat. But the traditional Hopi alkaline treatment with culinary ash hikes the calcium content three-hundredfold. Thus, a half cup of blue cornmeal (100 grams), which starts out with less than a milligram of calcium, winds up with 334 milligrams when mixed with ash, in one survey. Culinary ash treatment also triples the content of potassium and phosphorus, and doubles the magnesium.

Unfortunately, the blue cornmeal now being marketed in many health food stores isn't generally treated with culinary ash. So while it's a fine complex carbohydrate, it's not a great source of calcium.

To benefit from our native ancestors' customs, in fact, we need to eat tortillas. In almost all tortillarias (tortilla-making factories), whole corn is soaked in lime to make masa harina: tortilla flour. The process boosts calcium twenty to thirty times and renders the niacin much more available. Two enriched-corn tortillas, for example, have 84 milligrams of calcium, nearly 10 percent of the USRDA. (Too much protein and phosphorus, however, may interfere with the body's ability to retain calcium, so don't go filling your tortillas with lots of beef [protein, phosphorus] and chasing it with soda pop [phosphorus] if you want to benefit fully from the calcium.)

Lime-processing also explains why maize-dependent societies that use lime rarely develop pellagra, caused by niacin deficiency, whereas other corn-based cultures, by contrast, have suffered from it.

Grits

Grits—coarsely ground corn that's been boiled to loosen and remove the hulls—is another corn food that's alkali-treated. Unfortunately, though, the process destroys many of the nutrients. "Grits" can actually can be made from wheat, barley, and other grains as well, but in this country we prefer corn. Hominy grits, a specialty in the South, is made from Indian corn and is the most coarsely ground. As with any corn food, the yellow variety has more vitamin A. Grits also have a small amount of fiber.

Corn Bran

Corn bran, the outer portion of the kernel, has twice as much dietary fiber as does wheat bran. That's made it a popular addition to high-fiber breakfast cereals, helping the manufacturers boost their fiber claims.

Like wheat bran, corn bran is primarily insoluble. It appears to have the same beneficial stool-bulking effect as wheat bran, and may help treat or prevent constipation, diverticulosis, and other intestinal ills. Soluble fibers, such as those in oats and beans, tend to lower cholesterol. As with most nutrients, it's best to get our dietary fiber from as wide a variety of foods as possible.

Popcorn

One type of corn that only gains in popularity is popcorn. Americans munch more than 11 billion quarts a year, says the Popcorn Institute; that's 46 quarts per person. And when it's not drenched in fat and salt, it is one of nature's healthiest snacks.

Air-popped in an electric popper, unadorned with butter and salt, popcorn is an excellent low-calorie, high-carbohydrate, high-fiber snack. The National Cancer Institute recommends it as a moderately high-fiber food. Plain popcorn is a mere 31 calories a cup and contains about 1.4 grams of dietary fiber. An entire quart is about 120 calories, the same as a large apple or a medium-sized oatmeal cookie.

Popcorn is also good for your teeth and gums. Because eating popcorn massages the gums, it helps prevent plaque buildup—and it's low in plaque-promoting fermentable carbohydrates (such as sugar). That's why the American Dental Association endorses popcorn. One Minneapolis dentist even serves it in his waiting room.

But beware of movie popcorn: It's usually popped in highly saturated coconut oil, which is even more saturated than beef fat, and loaded with salt. Most microwave popcorns are also loaded with fat to prevent burning. A better bet: Get a hot air popcorn popper or microwave popping dish and use regular jarred popcorn in it. Fat: essentially none.

Cooking With Corn _____
by Ceri Hadda

A true corn-on-the-cob afficionado starts boiling the water before the corn is picked. Even if you're not fanatical, try to buy fresh corn near its source whenever possible, since its flavor quickly diminishes with each passing hour once it is picked. As soon as corn is picked, the sugars start turning to starches, so freshest is sweetest.

Fresh corn on the cob hardly needs anything to make it utterly delicious. Pop it in boiling water, and cook for 3 to 5 minutes after it returns to a boil; avoid overcooking. A little sugar and milk added to the water for boiling corn enhances its sweetness. Or steam for 5 minutes. Even quicker: wrap each ear in a wet paper towel and cook in the microwave on High for 2 to 3 minutes. And beyond conventional boiling and steaming, corn on the cob can be prepared in the coals of a barbecue (wrap it in aluminum foil). For a lower-cholesterol topping with lots of flavor, melt $1/3$ butter with $2/3$ corn oil; season with oregano, paprika, and/or a touch of cayenne.

Off the cob, fresh corn can be enjoyed as whole kernels, creamed, or mixed with lima beans as succotash. To get fresh corn off its cob, remove several rows of kernels at once with a special corn stripper or a knife. Make sure to get the nutritious germ (inner heart) of the kernels. If you can't get fresh, use frozen or well-drained canned corn.

Corn kernels cook quickly. They only need simple treatments to showcase their sweet savor. Toss them with sautéed onions, chopped ripe tomatoes, and shredded basil. Or purée a portion (the new small food processors are excellent for this) and mix with the rest of the kernels for a cream-style corn. When combined with beaten egg whites and a little grated Cheddar cheese, this makes a nice corn puff. You can also add corn kernels to cornbread batter for a double dose of flavor—and a moist crumb.

When cooking with cornmeal or grits, remember that the amount of liquid depends on the grind. In general, of course, the less liquid used, the thicker the end product. But for a given desired thickness, the coarser the grind, the less liquid is needed.

Spotlight: Corn Silk Tea

On every continent, corn silks are used to make diuretic teas. They do have proven diuretic activity. In experiments on animals, alcohol extracts of corn silks are effective diuretics at 1.5 mg/kg—that is, about the equivalent of 75 milligrams for a 110-pound adult. In animal studies, corn silks also lower blood pressure.

Frankly, if I needed a diuretic or a blood-pressure-lowering drug, I'd ask my doctor to let me try cornsilk tea before I resorted to the more conventional pill-a-day.

—James A. Duke, Ph.D.

Cornmeal

There's little difference between yellow and white cornmeal in flavor, but stoneground cornmeal does taste more like corn. Blue cornmeal has a hearty corn flavor, not to mention an intriguing purple color. Masa harina is a finely ground cornmeal used to make tortillas and other Mexican breads; you can also add it to pastry dough to make a crust for Mexican-style meat pies and turnovers.

Try adding whole cornmeal to regular cornbread and muffins and even to other batters and doughs for flavor and texture. About 1/3 cup gives a batch of pastry dough a pleasant crumble; the cornmeal also seems to interfere with the gluten formation in the dough, rendering it tender. Yeast doughs also benefit from the addition of cornmeal. Replace 1 cup of the flour called for with cornmeal. Also sprinkle the pans with cornmeal before placing the dough in or on them. After glazing the top of the bread, sprinkle with cornmeal.

Or add cornmeal to pancake and waffle batters. These are particularly nice with a bit of molasses added to them. When you add cornmeal to a regular pancake or waffle batter, start with about 1/2 cup per batch. Add the cornmeal along with the other dry ingredients called for in the recipe; you may have to add a bit more liquid than originally called for. Increase the cornmeal in suc-cessive batches of batter by increments of a tablespoon or so, until the waffle or pancake has a texture you like. For pastry doughs, add 1/2 cup cornmeal to a single-crust dough, increasing the ice water called for by a tablespoon or two, as needed.

Most baking recipes using cornmeal also rely on wheat flour, since the cornmeal has none of the gluten that is necessary to create structure to the bread, pastry dough, or batter. Some use cornmeal in a 1 to 1 ratio, while others (notably cornbreads with their characteristic crumbly texture) use 2 to 3 parts cornmeal for every 1 part flour.

Corn Grits

In consistency, grits are a cross between rice and mashed potatoes. You can eat them for breakfast, topped with Tabasco (liquid red pepper seasoning) or freshly grated pepper. Or they can be mixed with egg whites, grated onion or scallion, cheese and hot pepper sauce, then baked into a soufflélike mixture.

Corn and Banana Pancakes

by Ceri Hadda

1/2 cup unbleached all-purpose flour
3/4 teaspoon baking powder
1/2 teaspoon baking soda
1/4 teaspoon salt
1 cup stoneground yellow cornmeal
1 egg
1 egg white
2 tablespoons corn oil
1/2 teaspoon grated orange rind
1/4 cup orange juice
1 1/3 cups low-fat buttermilk
1 ripe banana, mashed (about 1/2 cup)
2 tablespoons sugar
  Vegetable oil
  Honey, reduced-sugar orange marmalade, or maple syrup for topping

PREPARATION TIME: 15 minutes
COOKING TIME: 20 to 25 minutes
YIELD: 4 servings (about 5 pancakes per serving)

In a medium bowl, sift together the flour, baking powder, baking soda, and salt; stir in the cornmeal until well blended. In another small bowl, beat together the egg, egg white, corn oil, orange rind, juice, buttermilk, mashed banana, and sugar. Add all at once to the dry ingredients. Stir with a wire whisk just until blended.

Brush a nonstick skillet with vegetable oil. Cook the pancakes, 2 tablespoons of batter per pancake, a few at a time, over moderate heat; turn when bubbles appear on the surface. Continue cooking until the pancakes are golden brown on the second side. Remove from pan and keep warm in the oven. Repeat with remaining batter, brushing the skillet with oil between batches. Serve with honey, reduced-sugar orange marmalade, or maple syrup.

NUTRITION INFORMATION: Cal: 351 Pro: 10g/11% Carb: 57g/64% Fat: 10g/25% (S:22% M:28% P:50%) Chol: 56mg Sodium: 416mg Potassium: 351mg Fiber: 3g C: 19% E: 34% B1: 21% B2: 22% B3: 11% B6: 15% Ca: 12% P: 17% Fe: 13% Mg: 10%
EXCHANGE: Med. Meat: ¼ Skim Milk: ¼ Bread: 2½ Fruit: ¾ Fat: 1½

Corn Chowder

by Ceri Hadda

½ cup chopped scallions
½ cup chopped green bell pepper
1 tablespoon soft margarine
1 tablespoon unbleached all-purpose flour
4 cups fresh corn kernels (about 8 to 10 ears) or 2 10-ounce packages frozen corn
2 cups low-fat milk
2 tablespoons dry sherry
2 teaspoons Worcestershire sauce
⅛ teaspoon cayenne
  Pinch ground nutmeg
½ cup low-fat plain yogurt
  Chopped green bell pepper for garnish (optional)
  Chopped scallion for garnish (optional)

PREPARATION TIME: 30 minutes
COOKING TIME: 30 minutes
YIELD: 4 servings

In a medium, heavy saucepan over moderate heat, sauté the scallions and green pepper in the margarine for 2 minutes. Cover and cook over low heat 5 minutes. Uncover; stir in the flour and cook 1 minute longer, stirring constantly. Add the corn; cover the pan. Cook over moderate heat 5 to 7 minutes. (If using frozen corn, uncover the pan during cooking to gently break up the kernels.) Add the milk, sherry, Worcestershire sauce, cayenne, and nutmeg. Bring to a boil, lower the heat, and continue cooking 5 minutes longer, or until the mixture thickens slightly. Reserve 1 cup corn mixture; puree the remaining mixture, one part at a time, in the food processor. Return all to saucepan and reheat gently. Serve with a dollop of yogurt, and a sprinkling of chopped green pepper and chopped scallion if desired.

NUTRITION INFORMATION: Cal: 224 Pro: 10g/17% Carb: 40g/65% Fat: 5g/18% (S:36% M:34% P:30%) Chol: 7mg Sodium: 152mg Potassium: 532mg Fiber: 3g A: 29% C: 60% D: 16% E: 13% B1: 13% B2: 24% B3: 11% B6: 11% B12: 10% Folic: 10% Panto: 10% Ca: 22% P: 24% Mg: 13% Cr: 47%
EXCHANGE: Skim Milk: ½ Bread: 2 Veg: ¼ Fat: ¾

MICROWAVE METHOD: In a 3-quart microwave-safe casserole or bowl cook the scallions, pepper, and margarine, covered, on High (100% power) until the pepper is tender, about 2 to 3 minutes. Stir in the flour. Cook on High 1 minute. Add the corn and remaining ingredients except the yogurt and garnishes. Cook covered on High to boiling, about 6 to 8 minutes (add 2 more minutes if using frozen corn). Stir. Reduce power to Medium (50% power) and cook until the mixture thickens slightly, about 5 minutes more. Reserve 1 cup corn mixture and purée as directed above. To reheat, cook covered on High until hot, about 3 to 4 minutes. Serve as above.

Polenta with Mushroom Sauté

by Ceri Hadda

Polenta can be served plain, topped with sliced or grated cheese, or topped with mushrooms, as here. It makes a wonderful side dish with any savory or sharply flavored vegetables.

1 cup minced onion
1 tablespoon margarine or unsalted butter
1 stalk celery, minced
1½ cups stoneground yellow cornmeal
3½ cups unsalted chicken broth or stock (see Page 28)
¼ teaspoon salt (optional)
Mushroom Sauté (recipe follows)

PREPARATION TIME; 15 minutes
COOKING TIME: 40 minutes
YIELD: 6 to 8 servings

In a medium, heavy saucepan over moderate heat, sauté the onion in the margarine 3 minutes; add the celery; continue sautéing, stirring often, 5 minutes longer, or until the onion and celery are tender but not brown. Meanwhile, soften the cornmeal in ¾ cup water in a small bowl for a few minutes. Add the chicken broth, and salt if desired, to the vegetables. Slowly whisk in the moistened cornmeal. Cook over low heat, stirring often, 30 minutes, or until the mixture is as thick as mashed potatoes. Meanwhile, prepare the Mushroom Sauté. To serve, top with the Mushroom Sauté.

Mushroom Sauté

3 tablespoons minced shallots or onion
1 pound mushrooms, sliced
4 teaspoons unsalted butter or margarine
1 tablespoon dry sherry or dry white wine
Salt and freshly ground black pepper
1 teaspoon minced fresh chives (optional)

PREPARATION TIME: 15 minutes
COOKING TIME: 10 minutes
YIELD: 6 servings

Sauté the shallot and mushrooms in the margarine in a small nonstick skillet over moderate heat 5 minutes, stirring constantly, or until juices begin to flow from the mushrooms. Add the sherry or wine, and continue sautéing, stirring constantly, 3 minutes. Taste, and add salt and pepper to taste. Sprinkle with chives if desired.

VARIATION: *To make baked polenta,* pour the thickened polenta into an 8- or 9-inch baking pan; refrigerate until firm, then cut into squares; top with thin slices of cheese and bake at 350°F until heated through, about 20 minutes.

NUTRITION INFORMATION: (polenta made with margarine, and mushroom sauté): Cal: 205 Pro: 6g/11% Carb: 33g/64% Fat: 6g/25% (S:20% M:36% P:44%) Chol: 1mg Sodium: 93mg Potassium: 440mg Fiber: 2g C: 10% E: 18% B1: 17% B2: 26% B3: 25% B6: 11% Panto: 18% P: 14% Fe: 15% Cu: 39% Se: 19% Cr: 22% EXCHANGE: Bread: 1¾ Veg: 1 Fat: 1

MICROWAVE METHOD (Polenta only): Soak the cornmeal as directed above. In a 3-quart microwave-safe casserole, cook the onion, margarine, and celery on High (100% power) until celery is tender, about 3 minutes. Stir the chicken broth and salt into the vegetables; then whisk in the soaked cornmeal. Cook covered on High 5 minutes. Stir. Reduce power to Medium (50% power); cook covered until thickened, about 9 to 11 minutes, stirring every 3 minutes. Let stand 5 minutes.

MICROWAVE METHOD (Mushroom Sauté): In a 1- to 1½-quart microwave-safe casserole, cook the shallots, mushrooms, and margarine, covered, on High (100% power) until the mushrooms give off juice, about 4 minutes. Add the sherry or wine and cook covered on High until the mushrooms are tender, about 2 minutes. Season as directed above.

Garlic Grits
by Ceri Hadda

Grits, that Southern breakfast staple, can be served as a side dish or used as a base for sautéed vegetables to make a main dish.

   3 cloves garlic, peeled and minced
   2 teaspoons olive oil
   1/8 teaspoon salt
   1/4 teaspoon liquid red pepper seasoning (like Tabasco)
   2/3 cup stoneground yellow corn grits

   PREPARATION TIME: 10 minutes
   COOKING TIME: 10 minutes
   YIELD: 3 servings

In a small saucepan over moderately high heat, sauté the garlic in the oil until tender but not brown. Add 2 cups water, salt and red pepper seasoning and bring to a boil. Slowly add the grits, stirring constantly with a wire whisk. Cover, lower heat, and simmer 5 minutes, or until the grits have thickened.

   NUTRITION INFORMATION: Cal: 64   Pro: 1g/6%
   Carb: 8g/50% Fat: 3g/44% (S:15% M:76% P:9%)
   Chol: 0mg Sodium: 86mg Potassium: 27mg
   Fiber: .1g
   EXCHANGE: Bread: 1/2 Veg: 1/4 Fat: 1/2

MICROWAVE METHOD: In a 2-quart microwave-safe casserole or measuring cup, cook the garlic and oil on High (100% power) until the garlic is tender, about 2 to 3 minutes. Add the water. Cook covered on High to boiling, about 4 to 6 minutes. Stir. Slowly add the grits, stirring constantly with a wire whisk. Reduce power to Medium (50% power); cook covered until the grits have thickened and the water is absorbed, stirring once, about 4 to 5 minutes. Let stand 5 minutes. Stir in the salt and pepper seasoning and serve.

Tamale Pie
by Ceri Hadda

This recipe combines the traditional ingredients of tamales but without their time-consuming preparations.

   1/2 pound beef round, coarsely chopped or ground
   1 1/2 cups chopped onions
   1 tablespoon olive oil
   1 green bell pepper, chopped
   1 clove garlic, peeled and minced
   1 to 2 tablespoons chili powder
   1/2 teaspoon dried oregano, crushed
   1 tablespoon red wine vinegar
   2 cups 1%-fat milk
   1/2 teaspoon salt
   1/2 cup stoneground yellow corn grits
   1 cup cooked fresh, frozen, or canned corn kernels (drained if canned)

   PREPARATION TIME: 30 minutes
   COOKING TIME: 1 hour
   YIELD: 4 servings

In a large nonstick skillet over moderately high heat, sauté the meat and onions in oil 5 minutes, or until the meat is no longer pink and the onions are tender but not brown. Add half the green pepper and garlic; sauté 3 minutes longer. Add the chili powder, oregano, 2 tablespoons of water and vinegar. Lower the heat, cover, and simmer, stirring occasionally, for 30 minutes. Stir in the remaining green pepper.

Preheat the oven to 350°F. When the beef is almost tender, heat the milk and salt in a small heavy saucepan over moderately low heat. Slowly add the grits, stirring all the time with a wire whisk. Simmer, stirring often, 3 to 4 minutes, or until the mixture comes to a full boil.

Pour the beef mixture into a 9-inch glass pie plate, cover with the corn, then spread grits mixture over the top. Bake for 20 minutes, or until the grits topping is firm and the beef mixture bubbles. Cut into wedges to serve. (The tamale pie will be like a deep-dish pie when it is spooned out of the dish; that is, the grits will be in wedge shapes, but the filling will spoon out.)

NUTRITION INFORMATION: Cal: 285 Pro: 18g/ 35% Carb: 26g/37% Fat: 13g/28% (S:40% M:53% P:7%) Chol: 45mg Sodium: 391mg Potassium: 568mg Fiber: 2g A: 29% C: 49% D: 13% B1: 13% B2: 24% B3: 17% B6: 17% B12: 23% Ca: 18% P: 24% Fe: 13% Mg: 12% Zn: 21% Se: 20% Cr: 26%
EXCHANGE: Med. Meat: 1¹/₂ Skim Milk: ¹/₂ Bread: 1 Veg: 1 Fat: ³/₄

MICROWAVE METHOD: In a 1¹/₂-quart microwave-safe casserole or bowl, cook the meat, onions, and only 1 teaspoon oil, covered with wax paper, on High (100% power) 5 minutes. Stir in the green pepper, garlic, chili powder, oregano, 2 tablespoons of water, and vinegar. Cook covered on High 5 minutes. Let stand. In a 4-cup microwave-safe measure, cook the milk with salt on High until just boiling, about 5 to 7 minutes. Slowly add the grits, stirring all the time with a wire whisk. Cook covered on High until mixture comes to a full boil, about 1¹/₂ to 2 minutes. Assemble in a 9-inch pie plate and bake as directed above.

Savory Corn Bread

by *American Health*

Vegetable oil
1 scallion, chopped
¹/₂ small red bell pepper, chopped
1¹/₄ cups unbleached all-purpose flour
³/₄ cup stoneground yellow cornmeal
2 tablespoons sugar
1 tablespoon double-acting baking powder
1 egg white
1 cup skim milk
¹/₄ cup margarine, melted

PREPARATION TIME: 20 minutes
COOKING TIME: 25 minutes
YIELD: 12 servings

Preheat the oven to 425°F.
Lightly grease an 8- by 8-inch square baking pan with vegetable oil. In a medium bowl, mix the next six ingredients. In a small bowl, combine the remaining ingredients; pour into the flour mixture, stirring just until moistened. Pour into the baking pan and bake 25 minutes, or until golden.

NUTRITION INFORMATION: Cal: 127 Pro: 3g/ 10% Carb: 19g/61% Fat: 4g/29% (S:19% M:37% P:44%) Chol: 1mg Sodium: 151mg Potassium: 67mg Fiber: .4g E: 12%
EXCHANGE: Bread: 1 Fat: 1

Anadama Bread

by Ceri Hadda

This classic New England yeast bread is made with cornmeal and molasses, two ingredients that help keep it fresh. The name is said to come from the expletive, "Anna, damn her," but whether it was muttered in affection or anger is unknown.

2¹/₂ to 3 cups unbleached all-purpose flour
³/₄ cup stoneground yellow cornmeal
1 teaspoon salt
1 package active dry yeast
¹/₂ cup skim milk
3 tablespoons corn oil
¹/₄ cup dark molasses
Vegetable oil
Vegetable cooking spray

PREPARATION TIME: 45 minutes plus rising time
COOKING TIME: 50 minutes
YIELD: 1 loaf (16 slices)

Combine 1¹/₂ cups of the flour with the cornmeal, salt, and undissolved yeast in a large bowl. Heat the milk, ¹/₂ cup water, oil, and molasses until very warm (120° to 130°F) in a small saucepan over low heat; then gradually add to the dry ingredients. Beat with an electric mixer at medium speed for 2 minutes, scraping the sides of the bowl occasionally. Add ¹/₂ cup more flour; beat at medium speed until the flour is absorbed, then increase mixer speed to high and continue beating 2 minutes longer, scraping the sides of the bowl occasionally. (If the dough gets too stiff for the mixer, knead until the flour is absorbed.) Knead in as much of the remaining flour as necessary to make a stiff dough.

Turn the dough out onto a floured surface. Knead 5 minutes, or until smooth and elastic. Place in a bowl lightly greased with vegetable oil; turn the dough so the greased side is exposed. Cover the bowl with a dish towel and let the dough rise in a warm place, away from drafts, 45 minutes, or until doubled in bulk. Punch down. Let rest 10 minutes.

Roll the dough out on a floured surface to a rectangle; roll up and pinch the seams to form a loaf. Place the dough, seam side down, in a 9- by 5-inch loaf pan sprayed with cooking spray. Cover the pan with a dish towel. Let the dough rise in a warm place, away from drafts, 45 minutes, or until almost doubled in bulk.

Preheat the oven to 375°F. Bake in the preheated oven 45 minutes, or until the top is golden brown and the loaf makes a hollow sound when the underside is lightly tapped. Invert onto a wire rack and let cool before slicing.

NUTRITION INFORMATION (per slice): Cal: 147 Pro: 3g/9% Carb: 26g/72% Fat: 3g/9% (S:6% M:25% P:59%) Chol: 1mg Sodium: 132mg Potassium: 253mg Fiber: .5g B1: 19% B2:11% B3:12%
EXCHANGE: Bread: 1 1/2 Fat: 1/2

Corn Biscuits

by Ceri Hadda

2/3 cup unsifted unbleached all-purpose flour
2/3 cup stoneground yellow cornmeal
1 1/4 teaspoon baking powder
1/4 teaspoon baking soda
1/4 teaspoon salt
1/4 cup margarine, softened
1/2 cup plain low-fat yogurt

PREPARATION TIME: 20 minutes
COOKING TIME: 15 minutes
YIELD: 16 biscuits

Preheat the oven to 425°F. Combine the flour, cornmeal, baking powder, baking soda, and salt in a medium bowl. With your fingertips, rub the margarine into the dry ingredients until the mixture resembles coarse crumbs. Add the yogurt all at once and stir with a fork just until the mixture forms a dough. Knead the dough lightly in the bowl seven or eight times. Pat into a 5- by 6-inch rectangle on an ungreased baking sheet. Score into sixteen pieces but do not separate the pieces. (This produces biscuits that are crunchy on top but soft on the sides; for very crunchy biscuits, cut dough before placing biscuits, 1 inch apart, on the baking sheet.) Bake in the preheated oven 15 minutes, or until the biscuits are golden.

NUTRITION INFORMATION: Cal. 69 Pro: 1g/ 8% Carb: 9g/51% Fat: 3g/41% (S:20% M:37% P:43%) Chol: 1mg Sodium: 116mg Potassium: 30mg Fiber: .1g
EXCHANGE: Bread: 1/2 Fat: 1/2

Honey Corn Muffins

by Ceri Hadda

1/2 cup unsifted unbleached all-purpose flour
1/2 cup fine whole wheat pastry flour
1 cup stoneground yellow cornmeal
2 teaspoons baking powder
1/2 teaspoon baking soda
1/4 teaspoon salt
1 egg
1 cup plain nonfat yogurt or buttermilk
1/3 cup honey
1/4 cup corn oil

PREPARATION TIME: 20 minutes
COOKING TIME: 20 minutes
YIELD: 12 muffins

Preheat the oven to 400°F. Lightly grease 12 nonstick muffin pan cups with vegetable spray. In a medium bowl, combine the flours, cornmeal, baking powder, baking soda, and salt until well blended. In a small bowl, mix the egg, yogurt or buttermilk, honey, and corn oil until well blended.

Add to the dry ingredients and beat just until moistened (do not overbeat the batter or the muffins will be tough and dry). Divide the batter evenly among the muffin cups. Bake in the preheated oven 15 to 20 minutes, or until the muffins are firm. Cool in the pan on a wire rack 2 minutes; remove onto the rack. Serve warm.

NUTRITION INFORMATION: Cal. 164 Pro: 4g/9% Carb: 26g/62% Fat: 5g/29% (S:16% M:27% P:57%) Chol: 18mg Sodium: 156mg Potassium: 97mg Fiber: .8g E: 21%
EXCHANGE: Bread: 1 Fruit: 1/2 Fat: 1

MICROWAVE METHOD: Prepare the batter as directed above. Lightly grease two microwave safe muffin pans of six cups each. Divide the batter evenly among the muffin cups. Let stand 10 minutes. Cook one pan on High (100% power) until the tops are firm, about 2 1/2 to 4 minutes, rotating once. Let cool 5 minutes. Remove from pan. Meanwhile, repeat with the remaining pan. Serve warm.

Indian Pudding

by Ceri Hadda

Vegetable oil
1/2 cup stoneground yellow cornmeal
1/4 teaspoon salt
4 cups low-fat milk
1 tart green apple, peeled and chopped
1/4 cup dark molasses
1/3 cup raisins
2 tablespoons sugar
1 teaspoon ground ginger
1/2 teaspoon ground cinnamon

PREPARATION TIME: 30 minutes
COOKING TIME: 1 1/2 hours
YIELD: 12 servings

Preheat the oven to 300°F. With vegetable oil, lightly grease a 1 1/2- to 2-quart baking dish and sprinkle with 1 teaspoon of the cornmeal. Combine the remaining cornmeal, the salt, and 1/2 cup of the milk in a small bowl. Scald the remaining milk in the top of a double boiler over direct heat; slowly add the moistened cornmeal, a little at a time, beating constantly with a whisk. Place over boiling water and cook, whisking often, 25 minutes, or until the mixture thickens. Remove from the heat and stir in the apple, molasses, raisins, sugar, ginger, and cinnamon. Pour the mixture into the prepared baking dish. Bake 1 1/2 hours, or until the pudding sets, stirring after 1 hour and then again at end of the baking time. Serve warm or chilled, with milk poured over each serving if desired.

NUTRITION INFORMATION: Cal: 96 Pro: 3g/13% Carb: 19g/78% Fat: 1g/9% Chol: 3mg Sodium: 87mg Potassium: 234mg Fiber: .5g Ca: 12%
EXCHANGE: Skim Milk: 1/4 Bread: 1/2 Fruit: 1/2

◇ RICE ◇

The Ubiquitous Staple: Rice

by Kevin Cobb

For much of the world, rice isn't a type of food; it simply *is* food. In some Asian languages, rice and food are the same word. For over a billion and a half people, rice constitutes as much as 80 percent of total calories; more than half of all rice is still consumed within eight miles of where it's grown.

In America, rice is just another food. Our indifferent response to this ubiquitous grain is bewildering when you look at what rice has to offer. Like that of any grain, rice protein needs the complement of other vegetable protein sources such as beans, or animal sources such as milk or meat, to form a complete protein. Rice has more protein than other grains, and its protein is more easily utilized.

The rice we do eat is mostly white and milled, the least nutritious type. But consumption of brown rice is on the rise. Like whole wheat, millet, and barley, brown rice is an excellent source of the complex carbohydrates that are the ideal replacement for the excess fat in our diets.

But rice has unique virtues: For example, it's one of the least allergenic foods known. That's one reason why rice cereals are often the first solid food a baby is given. "Rice is one of the most common components of hypoallergenic diets," says food scientist Steven Taylor of the University of Nebraska. "It's a safe dietary substitute for people with allergies to wheat, rye, barley, and oats; it's also a good substitute for people with celiac disease." Rice flour can be used to make baked goods for those on gluten-free diets. One possible explanation is that humans were eating rice earlier in our evolution than these other grains. In the humid tropics of Asia, for example, the gathering of wild-growing rices preceded the beginning of agriculture.

Rice is an easy food to digest, which makes it ideal for people at both ends of the age spectrum. Like most grains, its starch is amylopectin, which the body breaks down more readily than the starch in legumes, amylose. For the elderly, rice is easy to chew and digest.

Rice can also help us lose weight. When Dr. Walter Kempner of the Duke University Medical Center began prescribing a rice-and-fruit treatment to his patients with kidney disease half a century ago, he found they also lost weight. Many of the nutritional assumptions behind the rice diet were heretical to the medical establishment of the 1930s and 1940s. It was Dr. Kempner's belief that we eat too much protein and fat (particularly from animal sources), too little complex carbohydrates, and too much salt. He saw these as contributing to high blood pressure, diabetes, atherosclerosis, and obesity. People at Dr. Kempner's "Rice House" at Duke eat rice—but not *just* rice!—as often as twice a day, and lose weight.

While there are thousands of varieties of rice, there are only three general types: brown, white, and wild. All white rice begins life as brown; it becomes "white" when the outer bran layers are milled off, along with the husk, the polish (the inner bran layers), and the nutritious germ. After brown (unpolished) rice, enriched uncooked white rice is the most nutritious form of rice available. Wild "rice" is actually not a grain at all, but a grass; unlike true rices, it is native to America.

Although grain size (long, medium, or short) doesn't affect nutrition, precooking does. Rice is available uncooked, converted (parboiled), and precooked. Precooked is the "instant" or "minute" variety and is the worst choice nutritionally. It is cooked prior to packaging and then a second time at home. This double-cooking reduces much of the nutritional value. Although manufacturers add vitamins to enrich the rice, the nutrients are added to the surface and can be lost if you wash the rice first. Instant rice is usually more expensive as well, although quick to prepare.

Converted—or parboiled—rice is a better bet. Before it is milled, converted rice is soaked, steamed, and dried. This process pushes nutrients from the outer bran layer into the starchy "white" part of the rice. Uncooked white rice (the label may read "milled" or "polished") has simply had the hull and outer bran layers removed, without precooking or other treatment.

(Never buy rice that's labeled "coated"; this rice has been coated with sugar and talc, and may be contaminated with carcinogenic asbestos, according to food authors Nikki and David Goldbeck.)

Brown rice, the rice with the outer husk removed but most of the fiber-filled outer bran layer intact, is nutritionally superior to all white rice varieties. Whole and unpolished, it has a light brown grain with a chewy texture and a nutty taste. The bran layers that make it brown provide a boost in many nutrients, giving brown rice more protein, phosphorus, potassium, B vitamins, and much more fiber. (Enriched white rice has more iron and thiamin added back.) A half cup of uncooked brown rice, which cooks up to about a cup and a half, for example, gets 9 percent of its calories from protein (7 percent come from fat; 84 percent from carbohydrates), and provides a substantial 7.2 grams of dietary fiber. It also gives us about a quarter of the USRDA for vitamins B1, B3, and B6, about a sixth for magnesium, plus significant amounts of zinc, copper, and manganese.

Wild rice is sometimes called "the caviar of grains," both for its taste and its price. Nutritionally, though, it's a bargain. Compared to brown rice, an equal-sized serving has fewer calories and more protein than brown rice.

Rice polish and rice bran—the nutritious parts of the rice removed in milling—can be purchased in health food stores. Rich in B-vitamins, they can be added to foods to boost their nutritional value like wheat germ.

And maybe more: A few human studies suggest that rice bran may help lower elevated levels of blood cholesterol. Although an Australian study showed that rice bran wasn't as effective as oat bran in lowering cholesterol levels, two other studies—one at the University of California, Davis and another at Louisiana State University—found that 80 to 100 grams of rice bran (more than a cup's worth) a day was as effective as oat bran. In the California study, total cholesterol levels dropped an average of 8 percent after six weeks of eating 3 ounces of rice bran a day. The active component, however, may be the rice oil and not the fiber, researchers believe. They also stress that it's much too early to draw firm conclusions about these potential cholesterol-lowering properties. It's not too early, however, to eat more unpolished brown rice, naturally rich in bran.

Cooking Rice

by Joanna Bergmann and Ceri Hadda

With rice available in ever greater varieties, it can be easily incorporated into every meal of the day, from morning cereal to rice pudding for dessert. Most types of cooked rice are interchangeable, cup for cup, in recipes.

Most rice yields about 3 cups of cooked rice for every cup of raw rice used; shorter grain rices yield less, usually 2½ to 3 cups for every cup of raw rice.

When cooking rice, stir with a fork to minimize crushing the grains. As with pasta, rice should be given plenty of room to cook; otherwise as it expands, it will be crowded in the pot and the grains will mash against one another. For extra flavor, use broth, tomato juice, beet juice, or part water/part dry wine as the liquid for boiling the rice. (If you use canned broth, buy no-salt-added varieties.) Try sautéing a small onion, celery and/or pepper before adding rice and liquid to the pan.

A mixture of chopped fresh herbs such as parsley, dill, and basil, alone or in combination with a little minced garlic or scallions, can also be stirred into any cooked rice just before serving to give this grain flavor without added salt or fat; use a fork to stir and fluff up at the same time.

Leftover cooked rice is a versatile ingredient. Add it to muffin, quick bread, or pancake batters. To form the rice into croquettes, season with onions and add 1 egg white per 2 cups rice.

Certain kinds of rice are particularly well suited to specific cooking approaches. The grains of long-grain white rice remain separate when cooked, making this variety most appropriate when a fluffy rice is desired. Bring the rice, with twice its volume of water, to a boil; stir with a fork, cover and simmer 15 to 20 minutes or until the liquid has been absorbed and the rice is tender but not mushy.

For long-grain brown rice, follow the directions for long-grain white rice, but use $2\frac{1}{2}$ times as much liquid as raw rice, and increase the cooking time to 45 to 50 minutes.

For medium-grain rice, brown or white, follow the respective directions above, but decrease the amount of liquid by $\frac{1}{2}$ cup. It sticks together a little better than long-grain, and so works well in stuffings. Its stickier starch also helps to thicken soups.

Short-grain rice is the tenderest, softest, and stickiest rice. Most Chinese and Japanese rice is short-grain white rice; it's a denser-grain, moist, sticky rice that's perfect for eating in the traditional manner with chopsticks. Or chill the cooked rice and form into croquettes and other shapes that benefit from the rice's clinging personality. To cook short-grain rice, rinse it, then soak in a little more than the same volume of water for 10

minutes. Bring to a boil; lower heat; cover. Simmer 10 minutes, or until almost cooked. Remove from the heat; let stand 10 minutes.

For short-grain brown rice, cook as for white short-grain, but double the cooking time. (Glutinous rice, also known as sweet rice, also short-grain, nearly round, cooks to a tender, almost dissolved texture, making it most suitable for rice puddings and desserts. It's found in Asian markets.) Arborio rice is the Italian short-grain variety, used in risotto.

Aromatic rices have a distinctive smell and taste. Examples include Indian-grown basmati rice and Texas aromatic long-grain rice. Basmati rice is traditional in Indian cooking; it's great as a pilaf or biryani (India's answer to fried rice) base or side dish. Rinse imported basmati rice to remove all impurities, which can include dirt, pebbles, and other oddities. Add a few cardamon pods, slightly crushed, to the water as you cook basmati rice; the rice will acquire a delicate flavor. Basmati is so flavorful that a tablespoon or two is sometimes sautéed, along with other whole spices, in curry making.

Rice flour is milled rice, ground into flour. It's a good substitute for wheat flour, especially for those who are allergic to wheat. It imparts a pleasantly slippery texture to cookie doughs, much the way cornstarch does. Since rice flour has no gluten, it cannot be used in its entirety to replace wheat flour in bread baking; substitute rice flour for about $\frac{1}{3}$ of the flour called for in a bread recipe.

Finally, there is wild rice, which is no more a rice than ancho peppers are like black peppers. A grass rather than a grain, wild rice is a flavorful, nutty, and chewy treat. Simmer the rice for 30 to 40 minutes, until the grains split, revealing their soft gray interior, and look fluffy. Wild rice can be enjoyed alone or in combination with rice, as in a wild and brown rice pilaf. If you're mixing the wild rice with regular rice, cook each separately since the times may vary.

Brown Rice Cereal with Apricots

by Ceri Hadda and
Joanna Bergmann

³/4 cup chopped dried apricots
*1 cup brown rice cream cereal, packaged or
    homemade (see Note)*
4 cups skim milk
¹/2 teaspoon salt (optional)
¹/4 cup currants or raisins
1 tablespoon maple syrup
¹/2 teaspoon ground cinnamon
¹/2 teaspoon vanilla
3 tablespoons sliced almonds

PREPARATION TIME: 15 minutes
COOKING TIME: 10 minutes
YIELD: 4 servings

Soak the apricots in hot water to cover for 10 minutes. Drain. Mix the rice cream cereal with the milk, salt (if desired), currants, maple syrup, cinnamon, vanilla, and drained apricots in a saucepan and bring to a boil over medium heat. Reduce the heat and stir for at least 2 minutes, or until the mixture thickens. Add a bit more milk or water if it thickens too fast. Sprinkle with sliced almonds and serve immediately.

NOTE: *To make your own brown rice cereal,* wash 2 cups raw brown rice and spread on a baking sheet, bake at 350F° for 10 minutes, or until golden; and grind in a coffee grinder. Use right away or store in an airtight jar. Makes 2 cups.

NUTRITION INFORMATION: Cal: 277 Pro: 12g/17% Carb: 51g/70% Fat: 4g/13% Chol: 4mg Sodium: 134mg Potassium: 899mg Fiber: 5g A: 45% D: 26% E: 12% B1: 11% B2: 26% B3: 11% B12: 15% Panto: 10% Ca: 34% P: 37% Fe: 12% Mg: 15% Cu: 15% Mn: 27% Se: 25%
EXCHANGE: Skim Milk: 1 Bread: ³/4 Fruit: 1¹/2 Fat: ¹/2

Chicken Creole Soup

by Ceri Hadda and
Joanna Bergmann

This spicy soup makes a hearty main dish.

*1 3-pound fryer chicken, cut up, or 3 pounds
    chicken parts, skin and visible fat removed*
*5 cups unsalted chicken broth or stock (see
    page 28)*
*¹/2 cup raw long-grain brown, white, or
    converted rice*
2 large onions, coarsely chopped
1 tablespoon olive oil
¹/2 pound fresh mushrooms, thinly sliced
3 cloves garlic, finely minced
2 celery ribs, coarsely chopped
1 green bell pepper, coarsely chopped
*2 cups diced seeded fresh tomatoes, or when
    out of season, canned Italian plum tomatoes,
    no salt added*
*¹/2 teaspoon crushed red pepper flakes, or more
    to taste*
6 small green olives, chopped
¹/2 cup dry white wine
1 tablespoon brown sugar
Freshly ground black pepper
Rind of ¹/4 lemon, julienne cut, for garnish
*2 tablespoons finely chopped fresh parsley for
    garnish*

PREPARATION TIME: 40 minutes
COOKING TIME: 2 hours
YIELD: 6 servings

Place the chicken pieces in a medium stockpot, add the broth, and bring to a boil over medium heat. Reduce the heat and simmer until the chicken is fork-tender, about 30 minutes. Remove the chicken from the broth to cool slightly. Skim the surface of the broth and discard any impurities and fat. Remove 1¹/2 cups broth from the pot to a saucepan if using brown rice—1 cup if using white rice—and set the stockpot aside. In the saucepan, cook the rice in the broth, covered, until the rice is tender, about 40 minutes for brown rice or 20 minutes for white rice. When the chicken is cool enough to handle, discard the bones and cut the meat into bite-size pieces. Set aside.

In a skillet, sauté the onions in olive oil until translucent, about 5 minutes. Add ¼ cup broth from the pot and the mushrooms. Cook over medium heat until the liquid in the skillet is almost evaporated. Add the garlic and celery to the skillet and cook about 3 minutes longer. Add the pepper and cook another 2 minutes. Add the tomatoes and cook at least 5 minutes longer. Add the red pepper flakes, olives, and wine; over high heat cook until the alcohol from the wine evaporates, about 5 minutes.

To the remaining broth in the stockpot, add the cooked vegetables and rice, chicken pieces, and brown sugar. Heat through and season to taste with freshly ground pepper. Meanwhile, blanch the lemon rind in a strainer held in boiling water about 5 minutes, then pat dry with paper towels. Ladle the soup into bowls and sprinkle with lemon rind and parsley.

NUTRITION INFORMATION: Cal: 355 Pro: 35g/ 39% Carb: 28g/31% Fat: 12g/30% (S:27% M:51% P:22%) Chol: 88mg Sodium: 227mg Potassium: 997mg Fiber: 5g A: 28% C: 66% E: 10% B1: 18% B2: 26% B3: 70% B6: 42% Panto: 28% P: 35% Fe: 21% Mg: 14% Zn: 21% Cu: 27% Mn: 17% Cr: 45%
EXCHANGE: Lean Meat: 3½ Bread: ¾ Veg: 2¼ Fat ½

Raisin Rice
by *American Health*

This side dish also makes an excellent stuffing for roast chicken.

>   *2 cups raw enriched long-grain white or 1½ cups long-grain brown rice*
> *½ cup dark seedless raisins*
> *½ cup walnut pieces*
> *¼ teaspoon salt*
> *⅛ teaspoon ground ginger*
> *¼ teaspoon freshly ground black pepper*

PREPARATION TIME: 10 minutes
COOKING TIME: 20 minutes
YIELD: 5 servings

Prepare the rice as the package directs, omitting salt. To the hot cooked rice, add the remaining ingredients and combine well.

NUTRITION INFORMATION: Cal: 244 Pro: 5g/ 9% Carb: 46g/75% Fat: 4g/16% (S:7% M:24% P:69%) Chol: 0mg Sodium: 72mg Potassium: 153mg Fiber: 3g E: 11% B1: 14% B6: 34% Panto: 14% Fe: 10% Cu: 13% Mn: 58% Se: 45%
EXCHANGE: Bread: 2¼ Fruit: ½ Fat: 1

Rice and Peas
by Ceri Hadda and
Joanna Bergmann

This recipe illustrates how Japanese short-grain rice can be used in recipes traditionally calling for Italian arborio rice. Serve as a side dish, or as a main dish accompanied with pieces of cooked chicken or sprinkled with a small amount of grated cheese.

>   *2 teaspoons olive oil*
>   *1 cup chopped onion*
>   *1 cup raw Japanese short-grain rice*
> *1½ cups unsalted chicken or vegetable broth or stock (see pages 27 and 28)*
>   *½ teaspoon dried thyme, crumbled*
>   *½ teaspoon salt (optional)*
>   *1 cup fresh or frozen peas*

PREPARATION TIME: 10 minutes
COOKING TIME: 40 minutes
YIELD: 6 servings

In a medium, heavy saucepan, heat the oil and sauté the onion until transparent and golden. Add the rice; sauté 1 minute longer, stirring constantly. Add the chicken broth, thyme, and salt if desired and bring to a boil over moderate heat. Stir with a fork, lower heat, cover, and simmer 15 minutes. Add ⅓ cup water and the fresh peas. (If using frozen peas, add for the last 5 minutes of cooking only, so they don't overcook.) Cover and simmer 10 minutes longer, or until the peas are almost cooked and the rice is tender. Stir gently with a fork. Cover the saucepan and let stand 5 minutes before serving.

NUTRITION INFORMATION: Cal: 168 Pro: 5g/13% Carb: 31g/75% Fat: 2g/12% Chol: 1mg Sodium: 48mg Potassium: 186mg Fiber: 2g B1: 15% B3: 12% B6: 10% P: 11% Mn: 15% Cr: 15% EXCHANGE: Bread: 1³/₄ Veg: ¹/₄ Fat: ¹/₄

Dirty Rice

by Ceri Hadda and
Joanna Bergmann

This lightened version of the Cajun classic makes a quick main dish.

    4 teaspoons corn or peanut oil
    1 cup chopped scallions
    1 jalapeño pepper, seeded and chopped very
       fine
  ³/₄ pound raw chicken livers, finely chopped
    8 cups cooked long-grain brown or white rice,
       made with ¹/₂ broth or stock, ¹/₂ water
  ¹/₂ cup unsalted chicken broth or stock (see
       page 28)
  ¹/₂ cup chopped fresh parsley
    2 tablespoons chopped fresh coriander
       (optional)
       Salt
       Freshly ground black pepper

PREPARATION TIME: 25 minutes
COOKING TIME: 10 minutes
YIELD: 6 servings

In a large sauté pan, heat the oil. Add the scallions and cook 1 minute. Add the pepper and cook 1 minute. Add the livers and cook until browned. Add the cooked rice and stock and stir. Stir in the parsley and coriander if desired. Taste, and adjust seasonings.

NUTRITION INFORMATION: Cal: 399 Pro: 16g/ 17% Carb: 67g/70% Fat: 5g/13% (S:25% M:29% P:46%) Chol: 268mg Sodium: 64mg Potassium: 195mg Fiber: 3g A: 149% C: 23% E: 21% B1: 25% B2: 46%   B3: 25% B6: 71% B12: 137%

Folic: 92% Panto: 48% P: 22% Fe: 36% Zn: 19% Cu: 23% Mn: 88% Se: 121% EXCHANGE: Med. Meat: 1¹/₄ Bread: 4 Fat: ¹/₂

Chili-Bean Rice

by Ceri Hadda and
Joanna Bergmann

The beans and rice improve in flavor if cooked a day or two ahead, refrigerated and reheated to add to the vegetables. The recipe can be cut in half if you like.

    1 cup dried adzuki beans (see Note)
    2 cups dried kidney beans
    2 cups raw Texas long-grain basmati rice
    1 cup unsalted beef broth
    2 large onions, chopped
    4 cloves garlic, peeled and minced
    2 tablespoons corn oil
1¹/₂ cups chopped carrots
    1 cup chopped celery
    4 plum tomatoes, seeded and chopped
    1 28-ounce can tomatoes, no salt added
    2 tablespoons tomato paste, no salt added
    2 tablespoons chili powder
    1 tablespoon dried oregano
    1 teaspoon ground cumin
    1 teaspoon paprika
  ¹/₂ teaspoon cayenne
  ¹/₂ cup chopped fresh parsley

PREPARATION TIME: 30 minutes
COOKING TIME: 2¹/₂ hours, not including standing time
YIELD: 10 side-dish or 5 main-course servings

Cook the beans separately. Place the adzuki beans and 4 cups water in a saucepan, bring to a boil, cover, and simmer 1¹/₂ hours. At the same time, bring the kidney beans and 6 cups water to a boil in another saucepan, cook for 2 minutes, cover, turn heat off, and let stand for 1 hour. Resume cooking at moderate heat until tender, about 1 hour. At the same time also bring the rice, beef broth, and 2¹/₂ cups water to boiling in a saucepan; cover and simmer gently until all the liquid is absorbed, 15 to 20 minutes. (If you are cooking the beans and rice ahead of time, cool them and refrigerate in a covered container.)

Cook the onions and garlic in oil over low heat until the onions are translucent. Add the carrots and celery. Cover and cook for another 10 minutes. Add the tomatoes, canned tomatoes, tomato paste, chili powder, oregano, cumin, paprika, and cayenne. Continue to cook, uncovered, 20 minutes. Stir in the cooked beans and rice and cook over moderate heat, stirring occasionally, until heated through. Add the chopped parsley and stir.

NOTE: Adzuki beans are available at Asian food stores.

NUTRITION INFORMATION (per side dish serving): Cal: 379　Pro: 16g/17%　Carb: 72g/74%　Fat: 4g/ 9%　Chol: 1mg　Sodium: 87mg　Potassium: 826mg Fiber: 12g　A: 154%　C: 53%　E: 22%　B1: 22% B3: 17%　B6: 55%　Folic: 13%　Panto: 19% Ca: 12%　P: 18%　Fe: 24%　Mg: 12%　Zn: 10% Cu: 18%　Mn: 48%　Se: 43%　Cr: 31% EXCHANGE: Bread: 3¾　Veg: 2½　Fat: ¾

Wild Rice Salad

by Ceri Hadda and
Joanna Bergman

Serve this salad as a dinner side dish with turkey, game birds, chicken, or seafood—or by itself for lunch.

2 cups unsalted beef broth
2 medium carrots, julienne
2 ribs celery, julienne
½ pound snow peas, julienne
3 tablespoons corn or peanut oil
2 tablespoons cider vinegar
1 tablespoon reduced-sodium soy sauce,
　　or ½ tablespoon regular soy sauce
1 teaspoon dry sherry
½ teaspoon sesame oil
1 tablespoon chopped fresh coriander
1 cup raw wild rice
3 tablespoons chopped scallions (optional)

PREPARATION TIME: 20 minutes
COOKING TIME: 1 hour
YIELD: 4 servings

Bring the broth and 1½ cups water to a boil in a saucepan fitted with a steamer. Add the carrots, celery, and snow peas to the steamer, reduce heat, cover, and gently steam just until the carrots and celery have lost their hard crunch and the snow peas have brightened. Immediately remove the vegetables, refresh under cold running water to retain color and crispness, and place in a medium bowl. Reserve the cooking broth in the saucepan. Combine the oil, vinegar, soy sauce, sherry and sesame oil in a small bowl until blended. Pour this dressing over the vegetables and sprinkle with coriander. Refrigerate.

Rinse the wild rice in a sieve under cold water to remove impurities. Return reserved broth to boiling and add the rice. Reduce the heat and simmer uncovered 45 minutes, or until the rice is tender and the liquid is absorbed. (If the rice is tender before all the liquid is all absorbed, drain and reserve remaining liquid for another use.) Cool the rice. Combine the vegetables, wild rice, and chopped scallions, and mix well. Taste, and adjust seasoning if necessary. Serve cold or at room temperature.

NUTRITION INFORMATION: Cal: 303　Pro: 11g/ 14%　Carb: 40g/52%　Fat: 12g/35%　(S:14% M:27%　P:59%)　Chol: 1mg　Sodium: 251mg Potassium: 590mg　Fiber: 6g　A: 205%　C: 65%　E: 52%　B1: 12%　B2: 13%　B3: 26%　B6: 16%　Folic: 11%　Panto: 10%　P: 27%　Fe: 15%　Mg: 24%　Zn: 18%　Cu: 21%　Mn: 21%　Cr: 24% EXCHANGE: Bread: 2¼　Veg: 1　Fat: 2¼

MICROWAVE METHOD: In a 1-quart microwave-safe casserole, cook the carrots, celery, and ¼ cup water on High (100% power) until tender-crisp, about 3 to 4 minutes. Drain and cool as directed above. In the same casserole, cook the snow peas and 2 tablespoons water on High until brightened, about 2 minutes. Drain, cool, and continue as above, cooking the rice in broth and water.

Curried Chicken and Rice Salad

by Ceri Hadda and
Joanna Bergmann

*1 3-pound chicken, skin and visible fat
    removed, cut into pieces*
*3 cups unsalted chicken broth or stock
    (see page 28)*
1 cup raw long-grain brown rice
4 tablespoons chopped fresh parsley
2 medium onions, finely chopped
1 tablespoon corn oil
2 celery ribs, finely chopped
3 cloves garlic, peeled and finely minced
*1 medium tomato, seeded and finely
    chopped*
1 medium green Granny Smith apple
1 tablespoon curry powder, or to taste
*¾ to 1 cup plain nonfat yogurt
    Freshly ground black pepper*

PREPARATION TIME: 30 minutes
COOKING TIME: 1 hour
YIELD: 6 servings

Preheat the oven to 375°F. Arrange the chicken pieces in a single layer in a 9- by 13-inch baking dish and bake in the preheated oven until the juices run clear when pricked with a knife. Start checking after 30 minutes. Meanwhile, bring the chicken broth to a boil in a medium, heavy saucepan. Add the rice and lower the heat to simmer. Cook covered for 35 to 40 minutes. Set aside.

Remove chicken from oven and cool slightly. When the chicken is cool enough to handle, discard the bones and cut the meat into bite-size pieces. In a large serving bowl, combine the chicken and 3 tablespoons of the parsley.

In a sauté pan, cook the onions in oil over low heat 10 minutes or until tender. Add the celery and cook 10 minutes longer. Add the garlic and tomato and cook 5 minutes longer. Turn off heat.

Core the apple, cut it into quarters, and make ¼-inch cubes. Add to the vegetable mixture in the pan but do not cook. Add the curry powder and mix well.

Add the rice and the vegetable mixture to the chicken bowl. Add the yogurt and mix just until blended. Add pepper to taste. Sprinkle the remaining tablespoon parsley on top and serve at room temperature or chilled.

NUTRITION INFORMATION: Cal: 390 Pro: 34g/ 35% Carb: 37g/39% Fat: 11g/26% (S:27% M:38% P:35%) Chol: 88mg Sodium: 153mg Potassium: 684mg Fiber: 5g C: 22% E: 25% B1: 16% B2: 20% B3: 55% B6: 28% B12: 10% Panto: 15% Ca: 13% P: 30% Fe: 15% Mg: 11% Zn: 18% Se: 90% Cr: 22%
EXCHANGE: Lean Meat: 3½ Skim Milk: ¼ Bread: 1½ Veg: 1 Fruit: ¼ Fat: ½

MICROWAVE METHOD: Cook rice conventionally. In a 12- by 8-inch microwave-safe baking dish, cook the chicken, thicker portions toward the outside, covered on High (100% power) until tender, about 18 to 23 minutes, rotating the dish once and turning the pieces over. Cool and cut as above. In a 1½-quart microwave-safe casserole, cook the onions, garlic, and only 1 teaspoon oil on High until tender, about 3 to 4 minutes. Add the celery and tomato. Cook covered on High 5 minutes. Continue as directed above.

Chinese Fried Rice

by Ceri Hadda and
Joanna Bergmann

2 tablespoons peanut oil
*4 cups cold cooked long-grain brown or white
    rice*
3 cups very thinly sliced Chinese cabbage
½ pound mushrooms, sliced
1 red bell pepper, coarsely chopped
1 cup chopped scallions
1 celery rib, coarsely chopped
2 tablespoons reduced-sodium soy sauce
½ pound firm tofu, cut into 1-inch cubes

PREPARATION TIME: 25 minutes
COOKING TIME: 8 minutes
YIELD: 4 servings

Over high heat, heat the oil in a large sauté pan. Add the rice, cabbage, mushrooms, pepper, scallions, celery, and soy sauce. Cook about 5 minutes or until well heated, stirring constantly. Add the tofu and heat through, tossing gently. Serve immediately.

VARIATION: If desired, stir in 1/2 teaspoon minced fresh ginger and/or 1 clove garlic, minced, with the rice and vegetables.

NUTRITION INFORMATION: (with brown rice) Cal: 376 Pro: 13g/13% Carb: 60g/62% Fat: 11g/25% (S:18% M:47% P:35%) Chol: 0mg Sodium: 320mg Potassium: 692mg Fiber: 10g A: 58% C: 96% E: 30% B1: 22% B2: 20% B3: 30% B6: 11% Folic: 16% Panto: 17% Ca: 18% P: 17% Fe: 25% Cu: 16% Se: 117% Cr: 28%
EXCHANGE: Med. Meat: 1/2 Bread: 3 Veg: 2 Fat: 1 1/2

Cabbage Rolls Stuffed with Veal and Brown Rice

by Ceri Hadda and
Joanna Bergmann

  1 small head green cabbage (1 1/2 pounds)
  2 large onions, coarsely chopped
  1 small bulb fennel, coarsely chopped
  1 teaspoon strong Hungarian paprika
  1 tablespoon olive oil
3/4 pound extra-lean ground veal, cooked
  2 cups chopped fresh parsley
1/4 cup dry breadcrumbs
  2 tablespoons pignoli (pine nuts)
  2 teaspoons dried oregano
1/4 teaspoon freshly ground black pepper
  2 cups cooked short-grain brown rice
  1 cup unsalted beef broth
  2 tomatoes, seeded and coarsely chopped
  1 8-ounce can tomato sauce, no salt added
  1 teaspoon sugar
    Juice of 1/2 lemon

PREPARATION TIME: 40 minutes
COOKING TIME: 1 hour 15 minutes
YIELD: 4 to 6 servings

Preheat the oven to 350°F. Remove the core from the cabbage with a paring knife and separate as many of the large outer leaves as you can. Chop the inner leaves. Drop the outer leaves into boiling water. After 5 minutes, remove the cooked leaves and cut away the hard spine from each, leaving the leaves whole.

In a sauté pan, sauté the onions and fennel with the paprika in olive oil until tender, about 5 minutes. Put all but 1/4 cup of the onion and fennel into a very large bowl. Add the cooked veal, parsley, breadcrumbs, nuts, oregano, pepper, rice, and 1/2 cup of the broth; mix well.

Fill each cabbage leaf by spooning 3 tablespoons of the veal mixture into the middle of the leaf, then folding each side toward the middle and folding the end up. In the sauté pan with the remaining 1/4 cup onions, add the tomatoes, tomato sauce, sugar, lemon juice, and remaining 1/2 cup broth. Cook over low heat to reduce for at least 10 minutes. Spoon the mixture into a baking dish large enough to accommodate the cabbage rolls in a single layer. Arrange the chopped inner cabbage leaves over the sauce. Add the cabbage rolls, seam-side-down, cover with foil, and bake in the preheated oven for 50 minutes.

NUTRITION INFORMATION: (for 4 servings) Cal: 574 Pro: 39g/26% Carb: 70g/47% Fat: 18g/27% (S:35% M:31% P:34%) Chol: 77mg Sodium: 212mg Potassium: 1892mg Fiber: 13g A: 105% C: 213% E: 35% B1: 32% B2: 29% B3: 43% B6: 29% Folic: 33% Ca: 26% P: 36% Fe: 54% Mg: 27% Cu: 14% Mn: 20% Se: 57% Cr: 64%
EXCHANGE: Med. Meat: 3 Bread: 2 Veg: 3 1/4 Fat: 1 1/2

Italian Risotto with Shrimp

by Ceri Hadda and
Joanna Bergmann

Preparing a risotto requires constant stirring for at least 15 minutes, but the results are worth it.

  1 tablespoon olive oil
  2 medium onions, finely chopped

2 garlic cloves, peeled and finely minced
1 small bulb fennel or celery, finely chopped
1 medium carrot, finely chopped (½ cup)
1 cup raw Italian short-grain arborio rice
½ cup dry white wine
2½ cups unsalted chicken broth or stock (see page 28)
½ pound small shrimp, shelled and deveined
2 tablespoons chopped fresh parsley
2 tablespoons chopped watercress, parsley, or basil
Freshly ground black pepper

PREPARATION TIME: 30 minutes
COOKING TIME: 50 minutes
YIELD: 4 servings

Heat the oil in a heavy saucepan over medium heat. Add the onions and garlic. When the onion becomes translucent, add the fennel and carrot. Cover and let the vegetables steam a few minutes. Uncover, add the rice, and stir 5 minutes. Add the wine, stirring until it evaporates. Start adding the broth, ¼ cup at a time, stirring constantly until each successive amount is absorbed. (This step may take 15 to 20 minutes until the rice is tender and creamy.) Add the shrimp and cook only until they turn opaque. Add the parsley and watercress, season to taste with freshly ground pepper, and serve immediately.

NUTRITION INFORMATION: Cal: 244 Pro: 18g/30% Carb: 31g/51% Fat: 5g/19% (S:20% M:63% P:17%) Chol: 111mg Sodium: 220mg Potassium: 559mg Fiber: 3g A: 105% C: 22% B1: 13% B3: 25% B6: 31% B12: 17% Panto: 10% P: 22% Fe: 19% Zn: 11% Cu: 17% Mn: 37% Se: 36% Cr: 19%
EXCHANGE: Lean Meat: 1½ Bread: 1¼ Veg: 1½ Fat: ¾

MICROWAVE METHOD: In a 2-quart microwave-safe casserole, cook the oil, onion, garlic, fennel, and carrot on High (100% power) until tender, about 5 to 6 minutes. Stir in the rice; cook uncovered until rice is very hot but not browned, 3 or 4 minutes. Stir in the wine and broth; cook uncovered on High 9 minutes. Stir. Cook uncovered on High 8 minutes. Add the shrimp; cook on High until the liquid is almost all absorbed and the shrimp are opaque, about 3 to 4 minutes. Let stand 5 minutes. Stir in the parsley, watercress, and pepper.

Fish Fillets with Saffron Rice

by Ceri Hadda and Joanna Bergmann

1 tablespoon olive oil
2 large onions, chopped
¼ teaspoon ground saffron
¼ cup chopped fresh parsley
½ teaspoon fresh thyme
8 oil-cured black olives, pitted and chopped
1 cup raw converted rice
2 cups warm unsalted chicken or fish stock or fumet (see page 27)
2 tablespoons sliced almonds, lightly toasted (see Note)
4 4-ounce gray sole or red snapper fillets
¼ cup dry white wine

PREPARATION TIME: 30 minutes plus cooling time
COOKING TIME: 55 minutes
YIELD: 4 servings

In a medium saucepan, in hot oil, sauté the onions, saffron, parsley, thyme, and olives until the onions are translucent. Add the rice and stir until the rice is coated with oil and herbs. Add the warm stock and bring to a boil. Stir once with a fork, cover, and simmer 20 minutes, or until all the liquid is absorbed. Cool completely. Gently stir in the almonds. (This can be done a day ahead; cover the rice mixture and refrigerate.)

Preheat the oven to 400F°. Place about 2 tablespoons of the rice mixture in the center of each fillet, skin side out. Fold over to close the fish, enclosing the rice. Pour the wine into the bottom of a shallow oven-proof dish, add the fish, seam-side down, and spoon the remaining rice mixture over the fish. Cover the dish with aluminum foil and bake in the preheated oven for 10 minutes; uncover, and continue baking 10 minutes longer, or until the fish flakes easily with a fork. Serve immediately.

NOTE: To toast the nuts: Spread almonds in a small, heavy skillet; cook over medium-high heat, stirring often, until very lightly browned, about 3 minutes. Or on a paper plate, microwave the nuts on High (100% power) until toasted, about 1 to 2 minutes.

NUTRITION INFORMATION: Cal: 413   Pro: 31g/30%   Carb: 51g/50%   Fat: 9g/20%   (S:17% M:64% P:19%) Chol: 41mg Sodium: 140mg Potassium: 889mg Fiber: 5g   C: 28%   E: 12% B1: 22% B3: 19% B6: 46%   Folic: 15% Panto: 16% Ca: 12% P: 32% Fe: 16% Mg: 18% Zn: 10% Cu: 18% Mn: 60% Se: 54% Cr: 30%
   EXCHANGE: Lean Meat: 3   Bread: 2¼   Veg: 2 Fat: 1

MICROWAVE METHOD: Prepare the saffron rice and stuff the fillets as directed above. In a 9- to 10-inch round microwave-safe baking dish, cook the stuffed fillets, wine, and any remaining stuffing covered on High (100% Power) until the fish is opaque, about 5 minutes. Let stand 5 minutes.

Rice and Spice Muffins

by Ceri Hadda and
Joanna Bergmann

⅓ cup raw long-grain brown rice
¼ cup raisins
   Vegetable cooking spray
1⅔ cups unbleached all-purpose flour
1 tablespoon baking powder
2 teaspoons ground cinnamon
¼ teaspoon ground nutmeg
¼ teaspoon ground ginger
¼ teaspoon salt
3 tablespoons corn oil
½ cup skim milk
½ cup apple cider
1 egg
1 egg white
¼ cup firmly packed light brown sugar

PREPARATION TIME: 25 minutes
COOKING TIME: 1 hour 15 minutes
YIELD: 12 muffins

Combine the rice and 1 cup water in a small saucepan; bring to a boil over moderate heat; stir with a fork; continue boiling 5 minutes. Lower the heat, cover, and simmer 30 to 40 minutes, adding more water if necessary, or until rice is tender. Stir in the raisins with a fork; let stand 10 minutes.

Meanwhile, preheat the oven to 400°F.

Spray twelve muffin-pan cups with cooking spray, or use paper liners. Stir together the flour, baking powder, cinnamon, nutmeg, ginger, and salt in a large bowl. Combine the oil, milk, cider, egg, egg white, and sugar in a medium bowl; stir in the *warm* rice mixture. Add the rice mixture to the dry ingredients; stir just to blend (do not overmix). Spoon into the muffin-pan cups and bake in the preheated oven 20 minutes, or until muffins are golden brown and firm.

NUTRITION INFORMATION: Cal: 157   Pro: 3g/9%   Carb: 26g/68%   Fat: 4g/23%   (S:17% M:27% P:56%) Chol: 18mg Sodium: 147mg Potassium: 102mg Fiber: 1g E: 15% B1: 10%
   EXCHANGE: Bread: 1¼   Fruit: ¼   Fat: ¾

THE "NEW" GRAINS ◇

About the "New" Grains

by Jeanine Barone, M.S.

Oats

The health benefits of oats—first cultivated in North Africa, the Near East, and Russia around 2500 B.C.—are worth neighing about. A number of studies have shown that oats, rich in water-soluble fiber, decrease blood cholesterol in people both with near-normal and with highly elevated levels.

At the University of Kentucky College of Medicine in Lexington, for example, professor of medicine James Anderson gave men with high cholesterol levels 100 grams of oat bran (the outside of the oat kernel). That's one bowl of oat bran cereal and five oat bran muffins a day. Result: Total cholesterol decreased 19 percent. LDL cholesterol, the kind most closely linked to increased risk of heart disease, fell 24 percent. In another study also by Dr. James Anderson, a diet containing 100 grams (about 3½ ounces) of oat bran decreased blood cholesterol by 13 percent.

Even a bowl of oatmeal in the morning alone may help. Researchers at Northwestern University Medical School in Chicago put over 200 healthy men and women on low-fat, low-cholesterol diets. Some of them also ate two cups of oatmeal every day. Blood cholesterol fell for the group as a whole, but it fell slightly farther (about 3 percent more) for the oatmeal eaters. Oatmeal, the researchers concluded, can enhance the benefits of a low-fat diet.

One well-publicized study, however, found no significant benefit to oat bran. At Brigham Women's Hospital in Boston, 20 healthy subjects over 50 years old added either 3½ ounces of oat bran or low-fiber refined wheat products to their normal diet. Cholesterol levels dropped 7½ percent in either case. The conclusion: Oat bran has no special cholesterol-lowering properties. But the study has flaws. The subjects already had lower-than-average cholesterol levels (under 200 milligrams), and other studies have found that the lower the cholesterol level to start, the smaller the effect of oat bran. Even more surprising, the Brigham study *did* find an oat bran benefit: On the oat bran diet, artery-damaging LDL cholesterol dropped 9 percent; on wheat, it dropped only 6 percent. So it seems reasonable to expect a modest additional cholesterol-lowering benefit from oats in a low-fat diet, especially for people with elevated levels.

Even so, that's hardly the only reason to begin the day with this ancient, nourishing staple. It's digested slowly, yielding a slow, steady rise in blood sugar. And, lest we forget, it's also just plain nutritious: Oatmeal is rich in B vitamins, iron, magnesium, zinc, and manganese.

Harvested oats have an easily removed hull, yielding whole oat kernels, or groats. These can be cut with sharp blades, producing steel cut oats. Either kind can be cooked as hot breakfast cereal.

To make old-fashioned rolled oats, the oat kernel is rolled flat. This cuts cooking time. Quick cooking oats are cut several times and rolled. Because water can reach each oat faster, you can make oatmeal in about a minute. Instant oats are thinner yet, cutting cooking time even more—but also causing the oat flakes to quickly lose their texture and become mushy. Also, read the label: Many instant oat cereals add lots of salt.

Oats are usually associated with hot breakfast cereals. But oats and oat flour are versatile and can be added to stew, meat loaf, or soup, or combined with wheat flour to make bread, muffins, or cookies.

Barley

Poor barley. Oats and beans get all the attention, but barley may be just as helpful in lowering elevated levels of blood cholesterol.

It's certainly been popular throughout history. First used for food in Egypt as long ago as 6000 B.C., it shows up in sacred texts of the Chinese as well as in the Bible and was the chief bread plant of the Israelites, Romans, and Greeks. Today it's grown from Scandinavia to India and the Middle East, where it remains a staple. In America, about half goes to feeding livestock; much of the rest goes into making beer and other alcoholic beverages.

In a few small clinical studies, barley lowers blood cholesterol. In one such investigation at Montana State University, nutrition professor Rosemary Newman fed volunteers either oats or barley—two ounces of cereal, plus a muffin and a flatbread—every day for six weeks. Both the barley and the oat group found their cholesterol dropped by an average of 5 percent. (The subjects in the barley group with the lowest initial cholesterol level were the only ones who didn't experience a drop.)

The investigators hypothesize that two factors may be responsible for barley's benefit: the water-soluble fiber beta-glucans, and the oil-soluble compound tocotrienol. Beta-glucans, also abundant in oats and dry beans, appear to bind with cholesterol-containing bile acids, which are then harmlessly excreted. Because the body uses cholesterol to make bile, when it replaces these acids it uses up available cholesterol. Thus, blood cholesterol levels drop. Tocotrienol may lower cholesterol levels by affecting an enzyme key to cholesterol synthesis.

Diabetics might also benefit from the slow rise in blood sugar that barley produces compared to many other cereals, according to work done by Dr. David Jenkins of the University of Toronto.

But you can't drink to your health, unfortunately. The active substances, beta-glucans and tocotrienol, don't make it through the brewing process; they stay in the hops. Nor does beer contain any appreciable fiber. (For more on beer and wine, see Beverages, page 314)

Unlike the hull in oats, the hull adhering to the barley kernel is hard to remove and is often sanded (pearled) away. This process also removes some of the outer layers of the barley grain—that is, much of the dietary fiber. Beta-glucans, however, predominate in the inner endosperm layer, so they may survive pearling. At present, though, there's no standardization in commercial barley; some varieties have more beta-glucans than others.

Pearled barley is the most refined and most available form, but sometimes one can get Scotch or pot barley. Pot barley has been pearled two or three times, so the outer husk and much of the bran is removed. Pearled barley has been pearled an additional two or three times, removing the rest of the bran. Pot barley requires overnight soaking and longer cooking time compared with pearled barley.

Rye

Rye is a hardy and heart-healthy grain. Originating in central Asia about 4000 B.C., it thrives in severe, cold climates and has found a home in northern Europe.

It contains two substances our bodies might thank us for, if it could. One is tocotrienol, also found in oats and barley, which may help lower blood cholesterol, although rye hasn't been specifically tested for cholesterol-lowering.

It's a good grain to have when you're trying to cut back on the calories, too. That's because of the other substance, pentosans, a starch that absorbs water. More than other grains such as wheat, it retains more water and swells in the stomach, giving the grain a particularly filling quality. Rye is rich in pentosans. Rye also takes longer to break down into sugar, so it may help modulate blood sugar.

To get the most from this high-fiber grain, select dark, coarsely ground whole rye flour; that's the kind used for classic pumpernickel. Black bread is made from more finely ground rye flour and has a strong, slightly bitter taste.

The lighter the flour's color, the less fiber, iron, B vitamins, phosphorus, and protein. Thus light rye flour, which is sifted, is less nutritious than medium or dark rye; it's often combined with wheat flour to make bread. Rye doesn't have a hull, so kernels (berries) can also be eaten whole, but they first must be soaked, then cooked.

Buckwheat

Ah, buckwheat, the stuff pancakes are made of! More buckwheat is sold for pancake flour in this country than for any other purpose.

Unlike most grains, buckwheat, which resembles beechnut, isn't in the grass family. It's actually a relative of rhubarb. This anomaly is reflected in the origin of the word buckwheat from the Dutch "bockweit," which literally means beechwheat. Many people who are allergic to wheat can tolerate buckwheat well.

Nutritionally, though, it's similar to wheat, with a slightly more balanced protein content. It's a particularly rich source of magnesium, which may be important in keeping blood pressure in balance (see Nuts and Seeds, page 137), as well as dietary fiber.

Aside from its use in pancakes, buckwheat flour can be mixed with wheat in bread making. Kasha, another popular dish, is roasted whole buckwheat groats (hulled seeds) that are cooked into a dry porridge. It can then be eaten as cereal, served as a side dish with a meat entree, or used to stuff a knish.

Millet

Here's a delicious whole grain rich in protein, iron, phosphorus, and B vitamins (B-1, B-2, B-3) that, in this country at least, gets fed more to birds and cattle than humans.

It's different in other parts of the world. Often referred to as the "poor man's cereal," millet probably originated in Asia, where it's been cultivated to 6,000 years and remains a staple. It's a hardy grain that can withstand drought.

A little millet goes a long way. Its kernels swell enormously when water is added. Whole kernels can be cooked like kasha or, with more water, as a cereal. Millet flour has a nutty flavor and can be combined with wheat in breadmaking.

Triticale

Triticale is one of the oldest man-made crops. In the late 1800s, wheat (Triticum) and rye (Secale) were interbred. Triticale has more protein than wheat. It's a somewhat more balanced protein as well: Rye has good amounts of lysine, the amino acid that wheat is low in.

The gluten in triticale is delicate and must be handled gently or it will break down. Most bakers prefer to mix triticale with wheat to make bread rise. Rolled triticale kernels are now found in some breakfast cereals.

Quinoa

Pronounced "keenwa," quinoa (the "mother grain") was considered sacred by the Incas. An especially hardy seed, quinoa can survive and even thrive in extremely hot or cold temperatures, at high altitudes, with little rainfall, and in poor soil. It's not a true grain at all, but the fruit of the annual Chenopodium plant—a relative of a common weed.

Quinoa is valued not only for its hardiness but also its nutritional quality. It has more protein, iron, B-1, and B-2 than most conventional grains. Quinoa can be cooked whole like rice or the flour can be combined with wheat to make bread, muffins, or cookies.

Amaranth

Amaranth or amaranthus, derived from two Greek words meaning immortal (not withering), was commonly eaten as part of religious rituals by the Aztecs before Columbus sailed. Incas ate it too. It's no wonder. Amaranth is a hardy plant that grows quickly even under arid conditions. The edible parts of the plant include seeds eaten as a grain (cereal) and leaves eaten as a vegetable.

Amaranth seed contains more protein and minerals than most other grains, and its flour contains more iron, calcium, and zinc than wheat flour. One-half of a cup raw, which cooks up to a cup and a half, provides 41 percent of the USRDA for iron.

Use the flour, combined with wheat, to make bread, tortillas, or cookies. Also, rolled amaranth flakes are now in some breakfast cereals. The whole kernels can also be used in cooking and are purchased as pearled amaranth.

Teff

Teff, an Ethiopian grain, is the smallest of the grains. It's about the size of the period at the end of this sentence. It's the surface of grains that carry most nutrients, so teff, with a greater surface-to-center ratio, is quite nutritious. It's rich in iron and B vitamins. It also carries its own symbiotic yeast, so none needs to be added to make bread. In Ethiopia, teff is made into the unique spongy staple bread called *injera;* often lentils, stews, and other savory dishes are served atop the flat, floppy rounds of injera, turning the staff of life into a serving plate and an edible utensil too.

Job's Tears

It's only new to us. The Chinese cultivated it 4,000 years ago. It's reputed to be good for the complexion, though no evidence supports the folklore. An annual grass, Job's tears gets its name from its beadlike appearance. It can be used like rice or barley and is a good source of magnesium, zinc, and iron.

Cooking with the New Grains

by Mary Estella

In Scotland, oats are used in soups, cakes, breads, crackers, and mixed with ground meat and spices for the national dish called haggis. And we only eat them for breakfast!

Try breakfast oatmeal with the addition of dried fruits, sweet spices, grated orange peel, toasted coconut or seeds—or sweetened with barley or rice malt.

Oat flour has no gluten, but it can be combined with other flours to make bread. Cookies can be successfully made with oat flour by substituting 1 1/4 cups oat flour for 1 cup wheat flour. Oat bran is even easier to integrate into recipes; its light color and mild flavor makes it easy to add to cookies, muffins, pie crusts, pastries, or casseroles.

Barley, like rye, is more important in breweries than bakeries. The British make a malt from barley which is integral to making beer. Guinness, the rich dark stout, is made from barley that has been roasted black. The Japanese also roast barley, but instead of beer they make a fragrant, golden tea called "mugi-cha." The Japanese cook barley mixed with rice; or make "mugi-miso," a rich fermented paste of soy beans and barley, to season soups.

Pearled barley, which has most of its bran polished off, is a familiar ingredient in soups or stews from cream of mushroom to Scotch broth to beef and barley. To make a satisfying whole-grain breakfast cereal, simply simmer 1/2 cup of pearled barley in 3 cups of apple juice, a handful of chopped dried fruit, a cinnamon stick, and a pinch of salt; cover and simmer 1 1/2 hours. Add more liquid if needed.

Pearled barley can be used in many rice recipes such as stuffings, salads, and side dishes. To make a savory pilaf, sauté 1/2 pound mushrooms in 1 teaspoon olive oil. Add 3 cloves minced garlic, and a pinch each of cumin, thyme, and white pepper. Combine with 1 cup of rinsed barley in a baking dish; add 3 cups boiling water and a pinch of salt. Cover and bake at 375°F for 45 minutes to 1 hour or until the liquid is absorbed. Fluff with a fork and stir in 2 tablespoons of chopped parsley or coriander. Unpolished barley can be cooked the same way but must be presoaked for several hours.

Light and soft, barley flour can replace wheat flour in many recipes. Barley flakes or roasted ground barley make excellent breakfast cereals.

In America, rye is better known for brewing whiskey than baking bread. This northern European staple is low in gluten so it's made into crisp crackers or flat bread. For wheat-free bread crumbs, try grinding up rye crackers; use the crumbs for coating croquettes and in stuffings.

Whole rye "berries," like wheat berries, cook up chewy and delicious—with the benefit of fiber and germ. 1 cup of whole rye can be soaked overnight like beans (to shorten cooking time); pour off the soaking water, add 2 cups boiling water along with salt and seasonings, cover, and simmer for about 1 hour. Savory cooked rye is a nutritious addition to bread doughs, stuffings, sautéed vegetables, or salads.

Rye flakes can be used in muffins, bread mixes, or breakfast cereals, alone or combined with barley or oat flakes and sweetened with raisins, currants, or cinnamon. Low in gluten but high in flavor, rye flour is made into sourdough loaves with a long shelf life or combined with wheat flour to make pumpernickel bread. To return "just-baked" freshness to hearty rye bread, place slices in a vegetable steamer, cover and steam for 1 minute until warm and moist.

In Brittany, buckwheat crêpes are a traditional dish. In this French province crêpes are cooked on large round pans, and vendors sell them on street corners rolled up with a variety of fillings. Treat buckwheat like a cereal grain. It's available as groats, grits (partially ground), and flour; the flour is used more in pancakes than breads. Russians and East Europeans roast the groats, which are sold as kasha. Kasha cooks up fluffy when sautéed lightly to toast the grains and then simmered for about 20 minutes with twice the amount of boiling water. Started in cold water and simmered alone, or with diced potatoes and herbs, kasha makes a fabulous filling for knishes or cabbage rolls and can be shaped into croquettes. The small yeast-risen buckwheat pancakes called blinis are topped with sour cream and caviar—a deluxe Russian treat. Try blinis with yogurt instead of fat-laden sour cream.

International customs give a few clues to the many culinary uses of millet. Caribbean cooks mix millet with peas or beans and island spices; peasants of southwestern France make a porridge of millet; cooks in India combine millet flour with wheat and chick-pea flour to make chapatis. In Africa this golden arid-thriving grain remains a staple of life, consumed as a porridge and ground into flour for breads.

There are two basic ways to prepare millet and endless variations on these. First, for a soft, shapable grain, well-rinsed millet can be added to cold water or stock (about 3 cups liquid per 1 cup millet), seasoned, and simmered for 45 minutes or longer. While it is warm, the soft golden millet can be shaped into croquettes, stuffed into squash or cabbage leaves, or mixed with cooked beans and spices to make "burgers." Warm millet can be spooned into a loaf pan, allowed to cool and then sliced and fried, much like polenta or grits.

As an alternative to oatmeal, millet makes a delicious breakfast cereal. Simply combine 1/2 cup (well rinsed) millet with 3 cups apple juice or cider, 1/4 cup currants or chopped dried apricots, a pinch of cinnamon and sea salt; cover and simmer for 45 minutes, or until creamy. Serve with roasted sunflower seeds or almonds.

Millet swells to 4 or 5 times its size when added to soup or stew; add 1/3 cup to a pot of vegetable, chicken, or lentil soup, simmer with extra stock or water for 1 hour.

While millet melts into soups or breakfast cereals, it can also be prepared as a fluffy side dish pilaf. This is the second basic cooking technique. Uncooked millet for pilaf should be rinsed and drained in a mesh colander, spread on a baking pan and roasted in a 350°F oven until golden brown. Stir occasionally while it roasts. Place the millet in a heavy oven-proof casserole or pot. Add 1 teaspoon olive oil, a pinch of salt, and some thyme, basil, and rosemary per cup of millet and 2 cups boiling water. Stir, cover, and bake in the oven or simmer on the stove for 45 minutes to 1 hour.

When the millet has absorbed all the water, fluff with a fork and serve or use in another recipe. Millet cooked separately like rice can be marinated as a pasta salad (add some cooked chick-peas for extra protein), stir-fried as rice, or tossed with mint and tomatoes for a millet tabouli.

Heartier and more nutritious than rye or wheat alone, triticale is still mostly used for livestock. But it's delicious in baking, cooks quickly, and adapts well to familiar grain recipes.

Quinoa cooks in less time than rice or millet and can be added to salads, casseroles, stir-fries, or soups. According to Rebecca Wood, author of *Quinoa: The Supergrain* imported quinoa takes about 2 cups of water per cup of grain: domestic quinoas, about 1½ cups of water per cup. Cook in boiling water, seasoned water, or stock; bring back to a boil and simmer covered for 10 minutes or until all the liquid is absorbed. Fluff with a fork. "You can substitute quinoa for rice in any dish—fried rice, puddings, casseroles," says Wood. The flour, which can be made in a blender from the whole grain, is equally versatile. "Use it in any pastry, in pancakes, waffles, muffins, drop biscuits," she suggests. "It's got a lot of character." She suggests starting by substituting quinoa flour for half the flour in your favorite recipe and experimenting from there—up to 100 percent for dense fruitcakes. But if quinoa fits in, amaranth flour stands out, she notes. "It's got such a strong taste, I wouldn't put more than 20 percent into a bread recipe she says." Occasionally, I'll add a handful of amaranth grain to rice, just to give it a slightly different taste. But most people find it unpalatable plain."

Teff, an Ethiopian grain, is grown almost exclusively in the African highlands, where it is inextricably intertwined with the Ethiopian culture. The upland Ethiopians attribute their strength and prowess to this hardy grain. They grind teff into flour and make it into their national staple, injera, which is a fermented flat bread. Injera has a circumference of two feet, a spongy consistency, and a sour flavor. Injera pieces are torn from the bread and used as edible utensils to scoop up other—most often, spicy—foods. Teff is captivating interest in the American market, not only because injera is an exciting new flavor but also because the grain is delicious in other recipes. To make injera from teff, mix a cup of teff flour with 2 cups of spring or distilled water, loosely cover with a plate or damp towel, and set out at room temperature to ferment for 12 to 24 hours. Pour off the liquid which comes to the top, add a pinch of salt, and pour the batter, a half cup at a time, into a crêpe pan, over medium heat. Cover and cook for 3 minutes.

To prepare the grain called Job's tears, simply wash and drain 1 cup and bring to a boil in 2 cups of water with a pinch of salt. Cover; simmer for 1 hour; remove from heat and leave uncovered for 10 minutes. Try it in combination with other grains like rice.

Sesame-Maple Oat Crunch
by Mary Estella

Granola, with its rich assortment of seeds and nuts, is too caloric and high in fat to be an everyday breakfast cereal. But it packs a lot of nutrients per handful, so use it as a topping instead. This version tastes great with yogurt or over Gingered Pears (page 193). Or mix it with raisins for a trail mix to take on your next hiking adventure.

>   2½ cups rolled oats
>   ¼ cup sesame seeds
>   ½ cup whole wheat pastry flour
>   1 teaspoon ground cinnamon
>   ¼ teaspoon sea salt
>   1 teaspoon vanilla
>   ¼ to ½ cup maple syrup
>   ¼ cup safflower oil
>   3 to 4 tablespoons apple juice
>   Vegetable oil

PREPARATION TIME: 15 minutes
COOKING TIME: 30 minutes
YIELD: 10 servings (3 tablespoons each)

Preheat the oven to 350°F. Mix all the ingredients thoroughly in a bowl. Spread the mixture in a large baking dish or jelly roll pan lightly greased with vegetable oil. Bake in the preheated oven about 30 minutes, stirring occasionally. When the mixture is golden and smells great, remove from the oven. Allow to cool completely, then store in a glass jar or covered container in the refrigerator. Serve 3 tablespoons crunch with 1 cup plain nonfat yogurt.

VARIATIONS:
◆ Add raisins once the crunch has cooked and cooled.
◆ *Maple-Walnut Oat Crunch*: Replace the sesame seeds with ¼ cup walnuts.

NUTRITION INFORMATION (3 tablespoons crunch and 1 cup plain nonfat yogurt): Cal: 330 Pro: 17g/21% Carb: 45g/55% Fat: 9g/24% (S:15% M:22% P:63%) Chol: 4mg Sodium: 257mg Potassium: 680mg Fiber: 2g E: 14% B1: 21% B2: 35% B12: 23% Folic: 10% Panto: 15% Ca: 51% P: 48% Fe: 14% Mg: 22% Zn: 21% Cu: 15% Mn: 24%

EXCHANGE: Skim Milk: 1 Bread: 1¼ Fruit: 1 Fat: 1½

MICROWAVE METHOD: In a 12- by 8-inch microwave-safe baking dish, cook all the ingredients, well mixed, on High (100% power) until slightly crisp, about 13 to 16 minutes; stir once. Cool and store as directed above.

Gingered Squash and Millet Soup

by Mary Estella

Sweet orange squash and yellow millet are combined in this delicately spiced soup. It keeps for several days and can be frozen. It's a filling, but not heavy, first course.

1 to 2 teaspoons sesame oil
    2 onions, diced (about 2 cups)
    1 small butternut squash, or buttercup pared, seeded, and cubed (about 3 to 4 cups)
       Pinch of sea salt
   ½ teaspoon ground cumin
   ½ teaspoon ground coriander
   ¼ teaspoon cayenne
    2 bay leaves
   ½ cup raw millet
2 to 3 tablespoons mellow white or barley miso dissolved in ½ cup hot water or soup broth
   ½ teaspoon fresh ginger juice (from grating a small piece of fresh ginger on the small holes of a hand grater), or more to taste
    3 scallions, sliced, for garnish

PREPARATION TIME: 25 minutes
COOKING TIME: 50 minutes
YIELD: 5 servings

Heat the oil in a soup pot. Add the onions; sauté over medium heat until tender, stirring occasionally, about 5 minutes. Add the squash, stir, and sauté about 5 minutes longer. Add the salt, cumin, coriander, and cayenne, stir, and sauté for 1 minute. Cover the vegetables with 4 to 6 cups water and add the bay leaves. Rinse the millet in a fine-mesh strainer and add to the soup. Bring to a boil, lower the heat, and simmer for 20 to 30 minutes, until the squash is tender and the millet has swelled and is cooked. Stir the dissolved miso into the soup with the ginger juice. Discard the bay leaves.

Serve this soup chunky-style or puree it in a blender for a creamy golden soup or sauce. Garnish with scallions.

VARIATIONS:
♦ *Herbed Squash Soup:* In place of the cumin and coriander, add a sprinkle of your favorite soup herbs, such as basil, dill, thyme, savory, or marjoram.
♦ *Garlic and Squash Soup:* Sauté 3 to 4 cloves of minced peeled garlic with the onions and omit the ginger.
♦ *Quinoa-Squash Soup:* For an unusual soup that's quite delicious, use quinoa in place of millet, and season as you wish, using the suggestions given above.
♦ *Harvest-Millet Stew:* Use half the amount of squash and add a combination of carrots, parsnips, rutabagas, daikon, yams, or pearl onions to equal 1½ to 2 cups.

NUTRITION INFORMATION: Cal: 189 Pro: 5g/11% Carb: 38g/75% Fat: 3g/14% Chol: 0mg Sodium: 403mg Potassium: 606mg Fiber: 3g A: 205% C: 47% B1: 16% B3: 13% B6: 21% Folic: 10% P: 13% Fe: 12% Mg: 20% Cu: 16% Mn: 14% Cr: 14%

EXCHANGE: Bread: 1¾ Veg: 1½ Fat: ½

MICROWAVE METHOD: In a 3-quart microwave-safe casserole, cook the oil and onions on High (100% power) until tender, about 5 minutes. Add the squash, cumin, coriander, and red pepper and cook, covered, on High 3 minutes. Rinse the millet and add with 4 cups water and the salt and bay leaves. Cook covered on High to boiling, about 8 to 10 minutes. Stir. Reduce power to Medium (50% power); cook covered until the millet is tender, about 12 to 15 minutes; stir twice. Let stand 5 minutes. Stir in the miso and ginger, discard the bay leaves, and serve as above.

ABC Pancakes (Amaranth, Buckwheat, and Corn)
by Mary Estella

Try flavorful flours such as amaranth, buckwheat, and cornmeal in varying proportions in these pancakes. This basic dairy- and wheat-free recipe can be easily adapted using the flours you have on hand. Low-fat regular milk can be substituted for the soy milk.

  1 cup buckwheat flour
  1/2 cup amaranth flour
  1/2 cup yellow cornmeal
  1/4 teaspoon sea salt
  1 tablespoon baking powder
  2 cups soy milk
  1 egg
  2 tablespoons vegetable oil
  3 tablespoons maple syrup or applesauce for topping (optional)

  PREPARATION TIME: 15 minutes
  COOKING TIME: 20 minutes
  YIELD: 4 servings

Combine the flours, sea salt, and baking powder in a mixing bowl. Combine the soy milk, egg, and 1 tablespoon of the vegetable oil in a separate bowl. Pour the liquid ingredients into the dry and stir until the lumps disappear. Let sit for 5 minutes. Meanwhile, lightly oil a heavy skillet with the remaining 1 tablespoon oil, spreading the oil on the skillet with a paper towel. Set aside the greased paper towel to re-oil the skillet between batches. Heat the skillet until a drop of water flicked onto the skillet sizzles. Pour the batter with a small ladle, cooking spoon, or a quarter-cup measure, depending on the desired size of the pancakes. Flip the pancakes when bubbles form and break; cook until the undersides of the

pancakes are golden brown. Serve with applesauce or maple syrup if desired.

VARIATIONS:
♦ Blue cornmeal can be used in place of yellow.
♦ Add 3/4 cup blueberries to the batter.

NUTRITION INFORMATION: Cal: 354 Pro: 11g/12% Carb: 50g/55% Fat: 13g/32% (S:27% M:22% P:51%) Chol: 52mg Sodium: 425mg Potassium: 400mg Fiber: 5g E: 40% B1: 20% B2: 12% B6: 15% Panto: 10% Ca: 10% P: 32% Fe: 18% Mg: 25% Cu: 28% Mn: 37%
EXCHANGE: Med. Meat: 1/4 Whole Milk: 1/4 Bread: 3 Fat: 1 1/2

Stella's Greek Barley Salad
by Mary Estella

Marinated with black olives, sun-dried tomatoes, and crunchy cucumbers, barley never tasted so good! The flavors only improve if this side-dish salad is refrigerated overnight.

BASILY-GARLIC DRESSING:

    2 tablespoons olive oil
    2 tablespoons fresh lemon juice
  2 to 4 *cloves garlic, peeled and minced*
    1/4 teaspoon white pepper
    1/2 teaspoon dried oregano
    2 tablespoon chopped fresh basil (if available), or 1/2 teaspoon dried basil Salt (optional)

  PREPARATION TIME: 10 minutes
  YIELD: About 1/4 cup

Combine all ingredients in a small jar or blender and shake or blend for a few seconds.

SALAD

    2 cups cooked barley
   10 *black olives, pitted and chopped (about 1/4 cup)*
  6 to 7 *sun-dried tomato halves (no salt added), sliced*

2 to 3 tablespoons chopped fresh parsley
2 to 3 scallions, diced
    2 Kirby cucumbers, diced, or 1 regular
        cucumber, seeded and diced
3 to 4 radishes, sliced
    2 stalks celery, diced
        Green or red bell pepper for garnish

PREPARATION TIME: 25 minutes plus
refrigerating time
YIELD: 4 to 5 servings

Combine the barley with the olives, sun-dried tomatoes, parsley, and scallions. Pour the dressing over the barley mixture. Add the remaining vegetables, and garnish with the pepper. Refrigerate several hours or until ready to use.

VARIATIONS:
♦ Replace the barley with millet, couscous, or bulgur.
♦ Add ½ cup chopped dandelion greens or purslane and serve on a bed of watercress.

NUTRITION INFORMATION: **dressing only, per 1 tablespoon serving** Cal: 53 Pro: .2g/1% Carb: 1g/10% Fat: 5g/89% (S:15% M:76% P:9%) Chol: 0mg Sodium: 1mg Potassium: 22mg Fiber: 0g
EXCHANGE: Fat: 1¼

salad and dressing Cal: 246 Pro: 6g/8% Carb: 43g/66% Fat: 8g/26% (S:16% M:73% P:11%) Chol: 0mg Sodium: 70mg Potassium: 585mg Fiber: 10g A: 49% C: 73% E: 11% B1: 12% B3: 13% B6: 11% Folic: 10% P: 14% Fe: 13% Mg: 11% Se: 24% Cr: 41% Mo: 36%
EXCHANGE: Bread: 2 Veg: 2 Fat: 1½

Caraway, Rye, and Rice Pilaf
by Mary Estella

Rye berries add crunch to this savory pilaf with flavors from Scandinavia. If you love pumpernickel bread, try this whole grain dish with dinner or as a vegetable stuffing.

1 teaspoon sesame or olive oil
1 onion, diced

1 tablespoon caraway seeds
⅓ cup rye berries (see Note)
⅔ cup raw brown rice
2 tablespoons sauerkraut
2 tablespoons raisins
    Pinch sea salt
    Pinch white pepper
2 cups boiling water

PREPARATION TIME: 20 minutes
COOKING TIME: 1 hour 10 minutes
YIELD: 4 to 5 servings

Preheat the oven to 350°F. In a skillet heat the oil and sauté the onion 5 minutes, stirring occasionally. Add the caraway seeds and continue cooking 2 minutes. In a strainer, combine the rye berries and rice; rinse under running water. Place the washed grain in a small ovenproof dish. Add the sauerkraut, raisins, salt, and pepper. Spoon the sautéed onion and caraway over the grain mixture, add the boiling water, and stir. Cover tightly and bake in the preheated oven for 50 to 60 minutes, or until all the liquid is absorbed. Fluff with a fork, cover, and let the grain sit for 5 to 10 minutes before serving.

NOTE: Wheat berries can be substituted for the rye, but they must be presimmered in water to cover for 1 hour and drained before proceeding with the recipe.

VARIATIONS:
♦ Omit the raisins; dice a carrot and sauté it with the onion.
♦ Mix in 2 tablespoons chopped fresh parsley or sliced scallions just before serving.

NUTRITION: Cal: 181 Pro: 5g/10% Carb: 37g/80% Fat: 2g/10% Chol: 0mg Sodium: 118mg Potassium: 197mg Fiber: 4g E: 10% Mn : 10% Se: 51%
EXCHANGE: Bread: 2 Veg: ½ Fruit: ¼ Fat: ¼

MICROWAVE METHOD: On a paper plate or in a 9-inch microwave-safe pie plate, cook the caraway seeds on High (100% power) until toasted, about 1½ to 2 minutes. In a 1-quart microwave-safe casserole or bowl, cook the onion and oil on High until tender, about 2 to 3 minutes. Then proceed as directed above.

Kasha Pilaf

by *American Health*

3½ cups unsalted chicken broth or stock (see
     page 28)
  4 teaspoons olive oil
  1 medium onion, diced
  1 cup raw whole or medium kasha
     (buckwheat groats)
 ½ cup raw long-grain white converted rice
 ½ teaspoon salt (optional)
  1 cup frozen peas
    Freshly ground black pepper

PREPARATION TIME: 15 minutes
COOKING TIME: 25 minutes
YIELD: 8 servings

Bring the chicken broth to a boil in a saucepan.
Heat the oil in a large heavy skillet over medium
heat. Add the onion and cook, stirring often, until
tender, about 5 minutes. Add the kasha and cook,
stirring often, until lightly browned, about 2 minutes. Slowly add the boiling broth, rice, and salt
if desired. Reduce the heat, cover, and simmer 10
minutes. Add the peas; cook until the liquid is
absorbed and the rice is tender, about 5 minutes.
Add pepper to taste.

NUTRITION INFORMATION: Cal: 169 Pro: 6g/
15% Carb: 29g/67% Fat: 4g/18% (S:20% M:64%
P:16%) Chol: 1mg Sodium: 57g Potassium: 221mg
Fiber: 3g B1: 11% B3: 16% P: 13% Mg: 14%
Cu: 11% Mn: 19%
EXCHANGE: Bread: 1¾ Fat: ½

MICROWAVE METHOD: Heat the chicken
broth to boiling on the stove or in the microwave,
uncovered, on High (100% power). In a 2½- to 3-
quart microwave-safe casserole, cook only 2 teaspoons oil and the onion on High for 3 minutes.
Add the kasha; cook on High 1½ minutes. Add
the rice, broth, and salt. Cook covered on High
until most of the liquid is absorbed, about 8 to 10
minutes. Add the peas; cook covered on High until all the liquid is absorbed, about 6 to 8 minutes.
Let stand 5 minutes. Add pepper to taste.

Maria's Millet Polenta

by Mary Estella

Millet's creamy consistency (when simmered in
three times its volume of water) lends itself to
porridge-like breakfast cereals or pan-fried polen-
tas. Fragrant cinnamon sticks, cloves, and orange
peel add spice to millet's mild flavor here, making
this dish an excellent accompaniment to broiled
or roasted chicken.

      1 cup raw millet
7 to 10 whole cloves
      1 strip orange peel, 1 inch by 6 inches
      1 cinnamon stick
⅓ to ½ cup dried apricots, rinsed and diced
      Pinch sea salt
      1 teaspoon corn oil (optional)

PREPARATION TIME: 10 minutes plus
refrigerating time
COOKING TIME: 50 minutes
YIELD: 4 to 6 servings

Bring 3 cups water to a boil. Rinse and drain
the millet in a fine-mesh strainer. Poke the whole
cloves into the peel. Add the millet to the boiling
water and drop the cinnamon stick and clove-
studded peel in on top. Add the dried apricots to
the millet with the sea salt, cover, lower the heat,
and simmer for 35 to 45 minutes, or until the
millet is creamy and has absorbed all the water.
Remove the cinnamon stick and peel and stir.
Serve like oatmeal or refrigerate until solidified
(will keep for 2 to 3 days), slice, fry in the corn
oil in a nonstick skillet until gold and crispy, and
serve with a sauce or steamed vegetables.

NUTRITION INFORMATION: Cal: 156 Pro: 4g/10%
Carb: 30g/77% Fat: 2g/13% Chol: 0mg Sodium:
67mg Potassium: 193mg Fiber: 2g A: 13% P: 11%
Mg: 11% Cu: 14%
EXCHANGE: Bread: 1½ Fruit: ½

MICROWAVE METHOD: Rinse and drain the
millet and prepare peel with cloves as directed
above. In a 2-quart microwave-safe casserole heat
3 cups water covered on High (100% power) to
boiling, about 6 to 8 minutes. Add the millet, cinnamon stick, clove-studded peel, apricots, and sea

salt. Cook covered on High 5 minutes. Stir. Reduce power to Medium (50% power); cook covered until almost all water is absorbed, about 10 to 13 minutes. Remove the cinnamon and peel and continue as above.

Benjamin's Barley Stew

by Mary Estella

- 1 cup raw pearled barley
- 3 cups boiling water
  Pinch sea salt (optional)
- 1 onion, diced
- 2 carrots, sliced 1/4 inch thick
- 1 small rutabaga, cubed
- 2 large parsnips, diced
- 1 cup slivered cabbage, cauliflower, yams, or squash
- 2 bay leaves
- 1/4 teaspoon white pepper
- 1/2 teaspoon dried savory
- 1/2 teaspoon dried marjoram
- 1/2 teaspoon dried basil
- 1/4 teaspoon dried dill
- 3 tablespoons miso dissolved in 1/2 cup soup broth, or sea salt to taste
- 2 to 3 tablespoons chopped fresh parsley for garnish

PREPARATION TIME: 40 minutes
COOKING TIME: 1 hour, 25 minutes
YIELD: 4 to 6 main-dish servings

Add the barley to the boiling water, with salt if desired. Cover, return to a boil, lower the heat, and simmer 45 minutes. Add more water if needed; barley should be moist and fluffy. In a large soup pot, layer the vegetables in the order listed. Add just enough water to cover them. Add the bay leaves, pepper, and dried herbs. Cover the pot and slowly bring to a boil, lower the heat, and simmer 15 minutes. Add the cooked barley, simmer 5 to 10 minutes. Add the dissolved miso, stir, and adjust the seasoning. To serve, garnish with chopped parsley.

VARIATION: *Hot Garlicky Barley Stew:* Sauté the vegetables in 2 to 3 teaspoons olive oil in the soup pot. Begin with the onions, sauté until translucent, about five minutes, then add the remaining vegetables and sauté for 5 to 10 minutes. Add 3 to 4 cloves minced garlic, stir, and sauté for another minute. Cover with water and continue with the recipe.

NUTRITION INFORMATION: Cal: 210 Pro: 6g/ 10% Carb: 47g/85% Fat: 1g/5% Chol: 0mg Sodium: 333mg Potassium: 474mg Fiber: 8g A: 137% C: 26% B6: 11% Folic: 10% P: 15% Fe: 10% Mg: 12% Mn: 16% Se: 20% Cr: 10% Mo: 31%
EXCHANGE: Bread: 2 1/4 Veg: 2

MICROWAVE METHOD: In a 1 1/2- to 2-quart microwave-safe casserole, cook the water, barley, and salt on High (100% power) 12 minutes. Reduce the power to Medium (50% power) and cook covered until the barley is tender, about 17 to 22 minutes. Let stand. In a 2-quart microwave-safe casserole, layer the vegetables, only 1/2 cup water, and the bay leaves, pepper, and dried herbs. Cook covered on High until vegetables are just tender-crisp, about 12 to 15 minutes; stir once, then add the cooked barley. Season as directed above. Reheat if desired.

Roast Chicken with Oat Stuffing

by *American Health*

- 1 cup uncooked regular or quick-cooking oats
- 1 tablespoon unsalted butter or margarine
- 1 cup diced celery
- 1 cup diced onion
- 1 clove garlic, minced
- 4 ounces fresh mushrooms, sliced thin
- 1/4 cup minced fresh parsley
- 1/2 teaspoon dried thyme leaves
- 1/4 teaspoon dried rosemary
- 1/4 teaspoon dried sage
- 1 roasting chicken, (about 4 pounds)
- 1 1/2 cups unsalted chicken broth or stock (see page 00)
- 1 clove garlic, split

PREPARATION TIME: 40 minutes
COOKING TIME: 2½ to 3 hours
YIELD: 6 servings

Toast the oats in a large skillet over medium-low heat until lightly browned, stirring constantly. Pour into a medium bowl. Let the skillet cool for a few minutes, then melt 2 teaspoons of the butter or margarine. Stir in the celery, onion, and garlic. Cook over medium heat 5 minutes; cover and cook until the onion is wilted, about 10 minutes longer. Remove the vegetables from the skillet and add to the oats. Melt the remaining butter or margarine in the skillet; add the mushrooms and sauté 5 minutes. Add the mushrooms and the parsley, thyme, rosemary, and sage to the oats; stir well.

Preheat the oven to 325°F. Pull out and discard the fat from the chicken cavity. Rinse the chicken under cold running water and pat dry. Stir ½ cup of the chicken stock into the oat mixture. Loosely stuff the chicken with the oat mixture and skewer closed. Rub the chicken skin all over with the split garlic clove; discard the garlic. Place the chicken in a shallow roasting or baking pan on a rack and spoon any remaining stuffing around it. Spoon ¼ cup stock over the chicken. Roast in the preheated oven until the juices run clear when a thigh is pierced with a fork, about 2 to 2½ hours. Baste with the remaining stock and pan juices every 20 minutes for the first 1½ hours and every 10 minutes for the remainder of the roasting time.

Remove the stuffing to a serving dish. Let the chicken stand 10 minutes or so to allow the juices to settle. Carve the chicken, removing the skin from each serving. Spoon the pan juices over the chicken and serve.

NUTRITION INFORMATION: Cal: 348 Pro: 44g/
51% Carb: 13g/15% Fat: 16g/33% (S:36%
M:40% P:24%) Chol: 130mg Sodium: 176mg
Potassium: 610mg Fiber: 2g C: 11% B1: 16%
B2: 21% B3: 73% B6: 36% Panto: 19% P: 39%
Fe: 17% Mg: 16% Zn: 23% Cu: 10% Mn: 18%
Se: 50% Cr: 22%
EXCHANGE: Lean Meat: 5 Bread: ½ Veg: ¾
Fat: ½

MICROWAVE METHOD: On a large paper plate or a 9-inch pie plate, cook the oats on High (100% power) until lightly browned, about 3 to 4 minutes; stir once. In 1-quart microwave-safe casserole or bowl, cook the butter or margarine, celery, onion, and garlic on High until tender, about 3 to 4 minutes. Add the mushrooms; cook on High until wilted, 2 to 3 minutes. Add the mixture to the oats and complete the stuffing as directed above. Prepare the chicken and stuff as above. Rub the stuffed chicken with garlic and place, breast side down, in 2½- to 3-quart shallow microwave-safe casserole. Arrange the extra stuffing around the chicken; spoon 2 tablespoons of the broth over all. Cook uncovered on High for 15 minutes. Turn breast side up. Cook uncovered on High until done as above, about 10 minutes more.

Scottish Oat and Cauliflower Stew
by Mary Estella

Cracked or whole oats add creaminess to this Scottish stew. You can vary the vegetables and herbs; I find parsnips add sweetness, string beans provide crunch, and fresh dill accents the mild flavors of the cauliflower and oats.

    ½ cup whole or cracked oats
    2 teaspoons olive oil
    1 medium onion, diced
    2 carrots, chopped
1 to 2 parsnips, chopped
    2 ribs celery, chopped
    1 small cauliflower, chopped
    2 bay leaves
    ½ teaspoon dried basil
    ½ teaspoon dried marjoram
    ½ teaspoon white pepper
    ¼ teaspoon mace
1 to 2 cups string beans, cut in half crosswise
    3 tablespoons miso dissolved in ½ cup hot water, or sea salt to taste
    2 tablespoons minced fresh dill or parsley
    ½ red bell pepper, diced
    1 teaspoon sesame oil
2 to 3 cloves garlic, peeled and minced

PREPARATION TIME: 45 minutes
COOKING TIME: 50 minutes
YIELD: 6 main-course servings

Rinse the oats in a strainer. Bring 2 cups water to a boil in a saucepan, add the oats, and cover. Lower the heat and simmer 5 minutes. Let stand covered while you wash and chop the vegetables. In a large soup pot, heat the olive oil and sauté the onion. Add the carrots, parsnips, celery, and cauliflower. Continue sautéing 5 minutes, stirring occasionally. Add the oats and 4 more cups water. Add the dried herbs and spices, cover, and simmer 15 minutes, or until vegetables are tender. Discard the bay leaves. If you like creamy soup, puree the mixture (or part of it, if preferred) in a blender or food processor. Return to the pot and add the string beans. Simmer for another few minutes, until the beans are bright green.

Season the stew with the dissolved miso to taste. If the stew is very thick, add more water. Stir in the fresh dill or parsley. Sauté the diced red pepper in the sesame oil for 2 minutes; add the garlic and sauté another minute. Add to the stew, and adjust seasonings.

VARIATIONS:
♦ Replace the oats with millet.
♦ For a taste of India, replace the dried herbs with your favorite curry spices. Sauté the vegetables with the spices before you add the grain and water.
♦ Use 2 cups fresh or frozen peas in place of the string beans.

NUTRITION INFORMATION: Cal: 167   Pro: 6g/ 14% Carb: 30g/68% Fat: 4g/18% (S:16% M:66% P:18%) Chol: 0mg Sodium: 303mg Potassium: 645mg Fiber: 7g A: 133% C: 94% B1: 14% B6: 17% Folic: 20% P: 17% Fe: 11% Mg: 14% Mn: 17% Cr: 18%
EXCHANGE: Bread: 1¼ Veg: 2 Fat: ½

MICROWAVE METHOD: In a 4-quart microwave-safe casserole or bowl, cook 2 cups water on High (100% power) to boiling, about 3 to 5 minutes. Add the oats and let stand covered. In a 3-quart microwave-safe casserole or bowl, cook the oil and onion on High until tender, about 2 to 3 minutes. Add the carrots, parsnips, celery, and cauliflower. Cook covered on High 5 minutes. Add the oats, 3 cups water, and the dried herbs. Cook covered on High until the vegetables are tender, about 10 to 12 minutes. Puree as above if desired. Add the beans and cook covered until tender-crisp, about 3 minutes. Season as directed above.

Rita's Rye and Raisin Muffins
by Mary Estella

Rye flakes add a chewy texture to these light and spicy muffins.

2 cups rye flakes
1 cup whole wheat pastry flour
½ cup raisins
1 tablespoon baking powder
¼ teaspoon ground allspice
¼ teaspoon ground ginger
½ teaspoon ground cinnamon
  Pinch of sea salt
¾ cup apple cider or apple juice
¼ cup safflower oil
1 egg plus 1 egg white, lightly beaten
⅓ cup maple syrup
  Vegetable cooking spray

PREPARATION TIME: 20 minutes
COOKING TIME: 20 minutes
YIELD: 1 dozen muffins

Preheat the oven to 400°F. Combine the dry ingredients in a mixing bowl. Blend the liquid ingredients in a separate bowl. Combine the dry and liquid ingredients and stir just until mixed with no lumps. Grease muffin tins with cooking spray; spoon the batter into cups. Bake for 20 minutes or until golden.

VARIATIONS:
♦ Replace rye flakes with oatmeal and add ½ cup chopped walnuts.
♦ Use golden raisins, currants, or chopped dates instead of raisins.
♦ Add 1 teaspoon grated lemon or orange rind.

NUTRITION INFORMATION: Cal: 187   Pro: 4g/ 8% Carb: 32g/66% Fat: 6g/26% (S:13% M:15% P:72%) Chol: 18mg Sodium: 144mg Potassium: 128mg Fiber: 2g P: 11% Mn: 14%
EXCHANGE: Bread: 1¼ Fruit: 1 Fat: 1

◇ ROOTS ◇

Roots Revisited

by Madonna Behen and Robert Barnett

Potatoes nourish for pennies. So do fellow tubers and root vegetables: sweet potatoes, yams, jicama, celery root, carrots, beets, parsnips, and sunchokes (Jerusalem artichokes). All are high-fiber complex carbohydrates that help us feel full and control weight on a few calories.

Unadorned, a medium-sized baked potato contains about 110 calories; it's the butter and sour cream that add fat and calories. In Germany, a popular diet even calls for ten medium-sized potatoes a day. They're economical, too: Dime for dime, potatoes serve up protein, iron, potassium, and vitamin C much cheaper than even very rich sources do. A quarter's worth of spuds, roughly $3\frac{1}{2}$ ounces, yields 7 grams of iron, about 40 percent of the USRDA. One medium-sized potato plus a cup of low-fat milk provides about 11 grams of complete protein, about 23 percent of the RDA for a 130-pound woman, 18 percent for a 170-pound man. Cost for both: 14 cents.

Potatoes are the fourth largest world crop (rice, wheat, and corn are the first three). Take one home and bake it today; fewer than 1 percent of its calories come from fat. But an equal portion of fast-food french fries gets 47 percent of its calories from fat. And frying can be bad for other reasons as well.

Glycoalkaloids, colorless toxic substances, are more abundant in potato skins. So if you're planning on eating the skins, avoid all green-skinned potatoes. If you discard the skin, be sure to peel away all the green. The popular appetizer of fried potato skins—high in fat—can have high levels of glycoalkaloids. "The fat and salt in fried potato skins may mask the bitter taste of glycoalkaloids," says Cornell University nutritionist Nell Mondy.

Fortunately, most of the nutrients in a potato are in the flesh, not the skin. Even more so if you bake your spuds. In a recent Cornell University study, researchers found that baking concentrates nutrients in the pith (the fleshy center) while frying reduces the nutrients (as well as quadruples the calories!). Says Mondy, "Bake rather than fry, and beware of fried skins."

For optimum carbohydrates, serve potatoes hot. At the MRC Dunn Clinical Nutrition Centre in Cambridge, England, researchers Hans Englyst and John Cummings found that potatoes contain starches that are made digestible by heat. Cooling cooked potatoes (as when making potato salad) causes the starch to become less digestible. But reheating the potatoes makes them nearly as good as freshly cooked, they found. So if you're fond of potato salad, try serving it German-style: warm.

The root cellar, you'll find, holds many pleasant surprises. Native American sunchokes, the root of the sunflower plant, for example, are often made into a delicious pasta that's safe for people allergic to wheat. They may also benefit diabetics. Like beans, oats, and barley, sunchokes create only a slow rise in blood sugar after you eat them. They contain a polysaccharide called inulin, which is only slowly digested. Inulin, "digested" in the colon by bacteria, also traps urea, a kidney waste product. In diabetes, which often puts a strain on the kidneys, reducing blood sugar and urea levels may be a double bonus.

What many people call yams are actually sweet potatoes—orange-colored roots with a sweet taste. True yams are white-fleshed, tropical vegetables, seldom sweet and hardly ever available in this country. They contain a chemical similar to estrogen that some scientists believe may affect fertility; in Nigeria, where yam consumption is unusually high, so is the frequency of twins.

Sweet potatoes themselves are quite nutritious. One medium-sized baked sweet potato contains about almost five times the USRDA for vitamin A (white potatoes have nearly none). Their flavors are richer than white potatoes, partly due to their somewhat higher fat content; try them without butter.

Popular jicama is a newcomer to American kitchens. This brown, turnip-shaped native Mexican tuber is fast becoming an American favorite. The flesh of a jicama, crunchy and juicy, can be eaten chilled and raw in salads or cooked in stir-fries. Extremely low in calories (50 in a cup of sliced raw jicama), the jicama is a boon for weight control.

Carrots are famous for their namesake: beta-carotene. It's an antioxidant that may help protect against lung and other cancers (as well as heart disease). In a landmark study by the late Marilyn S. Menkes of Baltimore's Johns Hopkins University, published in the *New England Journal of Medicine* in 1987, smokers with the lowest blood levels of beta-carotene had four times the risk of getting a common form of lung cancer than smokers with the highest levels of beta-carotene. The difference is about what you'd get from eating an extra carrot a day. A carrot a day is about what we need to fill daily vitamin A requirements, too. (More recent research at the same university suggests a carotenoid-rich diet may also protect against melanoma, the deadly skin cancer.)

Paul Lachance, professor of nutrition at Rutgers University in New Brunswick, New Jersey, following the National Cancer Institute's guidelines, estimates that we should try to get about 6 milligrams of beta-carotene a day to minimize cancer risks. Current consumption: about 1½ milligrams a day. One medium carrot gives us about between 3 and 6 milligrams, so a carrot a day is a big step in the right direction. Cooking is okay, too; it destroys some of the carotenoids, but what's left is easier for the body to absorb.

But carrots may do more. They may help lower blood cholesterol. The key: calcium pectate, a fiber found in carrots. In Philadelphia, USDA researchers Peter D. Hoagland and Philip E. Pfeffer gave healthy volunteers seven ounces of carrots (about two medium ones) a day for three weeks. Result: blood cholesterol dropped an average of 11 percent. Calcium pectate, the researchers find, binds to bile acids. Because cholesterol is needed to make bile acids in the liver, less goes to the blood. Result: lower blood cholesterol. (Broccoli, onions, and cabbage also contain calcium pectate, they find; similar waste-soluble fibers can be found in oats, beans, barley, okra, apples, pears and the inner white part of grapefruit skins.)

So a carrot is a pretty sweet root. Literally: along with beets, they have among the highest sugar content of all vegetables. That makes them great for sweetening stews. Indeed, the Irish call carrots "underground honey."

Beets, celery root (a.k.a. celeriac), and parsnips are some of our more common roots. Beets are nutrient-dense; they are particularly rich in potassium. Steam the greens: A 3½-ounce serving provides over 10 percent of the USRDA for calcium and over 100 percent for vitamin A. The old-fashioned parsnip, cousin to the carrot, has large, fleshy white roots. Celery root, a relative of branch celery, is a turnip-shaped root that tastes like celery but has a hearty texture and few calories. Other roots, including turnips and rutabagas (both covered in the Cruciferous Vegetables chapter), the tropical cassava and taro root, the Oriental water chestnut and bamboo shoot, and the hoary American root salsify, are similarly high-carbohydrate, low-fat, low-calorie vegetables.

The Roots of Cooking ____

by Nao Hauser

Celebrate as we may diverse ethnic roots, Americans can all point to one set of culinary roots. Potatoes, sweet potatoes, carrots, and beets— these are the staples of American cookpots, whether they're served up at Thanksgiving feasts or scooped into sacks at McDonald's.

Roots transcend snobbery. Any backyard gardener and farmers' market shopper knows that the sweet-sour taste of a just-dug beet rivals fine wine in complexity, that the caramel-like sweetness of a roasted new sweet potato soothes as no bonbon can, that carrots are more suspenseful in their flavors than any dish conceived in nouvelle cuisine.

You have to sample roots from various soils and in all seasons to appreciate the spectrum of tastes they hold. But to a much greater extent than with other produce, you can experience the diversity through supermarket samplings, because roots don't have to be specially bred to withstand shipping and a store will draw on crops from many places to maintain a year-round supply.

There are regional differences, of course. White potatoes and beets are truer to cold climates, and thus better known to Yankees and Midwesterners. Sweet potatoes hold up better in the heat, and thus star in Southern cooking. But nationwide distribution has smoothed over such biases. What all Americans know is that roots are the vegetables you can count on in any season at reasonable prices.

Yet the realm is not without its bits of news and whiffs of intrigue. Jicama, a relative newcomer to produce bins, still surprises initiates with its winelike sweetness and refreshing crispness. Many people don't know what to make of gnarled celery root (celeriac) and knobby sunchokes (Jerusalem artichokes). Salsify rarely appears on menus, and cassava only gets smiles of recognition when identified as the starch in tapioca pudding. It's well worth getting acquainted with the more novel roots, if only to appreciate all the earth offers.

It's the tried-and-true roots, though, that warm a cook's heart. Potatoes, sweet potatoes, carrots, parsnips, and beets are readily available and wonderfully versatile. They can be roasted one day and boiled the next, simmered for hours in a soup or steamed in minutes in the microwave oven. They are about the only foods other than dairy products that you can find in the same form in a roadside diner or a fancy French restaurant.

Because most roots are naturally high in starch and minerals, they can be turned into rich-tasting fare with very little, if any, added fat. Here are some ways to accentuate the assets.

♦ *Potatoes.* If you want creamy potatoes, boil them in low-fat milk (rather than skim, to retain white color); then mash them into the liquid, which will thicken during the cooking from starch thrown off by the potatoes. For creamy low-fat potato salad, boil them in chicken stock and let them cool in the stock; here again, the starch will thicken the liquid, so that only a little yogurt is needed for satisfying consistency. If you crave a crispy, salty treat, cut potatoes lengthwise into 1/3- to 1/2-inch slices. Brush slices very lightly with a mixture of vegetable oil and low-sodium soy sauce; roast the slices in a covered barbecue grill or in a 400°F oven. To gild a baked potato, split it, mash the flesh with 1 to 2 tablespoons of plain, low-fat yogurt or milk, sprinkle with a mixture of 1 tablespoon fresh bread crumbs and 1 teaspoon grated Parmesan cheese, and place under the broiler to brown the topping; serve with a dollop of yogurt.

♦ *Sweet potatoes.* The custom of sweetening sweet potatoes with brown sugar or honey (to say nothing of marshmallows) is probably the most redundant in our cuisine. If you want to underscore the naturally high sugar content of sweet potatoes, simmer or bake slices in apple juice or milk. You can also set off the sweetness with touches of tartness and bitterness—as in a dollop of yogurt and a sprinkling of nutmeg on a whole baked sweet potato. Try this formula with a spectrum of yogurts, such as strawberry, orange, pineapple, and apple, and you'll see how the complexity of the potato plays to both sweet and tart elements. If you want to caramelize some of the sugar so that the potatoes taste like candy, rub thick slices with a little bit of vegetable oil and roast in a covered barbecue grill or a 400°F oven. Their sugar content makes sweet potatoes a marvelous foil for the spices that perfume a baker's kitchen, ranging from tangy ginger to sweet cinnamon. Because of their high moisture content, sweet potatoes can be mashed to a satiny puree. Cut into chunks, the deep orange potatoes brighten and sweeten pork and turkey casseroles and stews. Cut into matchsticks and steamed or sautéed, they are winter's elegant rejoinder to the vivid produce of a summer.

♦ *Carrots.* All chompers know the satisfaction of raw carrots. Refrigerating a pound of peeled, cut-up carrot sticks is probably a cook's simplest routine investment in good nutrition, especially in winter, when other raw vegetable snacks may be scarce. When cooked, carrots that start out sweet taste even sweeter, whether in pot roasts or cakes. The direct sweetness is considered essential in stocks and many soups, but it's also effective, when you grate the carrots, as an antidote to the acidity of tomatoes in sauces and casseroles. You can highlight the sugar in carrots by seasoning them with sweet spices, such as cardamom and ginger, or you can contrast the sweetness with slightly sour herbs, such as dill and tarragon.

♦ *Jicama.* The frog prince of roots, jicama enchants those who get past its homely, somewhat scaly skin. Pare away the brown covering, slice the moist, white flesh, and you have a crisp snack that pleases almost everyone with its gentle taste. Party-givers love jicama because it adds variety to crudité trays and won't wilt or discolor, no matter how many rounds of cocktails are passed. Sliced very thin or julienne cut, jicama adds a counterpoint of crunch to salads made with soft, intensely flavored ingredients, such as oranges and avocados.

Don't expect jicama to soften during cooking. It won't. What cooked jicama does beautifully is contribute body and winelike overtones to pureed soups. You have to grate the pared root to get it to release all of its flavor in the cookpot. It grates easily. Jicama's taste links especially well with others in the Mexican repertoire, such as corn, squashes, and sweet potatoes. Sweat the jicama with onions and/or a fruit to bring out its sweetness before you add other ingredients.

♦ *Sunchokes.* Although Native Americans roasted these nuggets long before Columbus arrived, they are a matter of novelty nowadays. As a change of pace, they can be commended for their unusual nutty taste and applelike texture. But they lack the sweetness of jicama and discolor quickly. So if you want to slice or julienne-cut them for use in salads, be sure to immerse them in a dressing or a lemon juice solution as soon as they're cut. To serve cooked sunchokes, sauté thin slices or add strips to a stir-fry (especially good with pork) for the last couple of minutes of cooking. Don't cook these roots too long; they turn to mush. Although quite low in calories, sunchokes are not as user-friendly as the other roots in low-fat, low-sodium cooking. They are more likely to beg for butter or cream and salt to compensate for their lack of richness.

♦ *Beets.* More than a few table wars have been fought over beets. Those who shun them shun them. Period. There's no reasoning with a beet-hater. But one could argue that the treatments accorded beets by those who evince some fondness have done little to further the cause. Beets don't take much treatment at all: They are the most self-contained of vegetables, offering definite sweet, sour, and bitter sensations. When these are in balance, just a pinch each of salt and

Spotlight: Beet Scares

Wild beets grow along the coasts of Asia and Europe, and in ancient times were prized for their green, leafy tops. The beet *(Beta vulgaris)* is a member of the Goosefoot or *Chenopodiaceae* family, which also includes such popular greens as Swiss chard and spinach. It wasn't until the Christian era that red and white beets began to be cultivated by the Romans for their roots.

Roots we prize today. But be forewarned: red beets contain strong water-soluble red pigments. If you eat large quantities, your urine may turn red. It's totally harmless. But it's nice to know: Before you run to the doctor, remember what you had for dinner!

—Marcella Barbour Fiacco, R.D.

pepper is all the seasoning beets will open up to—anything else overwhelms them. When these are not in balance, due to soil conditions or length of storage, you can tell what's missing and add accordingly: a pinch of sugar and a tiny bit of butter or some nut oil for sweetness; fruit or wine vinegar for sourness; and a pinch of mild spice, such as cardamom, if the taste is flat. Anything else is window-dressing; you can add it as long as it doesn't threaten the intrinsic harmony. Foods that are gently sweet and sour, such as yogurt, Port wine, and mild vinaigrettes, respect these ruby roots. But too much sugar or butter will violate both their delicate taste and their silky texture. The less you do to impair the high moisture content of beets, the less damage you have to repair. So although baked beets have their devotees, boiling is safer for low-fat preparations. Beet greens and Swiss chard are closely related; both have a mild taste and can be prepared like spinach.

♦ *Parsnips.* If you look at carrots, parsnips, and celery root as offspring of the same family, you can sympathize with the role of poor parsnips. Bright, sweet carrots always take center stage; celery root claims those who dote on crunchy celery taste with no strings attached. Parsnips—white, bland, and firm but not crisp to the bite—are, well, rarely brought out in company. But farmers and old-fashioned cooks know that you can steam parsnips like carrots or mash them like turnips, and accord them a welcome place on cold-weather tables. Parsnips are, above all, a cook's "secret" ingredient—the sweetener more subtle than carrots in a stock, soup, or stew, and the crisp accent much milder than turnips or celery root in stir-fried dishes and sautées. In fact, it's the nonstellar subtlety of parsnips that wins cooks' hearts. Where a pound of carrots would oversweeten a meat dish or soup, half a pound each of carrots and parsnips will contribute just the right flavor and texture. Moreover, parsnips yield a very smooth puree—quite nice by itself with a pinch of nutmeg, but also a good textural enhancement for soups based on other vegetables.

♦ *Celery Root.* Patience is the byword of celery root, or celeriac, as it is also known. You have to wait for late fall for this root to appear in edible condition, and you have to pare away every bit of its tough, gnarled skin; otherwise, it can be woody and quite bitter. It also takes diligence to slice, dice, or julienne-cut the hard roots, but such preparation is essential for serving them raw or quickly cooked. Why does anyone bother? Because raw celery root, served as a crudité or in a salad, can become a passion of sorts. It has a wonderful crunch and a delicate, yet pronounced, celery flavor. Cooked texture is almost velvety, making pureed celery root a fine accompaniment to meats or a base for a soup. Season with the root's herbal kin, parsley and dill.

♦ *Salsify.* If you should happen across salsify (also called oyster plant) at the market, you might take it home and give it a try, just for old times' sake. It was better known centuries ago, when cooks didn't come across other supermarket riches every day. It's not rich in sugar or starch, and discolors as soon as it's pared. But if you braise chunks in a bit of butter and some chicken stock, you may like its delicate taste, which some compare to oysters, others to artichokes.

♦ *Cassava (manioc).* The bland, cooked root is rarely found on menus, although it can be simmered in a stew like potatoes. You can also substitute it for potatoes, as Peruvians do, in the cheese-sauced dish called "Papas a la Huancaina" (see page 116). Cassava meal and flour are Latin American staples, frequently used in breads, puddings, and dumplings. Toasted cassava meal (called *farofa*) is a standard Brazilian condiment, served as an accompaniment to beans and meat. Its delicate, nutlike flavor gentles spices, while the meal thickens juices, making the food taste more satisfying.

♦ *Taro.* Like cassava, a tropical root. Cooked, mashed, and fermented, it becomes the Hawaiian staple poi, an essential condiment at any luau. Unfermented, it's extremely bland and used as baby food. Some Hawaiians prefer it very well-fermented, which yields a strong taste that may not appeal to people not raised on the island.

♦ *Yams.* True yams are rarely available in the United States. What's called a yam here is most likely a sweet potato, though true yams may be available in certain Latin American markets. The yam is a bland, starchy root that calls for spicy toppings.

♦ *Water chestnuts and bamboo shoots.* Add crisp texture to soups, stir-fries and stews. Fresh water chestnuts have a delectable sweetness that's lost in the canning process. They can be peeled and eaten raw like a fruit, sliced into a spinach or watercress salad, or stir-fried with chicken and red or green peppers for a sweet colorful trio of textural contrasts.

Aromatic Root Stew

by Nao Hauser

Roots play such an important role in stews that it seemed apt to include an especially savory sample here. The recipe calls for veal scallopine or pork tenderloin simply to save time. You can use veal or pork stew meat, cut into thin strips, instead, but be prepared to cook the meat with the leek 30 to 40 minutes longer, for tenderness, if necessary, before adding the other vegetables.

1 large leek (5 ounces trimmed weight)
2 teaspoons butter
4 oz. shiitake mushrooms, sliced
2 tablespoons Dijon-style mustard
2 tablespoons plain low-fat yogurt
1 teaspoon garam masala or curry powder
1/4 teaspoon ground cardamom
*   Pinch ground cinnamon*
3/4 pound veal scullopine or thinly sliced and flattened pork tenderloin, cut into 1/2-inch × 1 1/2-inch strips
2 cloves garlic, peeled and pressed
1 teaspoon grated fresh ginger
1/2 cup unsalted veal stock (see page 29) or unsalted unsalted beef broth, no salt added
2 teaspoons dry red or white wine
2 large carrots (8 ounces), julienne cut
2 parsnips or celery roots, pared, julienne cut
2 tablespoons port wine
1/4 teaspoon Chinese 5-spice powder (see Note)
1/4 cup finely chopped fresh parsley
4 cups hot cooked basmati or other rice

PREPARATION TIME: 45 minutes
COOKING TIME: 1 1/2 hours
YIELD: 4 servings

Cut the leek lengthwise and rinse under running water until free of dirt. Slice the white and light green parts very thinly. Set aside.

Spray a 9- or 10-inch skillet or saucepan with nonstick cooking spray; add 1 teaspoon of the butter and heat over medium heat. Add the mushrooms; sauté 5 minutes. Remove the mushrooms and reserve.

Mix the mustard, yogurt, garam masala, cardamom, and cinnamon in a bowl; add the meat and toss to coat. Melt the remaining teaspoon butter in the skillet over medium heat. Add the meat; cook, stirring often, about 5 minutes. Add the leek, garlic, ginger, 1/4 cup of the stock, and the wine. Simmer covered over low heat 50 minutes. Add the carrots and parsnips, the remaining stock, the Port, and 5-spice powder; simmer covered until all ingredients are very tender, about 30 minutes. Stir in the reserved mushrooms and the parsley; cook just to heat through. Serve over the rice.

NOTE: Five-spice powder can be found at Asian food markets and in many supermarket spice racks. If 5-spice powder is not available, substitute 1/8 teaspoon ground nutmeg, 1/8 teaspoon ground ginger, and a generous pinch of cinnamon.

NUTRITION INFORMATION: Cal: 511 Pro: 25g/ 20% Carb: 77g/62% Fat: 10g/18% (S:85% M:11% P:4%) Chol: 72mg Sodium: 243mg Potassium: 893mg Fiber: 10g A: 284% C: 30% B1: 27% B2: 24% B3: 41% B6: 55% Folic: 25% Panto: 31% Ca: 12% P: 35% Fe: 33% Mg: 19% Cu: 30% Mn: 81% Se: 67% Cr: 24%
EXCHANGE: Lean Meat: 2 1/2 Bread: 4 Veg: 2 Fat: 1/2

Borscht

by *American Health*

1 1/4 pounds beets
  2 tablespoons sugar
  2 tablespoons fresh lemon juice
1/2 teaspoon salt (optional)
  1 teaspoon grated lemon peel
1/8 teaspoon freshly ground black pepper
  1 8-ounce container plain 1%-fat yogurt

PREPARATION TIME: 30 minutes plus
refrigerating time:
COOKING TIME: 1 hour 10 minutes
YIELD: 6 cups, or 5 first-course servings

With a soft brush under cold running water,
scrub the beets well. In a 4-quart saucepan over
high heat, bring the beets, 5 cups of water, and
the remaining ingredients except the yogurt to a
boil. Reduce the heat to low, cover, and simmer
1 hour, or until the beets are tender. With a slotted spoon, remove the beets; set the broth aside.
Run the beets under cold water for easy handling;
peel, then shred. Return the shredded beets to
the saucepan and refrigerate until chilled, at least
4 hours.

To serve, spoon into soup bowls; top each with
some yogurt.

NUTRITION INFORMATION: Cal: 76 Pro: 3g/
17% Carb: 15g/74% Fat: .7g/9% Chol: 3mg
Sodium: 77mg Potassium: 400mg Fiber: 2g
C: 14% Folic: 14% Mag: 10%
  EXCHANGE: Skim Milk: 1/4 Veg: 1 Fruit: 1/4

MICROWAVE METHOD: Scrub the beets as
above. In a 2-quart microwave-safe casserole or
bowl, cook the beets and remaining ingredients
except the yogurt, tightly covered, on High (100%
power) until the beets are tender, about 19 to 22
minutes. Let stand 5 minutes. With a slotted
spoon, remove the beets and continue as directed
above.

Five-Vegetable Soup

by *American Health*

A fine first course for a hearty meal.

2 medium sweet potatoes
1 medium acorn squash
2 tablespoons fresh lemon juice
1 medium onion, diced
1 garlic clove, peeled and minced
1/2 medium head cabbage, coarsely shredded
1 teaspoon reduced-sodium soy sauce
1/4 teaspoon fennel seeds (optional)
1/8 teaspoon freshly ground black pepper
*1 15 1/4- to 20-ounce can chick-peas, drained
  and rinsed*

PREPARATION TIME: 25 minutes
COOKING TIME: 1 hour
YIELD: 7 cups, or 7 servings

Pare the sweet potatoes and cut into bite-size
pieces. Cut the acorn squash in half lengthwise;
discard the seeds. Cut into wedges along the
ridges, peel the wedges, and cut the wedges into
bite-size pieces. Set the sweet potatoes and squash
aside.

In a 4-quart saucepot, combine the lemon juice,
onion, and garlic and cook over medium-low heat
5 minutes, stirring occasionally. Add the sweet
potatoes, squash, and 1 cup water. Over medium-
high heat, bring to a boil. Reduce the heat to low,
cover, and simmer about 15 minutes or until the
vegetables are tender, stirring occasionally.

In a covered blender at low speed, blend half
the vegetable mixture until smooth; pour into a
small bowl. Repeat with the remaining vegetables
and liquid. Return the pureed vegetables to the
saucepot. Add the cabbage, soy sauce, fennel
seeds, pepper, and 2 1/2 cups water. Over high
heat, bring to a boil; reduce the heat to low,
cover, and simmer 30 minutes, or until the cabbage is tender. Add the chick-peas; heat through.

NUTRITION INFORMATION: Cal: 169 Pro: 5g/
12% Carb: 36g/81% Fat: 2g/7% Chol: 0mg
Sodium: 293mg Potassium: 669mg Fiber: 8g
A: 173% C: 63% E: 26% B1: 12% B6: 17%
P: 13% Fe: 15% Mg: 16%
  EXCHANGE: Bread: 2 Veg: 1

MICROWAVE METHOD: Prepare the sweet potatoes and squash as above. In a 4-quart microwave-safe casserole or bowl, cook the lemon juice, onion, and garlic on High (100% power) 2 minutes. Add the sweet potatoes, squash, and 1 cup water. Cook, covered, on High until the vegetables are tender, about 11 to 14 minutes. Puree as directed above and return to casserole. Add the cabbage, soy sauce, fennel seeds, pepper, and only 2 cups water. Cook covered on High until the cabbage is almost tender, about 6 to 9 minutes; stir once. Stir in the chickpeas. Cook covered on High until the beans are heated through, about 3 minutes. Let stand 5 minutes.

Jicama and Zucchini Soup

by Nao Hauser

> 1 tablespoon unsalted butter
> 2 medium onions, minced
> 1 red apple, cored and chopped
> 1 jicama, pared and shredded
> 1 rib celery with leaves, sliced thin
> 5 cups unsalted chicken broth or stock (see page 28)
> 1¼ pounds zucchini, sliced thin
> 1 tablespoon dried tarragon
> ⅛ teaspoon ground nutmeg
> 6 tablespoons fresh lime or lemon juice
> ¼ teaspoon chili powder
> ¼ cup minced fresh tarragon, dill, or parsley, or a combination
> ½ cup plain low-fat yogurt

PREPARATION TIME: 40 minutes
COOKING TIME: 1 hour, 10 minutes
YIELD: about 3 quarts, or 8 servings

Melt the butter in a 4-quart pot. Stir in the onions; cook covered over medium-low heat, stirring occasionally, 10 minutes. Add the apple, jicama, celery, and 1 cup of the broth; cook covered 35 minutes. Stir in the zucchini, tarragon, and nutmeg. Cook covered over medium heat until the zucchini is very soft, 15 to 20 minutes. Let cool slightly.

Process the mixture, a third at a time, in a blender until smooth. Return to the pot; stir in the remaining broth and the lime or lemon juice, chili powder, and fresh herbs. Cook until heated through; stir well. Ladle into serving bowls and stir 1 tablespoon yogurt into each serving.

NOTE: The soup may also be chilled and served cold; stir in the yogurt at serving time.

NUTRITION INFORMATION: Cal: 115 Pro: 6g/ 20% Carb: 17g/57% Fat: 3g/23% (S:52% M:36% P:12%) Chol: 6mg Sodium: 96mg Potassium: 624mg Fiber: 3g C: 45% B3: 13% P: 14% Mn: 10%
    EXCHANGE: Veg: 3 Fruit: ¼ Fat: ½

MICROWAVE METHOD: In a 4-quart microwave-safe casserole or bowl, cook the butter and onions covered on High (100% power) until the onions are tender, about 4 to 6 minutes. Add the apple, jicama, celery, and 1 cup broth. Cook covered on High 10 minutes. Add the zucchini, tarragon, and nutmeg. Cook covered on High until the zucchini is tender, about 5 to 7 minutes. Let cool and continue as above. Cook covered on High until heated through, about 7 to 10 minutes.

Carrot Vichyssoise

by Nao Hauser

Cooking the potatoes in milk gives this first-course soup a luscious creaminess.

> 2 leeks
> 3 carrots, shredded
> 3½ cups unsalted chicken broth or stock (see page 28)
> 1½ pounds potatoes (about 4 medium), sliced
> 1 cup 1%-fat milk
> ½ teaspoon ground cardamom
> ⅛ teaspoon ground mace
> ⅛ teaspoon ground nutmeg
> ½ cups fresh dill sprigs, minced
> Few drops red pepper sauce (like Tabasco)
> Freshly ground black pepper
> 1 carrot, grated, for garnish
> Sprigs of dill for garnish

PREPARATION TIME: 30 minutes plus refrigerating time
COOKING TIME: 1 hour
YIELD: about 2 quarts, or 8 first-course servings

Cut the leeks in half lengthwise and rinse under running water until clear of all dirt. Thinly slice the white and light green parts only.

Place the leeks, shredded carrots, and 1 cup of the broth in a 4-quart pot. Cook covered over medium heat 30 minutes. Add the potatoes, milk, 1/4 teaspoon of the cardamom, the mace and nutmeg; cook covered over medium heat until the potatoes are completely tender, about 25 minutes. Let stand covered to cool at least 10 minutes.

Puree the vegetable mixture in a blender, one half at a time, until smooth. Return to the pot. Stir in the remaining broth and cardamom, the minced dill and red pepper sauce, and black pepper to taste. Heat just to simmering, stirring often, over medium heat. Let stand to cool. Refrigerate until thoroughly chilled. Spoon into bowls; garnish with grated carrot and dill sprigs.

NUTRITION INFORMATION: Cal: 126 Pro: 5g/16% Carb: 24g/76% Fat: 1g/8% Chol: 2mg Sodium: 104mg Potassium: 533mg Fiber: 3g A: 156% C: 14% B3: 14% B6: 14%
EXCHANGE: Bread: 1¼ Veg: 1

MICROWAVE METHOD: In a 3-quart microwave-safe casserole or bowl, cook the leeks, shredded carrots, 1 cup of the broth, and the potatoes, covered, on High (100% power) until the potatoes are almost tender, about 8 to 10 minutes. Add the milk, 1/4 teaspoon of the cardamom, the mace, and nutmeg. Cook covered on High until the potatoes are completely tender, about 4 minutes. Let stand covered 10 minutes. Puree as above and return to the pot; add only 2 cups broth, the remaining cardamom, and the minced dill, red pepper sauce, and black pepper. Cook on High just to simmering, about 5 minutes; stir once. Let cool and continue as directed above.

Jicama-Sunchoke Salad with Mustard Dressing
by Barrie Kavasch

This colorful creation is a meal in itself and always a winner!

1 large jicama, peeled and julienne cut
2 cups sunchokes, julienne cut
1 pound dried red kidney beans, cooked and drained
1 large bunch watercress, coarsely cut
1 medium bunch fresh mustard leaves, coarsely cut
4 scallions, finely chopped
1 medium green bell pepper, julienne cut
1 medium yellow bell pepper, julienne cut
2 cloves garlic, peeled and diced
3 tablespoons sunflower oil
3 tablespoons apple cider vinegar
3 tablespoons spicy mustard (prepared)
3 tablespoons orange juice
1 teaspoon fresh dill
2 sprigs fresh parsley, finely chopped
2 sprigs fresh coriander, finely chopped
  Freshly ground black pepper
  Garnishes (optional):
    Chopped watercress
    Chopped fresh dill, parsley, and/or coriander
    Nasturtium blossoms

PREPARATION TIME: 40 minutes plus standing time
YIELD: 6 servings

Combine all the ingredients except the garnishes in a large bowl. Toss well. Cover and marinate at room temperature for 1 hour before serving. (Chill if desired.) Toss again, garnish with watercress and fresh herbs or nasturtium blossoms if desired, and serve.

NUTRITION INFORMATION: Cal: 292 Pro: 13g/18% Carb: 44g/60% Fat: 7g/22% (S:10% M:13% P:77%) Chol: 0mg Sodium: 121mg Potassium: 360mg Fiber: 11g A: 31% C: 117% E: 15% B1: 12% Fe: 17%
EXCHANGE: Bread: 1¾ Veg: 3½ Fat: 1½

Dill Potato Salad

by Nao Hauser

1/2 teaspoon dill seed
1/2 teaspoon fennel seed
1/4 teaspoon celery seed
1 1/2 pounds red-skinned potatoes, quartered and sliced 1/4 inch thick
1 cup unsalted chicken broth or stock (see page 28)
1 teaspoon dried dill
1/4 teaspoon ground allspice
1 red onion, very thinly sliced
1 rib celery, thinly sliced
1/2 cup pitted ripe olives, rinsed, drained, and sliced
1/2 cup fresh dill sprigs, minced
1/2 cup fresh parsley sprigs, minced
2 tablespoons tarragon vinegar
1/4 teaspoon chili powder
1/8 teaspoon salt
Freshly ground black pepper
3 tablespoons goat's milk yogurt, kefir, or whole milk yogurt

PREPARATION TIME: 30 minutes plus refrigerating time
COOKING TIME: 15 minutes
YIELD: 6 to 8 servings

Spread the seeds in a wide saucepan. Cover and toast over medium heat, stirring constantly, about 2 minutes. Stir in the potatoes, broth, dill, and allspice. Heat to simmering; simmer covered over medium heat, stirring several times, until the potatoes are tender, about 12 minutes. Let stand covered to cool to room temperature. Transfer the mixture to a medium bowl and refrigerate covered overnight.

Stir the onion, celery, olives, minced herbs, vinegar, chili powder, salt, and black pepper to taste into the potatoes. Spoon the yogurt over the mixture and stir well. Serve at room temperature.

NOTE: Refrigerating the potatoes overnight in the broth makes them very moist and almost creamy, so you don't need much yogurt to moisten the mixture. Use goat's milk yogurt for a very pleasant tanginess, or another whole milk yogurt for appropriate richness.

NUTRITION INFORMATION: (For 6 servings) Cal: 132 Pro: 4g/12% Carb: 28g/80% Fat: 1g/8% Chol: 1mg Sodium: 199mg Potassium: 647mg Fiber: 4g A: 13% C: 44% B3: 11% B6: 21% Cr: 16%
EXCHANGE: Bread: 1 1/2 Veg: 1/2 Fat: 1/4

MICROWAVE METHOD: In a 2-quart microwave-safe casserole, cook the dill, fennel, and celery seeds on High (100% power) until toasted, about 1 1/2 to 2 minutes. Add the potatoes, broth, dill, and allspice. Cook covered on High until potatoes are tender, about 7 to 9 minutes. Let stand covered to cool and continue as directed above.

Moroccan Carrot Salad

by Nao Hauser

This is a low-fat version of a spicy Moroccan classic. Serve it cold with other salads, such as diced sweet peppers and tomatoes and Sweet and Sour Beets (see page 114), as a prelude to a couscous entrée. It would also go well with tabouli on a cold buffet or in a picnic basket. Or you can serve it warm, as a side dish with roast poultry or broiled fish. If serving it warm, use the smaller amounts of the spices listed, because the seasonings taste stronger when hot.

1 pound carrots, sliced
1 cup unsalted chicken broth or stock (see page 28)
2 or 3 cloves garlic, peeled and pressed or minced
1 teaspoon sugar
2 tablespoons finely chopped fresh parsley
2 teaspoons fresh lemon juice
1/2 to 3/4 teaspoon ground cumin
1/2 teaspoon paprika
1/4 to 1/2 teaspoon ground cardamom
1/8 teaspoon ground cinnamon
1/8 teaspoon cayenne
1/8 teaspoon salt
Freshly ground black pepper

PREPARATION TIME: 20 minutes
COOKING TIME: 15 minutes
YIELD: 4 servings

Heat the carrots and broth to a boil in a medium saucepan. Reduce the heat; simmer covered until the carrots are tender, about 8 to 10 minutes. Remove the carrots to a serving bowl with a slotted spoon. Add the garlic and sugar to the broth; simmer until reduced by about half. Stir in the parsley, lemon juice, and spices (pepper to taste); simmer 1 minute. Pour over the carrots and stir. Serve hot or refrigerate and serve at room temperature on lettuce leaves as a salad.

NUTRITION INFORMATION: Cal: 71　Pro: 3g/15% Carb: 15g/77%　Fat: 1g/8%　Chol: .3mg　Sodium: 141mg　Potassium: 344mg　Fiber: 4g　A: 563% C: 11%　B6: 14%　Mn: 26%
EXCHANGE: Veg: 2½

Sweet and Sour Beets

by Nao Hauser

A very delicate version of a favorite flavor balance.

1 pound beets
2 scallions with tops, thinly sliced
1 tablespoon raspberry vinegar
2 teaspoons French walnut oil

PREPARATION TIME: 15 minutes
COOKING TIME: 40 minutes
YIELD: 4 servings

Cook the beets in 3 to 4 quarts of boiling water until tender when pierced with a fork, 30 minutes or more depending on size. Drain and let stand until cool enough to handle. Trim away the ends and slip off the skins; quarter lengthwise and slice. Toss the beets in a bowl with the remaining ingredients. Serve warm or refrigerate and serve cold as a salad.

NUTRITION INFORMATION: Cal: 56　Pro: 1g/ 9%　Carb: 8g/55%　Fat: 2g/36%　(S:18%　M:48% P:34%)　Chol: 0mg　Sodium: 56mg　Potassium: 363mg　Fiber: 2g　C: 12%　Folic: 15%　Mg: 11%
EXCHANGE: Veg: 1¼　Fat: ½

MICROWAVE METHOD: In a 1½-quart microwave-safe casserole, cook the beets and ½ cup water, covered, on High (100% power) until tender, about 15 to 20 minutes, stirring once. Continue as directed above.

Pot-Roasted Carrots and Parsnips

by Nao Hauser

Use the heaviest skillet or Dutch oven you have—preferably cast iron—and improvise a lid if necessary for this rich-flavored dish. If you're using a lightweight pan, you may have to add more broth during cooking to prevent burning.

1 tablespoon unsalted butter
2 large onions, sliced very thin
1 pound carrots, sliced
½ pound parsnips, sliced
½ to ⅔ cup unsalted veal stock (see page 29)
　　or unsalted beef broth
2 pinches ground allspice
　　Pinch ground cloves

PREPARATION TIME: 25 minutes
COOKING TIME: 1 hour 45 minutes
YIELD: 6 servings

Preheat the oven to 350°F. Melt the butter in a heavy 9-inch skillet over medium heat. Stir in the onions; cook over medium-low heat, stirring occasionally, 15 minutes. Stir in the carrots, parsnips, ½ cup of the stock, and the spices. Cover the skillet with aluminum foil, pressing down to place foil over the vegetables; place the pot lid over the foil. Bake in the preheated oven 1½ hours, stirring twice during the last half hour of cooking and adding the remaining stock if needed. (The vegetables will be tender after 1 hour; during the last half hour they begin to caramelize, yielding a very rich flavor.)

NUTRITION INFORMATION: Cal: 104 Pro: 2g/ 9% Carb: 20g/71% Fat: 3g/20% (S:58% M:31% P:11%) Chol: 6mg Sodium: 65mg Potassium: 430mg Fiber: 5g A: 373% C: 17% B6: 17% Mn: 22% Cr: 16%
EXCHANGE: Bread: ¹/₂ Veg: ¹/₂ Fat: ¹/₂

Comfort Potatoes

by Nao Hauser

Creamy mashed potatoes made irresistible with bits of browned onion and garlic.

        1 tablespoon unsalted butter
        1 medium onion, minced
     1¹/₂ pounds potatoes, unpeeled and cubed
        1 cup 1%-fat milk
  3 or 4 cloves garlic, peeled and minced
      ¹/₈ teaspoon salt
        Ground nutmeg
        Freshly ground black pepper
        About 2 tablespoons additional 1%-fat
        milk or plain low-fat yogurt (optional)

PREPARATION TIME: 25 minutes
COOKING TIME: 30 minutes
YIELD: 6 servings

Melt the butter in a medium skillet over medium heat. Add the onion; cooked covered, stirring often, until slightly browned, about 15 minutes. Reserve in the skillet.

Heat the potatoes, milk, and garlic in a medium saucepan to simmering; simmer covered over medium heat, stirring occasionally, until the potatoes are tender, about 12 minutes. Remove the potatoes with a slotted spoon and add to the skillet with the reserved onions; reserve the milk.

Mash the potatoes into the onions with a potato masher or fork. Add the reserved milk, mashing with a fork until smooth. Add the salt and the nutmeg and pepper to taste. If desired, stir in the additional milk or yogurt for a creamier texture.

NUTRITION INFORMATION: Cal: 133 Pro: 4g/ 11% Carb: 25g/71% Fat: 3g/18% (S:64% M:29% P:7%) Chol: 7mg Sodium: 71mg Potassium: 446mg Fiber: 4g C: 16% B6: 16%
EXCHANGE: Skim Milk: ¹/₄ Bread: 1¹/₄ Fat: ¹/₂ Veg: ¹/₄

Sweet Potato–Apple Puree

By Nao Hauser

This recipe yields a wonderful sweet-spicy side dish that's easy enough to serve any day.

        2 large sweet potatoes, pared, quartered,
          and sliced
      ³/₄ pound sweet apples (about 2 medium),
          pared, quartered, and thinly sliced
³/₄ to 1 cup skim milk
      ¹/₄ teaspoon ground cinnamon
      ¹/₄ teaspoon pumpkin pie spice
      ¹/₈ teaspoon ground nutmeg
          Freshly ground black pepper
          Pinch ground cloves
          Plain low-fat yogurt (optional)

PREPARATION TIME: 25 minutes
COOKING TIME: 30 minutes
YIELD: 6 servings

Cook the potatoes, apples, ³/₄ cup milk, cinnamon, and pumpkin pie spice in a medium saucepan, covered, over medium heat until the potatoes and apples are completely tender, about 30 minutes. Mash until smooth with a potato masher or fork. Stir in the nutmeg, pepper to taste, cloves, and 2 to 3 tablespoons yogurt or the remaining ¹/₄ cup milk if desired.

NUTRITION INFORMATION: Cal: 185 Pro: 4g/ 8% Carb: 43g/89% Fat: .7g/3% Chol: .7mg Sodium: 38mg Potassium: 375mg Fiber: 4g A: 453% C: 42% E: 32% B2: 14% B6: 18% Mn: 13%
EXCHANGE: Skim Milk: ¹/₄ Bread: 2 Fruit: ¹/₂

MICROWAVE METHOD: In a 2-quart microwave-safe casserole, cook the potatoes, apples, 1/2 cup of the milk, and the cinnamon and pumpkin pie spice, covered, on High (100% power) until tender, about 10 to 13 minutes. Mash and continue as directed above.

Sweet Potatoes Baked in Apples

by Nao Hauser

The sweet potato mixture is stiff—sturdy enough to bake in apples for a festive accompaniment to a holiday turkey.

> 1 cup plus 2 tablespoons skim milk
> 3 tablespoons dried currants
> 1/4 teaspoon ground cinnamon
>   Pinch ground allspice
> 1 1/2 pounds sweet potatoes, pared, quartered, and sliced
>   Freshly ground black pepper
>   Pinch ground cinnamon
>   Pinch ground nutmeg
> 1/4 cup plain low-fat yogurt
> 8 medium golden delicious or other sweet apples
> 1 tablespoon finely chopped pecans or walnuts

PREPARATION TIME: 30 minutes
COOKING TIME: 1 1/2 hours
YIELD: 8 servings

Heat 1 cup of the milk, the currants, the 1/4 teaspoon cinnamon, and the allspice to simmering in a medium saucepan; simmer 5 minutes. Remove any skin that forms on top of the milk. Add the potatoes; simmer covered until tender, about 25 minutes. Mash the potatoes into the liquid until smooth; stir in black pepper to taste, and the pinch of cinnamon, nutmeg, and yogurt. Stir in the remaining milk if needed for desired consistency.

Preheat the oven to 350°F. Cut a circle at the top of each apple, about 1 1/2 inches around the stem; cut to remove the caps from the tops and core the apples. Cut a very thin slice from the bottom of each apple, if necessary, to stand the apples upright. Fill the apples with the sweet potato mixture, mounding the tops; sprinkle with the nuts. Place the filled apples in a rectangular baking pan; pour 1 cup water into the pan. Bake in the preheated oven until the apples are tender when pierced with a knife tip, about 1 hour. Check after 45 minutes and cover the pan loosely with foil if the potatoes are getting too dry.

NUTRITION INFORMATION: Cal: 213   Pro: 4g/7%   Carb: 49g/87%   Fat: 2g/6%   Chol: 1mg Sodium: 35mg   Potassium: 411mg   Fiber: 6g A: 293%   C: 26%   E: 20%   B2: 12%   B6: 15% Mn: 15%
EXCHANGE: Skim Milk: 1/4   Bread: 1 1/4   Fruit: 1 1/2 Fat: 1/4

MICROWAVE METHOD: In a 2-quart microwave-safe covered casserole, cook 1 cup of the milk, and the currants, 1/4 teaspoon cinnamon, allspice, and potatoes, on High (100% power) until the potatoes are tender, about 9 minutes. Mash the potatoes and stuff the apples as directed above. In eight individual microwave-safe custard cups or a 10-inch shallow round pie plate, cook the apples, covered with wax paper, on High until tender, about 14 minutes. Let stand 5 minutes.

Papas a la Huancaina

By Nao Hauser

This chili-spiked potato dish is from Peru, where the potato first grew and where it still reigns supreme. The recipe is named for the region of Huancayo. Serve it as a main course with hard-cooked eggs and, if you wish, corn on the cob. Or arrange smaller portions on lettuce leaves as a first course. Use two chilies for real "hot potatoes," or none for a mild, creamy dish.

2 pounds potatoes (about 6 medium)

4 ounces fresh goat cheese

$^1/_2$ cup fresh parsley sprigs

$^1/_4$ cup skim milk

1 fresh or canned jalapeño pepper, seeded and sliced

1 tablespoon dried mint

Small pinch turmeric

Chopped red onion for garnish

Chopped fresh flat-leaf parsley for garnish

2 hard-cooked eggs, cut into wedges, for garnish (optional)

PREPARATION TIME: 10 minutes

COOKING TIME: 60 minutes

YIELD: 4 main-course servings, or 6 side-dish servings

Cook the unpeeled potatoes in a medium, heavy saucepan in water to cover over medium-high heat until tender when pierced with a knife, about 20 to 30 minutes. When cool enough to handle, slice $^1/_3$ inch thick.

Preheat the oven to 350°F. Arrange potatoes in an ungreased 8-inch square baking dish. Process the cheese, parsley, milk, pepper, mint, and turmeric in a blender until smooth; pour evenly over the potatoes. Bake in the preheated oven 15 minutes, or until heated through. Garnish each portion with onion, parsley, and egg if desired.

NUTRITION INFORMATION: (as main course) Cal: 335 Pro: 12g/15% Carb: 52g/61% Fat: 9g/24% (S:63% M:29% P:8%) Chol: 162mg Sodium: 480mg Potassium: 1017mg Fiber: 6g A: 14% C: 62% B1: 18% B3: 16% B6: 36% Folic: 12% Panto: 18% Ca: 20% P: 28% Fe: 12% Mg: 18% Zn: 13% Cu: 28% Cr: 24%

EXCHANGE: High Fat Meat: 1$^1/_2$ Bread: 2$^1/_2$ Veg: 1

(as side dish) Cal: 197 Pro: 6g/12% Carb: 34g/ 69% Fat: 4g/19% (S:73% M:22% P:5%) Chol: 17mg Sodium: 297mg Potassium: 656mg Fiber: 4g C: 42% B1: 11% B3: 11% B6 23% Ca: 12% P: 15% Mg: 11% Cu: 17% Cr: 16%

EXCHANGE: High Fat Meat: $^3/_4$ Bread: 2

MICROWAVE METHOD: In a microwave-safe baking dish, cook the sliced raw potatoes and $^1/_4$ cup water covered tightly on High (100% power) until tender, about 8 to 11 minutes. Drain well. Prepare the cheese mixture as directed above, pour over the potatoes, and cook covered with wax paper on Medium (50% power) until heated through, about 6 to 9 minutes.

◇ LEGUMES ◇

Full O' Beans

by Gail A. Levey, R.D.

Legumes, the edible mature seeds inside pods—beans, peas, and lentils—are nutritional wonders. (Peanuts, botanically a legume, are covered in Nuts and Seeds, page 137.)

High in protein, fiber, and complex carbohydrates, chock-full of iron and B vitamins, legumes are low in sodium and, with few exceptions, fat and calories. They form an essential part of nearly any strategy to replace some animal sources of protein with plant sources.

And they have special qualities. Beans are a boon to diabetics—and to anyone worried about weight control. Their fiber is especially good at lowering blood cholesterol. Other agents in legumes, researchers are now reporting, may even offer protection against cancer.

Green beans, including wax beans and French green beans (*haricot verts*), are not true legumes, so don't expect these specific benefits. But they are good sources of fiber, carotenoids (the darker the green, the better), and potassium. They've got some folic acid, too. For best taste and vitamins, try them steamed quickly until they're just-crisp.

Low-Fat Protein

Although soybeans (covered in the next chapter) get 40 percent of their calories from fat, the percentage of calories most legumes get from fat hover around the 3 percent mark. Instead of fat, they have protein. Indeed, legumes are so rich in protein, you'll find them alongside meat, poultry, fish, eggs, and cheese in most nutrition guides.

A cup of boiled chick-peas, for example, provides about 15 grams of protein, but only about 4 grams of fat and 269 calories. A 3½-ounce pan-fried regular hamburger, by contrast, which gives us about 24 grams of protein, also gives us about *24 grams* of fat (mostly saturated) and 306 calories.

Technically, legume protein is incomplete, lacking in at least one essential amino acid. But combine legumes with grains or seeds in a meal—rice and beans, or a corn tortilla/bean taco, or hummus (a chick-pea/sesame seed combo)—and you've got complete protein. Adding a little red meat, poultry, fish, or dairy food to a bean dish also completes the protein.

You don't have to eat a perfect combination at every meal. It's a balance over days and weeks, not hours.

Essential Minerals

Unusual among plant foods, most legumes provide good portions of iron. One raw quarter cup of beans will on average satisfy nearly 20 percent of the USRDA for iron. Legumes also supply zinc, another essential mineral often hard to find in plant foods; a half cup of cooked beans fills 7 to 10 percent of your daily need for zinc.

Legumes are low in sodium and high in potas-

118

sium, a winning combination for those with high blood pressure. They contain good amounts of other minerals, too—especially magnesium, which many Americans don't get enough of, and copper, another important nutrient that some surveys suggest is low in our diets. Too little copper, both animal and human studies suggest, may raise blood cholesterol levels.

As for vitamins, legumes are high in folic acid, important for red blood cell activity, and contain a smattering of other B vitamins, notably B-6 and thiamine. Bean sprouts have much more vitamin C than unsprouted beans, but less iron and vitamin A (beta-carotene). Bean sprouts served with the bean itself are nutritionally similar to unsprouted beans.

Legumes and Diabetes

Beans are slow guys. Full of fiber and complex carbohydrates, they take a long time to digest, causing a very gentle rise in blood sugar. As a result, you need less insulin to control blood sugar after eating beans than you do after a meal of other carbohydrates such as white bread.

That's potentially life-saving news to diabetics. At the University of Toronto, Drs. Thomas Wolever and David Jenkins developed a diet for diabetics that's full of legumes, whole grains, vegetables, and fruit.

For Type-I diabetics, all of whom need daily insulin shots, this high-fiber diet reduces daily insulin needs by 38 percent, finds Dr. James Anderson of the University of Kentucky. For Type-II diabetics, whose bodies retain the ability to manufacture some insulin, the bean-rich diet reduces the need for injected insulin a whopping 98 percent. The American Diabetes Association now recommends such a diet for diabetics.

Going slow on the insulin is a good idea for healthy eaters in search of the body beautiful, too. Because a rise in insulin may trigger hunger, a bean lunch may ward off those 3 o'clock munchies. And because insulin turns on fat production and storage, a bean-rich diet that keeps insulin low can help us stay lean.

The insulin-sparing effect of legumes lasts for hours, too. In one study, Drs. Jenkins and Wolever fed subjects either a breakfast of bread and cheese or one of lentils. Four hours later, both

groups were given the same lunch. Result: Those who had eaten lentils for breakfast produced 25 percent less insulin after lunch.

Legumes and Cholesterol

Dropping the amount of cholesterol in your blood lowers your risk of heart disease. And beans can help lower your blood cholesterol. One reason is that they're so low in total fats and saturated fats. But the big reason is soluble fiber.

All fiber helps speed food through the gut, but legume fiber has special qualities. It dissolves in water, forming a gel that binds with cholesterol. Together they pass harmlessly out of the body.

New research suggests another mechanism that may be even more important. Bacteria in the colon feed on the fiber in beans, producing short-chain fatty acids that suppress cholesterol production in the liver.

But however it works, it works. Kentucky's Dr. Anderson dropped his patients' cholesterol levels 19 percent with a diet containing a pint of pinto or navy beans daily. Jenkins reports similar results.

Says Anderson, "When I practice what I preach—staying lean, exercising and eating a high-carbohydrate, high-fiber, low-fat diet—my blood cholesterol runs a hundred eighty milligrams per deciliter, down from two eighty-five."

Legumes and Cancer

Humble beans may even help protect against certain cancers. One reason may be their protease inhibitors, substances that can interfere with protein-digesting enzymes.

Raw legumes are rich in protease inhibitors. When you cook legumes, some protease inhibitors remain—not enough to ruin your digestion, but just enough to give a possible anti-cancer benefit. At the Harvard School of Public Health, cancer biologist Ann Kennedy recently gave lab animals a chemical that normally causes oral cancers. But "when protease inhibitors are brushed onto the inner cheek surfaces of hamsters, fewer cancers developed." Added to the animals' diets, protease inhibitors also helped prevent colon cancer.

How it works is still a mystery, admits Kennedy, though she suspects that tumors need particular proteases to develop. Protease inhibitors are richly represented in soybeans (which also contain cancer-protective isoflavones; see next chapter), but can be found in chick-peas, lima beans, black-eyed peas, kidney beans, and lentils. Because legumes also have phytic acid, a substance some reports suggest may also fight cancer, these humble vegetables are looking more and more like allies in cancer prevention.

Taking the Wind Out of Beans

The nutrition in beans doesn't mean beans if you don't eat them. And a lot of would-be bean eaters don't because of gas. But the proper soaking technique can reduce the gas-producing potential of dried legumes.

Humans can't digest two things in legumes: fibers and certain complex sugars called alpha-galactosides. Arriving undigested in the lower intestine, these do get broken down by bacteria there. But that process produces carbon dioxide, hydrogen, and other gases.

You can't take the fiber out of beans. Nor would you want to. Bean fibers far outweigh the discomforts they cause. But "you can get rid of ninety percent of the gas-forming *sugars* in legumes," says USDA research chemist Alfred Olson of the Western Regional Research Center in California. First, rinse the beans, picking out foreign matter such as tiny pebbles. Pour boiling water over the legumes and let them soak for at least four hours. Then throw out this water and cook in fresh water.

Quite apart from gassiness, though, overnight soaking in the refrigerator is essential if you want firm beans. Firmness is especially desirable for salads. But if you're worried about gas and don't have much time, quick-soaking is just as good for stews and casseroles. Gently boil 2 minutes; remove from heat; soak 1 hour, replace water, and proceed. Lentils and split peas for soup don't need to be soaked. In the Southwest, many cooks add the Mexican herb epazote to their beans; by reputation, it reduces flatulence.

Cooking Beans———
by Ceri Hadda and Nao Hauser

Legumes come into American kitchens in such classics as Boston baked beans, the Southern combination of rice and black-eyed peas called "hopping John," the white bean soup featured in the U.S. Senate dining room, Louisiana's red beans and rice, Cincinnati chili, and Tex-Mex tacos. Rejected for a while as poor man's fare, they are now gaining favor again—not only for their wealth of low-fat nutrients but also for their cosmopolitan culinary status. As Americans discover the joys of French cassoulet, Brazilian feijoada (a stew of black beans and smoked meats), Mediterranean salads, Italian pasta e fagioli (pasta and beans), and the curry-spiced legumes served from India to Ethiopia to Jamaica, they learn to celebrate the humble bean.

The most opulent bean flavor comes fresh, in the pod, when the spring and summer harvests come in. Not many varieties are marketed this way, but it is well worth the work of shelling sweet peas (and some varieties, often called "sugar snap peas," don't even need shelling), limas, cranberry beans, fava beans, or black-eyed peas to get at the treasure within. Simmer shelled limas in just enough vegetable or chicken broth to cover, add corn kernels cut fresh from the cob for the last few minutes of cooking, and you'll have a summer succotash fit for the gods. Fresh cranberry and fava beans can also be simmered to tenderness with just enough broth or water to cover in 20 to 30 minutes; black-eyed peas will take at least twice as long and therefore require more liquid. Fava beans must be shelled twice—first to remove the pod, and then to peel off the skin; so you may want to add them to pasta for a delicate-flavored dish. Limas, butter beans (larger and sometimes multicolored lima varieties), and black-eyed peas are also sold frozen, providing quick-cooking nutrition without the salt of canned beans. Frozen baby limas and peas (and small fresh peas, too) need not be cooked; once they've been completely thawed, they are tender enough to toss into salads without further heating.

Most other legumes are only available canned or dried. The convenience of canned products is offset by the salt required for, and the softened texture resulting from, the canning process. Thorough rinsing will remove some of the salt, and certain brands of beans (not necessarily indicated by price) have better texture than others. If salt reduction isn't your biggest priority, you may not even want to rinse canned beans, since much of the soluble fiber is in the "sauce" that you wash away. (In one of Anderson's studies, eating one can of beans with the sauce was more effective in lowering cholesterol than eating nearly two cans that had been rinsed.) Beans jarred by the retort method are spared much of the salt and overcooking of conventional canning and may be found in some health and gourmet food stores. Enjoy, sauce and all.

Spotlight: Okra

Okra, introduced into Louisiana by French colonists, was grown in the Nile Valley during the reign of the Pharaohs more than 3000 years ago. It looks like a legume, and so is included here, but actually it's a member of the hibiscus family and is closely related to cotton.

It's a surprising vegetable. Full of gummy type of fiber, it has remarkable thickening power in soups and stews, witness gumbo. But don't cook your filé gumbo in pots or use utensils made of iron, copper, or brass. A chemical reaction occurs, which, while harmless, turns both pods and utensils black.

Cook up a raw cupful, about 8 pods, and you'll get only 38 calories, but you'll get plenty of vitamins A, C, thiamin, B-6, magnesium, manganese, potassium, and protein. The fiber is water-soluble, so it may lower blood cholesterol, though that hasn't been studied. You'll also get a nice bit of calcium: 81 milligrams, nearly 10 percent of the USRDA. It just goes to show: You never know what wonders your body is getting when you widen your culinary habits.

—Lisa Chobanian

But there are other ways around the tedium of preparing dried beans. The simplest is to start with lentils or split peas, which are small enough to simmer to tenderness in 20 to 45 minutes without prior soaking; the timing will depend not only on variety but also on how dry the beans were to begin with and how soft you want them.

Other dried legumes should be presoaked to reduce cooking time. After washing them and checking for the presence of small stones or other foreign matter, place the beans in a bowl or pot, add twice the volume of water (1 quart water for 1 pound beans), and let stand eight hours or overnight; if your kitchen is very warm, refrigerate the beans for overnight standing to prevent fermentation from starting. Alternatively, heat the beans and liquid to boiling, conventionally or in the microwave, reduce heat and simmer two minutes (Medium microwave setting), and let stand, covered, 1 hour.

To continue cooking, drain the beans, add 4 to 6 cups fresh water (depending on degree of desired softness, and therefore length of cooking time), and heat to boiling for at least ten minutes (this is important; boiling breaks down the lectins that our bodies can't digest); reduce heat and simmer, loosely covered, until the beans are tender. Pre-soaked black-eyed peas may be done in as little as 30 minutes; black and pinto beans may take more than 2 hours. If you're making soup, you'll need about twice as much water with the beans, along with other ingredients, and the cooking time will be lengthened somewhat by the extra volume. To microwave, heat the beans and liquid to boiling (10 to 15 minutes) at High in a covered casserole; reduce setting to Medium and cook covered until tender, about 30 to 45 minutes; let cooked beans stand covered 5 minutes. Pre-soaked whole beans can also be pressure-cooked in 20 to 40 minutes; use 6 cups of water per pound of beans and don't fill the cooker more than half full. (Many pressure cooker manufacturers recommend against cooking lentils and split peas under pressure because of the danger of clogging the steam vent.)

One cup of dried beans yields about 2½ cups cooked; one pound yields four to six servings. The most flavorful beans are seasoned at least twice—once with onion, spices and herbs (but not salt or acidic ingredients, which will toughen the skin) as they simmer, and then again after they've been cooked and drained. The creamiest beans, as in French cassoulet and traditional baked beans, are cooked twice—simmered first until just tender and then baked with additional liquid and seasonings in a slow oven for two hours or longer. Cooked beans keep a week in the refrigerator and can be frozen for longer storage.

Spotlight: The Well-Seasoned International Bean

Americans need little introduction to the chilies, cumin, garlic, and onions common to most Tex-Mex chili recipes. But the customs of other countries differ. In Italy, white beans are cooked with sage and garlic, chick-peas with rosemary and garlic. In France, fava beans are flavored with savory, while white beans are simmered with a clove-studded onion.

Greeks season white or lima beans with garlic, tomatoes, and mint, or with garlic, parsley, bay leaf, oregano, and thyme. In the Arab world, lentils go with garlic, cumin, and lemon. In India lentils or chick-peas can be paired with any of the garam masala spices, such as cinnamon and cumin, as well as garlic and ginger. In Japan, soybeans connect with kelp, sugar, and soy sauce. Finally, in the glorious mix of cultures in the Caribbean, black beans are often cooked with onion, garlic, fresh chili, bay leaf, oregano, cumin; red beans with onion, garlic, fresh chili, bay leaf, and thyme.

Whichever culture is your inspiration, season beans while they simmer with the strongest herbs, such as dried thyme, bay leaves, sage, and rosemary, and the sweet spices, such as cinnamon and cloves. Add mild fresh herbs, such as thyme, mint, savory, and parsley, close to the end of cooking time or when serving the beans cold as a salad; also refresh the sweet spices, if desired.

—Nao Hauser

Minestrone
by Ceri Hadda

Use the following vegetables as a guide, but add whatever vegetables you have on hand. This "add what you have" combination adds up to a soup that can stand by itself as a complete-protein entrée.

> 1/2 pound dried chick-peas, soaked overnight
> 3 cups chopped onions
> 1 cup chopped celery
> 1/2 cup chopped carrot
> 2 cloves garlic, peeled and minced
> 2 tablespoons olive oil
> 6 cups unsalted beef broth
> 1 can (16 ounces) crushed tomatoes with juice, no salt added
> 1/2 teaspoon dried oregano, crushed
> 1 large potato, diced
> 1 large zucchini, halved or quartered lengthwise, and sliced
> 1/2 pound green beans, cut into 1- to 2-inch lengths
> 1/2 cup dried ditalini or elbow macaroni
> 1/2 cup fresh or frozen peas
> 2 to 4 tablespoons Dijon-style mustard (optional)
> 2 tablespoons red wine vinegar (optional)
> Freshly ground black pepper
> Chopped fresh parsley for garnish

PREPARATION TIME: 40 minutes plus overnight soaking
COOKING TIME: 3 1/2 hours
YIELD: 6 servings

Drain the chick-peas, place in a 3-quart saucepan with enough water to cover the chick-peas by 1 1/2 inches, and simmer 1 1/2 hours, or until almost tender, adding water, if necessary, to keep beans covered, and skimming the surface to remove impurities that collect.

Meanwhile, sauté the onions, celery, carrot, and garlic in the oil in a 6-quart saucepan until tender but not brown. Add the chick-peas and their liquid to the sautéed vegetables. Add the beef broth, tomatoes, and oregano. Cover and simmer 1 hour, or until the chick-peas are tender. Uncover. Add the potato and simmer 15 minutes. Add the zucchini, green beans, and pasta and simmer 15 minutes longer, or until the potato and pasta are tender. Add the peas; simmer 5 minutes longer. Season to taste with mustard, vinegar, and pepper. Serve sprinkled with chopped parsley.

NUTRITION INFORMATION: Cal: 363 Pro: 18g/ 19% Carb: 57g/61% Fat: 8g/20% (S:19% M:66% P:15%) Chol: 1mg Sodium: 150mg Potassium: 1254mg Fiber: 4g A: 93% C: 57% E: 14% B1: 26% B2: 16% B3: 31% B6: 23% Folic: 14% Ca: 14% P: 32% Fe: 28% Mg: 15% Cu: 21% Mn: 26% Cr: 53%
EXCHANGE: Lean Meat: 1 Bread: 2½ Veg: 3 Fat: 1

MICROWAVE METHOD: In a 6-quart microwave-safe casserole, cook the chick-peas and water to cover, tightly covered, on High (100% power) to boiling, about 10 to 13 minutes. Stir. Reduce to Medium (50% power); cook covered until chick-peas are almost tender, about 25 to 30 minutes. Let stand. In a 4-quart microwave-safe casserole, cook the onion, celery, carrot, garlic, and oil, covered, on High about 5 minutes. Add the potato and ½ cup beef broth; cook covered on High until just tender, about 5 minutes. To the cooked chick-peas, add the onion mixture, 4½ cups broth, and the tomatoes and oregano. Cook tightly covered on High to boiling, about 10 to 15 minutes. Stir in the zucchini, green beans, and macaroni. Cook tightly covered on High until the macaroni is almost tender, about 15 to 17 minutes. Add the peas. Cook tightly covered on High until the vegetables and macaroni are tender, about 5 to 6 minutes. Stir in the mustard, vinegar, and pepper to taste. Let stand 10 minutes. Serve as above.

Three-Bean Goulash Soup

by Ceri Hadda

1 *pound dried kidney beans, soaked overnight*
1 *pound dried baby lima beans, soaked overnight*
½ *pound dried yellow split peas, rinsed*
½ *pound lean stewing veal, cut into ¼-inch pieces*
¼ *cup olive oil*
3 *cups chopped onion*
¾ *cup chopped carrot*
1 *large green bell pepper, chopped*
¼ *cup sweet paprika*
¼ *cup tomato paste, no salt added*
2 *cups unsalted chicken broth or stock (see page 28)*
Salt (optional)
Freshly ground black pepper (optional)
Plain nonfat yogurt for garnish
Sweet paprika for garnish
Julienne strips of green bell pepper for garnish

PREPARATION TIME: 40 minutes plus overnight soaking
COOKING TIME: 3½ hours
YIELD: 15 servings

Drain the kidney beans and lima beans and place in a 7- or 8-quart stock pot with enough water to cover beans by 1½ inches. Simmer 1½ hours, or until almost tender, adding water if necessary to keep the beans covered. Add the yellow split peas and continue simmering until the beans are tender and the peas have begun to dissolve, about 30 minutes.

Meanwhile, sauté the veal in oil in a large sauté pan; remove and reserve. Add the onion and carrot to the drippings in pan; sauté over medium heat until tender but not brown, about 15 minutes. Add the green pepper and sauté 3 minutes longer. Add the paprika; sauté 1 minute, stirring constantly so paprika does not burn. Add the sautéed vegetables, veal, tomato paste, and chicken broth to the bean mixture; stir to combine. Cover and simmer 1 hour, or until the veal is tender and mixture has begun to thicken.

Reserve 8 cups of the bean mixture; puree the remaining mixture in batches in the food processor and return to the saucepan with the reserved bean mixture. Gently reheat. Taste, and add salt and pepper if necessary. Serve with dollops of plain yogurt, a sprinkling of paprika, and julienne strips of green pepper.

NUTRITION INFORMATION: Cal: 277 Pro: 17g/ 25% Carb: 41g/57% Fat: 6g/18% (S:23% M:64% P:13%) Chol: 12mg Sodium: 59mg

Potassium: 782mg Fiber: 9g A: 67% C: 33% E: 35% B1: 15% B3: 13% B6: 12% P: 21% Fe: 20% Mg: 17% Zn: 12% Cu: 21% Mn: 30%
   EXCHANGE: Lean Meat: 1 Bread: 2½ Veg: ¾ Fat: ¾

Italian Bean Salad

by Ceri Hadda

This main-dish salad is great in summer, and it's quickly made if you use canned beans.

2 cups cooked cannellini, chick-peas, or kidney beans (about 1 cup dried), drained, or a 1-pound can cannellini, chick-peas, or kidney beans, rinsed and drained
1 6½-ounce can solid white-meat tuna packed in spring water, drained and flaked
½ medium red bell pepper, chopped or diced
¼ cup finely chopped red onion
2 tablespoons chopped fresh parsley
2 tablespoons chopped fresh basil, if available
1½ tablespoons red wine vinegar
¼ teaspoon dry mustard
  Freshly ground black pepper
2 tablespoons olive oil
  Lettuce

PREPARATION TIME: 20 minutes plus refrigerating time
YIELD: 3 servings

Combine the beans, tuna, red pepper, onion, parsley, and basil in a medium bowl. Stir together the vinegar, mustard, and pepper in a small bowl; add the olive oil in a slow stream, beating constantly. Pour the dressing over the bean mixture and toss lightly to combine. Refrigerate for several hours to allow the flavors to blend; then toss again before serving. Serve over lettuce.

NUTRITION INFORMATION: Cal: 296 Pro: 26g/ 35% Carb: 24g/33% Fat: 11g/32% (S:17% M:70% P:13%) Chol: 25mg Sodium: 273mg Potassium: 276mg Fiber: 9g C: 33% B3: 19%
   EXCHANGE: Lean Meat: 2½ Bread: 1¾ Veg: ½ Fat: 2½

Persian Lentils and Rice

by Ceri Hadda

Serve as an entrée with plain yogurt, or use to stuff eggplant or peppers and accompany with a tomato sauce. The small amount of ground beef acts as a seasoning, lending a meaty flavor to the dish.

½ pound lean ground beef
3 tablespoons olive oil
3 large onions, finely chopped
1 cup raw brown rice
1 teaspoon ground cinnamon
1 teaspoon ground cumin
1 teaspoon salt
  Freshly ground black pepper
¼ cup chopped fresh parsley
1 pound dried lentils, rinsed
  Juice of 1 lemon
  Plain nonfat yogurt

PREPARATION TIME: 30 minutes
COOKING TIME: 1 hour 15 minutes
YIELD: 8 servings

Brown the beef in a large skillet or Dutch oven. Remove with a slotted spoon and reserve. Wipe out the skillet, heat the oil, and sauté the onions until golden brown and translucent, about 20 minutes. Remove a quarter of the onions and set aside. Add the rice to the skillet; sauté 1 minute. Add the cinnamon and cumin; sauté 1 minute. Add 2½ cups water, salt, pepper to taste, and half the parsley. Bring to a boil; cover; lower heat. Simmer 40 minutes, or until almost all the liquid is absorbed and the rice is almost tender.

Meanwhile, combine the lentils and 4 cups water in a medium saucepan. Bring to a boil; lower the heat and simmer, partially covered, 20 minutes or until just tender. Turn off the heat and let stand. When the rice is done, add the lentils and their liquid and the browned beef to the rice mixture. Cook over low heat, stirring occasionally with a fork, 5 minutes. Cover; let stand 10 minutes. Stir the reserved onions, the remaining parsley, and the lemon juice into the mixture. Serve topped with yogurt.

NUTRITION INFORMATION: Cal: 382   Pro: 21g/ 22%   Carb: 56g/57%   Fat: 9g/21%   (S:26% M:66%   P:8%)   Chol: 18mg   Sodium: 341mg Potassium: 666mg   Fiber: 11g   C: 23%   E: 22% B1: 16%   B2: 12%   B3: 16%   B6: 54%   Folic: 19%   Panto: 24%   Ca: 10%   P: 26%   Fe: 27%   Zn: 20%   Cu: 23%   Se: 50%   Cr: 21%   Mo: 66%

EXCHANGE: Lean Meat: 1   Bread: 3½   Veg: 1 Fat: ¾

Cassoulet-Style Beans

by Ceri Hadda

   1 pound turkey breast fillets, cut into 1½-inch cubes
   5 cloves garlic, peeled and pressed
¼ teaspoon salt (optional)
¼ teaspoon ground thyme
   Pinch ground allspice
   3 tablespoons olive oil
   1 large onion, chopped
¼ cup tomato paste, no salt added
   1 cup unsalted chicken broth or stock (see page 28)
½ cup dry white wine
   1 teaspoon dried thyme leaves
   1 bay leaf
   4 cups cooked navy, baby lima, or Great Northern beans (about 1 pound dried), drained (see Note), or 2 1-pound cans white or Great Northern beans, rinsed and drained
½ cup dry breadcrumbs

PREPARATION TIME: 30 minutes plus 1 hour marinating time
COOKING TIME: 1 hour 25 minutes
YIELD: 5 servings

Toss the turkey cubes with 1 clove of the pressed garlic and the salt (if used), ground thyme, and allspice. Let stand 1 hour (or refrigerate covered overnight).

Preheat the oven to 375°F. Sauté the turkey in olive oil in a medium heavy Dutch oven over medium-high heat until lightly browned, about 3 to 5 minutes; remove with a slotted spoon. Sauté the onion until golden, about 7 to 10 minutes. Add the remaining pressed garlic and the tomato paste, chicken broth, wine, thyme, and bay leaf. Bring to a boil. Return the turkey to the pot along with the beans, pushing the turkey under the beans; stir to blend; sprinkle with breadcrumbs. Bake 1 hour, breaking up the crust once or twice with a spoon and adding some of the cooking liquid from the beans or water if the beans get too dry. Discard bay leaf before serving.

NOTE: When cooking the beans, add 1 small onion, halved and studded with 2 cloves, 4 cloves garlic, unpeeled, and ½ teaspoon thyme to the water. Drain, reserving cooking liquid.

NUTRITION INFORMATION: Cal: 431   Pro: 35g/ 32%   Carb: 46g/42%   Fat: 12g/25%   (S:21% M:65%   P:14%)   Chol: 47mg   Sodium: 154mg Potassium: 1101mg   Fiber: 8g   C: 20%   E: 22%   B1: 23%   B2: 16%   B3: 37%   B6: 66%   Folic: 17% Panto: 17%   Ca: 13%   P: 43%   Fe: 36%   Zn: 21% Cr: 13%

EXCHANGE: Lean Meat: 3¼   Bread: 2½   Veg: 1 Fat: ¾

Chili Con Carne

by Ceri Hadda

Bulgur (cracked wheat) extends the beef in this recipe, so only half a pound of meat imparts its flavor to ten servings.

   1 pound dried kidney beans
   4 cups chopped onions
½ pound lean ground beef
   1 tablespoon corn oil
   1 cup chopped green bell pepper
   1 cup chopped carrot
   3 cloves garlic, peeled and minced
¼ to ⅓ cup chili powder (to taste)
½ cup bulgur wheat
½ cup canned crushed tomatoes, no salt added
   Salt (optional)
   Freshly ground black pepper

PREPARATION TIME: 30 minutes plus 1 hour standing time
COOKING TIME: 2 hours
YIELD: 6 servings

Place the kidney beans and water to cover in a medium saucepan. Bring to a boil over moderate heat; remove from heat, cover, and let stand 1 hour. Drain; cover the beans with fresh water and simmer over moderate heat 1 hour or until tender.

Meanwhile, sauté the onions and beef in the oil in a large saucepan over moderately high heat until the beef is no longer pink and the onion is tender, about 10 minutes. Add the pepper, carrot, and garlic; sauté 2 minutes. Add the chili powder; sauté 1 minute longer, stirring constantly so the chili powder doesn't burn. Add the beans and their liquid and the bulgur, tomatoes, and 1 cup water to the beef mixture, stirring well to blend. Bring to a boil; lower the heat. Simmer 45 minutes, stirring often and adding additional water if necessary so the mixture doesn't dry out. Taste, season with salt and pepper if desired.

NUTRITION INFORMATION: Cal: 361 Pro: 21g/22% Carb: 50g/54% Fat: 10g/24% (S:34% M:42% P:22%) Chol: 25mg Sodium: 105mg Potassium: 520mg Fiber: 12g A: 167% C: 49% B1:11% B3:16% 16% Fe: 16% Cr: 24%
EXCHANGE: Lean Meat: 1¼ Bread: 2½ Veg: 2¼ Fat: 1

MICROWAVE METHOD: In a 4- to 5-quart microwave-safe casserole, cook the beans and water to cover, tightly covered, on High (100% power) to boiling, about 10 to 13 minutes. Stir. Reduce to Medium (50% power); cook covered 2 minutes more. Let stand covered 1 hour; drain. Meanwhile, in a 2-quart microwave-safe casserole, cook the onions, oil, pepper, carrot, and garlic uncovered on High until tender, about 6 to 7 minutes. Stir in the chili powder. Cook uncovered on High 1 minute. Stir the chili mixture, ground beef, bulgur, tomatoes, and 2 cups water into the beans. Cook covered on High 10 minutes. Reduce to Medium; cook tightly covered until beans are tender, about 45 to 50 minutes; stir twice. Season as desired.

Curried Chick-Peas
by Ceri Hadda

This is a spicy dish, so use the smaller amount of cayenne if you want a milder taste. Serve hot with rice or enjoy it cold with bread—either way, the grain makes it a complete-protein main course.

> 1 cup chopped onion
> 1 teaspoon minced fresh ginger
> 2 tablespoons olive oil
> 1 large tomato, chopped
> 2 tablespoons tomato paste, no salt added
> 1 teaspoon ground coriander seeds (see Note)
> 1 teaspoon ground cumin (see Note)
> ¼ teaspoon ground turmeric (see Note)
> ½ to 1 teaspoon cayenne (see Note)
> 4 cups cooked chick-peas (about 2 cups dried), drained, or 2 1-pound cans rinsed and drained
> Plain nonfat yogurt for garnish
> Chopped fresh coriander or parsley for garnish

PREPARATION TIME: 20 minutes
COOKING TIME: 30 minutes
YIELD: 4 servings

Sauté the onion and ginger in oil in a wok or large deep skillet. Add the tomato and cook 1 minute, stirring. Add ⅔ cup of water, tomato paste, coriander, cumin, turmeric, and cayenne. Simmer 3 minutes. Stir in the chick-peas, cover, and simmer 20 minutes. Serve with dollops of yogurt and chopped coriander.

NOTE: If desired, substitute 2 to 3 teaspoons curry powder for the ground spices in this recipe.

NUTRITION INFORMATION: Cal: 459 Pro: 23g/19% Carb: 69g/58% Fat: 12g/23% (S:15% M:74% P:10%) Chol: 1 mg Sodium: 49mg Potassium: 1082mg Fiber: 13g A: 19% C: 29% E: 21% B1: 25% B2: 14% B3: 13% Ca: 21% P: 38% Fe: 45% Cr: 12%
EXCHANGE: Lean Meat: 1¼ Bread: 3¾ Veg: 1 Fat: 1½

MICROWAVE METHOD: In a 1½-quart micro-wave-safe casserole, cook the onion, ginger, and only 1 tablespoon oil uncovered on High (100% power) until onion is tender, about 3 to 4 minutes. Add the tomato, only ½ cup water, and the to-mato paste, coriander, cumin, turmeric, and cay-enne. Cook covered on High to boiling, about 4 to 5 minutes. Stir in the chick-peas. Reduce power to Medium (50% power); cook covered 10 min-utes or until heated through. Serve as directed above.

Tomato Succotash

by Ceri Hadda

A traditional combination of lima beans and corn is highlighted with the addition of tomatoes and basil.

1 10-ounce package frozen baby lima beans
1 small onion, chopped
2 tablespoons tomato puree, no salt added
2 cups fresh corn kernels or 1 10-ounce
  package frozen corn
1 small ripe tomato, chopped
¼ cup buttermilk
2 tablespoons chopped fresh basil
  Salt (optional)
  Freshly ground black pepper (optional)

PREPARATION TIME: 20 minutes
COOKING TIME: 20 minutes
YIELD: 6 servings

Combine the lima beans, onion, ½ cup water, and tomato puree in a medium, heavy sauce-pan. Bring to a boil over moderate heat; lower heat and cover. Simmer 5 minutes. Add the corn and tomato. Cover and simmer 5 minutes longer. Uncover; continue cooking, stirring, 2 to 3 min-utes longer, or until most of the water has evap-orated. Add the buttermilk and basil. Heat 1 to 2 minutes longer but do not allow the mixture to boil. Taste, and season with salt and pepper if necessary.

NOTE: This dish improves if made ahead and very gently reheated.

NUTRITION INFORMATION: Cal: 106 Pro: 5g/ 19% Carb: 23g/79% Fat: .4g/3% Chol: 1mg Sodium: 41mg Potassium: 375mg Fiber: 4g A: 12% C: 23% E: 21% Folic: 11% Cr: 22% EXCHANGE: Bread: 1¼ Veg: ¼

MICROWAVE METHOD: In a 1½-quart micro-wave-safe casserole, cook the lima beans, onion, only 2 tablespoons water, and the tomato puree covered on High (100% power) until the lima beans are almost tender, about 4 to 5 minutes. Stir in the corn, tomato, buttermilk, and basil. Cook covered on Medium (50% power) until heated through, about 6 to 8 minutes. Season if necessary.

Braised Lentils

by *American Health*

1 tablespoon vegetable oil
1 small onion, chopped
1 large stalk celery, chopped
2 tablespoons sun-dried tomatoes, drained and
  finely chopped
1 clove garlic, peeled and minced
1 fresh jalapeño pepper, seeded and minced
½ cup chopped fresh parsley
¾ cup dried lentils, rinsed
3 cups unsalted chicken broth or stock (see
  page 28)

PREPARATION TIME: 20 minutes
COOKING TIME: 1 hour 45 minutes
YIELD: 6 servings

In a medium saucepan warm the oil over mod-erately high heat until it shimmers. Add the next six ingredients. Sauté, stirring occasionally, until the onion and celery are softened but not browned, about 5 minutes. Stir in the lentils and chicken broth. Bring to a boil; cover and simmer until tender and most of the liquid is absorbed, about 1¼ to 1½ hours.

NUTRITION INFORMATION: Cal: 118 Pro: 8g/ 27% Carb: 15g/50% Fat: 3g/23% (S:18% M:30% P:52%) Chol: 1mg Sodium: 109mg

Potassium: 356mg Fiber: 4g C: 13% E: 15% B3: 11% B6: 22% Panto: 10% P: 13% Fe: 12% Cu: 13%
EXCHANGE: Lean Meat: ½ Bread: 1 Veg: ¼ Fat: ½

MICROWAVE METHOD: In a 2-quart microwave-safe casserole, cook only 1 teaspoon of the oil and the next six ingredients on High (100% power) until tender, about 3 to 4 minutes. Add the lentils and 2 cups broth. Cook covered on High to boiling, 8 to 10 minutes; stir once. Reduce to Medium (50% power); cook covered until tender and most of the liquid is absorbed, about 30 to 32 minutes; stir twice. Let stand 5 minutes.

Easy Baked Beans

by Ceri Hadda

½ cup canned tomato puree, no salt added
⅓ cup dry white wine
¼ cup light molasses
2 teaspoons dry mustard
1 teaspoon ground ginger
2 1-pound cans pinto beans, rinsed and drained
2 whole cloves
1 medium onion, quartered

PREPARATION TIME: 15 minutes
COOKING TIME: 1½ hours
YIELD: 6 servings

Preheat oven to 325°F. Combine the tomato puree, wine, molasses, mustard, and ginger in a 1½- to 2-quart baking dish until well blended. Add the beans; stir well to combine. Stick the cloves into 2 onion quarters; press all 4 quarters into the bean mixture. Bake in the preheated oven 1½ hours, or until the beans are richly glazed, stirring every 30 minutes and adding water if the beans appear to be drying out. Remove the cloves from the onion quarters before serving.

NUTRITION INFORMATION: Cal: 295 Pro: 15g/ 19% Carb: 59g/78% Fat: 1g/3% Chol: 0mg Sodium: 31mg Potassium: 245mg Fiber: 8g C: 16% B1: 30% B2: 11% Ca: 11% Fe: 28%
EXCHANGE: Bread: 3¾ Veg: ½

MICROWAVE METHOD: Stick the cloves into 2 onion quarters. In a 1½- to 2-quart microwave-safe casserole, stir the remaining ingredients; press the onion quarters into the bean mixture. Cook, covered with wax paper, on High (100% power) 10 minutes. Reduce to Medium (50% power); cook until beans are glazed, about 13 to 15 minutes. Stir twice. Remove cloves before serving.

◇ SOYFOODS ◇

*The Generous Soybean*___

by Jeanine Barone, M.S.

Let us pause a moment to admire the generous soybean. It gives more than it takes. To the soil, it gives back nitrogen. To the human body, it contributes a rich store of protein, iron, and often calcium with just a small amount of mostly unsaturated fat.

In its many forms—particularly its most popular, tofu or bean curd—it gives the artist in each cook a mild sweet canvas that yields to a wide palette of seasonings. As tempeh (fermented soy cakes), it's got the texture of meat for those who like to go vegetarian but still like a hunk of something to chew. Soymilk can take the place of milk for some. And miso (soybean paste), usually made from fermented soybeans, adds a rich savory flavor to many dishes—even tofu.

Soy's balance of amino acids is so nearly perfect that it is almost a complete protein source by itself, though you'll improve the balance by combining it with grains or dairy products, which contain more of the two amino acids it's low in. That protein is easy to digest: Researchers at the Veterans' Administration Medical Center in Dallas report that soy protein stimulates less stomach acid than does beef protein.

Tofu is made much as cheese is, but without the fermentation. Soaked soybeans are ground up, heated, filtered; the resulting soymilk is made to curdle by the addition of calcium salts. The product is then placed in a mold to form the now-familiar white bean cakes found in many markets.

The result is a low-calorie, high-protein food. It contains no cholesterol, and, although it's high in fat, four-fifths of the fat it does contain is unsaturated; it also contains some Omega 3 linolenic acid, which *may* confer some of the benefits of fish-derived Omega 3 fats (see Fish, page 212).

There also appears to be something specific to soy protein that helps lower blood cholesterol, perhaps by altering our metabolism of cholesterol. In 1985, at the University of Naples, volunteers given soy protein supplements plus a low-fat diet had lower cholesterol than volunteers who had a low-fat diet alone. In another study, twelve men who were vegetarians who also ate eggs and cheese were asked to maintain their normal diets but eat either cheese every day or tofu. After three weeks, the tofu eaters dropped their blood cholesterol by 16 milligrams/deciliter, most of that in the "bad" LDL cholesterol. The cheese eaters registered no change in cholesterol status.

Soybeans also contain substances called isoflavones that may possibly help protect women from breast cancer by lowering levels of estrogen. (In large doses in animals, isoflavones are contraceptives.) At the University of Alabama in Birmingham, pharmacologist Stephen Barnes has found that soybeans can lower the risk of breast cancer in animals by as much as 70 percent. Some researchers speculate soybeans may help protect women in Japan, where incidence is low, from the disease.

Tofu is also rich in iron. A 3-ounce serving of tofu has 10.5 grams of iron, about 58 percent of the USRDA. While the iron in vegetable sources isn't as available for use by our bodies as that in animal sources such as beef, a recent study at the University of Kansas reveals that the iron in tofu is three times as bioavailable as the iron in other soy products. Something in the grinding, hulling, boiling, filtering, or straining seems to liberate the iron in tofu.

Calcium is trickier. That same serving of tofu provides 21 percent of the USRDA for calcium, a boon to people who don't like milk. But only tofu processed with calcium salts will contain much calcium. Tofu processed the traditional way with the sea salt nigiri will have much less calcium. Here is one case where the old-fashioned way is not always better.

Soymilk, which must be refrigerated like regular milk and is as perishable, can be used like cow's milk, though it is not a dairy product. It even contains approximately the same amount of protein and has an amino acid composition similar to that of milk. But though it's a good protein source for the lactose-intolerant, who can't digest milk, and for people with milk allergies, soymilk has little calcium or vitamin D; cows' milk is rich in both. Also, be careful of brands that have added oil and sugar, which add calories without nutrition.

Tempeh is a cultured soy cake with a spongy texture and somewhat nutty flavor. Boiled soybeans are cooled and then inoculated with a mold (Rhizopus) and allowed to ferment in a process that resembles the production of cheese or yogurt. Quite a nutritious food, this. Tempeh's not only a good source of protein with less fat than tofu, it also provides rich amounts of vitamin A, B-6, iron, magnesium, and zinc.

Vegans, who eat no animal products at all, should be aware that tempeh is not a reliable source of B-12, which is found only in animal products. Thus, they are at great risk for B-12 deficiency. B-12 is especially important for a healthy pregnancy and for young children. In the elderly, low blood levels of B-12 can lead to for-getfulness, confusion, and irritability, and can be confused with Alzheimer's disease, University of Cincinnati Medical Center researchers have found.

It may sound surprising that B-12 is so hard for vegans to get. After all, the main diet of most people in the world is primarily if not completely vegan. The difference is hygiene. In the Far East, for example, tempeh often does contain good amounts of B-12, but that's mostly from the bacteria that "contaminate" production. Here, immaculate production methods provide little opportunity for such unintended fortification. Sometimes tempeh culture is also inoculated with a benign bacterial culture to increase B-12 content, but this isn't standard in the United States.

Miso is fermented bean paste that is primarily used to season soup. There are many kinds of miso, which differ depending on the ingredients and the amount of salt used. Rice and soybeans are the most common types but barley can also be used. Cooked soybeans are mixed with steamed koji rice and a mold (Aspergillus) to start fermentation. Salt is added to prevent the growth of other molds. Again, as in tempeh, little B-12 is produced in miso. Miso may have some anticancer potential. In a 13-year study of a quarter million Japanese done by Japan's National Cancer Center, those who drank a bowl of miso every day had a third less stomach cancer than those who didn't drink it at all. Miso does have a lot of sodium, so be careful: A teaspoon has 215 milligrams. Try making your miso soup fairly light, not rich and salty.

Cooking with Soyfoods ___
by Mary Estella

Fresh, pure, white, and milky-sweet, tofu—also called dofu or bean curd—is cheap, nutritious, and quick and versatile in cooking. For years, however, the very qualities that endeared tofu to the hearts of Asian chefs (they call it "meat-without-the-bone") confused us: its mild taste, smooth texture, and ability to absorb seasonings. Now we're beginning to understand that what at first may appear bland and boring can be an elegant food.

Traditionally, tofu was made and sold every day to ensure its fresh, sweet flavor. Today, tofu can still be bought fresh (unpasteurized) by the piece from large, water-filled buckets at natural food or Asian markets. Packed (pasteurized) tofu is usually sold in one-pound blocks with a two- to four-week shelf life. Fresh or packed (after opening), tofu should be used within several days and kept refrigerated in water that's changed daily. Freezing tofu changes its texture, giving it a slightly chewy consistency appropriate for "meaty" dishes.

Firm tofu has more water pressed out while setting than medium or soft tofu. Use it for cutlets or kebabs; it holds together when sliced. Silken tofu is a very soft, custardy tofu that's set directly in the container. Slice and cube it carefully and use it as a garnish on noodles and in soup, or serve it simply seasoned with ginger and soy sauce.

Tofu can be eaten straight from the package, but it tastes better if you steam it a few minutes, even if you want to use it to make salad dressings or sauces that require no further cooking. For pan-frying or sautéing, simply drain sliced tofu on unprinted, white paper towels for a few minutes to absorb excess liquid—which would cause the hot oil to splatter.

The secret of tofu cookery isn't in the technique, though; it's in the seasoning. Try tofu marinated with mustard and herbs, broiled with barbecue sauce, pan-fried with garlic, stir-fried with rice and spices, or simply and elegantly diced and used as a garnish.

Tempeh (pronounced TEM-pay), like tofu, is made from soybeans. But the similarity stops there. A popular food in Indonesia, tempeh is one of the few soyfoods made without salt. Unlike tofu, tempeh contains dietary fiber and has a meatier quality that lends itself to substituting in chicken, fish, and meat cutlet recipes.

When you buy tempeh, look for a freshness date. White mold is natural; harmless delicate black mold may also appear on the tempeh and it enhances the flavor. But if red, yellow, or green mold appears with an ammonia odor, return the package to the store. Tempeh should stay fresh for about a week from purchase.

Due to the precooking and incubation of the soy beans, tempeh requires only a short cooking time. Traditionally, tempeh is simmered in coconut milk with spices. Cut into strips or triangles, tempeh is delicious simmered in a savory broth, or sliced and pan-fried in sesame or olive oil, then seasoned with garlic, grated ginger, or soy sauce. Seasoned, cooked tempeh can add protein and flavor to stir-fries or noodle or rice dishes. Try it in your favorite sweet-and-sour recipe; marinate and skewer it on kebabs; sauté small cubes and add it to stew or casseroles. Cooked, it's great in sandwiches, too. Try a T.L.T.!

Made by a natural fermentation of soybeans and grains, miso is a paste used throughout Asia to season soups, sauces, dressings, marinades, and entrees. It will keep unrefrigerated, but for long storage it's best to store containers in a cold place.

Miso is characterized by color and taste. Light-colored "sweet miso" is often beige, cream, or yellow. High in carbohydrates and low in salt, sweet miso is made with a greater percentage of koji (the grain inoculated with Aspergillus mold) and is aged from two weeks to a few months.

Shiro or white miso, made from rice, is smooth and sweet with a cream-like flavor. Creative cooks often use white miso in recipes that call for butter, milk, or cream. For dairy-free soups, sauces, and spreads, add a few tablespoons of white miso dissolved in a cup of warm water or stock. (Miso is usually blended in a small amount of liquid before adding to soups, or by the spoonful when combining in thicker marinades or spreads.)

Red miso, darker and saltier, is made with less koji and more soybeans and is aged longer, from one to three years. Some red misos are made from rice, some from barley. Hatcho miso, made from soybeans, is the strongest and saltiest.

Rich red misos are perfect for marinades on chicken, fish, or tofu. The enzymatic action of unpasteurized miso acts as a natural meat tenderizer. Try some in barbecue or tomato sauce. While soy sauce may have a strong, even overpowering taste, miso enhances and blends with the flavor of many a dish.

Hot and Sour Miso Soup with Cabbage and Tofu

by Mary Estella

Cabbage becomes sweet when sautéed. Seasoned with hot pepper and lemon juice, this simple miso soup is rich and satisfying.

>   2 teaspoons sesame oil
>   2 onions, diced
> 3¹/₂ cups very finely sliced green or napa
>   cabbage
>   1 medium carrot, julienne cut
>   Pinch sea salt
>   2 cloves garlic, peeled and minced
> ¹/₂ to 1 teaspoon hot pepper oil or ¹/₈ to ¹/₄
>   teaspoon cayenne (to taste)
>   ¹/₄ pound tofu, cut into small cubes
> 2 to 3 tablespoons rice or barley miso
>   dissolved in ¹/₂ cup water or soup broth
>   1 tablespoon fresh lemon juice
>   1 tablespoon red wine or rice vinegar
>   (optional)
> 2 to 3 scallions, sliced
>   Garnishes (optional):
>   Nori (sea vegetable) flakes, or nori
>   sheets cut into ¹/₈ by 1-inch strips
>   Toasted or black sesame seeds
>   (see Note)
>   Snow peas, steamed
>   Red bell pepper, cut into strips

PREPARATION TIME: 35 minutes
COOKING TIME: 35 minutes
YIELD: 4 to 6 servings (about 1¹/₂ quarts)

Heat oil in a 4-quart soup pot. Sauté the onions in the oil about 5 minutes. Add the cabbage, carrot, and sea salt; sauté 5 to 10 minutes, until vegetables become sweet-smelling. Add the garlic and hot pepper oil to taste. Stir. Add 4 cups water, bring to a boil, cover, lower heat, and simmer 15 to 20 minutes. Add the tofu. Stir in the dissolved miso and the lemon juice. Taste, and add vinegar, if desired. Adjust seasoning. Sprinkle with sliced scallions. Serve with the garnish of your choice.

VARIATION: *Gingery Miso Soup:* Add 1 teaspoon fresh ginger juice (from grating a small piece of fresh ginger on the small holes of a hand grater) along with the miso.

NUTRITIONAL INFORMATION: Cal: 79 Pro: 4g/ 17% Carb: 12g/53% Fat: 3g/30% (S:15% M:38% P:47%) Chol: 0mg Sodium: 286mg Potassium: 328mg Fiber: 4g A: 133% C: 43% E: 10% B6: 10% Cr: 16%
EXCHANGE: Med Meat: ¹/₄ Veg: 2 Fat: ¹/₄

MICROWAVE METHOD: In a 3-quart microwave-safe casserole or bowl, cook only 1 teaspoon oil and the onions on High (100% power) until tender, about 3 to 4 minutes. Add the cabbage, carrot, and sea salt. Cook covered on High 5 minutes. Add only 3¹/₂ cups water and the garlic and hot pepper oil. Cook covered on High to boiling, about 8 to 10 minutes. Reduce to Medium (50% power); cook 7 minutes more. Add the tofu and continue as directed above.

Tofu-Spinach Dip

by *American Health*

This dip tastes great with crudités.

>   8 ounces tofu, well drained
>   2 cups lightly packed, finely chopped spinach
>   2 tablespoons fresh lemon juice
>   1 teaspoon sugar
> ¹/₂ teaspoon salt
> ¹/₂ teaspoon paprika
> ¹/₂ teaspoon garlic powder
> ¹/₄ teaspoon onion powder
> ¹/₄ teaspoon Italian seasoning

PREPARATION TIME: 20 minutes plus refrigeration time
YIELD: about 1¹/₃ cups

Crumble the tofu. In a food processor with the metal blade or in a blender at medium speed, blend all the ingredients until smooth, stopping occasionally to scrape container down with a rubber spatula. Pour the mixture into a serving bowl. Cover and refrigerate at least 4 hours to blend the flavors. Stir, and serve with vegetable sticks.

NUTRITION INFORMATION: (for a 2-tablespoon serving): Cal: 22 Pro: 2g/35% Carb: 2g/29% Fat: 1g/36% (S:22% M:8% P:70%) Chol: 0mg Sodium: 117mg Potassium: 79mg Fiber: .4g A: 16%
EXCHANGE: Med. Meat: ¼ Veg: ¼

Marie's Mushroom-Leek Soup

by Mary Estella

Soy milk and oatmeal are used to add a creamy texture and to thicken this adaptation of a French-style soup.

> 1 tablespoon plus 2 teaspoons olive oil
> 2 cups diced leeks (2 to 3 leeks) (see Note)
> 1 pound fresh mushrooms, sliced
> 2 stalks celery, chopped
> 1 small carrot, diced
>   Pinch sea salt
>   Freshly ground black pepper
> ⅓ cup oatmeal
> 2 bay leaves
> ½ teaspoon dried dill
> ½ teaspoon dried basil
> ¼ teaspoon dried marjoram
> 2 to 3 cloves garlic, peeled and minced
> 2 tablespoons white or barley miso, or sea salt to taste
> ¾ cup soy milk
> ¼ cup mirin (sweet rice wine) or dry white wine (optional)
> 2 scallions, sliced, for garnish
>   Freshly grated nutmeg

PREPARATION TIME: 25 minutes
COOKING TIME: 45 minutes
YIELD: 5 servings

In a 4-quart soup pot, heat the 1 tablespoon olive oil. Add the leeks and sauté 5 to 7 minutes over medium heat, stirring often. Add half of the sliced mushrooms and the celery, carrot, salt, and pepper to taste. Sauté for 5 to 10 minutes, until the vegetables cook down, stirring to prevent sticking. Add 3¾ cups water, the oatmeal, bay leaves, and dried herbs. Cover and simmer 20 minutes over medium-low heat. While the soup simmers, heat 2 teaspoons olive oil in a sauté pan. When the oil is hot, add the remaining mushrooms and stir. Add the garlic and sauté for about 2 minutes, until the mushrooms have "seared" in the garlic flavor. Set aside.

When the soup vegetables are tender, discard the bay leaves. Puree the soup in a blender or food processor in batches with the miso (the soup should be very thick). Pour into a large serving dish. Stir in the soy milk. For extra flavor, add the wine and mix well. Stir in the sautéed mushrooms and adjust seasonings to taste. Garnish each serving with sliced scallions and a pinch of freshly grated nutmeg.

NOTE: Slice off the root end of the leeks, then slice the leeks in half lengthwise. Separate and rinse them carefully under running water as sand can be caught between the layers; then dice.

VARIATIONS:
♦ Instead of oatmeal, add 2 peeled and diced potatoes for thickness.
♦ *Asparagus-Leek Soup:* Use 1 pound fresh asparagus in place of the mushrooms.

NUTRITION INFORMATION: Cal: 146 Pro: 6g/ 14% Carb: 20g/49% Fat: 7g/37% (S:17% M:64% P:19%) Chol: 0mg Sodium: 331mg Potassium: 574mg Fiber: 5g A: 81% C: 16% B1: 14% B2: 21% B3: 23% Panto: 21% P: 16% Fe: 19% Cu: 29% Cr: 26%
EXCHANGE: Bread: ¼ Veg: 3 Fat: 1

MICROWAVE METHOD: In a 2-quart microwave-safe casserole or bowl, cook only 1 teaspoon oil and the leeks on High (100% power) until tender, about 4 to 5 minutes. Add half the sliced mushrooms, celery, carrot, salt, and pepper to taste. Cook covered on High until almost tender, about 4 to 5 minutes. Add 3¾ cups water, the oatmeal, bay leaves, and dried herbs. Cook covered on Medium (50% power) 10 minutes. Let stand 5 minutes. In a 1-quart microwave-safe casserole or bowl, cook 1 teaspoon oil, the remaining mushrooms, and the garlic on High until tender, about 3 to 4 minutes; set aside. Puree the soup and continue as directed above.

Tempeh with Pineapple and Snow Peas
by Mary Estella

Tempeh, a soyfood from Indonesia, is usually simmered with spices in coconut milk. In this recipe, pineapple and lemon juice are combined for a tempting sweet-sour taste. Serve over noodles instead of rice, if you like.

    2 to 3 tablespoons vegetable oil
      ½ pound tempeh, sliced into bite-size
          triangles
      1 teaspoon sesame oil
      1 medium onion, sliced into half moons
      2 medium carrots, julienne cut
          A few drops hot pepper oil or pinch
          cayenne (optional)
      3 cloves garlic, peeled and minced
  ½ to 1 teaspoon grated fresh ginger
      3 cups pineapple juice
      ¼ cup fresh lemon juice
      2 tablespoons reduced-sodium soy sauce
      1 cup pineapple chunks
  1 to 2 tablespoons arrowroot or kudzu,
          dissolved in ¼ cup cold water until
          there are no lumps
      4 ounces snow peas
      2 cups hot cooked brown rice, or noodles
      ½ red bell pepper, sliced into thin strips,
          for garnish

PREPARATION TIME: 35 minutes
COOKING TIME: 30 minutes
YIELD: 4 servings

Heat the vegetable oil in a skillet, and pan-fry the tempeh pieces until golden brown on each side; drain on paper towels. Set aside.

Heat the sesame oil in a saucepan. Add the onion and carrots and sauté over medium heat about 5 minutes, stirring to prevent sticking. If desired, stir in the hot pepper oil or cayenne. Add the garlic and ginger; sauté for another minute. Add the pineapple juice and pan-fried tempeh pieces. Cover and simmer 10 to 15 minutes. Add the lemon juice, soy sauce, and pineapple chunks. Pour the dissolved arrowroot into the sauce and stir carefully until thick. Lower the heat and gently simmer for a minute or two, until the sauce is shiny and clear again. Add the snow peas to the sauce (or steam them for 30 seconds until bright green and crisp, then mix them into the sauce). Serve over rice, garnished with sliced red bell pepper.

VARIATIONS:
♦ Use an equal amount of water chestnuts in place of pineapple chunks.
♦ Add mung sprouts to the sauce with the snow peas.
♦ If you don't have snow peas, substitute celery strips and scallions sliced on the diagonal. Or use blanched broccoli flowerets.
♦ In place of tempeh, use firm tofu or skinless chicken breasts, cut into bite-size pieces and sautéed.
♦ For a special treat, garnish with shiitake mushrooms sautéed in sesame oil.

NUTRITION INFORMATION (with ½ cup brown rice): Cal: 436 Pro: 11g/9% Carb: 73g/65% Fat: 13g/26% (S:14% M:27% P:59%) Chol: 0mg Sodium: 337mg Potassium: 703mg Fiber: 7g A: 194% C: 121% E: 52% B1: 24% B2: 10% B3: 14% B6: 25% Folic: 16% Ca: 16% P: 15% Fe: 20% Mg: 14% Cu: 19% Mn: 82% Se: 60% Cr: 22%
EXCHANGE: Med. Meat: ½ Bread: 2 Veg: 1½ Fruit: 2¼ Fat: 1¾

Curry-Sesame Tofu with Steamed Vegetables and Rice
by Mary Estella

A quick, crunchy tofu recipe. Serve plain or with your favorite dip or sauce—a ginger-soy sauce is delicious. Or you can use the crispy cutlets alone to make a sandwich.

      1 pound firm tofu
      ⅓ cup hulled sesame seeds
      2 tablespoons all-purpose unbleached white
          or whole wheat pastry flour

2 teaspoons curry powder
1 teaspoon ground cumin
1/4 teaspoon ground turmeric
1/2 teaspoon salt
    Pinch cayenne (optional)
1 to 2 tablespoons sesame oil
1 egg white, beaten
2 stalks broccoli, cut into 1-inch pieces, or
    4 ounces snow peas
1/2 red bell pepper, sliced
2 cups hot cooked brown rice

PREPARATION TIME: 15 minutes
COOKING TIME: 10 minutes
YIELD: 5 servings

Slice the tofu into rectangular 1/4-inch cutlets (approximately 12), and drain on paper towels for 10 minutes. Leave as cutlets or cut into bite-size triangles.

Combine the sesame seeds, flour, spices, salt, and cayenne in a plastic bag. Close and shake to mix evenly. Empty the contents of the bag onto a dinner plate and spread evenly. Heat the sesame oil in a heavy skillet. Dip a quarter to a third of the tofu pieces into the egg white, shaking off any excess, and then into the seasoning mix to coat both sides. Place the coated tofu pieces in the frying pan and fry until golden and crisp on both sides. Drain on paper towels. Repeat with the remaining tofu.

Steam the broccoli or snow peas and the sliced red pepper until the broccoli or snow peas are bright green. Combine with the tofu and serve over the hot rice.

NUTRITION INFORMATION: Cal: 289 Pro: 14g/ 18% Carb: 32g/42% Fat: 13g/40% (S:15% M:40% P:45%) Chol: 0mg Sodium: 220mg Potassium: 285mg Fiber: 7g A: 18% C: 79% E: 27% B1: 19% B2: 13% B3: 12% B6: 11% Folic: 14% Ca: 30% P: 22% Fe: 26% Mg: 20% Cu: 23% Se: 47%
EXCHANGE: Med. Meat: 1 Bread: 1 1/2 Veg: 1 Fat: 2

Pan-Fried Tofu and Noodle Dinner
by Mary Estella

A convenient supper—flavorful, well-balanced, and less than an hour to prepare.

1 small bunch broccoli
1 8-ounce package udon, somen, or soba
    noodles
1 pound firm tofu
2 tablespoons sesame oil
2 to 3 cloves garlic, peeled and minced
   1/2 teaspoon fresh ginger juice (from grating
    a small piece of fresh ginger on the small
    holes of a hand grater)
2 tablespoons reduced-sodium soy sauce
3 tablespoons mirin (sweet rice wine) or
    dry white wine
1 tablespoon fresh lemon juice
2 carrots, julienne cut
1 to 2 teaspoons sesame oil (optional)
1 teaspoon hot pepper oil (optional)
   1/3 cup roasted sunflower seeds for garnish
    (optional)
2 or 3 scallions, sliced, for garnish

PREPARATION TIME: 25 minutes
COOKING TIME: 25 minutes
YIELD: 4 servings

In a large saucepot, bring 2 quarts of water to a boil. Meanwhile cut the broccoli into flowerets and add to the boiling water. When the water returns to a rolling boil, remove the broccoli with a slotted spoon and set aside. Use the water to cook the noodles, according to package directions. Rinse, drain, and set aside. Keep warm. While the noodles are cooking, slice the tofu into 1/4- to 1/2-inch pieces. Slice each rectangle into bite-size triangles and place on a double layer of plain white paper towels to absorb excess water before frying.

Heat the sesame oil in a large cast-iron skillet. Pan-fry the tofu pieces on each side for 2 to 3 minutes, until golden and crisp. (Some pieces of tofu may break, so be careful when turning them over with the spatula.) Add the garlic; fry 30 seconds. Add the ginger, soy sauce, mirin, and lemon juice; cover and lower the heat. After 2 to 3 minutes, add the carrots, placing them on top of the tofu. Cover and steam until the carrots are bright and crisp, about 2 minutes. The tofu should absorb all the juices with little liquid left in the pan. (Add more mirin, white wine, lemon juice, or soy sauce if it appears too dry.)

In the skillet or a large bowl, combine the tofu mixture with the cooked and drained noodles. Add sesame and/or hot pepper oil for extra flavor if desired. Adjust the seasonings. Toss broccoli with the noodles and tofu or arrange it around the outside of the serving dish. Garnish with sunflower seeds and sliced scallions.

VARIATIONS:
♦ Use 2 cups snow peas in place of broccoli; add with the carrots.

♦ Add a teaspoon or two of rice or umeboshi vinegar instead of roasted sesame oil or hot pepper oil at the end for extra flavor.
♦ Use shelled and deveined shrimp in place of tofu. Pan-fry the shrimp with the seasonings until they turn pink and curl.

NUTRITION INFORMATION: Cal: 396   Pro: 19g/18%   Carb: 56g/54%   Fat: 13g/28%   (S:15% M:40%   P:45%)   Chol: 0mg   Sodium: 341mg Potassium: 316mg   Fiber: 8g   A: 218%   C: 91%   E: 13%   B2: 14%   B6: 13%   Folic: 15%   Ca: 24%   P: 20%   Fe: 32%   Mg: 27%   Mn: 14%   Cr: 15%
EXCHANGE: Med. Meat: 1   Bread: 2¾   Veg: 2 Fat: 1½

MICROWAVE METHOD: In a 2-quart microwave-safe casserole or bowl, cook the broccoli and ¼ cup water tightly covered on High (100% power) until just tender-crisp, about 4 to 7 minutes. Drain. Continue as directed above.

◇ Nuts and Seeds ◇

A Little Goes a Long Way—

By Robert Barnett

NUTS

Pliny, the ancient Greek philosopher, was a little perplexed. "Hazelnuts," he wrote, "put more fat on the body than one would think at all likely."

If he had had a modern lab, he'd have known why. With few exceptions, nuts are mostly fat. Most are 50 to 60 percent fat—by *weight*. As a percentage of calories, a more appropriate nutritional guide, they're even higher. Cashews, for instance, are 50 percent fat by weight but 68 percent of their calories are from fat. Macadamias are the highest: 88 percent of their calories come from fat. Brazil nuts, hazelnuts, pecans, pine nuts (pignoli), and English walnuts all have at least 80 percent of their calories from fat. Pistachios, peanuts, and almonds are in the 70 percent range.

Chestnuts are one of the few low-fat nuts we eat. Along with less commercial ginkgo nuts and acorns, chestnuts are mostly carbohydrate: An ounce of roasted chestnuts has 70 calories, 88 percent from carbohydrates, 7 percent from fat. No wonder chestnut flour often takes the place of wheat flour in parts of France, Italy, Portugal, and Spain.

Fortunately, the fat in most nuts is mostly monounsaturated and polyunsaturated, not the saturated fats that have been implicated in heart disease. Hazelnuts, macadamia nuts, pecans, pis-tachio nuts, and almonds are highest in monoun-saturates; pignoli, English walnuts, and chestnuts are rich in polyunsaturates. Some nuts, particularly butternuts and walnuts, are even good sources of heart-healthy Omega 3 oils, similar to though less active than the kind found in fish oils. But even a "healthy" fat is still a fat. It's best to limit our intake of fat to 30 percent of total calories or less, if only to keep from getting fat ourselves.

Nuts may be a little too rich to play a major role in a healthy diet. But they are versatile bit players, enriching the taste of a dish with just a walk-on. Their flavor is superb, and a little goes a long way.

Nuts do have a lot to offer, of course, even in the small amounts nutritionists recommend. They're rich in protein and minerals, as well as some vitamins. They also provide some dietary fiber, especially when eaten with the husks or skins.

For vegetarians who otherwise are eating a low-fat diet, and certainly for vegans who shun all meat and dairy, nuts can provide protein; combine them with grains for a complete protein. Perhaps more important, some are good sources of minerals such as magnesium, manganese, and zinc. Vegans might have a particularly tough time getting the latter two. And if you don't like dark green leafy vegetables, whole grains, and legumes, you could be low in magnesium.

Lots of Americans—especially children, teenage girls, and adult women—have diets that leave them chronically short of iron, calcium, magnesium, zinc, copper, and manganese, according to the FDA's Total Diet Study, published in 1986. The USDA's latest Nationwide Food Consumption Survey (1986) confirms that many women get less-than-recommended amounts of iron, calcium, magnesium, and zinc.

Getting enough of these minerals could be more important than we know. Biologist Paul Saltman of the University of California at San Diego and colleagues in Belgium have found that women with serious osteoporosis have very low levels of manganese in the blood, and animal studies show that low manganese diets can lead to porous bones. So manganese, which helps our bones utilize calcium, may turn out to be a key to strong bones.

Nuts, even in small amounts, can help. A half-ounce of dry roasted pecans, for example, provides 17½ percent of the midrange of the USDA recommended "estimated safe and adequate" amount of manganese. A half-ounce—that's what you'll find in most of our recipes, per serving. It's enough for taste and texture, good amounts of some nutrients, but not much fat and calories.

A half-ounce of dry roasted hazelnuts will give you about 11 percent of the USRDA of magnesium. It's an increasingly appreciated nutrient. Low intakes of magnesium, along with excess sodium and perhaps too little calcium, may contribute to high blood pressure. Many nuts are also excellent sources of vitamin E, the body's main antioxidant, which protects against free radicals implicated in many diseases and aging; supplemental vitamin E has been shown to boost the immune systems of the elderly and reduce symptoms of disease as diverse as Parkinson's and PMS.

Most of what we think of as nuts are not, botanically speaking, true nuts. Botanists define nuts as those one-seeded edible kernels in a dry or hard shell that are indehiscent, i.e., they won't open by themselves. Pistachios will open by themselves, so they're not nuts; peanuts don't have a hard shell, and in fact are legumes. True nuts include walnuts, almonds, hazelnuts, filberts, Brazil nuts, and chestnuts.

Preservatives and Contaminants

If you're sensitive to sulfites, avoid dried nuts or nut mixes, says the FDA. Many are preserved with sulfites. As for aflatoxin, a carcinogenic toxin produced by a mold, it doesn't appear to be much of a problem in commercial products. Warmth and a humid environment encourages production of this deadly toxin; it develops usually after harvest and can spread easily. Major nut producers have high quality control standards and are quite careful.

Commercial peanut butter appears to be safe. A *Consumers Union* survey of peanut butters found that the average aflatoxin level was a very low 0.85 parts per billion. The FDA safety standard is 20 parts per billion. But peanut butter ground in the store may not be as safe as commercial brands, warns the FDA. Peanuts that sit around have more of an opportunity to pick up mold; freshly ground peanut butter is often missing the preservative, salt. Throw out any peanut butter (from any source) that's become moldy; skimming the mold off just won't do.

As you shell or eat nuts, look at each one and discard any moldy, discolored, or shriveled ones. If you bite into a nut that tastes bad, spit it out. Discreetly!

SEEDS

Seeds are the capsules that contain the plant embryo and the concentrated nutrients needed for germination. So it's not surprising that, like nuts, they are rich in certain minerals—as well as in calories and fat.

Pumpkin seeds derive 76 percent of their calories from fat; sesame, 78 percent; and so on down the line. As is true in the case of nuts, the fat is primarily unsaturated. And good nutrients—including zinc, phosphorus, magnesium, and iron—come along, too.

One exception to the high-fat seed is the caraway seed. It's got lots of protein and carbohydrates, but has only 37 percent of its calories from fat. But who ever ate more than a few caraway seeds at a time?

Spotlight: Brazil Nuts

The Brazil nut travels many miles from its home in the foothills of the Andes in Brazil, Venezuela, or Colombia to your coffee table nut bowl. But it doesn't forget Andean earth. From that soil it picks up enough selenium—a trace mineral now being studied for its potential to protect against cancer—to send blood levels soaring.

When Cornell University toxicologist Donald J. Lisk and three colleagues ate six Brazil nuts a day—about an ounce—for about three weeks, their blood levels of selenium rose a dramatic 100 to 350 percent.

It's not surprising. The selenium level in Brazil nuts is astonishingly high. According to Lisk's lab analysis of supermarket Brazil nuts, six large nuts average about 700 micrograms of selenium. Though the USDA hasn't yet set a USRDA, the 1990 RDA for an adult man is 70 micrograms; for an adult woman, 50 micrograms.

Does that mean Brazil nuts have *too* much selenium? "If an ounce has seven hundred micrograms, that's more than I would want to take every day. Signs of toxicity can show up at a thousand micrograms a day," says USDA research chemist Orville Levander of the Human Nutrition Research Center in Beltsville, Maryland. "But I wouldn't be too concerned," he says. "No one sits down and pigs out on five pounds of Brazil nuts. Of course, if you eat too much of anything it could be a problem."

To Lisk, the news that Brazil nuts raise blood levels of selenium is exciting because a number of studies reveal a link between relatively high blood selenium and lowered risk of cancer.

"It's promising, but not proven," says Harvard School of Public Health epidemiologist Walter Willett. "Some studies show that people with low levels have greater risk, others don't show the connection." Willett and colleagues are now studying the diets of 60,000 nurses, and should have some data on the potential selenium/cancer hypothesis within a few years.

If animal studies are any indication, adequate dietary selenium may also protect against certain toxic metals, says Lisk. In one study, he gave toxic methyl mercury to Japanese quail, and all died within three weeks; when he gave quail the same amount of mercury but also selenium, "there was no effect—not even weight loss." In animal studies, to get a benefit, both in terms of cancer and toxic metals, "it has to be simultaneous," says Lisk. "You can't just have a bushel of Brazil nuts ready to go in case you have a tumor."

The American diet, notes Levander, currently provides about 100 micrograms of selenium a day. Eat an ounce of Brazil nuts a week and you'll probably boost that to 200 micrograms a day—a safe level. So crack open a few—just a few.

—Robert Barnett

Cooking With Nuts

by Nao Hauser

The fat caveat issued with nuts should signal a change of venue: take them off the coffee table and toss them in the cookpot! For the same fat level that can make nuts hazardous by the handful also makes them extremely flavorful by the spoonful. And the same caloric comfort they offer on their own bestows a certain generosity of taste on leaner ingredients. Seeds, while less versatile, can play a similar role.

Every supermarket stocks raw almonds, pecans, and walnuts, usually near other baking supplies; buy these chopped or sliced, if you wish, for maximum time savings. Most stores carry raw hazelnuts, pignoli, and unsalted, dry-roasted peanuts, too. When available, Brazil nuts and chestnuts are sold in the shell in produce departments. Only unsalted cashews and pistachio nuts might require a trip to a health food store.

Choose nuts in the shell that are clean and free of splits, cracks, stains, or holes; shelled nuts should be plump with a bright color and no off odors.

Store nuts in a tightly sealed container in a cool, dark place for several months. They will keep longer in the refrigerator in a sealed can, plastic bag, or jar with a tight fitting lid. They may also be frozen up to two years. The closer a nut is to its original form, the longer it will last: Nuts in the shell last longer than shelled, whole longer than chopped, unroasted longer than roasted. Nuts higher in fat—macadamias, English or black walnuts, Brazil nuts, pignoli—turn rancid more quickly.

Purchase blanched nuts if the appearance of the skins in a dish bothers you; otherwise, don't worry about blanching—the skins hardly affect taste or texture when you're using only small quantities of nuts.

Sharing the Riches

All nuts seem to taste like more than the sum of their calories after they have been roasted. Perhaps this is an evocation of smell, because few fragrances are more seductive than that of nuts on the stove.

To spread the taste throughout a dish, chop nuts into small pieces or slice them thinly. If you use a food processor, chop with on/off turns and stop well before you grind the nuts to a paste or powder. If you don't have a food processor or nut grinder, wrap nuts in a dish towel and lightly crush them with a rolling pin, or chop with a knife on a board.

To toast a small quantity of nuts or seeds, spread them in a heavy skillet and cook over medium heat, stirring often, just until they smell toasted and begin to deepen in color. Keep the heat low to medium for sesame seeds and stir constantly.

To toast nuts in the microwave oven, spread them in a glass baking dish or on a paper plate and microwave at High, stirring or rotating the dish every minute, until the color begins to deepen. You won't save much time, though: stove-top or microwave, a small quantity requires about two minutes. Roast a pumpkin's worth of pumpkin seeds or a pound of chestnuts in a hot oven, which works more efficiently than stovetop cooking with large quantities.

Think of nuts as a substitute for butter or oil—and think in similar quantities. Three to four tablespoons of chopped nuts is about one ounce (it varies among types of nuts); about half of that is fat. So you might toss that amount of toasted chopped walnuts with four to six servings of cooked chopped broccoli, for example, instead of using a large pat (about a half-ounce) of butter. An ounce of finely chopped nuts mixed with greens in a salad will diminish proportionately the need for oil in the dressing—making one tablespoon of oil (a half-ounce) taste as satisfying as two.

The seasoning power of nuts is especially effective with grains, which are enhanced by the textural contrast as well as the richness. Toasted almonds or pignoli are delicious with white rice, pecans go well with brown rice, and hazelnuts befit the elegance of wild rice.

Pignoli and couscous, cashews or pistachio nuts with white or basmati rice, and walnuts with bulgur are all time-honored combinations in Mediterranean and Indian cuisines.

But matings can be as eclectic as toasted Brazil nuts with polenta or pecans with kasha as long as you like the taste of nuts, which will dominate the blander grain. Don't hesitate to add dried fruit, such as currants or chopped apples, to a grain and nut mixture, because nuts go especially well with sweet flavors.

Vegetables native to the Americas seem to have a natural kinship with native nuts: witness sweet potatoes or grits with pecans, pumpkin bread or acorn squash with black walnuts, and corn off the cob with chopped filberts. Geographic affinity applies also to tropical fruits and nuts, such as mango with sliced Brazil nuts and pineapple with macadamia nuts.

Unless you're baking nuts into a bread, cake, or pudding, it's best to stir them into a dish just before serving, so that they stay crunchy (and, in the case of walnuts, don't discolor pale foods).

Or pass a dish of toasted chopped nuts at the table to enrich simpler fare. A sprinkling of peanuts hits the spot with chili-spiked black beans and rice. Hazelnuts, pecans, or walnuts can turn a pureed vegetable soup into a meal, especially if you pass rice to stir into the soup, too. Lentil soup tastes great with pistachio nuts, squash soup with sunflower seeds. Sunflower seeds are also delicious sprinkled on salads, especially those made with spinach. Pumpkin seeds are a delightful addition to sweet potatoes—just mash a baked sweet potato with low-fat yogurt and sprinkle toasted pumpkin seeds over it.

Peanut soup, a classic Southern dish made by thickening chicken broth with ground peanuts, is extremely rich, but you can appreciate the taste sensation, in leaner form, by garnishing clear chicken broth with strips of chicken, corn kernels, and toasted chopped peanuts.

A Fine Carbohydrate

Chestnuts, primarily carbohydrate, can be roasted, peeled, chopped, and stirred into grains like other nuts—but they can also be treated like a vegetable. Peel and cook them as directed in the recipe for Glazed Onions and Chestnuts (see page 142); then cut them into halves or quarters and combine them with Brussels sprouts, chopped broccoli, or green beans.

To make the base for a very good soup, simmer about a cup and a half of shelled chestnuts in a quart of chicken stock until they are very soft; then puree in a blender and thin to desired consistency with low-fat milk. Season with pepper and nutmeg. For sweet flavor, cook one or two chopped leeks in a spoonful of butter and just enough stock to cover, over medium low heat, until they are limp before adding the chestnuts and remaining stock.

Pignoli-Stuffed Mushrooms

by Debbie Maugans

20 large fresh mushrooms
 1 teaspoon margarine
 1 teaspoon minced peeled garlic
 3 tablespoons minced fresh parsley
 2 tablespoons minced scallion
 1 teaspoon fresh lemon juice
 1/3 cup fresh breadcrumbs

 2 teaspoons freshly grated Parmesan cheese
 2 tablespoons pignoli (pine nuts), lightly
    toasted (see note), or finely chopped pecans

PREPARATION TIME: 25 minutes
COOKING TIME: 35 minutes
YIELD: 20 appetizers

Clean the mushrooms with a damp cloth. Remove the stems and mince them. Set the caps aside. Preheat the oven to 350°F. Melt the margarine in small nonstick skillet over low heat. Add the garlic and mushroom stems; sauté 15 minutes over low heat, or until all the liquid in the skillet evaporates. Stir in the parsley and scallion; sauté 2 minutes. Remove from heat, and stir in the lemon juice. Cool slightly. Stir in the breadcrumbs, cheese, and pignoli. Spoon the mixture into the mushroom caps; place in an ungreased baking dish. Bake in the preheated oven for 15 minutes. Serve warm.

NOTE: *To toast the nuts,* spread them in a heavy skillet and cook over medium heat, stirring often, just until they smell toasted and begin to deepen in color.

NUTRITION INFORMATION: Cal: 20   Pro: .9g/ 16%   Carb: 3g/47%   Fat: .9g/37%   (S:19%   M:52% P:29%) Chol: 1mg   Sodium: 19mg   Potassium: 96mg Fiber: .5g
EXCHANGE: Veg: 3/4

MICROWAVE METHOD: Prepare the mushrooms as above. On a paper plate, cook the pignoli on High (100% power) until toasted, about 1 1/2 to 2 minutes; set aside. In a 1-quart microwave-safe casserole or bowl, cook the margarine, garlic, and mushroom stems on High 2 minutes. Drain off any liquid. Add the parsley and scallion and cook covered on High 1 minute. Stir in the remaining ingredients. Stuff the mushrooms as directed above. In a 10-inch round microwave-safe dish or pie plate, place half the mushrooms around the edge. Cook on High until heated through, about 3 to 5 minutes. Repeat to cook the remaining mushrooms.

Glazed Onions and Chestnuts

by Debbie Maugans

1/2 pound chestnuts (shell on)
1 pound pearl onions
3/4 cup unsalted beef broth
1/3 cup orange juice
2 tablespoons brown sugar
2 teaspoons balsamic vinegar
1/4 teaspoon salt
1 tablespoon minced fresh parsley

PREPARATION TIME: 30 minutes
COOKING TIME: 25 minutes
YIELD: 4 servings

Cut an X on the flat side of each chestnut. Place them in a pan, cover with cold water, and bring to a boil. Boil 1 minute. Remove from heat and lift out the nuts one by one, peeling off the shell and inner skin. Hold them in a cloth while peeling. Chop the chestnuts coarsely.

Trim and peel onions, and cut an X in the root end of each. Combine the broth, orange juice, brown sugar, vinegar, and salt in a medium, heavy, saucepan; add the onions, and bring to a boil. Cover, reduce the heat, and simmer 8 to 10 minutes, or until just tender when pierced with the tip of a sharp knife. Remove the onions with a slotted spoon and set aside. Boil the cooking liquid over high heat until reduced to 1/4 cup. Reduce the heat to low and stir in the chestnuts and onions. Cook, stirring frequently, 4 minutes, or until the chestnuts are tender. Transfer to a serving dish, and sprinkle with parsley.

NUTRITION INFORMATION: Cal: 228 Pro: 5g/8% Carb: 50g/87% Fat: 1g/5% Chol: 1mg/Sodium: 166mg Potassium: 592mg Fiber: 4g C: 29% B6: 11% P: 11% Mg: 18% Cu: 18% Mn: 37% Cr: 18%
EXCHANGE: Bread: 2 3/4 Veg: 1 1/2

Fragrant Wild Rice with Black Walnuts

by Debbie Maugans

Black walnuts contain fewer calories and less fat than English walnuts. The flavor is quite distinctive, and adds a spicy touch to this recipe. Substitute pecans if black walnuts are unavailable.

1 cup raw wild rice
1/2 cup orange juice
1/4 cup dry sherry or water
1 packet low-sodium chicken broth
1/2 teaspoon ground ginger
1 cup thinly sliced fresh mushrooms
1/2 cup grated carrots
2 tablespoons minced fresh parsley
3 tablespoons minced fresh chives
1/3 cup finely chopped black walnuts

PREPARATION TIME: 30 minutes
COOKING TIME: 50 minutes
YIELD: 6 servings

Rinse the rice well; drain. Combine 1 1/4 cups water, the orange juice, sherry or water, packet of broth, and ginger in a heavy saucepan. Bring to a boil. Add the rice; cover, reduce the heat, and simmer 35 minutes. Layer the mushrooms, carrots, and parsley on the top of rice; cover and simmer 5 to 10 minutes longer or until the rice is tender and all the liquid is absorbed. Stir in the chives; remove from heat. Stir in the walnuts and serve immediately.

NUTRITION INFORMATION: Cal: 161 Pro: 7g/17% Carb: 25g/59% Fat: 5g/24% (S:9% M:24% P:67%) Chol: 1mg Sodium: 20mg Potassium: 312mg Fiber: 2g A: 56% C: 23% B3:15% Folic: 11% P: 18% Mg: 17% Zn: 13% Cu: 13% Mn: 20%
EXCHANGE: Bread: 1 1/2 Veg: 1/2 Fat: 1

MICROWAVE METHOD: Rinse and drain the rice. In a 2-quart microwave-safe casserole, heat 1 1/4 cups water, the orange juice, sherry or water, broth, ginger, and rice on High (100% power) to boiling, about 6 to 7 minutes. Reduce power to Medium (50% power); cook tightly covered 15 minutes. Add the mushrooms, carrots, and parsley over rice. Cook covered on Medium until the rice is tender and all liquid is absorbed, about 8 to 10 minutes. Let stand for 5 minutes, then continue as directed above.

Lentil Salad with Peanuts

by Debbie Maugans

1 1/2 cup finely chopped raw peanuts or cashews
1 1/2 cups dried brown lentils
8 whole cloves
2 whole peppercorns
2 bay leaves
2 cloves garlic, peeled and sliced
2 tablespoons olive oil
2 tablespoons red wine vinegar
1 tablespoon Dijon mustard
1/4 teaspoon cayenne
1/4 teaspoon plus 1/8 teaspoon ground cumin
1/2 cup finely diced red bell pepper
1/2 cup minced fresh parsley
1/3 cup minced scallion
  Assorted salad greens
8 ounces plain nonfat yogurt

PREPARATION TIME: 30 minutes
COOKING TIME: 30 minutes
YIELD: 6 servings

Spread the nuts in a heavy skillet and cook over medium heat, stirring often, just until they smell toasted and begin to deepen in color. Or place in a microwave-safe dish or on a paper plate and microwave on High, stirring or rotating the dish every minute, until the color begins to deepen.

Place the lentils in a large saucepot; cover with 2 inches of cold water. Tie the next four ingredients in a cheesecloth bag; add to the lentils. Bring to a boil, cover, and remove from heat. Let stand 30 minutes. Add additional water, if necessary, to cover lentils by 1 inch. Bring to a simmer over low heat; simmer 1 to 2 minutes, or until tender. Drain the lentils and discard the spice bag. Place the lentils in a bowl. Combine the olive oil, vinegar, mustard, cayenne, and the 1/4 teaspoon cumin; stir into the warm lentils. Add the bell pepper, parsley, and scallion. Cover and refrigerate until chilled. To serve, stir the peanuts into the lentils and spoon onto plates lined with salad greens. Stir the 1/8 teaspoon cumin into the yogurt; serve with the lentils.

NUTRITION INFORMATION: Cal: 283 Pro: 16g/ 22% Carb: 34g/44% Fat: 11g/34% (S:16% M:61% P:23%) Chol: 1mg Sodium: 115mg Potassium: 648mg Fiber: 8g A: 16% C: 33% E: 20% B1: 15% B2: 13% B3: 14% B6: 42% Folic: 23% Panto: 24% Ca: 16% P: 28% Fe: 23% Mg: 11% Zn: 15% Cu: 24% Cr: 34%
EXCHANGE: Lean Meat: 1 Bread: 2 Veg: 1/2 Fat: 1 1/2

Chinese Steamed Fish with Cashews

by Debbie Maugans

12 ounces swordfish steak or 16 ounces halibut,
  3/4 inch thick
2 teaspoons reduced-sodium soy sauce
1 teaspoon fresh lemon juice
1 teaspoon sesame oil
1 clove garlic, minced
1/8 teaspoon cayenne
2 scallions, cut into thin 1-inch strips
2 teaspoons thinly sliced cashews
2 tablespoons minced fresh coriander

PREPARATION TIME: 15 minutes
COOKING TIME: 15 minutes
YIELD: 2 servings

Rinse the fish and pat dry. Cut into serving portions if necessary. Combine the next five ingredients in a small bowl; set aside. Boil water in the bottom half of a steamer (see Note). Arrange the fish on the top rack of the steamer; brush with the soy sauce mixture. Scatter the scallions on top of the fish. Position the rack over the boiling water and cover the steamer tightly. Steam 5 to 6 minutes or until the fish is opaque. Using a spatula, gently transfer the fish to a serving platter. Sprinkle with cashews and coriander.

NOTE: A steam cooker is ideal for steaming, but any deep saucepan (or electric skillet) with a tight-fitting lid will work. Improvise by setting a wire rack on empty tuna cans, tops and bottoms removed, inside the saucepan.

NUTRITION INFORMATION: Cal: 256 Pro: 36g/ 58% Carb: 2g/4% Fat: 11g/38% (S:26% M:45% P:29%) Chol: 69mg Sodium: 358mg Potassium: 564mg Fiber: .3g A: 10% B2: 11% B3:81% B6: 27% B12: 46% P: 49% Fe: 10% Mg: 15% Cu: 15%
EXCHANGE: Lean Meat: 4½ Fat: ½

MICROWAVE METHOD: Rinse the fish and pat dry. Combine the next five ingredients in a small bowl. Arrange the fish in a 12- by 8-inch microwave-safe baking dish. Brush with the soy mixture and scatter scallions on top. Cook tightly covered on High (100% power) until the fish is opaque, about 3 to 5 minutes. Transfer to a serving platter and serve as directed above.

Circassian Chicken

by Nao Hauser

This classic Turkish dish—chicken in a walnut-thickened sauce—can be served many ways, such as: (1) a salad, on top of or rolled up in romaine leaves; (2) a sandwich, spooned into whole wheat pita pockets and garnished with chopped cucumber and shredded radishes; (3) a warm entrée with a mushroom or fruited rice pilaf. It tastes great at room temperature but also reheats well over low heat.

1 cup unsalted chicken broth or stock (see page 28)
1 medium onion (4 ounces), chopped
1 small carrot (2 ounces), sliced thin
1 cup parsley sprigs

¼ teaspoon ground cinnamon
   Pinch cayenne
2 whole chicken breasts (about 1 pound each), skin and visible fat removed
2 ounces (¼ cup chopped walnuts Paprika and chopped fresh parsley for garnish

PREPARATION TIME: 30 minutes
COOKING TIME: 45 minutes
YIELD: 5 to 6 servings

Heat the broth, onion, carrot, parsley, cinnamon, and cayenne to simmering in a wide saucepan. Add the chicken; simmer over medium-low heat, covered, turning over once, until fully cooked, 35 to 40 minutes. Remove the chicken; let stand until cool enough to handle. Strain the broth into a saucepan, reserving the vegetables. Boil the broth until reduced to ½ cup. Bone the chicken, cut into thin 1½-inch-long strips, and place in a bowl. Place the reserved vegetables, reduced broth, and walnuts in a blender and process until smooth. Spoon the walnut sauce over the chicken; stir gently to coat. Sprinkle with paprika and parsley.

NUTRITIONAL INFORMATION (served with ½ cup brown rice): Cal: 401 Pro: 37g/38% Carb: 29g/ 29% Fat: 15g/33% (S:22% M:36% P:42%) Chol: 86mg Sodium: 98mg Potassium: 463mg Fiber: 5g A: 60% C: 18% E:24% B1:12% B2: 11% B3: 55% B6: 20% P: 25% Fe: 15% Mg: 13% Zn: 11% Cu: 10% Mn: 16% Se: 98% Cr: 27%
EXCHANGE: Lean Meat: 4¼ Bread: 1½ Veg: ½ Fat: 1

MICROWAVE METHOD: In a 2-quart microwave-safe casserole or bowl, cook the broth, onion, carrot, parsley, cinnamon, and cayenne, covered, on High (100% power) to boiling, about 2½ to 3 minutes. Add the chicken and cook covered on High until tender, about 12 to 14 minutes. Remove the chicken, cool, and continue as directed above.

Mulled Fresh Fruit with Hazelnuts

by Debbie Maugans

Serve this fruit dish in large bowls for breakfast or dessert. It has more body than stewed fruit, without the solidity of gelatin.

1 tablespoon arrowroot
1/2 teaspoon ground cinnamon
1/2 cup orange juice
1 1/2 pounds mixed fresh fruits: chopped apricots, peaches, or plums; whole berries, currants, or cherries
1 tablespoon honey
1 1/2 cups vanilla-flavored nonfat yogurt
1/2 cup finely chopped hazelnuts or Brazil nuts
3/4 cup uncooked rolled oats, toasted (see Note)

PREPARATION TIME: 25 minutes plus refrigerating time
COOKING TIME: 2 minutes
YIELD: 6 servings

In a saucepan, mix the arrowroot, cinnamon, and enough water to form a smooth paste. Stir in the orange juice and a bit more water until smooth. Add the fruit. Over medium heat, simmer, stirring gently, 2 minutes or just until the fruit is tender. Remove from heat and stir in the honey. Pour into a serving dish and refrigerate until thoroughly chilled. To serve, spoon the fruit into bowls, top with yogurt, and sprinkle with hazelnuts and oats.

NOTE: *To toast the oats,* spread them on a baking sheet and bake in a preheated 350° oven, stirring once or twice with a spatula until golden brown, about 10 minutes.

NUTRITION INFORMATION (per 1/2-cup serving):
Cal: 212 Pro: 7g/13% Carb: 32g/57% Fat: 7g/30% (S:10% M:75% P:15%) Chol: 1mg Sodium: 45mg Potassium: 503mg Fiber: 4g A: 16% C: 55% B1:14% B2: 13% Ca: 16% P: 19% Mg: 16% Cu: 13% Mn: 20%
EXCHANGE: Skim Milk: 1/2 Bread: 1/2 Fruit: 1 Fat: 1 1/2

◇ MUSHROOMS ◇

Mysteries of the Mushroom

by Andrew Weil, M.D.

Even people who like mushrooms are apt to write them off as an interesting garnish rather than a primary food. Our culture has downgraded mushrooms, and even feared them, for centuries.

In China and Japan, a very different attitude prevails. There, these fruits of the earth—mushrooms are the fruit bodies of underground fungal organisms—are highly esteemed as both foods and remedies. The symbol for Shoulau, the Chinese god of longevity, is a walking stick that branches out into mushroom finials.

The East has its wisdom. Today, scientists find that certain mushrooms may protect against tumors, while others are good for the heart. These magic medicinals include shiitake, enoki, wood ears, matsutake, and oyster mushrooms.

If mushrooms seem low in nutritional content, perhaps it's because they're so high in water and low in fat, carbohydrates, and calories (a fresh *pound* has only about 125 calories). But when they're dried, mushrooms have almost as much protein as veal, ounce for ounce. Cooking also removes moisture, concentrating the protein. Like beans, mushrooms are low in certain amino acids found in abundance in grains. A main dish of mushrooms and rice or pasta creates a balanced protein meal.

Both the common supermarket button mushroom and the oyster mushroom are good protein sources. So are enoki and straw mushrooms. High in fiber, mushrooms are also good sources of B vitamins, vitamin C, and potassium (see Food Profiles, page 338).

But fungi nutrition isn't all rosy. Tough mushroom cell walls are not easily broken down in the digestive tract, so the nutrients within may be unavailable to the body. Mushrooms also contain unusual chemical compounds that inhibit digestive enzymes, others that block absorption of proteins, and a number of natural toxins.

All these problems have a common solution: thorough cooking. Heat breaks down the cell walls and destroys antinutrients and toxins. Drying has a similar effect. No mushrooms should be eaten raw in quantity—even the familiar supermarket variety.

Pesticide residues, in fact, are a more worrisome problem with this most popular variety. Grown in the dark on composted manure, button mushrooms must compete with insect larvae. Commercial growers use chemical poisons to deter the flies. Many of these chemicals are intended for crops outdoors, where sunlight breaks them down. But mushrooms grown in the dark probably reach the market with significant residues of pesticides that can't be washed off.

Mushrooms Against Disease

In a Mushroom Research Institute of Japan study in 1986, scientists gave mice carcinogens, then added a mixture of several varieties of dried mushrooms to their feed. These included common button, shiitake, wood ear, enoki, oyster, and straw mushrooms. The result was that tumor growth was 40 to 50 percent lower than among mice fed no mushrooms.

A number of mushroom species have antiviral, antitumor properties, lab scientists find. The probable active ingredient—long chain sugars called polysaccharides. Unlike current antiviral and anticancer drugs, the mushrooms have no toxic effects in animals. Instead they appear to work by boosting the immune system.

Physicians in Japan have found lower-than-average cancer rates in a region where enoki are produced commercially. The difference may be that growers and their families eat this mushroom regularly.

Another species with a powerful antitumor effect is the Japanese wild matsutake or pine mushroom.

American mushroom hunters have learned to collect a close relative with the same haunting, spicy, resinous aroma—the American matsutake from the Pacific Northwest. Much cheaper and much more widely available, oyster mushrooms also have a similar antitumor effect.

Shiitakes, now cultivated throughout the United States, appear to stimulate production of the powerful natural immune substance interferon. The shiitake polysaccharide called lentinan also has "remarkable antitumor effects in mice," report scientists from Japan's National Cancer Center.

Another study reported that the "high level of activity in shiitakes in experimental animals was comparable to that of Amantadine," a powerful antiviral prescription drug with potentially serious side effects.

Shiitakes also contain eritadenine, which may lower blood cholesterol. In one human experiment, 30 healthy young women were given different amounts. One group that ate about 3 ounces of fresh shiitakes a day had 12 percent lower cholesterol after a week.

Mushrooms may even help counterbalance animal fats. In a second experiment, one group ate 2 ounces of butter daily for a week; another, 2 ounces of butter and 3 ounces of shiitake mushrooms. The butter eaters' cholesterol shot up 14 percent, but the butter-and-mushroom eaters' cholesterol actually fell 4 percent. The little wood ear fungus of Chinese cookery inhibits blood clotting, an effect discovered serendipitously in 1980 by a team of researchers in Minnesota. Regular eating of wood ears may be one factor contributing to the low incidence of heart attacks in China.

Mushrooming Opportunities

Americans are discovering the pleasures of once-exotic mushrooms, and that change should be good for us. One caution: The health benefits of mushrooms can be largely undone by serving them underneath blankets of butter, oil, cream, or high-fat cheese. Learn to appreciate their distinctive flavors and textures in other ways by adding them to soups, Oriental stir-fries, and simple but elegant grain dishes.

Cooking with Mushrooms

by Jane Merrill

The last become first, the low are brought high. Over the past fifteen years, the mushroom has sprouted into the chic, natural symbol of eating *haut* and light.

The Romans sought mushrooms, calling them *cibus deorum,* food of the gods, as many cookbooks attest. But that's a joke, according to *Laroussem of the Champignon.* Agrippina, wife of Emperor Claudius, the story goes, slipped her husband a poisonous toadstool in a dish of culinary mushrooms, thus assuring imperial succession to her son Nero. So many emperors were rendered divine by poisonous mushrooms, the deadly Nero later quipped, that they were *cibus deorum.*

Even without the extra spice of poison, however, exotic mushrooms have a heavenly taste.

Even common buttons, prepared right, can be reborn. Once served mostly in cream-based white sauces and as a garnish, mushrooms are now featured in recipes, as cooks take advantage of their diminutive calorie count.

"It's as though Americans were brought up monochromatically and now are discovering colors," says John Gottfried. A major East Coast purveyor of wild mushrooms, he traces his interest to a broth of matsutake mushrooms a Buddhist priest gave him in southern Japan in the 1970s. He now sells half a ton of fresh "esoterics" (everything except common buttons) a week. "Mushrooms grow all over the United States but regional differences affect quality," he says. "As a rule, the farther west you go the more flavor." The exception, he says, are Pacific and Northwest area mushrooms, "which are beautiful but less intense in flavor.

"Morels are like thick, crisp slices of London broil, chanterelles have a sweet perfume of apricots, and cèpes are woody and almost chocolatey, while matsutakes have a clear pine flavor. The shiitake is the sexiest mushroom," adds Gottfried. "When you grill it—cutting off the stem, lightly buttering the cap, and broiling until the gills are crisp—then bite in—it's like nibbling on an earlobe."

To Japanese cookbook author Sonoko Kondo, shiitakes "bring the message of fall. We go mushroom hunting in the fall on farms where they are cultured, and try to bring the taste of the season to the table with the mushrooms."

Shiitakes are the most popular of all mushrooms worldwide, with total sales estimated at a billion dollars a year. With domestic cultivation, the price of shiitakes is falling, so go ahead and form a taste!

Finding the Best

Some mushrooms lovers find it a thrill to forage for their fungi. "Looking for wild mushrooms," writes Sara Ann Friedman in her book *Celebrating the Wild Mushroom* "allows us to satisfy without dire consequences those childhood urges that we are encouraged to bury. It allows us to get dirty. It gratifies our urge to steal. Crawling furtively through the woods, guarding our secret places, we fulfill our primal, competitive, and territorial drives." To try your hand at foraging safely, contact your local mushroom club.

For nonforaging types, the good news is that exotic mushrooms are increasingly available at reasonable prices. Campbell Soup Company, for example, is now selling shiitake and oyster mushrooms at competitive prices in many markets.

Neither pickled nor canned varieties have much mushroom taste, experts agree. They may contain sulfites (now banned in fresh mushrooms), and canned varieties are high in sodium.

Using preserved mushrooms, however, isn't always a compromise, Guiliano Bugialli, a dean of Italian cookery, points out. In Italy, porcini—what the French call cèpes—are inexpensive, but here, where "the price seems to move up daily, I find the canned decent and also rely on the dried. Some sauces and meat stuffings *call* for the dried. The dried flavor is much stronger."

Dried mushrooms, with their intense flavor, are particularly suited to soups, stews, and long-simmered dishes. To reconstitute them, soak in warm water for 20 to 30 minutes. Remove mushrooms from liquid, then strain the liquid through a coffee filter. Add the mushrooms and the liquid to the dish being made.

Mixing Commons with Exotics

Stretching the pricey esoterics with fresh little buttons can be frugal and savvy. Bruce Marder, chef/owner of the West Beach Café in Venice, California, says of common buttons, "These mushrooms have lots of water. I cook them separately and add them to a dish. The only method to keep flavor in and not release the water is to cook them in small amounts on a very hot surface with a little oil." Get the pan "too hot," the chef recommends, then toss in mushrooms and oil together. "The hot pan lessens the absorption of the oil in cooking." Then discard the oil. Button mushrooms can also be delicious steamed.

According to top-notch Manhattan caterer Takis Petrakos, the best preparations of mushrooms don't "do" too much. "As with veal, too often the attempt is to make them taste strong. But as a natural, whole food, mushrooms deserve to be left alone now and again."

Spotlight: The Secret of Mushroom Flavors

Jack Czarnecki is the chef and owner of the only mushroom specialty restaurant in America—Joe's Restaurant, in Reading, Pennsylvania—and the author of *Joe's Book of Mushroom Cookery*. He dries his own mushrooms to concentrate their flavor. "Mushrooms must truly be freshly picked to be best," he maintains. "But drying properly concentrates the full flavor.

"When dried mushrooms are reconstituted in water or stock," he goes on, "the liquor that remains—and not the reconstituted mushroom itself—retains most of the character and flavor of the mushroom. Whatever flavor is left in the mushrooms can be utilized by pureeing them and adding the puree to the dish along with the extract. But the liquor is really the key to fabulous and surprisingly simple sauces.

"The best extracts, by far, come from cèpes (also called porcini) and morels. After these, in quality, are the extracts from black trumpet mushrooms, forest mushrooms, and shiitake. Bringing up the rear, as far as extracts go, are dried chanterelles and wood ears.

"To maximize the amount of color and flavor transferred from the dried mushrooms to the liquid, follow this technique: bring three cups of water and one to one-and-a-half ounces of dried mushrooms to a rapid boil. Then reduce the heat so that the liquid just simmers and cook it for 20 to 30 minutes. At this point, the liquid can be used for soups or for cooking meats, grains, or vegetables. But to make a richer extract for sauces or to store as a concentrated essence for seasoning other dishes, you should continue simmering the mushrooms until the liquid is reduced by about half.

"Mushroom extracts can be refrigerated for up to a week or kept frozen without loss of character for months. You can use them as you would meat or poultry stocks, and you can combine them with those stocks.

"I season the extracts with . . . salt, sugar, and soy sauce. Balanced use of these three ingredients gives the desired palate impression of full mushroom flavor. You can use as little of each one as you wish, but even a pinch each of salt and sugar and a dash of reduced-sodium soy sauce will underscore the mushroom essence.

"To turn an extract into a sauce, thicken it with arrowroot or cornstarch. Arrowroot is expensive but better because it yields a clear, elegant sauce, whereas cornstarch makes the sauce shiny but opaque. Stir either thickener into a small amount of cold water. Heat the mushroom extract to boiling. Add about 1 teaspoon of the thickening solution, stirring until the milky white of the thickener disappears. Repeat until you achieve the desired consistency."

— Nao Hauser

Stuffed Morels

by Pino Luongo

6 *small new potatoes*
1 *clove garlic, peeled and finely chopped*
1 to 2 *tablespoons finely chopped fresh parsley*
½ teaspoon salt
Freshly ground black pepper
4 *large morels, stems removed*

PREPARATION TIME: 30 minutes
COOKING TIME: 20 to 25 minutes
YIELD: 4 appetizers or first-course servings

Peel, boil, and puree the potatoes with a potato ricer, masher, or food mill. (They will be less liquid than mashed potatoes because you do not add milk.) Mix the potatoes with the garlic and parsley. Season with salt and pepper to taste.

Wash the mushrooms inside and out; pat dry with paper towels.

Fill each cap with the potato mixture using your fingers or the side of a knife. Be careful not to break the cups, stuffing them adequately but lightly.

Lay the morels flat on a baking sheet. Broil them until tender (test with a fork), about 5 to 6 minutes.

NUTRITION INFORMATION: Cal: 153 Pro: 4g/ 9% Carb: 36g/89% Fat: .3g/2% Chol: 0mg Sodium: 253mg Potassium: 672mg Fiber: 2g C: 25% B1: 12% B3: 17% B6: 24% Panto: 15% Cu: 21% Cr: 24%
EXCHANGE: Bread: 2

Grilled Shiitakes on Thyme Toast

by Lee Grimsbo

8 slices sourdough or Italian semolina bread
1 bunch fresh thyme
1/2 clove garlic, peeled and crushed
1/8 teaspoon salt
3 tablespoons olive oil
2/3 pound fresh shiitake mushrooms

PREPARATION TIME: 20 minutes
COOKING TIME: 8 minutes
YIELD: 8 appetizers or first-course servings

Remove the crust from the bread. Cut into slices 1/2 inch thick. Toast the bread.

Preheat oven to 400°F. Tear the thyme leaves off the stalk; mince, to yield about 6 teaspoons. Combine the thyme, garlic, salt, and all but 1 teaspoon of the olive oil. Spoon the mixture onto the toasted bread; spread immediately to distribute oil evenly.

Snip off the shiitakes' stems; discard or save for stock. Arrange the mushrooms in a single layer on a baking sheet. Brush the caps with the remaining olive oil. Bake in a preheated oven until softened, about 5 to 8 minutes. Let stand to cool slightly.

Arrange a few of the shiitakes, overlapping, caps up and gills down, on each piece of toast. Place under the broiler until lightly browned, about 5 minutes. Serve immediately.

NUTRITION INFORMATION: Cal: 141 Pro: 4g/ 12% Carb: 19g/54% Fat: 5g/34% (S:15% M:76% P:9%) Chol: 0mg Sodium: 187mg Potassium: 179mg Fiber: .9g B1: 18% B2: 19% B3: 13%
EXCHANGE: Bread: 1 Veg: 1 Fat: 1

Shiitake Mushroom Soup with Tofu

by Sonoko Kondo

4 dried shiitake mushrooms
1 teaspoon vegetable oil
1 teaspoon sesame oil
1 scallion, chopped
1 10-ounce cake firm tofu, cut into 1/2-inch cubes
4 ounces canned bamboo shoots
2 1/4 cups unsalted chicken broth or stock (see page 28)
1 teaspoon reduced-sodium soy sauce
    Dash of freshly ground black pepper

PREPARATION TIME: 15 minutes plus soaking time
COOKING TIME: 10 minutes
YIELD: 4 servings

Soak the mushrooms in warm water for 20 minutes to soften. Slice the mushrooms into thin strips, 2 inches long.

Heat the oil in a wok or skillet over medium heat, add the scallion, and sauté until fragrant, about 1 minute. Add tofu, shiitake mushrooms, bamboo shoots, chicken broth, and seasonings and bring to a boil. Before serving, remove surface film with a kitchen spoon or ladle.

NOTE: You may use the soaking liquid of the shiitake mushrooms in place of the chicken broth if you are a vegetarian.

NUTRITION INFORMATION: Cal: 102 Pro: 9g/ 34% Carb: 4g/15% Fat: 6g/51% (S:19% M:54% P:27%) Chol: 1mg Sodium: 118mg Potassium: 221mg Fiber: 3g B3: 13% P: 15% Fe: 11%
EXCHANGE: Med. Meat: 1 Veg: 1

MICROWAVE METHOD: Prepare the mushrooms as above. In a 2-quart microwave-safe casserole, cook the oil and scallion on High (100% power) until tender, about 1 1/2 to 2 minutes. Add the broth and the remaining ingredients. Cook covered on High to boiling, about 6 to 8 minutes; stir once. Let stand 5 minutes. Serve as directed above.

Pasta ai Funghi alla Chiantigiana (Pasta with Mushrooms, in the Style of Chianti)

by Giuliano Bugialli

    2 ounces dried porcini mushrooms (also called
        cèpes)
    1 medium red onion
    2 cloves garlic, peeled
   20 fresh flat-leaf Italian parsley sprigs, leaves
        only
    2 tablespoons olive oil
  1/2 cup dry Vinsanto or dry Marsala wine
    5 tablespoons tomato paste, no salt added
        Salt (optional)
        Freshly ground black pepper
        Coarse-grained salt
    1 pound dried spaghetti
    2 teaspoons unsalted butter

PREPARATION TIME: 35 minutes plus soaking
time
COOKING TIME: 1 1/2 hours
YIELD: 6 servings

Soak the mushrooms in lukewarm water for 30 minutes. Drain, reserving 2 cups water. Strain the sand out of the water by passing it through several layers of paper towels; set aside. Clean the mushrooms very well to remove all the sand attached to the stems. Finely chop the mushrooms, onion, garlic, and parsley all together on a board.

Heat the oil in a medium saucepan over medium heat, add the chopped vegetables, and sauté 15 minutes, stirring occasionally with a wooden spoon. Add the wine and let it evaporate for 5 minutes.

Meanwhile dissolve the tomato paste in the 2 cups strained mushroom water and add this liquid to the pan. Cover and cook over low heat for 1 hour, stirring occasionally with a wooden spoon. Season with salt and pepper to taste, raise heat, and reduce for 10 minutes more.

Meanwhile, bring a large pot of cold water to a boil, add coarse-grained salt to taste, and the pasta. Cook from 8 to 11 minutes, depending on brand. Drain the spaghetti, put into a large bowl

with the butter, mix well, then transfer to a large skillet together with the sauce and sauté over high heat for 1 minute more. Place on a warmed serving dish and serve immediately.

NUTRITION INFORMATION: Cal: 304 Pro: 10g/ 12% Carb: 52g/67% Fat: 7g/21% (S:26% M:65% P:9%) Chol: 4mg Sodium: 115mg Potassium: 361mg Fiber: 2g C: 15% E: 13% B1: 22% B2: 16% B3: 17% P: 14% Fe: 14% Se: 141% EXCHANGE: Bread: 3 Veg: 1 Fat: 1 1/4

Enoki and Cucumber Salad

by Nao Hauser

    1 large or 2 small cucumbers
    2 teaspoons rice wine vinegar
    2 teaspoons minced fresh ginger
    1 clove garlic, peeled and pressed
        (optional)
  1/2 teaspoon sugar
  1/2 teaspoon reduced-sodium soy sauce
    1 small head red leaf lettuce, torn
    1 3.5-ounce package enoki, trimmed
  1/2 cup raw fresh or thawed frozen baby
        peas
 4 to 6 radishes, shredded fine
    1 tablespoon vegetable oil
    2 teaspoons fresh lemon juice
        Freshly ground black pepper

PREPARATION TIME: 25 minutes
YIELD: 5 servings

Peel and seed the cucumber and thinly slice it.

Mix the vinegar, ginger, garlic (if used), sugar, and soy sauce together in a small bowl; add the cucumber and toss to coat. Let stand while preparing the rest of the ingredients.

Combine the lettuce, enoki, peas, and radishes in a salad bowl. Toss with the oil, lemon juice, and black pepper to taste. Add the cucumbers; toss again.

NUTRITION INFORMATION: Cal: 62 Pro: 2g/ 14% Carb: 8g/44% Fat: 3g/42% (S:14% M:24%

P:62%) Chol: 0mg Sodium: 38mg Potassium: 352mg Fiber: 3g A: 11% C: 20% E: 15% Folic: 14% Cr: 24%
  EXCHANGE: Veg: 1 Fat: ½

Chicken Provençal with Wood Ear Mushrooms
by John Major

6 dried wood ear mushrooms
2 tablespoons olive oil
1 frying chicken, cut up and skin and bones removed
2 medium onions, halved and thinly sliced
1 pound plum tomatoes, peeled and seeded
  Green tops of 2 stalks celery, finely chopped
1 bay leaf
½ teaspoon dried thyme
½ teaspoon dried oregano
½ teaspoon dried marjoram
½ cup unsalted chicken broth or stock (see page 28)
  Salt (optional)
  Freshly ground black pepper
½ pound green beans, cut into 1-inch pieces
10 black olives, pitted and cut into pieces
4 cups hot cooked rice

PREPARATION TIME: 30 minutes
COOKING TIME: 1 hour
YIELD: 4 servings

Soak the mushrooms in warm water for 20 minutes. Remove and discard the stems, slice tops into thin julienne strips. Set aside.

In a heavy, deep skillet, heat the olive oil. Over medium heat, cook the chicken and onions until golden. Add all the remaining ingredients except the salt, pepper, green beans, olives, and rice; simmer for 40 minutes, covered. Season to taste with salt and pepper. Add the green beans and olives and continue cooking over low heat until the beans are tender-crisp, about 5 minutes more. Discard the bay leaf. Serve over rice.

NOTE: If fresh wood ear mushrooms are available, substitute an equal number of them for the

dried. If they are more than three inches in diameter, use only 3 or 4. Omit soaking.

NUTRITION INFORMATION: Cal: 542 Pro: 32g/ 23% Carb: 67g/49% Fat: 17g/28% (S:35% M:53% P:12%) Chol: 30mg Sodium: 168mg Potassium: 935mg Fiber: 7g A: 39% C: 57% E: 16% B1: 30% B2: 24% B3: 59% B6: 85% Folic: 17% Panto: 36% Ca: 11% P: 35% Fe: 33% Mg: 14% Zn: 17% Cu: 25% Mn: 78% Se: 57% Cr: 72%
  EXCHANGE: Lean Meat: 3 Bread: 3 Veg: 3 Fat: 1½

Steamed Chicken with Shimeji Mushrooms
by Sonoko Kondo

½ teaspoon salt
1 pound boneless chicken breasts, skin removed
2 tablespoons sake
1 teaspoon reduced-sodium soy sauce
4 ounces oyster mushrooms
2 tablespoons grated fresh ginger root
1 lemon wedge
  Reduced-sodium soy sauce

PREPARATION TIME: 10 minutes plus standing time
COOKING TIME: 25 minutes
YIELD: 4 servings

Rub salt over the chicken breasts and put them in a soup bowl in a single layer. Sprinkle sake over the chicken.

Cook the chicken in the bowl in a steamer over high heat for 15 minutes, or until chicken is thoroughly cooked. Remove the chicken, pour off the broth, and reserve it to cook the mushrooms in.

Let the chicken stand for 15 minutes and then slice into ¼-inch pieces.

Transfer the chicken broth to a small saucepan and season with the soy sauce. Add ½ cup of water; heat to simmering. Add the mushrooms;

simmer 2 to 3 minutes or until tender. Serve the mushrooms with the chicken.

Serve the grated ginger, lemon wedge, and soy sauce as condiments on the side.

NUTRITION INFORMATION: Cal: 184 Pro: 33g/ 75% Carb: 3g/6% Fat: 4g/19% (S:33% M:41% P:25%) Chol: 87mg Sodium: 368mg Potassium: 391mg Fiber: .4g B1: 11% B2: 23% B3: 77% B6: 30% P: 27% Se: 29% Cr: 16%
EXCHANGE: Lean Meat: 4 Veg: ½

MICROWAVE METHOD: Prepare the chicken as above in an 8-inch square microwave-safe baking dish. Cook tightly covered on High (100% power) until tender and cooked, about 6 to 8 minutes; turn the chicken over and rotate dish halfway through. Remove; let stand 15 minutes, then slice into ¼-inch pieces. To the chicken broth add the soy sauce, only ¼ cup of water and the mushrooms. Cook covered on High until mushrooms are tender, about 2 to 3½ minutes. Serve as above.

Pork with Red Peppers and Morels

by Jack Czarnecki

1½ ounces dried morels (shiitake or cèpes—also called porcini—mushrooms can also be used)
1¼ pounds pork butt or tenderloin, fat trimmed
2 large red bell peppers
¼ teaspoon salt
¼ teaspoon sugar
1 teaspoon reduced-sodium soy sauce
1 tablespoon cream sherry
Salt (optional)

1½ tablespoons arrowroot or cornstarch mixed with ¼ cup water
2 cups hot cooked rice

PREPARATION TIME: 20 minutes
COOKING TIME: 1 hour 10 minutes
YIELD: 4 servings

In a large saucepan, bring 3 cups of water and the mushrooms to a boil; simmer uncovered for 30 minutes.

Cut the pork into 1-inch squares. Chop the peppers into 1-inch squares. Add the pork and peppers and the rest of the ingredients except the arrowroot and rice to the saucepan, bring to a rapid boil, reduce heat, and let simmer for another 30 minutes. Season to taste with salt. There should be about 2 cups of liquid.

Heat the stew to boiling. Stir in the arrowroot or cornstarch mixed with water until the milky color disappears and the mixture thickens. Serve on a bed of rice.

NUTRITION INFORMATION (without rice): Cal: 253 Pro: 40g/65% Carb: 6g/10% Fat: 7g/25% (S:36% M:48% P:16%) Chol: 126mg Sodium: 258mg Potassium: 883mg Fiber: 1g C: 103% B1: 88% B2: 37% B3: 37% B6: 32% B12: 13% Panto: 14% P: 42% Fe: 16% Zn: 28% Se: 57%
EXCHANGE: Lean Meat: 5 Veg: 1

MICROWAVE METHOD: In a 2-quart microwave-safe casserole or bowl, cook only 2½ cups water and morels covered on High (100% power) 10 minutes. Reduce power to Medium (50% power); cook covered 10 minutes more. Add all the remaining ingredients except the arrowroot or cornstarch. Cook covered on Medium until meat is tender, about 18 to 22 minutes. Stir in the thickening mixture. Cook covered on High until thickened, about 2 minutes.

◊ SQUASH ◊

Squash: The Colors, of Health

by Marci Fiacci and Robert Barnett

Squash was a gift from the New World to the Old—the name comes from the language of the Narragansett Indians. The earthy fruit of gourd plants, squash has a sweet, rich taste that's hearty enough to anchor a main dish—meaty or meatless.

An acorn squash, halved and baked and topped with nutmeg, offers reason enough for our devotion to squash. The glistening puree of butternut, warmed with naturally low-fat buttermilk into soup, speaks for itself. In a vegetarian dinner, winter squash can become a centerpiece.

Winter squash is low in fat and sodium, rich in potassium, a moderately good source of vitamin C, and an excellent source of carotenoids, the pigments that give it color. Carotenoids serve as essential building blocks for vitamin A and may also independently protect against potentially carcinogenic cell damage. A half cup of cooked summer squash provides only 4 percent of the USRDA for vitamin A, but winter varieties have as much as 156 percent in a half cup. That serving has only about 40 calories.

There are hundreds of different carotenoids that give squash its bright colors. Until recently, nutritionists didn't distinguish between these plant precursors of vitamin A and the preformed type found in dairy foods. Now many believe carotenoids themselves may be essential. What new essential anticancer or heart-healthy "nutrients" will they discover tomorrow? It may not really matter: If you eat a balanced diet of whole foods, you're probably already getting them—a good illustration of the principle that health protection comes from an emphasis on whole foods, not individual nutrients.

Only about 50 of the 500 different carotenoids, notably beta-carotene, get converted in our bodies into vitamin A. But many unconverted carotenoids are strong antioxidants; vitamin A is not. Antioxidants protect us against the damage that highly reactive free radical molecules can do. These free radicals, implicated in many chronic diseases, are created by natural metabolic processes, but also by dietary toxins such as rancid fat, environmental ones such as pollution, personal habits such as smoking, and conditions such as infectious illness. Unchecked, free radicals can attack cells or DNA, causing damage that may eventually, many years later, lead to cancer.

Antioxidant chemicals, like the carotenoids—including alpha-carotene, beta-carotene, lycopene, and beta-cryptoxanthen—put up a natural defense against free radicals. Of ten studies conducted by the National Cancer Institute between 1977 and 1989, all showed that cancer risk was less likely (up to 50 percent less likely for lung cancer) in people who took in more carotenoid-

154

rich foods such as green and yellow vegetables. Eating dark-green leafy vegetables and yellow ones such as squash is also associated with lower rates of cancers of the mouth, larynx, esophagus, stomach, bladder, and cervix. (Increasing evidence supports the hypothesis that dietary antioxidants may also help protect against heart disease, by slowing the creation of oxidized blood cholesterol, which forms artery-clogging plaque.)

But preformed vitamin A, found in animal products like milk, appears to have very little antioxidant power. In one study in a region of France known for high alcohol consumption and high rates of esophageal cancer, for example, a dietary study found a protective effect associated with dietary carotenoids, but no clear effect associated with vitamin A.

"When the intake of foods rich in carotenoids is estimated separately from those containing preformed vitamin A, the former, but usually not the latter, is associated with a protective effect," says nutrition professor James Olson of Iowa State University in Ames. Advises Ritva Butrum, acting chief of the National Cancer Institute's diet and cancer branch, "The public's safest and most effective way of reducing cancer risk is, among other things, to eat a balanced diet including foods rich in natural carotenoids."

Winter squash and pumpkins are especially rich sources of carotenoids. Summer squash, including zucchini, yellow crookneck, pattypan, and chayote, aren't nearly as rich in carotenoids as are winter varieties such as acorn, although some varieties do have some quercetin, another cancer-protective antioxidant. Cucumber, another member of the squash family, has hardly any, as could be guessed from its pale flesh. But cucumbers do have some potassium and small amounts of vitamin C, folic acid, and fiber. Eggplant is from a different botanical family but is nutritionally similar to summer squash.

Try summer squashes and eggplants lightly steamed in a salad—cooking breaks down fiber, so the less you cook them, the more fiber they'll keep. Indeed, to preserve water-soluble nutrients such as vitamin C, potassium, and folic acid, cook all squash, summer or winter, in a minimum of water and not too long. Carotenoids are fat-soluble, so they won't dissolve in water, though you can lose some in butter or oil or by heating the vegetable in the presence of vinegar or citrus fruits, if you discard the cooking liquid.

Cooking Squash

by Ceri Hadda and Nao Hauser

Summer squash, light in taste and calories, is extremely versatile—as any gardener overwhelmed by a harvest soon learns! The three most common varieties are zucchini, yellow squash (straight or crookneck), and pattypan (also called cymling). All taste best if harvested before they become too large, water-laden, and thick-skinned. None needs paring or much preparation at all: Just rinse, slice off the stem end, and cut the squash any way you wish. Sliced thin or julienne-cut, zucchini and yellow squash can be served raw as crudités or in salads. The tiniest pattypan squash, disc-shaped and scallop-edged, make novel canapés when hollowed slightly at the stem end to hold a dab of dip or a tiny marinated shrimp.

Steaming is the simplest cooking method for summer squash. Squash contains so much water that if sliced, diced, or cut into strips, it will steam in its own juice in a tightly covered pan over medium heat (or in the microwave oven; cover with plastic wrap and cook at High for 4–5 minutes per pound); coat the pan lightly with olive oil or sauté an onion in oil and then place the squash over it to prevent scorching. Cooks whose backyard gardens are overrun simultaneously by squash and basil appreciate the taste affinity between the two; tarragon, parsley, summer savory, and dill also go well with the steamed vegetable.

It takes more time to steam whole summer squash in a steamer or bake it in the oven, but the process does yield more intense flavor. For summer ease and great taste, halve or slice squash lengthwise, brush cut sides with a mixture of balsamic vinegar and olive oil, and bake in a covered grill. If you can't keep up with your own zucchini or yellow summer squash harvest, cut up the surplus, simmer it in vegetable or chicken broth, and puree—you'll have a soup base to stow in the freezer, ready to thin to desired consistency and season in any of a variety of ways whenever you're ready to serve it.

Eggplant is a slightly different matter. Salting and draining purges the eggplant of bitter juices, but this procedure is not necessary for baby eggplants, which are sweeter. Cut the mature vegetable into slices or cubes, sprinkle with salt, set in a colander inside a bowl, and put a plate on top to weight it down. Let sit an hour. Drain, rinse, and pat dry with a paper towel. Once "purged," eggplants have nearly infinite uses. Broil them brushed lightly with olive oil, and season with salt, pepper, and lemon juice. Endless recipes marry the meaty taste of eggplant with tomatoes, onions, garlic, and herbs. Cook them thoroughly with zucchini, tomatoes, onions, and garlic for a classic ratatouille. Or broil an eggplant, then combine in a food processor with a little tahini dressing, lemon juice, olive oil, and garlic for a Middle Eastern baba ghannoush.

Winter squash, rich and sweet, brings brilliant color to late-fall and winter tables. The most common varieties are acorn, butternut, hubbard, pumpkin, and spaghetti squash. All can be baked whole (be sure to pierce rind with a knife tip in several places), halved, or quartered in a 375°F oven, on a baking sheet to catch juices, until tender enough to pierce easily with a fork (about 45 minutes for small squash and twice as long for large ones). To microwave, place pierced whole squash on paper toweling or halves or pieces in a baking dish covered with plastic wrap, and cook at High for 6 to 8 minutes per pound; let stand 5 minutes. Any of the squash can then be served as a side dish with seasoned, plain, or fruit yogurt, or a little bit of butter. But the most popular winter squash also have distinctive identities that can be flattered in these separate ways:

♦ *Acorn.* Pick-of-the-crop acorn squash is so meaty and sweet that you can't do much to improve on it—ground pepper and nutmeg or allspice and a small dab of yogurt suffice for seasoning. Acorn squash make attractive cook-and-serve containers for main or side dishes: You can fill the halves with cooked green vegetables, rice, bulgur, or barley, with or without some ground meat, and the sweetness of the squash will enhance everything else.

But not all acorn squash is created equal; as the season wanes, some samplings are not very sweet. Help them along by serving them with warm applesauce or a chopped pear briefly sautéed in a teaspoon of butter and sprinkled with cinnamon.

♦ *Butternut.* Butternut is the most versatile winter squash. Pare it, cut it into strips, and braise it in a small amount of chicken broth, with some chopped parsley, for an attractive side dish. Remove the thin rind with a vegetable parer; if the rind is very tough, piece the whole squash and microwave it at High for 2 minutes to make the rind easier to remove, or cut the squash into sections and use a paring knife to cut away the rind.

The long, beige-skinned butternut squash yields a delicious satiny puree. You can bake the whole squash, scoop out and discard the seeds, and mash the flesh with fruit juice, milk or yogurt, and spices to make the puree. Or you can pare the squash, discard the seeds, and cut up the flesh and simmer it with chopped pears or apples (which will usually give off enough juice for simmering) until soft; mash the squash and fruit together and season with cinnamon, nutmeg, or grated ginger root. If you simmer the squash in water or broth and then puree it, you'll have an elegant soup base. The puree is also excellent when blended with other cooked purees, such as potato or turnip. Hubbard squash, if bought by the piece and cut up, can be prepared the same way.

♦ *Spaghetti.* The surprise inside baked spaghetti squash is flesh that separates into noodlelike strands when fluffed with a fork. The delicately flavored strands, less sweet than butternut or acorn squash, hold their own with tomato, cheese, herb, and other not-too-heavy spaghetti sauces.

Butternut Squash Bisque
by Ceri Hadda

2 cups chopped yellow onions
1 green apple, peeled, cored, and chopped
2 tablespoons corn oil

1 butternut squash (about 2¹/₂ pounds),
   pared, seeded, and chopped
2 large plum tomatoes, cored and chopped
5 cups unsalted chicken broth or stock (see
   page 28)
   Juice of 2 oranges
1 cinnamon stick
1¹/₂ cups low-fat buttermilk
¹/₂ cup raw long-grain rice

PREPARATION TIME: 40 minutes
COOKING TIME: 1 hour 20 minutes
YIELD: 8 main-course servings, or 12 first-course
   servings

Sauté the onions and apple in the corn oil in a
large saucepan over moderate heat 3 minutes.
Add the chopped squash and tomatoes; sauté 1
minute longer. Cover the saucepan, lower the
heat, and sweat 15 minutes. Uncover the saucepan; add two thirds of the broth, the orange juice,
and the cinnamon stick. Bring to a boil over moderate heat, lower the heat, cover, and simmer 30
minutes, or until the squash is very tender.

Cool, remove the cinnamon stick, and puree in
batches in a food processor or blender. Return
the mixture to the saucepan and add the remaining broth and the buttermilk. Bring to a boil over
moderate heat. Stir in the rice, cover, lower the
heat, and simmer 15 to 20 minutes, or until the
rice is soft but not mushy.

NOTE: If you make the bisque in advance, don't
add the rice until 20 minutes before you're ready
to serve, or it will absorb all the bisque.

NUTRITION INFORMATION: **as first course** Cal:
136 Pro: 5g/14% Carb: 23g/65% Fat: 3g/21%
(S:21% M:30% P:49%) Chol: 2mg Sodium:
59mg Potassium: 483mg Fiber: 2g A: 106%
C: 43% E: 11% B3: 13% B6: 15%
EXCHANGE: Bread: 1¹/₄ Veg: ¹/₂ Fat: ¹/₂

   as main course Cal: 205 Pro: 7g/14% Carb:
35g/65% Fat: 5g/21% (S:21% M:29% P:50%)
Chol: 2mg Sodium: 90mg Potassium: 740mg
Fiber: 4g A: 166% C: 66% E: 17% B1: 14%
B3: 20% B6: 23% Folic: 13% Ca: 13% P: 15%
Mg: 14% Mn: 20%
EXCHANGE: Skim Milk: ¹/₄ Bread: 1³/₄ Veg: ³/₄
Fat: ³/₄

MICROWAVE METHOD: In a 5-quart microwave-
safe casserole, cook the onion, apple, and only 2
teaspoons of the oil on High (100% power) until
tender, about 4 to 6 minutes. Add the squash and
tomatoes. Cook covered on High 1 minute. Reduce to Medium (50% power); cook 7 minutes
more. Add two thirds of the broth and the orange
juice and cinnamon stick. Cook covered on High
until the squash is tender, about 16 to 18 minutes;
stir once. Cool, puree in batches, and return to
the casserole. Add the remaining broth and the
buttermilk. Cook covered on High until just boiling (time depends on how long it has cooled). Add
the rice; stir. Cook covered on Medium until rice
is tender but not mushy, about 10 to 15 minutes.
Let stand 5 minutes.

Apple-Stuffed Acorn Squash
by Ceri Hadda

Small acorn squash halves are ideal containers
for other vegetable side dishes; larger ones can
be used to hold entrées such as stew.

1 small acorn squash (¹/₂ to ³/₄ pound)
¹/₂ tablespoon unsalted butter
1 tart apple, peeled, cored, and sliced
1 tablespoon chopped pecans or walnuts
1 tablespoon raisins
¹/₃ cup natural apple juice
¹/₂ teaspoon ground cinnamon

PREPARATION TIME: 15 minutes
COOKING TIME: 1 hour
YIELD: 2 servings

Preheat the oven to 375°F. Halve the squash
but do not clean it out; place the squash halves,
cut side down, in a baking pan; add ¹/₂ inch of
water; cover the pan. Bake 35 to 45 minutes, or
until tender. Meanwhile, in a nonstick skillet over
moderate heat, melt the butter. Add the apple
slices; sauté about 5 minutes, stirring frequently,
until soft. Add the nuts; sauté 1 minute. Add the
raisins and apple juice and simmer until the juice
thickens slightly, about 3 minutes. Stir in the cinnamon.

Let the squash stand until cool enough to handle; remove the seeds and fiber. Scoop out the flesh into a small bowl, leaving a 1/4-inch shell. Reserve about 1/4 cup of the apple mixture. Add the rest of the apple mixture to the squash; mix well. Stuff the squash shells with the mixture; top with the reserved apple mixture. Return the stuffed squash halves to the oven for about 10 to 15 minutes. Or cover, refrigerate, and reheat at serving time.

NUTRITION INFORMATION: Cal: 169 Pro: 3g/6% Carb: 36g/76% Fat: 4g/18% (S:26% M:25% P:49%) Chol: 3mg Sodium: 8mg Potassium: 743mg Fiber: 5g A: 13% C: 25% B1: 17% B6: 16% Mg: 17%
EXCHANGE: Bread: 1 1/2 Fruit: 1 Fat: 1

MICROWAVE METHOD: In a 12- by 8-inch microwave-safe casserole, cook the squash halves and 2 tablespoons water covered on High (100% power) until tender, about 5 to 7 minutes. Let stand. Meanwhile, in a 1-quart microwave-safe casserole, cook the butter on High until melted, about 20 to 30 seconds. Add the apples, nuts, raisins, and only 2 tablespoons of the apple juice. Cook covered on High until apple is tender, about 3 to 5 minutes. Stir in the cinnamon. Remove the seeds from the squash and stuff as directed above. Place the stuffed squash in the casserole, cover with wax paper, and microwave at High until hot, about 2 minutes.

Spaghetti Squash with Pepper Sauce

by Ceri Hadda

Although sweeter than pasta, spaghetti squash can be used in almost any recipe calling for spaghetti.

1 spaghetti squash (about 3 pounds), halved lengthwise
2 teaspoons olive oil
1 large onion, cubed
2 cloves garlic, peeled and minced
1 pound red bell peppers, cubed

1/2 cup unsalted chicken broth or stock (see page 28)
1/2 teaspoon dried oregano, crumbled
1/2 teaspoon dried basil, crumbled
1/8 teaspoon red pepper flakes
1/2 cup shredded part-skim mozzarella cheese
1/2 cup part-skim ricotta cheese
Freshly ground black pepper (optional)

PREPARATION TIME: 30 minutes
COOKING TIME: 45 minutes
YIELD: 4 servings

Preheat the oven to 375°F. Place the spaghetti squash, cut side down, in a 9- by 13-inch baking pan. Add 1/2 inch water; cover the pan. Bake in the preheated oven 45 minutes, or until tender.

Meanwhile, heat the oil in a large nonstick skillet. Add the onion and garlic; sauté 5 minutes. Add the pepper cubes; sauté 5 minutes. Add the chicken broth, oregano, basil, and pepper flakes. Bring to a boil, lower the heat, and simmer 10 minutes, or until the pepper cubes are tender. Transfer the mixture to a food processor; cover and process with the metal blade with pulses until the mixture forms a chunky sauce. Return to the skillet; keep warm over low heat.

Discard the seeds and fiber from the squash. Fluff the spaghetti-like strands with a fork and divide among four heated plates. Spoon the pepper sauce over each portion, then add a sprinkling of mozzarella and a dollop of ricotta to each. Season with ground black pepper if desired.

NUTRITION INFORMATION: Cal: 200 Pro: 12g/21% Carb: 23g/43% Fat: 9g/36% (S:46% M:41 P:13%) Chol: 18mg Sodium: 121mg Potassium: 885mg Fiber: 8g A: 31% C: 243% B1: 15% B2: 16% B3: 12% B6: 21% Folic: 20% Ca: 28% P: 27% Fe: 14% Mg: 25% Zn: 15% Cu: 22% Mn: 23% Cr: 24%
EXCHANGE: Med. Meat: 1 1/4 Bread: 1 Veg: 1 1/2 Fat: 1/2

MICROWAVE METHOD: In a 2 1/3- to 3-quart microwave-safe baking dish, cook the squash and 1/4 cup water tightly covered on High (100% power) until tender, about 13 to 18 minutes. Let stand. In a 1-quart microwave-safe casserole, cook the oil, onion, and garlic on High until tender, about 3 to 4 minutes. Add the bell peppers, only

¼ cup of the broth, and the oregano, basil, and pepper flakes. Cook covered on High until the pepper is tender, about 4 to 6 minutes. Process in a food processor as directed and continue as above.

Tian of Zucchini and Tomatoes
by Ceri Hadda

A traditional method of baking vegetables from the Provence region of France. This recipe reduces the olive oil traditionally used by extending it with white wine and fresh lemon juice.

    1 pound small zucchini (about 3)
    2 ripe plum tomatoes
    2 cloves garlic, minced
    2 tablespoons dry white wine
    1 tablespoon olive oil
    1 tablespoon fresh lemon juice
¹/₁₆ to ⅛ teaspoon cayenne
    ¼ teaspoon dried thyme, crushed
    1 tablespoon minced fresh basil
    1 tablespoon minced fresh flat-leaf
      parsley

PREPARATION TIME: 20 minutes
COOKING TIME: 1 hour
YIELD: 4 servings

Preheat the oven to 350°F. Slice the zucchini ⅓ inch thick. Cut the tomatoes in half lengthwise and slice ⅓ inch thick. Arrange the zucchini and tomato slices in rows in a 9-inch square ungreased baking dish; sprinkle with the garlic.

Combine the wine, olive oil, lemon juice, cayenne, and thyme in a small bowl; drizzle over the vegetables. Cover the dish with aluminum foil and bake 30 minutes. Uncover and baste the vegetables with the liquid in the dish. Sprinkle with the fresh herbs and continue baking 30 minutes longer, basting once or twice, until the zucchini is tender but not overbaked.

NOTE: Yellow summer squash may be substituted for all or part of the zucchini in this recipe.

NUTRITION INFORMATION: Cal: 75   Pro: 2g/ 9%   Carb: 11g/51%   Fat: 4g/40%   (S:13%   M:79% P:8%)   Chol: 0mg   Sodium: 13mg   Potassium: 551mg   Fiber: 4g   A: 32%   C: 46%   Cr: 16%
EXCHANGE: Veg: 1¼   Fat: ¾

Butternut Squash Soufflé
by Ceri Hadda

    2 small butternut squash (about 1 pound
      each), halved lengthwise
    2 tablespoons orange juice
    2 tablespoons low-fat milk
2½ tablespoons reduced-sugar orange
      marmalade
    2 egg whites
    2 teaspoons toasted wheat germ

PREPARATION TIME: 25 minutes
COOKING TIME: 1 hour
YIELD: 4 servings

Preheat the oven to 375°F. Place the squash, cut side down, in a roasting pan. Fill the pan with ½ inch of water and bake 30 minutes. Turn cut sides up and bake 15 minutes longer, or until the flesh is very soft. Let cool until handleable. Increase the oven heat to 400°F.

Carefully scoop out the flesh from the squash skins, leaving a ¼-inch shell. Place the flesh in a food processor fitted with the metal blade. Add the orange juice, milk, and marmalade, cover, and process on high speed until smooth. Transfer the squash puree to a medium bowl.

Beat egg whites in a small bowl with an electric mixer at high speed until stiff, but not dry. Quickly but thoroughly fold the egg whites into the puree. Spoon the puree into the squash skins, dividing evenly. Place squash on baking sheet. Sprinkle ½ teaspoon wheat germ over each portion and bake for 15 minutes, or until soufflés are risen and golden on top.

NOTE: The soufflé mixture can also be baked in individual ramekins or a 1-quart soufflé dish.

NUTRITION INFORMATION: Cal: 103   Pro: 4g/14% Carb: 24g/83%   Fat: .4g/3%   Chol: 1mg   Sodium:

45mg Potassium: 545mg Fiber: 3g A: 239%
C: 49% B6: 11% Folic: 11% Mg: 14%
Mo: 14%
    EXCHANGE: Bread: 1½

MICROWAVE METHOD: In a 2½- to 3-quart shallow microwave-safe casserole, place the squash cut side up. Cook tightly covered on High (100% power) until soft, about 10 to 12 minutes. Cool and continue as directed above.

Chayote Latkes
by Ceri Hadda

Chayote, sweet and apple-like when raw, takes on a potato-like flavor when cooked, so it's a logical choice to replace potatoes in latkes—traditional potato pancakes. Serve the latkes with plain yogurt or a tomato sauce.

>   2 chayotes
>   1 small onion, grated
>   3 eggs, lightly beaten, or 2 eggs plus two
>   egg whites
>   1 tablespoon snipped fresh dill (optional)
> ½ to ¾ cup dry breadcrumbs
>   Salt (optional)
>   Freshly ground black pepper
>   1 teaspoon vegetable oil

PREPARATION TIME: 20 minutes
COOKING TIME: 30 minutes
YIELD: 4 servings (about 20 latkes)

Peel, halve, pit, and shred the chayotes. Squeeze or press the shredded chayote on a strainer to remove the excess moisture. Combine the chayote, onion, eggs, and dill in a large bowl until well blended. Add ½ cup breadcrumbs, or more if needed for batter consistency, and salt and pepper to taste.

Brush a large nonstick skillet with a light coating of oil and place over moderately high heat. When the skillet is hot, drop in batter by the tablespoon, flattening slightly with the back of a spoon. Stir batter each time before using.

Sauté the latkes 2 to 3 minutes, or until golden brown; turn and sauté the second side. Remove to a heated platter; keep warm while cooking the remaining latkes.

NUTRITION INFORMATION: Cal: 191 Pro: 8g/16% Carb: 28g/56% Fat: 6g/28% (S:32% M:40% P:28%) Chol: 160mg Sodium: 156mg Potassium: 342mg Fiber: 2g C: 76% B1: 11% B2: 13% B12: 10% P: 15% Fe: 14%
    EXCHANGE: Med. Meat: ¾ Bread: 1 Veg: 2 Fat: ¼

Stir-Fried Shrimp and Pattypan Squash
by Ceri Hadda

This summer squash turns a delicate green when cooked.

>   1 pound shrimp, shelled and deveined
>   1 tablespoon dry white wine
>   1 quarter-size slice fresh ginger, pared and
>   minced
>   2 cloves garlic, peeled and minced
>   4 scallions
>   2 pattypan squash (about 1 pound)
> ¾ cup unsalted chicken broth or stock (see
>   page 28)
>   1 tablespoon red wine vinegar
>   1 tablespoon cornstarch
>   1 teaspoon sesame oil
>   1 teaspoon reduced-sodium soy sauce
> ½ teaspoon chili oil
>   2 tablespoons peanut oil
> ½ pound fresh mushrooms, sliced
>   4 cups hot cooked brown rice

PREPARATION TIME: 30 minutes plus marinating time and time to prepare shrimp
COOKING TIME: 20 minutes
YIELD: 4 servings

Combine the shrimp, wine, ginger, and garlic in a medium bowl: toss to blend. Cover and let stand at room temperature 1 hour, stirring occasionally, or refrigerate overnight.

Trim the scallions so that 2 inches of green are left on; then slice. Set aside. Quarter and trim the squash and slice ⅓ inch thick.

Steam the squash slices 3 minutes, or just until barely cooked. Refresh in cold water; drain well. Combine the chicken broth, vinegar, cornstarch, sesame oil, soy sauce, and chili oil in a cup; set aside.

At serving time, heat 1 tablespoon of the peanut oil in a wok over moderately high heat. Stir-fry the shrimp with their liquid 3 to 5 minutes, or until almost cooked. Remove and reserve. Add the remaining 1 tablespoon peanut oil to the wok. Stir-fry the squash, mushrooms, and scallions 1 minute, or until coated. Add the broth mixture; cover. Simmer 5 to 10 minutes, or until the squash is almost tender. Uncover, return the shrimp to the wok, and cook, tossing constantly, until the squash and shrimp are heated through. Serve over the rice.

NOTE: Zucchini or yellow summer squash can be substituted for the pattypan squash; it is not necessary to steam these squash.

NUTRITION INFORMATION: Cal: 434 Pro: 22g/ 20% Carb: 62g/57% Fat: 11g/23% (S:17% M:45% P:38%) Chol: 94mg Sodium: 179mg Potassium: 795mg Fiber: 7g A: 12% C: 19% E: 33% B1: 19% B2: 18% B3: 45% Panto: 14% Ca: 11% P: 23% Fe: 22% Mg: 17% Cu: 21% Se: 114% EXCHANGE: Lean Meat: 1½ Bread: 3¼ Veg: 1¾ Fat: 1¼

Autumn Beef Stew

by Ceri Hadda

Serve this hearty dish with rice.

¾ *pound lean stewing beef, cut into 1½-inch*
    cubes
1 *cup red wine*
1 *tablespoon ground cumin*
¼ *teaspoon cracked pepper*
2 *cloves garlic, peeled and crushed but left*
    whole
1 *teaspoon grated orange rind*
    Vegetable cooking spray

1 *teaspoon olive oil*
1 *large onion, diced*
1 *cup tomato juice*
1 *dumpling squash or other winter squash*
    (about 1½ pounds)

PREPARATION TIME: 25 minutes plus marinating time
COOKING TIME: 1½ hours
YIELD: 4 servings

Combine the beef, ½ cup of the wine, and the cumin, cracked pepper, garlic, and orange rind in a medium bowl until well blended. Cover and let stand at room temperature 1 or 2 hours or refrigerate overnight.

Pat the meat dry, reserving the marinade. Coat a medium Dutch oven or saucepot with vegetable cooking spray; add the oil and heat over moderate heat. Sauté the beef on all sides; remove and reserve. Add the onion to the drippings in the pan and sauté 3 to 5 minutes, or until golden. Return the beef to the pot with the reserved marinade. Add the remaining wine and the tomato juice. Bring to a boil, cover, lower the heat, and simmer 45 minutes.

Cut the squash into thirds, remove the seeds, and steam 5 minutes. When cool enough to handle, peel and cube the squash. Add to the pot. Cover and simmer 30 minutes longer, or until the beef and squash are tender. Serve over rice.

NUTRITION INFORMATION (with ½ cup cooked rice): Cal: 376 Pro: 24g/25% Carb: 41g/44% Fat: 9g/21% (S:39% M:52% P:9%) Chol: 57mg Sod: 312mg Pot: 985mg Fiber: 4g Vit A: 70% Vit C: 40% B1: 21% B2: 14% B3: 25% B6: 47% B12: 29% Folic: 16% Panto: 17% Phos: 25% Iron: 28% Mag: 15% Zinc: 36% Cop: 19% Chrom: 18% Sel: 57% Mang: 51% EXCHANGE: Lean Meat: 2¼ Bread: 2½ Veg.: 1 Fat: ½

MICROWAVE METHOD: Marinate the beef as above. Prepare the squash as above without steaming. In a 2-quart microwave-safe casserole, cook the oil and onion on High (100% power) until tender, about 2 to 3 minutes. Add the beef with the marinade, tomato juice, and squash; omit the remaining wine. Cook covered on High 10 minutes. Stir. Reduce to Medium (50% power);

cook covered until the beef and squash are tender, about 20 to 26 minutes, rotating the dish and stirring twice. Let stand 5 minutes.

Lemon-Zucchini Muffins

by Ceri Hadda

    Vegetable cooking spray
 1 cup whole wheat pastry flour
 1 cup unbleached all-purpose flour
 1 tablespoon baking powder
 1/4 teaspoon salt
 1/4 teaspoon ground nutmeg
 1 cup firmly packed shredded zucchini
   Grated rind of 1/2 to 1 lemon
 1/2 cup plain low-fat yogurt
 1/2 teaspoon baking soda
 1 egg, beaten
 1/4 cup corn oil
 1/2 cup honey
 1/2 cup 1%-fat milk

    PREPARATION TIME: 30 minutes
    COOKING TIME: 35 minutes
    YIELD: 12 muffins

Preheat the oven to 375°F. Spray 12 muffin pan cups with cooking spray or use paper cupcake liners. Sift the flours, baking powder, salt, and nutmeg together into a large bowl. Add the zucchini and lemon rind.

Mix the yogurt with the baking soda in a small bowl. Add to it the egg, oil, honey, and milk; add all at once to the dry ingredients. Mix just to moisten the dry ingredients. (Do not overmix or the muffins will be tough.) Spoon the batter into the prepared muffin pan cups and bake 30 to 35 minutes, or until golden and firm. Cool in the pan on a wire rack 5 minutes before unmolding.

    NUTRITION INFORMATION: Cal: 172 Pro: 4g/ 9% Carb: 28g/63% Fat: 6g/28% (S:18% M:27% P:55%) Chol: 19mg Sodium: 175mg Potassium: 121mg Fiber: 2g E: 21% P: 16%
    EXCHANGE: Bread: 1³/₄ Fat: 1

Honeyed Squash Custard

by Ceri Hadda

A soothing dessert, reminiscent of pumpkin pie. Use any winter squash, such as pumpkin, acorn, butternut, or hubbard.

 1/2 to 1 pound acorn or other winter squash
   1/2 teaspoon ground cinnamon
   1/4 teaspoon ground ginger
   1/8 teaspoon ground nutmeg
      Large pinch ground cloves
 1 1/4 cups low-fat milk
   1/3 cup light honey
   1 egg and 2 egg whites beaten together

    PREPARATION TIME: 25 minutes
    COOKING TIME: 2 hours
    YIELD: 6 servings

Preheat the oven to 350°F. Halve the squash but do not clean it out. Place the squash halves, cut side down, in a baking pan; add 1/2 inch of water; cover the pan. Bake 35 to 45 minutes, or until tender. Let squash stand until cool enough to handle. Remove and discard the seeds and fiber. Scoop out the flesh and puree it in a blender or food processor. Measure 3/4 cup puree (reserve any extra for other use).

Preheat the oven to 350°F. In a large bowl, combine the squash puree with the cinnamon, ginger, nutmeg, and cloves, using a wire wisk. Slowly beat in the milk, honey, and eggs until well blended. Pour the mixture into an ungreased 1- to 1 1/2-quart ovenproof dish. Place the dish in a roasting pan, place the pan on the oven rack, and pour boiling water into the pan to halfway up the side of the dish. Bake for about 1 to 1 1/4 hours, or until a narrow knife inserted halfway between the center of the custard and the edge of the dish comes out clean. Serve warm or refrigerate until serving time.

    NUTRITION INFORMATION: Cal: 113 Pro: 4g/ 14% Carb: 20g/69% Fat: 2g/17% (S:48% M:35% P:17%) Chol: 42mg Sodium: 56mg Potassium: 232mg Fiber: .6g A: 21%
    EXCHANGE: Lean Meat: 1/4 Low-fat Milk: 1/4 Bread: 1/4 Fruit: 1

MICROWAVE METHOD: In a 12- by 8-inch microwave-safe casserole, cook the squash halves and 2 tablespoons water covered on High (100% power) until tender, about 5 to 7 minutes. Proceed as directed above to make the puree. Prepare the custard mixture and pour into a microwave-safe casserole as above. Cook on Medium (50% power) 10 minutes; stir. Cook on Medium until a knife inserted in center comes out clean, about 7 to 10 minutes.

Poor Man's Caviar

by Nao Hauser

This eggplant dish is a Middle Eastern classic, named for its role as an appetizer on belugaless tables. Some versions are seasoned with tomato paste; this one features the mellowed tang of roasted garlic. Serve it as a dip with crudités and crackers, or with lettuce and sliced tomato as a salad, adding any or all of the garnishes listed below. Roasting whole eggplant is not only an easy way to cook the vegetable but one that doesn't require prior salting to remove bitterness.

  1 medium eggplant (1 to 1 1/2 pounds)
  12 unpeeled garlic cloves
  3 tablespoons fresh lemon juice

  1 tablespoon olive oil
  1/4 teaspoon salt
  6 to 8 fresh parsley sprigs, thick stems removed, chopped fine
    Thinly sliced green onion, black olives, and/or chopped hard-cooked egg for garnish (optional)

PREPARATION TIME: 15 minutes
COOKING TIME: 1 hour 15 minutes
YIELD: 4 to 6 servings

Preheat the oven to 400°F. Pierce the eggplant deeply in 10 places with fork tines. Place in a metal pie or baking dish with the garlic cloves. Bake in preheated oven until the garlic is completely soft, 20 to 25 minutes. Remove the garlic. Bake until the eggplant is completely soft and beginning to collapse, 40 to 50 minutes longer.

Peel the eggplant and garlic cloves. Puree in a food processor or blender with the lemon juice, oil, and salt; add parsley and process to combine. Refrigerate until cold. Garnish as desired to serve.

NUTRITION INFORMATION (for 4 servings):
Calories: 52 Pro: 1g/8% Carb: 8g/55% Fat: 2g/ 37% (S:16% M:72% P:12%) Chol: 0mg Sodium: 92mg Potassium: 250mg Fiber: 2g C: 18%
  EXCHANGE: Veg: 1 1/4 Fat: 1/2

◇ CRUCIFEROUS VEGETABLES ◇

King Cabbage and His Noble Kin

by Gail A. Levey, M.S., R.D.

Cruciferous vegetables—recommended by the National Cancer Institute, the National Academy of Sciences, and the American Cancer Society for their alleged ability to protect against cancer—have had a good press for a long time.

The Roman consul Cato the Elder wrote of cabbages 2,000 years ago: "The cabbage surpasses all other vegetables. If, at a banquet, you wish to dine extravagantly and enjoy your dinner, then eat as much cabbage as you wish, seasoned with vinegar, before dinner, and likewise after dinner eat some half-dozen leaves. It will make you feel as if you had not eaten, and you can drink as much as you like."

Cato may have overstated his case: Few good habits are powerful enough to entirely undo overindulgences. But cabbage-family vegetables do contain substances that speed the liver's ability to inactivate certain toxins. Today some scientists may be, like Cato, a little too enthusiastic about the potential of these vegetables—in this case, to prevent cancer. But make no mistake about it: Cruciferous vegetables are *extraordinarily* nutritious. Free of fat and cholesterol, rich in fiber, a cup of cooked cruciferae supplies at most 60 calories.

Quite a contribution, especially from a botanical family that traditionally does well in produce-starved winter months. And it's a huge family. Cruciferous vegetables—the name comes from the cross, or crucifer, their four-petaled flowers form—include arugula, bok choy, broccoli, Brussels sprouts, cabbage, cauliflower, collard greens, horseradish, kale, kohlrabi, mustard, mustard greens, radishes, rutabaga, turnip, turnip greens, watercress, and garden cress. All are members of the cabbage family.

The Cancer Connection

Even though some prestigious scientific organizations claim cruciferae help fight cancer, the case is far from proven. Still, "The evidence is clear enough to let the public in on what scientists know," says biochemistry professor Sidney Weinhouse of Temple University. "These vegetables may do some good, and certainly do no harm. The danger is treating them as panaceas."

The man in charge of prevention at the National Cancer Institute, epidemiologist Peter Greenwald, agrees. But he adds, "One thing we look for is different investigators doing different studies and coming up with the same conclusions. The evidence is suggestive, but we need more research."

Lab research suggests cabbage chemicals block carcinogens. Yet, although population studies suggest that people who eat plenty of vegetables in general have less cancer, few draw a clear link with cruciferae specifically. Says epidemiologist

Jim Marshall of the State University of New York at Buffalo Medical School, "Cruciferous vegetables are very complicated, so the total range of their effects remains to be assessed."

One reason cancer experts recommend cruciferae, though, is that they are rich in nutrients as well as other compounds that some studies suggest may protect against cancer. Among them:

♦ Beta-carotene. Some scientists believe carotenoids protect by suppressing the cancer process in cells already exposed to carcinogens. Major studies are testing that hypothesis (see Squash, page 154). Many cruciferae are rich in carotenoids.

♦ Vitamin C. Plentiful in all family members, it may prevent formation of nitrosamines and other cancer-causing chemicals in the stomach. How significant such an effect is remains unknown.

♦ Calcium. Many cruciferae are good sources of this element, which may protect against rapid turnover of colon cells, a precancerous condition.

♦ Fiber. Cruciferous vegetables are a good source of dietary fiber and are virtually fat-free, a combination associated with a reduced risk of colon cancer.

♦ Indoles, aromatic isothiocyanates, and other related chemicals. Cruciferae's unique claim. By revving up certain enzymes, these chemicals may enhance the detoxification of active ingredients. In a typical experiment, rats or mice are given known carcinogens. Those also given the chemicals cruciferae provide get fewer tumors. Some evidence also suggests cruciferae may, like soybeans, interfere with excess estrogen production, possibly lowering the risk of breast cancer in susceptible women.

In two of the few human experiments done on metabolic effects, researchers compared how two groups of volunteers utilized three common drugs—acetaminophen, antipyrine, phenacetin—when the volunteers were divided into groups on cruciferous and noncruciferous diets. Those eating the cruciferous vegetables metabolized the drugs faster. Some people have leaped to the conclusion that the vegetables also destroy carcinogens faster, too. But Carl Anderson, professor of medicine at New York Medical College and a member of the team that did the original studies, thinks it is too soon for a conclusion to be drawn.

And speeding up enzymes may not always help. "Similar enzyme systems that inactivate some harmful substances can also *enhance* the toxicity of other substances," says pharmacology professor Paul Talalay of Johns Hopkins Medical School in Baltimore. The goal of future research may be to help us balance enzymes—through our diets, among other ways—but we're far from reaching that capability, says Talalay.

Still, all of the experts we consulted believe that cruciferae are so nutritious that they should be an important part of any healthy diet. (Broccoli and cabbage may also lower blood cholesterol; see Roots Revisited, page 104.)

Rich in Minerals

While cross-petaled plants share many nutritious qualities, some have more of some nutrients than others.

Kale's vibrant color clues you in to its love of the sun and thus its abundance of carotenoids, some of which your body turns into vitamin A. Ditto for turnip greens, mustard greens, collard greens, broccoli, watercress, savoy cabbage and Brussels sprouts. In fact, one cup of cooked kale or turnip greens more than fills your daily vitamin A quota.

As for vitamin C, only citrus fruits and green peppers have as much as cruciferae. A cup of broccoli, Brussels sprouts, kohlrabi, or cauliflower gives you all the C you need in a day—as much or more than you get in an orange.

Many supply calcium, too. Four cruciferae—turnip greens, broccoli, bok choy, and collard greens—give you more calcium in a cup than you would find in a half glass (4 ounces) of milk.

For blood-building iron, it's Brussels sprouts, broccoli, and bok choy. A cup of any of them meets 10 percent of your daily needs. Also, cruciferae's vitamin C boosts your body's absorption of iron. It's a double bonus.

Folic acid, as important for healthy blood as iron, abounds in turnip greens, broccoli, Brussels sprouts, celery cabbage, and cauliflower.

As a nutritionist, I vote for broccoli, Brussels sprouts, and turnip greens as the best all-around cruciferae, although all have superb nutritional qualities.

Cooking the Cruciferous Vegetables

by Nao Hauser

Unlike gentler vegetables, the members of the cruciferous family tend to be known by their smell—and rarely in a positive sense! But behind each assertive personality, there lies a delicate balance of sweet, sour, salty, and bitter flavor. The key to unlocking these is in the preparation and cooking.

Although many types can be used interchangeably in recipes, each species reveals its complexity in different ways. Brief cooking, for example, reduces the sourness of broccoli and brightens its color, while prolonged cooking will make it look dull and taste unpleasantly strong.

Similarly, the sharpness of radishes and turnips dissipates quickly in a saucepan. Cook radishes overlong, though, and they become too strong. Turnips, by contrast, taste very mild even when soft enough to mash. Raw arugula (rocket salad, rucola) adds a sharp, peppery, mustard accent to green salads but becomes milder stir-fried or cooked into a thick Tuscan soup with potatoes and bread. Cabbages reveal perhaps the most interesting spectrum, starting with a definite sourness when raw and becoming quite sweet when thoroughly cooked.

The complex and strong characters of these vegetables yield natural links with fruits and nuts. You can draw on the palette of winter produce bins to create such pleasing combinations as cabbage and apples, Brussels sprouts and grapes, and broccoli and citrus.

It is a joy, too, to have the cold-weather crucifers available for garnishes and crudités when the colors of summer are gone. Use the ruffles of red kale or the rosiness of shredded radishes to accent salads when tomatoes look bleak. Compose a platter of pale green kohlrabi slices and broccoli and cauliflower florets on a bed of red cabbage leaves to serve with dips.

The sturdiness of the crucifers, however, can be somewhat deceptive. Like warm-weather vegetables, they taste best if cooked soon after purchase. Though cabbages and turnips are among the traditional "cellar vegetables," meaning that people used to rely on them for nutrients during the winter, refrigerators have a much higher moisture level than old-fashioned root cellars; so don't count on prolonged storage. And don't keep cooked leftovers around for more than a day, either, because the crucifers, to put it mildly, do not grow more fragrant with age!

Cook cruciferous vegetables in a nonreactive pot (uncoated aluminum can intensify odors). The color pigments in the vegetables—chlorophyll green, anthocyanin red, and flavone ivory—will respond to the natural acids released into the cooking water as the vegetables soften and to any acids you might add. Lemon juice, vinegar, or wine can make cauliflower whiter and red cabbage ruddier, but they will turn broccoli olive drab. (The slightly alkaline nature of tap water will balance the acids when you're making soup, but otherwise you don't want to use much water or you risk leaching out vitamins.)

Spotlight: Cauliflower Against Appendicitis?

Scientists are often surprised by their own data. When British researchers examined weekly diet records of 8,600 households, they found a clear link between consumption of certain vegetables and lower rates of potentially fatal appendicitis. The protector vegetables: cauliflower, tomatoes, peas, green beans, and Brussels sprouts. The vegetables not only have fiber that whisks foods through the intestines and appendix before it can collect bacteria, the researchers suggest, but may directly affect the bacteria, inhibiting "bad bugs" and promoting "good bugs." Eat your peas, honey, you wouldn't want to get appendicitis.

—Robert Barnett

Cauliflower Soup with Lemon-Broccoli Puree

by Nao Hauser

The soup can be made a day ahead and refrigerated, or frozen for several months. But make the Lemon-Broccoli Puree close to serving time for the brightest color.

1 large onion, minced
2 ribs celery with leaves, sliced
2 carrots, thinly sliced
5½ cups unsalted chicken broth or stock (see page 28)
1 head cauliflower (about 2 pounds), cored and broken into flowerets
1 tablespoon dried dill
½ teaspoon dried thyme
2 tablespoons tarragon vinegar
½ teaspoon ground allspice
Dash cayenne
Lemon-Broccoli Puree (recipe follows)

PREPARATION TIME: 25 minutes
COOKING TIME: 1 hour 5 minutes
YIELD: 8 servings

Place the onion, celery, carrots, and ½ cup of the chicken broth in a large saucepan; cook, covered, over medium-low heat 30 minutes. Add the remaining 5 cups broth, cauliflower, dill and thyme; heat to boiling. Reduce the heat and simmer covered until the cauliflower is very tender, about 30 minutes.

Strain the soup, reserving the liquid. Puree the vegetables with a small amount of liquid, in batches, in a food processor or blender until smooth. Return the vegetables and liquid to the pot; stir in the vinegar, allspice, and cayenne. Heat to simmering before serving. To serve, ladle into bowls, add a large dollop of Lemon-Broccoli Puree to each, and garnish with reserved broccoli flowerets if desired.

LEMON-BROCCOLI PUREE

1 bunch broccoli (about 1 pound)
Grated rind and juice of 1 small lemon
⅓ to ½ cup unsalted chicken broth or stock (see page 28)

PREPARATION TIME: 15 minutes
COOKING TIME: 10 minutes
YIELD: about 2 cups

Cut off the broccoli flowerets in small pieces; slice the stems. Add the broccoli to a large pot of boiling water; let the water return to a boil. Rinse the broccoli immediately under cold water; drain well. Reserve some broccoli flowerets for garnish, if desired. Place the remaining broccoli in a food processor or blender in batches, add some lemon rind, lemon juice, and broth with each batch, and process to a puree (the puree will not be absolutely smooth).

NUTRITION INFORMATION: Cal: 112 Pro: 9g/28% Carb: 18g/59% Fat: 2g/12% Chol: 1mg Sodium: 111mg Potassium: 899mg Fiber: 8g A: 209% C: 183% B1: 11% B2: 16% B3: 20% B6: 26% Folic: 27% Ca: 15% P: 18% Fe: 14% Mg: 16% Cu: 16% Mn: 25% Cr: 20% EXCHANGE: Veg: 4

MICROWAVE METHOD (soup): In a 4-quart microwave-safe casserole or bowl, cook the onion, celery, carrot, and ½ cup of the broth covered on High (100% power) 7 minutes. Stir in only 4 cups broth and the cauliflower, dill, and thyme. Cook covered to a boil, about 10 to 12 minutes. Reduce to Medium (50% power); cook until cauliflower is very tender, about 18 minutes. Strain and continue as directed above.

MICROWAVE METHOD (puree): Prepare the broccoli as directed. In a 2-quart microwave-safe casserole, cook the broccoli and ¼ cup water on High (100% power) until tender-crisp, about 4 to 6 minutes. Rinse and continue as directed above.

Turnip-Corn Soup

by Nao Hauser

This is a very hearty soup you can easily make a meal of. Substitute rutabaga for the turnips, if you wish. Be careful to wash the turnip greens like spinach, in several changes of cold water. If they are very young and mild-tasting, you can just chop and add them to the soup without prior cooking.

2 teaspoons ground coriander
1 teaspoon ground cumin
1/2 teaspoon chili powder
8 ounces lean boneless pork, cut into 1/2-inch pieces
5 cups unsalted beef, veal, pork, or vegetable broth or stock (see page 27)
1 large onion, minced
2 carrots, shredded
1 tablespoon brandy
1 pound turnip or mustard greens, washed, stems removed, torn into pieces
1 cup red wine
2 10-ounce packages frozen corn kernels, thawed, or 1 package corn and 1 package baby lima beans
12 ounces turnips, pared and diced
6 cloves garlic, peeled and chopped
1 tablespoon dried oregano
1 teaspoon dried marjoram
2 bay leaves
1/4 cup red wine vinegar

PREPARATION TIME: 30 minutes
COOKING TIME: 50 minutes
YIELD: 8 servings

Combine the coriander, cumin, and chili powder on a plate. Toss the pork in the spices to coat. Heat a large, heavy Dutch oven over high heat and add the pork; cook, stirring constantly, until lightly browned, about 2 minutes. Remove and reserve.

Add 1 cup of the broth, stirring to scrape up the spices; reduce the heat. Stir in the onion, carrots, and brandy; cook over medium-low heat 15 minutes.

Cook the turnip greens with water that clings from washing in a large saucepan, covered, over medium-low heat until wilted, about 10 minutes.

Add the remaining 4 cups broth, the wine, reserved pork, turnip greens, corn, turnips, garlic, oregano, marjoram, and bay leaves to the Dutch oven. Simmer covered 25 minutes. Stir in the vinegar; simmer 5 minutes. Remove bay leaves before serving.

NUTRITION INFORMATION: Cal: 200 Pro: 15g/ 29% Carb: 26g/50% Fat: 5g/21% (S:36% M:46% P:18%) Chol: 27mg Sodium: 123mg Potassium: 643mg Fiber: 5g A: 255% C: 42% E: 11% B1: 26% B2: 15% B3: 26% B6: 25% Folic: 23% Ca: 12% P: 19% Mg: 11% Cu: 18% Mn: 23% Se: 26% Cr: 29%
EXCHANGE: Med Meat: 1 1/4 Bread: 1 Veg: 2

Watercress-Mushroom Salad

by Nao Hauser

Mushrooms are the perfect counterpoint to the spiciness and crunch of watercress. Use French walnut oil if possible; it's more flavorful.

8 ounces fresh mushrooms, very thinly sliced
1/2 small red onion, very thinly sliced
Freshly ground black pepper
1 bunch watercress, torn into pieces
1/2 cup white wine
3 tablespoons fresh lime juice
1 tablespoon French walnut oil
2 teaspoons Dijon-style mustard
1 teaspoon dried tarragon
1/2 teaspoon raspberry vinegar
1/2 teaspoon reduced-sodium soy sauce

PREPARATION TIME: 20 minutes
YIELD: 4 servings

Place the mushrooms and onion in a large salad bowl; sprinkle with black pepper to taste. Arrange the watercress over the mushrooms. Combine the remaining ingredients in a blender or food processor and blend until smooth. Pour over the salad and toss well.

NUTRITION INFORMATION: Cal: 60 Pro: 2g/ 15% Carb: 6g/34% Fat: 4g/51% (S:18% M:46% P:36%) Chol: 0mg Sodium: 74mg Potassium: 376mg Fiber: 2g A: 32% C: 35% B2: 18% B3: 12% Panto: 14% Cr: 17%
EXCHANGE: Veg: 1 Fat: ¾

Susan's Calico Coleslaw

by *American Health*

Don't fret that this recipe appears to have a high percentage of calories from fat. It's actually low in quantity of fat: only 5 grams. Cruciferous vegetables are so low in calories that the percentages can be misleading.

  5 *cups shredded cabbage*
  2 *tablespoons sugar*
 ½ *teaspoon dry mustard*
 ¼ *teaspoon freshly ground black pepper*
  1 *small green bell pepper, chopped*
  1 *carrot, shredded*
 ¼ *cup coarsely diced pimentos*
 ½ *teaspoon grated onion*
  2 *tablespoons vegetable oil*
 ⅓ *cup vinegar*

PREPARATION TIME: 30 minutes
YIELD: 6 servings

Toss the cabbage with the sugar, mustard, pepper, green pepper, carrot, pimentos, and onion in a serving bowl. In a small bowl, combine the oil and vinegar; pour over the cabbage mixture and toss well.

NUTRITION INFORMATION: Cal: 90 Pro: 1g/ 6% Carb: 12g/49% Fat: 5g/45% (S:13% M:27% P:61%) Chol: 0mg Sodium: 20mg Potassium: 271mg Fiber: 2g A: 111% C: 103% E: 25% Folic: 12%
EXCHANGE: Veg: 1 Fruit: ¼ Fat: 1

Kohlrabi-Beet Salad with Port and Walnuts

by Nao Hauser

If you love the delicate sweetness of kohlrabi, use up to 1½ pounds in this salad. Increase the portion size and add 2 to 3 ounces of sliced cooked chicken per serving for a delicious main course.

   Red-leaf or romaine lettuce leaves
  4 *kohlrabi bulbs, pared and very thinly sliced*
  4 *beets (about ¾ pound), cooked, pared, and sliced thin*
  1 *ounce chopped walnuts*
 ½ *cup port wine*
  1 *tablespoon fresh lemon juice*
 ¼ *teaspoon sugar*
 ¼ *teaspoon ground ginger*

PREPARATION TIME: 30 minutes
COOKING TIME: 1 hour and 7 minutes
YIELD: 4 servings

Line four salad plates with lettuce leaves. Arrange the kohlrabi and beets on the lettuce. Spread the walnuts in a small skillet and cook over medium heat, stirring constantly, until toasted, about 5 minutes. Spoon over the salads. To the skillet, add the port, lemon juice, sugar, and ginger, stirring to dissolve the sugar. Simmer until reduced by about half. Spoon over the salads.

NOTE: *To cook beets:* Scrub well under cold running water. Place in a quart of warm water in a medium saucepan; bring to a boil; lower heat and simmer until tender, about 1 hour. Trim ends, slip off the skins, and slice the beets thin. Or use canned beets and rinse well to remove as much sodium as possible.

NUTRITION INFORMATION: Cal: 118 Pro: 6g/ 17% Carb: 18g/54% Fat: 4g/29% (S:7% M:23% P:70%) Chol: 0mg Sodium: 78mg Potassium: 982mg Fiber: 6g C: 190% B6: 14% Folic: 16% P: 14% Mg: 20% Cu: 18% Mn: 23%
EXCHANGE: Veg: 3 Fat: 1

MICROWAVE METHOD: In a 1½-quart microwave-safe casserole, cook the beets and ½ cup water covered on High (100% power) until tender, about 12 to 13 minutes.

Mashed Turnips with Thyme

by *American Health*

    2 pounds turnips, pared and diced
 ⅓ cup orange juice
 ½ teaspoon salt
 ½ teaspoon dried thyme

PREPARATION TIME: 10 minutes
COOKING TIME: 20 minutes
YIELD: 6 servings

In a covered 2-quart saucepan over high heat, cook the turnips in 1 inch of boiling water for 20 minutes, or until tender. Drain, then mash slightly. Stir in the orange juice, salt, and thyme.

NUTRITION INFORMATION: Cal: 29   Pro: 1g/11% Carb: 8g/86%   Fat: .1g/3%   Chol: 0mg   Sodium: 224mg   Potassium: 196mg   Fiber: 2g   C: 35%
EXCHANGE: Veg: 1

MICROWAVE METHOD: In a 1½-quart microwave-safe casserole, cook the turnips and ¼ cup water covered on High (100% power) until tender, about 8 to 10 minutes. Drain; continue as directed above.

Brussels Sprouts with Hazelnuts and Grapes

by Nao Hauser

This is a very festive combination—perfect for any celebration that features turkey, chicken, duck, or roast pork. Be careful not to overcook the Brussels sprouts; they should be tender but still green enough to contrast with the grapes.

1½ pounds Brussels sprouts, trimmed
    1 ounce blanched hazelnuts, chopped
1½ cups halved seedless red grapes (about 8
       ounces)
  ⅛ teaspoon ground cardamom

PREPARATION TIME: 15 minutes
COOKING TIME: 10 minutes
YIELD: 6 servings

Steam the Brussels sprouts over simmering water until tender, 7 to 10 minutes. Spread the hazelnuts in a wide saucepan or skillet and cook over medium heat, stirring constantly, until toasted, about 5 minutes. Reduce heat to low; stir in the grapes and cook covered 5 minutes (don't be alarmed by the slight popping sound the skins make!). Stir in the Brussels sprouts and cardamom. Serve hot.

NUTRITION INFORMATION: Cal: 97   Pro: 4g/ 13%   Carb: 17g/59%   Fat: 4g/28%   (S:10%   M:71% P:19%)   Chol: 0mg   Sodium: 26mg   Potassium: 452mg   Fiber: 6g   A: 17%   C: 119%   B1: 11% B6: 13%   Folic: 18%   Mn: 18%   Cr: 12%
EXCHANGE: Veg: 2   Fruit: ½   Fat: ½

Cauliflower with Pignoli and Currants

by Nao Hauser

Currants sweeten the cauliflower and pignoli nuts complement its texture. You can substitute 1½ pounds Brussels sprouts for the cauliflower if you wish.

 ¼ cup dry Marsala wine
    2 tablespoons balsamic or red wine vinegar
    1 ounce dried currants
    1 ounce pignoli (pine nuts)
    1 teaspoon unsalted butter or margarine
    1 head cauliflower (about 2 pounds) cut into
       small flowerets
 ¼ teaspoon garlic powder
 ⅛ teaspoon ground nutmeg
    Dash ground cinnamon

PREPARATION TIME: 15 minutes
COOKING TIME: 20 minutes
YIELD: 6 servings

Pour the wine and vinegar over the currants in a small bowl; let stand 15 minutes. Spread the nuts in a small skillet and cook over medium heat, stirring constantly, until golden, about 4 minutes.

Melt the butter in a wide saucepan over medium heat. Stir in the cauliflower and spices; sauté 5 minutes. Stir in the currants with the liquid and the nuts. Cover and cook over medium-low heat, stirring occasionally, until the cauliflower is tender, about 10 minutes.

NUTRITION INFORMATION: Cal: 77 Pro: 4g/ 20% Carb: 10g/46% Fat: 3g/34% (S:55% M:25% P:20%) Chol: 2mg Sodium: 16mg Potassium: 495mg Fiber: 5g C: 127% B6: 13% Folic: 17%
EXCHANGE: Veg: 2 Fat: ½

MICROWAVE METHOD: In a 2-cup glass measure, cook the currants, wine, and vinegar on High (100% power) to boiling, about 1½ to 2 minutes. Let stand covered. On a large paper plate, spread the nuts. Cook on High until toasted, about 2 to 3 minutes, stirring once. In a 2½- to 3-quart microwave-safe casserole, cook the butter, cauliflower, and spices on High until just tender-crisp, about 5 to 7 minutes. Stir in the currants, any liquid, and the nuts. Cook covered 2 to 3 minutes, until the cauliflower is tender.

Orange-Sesame Broccoli

by Nao Hauser

If you wish to substitute bok choy for the broccoli in this stir-fry, slice the stems about ¼ inch thick and cut the leaves into small strips.

1 bunch broccoli (about 1 pound)
2 teaspoons sesame oil
1 tablespoon orange juice
2 teaspoons grated orange rind
2 teaspoons reduced-sodium soy sauce
2 cloves garlic, peeled and minced
1 teaspoon minced fresh ginger
1 tablespoon sesame seeds, toasted (see Note)

PREPARATION TIME: 15 minutes
COOKING TIME: 6 minutes
YIELD: 4 servings

Pare the broccoli stalks. Cut off the flowerets in small pieces; slice the stems thinly on the diagonal. Heat the oil briefly in a wok over medium-high heat. Stir in the broccoli; stir-fry 3 minutes. Stir in the orange juice, orange rind, soy sauce, garlic, and ginger. Stir-fry until the broccoli is tender, about 2 minutes. Stir in the sesame seeds.

NOTE: To toast the sesame seeds, spread in small skillet; heat covered over medium-low heat, stirring constantly, until lightly browned, about 3 minutes.

NUTRITION INFORMATION: Cal: 72 Pro: 4g/ 20% Carb: 8g/40% Fat: 4g/40% (S:15% M:38% P:47%) Chol: 0mg Sodium: 98mg Potassium: 225mg Fiber: 5g A: 32% C: 125% B2: 14% B6: 13% Folic: 20% Ca: 13% Mg: 19% Cr: 16%
EXCHANGE: Veg: 2 Fat: ½

Onion-Braised Broccoli de Rabe

by Nao Hauser

Italian-style "boiled greens" usually means boiled broccoli de rabe, a non-heading form of broccoli, sautéed in olive oil. The following method produces similar flavor with much less oil. Cook the greens just until the stems are tender and serve immediately.

2 teaspoons olive oil
1 small red onion, very thinly sliced
¼ cup unsalted chicken broth or stock (see page 28)
2 teaspoons balsamic vinegar
2 cloves garlic, peeled and minced
1 bunch broccoli de rabe (about 1 pound)

PREPARATION TIME: 15 minutes
COOKING TIME: 25 minutes
YIELD: 4 servings

Heat the oil in a 9-inch skillet over medium heat. Stir in the onion; cook covered over medium heat, stirring occasionally, until limp and lightly browned, about 10 minutes. Reduce the heat to medium-low. Stir in the broth, vinegar, and garlic; cook uncovered 5 minutes. Slice the broccoli de rabe stems into $1/4$-inch pieces; cut the leafy parts about $3/4$ inch thick. Stir the stems and leaves into the onion mixture and cook, covered, until the leaves are wilted and the stems are tender, about 10 minutes.

NUTRITION INFORMATION: Cal: 62   Pro: 4g/ 22%   Carb: 8g/44%   Fat: 3g/34%   (S:16%   M:69% P:15%)   Chol: 1mg   Sodium: 16mg   Potassium: 226mg   Fiber: 5g   A: 32%   C: 121%   B2: 14% B6: 12%   Folic: 20%   Ca: 13%   Mg: 17%   Cr: 16% EXCHANGE: Veg: $1^1/2$ Fat: $1/2$

Hot and Sour Chinese Greens
by Nao Hauser

Using caraway seeds in this recipe is not Chinese at all, but it intensifies the hot and sour tastes. Serve the spicy greens over rice or thin noodles.

   1 small bunch bok choy or Chinese
      cabbage (1 to $1^1/4$ pounds)
 $1^1/2$ teaspoons caraway seeds
  $1/4$ teaspoon dry mustard
$1/8$ to $1/4$ teaspoon red pepper flakes
   1 teaspoon vegetable oil
   2 cloves garlic, peeled and minced
  $1/4$ cup unsalted chicken broth or stock
     (see page 28)
   1 tablespoon rice wine vinegar
  $1/2$ teaspoon reduced-sodium soy sauce
  $1/2$ teaspoon sugar

PREPARATION TIME: 15 minutes
COOKING TIME: 20 minutes
YIELD: 4 servings

Slice the bok choy or cabbage stalks about $1/4$ inch thick. Slice the leaves about $3/4$ inch thick. Reserve.

Spread the caraway seeds in a 9-inch heavy skillet over medium heat; cook, stirring constantly, until toasted, about 2 minutes. Add the mustard and pepper flakes; cook, stirring, 2 minutes. Stir in the oil and garlic; cook 1 minute. Add the bok choy or cabbage; stir to coat. Combine the broth, vinegar, soy sauce, and sugar and add to skillet. Cook covered over medium heat, stirring occasionally, until the stems are tender, about 10 minutes. Remove cover; cook 5 minutes longer.

NUTRITION INFORMATION: Cal: 42   Pro: 2g/ 19%   Carb: 6g/52%   Fat: 2g/29%   (S:17%   M:27% P:56%)   Chol: 1mg   Sodium: 48mg   Potassium: 370mg   Fiber: 3g   A: 37%   C: 64%   B6: 16% Folic: 27%   Ca: 11%   Cr: 16% EXCHANGE: Veg: 1   Fat: $1/4$

Braised Kale
by Nao Hauser

Long, slow cooking tenderizes kale and softens its taste. Stir a quarter pound sautéed mushrooms and a bit more yogurt into this dish, if you wish.

 1 leek
 1 pound kale
 2 teaspoons unsalted butter
$1/2$ cup unsalted chicken broth or stock (see
   page 28)
$1/3$ cup plain nonfat yogurt
 1 teaspoon Dijon-style mustard
  Pinch salt
  Freshly ground black pepper
  Ground nutmeg

PREPARATION TIME: 20 minutes
COOKING TIME: 1 hour and 15 minutes
YIELD: 4 servings

Slice the leek lengthwise and rinse under running water until clear of dirt. Very thinly slice the white and light green parts and set aside.

Remove and discard the tough center stems from the kale leaves. Tear the leaves into small pieces; rinse well in a large bowl of cold water and drain.

Melt the butter in a wide, heavy saucepan over medium heat. Stir in the leek and broth; cook covered, stirring occasionally, until the leek is completely wilted, about 15 minutes. Add about half of the kale; cook covered until the kale wilts enough to fit the remaining kale in the pan, about 5 to 10 minutes. Add the remaining kale; cook until all the kale is thoroughly wilted and tender, stirring occasionally, about 50 minutes. (If mixture begins to stick, add a little more broth.)

Remove from heat. Stir in the yogurt, mustard, salt, and the pepper and nutmeg to taste; let stand covered 1 to 2 minutes for the flavors to blend.

NUTRITION INFORMATION: Cal: 79 Pro: 4g/ 20% Carb: 10g/49% Fat: 3g/31% (S:55% M:29% P:16%) Chol: 6mg Sodium: 184mg Potassium: 350mg Fiber: 1g A: 169% C: 79% Ca: 13% Mn: 14%

EXCHANGE: Veg: 1½ Fat: ½

MICROWAVE METHOD: Prepare the leek and kale as directed above. In a 3- to 4-quart microwave-safe casserole or bowl, cook the leek and broth on High (100% power) until tender, about 4 to 5 minutes. Add the kale and cook covered on High until tender, about 10 to 12 minutes. Stir once. Continue as directed above.

Vegetable Curry on Rice

by *American Health*

2 tablespoons olive oil
2 cups chopped onions
1 cup chopped celery
2 garlic cloves, peeled and minced
1 medium head cauliflower
1 16-ounce can tomatoes, no salt added
1 10-ounce package frozen peas
1 large potato, pared and cut into ¾-inch cubes
2 tablespoons curry powder
1 tablespoon sugar
¼ teaspoon ground ginger
⅛ teaspoon cayenne
4 cups hot cooked brown rice
2 tablespoons sesame seeds

PREPARATION TIME: 30 minutes
COOKING TIME: 40 minutes
YIELD: 5 servings

In a 12-inch skillet over medium heat, heat the oil; cook the onions, celery, and garlic until tender, about 10 minutes, stirring occasionally. Meanwhile, break the cauliflower into small flowerets and add to the skillet with the tomatoes and their liquid and the remaining ingredients except the rice and sesame seeds. With a spoon, break the tomatoes into pieces; heat the mixture to boiling. Reduce the heat to low, cover, and simmer 30 minutes, or until the vegetables are tender, stirring occasionally. To serve, spoon the mixture onto the rice and sprinkle with sesame seeds.

NUTRITION INFORMATION: Cal: 417 Pro: 12g/ 11% Carb: 73g/67% Fat: 10g/21% (S:14% M:58% P:28%) Chol: 0mg Sodium: 98mg Potassium: 1059mg Fiber: 11g A: 20% C: 156% E: 30% B1: 33% B2: 11% B3: 24% B6: 27% Folic: 28% Ca: 18% P: 19% Fe: 26% Cu: 22% Mg: 20% Mn: 21% Se: 91%

EXCHANGE: Bread: 3½ Veg: 2½ Fat: 1¾

◇ SALAD AND GREENS ◇

Green Power

by Eileen Behan, R.D.

Crisp, delicate, tangy, sometimes a touch bitter, salad greens taste like lightweights. But they're not. Arugula to romaine, they are, with few exceptions, nutritional powerhouses.

Incredibly low in calories, salt, and fat, they're a good source of fiber and water and are loaded with vitamins, including C, A, and folic acid. A salad's worth of romaine lettuce, about 10 inner leaves, for example, is only 16 calories but provides over 50 percent of the USRDA for vitamin A, 40 percent for vitamin C, and 25 percent for folic acid.

Most dark greens are similarly nutritious. But pale greens like iceberg are light on nutrients. The only vitamin or mineral in five whole leaves worth noting is folic acid—15 percent of the USRDA. It's got minuscule amounts of vitamins A and C.

Need iron? Go for the darkest greens. Though not as rich a source as meat, dark leafy greens—especially spinach, beet greens, Swiss chard, collards, and dandelion greens—contain good amounts, and should be part of every vegetarian's diet. Just under two cups of raw spinach, which wilts down to one serving, provides 15 percent of the USRDA for iron. It also provides 47 percent for vitamin C, which helps our bodies use the iron in vegetables. (So does a little chicken, fish, or red meat in a salad.)

So, a salad of spinach (dark green), tomatoes (vitamin C) and chicken (meat) gives you more iron than, say, a salad of iceberg lettuce (light green) and sliced cheese or egg. And don't worry about cooking your spinach: Dark greens retain 95 percent of their iron after cooking.

Some greens are also high in calcium, but many also contain oxalic acid, which can bind with calcium and make it unavailable to the body. Spinach, which contains nearly a gram of oxalic acid per 100 grams, is very high in the acid. Chives (1.48 gram/100 gram) and parsley (1.70 gram/100 gram) are even higher. Beet leaves (0.61) and

Spotlight: Avocados

Ever since the first Californian sliced an avocado into a sprout salad, the rich green fruit has had a health reputation. Odd, for such a fatty food: An avocado is nearly 80 percent fat by calories. But that fat is mostly monounsaturated fat, the kind that may lower blood cholesterol. And the avocado is a good source of vitamins A, C, E, and folic acid, of potassium, of fiber, of copper and other minerals. The taste is sweet and rich. So enjoy it in moderation—in thin slices, in salads, where it can mingle with lettuce and citrus tastes.

—Robert Barnett

collards (0.45) are fairly high. Cooking, some experts believe, may lessen oxalic acid's calcium-binding effect. Nor is it a pervasive effect: although oxalic acid renders calcium unavailable in the food it's in, it doesn't appear to block other foods' calcium, according to University of Connecticut nutrition professor Lindsay Allen. In one study of 10 children fed canned spinach for 60 days in addition to their regular diets, there was no negative effect on calcium balance.

Still, best bets are greens that are high-calcium but low-oxalic. A 3½-ounce serving of turnip greens provides 19 percent of the USRDA for calcium but only 0.05 gram of oxalic acid. Kale—like turnips, a cruciferous vegetable—gives us 14 percent for calcium but only 0.02 gram of oxalic acid for the same amount. Curly endive gives us 10 percent for calcium but only 0.21 gram of oxalic acid—about a fifth of what's in spinach.

Greens have fiber and water, too; both can help keep us regular. Greens' fiber is primarily insoluble—cellulose, lignin—the kind that can help increase stool bulk and help relieve constipation and diverticulosis. (They contain only small amounts of water-soluble fiber.) The National Cancer Institute recommends we boost our daily dietary fiber intake to 20 to 30 grams a day. Greens help us reach that goal; a half cup of chopped curly endive (chicory greens) gives us about 4 grams of dietary fiber.

Pale blood? Try greens, the darker the better. They're bursting with the B vitamin folic acid, needed to keep red blood cells healthy and prevent anemia. Most Americans don't get enough folic acid. Many elderly people in particular are deficient in folic acid; antibiotics can reduce gut bacteria needed to metabolize it.

On the Pill? Greens again. Folic acid deficiency can be a side effect of oral contraception. Some physicians now routinely prescribe folic acid-containing supplements for women on the Pill. But high doses of folic acid can interfere with absorption of iron, zinc, and copper. Better to eat greens.

If you're pregnant, or thinking of becoming so, greens are even more crucial for you and your baby. Folic acid helps build genetic material, and a deficiency during pregnancy can lead to birth defects, including neural tube defects. These days,

pregnant women who get good prenatal care are routinely given folic acid–rich supplements. But if you eat lots of leafy greens every week, you won't wait until you know you're pregnant before you get enough folic acid—and your fetus will be getting the gene-building vitamin from the first day of conception.

Men need folic acid, too. Everyone does. It's needed for the synthesis of DNA, the genetic building block of life. Damage to DNA can contribute to cancer. So it's not surprising that folic acid may protect against cancer. One study looked at 73 male smokers with precancerous lung cells. Those who took folic acid supplements were more than twice as likely to have lung cells that returned to normal than those who didn't. In another study, potentially precancerous cervical cells (dysplasia) returned to normal in women who took folic acid supplements, but not in the unsupplemented.

Spotlight: The Wildest Salad Greens, the Sweetest Flowers

When is a wild green tame? Purslane, a wild succulent popular in Europe, is a mildly tart salad green that marries well with sweeter greens, tomatoes, onions, olive oil, and vinegar. Gardeners in America know it as a prolific weedy thing that sprouts up in newly disturbed earth. But it's been spotted in farmers' markets on both coasts, and seed catalogues now sell seeds for vegetable gardens. Perhaps it's on its way to becoming a tamer part of our diet. Sorrel, also called sourgrass or dock, is another wild thing going tame. Dandelion greens are already so tame we've included them in the Greens profile, page 357.

The more, the merrier. Wild greens, or potherbs, have been part of the human diet since paleolithic times. Many are extraordinarily nutritious.

A cup of cooked purslane, for example, at 21 calories, provides about 9 percent of the USRDA for calcium, 5 percent for iron, 19 percent for magnesium, 17 percent for vitamin C, and 43 percent for vitamin A, as well as 561 milligrams of potassium. (As in all vegetables, the vitamin A figures refer primarily to beta-carotene, an antioxidant in addition to a vitamin precursor.) But that's not the whole of it. Purslane, a sticky succulent, is a rich source of Omega 3 fatty acids, similar to the kind found in fish (tofu, wheat germ, walnuts, and navy beans are also good sources). Fish-type Omega 3 fatty acids are more active than those from vegetable sources—they act differently—but our bodies can to a limited degree make the former from the latter, so eating purslane may do the heart some good.

Other greens are even more nutrient-packed. A cup of cooked lamb's quarters—you can cook it like spinach—provides 350 percent of the USRDA for vitamin A, 111 percent for vitamin C, and 46 percent for calcium. It also gives us 7 percent for iron, 12 percent for thiamin, 28 percent for riboflavin, and 8 percent for niacin. Not bad for 58 calories! Lamb's quarters (not to be confused with mâche, sometimes called lamb's lettuce) is also known as pigweed, goosefoot, or wild spinach. Plants growing in fertilized fields may have high levels of nitrates and should be avoided.

Garden or French sorrel, often found growing wild (also known as curly dock in some quarters), is a nourishing little weed as well. One cup of the chopped, raw vegetable, at 29 calories, gives us 18 percent of the USRDA for iron, 34 percent for magnesium, 106 percent for vitamin C, plus 519 milligrams of potassium, and only 5 milligrams of sodium. It's quite high in oxalic acid, which fights calcium, so it's better as a delicious tart accent in salads or a versatile seasoning puree than as a daily vegetable. Just simmer clean, shredded leaves in a small amount of water; the French pair shad and sorrel, and it's delicious with potatoes, too. A lot of sorrel simmers down to a little puree.

Maybe a cup of greens is too much for you. Just a half cup of cooked garden cress, a cabbage-family cousin of watercress, provides 26 percent of the USRDA for vitamin C and 104 percent for vitamin A—for a mere 16 calories. A half cup of cooked New Zealand spinach, sometimes called summer spinach, silver beet, or Swiss chard, provides 24 percent of the USRDA for vitamin C and 65 percent for vitamin A; use it raw in salads or in any recipe that calls for spinach. A half cup of cooked water spinach, sometimes known as swamp cabbage, has only 10 calories but yields 13 percent of the USRDA for vitamin C and 51 percent for vitamin A. Young leaves can substitute for spinach. A half cup of amaranth greens, a.k.a. redroot, provides 14 percent of the USRDA for calcium, 8 percent for iron, 9 percent for magnesium, 45 percent for vitamin C, 37 percent for vitamin A, 423 milligrams of potassium, and 14 milligrams of sodium. Ed Giobbi, the cookbook author and artist, likes delicate-flavored redroot cooked by itself or along with potatoes, lamb's quarters, dandelion, or purslane.

Or maybe you want flowers. Human beings have been munching on them for millennia. Some flowers are poisonous, but the edible ones are nutritious. A third of a cup of bright yellow marigolds provides nearly 20 percent of the USRDA for vitamin A. The same amount of chrysanthemums, yellow and aromatic, gives us about 10 percent of the USRDA for vitamin C. Rose petals flavor jellies, but rose hips, brewed into tea, provide vitamin C; it's not known how much gets into the tea, but 3½ ounces of rose hips, the red berries, provide over 2,000 percent of the USRDA! In Italy, squash flowers, with their sweet, delicate taste, are lightly sautéed and added to pasta. A third of a cup raw will provide about 15 percent of the USRDA for vitamin C.

One note of caution: With any wild food, pick only in the company of an experienced forager; avoid any field, such as those near highways, that may have been sprayed with pesticides. And when you find a good local source of wild greens, treasure it!

—R.B.

Cooking with Salad Greens

by Nao Hauser

The best salads are true to their seasons: spring and early fall for delicate lettuces, summer for tomatoes and peppers, and the cold months for cabbages and kale. Year-round supplies of iceberg and romaine lettuces in most supermarkets blur the seasons somewhat, but it is always easier to make a flavorful salad with minimal dressing if you rely on ingredients at peak harvest time.

The main challenge to a salad-maker, then, is flexibility. For a simple side dish of something fresh, let the contents of produce bins dictate the recipe. In October, for example, nothing's better than a salad bowlful of Boston or Bibb lettuce spiced with arugula and radicchio and a small amount of a nut-oil dressing (fall is the season of walnut and hazelnut harvests, too). In August, you'd best forget heat-shy lettuces and feast on tomatoes and cucumbers dressed with nothing but their own juices and perhaps a splash of vinegar (see also Summer Garden Salad, page 208). In January, a juicy salad will feature oranges and/or grapefruit (see Orange and Avocado Salad with Tender Greens, page 180), a crisp one carrots or jicama (see Moroccan Carrot Salad, page 113, and Jicama-Sunchoke Salad with Mustard Dressing, page 112), an imaginative one cooked beets and raw kohlrabi (see Kohlrabi-Beet Salad with Port and Walnuts, page 169).

Most of the year, a salad implies some presence of greens. And here, again, flexibility is the key to both flavor and nutrition. Use the tender beet greens of spring, the inner leaves of winter kale, young dandelions and small broccoli de rabe leaves as you would spicy arugula and radicchio—by mixing them with milder lettuces. Virtually all greens other than lettuces can lead two culinary lives: the younger and smaller leaves are good raw, the older and tougher ones should be cooked (see Braised Kale, Onion-Braised Broccoli de Rabe, and Turnip-Corn Chowder in the Cruciferous Vegetables chapter for methods that will work with any sturdy, dark leafy greens; see Garlicky Spinach and Pasta with Garlic and Greens in the Garlic chapter for methods especially apt for spinach and Swiss chard leaves). During months when there isn't much harvesting of tender greens, choose the firmest head lettuces and cabbages, which hold up fairly well in commercial cold storage. Ideally, salad leaves should be individually rinsed, quickly, before serving, and dried in a salad spinner. But spinach and turnip greens tend to hold so much silt that it is only practical to immerse them in several changes of cold water in a sink or large bowl. Tear strong-tasting greens into small pieces and milder ones into larger pieces for flavor balance in a mixed salad. The rule that greens should be torn and never cut with a knife is meant to be broken from time to time: very thinly sliced red, green, and Napa cabbages, as well as iceberg lettuce, make

Spotlight: The Sweet Smell of Tomatoes

What would salads be without tomatoes? A simple tomato slice, aromatic and fire-engine red, perfectly complements a plate of mixed greens when lightly tossed with olive or walnut oil, vinegar, and freshly ground pepper.

Cherish the fiery red: It's the red of lycopene, a pigment related to the carotenoids that give carrots their orange, and it may furnish similar protection against cancer.

Safeguard the aroma: Don't refrigerate fresh tomatoes, and don't slice them until moments before you want to eat them. Much of the fresh aroma comes from a chemical, z-3-hexenal, that's released upon slicing and disappears within three minutes. That's why tomato slices on your lunchbox turkey sandwich taste faded by noon. Says USDA research chemist Ron Buttery, PH.D., of Albany, California, "Refrigerating a tomato turns off the enzyme that produced z-3-hexenal." The worst idea: cutting a cold tomato. "If you do refrigerate a tomato, let it warm up a bit before you slice it," he says. Cooked tomatoes, with their rich flavors, rely on entirely different and quite complex compounds, he notes.

—Robert Barnett

not only good slaws and sandwich toppings but also nutritious beds, full of crunchy contrast, for sautéed or broiled meats and poultry and soft-cooked vegetables, such as potatoes and beets.

The best embellishments for spring lettuces are the small sweet peas (uncooked), green onions, and chives harvested at the same time; there is an affinity, too, in the sweetness of tiny beets (cooked, of course) and the delicacy of thinly sliced mushrooms and cucumber. Summer's

Spotlight: Parsley for Wombs?

Parsley's the chef's mystery
Important in "bouquet garni."
And parsley is made
Into French persillade.
And French soldiers drank parsley tea.
         —James Duke

Parsley, a member of the carrot family, is reported in animal studies to lower blood pressure and work as a mild uterine tonic. Parsley oil is rich in apiol and myristicin, both pharmacologically proven uterine stimulants. The oil has been used to bring on periods, and misused to bring on abortions, so it should never be given to pregnant women. But parsley itself contains only a small amount of essential oil.

Its main contribution is taste. It's served as a condiment, a garnish, a grace note on top of soups. But it can be a vegetable or salad green, too. It's central to tabouli. Moroccans eat parsley as a salad, seasoned with cumin and paprika. It can be steamed as well. Eat it in quantity and you'll reap a bounty of nutrients. A raw half-cup, chopped, has only 10 calories and 39 milligrams of sodium, but provides 536 milligrams of potassium, 11 percent of the USRDA for iron, 45 percent for vitamin C, 15 percent for folic acid, and 16 percent for vitamin A. It's also rich in chlorophyll, reputed to freshen breath.

         —J.D. and R.B.

lettuce-less salads call for the bitter spark of basil, tarragon, chervil, and other herbs picked with the tomatoes, zucchini, and peppers. Fall is the time to explore juxtapositions of briefly sautéed wild mushrooms and greens, as well as salad garnishes of sliced ripe pears and purple plums and chopped nuts. Winter salads can be as bright as those of any other season if you pair the assertive cruciferous greens, such as kale and red cabbage, with such mild counterpoints as diced cooked potatoes, frozen corn kernels or lima beans, shredded carrots, and canned kidney beans or chick-peas; a chopped hard-cooked egg will both add dramatic color and mellow the bite of the cabbage.

Once a salad has grown from a simple side dish into a complex tossing, many busy cooks will be tempted to add a little protein and call it a meal (with only bread needed to supplement calories and carbohydrates). Canned tuna and sardines, as well as cooked beans and eggs, will flatter the sturdier greens, as will diced leftover poultry and grated or shredded cheeses. But the most luxurious main course salads feature meat, poultry, or seafood with dressings made from cooking juices. The meat may be cooked in any way that provides some liquid for the dressing. With poached chicken, salmon, shrimp, or scallops, for example, the poaching liquid can be reduced by one-third to one-half, as desired, and seasoned to dress the greens (see Oriental Chicken Salad, page 180, for the precise method). With sautéed pieces of boneless meat, poultry, or seafood, the pan can be deglazed with broth or fruit or vegetable juice to make a low-fat dressing. With roasted or broiled meat, poultry, or fish, the pan juices provided by basting with broth or a marinade should be defatted and then seasoned with vinegar or citrus juice to make the dressing. In all cases the salad should be served at once, before the juices congeal.

Salad Dressings

The word "salad" comes from the Latin for salt, implying an ancient link between greens and the most basic seasoning. A good pinch of salt is still the best way to bring out the best flavor of delicate greens. But there are ways to minimize the amount of salt needed in any salad. First among these is to tear greens and cut other salad ingredients into small pieces to release their savory juices. Secondly, mince any kind of onion with parsley and other herbs and add lemon juice or another acid; this basic seasoning mix flatters all salads made with lettuces and mild greens. With salads that include such spicy cruciferous greens as watercress and arugula, the parsley is superfluous, but the onion and acid are still good complements. Greens seasoned thus need very little additional dressing—just two or three teaspoons per serving—to taste moist and satisfying.

A vinaigrette is the basic salad dressing of most cooking repertoires, and it can remain so in a healthy diet as long as you apply it quite sparingly. To reduce fat, you can alter the classic ratio of three or four parts oil to one part acid with little diminishment of flavor; indeed, if you use a mild, somewhat sweet acid, such as orange with lime or grapefruit juice or balsamic vinegar, and a sweet olive or nut oil for part of the oil, you can invert the proportions to two parts acid to one part oil. Whisk in some prepared mustard and if you wish to create a thicker emulsion.

Low-fat or nonfat yogurt (choose according to taste; some brands of nonfat yogurt satisfy, others taste chalky) provides the answer to cravings for a creamy dressing. Season and thin yogurt to taste with fresh lemon juice, minced parsley, green onion, garlic, and dried dill or tarragon for an all-purpose dressing. For specific formulas, see Blue Cheese Salad Dressing (Milk and Yogurt, page 286), Yogurt, Dill, and Lemon Sauce, or Cucumber, Yogurt, Mint, and Dill Sauce (Fish, page 212), and Curried Yogurt Dressing (Fruit, page 296). You may want to process the yogurt sauces to smoothness in a blender or food processor and thin with a little milk to use them as salad dressings.

The most fascinating range of low-fat dressings comes from smooth purees of vegetables and fruits. Examples include Fresh Tomato-Parmesan Dressing, Tangy Cucumber Dressing, Strawberry Dressing, Artichoke Dressing, and Avocado Dressing in this chapter as well as Roasted Pepper Dressing in the Peppers chapter, page 204. All of these are easy to make with a blender or food processor and can be refrigerated in a covered container for up to a week. They add not only

another nutritional dimension to green salads but also flavors much fresher than those poured from commercial jars.

Antipasto Green Salad with Artichoke Dressing
by Nao Hauser

This recipe makes a fine first course, or, if you double the serving size, a main dish for a family of four.

12 ounces cauliflower, broken into very small flowerets
 2 tablespoons olive oil
 1 tablespoon balsamic or red wine vinegar
 1 small clove garlic, peeled and minced
 1 teaspoon dried oregano leaves
¼ teaspoon ground coriander
½ cup dry white wine
 1 13¾-ounce can artichoke hearts, drained
 1 small red onion, thinly sliced
 1 green bell pepper, thinly sliced
 2 stalks celery, thinly sliced
 1 3¼-ounce can pitted ripe olives, rinsed, drained, and sliced (optional)
12 ounces combined escarole, romaine, curly endive, dandelion greens, radicchio, and/or arugula, torn into bite-size pieces
 1 6½-ounce can tuna in water, drained and flaked
 8 ounces cherry tomatoes, halved
   Freshly ground black pepper

PREPARATION TIME: 30 minutes
COOKING TIME: 10 minutes
YIELD: 8 servings

Add the cauliflower to a large pot of boiling water; let water return to boil (cauliflower should be tender-crisp). Drain well.

Place the oil, vinegar, garlic, oregano, coriander, and wine in a blender with 5 of the artichoke hearts, broken into pieces, and process until smooth.

Combine the onion, green pepper, celery, olives, and remaining artichoke hearts, broken into pieces, in a large salad bowl. Toss with the greens, tuna, cauliflower, tomatoes, and black pepper to taste. Spoon artichoke dressing over the salad; toss well.

NUTRITION INFORMATION: Cal: 140 Pro: 11g/28% Carb: 11g/40% Fat: 4g/24% (S:15% M:64% P:21%) Alc: 8% Chol: 18mg Sodium: 182mg Potassium: 746mg Fiber: 5g A: 57% C: 113% B1: 11% B6: 16% Folic: 26% Ca: 10% P: 14% Fe: 17% Mg: 13% Mn: 18% Cr: 18%
EXCHANGE: Lean Meat: ³/₄ Veg: 2¹/₂ Fat: ³/₄

MICROWAVE METHOD: In a 1¹/₂-quart microwave-safe casserole or bowl, cook the cauliflower and 2 tablespoons water covered on High (100% power) until tender-crisp, about 4 to 6 minutes. Drain and continue as directed above.

Spinach Salad with Lemon

by *American Health*

10 ounces fresh spinach
 1 4-ounce jar sliced pimentos, drained
 2 tablespoons fresh lemon juice
¹/₄ teaspoon salt
¹/₄ teaspoon sugar
     Dash freshly ground black pepper

PREPARATION TIME: 15 minutes
YIELD: 6 first-course servings

Tear the spinach into bite-size pieces. Put the spinach into a large salad bowl. Add the pimentos and toss to mix well. In a small cup, mix the lemon juice, salt, sugar, and pepper. Pour over the salad; toss well.

NUTRITION INFORMATION: Cal: 18 Pro: 2g/28% Carb: 3g/61% Fat: .3g/11% Chol: 0mg Sod: 123mg Pot: 275mg Fiber: 2g Vit A: 73% Vit C: 56% Folic: 23% Mang: 12%
EXCHANGE: Veg: ¹/₂

Orange and Avocado Salad with Tender Greens

by *American Health*

 3 tablespoons orange juice
 2 tablespoons fresh lemon juice
 1 tablespoon olive oil
1¹/₂ teaspoons sugar
 ¹/₄ teaspoon salt
 3 large oranges, peeled and sectioned
 1 medium avocado, peeled and sliced
¹/₂ small onion, thinly sliced
¹/₂ medium head romaine lettuce
 1 small head Boston lettuce

PREPARATION TIME: 30 minutes plus refrigerating time
YIELD: 6 first-course servings

In a large bowl, mix the first five ingredients. Stir in the oranges, avocado, and onion; cover and refrigerate at least 1 hour to blend flavors. Tear the lettuce into bite-size pieces; place in a plastic bag, seal, and refrigerate until ready to serve. To serve, combine lettuces and fruit mixture and gently toss to mix well.

NUTRITION INFORMATION: Cal: 129 Pro: 3g/27% Carb: 17g/49% Fat: .7g/44% (S: 16% M: 71% P: 13%) Chol: 0mg Sodium: 92mg Potassium: 540mg Fiber: 4g A: 29% B1: 12% C: 120% Folic: 29%
EXCHANGE: Veg: ¹/₂ Fruit: 1 Fat: 1¹/₂

Greens with Hazelnuts and Goat Cheese Dressing

by Nao Hauser

³/₄ cup skim milk
 3 ounces fresh goat cheese
 3 tablespoons chopped fresh parsley
 2 tablespoons fresh lemon juice
 1 tablespoon dried tarragon
¹/₄ teaspoon ground cardamom
 8 ounces romaine, Boston, or loose-leaf
     lettuce, torn into bite-size pieces

6 ounces arugula, dandelion greens, radicchio, watercress, or Belgian endive, torn into bite-size pieces
8 ounces fresh mushrooms, sliced
2 cups croutons
1 small red onion, thinly sliced
1/4 teaspoon salt (optional)
  Freshly ground black pepper
1 ounce coarsely chopped hazelnuts

PREPARATION TIME: 30 minutes
COOKING TIME: 5 minutes
YIELD: 6 servings

Place the milk, cheese, parsley, lemon juice, tarragon, and cardamom in a blender; process until smooth.

Combine the greens, mushrooms, croutons, and onion in a large salad bowl; sprinkle with the salt if desired and black pepper to taste. Spread the hazelnuts in a small skillet and cook over medium heat, stirring constantly, until golden, about 2 to 3 minutes. Sprinkle the nuts over the salad, spoon the dressing over the top, and toss well.

NUTRITION INFORMATION: Cal: 139 Pro: 7g/ 20% Carb: 16g/44% Fat: 6g/36% (S:45% M:47% P:8%) Chol: 13mg Sodium: 318mg Potassium: 477mg Fiber: 3g A: 90% C: 35% B1: 12% B2: 22% B3: 12% Folic: 17% Ca: 19% P: 19% Fe: 14% Cr: 16%
EXCHANGE: Med. Meat: 1/2 Bread: 1/2 Veg: 1 Fat: 3/4

Oriental Chicken and Greens Salad

by Nao Hauser

The addition of chicken turns greens into a main course, and the greens balance the sweet, sour, and salty tastes of the Oriental seasonings, carrot, and red pepper.

1 1/2 cups unsalted chicken broth or stock (see page 28)
2 teaspoons grated fresh ginger
1 teaspoon reduced-sodium soy sauce

1/4 teaspoon Chinese 5-spice powder (see Note)
2 whole chicken breasts (about 1 pound each), skin and visible fat removed
1 tablespoon sesame oil
1 tablespoon rice wine or cider vinegar
6 scallions, sliced
2 carrots, grated
1 red bell pepper, julienne cut (optional)
4 teaspoons chopped walnuts, toasted
8 to 10 ounces romaine or celery cabbage, torn into bite-size pieces
8 to 10 ounces spinach, turnip greens, Swiss chard, kale, or beet greens, stems removed, torn into bite-size pieces
  Freshly ground black pepper

PREPARATION TIME: 40 minutes
COOKING TIME: 45 minutes
YIELD: 6 servings

Heat the broth, ginger, soy sauce, and 5-spice powder to boiling in a large saucepan; reduce the heat. Add the chicken and simmer, covered, turning once, until the juices run clear when the thickest part is pierced with a fork, 25 to 30 minutes. Remove the chicken; let stand until cool enough to handle. Discard the bones; cut the meat into small pieces.

Skim the fat from the pan liquid and boil until reduced to 3/4 cup; whisk in the oil and vinegar to make the salad dressing. Return chicken pieces to dressing in pan; simmer 3 minutes. Combine the scallions, carrots, red pepper, and walnuts in a large salad bowl; toss with the greens. Add black pepper to taste. Spoon the warm dressing and chicken over the greens and toss well.

NOTE: You can purchase 5-spice powder at Asian food markets and in many supermarkets. If 5-spice powder is not available, substitute 1/8 teaspoon ground cinnamon and 1/8 teaspoon ground nutmeg.

NUTRITION INFORMATION: Cal: 260 Pro: 39g/ 60% Carb: 7g/11% Fat: 8g/29% (S:23% M:38% P:39%) Chol: 97mg Sodium: 165mg Potassium: 723mg Fiber: 3g A: 207% C: 51% E: 13% B2:

14% B3: 85% B6: 44% Folic: 21% Panto: 13%
P: 33% Fe: 14% Mg: 18% Mn: 15% Se: 43%
Cr: 32%
EXCHANGE: Lean Meat: 4 Veg: 1½

MICROWAVE METHOD: In a 12- by 8-inch microwave-safe baking dish, cook the broth, ginger, soy sauce, and spice powder, covered, on High (100% power) to boiling, about 3½ to 4 minutes. Add the chicken, thickest portion toward the outside, and cook covered on High until the chicken is fork-tender, about 10 to 12 minutes. Let stand 5 minutes. Remove the chicken; cool and continue as directed above.

Confetti Salad with Avocado Dressing
by Nao Hauser

  1 ripe avocado, peeled and cut into chunks
  2 tablespoons cider vinegar
    Juice of 1 lime
  1 clove garlic, peeled and minced
  ½ teaspoon ground cumin
  ½ teaspoon chili powder
  ¾ to 1 cup vegetable or tomato juice, no salt added
  1 small, sweet white onion, thinly sliced
  1 green bell pepper, diced
  1 small zucchini, diced
  1 10-ounce package frozen corn kernels, thawed and thoroughly drained
  1 cup canned chick-peas, rinsed and drained
  1 large tomato, chopped
  1 small bunch fresh parsley or coriander, chopped
    Freshly ground black pepper
 12 ounces assorted greens (any combination of mild lettuces with turnip greens, beet greens, dandelion greens, and/or spinach)

PREPARATION TIME: 40 minutes
YIELD: 6 servings

Place the avocado, vinegar, lime juice, garlic, cumin, and chili powder in a blender; puree. Add ¾ cup vegetable juice; process until smooth. (If

dressing is too thick, add the remaining juice and process to blend.)
Combine the onion, green pepper, zucchini, corn, chick-peas, tomato, and parsley in a large salad bowl. Sprinkle with black pepper to taste. Add the greens to the bowl, spoon the dressing over the salad, and toss well.

NUTRITION INFORMATION: Cal: 173 Pro: 6g/ 12% Carb: 27g/55% Fat: 7g/33% (S:17% M:67% P:16%) Chol. 0mg Sodium: 166mg Potassium: 788mg Fiber: 6g A: 42% C: 86% B1: 13% B3: 12% B6: 16% Folic: 33% P: 11% Fe: 16% Mg: 12% Cr: 27%
EXCHANGE: Bread: 1 Veg: 2 Fat: 1½

Tangy Cucumber Dressing
by Nao Hauser

A light, all-purpose dressing, this blend adds zest to mild greens such as Boston lettuce and spinach, but also complements the tanginess of mustard greens, curly endive, and Chinese cabbage.

  1 medium cucumber
  ½ cup fresh parsley sprigs
  ¼ cup plain low-fat yogurt
  1 small scallion with top, sliced
  1 tablespoon tarragon vinegar
  1 tablespoon Dijon-style mustard
  1 clove garlic, peeled and sliced
  ½ teaspoon celery seed
  ½ teaspoon dried dill
    Few drops Worcestershire sauce

PREPARATION TIME: 10 minutes plus refrigerating time
YIELD: 1 cup

Peel, seed, and coarsely chop the cucumber.
Place all the ingredients in a blender and process until smooth. Refrigerate in a covered container several hours to blend flavors and up to 1 week.

NUTRITION INFORMATION (per 2-tablespoon serving): Cal: 17 Pro: 1g/22% Carb: 2g/51% Fat: 1g/27% (S:63% M:29% P:8%) Chol: 1mg Sodium: 32mg Potassium: 79mg Fiber: 1g
EXCHANGE: Veg: ½

Fresh Tomato-Parmesan Dressing

by *American Health*

Serve with any kind of greens.

   1 *large tomato, cut up*
   3 *tablespoons red wine vinegar*
1 to 2 *tablespoons freshly grated Parmesan cheese*
   2 *cloves garlic, peeled and minced*
   ¼ *teaspoon onion powder*
   ¼ *teaspoon dried basil*
   ⅛ *teaspoon freshly ground black pepper*
   ½ *teaspoon sugar (optional)*

PREPARATION TIME: 10 minutes
YIELD: about ¾ cup

In a blender at medium speed, blend all the ingredients except the sugar until smooth. Taste, and add sugar if desired. Refrigerate in a covered container up to a week.

NUTRITION INFORMATION (per 2-tablespoon serving): Cal: 15 Pro: 1g/21% Carb: 2g/66% Fat: .2g/13% Chol: 1mg Sodium: 34mg Potassium: 114mg Fiber: 1g C: 11%
EXCHANGE: Veg: ½

Strawberry Dressing

by Nao Hauser

This very delicate, sweet-sour blend goes beautifully with salads of spinach or watercress and mushrooms. Its rosy color highlights arranged salads of Belgian endive and Boston or Bibb lettuce. Substitute hulled fresh strawberries for the frozen only when the fresh are very sweet and juicy.

   8 *ounces frozen unsweetened strawberries (about 1¼ cups), thawed*
2½ to 3 *tablespoons balsamic or red wine vinegar*
   1 *tablespoon unsalted chicken broth or stock (see page 28) or water*
   1 *tablespoon olive oil*
   1 *teaspoon dried tarragon*
   ⅛ *teaspoon ground cardamom*

PREPARATION TIME: 5 minutes
YIELD: 1 cup

Place the strawberries, 2½ tablespoons of the vinegar, and the remaining ingredients in a blender and process until smooth. Taste, and add the additional vinegar if desired.

NUTRITION INFORMATION (per 2-tablespoon serving): Cal: 38 Pro: .2g/2% Carb: 6g/60% Fat: 2g/38% (S:14% M:76% P:10%) Chol: 0mg Sodium: 3mg Potassium: 30mg Fiber: 1g C: 19%
EXCHANGE: Fruit: ¼ Fat: ½

Citrus Salad Dressing

by Nao Hauser

For all kinds of green salads or cole slaw. Use fresh-squeezed juice for best taste.

¼ *cup fresh orange juice*
¼ *cup fresh grapefruit juice*
2 *tablespoons vegetable oil*
2 *tablespoons walnut or fruity olive oil*
4 *teaspoons coarse-grain mustard*

PREPARATION TIME: 5 to 10 minutes
YIELD: ¾ cup (about 6 servings)

Whisk together all the ingredients in a small bowl or shake well in a covered jar. Refrigerate up to 10 days.

NUTRITION INFORMATION (per 2-tablespoon serving): Cal: 92 Pro: .3g/1% Carb: 2g/9% Fat: 9g/89% (S:12% M:45% P:43%) Chol: 0mg Sodium: 46mg Potassium: 42mg Fiber: .1g C: 15% E: 12%
EXCHANGE: Fat: 2

◇ SEA VEGETABLES ◇

A Sea of Vegetables

by Jeanine Barone, M.S.

Once we called them seaweed. Now we appreciate them more and call them sea vegetables. They have plenty to offer.

Nori, the most popular sea vegetable, is also the richest in protein. Ounce for ounce, it has almost twice the protein of an equal serving of whole milk, five times the vitamin A (as beta-carotene), and double the vitamin C of raw tomatoes. Kombu and wakame are brown algae; they are close relatives. Also known as kelp, kombu is one of the richest sea vegetable sources of iodine, so be careful of it if you're concerned about high iodine intake. It contains over 400 times the iodine found in an equal serving of oysters.

Wakame, also a good source of iodine, is rich in calcium and the trace minerals magnesium, manganese, and copper. Ounce for ounce, it contains over twice the calcium of milk with less fat and fewer calories. Arame is an even richer calcium source with twice the calcium of whole milk but less than 1 percent of the fat. Hijiki, the richest sea vegetable calcium source, contains over twice the calcium of milk, and 24 times the potassium found in an equal amount of pears. It is also a good source of iron. Dulse, the best iron source of any sea vegetable, contains, ounce for ounce, 30 times the iron found in a hard-boiled egg and

approximately 7 times that in sirloin beef.

Agar, made from algae such as gelidium, as the name indicates, helps things gel. This natural gelatin produces a firm jelly, jam, or marmalade without the additional sugar found in sweetened gelatins. It's also a good source of calcium, iron, iodine, and phosphorus, with essentially no fat.

Cooking with Sea Vegetables

by Mary Estella

Walk along any ocean beach and tossed up on shore, along with shells and driftwood, is seaweed. These stringy, salt-coated, brown or black strands seem a far-fetched ingredient for tonight's soup. Never fear! These "weeds" can be eaten. Like vegetation above sea level, sea vegetables are harvested while they grow, attached to rocks or other surfaces on the ocean floor.

Like land vegetables, sea vegetables have seasons. They are cut, dried, and packaged for future use. If stored in a cool, dry place, sea vegetables keep indefinitely, ready to be prepared in a variety of ways. Japan, an island nation, turns to the sea for nourishment, combining the fruits of the sea with the rice of terraced fields for a refined cuisine. In Japan, billions of 8- by 10-inch, paper-thin black sheets of nori are used each year as wrappers for rice, noodles, vegetables, and fish.

Nori rolls or nore-make (rice rolled in nori) are as popular in Japan as sandwiches are in America. Nori need only be "toasted" by gently passing over a gas flame or electric burner. The sheets will become crisp and their color more green. Tasty and crisp, it's often cut into strips for a garnish or shredded and mixed with sesame seeds for a condiment. Sushi nori is sold pretoasted and ready to use.

Kombu grows in the cold, deep water off Japan's northern islands. Up to forty feet long, the leaflike fronds are harvested on long hooks, spread out to dry, and cut into 6- to 12-inch lengths for packaging. Atlantic kombu, or kelp as it's sometimes called, is being harvested off Maine's rocky coast and can be prepared in ways similar to Japanese kombu. Traditionally, kombu is used to flavor soup stocks called "dashi" in Japan. It is often added to dried beans as they cook for flavor and to aid in their digestibility. It is also roasted and ground into a powder used for seasoning.

Wakame, a feathery dark green sea vegetable, grows in shallow, cold ocean currents. A favorite ingredient in soup or salad, wakame must be reconstituted first by soaking for 10 to 15 minutes. The outer tough "rib" is cut away and the soft, flavorful, sliced wakame is added to other dishes. A delicate vegetable, wakame requires little cooking time and is often added to a cucumber salad seasoned with vinegar or lemon. "Instant" wakame is now available in sealed envelopes. Simply add to a bowl of water and it quickly swells and is ready to be used in your favorite recipe.

Hijiki and arame are both delicate black strands of sea grass. High in calcium, protein, and other nutrients, hijiki is slightly thicker and requires more cooking time than arame. Shredded from a wide sea grass, arame has a more delicate flavor and is a good choice for introducing sea vegetables into one's diet. Both need to be rinsed and soaked in water for 5 to 10 minutes before cooking to remove any sand or tiny shells. These sea grasses can be sauteed and seasoned with ingredients such as soy sauce, dark sesame oil, ginger, garlic, lemon juice, or mirin. The shimmering black strands are attractive in mixed vegetable dishes or as a dramatic garnish to seafood or soyfood entrées. Cooked, they keep several days in the refrigerator and can be chopped and added to grain or noodle dishes.

From Maine to the Mendocino region of California, America is experiencing a revival in the sea vegetable industry. Small companies along both coasts are gathering and shipping sea vegetable products to local and national markets. Dulse, for example, a reddish-purple, feathery sea vegetable traditionally used in the British Isles, is now harvested in Maine. Snack on it right out of the bag; roasted, dulse is crisp and slightly salty like chips. Dulse can be added to sandwiches with lettuce, tomato, and sprouts; tossed into salads; blended in dressings; or chopped and mixed into bread dough. A small handful of dulse adds a rich purple color to soups or stews.

Sea vegetables have long been used as thickeners or stabilizers in frozen foods or desserts. Irish moss, or agar, is used in many gourmet ice creams and gelatins. Easy to prepare, agar comes packaged in bars, flakes, or powder. It adds no flavor of its own to sweet fruit gelatins or vegetable aspics. It sets quickly at room temperature and is perfect for jelling jams, fruit sauces, puddings, or pie fillings. The cooking instructions vary for the bars, flakes, or powdered form of agar. Follow package directions.

California Nori Rolls

by Mary Estella

Rice and avocado are rolled up in nori, a black sheet of sea vegetable. Easy to make with a sushi mat (the bamboo rolling mat), nori rolls can be filled with a variety of steamed or raw vegetables—such as carrot, cucumber, or bell pepper—and seasonings. Avocado rolls should be eaten the same day because avocado will turn brown, but other vegetable fillings can keep two to three days.

1 cup raw brown rice or brown basmati
    rice
2 tablespoons mirin, or 1 tablespoon rice
    syrup (optional) (see Note)
1 tablespoon rice vinegar
1/4 teaspoon sea salt
4 sheets nori (toasted or regular)
1 ripe avocado
    Juice of 1 lemon
2 teaspoons stone-ground mustard
4 scallions, cut to equal length of nori
    sheets
4 to 6 sun-dried tomatoes, no salt added, or 1
    small red pepper, sliced into thin strips

PREPARATION TIME: 45 minutes
COOKING TIME: 50 minutes
YIELD: 6 appetizer or 4 main-course servings

Rinse the rice in a strainer. Bring 2 cups water to a boil in a 1-quart saucepan; add the rice, mirin, vinegar, and sea salt; cover and simmer on very low heat 45 minutes, or until liquid is absorbed. Do not stir the rice as it simmers. Let rice stand until cool enough to handle.

Toast the nori sheets over medium flame or hot electric burner by waving the sheet back and forth—almost like fanning the heat. The nori should change color slightly and become crisp. Peel the avocado and cut into thin slices; sprinkle with lemon juice to prevent discoloring.

Place 1 nori sheet on a sushi mat (shiny side down). Arrange the mat so that the short end is toward you. Make sure the table, the sushi mat, and fillings are dry—any excess moisture will soften the nori and it will tear.

Spoon 1/2 cup of the rice onto the nori sheet. Lightly moisten your fingers with water and press the rice to cover the lower three-fourths of the nori. Press the rice firmly to about 1/3-inch thickness, leaving 1 inch nori uncovered along the top. About 1 inch from the bottom of the nori sheet, spread 1/2 teaspoon of mustard. Place a scallion on the mustard, then place 2 slices of avocado on top, overlap if necessary, and add a few thin strips of sun-dried tomato or red pepper.

To roll, lift the sushi mat and begin to roll, holding the filling in place with your index fingers.

Roll the nori, neatly and firmly, like a jelly roll, almost to the end, then moisten the top strip of nori with water to seal the roll. Fill and roll the remaining nori. Store nori rolls uncut in the refrigerator, wrapping each roll tightly in plastic wrap.

To slice, use a sharp knife (not serrated), to cut into 1/2- to 1-inch rounds as you prefer. Wipe the blade with a sponge to remove any rice after each slice.

Serve as an appetizer with ginger-soy sauce or as a side dish with chicken, fish, or tofu; or pack in a lunch box.

NOTE: Mirin or rice syrup can be found at Asian food stores.

The rice needs to be on the sticky side to hold together. If your nori roll falls apart, the rice may be too dry. Pressure cooking brown rice will ensure its stickiness. Or use basmati rice. Do not add oil or butter to the rice as it cooks, as this will make it separate, not sticky.

VARIATION:

♦ Salmon-Cucumber Rolls: Slice lox into long thin strips about 1/2-inch wide. Peel and slice cucumber into long thin strips. Spread a small amount of horseradish (Japanese wasabe) on rice, add strips of salmon and cucumber, roll and complete as directed above.

NUTRITION INFORMATION (per 1 appetizer roll): Cal: 154 Pro: 4g/9% Carb: 24g/59% Fat: 6g/32% (S:17% M:70% P:13%) Chol: 0mg Sodium: 125mg Potassium: 359mg Fiber: 4g A: 26% C: 59% Se: 41%
EXCHANGE: Bread: 1 1/2 Fat: 1

Cucumber-Dulse Salad with Lemon Vinaigrette
by Mary Estella

Dulse—a feathery soft, dark purple sea vegetable—needs no cooking. Simply add a few tablespoons of rinsed, soaked, and drained dulse to sliced vegetables and season with lemon juice for a quick, vitamin-rich salad. This salad can be refrigerated for 2 to 3 days. Serve with a bean or thick vegetable stew or with a fish entrée and a pilaf.

> 1 red onion
> 1 cucumber
> 1/2 cup lightly packed dried dulse (about 1/2 ounce)
> 1 tablespoon fresh lemon juice
> 1 teaspoon red wine vinegar
> 1 tablespoon olive or sesame oil
> Pinch sea salt
> White pepper
> 1 small bunch watercress or red leaf lettuce
> Lemon wedges for garnish

PREPARATION TIME: 20 minutes plus standing time
YIELD: 4 to 5 servings

Quarter the onion lengthwise and slice. Peel the cucumber, quarter it lengthwise, and slice.

Place the dulse in a bowl, cover with cool water, and soak 2 to 3 minutes. Place the sliced onion and cucumber in a mixing bowl. Drain the dulse in a strainer to remove all water. There should be about 2 to 3 tablespoons of dulse.

Add the dulse, lemon juice, vinegar, oil, sea salt, and pepper to vegetables; stir to coat. (The dulse will break apart and become part of the dressing.)

Cover and allow salad to stand 1 to 2 hours before serving. Serve on a bed of watercress or red leaf lettuce. Garnish with lemon wedges.

VARIATIONS: Add celery, radish, scallions, or parsley to the salad. Add extra herbs, lemon juice, mustard, or garlic to the seasoning.

NUTRITION INFORMATION: Cal: 48 Pro: 1g/8% Carb: 5g/41% Fat: 3g/51% (S:15% M:74% P:11%) Chol: 0mg Sodium: 58mg Potassium: 226mg Fiber: 1g C: 16%
EXCHANGE: Veg.: 1 Fat: 1/2
(with 1 breadstick) Cal: 153 Pro: 4g/11% Carb: 25g/66% Fat: 4g/23% (S:15% M:74% P:11%) Chol: 0mg Sodium: 606mg Potassium: 259mg Fiber: 1g C: 16%
EXCHANGE: Bread: 1 Veg: 1 Fat: 1

◇ GINGER ◇

The Joy of Ginger

by James Duke, Ph.D.

I hardly think you can injure
A seasick sailor with ginger.
And they say that you can
Overstimulate man,
Yet tenderize meat in the pan!

—James Duke

Ginger—a tropical spice—does more than add a sweet pungent heat in the kitchen. It's an important medicinal spice as well. Only garlic is better represented in my international collection of herb and spice studies. About half of all Oriental herbal medicine includes ginger root.

In China, ginger tea, made by boiling fresh ginger root in water, has long been prescribed for colds, coughs, flu, and hangovers. In Japanese animal studies conducted at Tsumara Research Institute for Pharmacology and reported in 1984, ginger exhibited an "intense antitussive [cough-suppressing] effect," even when compared with codeine. It also lowered fever and reduced pain.

Other animal studies, conducted in Montreal in 1955 and in Tokyo in 1979, find that ginger oil may have a mild stimulating effect on the immune system.

Ginger has also had a folk reputation as a motion-sickness antidote. Chinese commercial fishermen at sea would chew on a slug of ginger root to ward off decidedly unprofitable bouts of seasickness.

It's not just folklore. A 1982 study from Brigham Young University and Mount Union College in Ohio found that powdered ginger root was more effective than the common antinausea drug Dramamine in blocking motion sickness. (It's also a wee bit cheaper.)

Ginger most likely works against motion sickness by "interrupting the feedback between the stomach and the nausea center of the brain," says Daniel Mowrey, who coauthored the study while at Brigham Young. It does so, he believes, by increasing stomach activity and absorbing stomach acids.

Researchers at Odense University in Denmark believe that it may also work on the inner ear, another mechanism involved in motion sickness. In a 1986 double-blind study, powdered ginger root inhibited vertigo in each of the eight volunteers.

Like garlic, ginger may be good for the cardiovascular system. But since studies have been done primarily on animals, not people, it's impossible to draw firm conclusions. A Danish study published in 1986, for example, revealed that ginger extracts inhibit a blood-clotting compound in the lab.

Finally, ginger appears to have a direct effect on the heart. Animal research at Tsumura indicates that it decreases the heart rate. Other Japanese researchers find that ginger also increases the force of contractions in the upper or atrial chamber of the heart. Digitalis, the heart drug, has similar effects.

In the kitchen, ginger is a great natural preservative, bacteriacide and meat tenderizer. Nigerian test tube studies show that ginger extract is very effective in killing salmonella. And Indian studies report that ginger extracts inhibit the fungi that produce aflatoxin, a potent carcinogen.

Ginger is a strong antioxidant. It contains two phenolic compounds, shogaol and zingerone, that protect fats from being damaged by highly destructive forms of oxygen known as free radicals. In short, it protects oils and fats from rancidity.

It's clear that ginger helps preserve pork. At the University of California at Davis, researchers cooked and then refrigerated pork patties. Some were unspiced, some mildly spiced with ginger, some more strongly spiced. Patties made with ginger stayed fresh as much as a third longer than unspiced pork.

Conceivably, it could help people as well: Since body fat, just like any fat, is subject to oxidative damage—a process that plays a role in initiating certain cancers, coronary heart disease, and perhaps even aging—antioxidants like ginger may help "preserve" us as well.

Cooking with Ginger

by Nao Hauser

Ginger is a coy character in the kitchen. It doesn't have the eye-tearing, lip-searing impact of chilies, but it definitely heats up a dish. Yet there is a faint floral edge to the pungency that also serves to underscore the sweetness of fruit and the delicacy of chicken and fish.

The two sides of ginger root are reflected in its diverse uses in Oriental cuisines. Pickled in vinegar with soy sauce and sugar, and then sliced paper thin, it is the essential accompaniment to Japanese sushi. Parboiled to reduce its bite and then cooked in a sugar syrup, it becomes a popular candy in China and Korea. The minced root is an essential counterpoint to the "fishiness" of steamed fish. It is also the standard bittering agent used to balance the sweetness of sugar, the saltiness of soy sauce or nam pla, and the acidity of vinegar in sauces and salad dressings.

The problem posed by such formulas is that they make ginger the foil for much sodium, sugar, and fat. If you eliminate one or two parts of the equation, the ginger can taste unbearably bitter. So it's easier to create new contexts for the seasoning than to try to tinker with the most tried-and-true Oriental recipes. Seek other taste-mates for ginger, and you'll discover its affinity for the natural sugars of tropical fruits and vivid root vegetables, such as carrots and beets. The intrinsic fat and salinity of nuts and such ocean fish as tuna and swordfish also welcome ginger (see recipe for Steamed Fillets with Black Bean Sauce, Cucumber, and Scallion, page 229). The heat and bitterness of the root can be just what's needed to spark the minerals, starches, and sugars of stock-based soups and stews.

When you're experimenting, start with no more than 1/2 teaspoon of minced ginger root per serving. You can always up the amount to taste. The ginger will get somewhat milder when allowed to simmer (though it never becomes as gentle as cooked garlic does), so you may want to reinforce the flavor by adding more just before serving. There is only one caveat: Don't allow fresh ginger to burn or it will become acrid. If you want the taste of ginger in a broiled, roasted, or sautéed dish, either use the ground dried spice or marinate the food with fresh ginger and then turn the marinade into a sauce.

Ginger is sold in many forms. The most common is the ground dried ginger on spice shelves. This is a convenient product for sprinkling on meats and fruits and dissolving in beverages and batters. The crystalized ginger also found on spice racks is most often used in ice cream, mousses, and other sweets that can accommodate the sugar coating. You may find dried ginger root, for brewing into a tea, in Oriental and other specialized markets. The refrigerator cases of Japanese groceries usually feature several brands of pickled ginger, some of them dyed bright red to accentuate the natural blush the roots acquire when bathed in vinegar. To avoid the dye and excess salt of such products, pickle ginger at home in a solution of equal parts of rice wine vinegar and water with sugar to taste; it will keep in the refrigerator for several months, ready to slice thin and serve with sushi or broiled fish. The most delicate ginger pickles start with the fresh ginger shoots that signal springtime in some Oriental markets. Clean these well and stand them in a hot vinegar solution; they will turn pink and be ready to eat in a few hours. Some cookbooks recommend blanching ginger root or shoots very briefly before pickling to reduce bitterness and help prevent spoilage.

None of these products is as versatile or as intriguingly flavored as fresh ginger root. Choose young roots with very smooth skin to avoid a woody texture. If the skin is thin, it needn't be pared. A very fine grater is the best tool for minced ginger, especially for use with fruits or in beverages or salad dressings. But it's much easier to mince ginger in a food processor or electric spice grinder, and the difference won't be noticeable in most dishes.

To store ginger root for just a few days, wrap it in paper toweling and refrigerate it in a plastic bag. You can freeze the root for longer storage and cut off pieces as needed, but the quality will diminish over time. Some people bury the root in a pot of soil (where it may send up new shoots), dig it up, and cut off pieces as needed, but this approach is rather messy. A far pleasanter way to keep ginger is immersed in dry sherry in a covered container. The sherry will preserve it indefinitely without refrigeration. You can cut off pieces, wipe dry, and mince as needed. Use the sherry as a seasoning or basting liquid and replace it.

The simplest ways to savor freshly minced ginger are in hot liquids, such as tea, mulled cider, and chicken broth, and in foods cooked with a lot of liquid, such as brown rice, beans, braised meats, fish stews, and root vegetables. The liquid tames the heat. The ginger, in turn, brings distinction even to hot water.

Double-Ginger Chicken
by Nao Hauser

Ginger in two forms doubles the deliciousness of this dish. Ground ginger is used to coat the chicken because it doesn't burn as readily as fresh ginger root does.

About 1/4 ounce Chinese black or other dried mushrooms
4 boneless chicken breast halves (about 1 pound), skin removed
1 teaspoon ground ginger
1/8 teaspoon ground cinnamon
1/8 teaspoon ground nutmeg
1/2 cup plus 2 tablespoons dry red wine
1 teaspoon reduced-sodium soy sauce
1/2 teaspoon sugar
1 teaspoon Chinese sesame oil
2 teaspoons minced fresh ginger
1 red bell pepper, julienne cut
3 scallions, sliced on the diagonal, white and green parts separated
Cayenne
4 cups hot cooked brown rice

PREPARATION TIME: 30 minutes
COOKING TIME: 15 minutes
YIELD: 4 servings

Place the mushrooms in a bowl and pour hot water over them to cover; let stand 30 minutes.

Meanwhile, cut the chicken into 1/3-inch-wide strips. Mix together the ground ginger, cinnamon, and nutmeg in a shallow baking dish; stir in 2 tablespoons wine, the soy sauce, and sugar. Add the chicken and toss to coat with spice mixture; let stand 15 minutes.

Drain the mushrooms, cut them into thin strips, and reserve.

Heat a large, heavy skillet over high heat; add oil. Add a third of the chicken strips; cook, turning over once, until browned on both sides, about 1 minute. Remove and repeat with the remaining chicken.

Pour the 1/2 cup wine into the skillet, stirring to scrape the bottom; reduce heat to medium. Stir in the minced ginger, red bell pepper, reserved mushrooms, and white part of scallions; simmer, stirring occasionally, 3 minutes. Stir in the chicken; cook, stirring occasionally, until chicken is cooked through, about 5 minutes. Stir in scallion tops and cayenne to taste. Serve hot over rice.

NUTRITION INFORMATION (with rice): Cal: 423 Pro: 32g/31% Carb: 53g/57% Fat: 6g/12% Chol: 72mg Alc: 6% Sodium: 138mg Potassium: 494mg Fiber: 7g C: 64% E: 24% B1: 18% B2: 10% B3: 74% B6: 28% P: 21% Fe: 15% Se: 141% Cr: 23%
EXCHANGE: Lean Meat: 3 Bread: 3 Veg: 1

MICROWAVE METHOD: Prepare mushrooms and chicken as above. In a 12- by 8-inch microwave-safe baking dish, cook the chicken and oil, covered, on High (100% power) 3 minutes. Stir. Add all the wine, minced ginger, red pepper, reserved mushrooms, and white part of scallions. Cook covered on High until the chicken is cooked, about 3 to 5 minutes; stir once. Stir in the scallion tops and cayenne. Let stand 5 minutes.

Ginger-Hot Black Beans and Pork

by Nao Hauser

The flowery scent of the ginger cooks off in the simmering, leaving just the heat that goes so well with beans and pork. Serve this main course with rice and/or warm tortillas and sprinkle with chopped coriander, if you wish.

1½ teaspoons ground cumin
    Pinch ground cloves
    Pinch ground nutmeg
¾ pound lean boneless pork, diced
½ cup dry red wine
1 medium onion, minced
4 cloves garlic, peeled and minced
2 tablespoons minced fresh ginger
1 green bell pepper, chopped
1 red bell pepper, chopped

1 14-ounce can peeled plum tomatoes, no salt added, with juice
4 cups cooked black beans
¼ teaspoon chili powder

PREPARATION TIME: 30 minutes
COOKING TIME: 35 minutes
YIELD: 5 servings

Mix the cumin, cloves, and nutmeg together on a plate. Toss the pork with spices to coat; let stand 5 minutes. Heat a large, heavy skillet over high heat until very hot. Add the pork; cook, stirring constantly, until browned on all sides. Remove the pork and reserve.

Pour the wine into the skillet, stirring to scrape the bottom. Stir in the onion, garlic, and 1 tablespoon fresh ginger; cook over medium heat, stirring occasionally, 5 minutes. Stir in the peppers; cook, covered, 5 minutes.

Chop the tomatoes coarsely, reserving juice. Add the tomatoes and juice, beans, and reserved pork to skillet. Cook, covered, over medium heat 10 minutes. Stir in remaining 1 tablespoon fresh ginger and chili powder; simmer uncovered, stirring occasionally, 10 minutes.

NUTRITION INFORMATION: Cal: 356 Pro: 29g/ 32% Carb: 42g/47% Fat: 8g/21% (S:37% M:44% P:15%) Chol: 48mg Sodium: 51mg Potassium: 1145mg Fiber: 7g A: 16% C: 122% B1: 61% B2: 16% B3: 23% B6: 26% Folic: 55% P: 35% Fe: 28% Mg: 33% Zn: 20% Cu: 24% Se: 24% Cr: 12% Mo: 115%
EXCHANGE: Lean Meat: 2½ Bread: 2½ Veg: 1½

MICROWAVE METHOD: Coat the pork with spices as above. In 2-quart microwave-safe casserole cook the wine, onion, garlic, and ginger, covered, on High (100% power) until the onion is tender, about 2 to 3 minutes. Add the pork. Cook covered on High 3 minutes. Chop the tomatoes coarsely, reserving juice. Add the peppers, chopped tomatoes with liquid, beans, and chili powder. Cook covered on High 5 minutes. Reduce power to Medium (50% power); cook 10 minutes more, until pork is tender.

Gingered Carrots and Turnips

by Nao Hauser

A hint of ginger brings out the delicate sweetness of carrots and turnips.

1 teaspoon unsalted butter
2 teaspoons minced fresh ginger
*1 cup unsalted chicken broth or stock (see
   page 28)*
1 teaspoon dry sherry
4 carrots, julienne cut or sliced
*2 turnips, pared, julienne cut or quartered, and
   sliced*
*8 sprigs fresh parsley, thick stems removed,
   minced*

PREPARATION TIME: 25 minutes
COOKING TIME: 15 minutes
YIELD: 5 servings

Melt the butter in a medium saucepan over medium heat. Add the ginger; sauté 2 minutes. Pour in the broth, stirring to scrape the bottom. Stir in the sherry, carrots, and turnips. Cook covered over medium heat until vegetables are tender, about 10 minutes. Remove the vegetables to a serving bowl with a slotted spoon. Stir the parsley into the broth; simmer until reduced to about 1/4 cup. Pour the broth over the vegetables.

NUTRITION INFORMATION: Cal: 45 Pro: 2g/
15% Carb: 7g/62% Fat: 1g/23% (S:54% M:33%
P:13%) Chol: 2mg Sodium: 79mg Potassium:
221mg Fiber: 2g A: 225% C: 14% Mn: 12%
   EXCHANGE: Veg: 1¼ Fat: ¼

MICROWAVE METHOD: In a 2-quart microwave-safe casserole cook the butter and ginger on High (100% power) 1 minute. Add only ¼ cup broth, the sherry, carrots, and turnips. Cook covered on High until the vegetables are tender, about 6 to 8 minutes; stir once. Sprinkle with parsley.

Gingered Pears

Mary Estella

Serve these pears warm with a crunchy topping or cookies. Or spoon them over gingerbread or cake. For a festive touch, add about half a cup of rinsed cranberries to the simmering pears and cook until they're soft.

4 to 5 firm, ripe pears
   1 quart pear juice or apple cider
   Pinch salt
   Pinches of cinnamon
   Pinch of allspice
   Pinch of nutmeg
   3 tablespoons arrowroot starch (see Note)
   1 teaspoon vanilla extract
*½ teaspoon fresh ginger juice (grate fresh
   ginger on a hand grater), or a pinch each
   of ground ginger and cloves*

PREPARATION TIME: 15 minutes
COOKING TIME: 25 minutes
YIELD: 5 servings

Rinse the pears and quarter them lengthwise. Remove the seeds and slice the pears thinly on a slight diagonal. Place the sliced pears in a medium saucepan. Cover with the juice or cider; add the salt and the spices. Bring to a boil; lower flame and simmer until the pears are soft, about 15 minutes.

Dissolve the arrowroot starch in ⅓ cup of cold water. Add to the pears, and simmer, stirring, until the sauce is thick and clear. Add the vanilla extract and ginger juice. Stir and adjust the spices, if desired. Serve warm or cool.

NOTE: Arrowroot starch is available at natural food stores.

NUTRITION INFORMATION: Cal: 155 Pro: .4g/
1% Carb: 39g/96% Fat: .5g/3% Chol: 0mg
Sodium: 53mg Potassium: 333mg Fiber: 3g
Cr: 11%
   EXCHANGE: Bread: ¼ Fruit: 2½

MICROWAVE METHOD: Prepare the pears as directed above and arrange them in a 2½- to 3-quart shallow microwave-safe casserole. Pour in only 3 cups juice or cider, the salt, and spices.

Cook covered on High (100% power) until almost tender, about 5 to 6 minutes, stirring once. Dissolve the arrowroot starch in 1/3 cup cold water. Add to the pears. Cook on High until thickened, about 3 to 4 minutes. Add the vanilla and ginger juice; stir and continue as directed above.

Pineapple in Gingered Plum Wine

by Nao Hauser

Add fresh orange segments or sliced kiwi to this dessert, if you wish. The heat of the ginger underscores the sweetness of the pineapple, making it all the more refreshing. Be sure to cut the pineapple over a dish to catch the juice; then add the juice to the fruit.

 1 pineapple
 1 cup plum wine
 2 teaspoons finely grated or minced fresh
    ginger
 1 teaspoon sugar
 1/8 teaspoon ground cinnamon
    Chopped fresh mint (optional)

PREPARATION TIME: 15 minutes plus
refrigerating time
COOKING TIME: 10 minutes
YIELD: about 5 servings, depending on size of
pineapple

Pare and core the pineapple. Cut it into chunks and set aside.

Heat the wine, ginger, sugar, and cinnamon to simmering in a small saucepan over medium heat. Simmer uncovered until reduced by about one-third. Pour over pineapple in a medium bowl; refrigerate until thoroughly chilled.

To serve, spoon pineapple with liquid into dessert dishes; sprinkle with mint if desired.

NUTRITION INFORMATION: Cal: 127   Pro: .8g/
2% Carb: 25g/72% Fat: .8g/5% Alc: 21% Chol:
0mg Sodium: 2mg Potassium: 208mg Fiber: 3g C:
47% B1: 11% Cu: 11% Mn: 88%
   EXCHANGE: Fruit: 1½ Fat: ¾

Mashed Gingered Sweet Potatoes

by Nao Hauser

Ginger lightens the starchy taste of sweet potatoes, giving them a wonderful zing.

 1 cup apple juice
 1 tablespoon minced fresh ginger
 1/8 teaspoon ground nutmeg
 4 large sweet potatoes pared (about 2 pounds)
 2 tablespoons plain low-fat yogurt
    Freshly ground black pepper

PREPARATION TIME: 15 minutes
COOKING TIME: 25 minutes
YIELD: 5 servings

Heat the apple juice, ginger, and nutmeg to simmering in a medium saucepan. Cut the potatoes in half lengthwise and slice them 1/4 inch thick. Add the potatoes; simmer covered over medium heat until tender, about 20 minutes. Using a potato masher or fork, mash the potatoes into the liquid until smooth. Stir in the yogurt and add pepper to taste.

NUTRITION INFORMATION: Cal: 218   Pro: 3g/
6% Carb: 50g/91% Fat: .7g/3% Chol: 1mg
Sodium: 29mg Potassium: 412mg Fiber: 3g
A: 619% C: 52% E: 41% B2: 16% B6: 23%
Panto: 10% Cu: 15% Mn: 19%
   EXCHANGE: Bread: 2½ Fruit: ½

MICROWAVE METHOD: In 2-quart microwave-safe casserole cook only 2/3 cup apple juice, ginger, nutmeg, and sweet potatoes, covered, on High (100% power) until potatoes are tender, about 9 to 11 minutes. Let stand 5 minutes. Using a potato masher or fork, mash the potatoes into the liquid until smooth. Stir in the yogurt and add pepper to taste.

◇ GARLIC AND ONIONS ◇

Extravagant Praise for the Stinking Rose

by Kevin Cobb

Garlic then have power to save from death
Bear with it though it maketh unsavory breath
—Sir John Harington,
The Englishman's Doctor, 1609

I had a garlic-deprived childhood.
—Alice Waters, in
The Official Garlic Lovers Handbook

Strong vegetables elicit strong opinions. Take garlic and onions, members of the *Allium* genus in the Amaryllidaceae family. For more than 3,000 years they have been praised as the food of the gods and reviled as offspring of the Devil. A Muslim legend even claims that as Satan was cast to earth, garlic appeared from the ground where his left foot rested and an onion sprouted at his right foot. Ancient Greeks, on the other hand, made broad claims for their healing power.

Little has changed: You love these forceful bulbs or you hate them. If you enjoy them, there's now good evidence that your affection will be returned.

Onions, scallions (also called green onions), shallots, leeks, and garlic are low in calories, rich in potassium, nearly fat free, and a reasonable source of fiber and vitamin C. Raw, an onion's got plenty of culinary bite with hardly any sodium; cooked, it sweetens a dish. But the healing rather than nourishing properties of onions and garlic get our attention.

Raw garlic and onions have antibiotic properties in animal and lab studies, according to Loma Linda University microbiologist Moses A. Adetumbi in California. They can prevent the growth of a wide range of bacteria, and perhaps fungi and yeast as well. In one test-tube study, for example, garlic diluted to 1 part per 128 killed *Candida albicans*, the organism responsible for vaginal yeast infections. Both garlic and onions have been used, both externally and internally, as antibiotics in traditional medicine.

Onions and onion juice may also help some allergy sufferers. At the University of Munich in Germany, researcher Walter Dorsch reported that onion juice applied topically to allergy-inflamed skin cools the reaction. He also found that onion juice reduced observable symptoms of asthma in guinea pigs.

Onions and garlic benefit the heart three ways: By reducing the tendency of blood to form artery-damaging clots, lowering levels of "bad" cholesterol (LDL), and raising "good" cholesterol (HDL). Garlic is antithrombotic; that is, it may inhibit blood clotting—and a pronounced tendency to form clots is a major risk factor in heart attacks and stroke. At the State University of New York (SUNY) at Albany, biochemist Eric Block and his colleagues have discovered one of garlic's secrets—a substance they've dubbed "ajoene," which acts by "inhibiting fibrogen receptors on platelets." A SUNY/Venezuelan co-study found that the garlic-derived ajoene compound is at least as effective an antithrombotic agent as aspirin. They hope ajoene might soon prove useful as a drug. Garlic is already at the supermarket, of course.

The secret to the heart benefits is the stink, released when the fresh bulbs are cut or sliced or crushed. The process, which probably protects the plant from fungal invaders and pests, starts with an unusual chemical called alliin. Soon after release, alliin is converted to allicin by an enzyme in garlic; in onions the same enzyme transforms a related substance that get tears flowing.

Onions have different compounds but may have similar effects. They may even help undo some of the negative effects of a high-fat meal. In London's Queen Elizabeth College, healthy volunteers who ate a high-fat breakfast with a little over two ounces per person of fried onions had less platelet aggregation than those who ate the high-fat meal without the onions.

Garlic may also lower levels of blood cholesterol and triglycerides, while simultaneously raising beneficial HDL cholesterol. In India, at the Tagore Medical College in Rajasthan, 20 healthy people ate lab-extracted garlic oil for six months, and then abstained for two months. To get the same amount of oil from fresh garlic, you'd have to eat about one ounce (around 10 cloves) a day, the authors calculate. Result: Blood cholesterol went down 18 percent, triglycerides 17 percent. LDLs went down significantly, while HDLs actually increased. Another group of 62 patients with coronary heart disease had similar results. (Onions may also lower blood cholesterol, perhaps because of their fiber.)

In southern Italy, a land fond of garlic, the incidence of heart attacks and stroke is much lower than in the United States. It's not just garlic, of course. Pasta, rice, whole grain breads, beans, vegetables, greens both wild and tame, fish, wine, olive oil—and little reliance on red meat or high-fat dairy foods—are believed to contribute to Italians' low rate of cardiovascular disease. But the stinking rose may be a contributor, too.

Cancer Prevention

One of the most tantalizing areas of research is cancer protection. The same chemicals that may protect the heart block the synthesis of prostaglandins and thromboxane, hormone-like substances that may promote tumors. At New York University Medical Center, professor of environmental medicine Sidney Belman finds that applying garlic and onion oils directly to the skin of mice inhibits tumor growth. In Houston, University of Texas cell biologist Michael Wargovich found that a single dose of a specific component of garlic oil (diallyl sulfide, or DAS) given to mice that then got a carcinogen inhibited colon cancer in 75 percent of the mice. DAS, he says, "seems to work in the very early stages of carcinogenesis, before cells can go into the cancer sequence." Another compound of garlic oil, allyl methyl trisulfide (AMT), may promote an enzyme linked to tumor inhibition, finds cancer researcher Lee Wattenberg of the University of Minnesota.

One report of two counties in the Shandong province of China supports the idea that garlic may be part of a cancer-protective diet. In one county, the rate of gastric cancer was 10 times greater than in the other—40 cases per 1000 as opposed to 4. Mei Xing, a researcher at Shandong Medical College, discovered that those in the low-cancer county ate an average of three-fourths of an ounce of garlic a day, about 7 cloves. Those in the high-cancer county rarely ate any. A recent Chinese study conducted in cooperation with the U.S. National Cancer Institute reports that people who ate onions and garlic regularly had about a four-fold lower risk of stomach and colon cancers than those who ate them rarely. Population studies in Japan and Korea find similar associations.

Garlic's Place

Clearly, garlic and onions can play a role in a healthy diet. But not for everyone. "People with hiatus hernias may be adversely affected by garlic and onions, and elderly people often find garlic and onions difficult to tolerate," says SUNY biochemist Block.

But if garlic agrees with you, enjoy it. You may

have to enjoy quite a lot of it to get its full health benefits, though, says nutrition researcher David Kritchevsky of the Wistar Institute in Philadelphia. "You'd have to eat fifteen grams of garlic a day [about five cloves]," he says. "But that's antisocial."

We're learning the active ingredients in garlic, notes Kritchevsky, so we should be able to synthesize them. Perhaps someday even garlic haters can benefit, indirectly, from the stinking rose.

In the meantime, those of us who love its punch and power do well by eating as much as our stomachs (and friends) can handle. "If you're a hermit, the more the merrier," says Block. "If you're a salesman working nose-to-nose with other people, you may have to put up with eating small amounts to keep your job."

Cooking with Garlic and Onions

by Kevin Cobb

At the store you're likely to find several varieties of onions, but only one or two types of garlic. Aside from the usual assortment of white and yellow onions, there are the purple-red Italian, the squat sweet Bermuda (an old-fashioned name), and the tiny pearl. There are also scallions, called green onions in many parts of the country, leeks, and shallots. Chives, an herb used to season, is also in the *Allium* family.

A very well stocked store might also have the sublime Vidalias of Georgia, the expensive imports from Maui, the Walla Walla from Washington state, and the 1015 from the Rio Grande Valley in Texas. These are mild enough to eat raw.

Varieties of garlic are of more interest to farmers than shoppers. In the store you may find heads with white or pink skins; some prefer the pink, which is slightly sweeter in flavor. In recipes, they are interchangeable. There is also elephant garlic, the Baby Huey of the bulb world. It's milder than regular garlic, and best for roasting whole.

To peel an onion, cut the top off and peel down

without trimming off the bottom until the last possible moment. If you want to avoid tears, peel the onion under cold water. Sliced, diced, minced, or crushed, garlic and onions release their pungent chemicals.

How garlic is cut helps determine how strong the taste will be. Barbara Batcheller, author of *Lilies of the Kitchen,* claims that "one clove of garlic is ten times stronger pushed through a garlic press than one clove minced fine with a good sharp knife." The press crushes the garlic, releasing a big dose of allicin. Use pressed garlic for extra sharpness, minced for tanginess, and sliced or cut garlic, slowly simmered in soups and stews, for a mild, subtle flavor.

Raw garlic is a fine ingredient in a seasoning garnish for braised meat or soup. Just combine a half cup of finely chopped parsley, two cloves of minced garlic, two teaspoons of grated lemon rind, and a pinch of nutmeg. This is the classic Italian garnish for osso bucco.

To replace salt in salad dressings, try mincing together two scallions, one clove of garlic, and one-half cup of parsley sprigs. Double or triple the garlic and mix with prepared mustard, and you have a paste to spread on poultry or meat prior to roasting.

The *Official Garlic Lovers Handbook,* a compendium of advocacy and advice compiled by the Lovers of the Stinking Rose, summarizes these points quite nicely in three rules:

Garlic Rule No. 1: When preparing garlic for cooking, the more you do to it, the more it will do to you.

Garlic Rule No. 2: When cooking garlic, the more you do to it, the *less* it will do to you.

Garlic Rule No. 3: Burning garlic cancels Garlic Rule No. 2.

Long moderate heat renders garlic mild. Hot direct heat—such as frying—can burn the garlic, producing an undesirable acrid taste.

To remove the odor of garlic or onions from your hands and from kitchen equipment, rub them with lemon juice or salt.

To get the full range of their health benefits and culinary versatility, try garlic and onions raw as well as cooked. Salsa made with raw garlic and onions is one way. The hot peppers are heart-healthy, too.

For the mildest taste, cook whole cloves of garlic, uncut, for a good long time. Garlic loses its pungency the longer it is cooked, so add it early to a dish for mild flavor, late for heat. James Beard introduced this classic idea to Americans more than a quarter century ago with his disarmingly mild "40 Clove Chicken"—made with forty unchopped garlic cloves, placed inside the chicken's abdominal cavity before baking. Microwaves make it possible to attain a similarly sweet, mild nutty taste from garlic in just a few minutes.

Onions, well cooked, are more than just mild; they're sweet. Indeed, they are classically added to meat stews and other dishes as a sweetening agent. That's not surprising, since cooking temperatures convert some of their odiferous compounds into another complex molecule that is fifty to seventy times sweeter than a molecule of table sugar.

That may not come in handy when you're making dessert, but it could be a good thing to remember when you want to sweeten your tomato sauce without a lot of sugar.

To cleanse your breath from the bracing and lasting odor of raw garlic and onions, there are many suggestions. Try munching on fresh parsley; its rich endowment of chlorophyll makes it a natural breath freshener. Other possibilities to munch on: citrus peel, a roasted coffee bean, fresh mint, an apple.

Even when you eat it cooked, though, garlic tends to leave its mark. If the odor of garlic or onions offends your friends, perhaps it's time to get new friends. Or feed them garlic: Fellow indulgers in the stinking rose tend to notice it less on each other.

Spotlight: Raw Garlic, Cooked Shallots?

When Tufts University Medical School professor of medicine Victor Gurewich asked 20 of his patients with high cholesterol levels to eat a medium, raw white onion each day, their heart-healthy HDL cholesterol shot up by an average of 30 percent.

But when they ate milder red onions, or white or yellow onions that had been thoroughly cooked, there was little or no effect. Similarly, the antibiotic effects of raw onions and garlic are destroyed by cooking, and the high-heat methods needed to prepare some "odorless" garlic preparations may destroy many of their bioactive compounds. The garlic oil that New York University professor Sidney Belman has shown to inhibit colon cancer in animals, for example, comes from *raw* garlic. "We don't know if the same effect would occur if the garlic and onion were cooked," he says. "We don't heat the oils." University of Texas cell biologist Michael Wargovich notes that the potential cancer-protective garlic compound DAS is highly volatile—it's easily destroyed by heating.

Does that mean we have to go around eating raw onions and garlic and losing our friends? Not necessarily. Cooked onions and garlic retain a few powers. Garlic preparations may not be antibiotic, but they "retain antimutagenic activity," according to University of California, Berkeley professor of biochemistry Terrance Leighton. That is, they retain the power to block potential mutations in DNA, which can be a small early step toward cancer.

Which kind of onion and garlic is healthiest, and whether it retains its effects through the normal range of cooking temperatures, depends in large part on which substance is being studied.

Take quercetin, the potent cancer-protective compound that Leighton is investigating. It's an excellent candidate for providing some of onion's anticancer, and possibly heart-protective, potential. In animal studies, quercetin reduces the risk of breast tumors by 25 percent. Researchers in Austria have begun clinical trials of quercetin as an anticarcinogen; it also appears to enhance the activity of anticancer drugs.

"Quercetin has two potential protective modes of action," says Leighton. Like allicin (the blood-thinning, garlic compound), quercetin is a potent antioxidant—it helps protect DNA from oxidative assaults from pollution, smoking, and dietary toxins. Secondly, quercetin appears to inhibit an enzyme system that promotes rapid cell growth, and, under certain conditions, tumor growth. Says Leighton, "It's one of the most active blockers of this system."

If you want to get quercetin in your diet, you can eat broccoli, yellow Italian squash, red grapes or red wine, but the best source is certain onions. "It's not found in significant concentrations in garlic," says Leighton. "Yellow and red onions and shallots have high concentrations; white onions and scallions seem to have low levels." Indeed, it's quercetin that

gives yellow onion skins their color, he notes. The highest levels he's ever seen come from yellow globe onions grown primarily in Utah— as much as 5 percent of dry weight.

Cooking doesn't destroy it. "Normal sautéing of yellow onions doesn't seem to affect quercetin content, or its chemical state," he says. "It's a reasonably stable molecule."

What to eat? So little is known about these potential health-promoting compounds in our foods, and the growing conditions that affect their concentration, that prudence is the wisest policy.

Until we know better, *our* shopping bags will brim with the widest variety of onions (yellow, red, and white), shallots, scallions, leeks, and garlic. And we'll eat them, raw in salsa and salads, lightly steamed, sautéed in a couple of teaspoons of olive oil (that first step toward a thousand dishes), baked for hours, and in any other way we find.

—Robert Barnett

French Onion Soup

by Robert Grenner

1½ pounds onions, thinly sliced
 2 tablespoons soybean oil
 ¾ teaspoon salt
 ½ teaspoon sugar to caramelize the onion
    (optional)
 1 teaspoon flour
 2 quarts hot unsalted veal or beef broth or
    stock (see page 29)
 ½ cup dry vermouth
    White pepper
 3 teaspoons cognac
 ½ cup freshly grated imported Parmesan
    cheese
 8 slices French bread, toasted

PREPARATION TIME: 30 minutes
COOKING TIME: 1 hour 20 minutes
YIELD: 8 servings

Over low heat cook the onions in the oil for 15

minutes, using a covered 4-quart saucepan. Uncover and raise the heat to medium; stir in the salt and sugar if used. Cook for 30 minutes, stirring frequently, until the onions have turned an even deep golden brown.

Sprinkle in the flour and stir for 3 minutes. Turn off the heat and stir in the hot veal or beef stock. Add the vermouth; simmer partially covered for 30 minutes, skimming occasionally. Adjust seasoning with white pepper if necessary.

Divide the soup equally into 8 warm, heatproof bowls, add ½ teaspoon cognac and 2 teaspoons of cheese to each. Float a toasted bread round on top and add more cheese. Put bowls under broiler until cheese is golden.

NUTRITION INFORMATION: Cal: 220 Pro: 12g/21% Carb: 24g/45% Fat: 8g/34% (S:35% M:40% P:25%) Chol: 6mg Sodium: 600mg Potassium: 376mg Fiber: 1g E: 21% B1: 14% B2: 13% B3: 24% B6: 10% Ca: 16% P: 17% Fe: 10% Cu: 12% Mn: 10% Se: 31% Cr: 26%

EXCHANGE: Med. Meat: ½ Bread: 1½ Veg: 1 Fat: ¾

Café Venezia's Baked Garlic

by Janis Wilcox

Baked garlic tastes better than it sounds. It's as savored by garlic fans as truffles are among chocolate lovers. Basted with wine and butter, the garlic becomes sweet and spreadable. Fabulous as an appetizer, or with roast chicken or grilled fish.

4 large heads garlic, unpeeled
2 tablespoons olive oil
2 tablespoons unsalted butter
Pinch sea salt
Freshly ground black pepper
1/2 cup dry white wine (stock or water may be substituted)

PREPARATION TIME: 10 minutes
COOKING TIME: 1 hour 20 minutes
YIELD: 4 to 8 appetizer or first-course servings.

Preheat oven to 300°F. Remove the outer layer of peel from the garlic with a paring knife. Remove any dry or discolored cloves. Slice around the base of the garlic and peel carefully to reveal the cloves.

Rinse any sand or dust off garlic and place in a small baking dish which will hold garlic heads snugly. Drizzle with the olive oil and place some butter on each one. Sprinkle with salt and pepper. Pour white wine or stock in baking dish.

Cover and bake in oven 20 minutes. Baste the bulbs and bake for about 1 hour more or until the cloves are soft and tender when pierced with a fork.

Squeeze the garlic cloves from one end onto bread, then spread with a knife.

Baked garlic can be made ahead of time and reheated on a grill or in the oven.

SERVING SUGGESTIONS: Serve with roasted or oven-baked chicken or grilled fish dishes and salad. As an appetizer, serve with goat cheese, roasted peppers, sun-dried tomatoes, sliced avocadoes, and a basket of fresh, crusty bread.

NUTRITION INFORMATION (garlic with one slice Italian bread): Cal: 162 Pro: 4g/10% Carb: 22g/54% Fat: 7g/36% (S:38% M:54% P:8%) Chol: 8mg Sodium: 205mg Potassium: 83g Fiber: .3g B1: 10% Cr: 12%
EXCHANGE: Bread: 1 Veg: 1 Fat: 1 1/2

Roasted Garlic Vinaigrette

by Robert Grenner

1/2 cup plus 1/2 teaspoon vegetable oil
1 small head garlic (remove the husks but leave the skin on the cloves), separated into cloves
1/4 cup red wine vinegar
3 teaspoons chopped fresh parsley
1/2 teaspoon Worcestershire sauce
White pepper

PREPARATION TIME: 15 minutes
COOKING TIME: 30 minutes
YIELD: About 1 cup

Preheat oven to 275°F. In a sauté pan, heat 1/2 teaspoon of oil and add the garlic cloves. Place in the preheated oven and roast until soft, about 30 minutes, shaking the pan occasionally to ensure uniform cooking. Remove from the oven and cool. Peel the skin off the garlic.

Place the garlic, vinegar, parsley, Worcestershire sauce, and white pepper to taste in a blender and combine. With the blender on, drizzle 1/2 cup oil slowly into the other ingredients; process until thickened.

NUTRITION INFORMATION (per 1 tablespoon serving): Cal: 65 Pro: .1g/1% Carb: .9g/5% Fat: 7g/94% (S:13% M:25% P:62%) Chol: 0mg Sodium: 2mg Potassium: 10mg Fiber: 0g E: 29%
EXCHANGE: Fat: 1 1/2

Garlic-Sauced Pasta with Greens

by Nao Hauser

1 head garlic, cloves peeled and split
1 cup unsalted chicken broth or stock (see page 28)
1 teaspoon dried oregano leaves
1/4 teaspoon ground cinnamon
   Pinch ground nutmeg
2 teaspoons Dijon-style mustard
2 tablespoons plain low-fat yogurt
1 pound spinach, well washed
2 teaspoons olive oil
1 large red bell pepper, chopped
6 ounces (about 1 1/2 cups dried) tubettini, penne, or other pasta, cooked and drained

PREPARATION TIME: 30 minutes
COOKING TIME: 50 minutes
YIELD: 4 servings

Cook the garlic, broth, oregano, cinnamon, and nutmeg in a small covered saucepan over medium heat 25 minutes. Remove the cover; simmer another 10 minutes. Let cool at least 5 minutes. Process the garlic mixture with the mustard in a blender until smooth; add yogurt and process until smooth.

Cook the spinach with only the water that clings from washing in a large covered saucepan over medium heat just until wilted, about 5 minutes. Rinse under cold water; squeeze out excess moisture. Chop coarsely.

Heat the oil in a large skillet over medium heat. Add the pepper; sauté 5 minutes. Stir in the spinach, pasta, and garlic sauce. Cook over low heat to heat through.

NUTRITION INFORMATION: Cal: 220 Pro: 11g/
19% Carb: 38g/65% Fat: 4g/16% (S:20% M:64%
P:16%) Chol: 1mg Sodium: 143mg Potassium:
738mg Fiber: 3g A: 188% C: 56% E: 20% B1:
21% B2: 24% B3: 14% B6: 14% Folic: 41% Ca:
20% P: 17% Fe: 32% Mg: 31% Zn: 10% Cu:
14% Mn: 33% Se: 39% Cr: 41%
EXCHANGE: Bread: 2 Veg: 1 1/2 Fat: 3/4

MICROWAVE METHOD: In a 1-quart microwave-safe casserole or bowl cook the garlic, only 3/4 cup broth, oregano, cinnamon, and nutmeg, covered, on High (100% power) 5 minutes. Reduce power to Medium (50% power); cook 6 minutes more. Let cool. Process with mustard and yogurt as above. Pour into a large serving bowl.

While the garlic broth is cooling, in a 3-quart microwave-safe casserole cook the spinach with the water that clings to it from washing, loosely covered, on High until wilted, about 4 to 5 minutes. Rinse, squeeze dry, and chop coarsely. In a 1-quart microwave-safe casserole or bowl, cook the oil and pepper on High until the pepper is tender, about 4 to 5 minutes. To pureed garlic mixture add spinach, peppers, and pasta. Toss to coat. If desired, cook covered on Medium-High until heated through, about 5 minutes.

Garlicky Spinach

by Nao Hauser

2 teaspoons olive oil
10 cloves garlic, peeled and minced
1 1/2 pounds spinach, well washed
2 teaspoons balsamic vinegar

PREPARATION TIME: 20 minutes
COOKING TIME: 20 minutes
YIELD: 6 servings

Heat the oil in a large heavy skillet over medium heat. Stir in the garlic; sauté until golden, about 4 minutes. Increase the heat to high. Add one sixth of the spinach, tossing to distribute garlic. Cook until the spinach wilts; push to the side of the pan. Repeat, adding one-sixth of the spinach at a time, pouring off liquid after every two batches. Stir in vinegar; cook, stirring constantly, 2 minutes. Serve immediately.

NUTRITION INFORMATION: Cal: 46 Pro: 4g/
27% Carb: 6g/43% Fat: 2g/30% (S:16% M:66%
P:18%) Chol: 0mg Sodium: 81mg Potassium:
548mg Fiber: 2g A: 186% C: 21% E: 18% B2:
16% B6: 14% Folic: 41% Ca: 16% Fe: 23% Mg:
25% Cu: 11% Mn: 28% Cr: 18% Mo: 18%
EXCHANGE: Veg: 1 1/2 Fat: 1/4

Garlic-Marinated Pork with Leek and Spinach Stuffing

by Ceri Hadda

A marvelously festive offering, this is a good alternative to a holiday ham, with less salt, fat, and none of the additives (such as nitrates). See Note below to prepare the pork for fewer diners.

1 crown roast of pork (about 10 pounds)
8 very large cloves garlic, peeled
2 jalapeño peppers, halved and seeded
3/4 cup dry white wine
1/4 cup red wine vinegar
1 tablespoon dried oregano, crumbled
1 teaspoon salt (optional)
   Leek, Rice, and Spinach Stuffing (recipe follows)

PREPARATION TIME: 15 minutes plus marinating time
COOKING TIME: 2 1/2 to 3 hours
YIELD: 20 servings

Place the pork in a very large plastic bag, set in a roasting pan.

With the motor of the food processor running, drop the garlic cloves, then jalapeño pepper halves, through the feed tube. (If you don't have a food processor, just chop the garlic and pepper very fine.)

Stop the processor. Add the wine, vinegar, oregano, and salt (if used). Cover and process until blended. (Without a food processor, put the garlic and pepper in a bowl, add liquids and spices, and blend with a whisk.) Pour marinade over the pork in the bag. Seal the bag tightly. Turn the bag to distribute the marinade. Refrigerate pork 8 hours or overnight, turning bag several times.

Preheat the oven to 350°F. Remove the pork from the plastic bag to a roasting pan; pour the marinade over. Place pieces of aluminum foil on the ends of the pork ribs, to prevent charring. Stuff a wad of aluminum foil in the center of the roast, to retain shape.

Roast the pork 2 1/2 to 3 hours, or until a meat thermometer inserted in the meat, away from any bones, registers 165°F. Remove the foil from center of the roast and rib ends. Remove any fat drippings from center. Fill the center with part of the Leek, Rice, and Spinach Stuffing. Serve the remainder as a side dish. Skim off fat from pan juices. Serve the juices with the roast and stuffing.

LEEK, RICE, AND SPINACH STUFFING

4 bunches leeks (about 6 pounds)
4 bunches scallions
3 tablespoons olive oil
1 cup chopped shallots
4 10-ounce packages chopped frozen spinach
9 1/2 cups unsalted chicken broth or stock (see page 28), or water, or a combination
4 cups raw rice
   Salt (optional)
   Freshly ground black pepper

PREPARATION TIME: 25 minutes
COOKING TIME: 45 minutes
YIELD: 20 servings

Trim the leeks; slice them in half lengthwise. Rinse the leeks very well to remove all traces of sand. Slice the leek halves into 1/4-inch pieces, discarding the tough green ends. Trim the scallions and chop them, including the green part.

Sauté the leeks in oil in a 4 to 6-quart saucepan or casserole for 5 minutes. Cover the saucepan; lower heat, cook 10 minutes. Uncover pan. Add shallots and scallions; sauté 5 minutes longer.

Add the spinach and stock and/or water to pan. Bring to a boil, breaking up the spinach with a fork. Add the rice; cover pot; lower heat.

Simmer 15 to 20 minutes, or until rice is tender and most of the liquid has been absorbed. If too dry, add 1/3 cup more liquid and continue cooking 5 minutes longer.

Taste the mixture and add salt and pepper if necessary.

NOTE: If your gathering is smaller—say only ten people—prepare just one loin of pork (the crown is actually two loins sewn together). Marinate as above. Place, fat-side up, in the roasting pan. Bake about 2 1/2 hours or until a meat thermometer registers 165°F. Prepare half the amount of stuffing—or prepare the whole amount for delicious leftovers! Serve the stuffing on the side.

NUTRITION INFORMATION (pork only): Cal: 289 Pro: 34g/48% Carb: 1g/2% Fat: 16g/50% (S:38% M:49% P:13%) Chol: 107mg Sodium: 83mg Potassium: 461mg Fiber 0g C: 32% B1: 72% B2: 19% B3: 33% B6: 28% B12: 12% P: 26% Zn: 18% Se: 53% Mo: 257%
EXCHANGE: Lean Meat: 5

(leek stuffing only) Cal: 211 Pro: 7g/14% Carb: 39g/74% Fat: 3g/12% Chol: 1mg Sodium: 102mg Potassium: 382mg Fiber: 5g A: 89% C: 17% E: 12% B1: 13% B3: 16% B6: 31% Folic: 22% Panto: 12% Ca: 12% P: 11% Fe: 16% Mg: 15% Cu: 13% Mn: 57% Se: 41% Cr: 11%
EXCHANGE: Bread: 1³/₄ Veg: 2 Fat: ¹/₂

(pork and stuffing) Cal: 501 Pro: 41g/33% Carb: 41g/33% Fat: 18g/34% (S:34% M:52% P:14%) Chol: 108mg Sodium: 185mg Potassium: 843mg Fiber: 5g A: 90% C: 49% E: 15% B1: 85% B2: 28% B3: 49% B6: 59% B12: 14% Folic: 23% Panto: 19% Ca: 13% P: 38% Fe: 25% Mg: 22% Zn: 24% Cu: 19% Mn: 58% Se: 94% Cr: 11% Mo: 265%
EXCHANGE: Lean Meat: 5 Bread: 1³/₄ Veg: 2 Fat: ¹/₂

MICROWAVE METHOD (for stuffing): Prepare half the recipe at a time, using half the amount of ingredients called for above. Prepare the leeks as directed above. In a 4- or 5-quart microwave-safe casserole, cook the leeks and only 2 teaspoons of oil on High (100% power) until tender, about 6 minutes; stir twice. Add the shallots and scallions; cook on High 2 minutes. Add the spinach and stock. Cook covered on High to boiling, about 10 minutes. Add the rice; cook tightly covered until rice is cooked, about 15 to 20 minutes, stirring twice. Season with salt and pepper to taste.

Garlic Potato Gratin
by Nao Hauser

  1 tablespoon olive oil
10 cloves garlic, peeled and minced
  2 pounds potatoes
2¹/₂ cups unsalted chicken broth or stock (see page 28)

PREPARATION TIME: 20 minutes
COOKING TIME: 1 hour 35 minutes
YIELD: 6 servings

Preheat oven to 350°F. Heat the oil in a heavy 10-inch skillet over medium heat. Add the garlic; sauté until golden, about 4 minutes. Remove the garlic.

Scrub the potatoes and thinly slice them. Arrange a single layer of potatoes in the skillet; dot with some of garlic. Continue layering, ending with potatoes. Pour in broth. Bake in oven until the broth is absorbed, about 1¹/₂ hours. Turn the top layer of potatoes over after 45 minutes to keep them from drying out.

NUTRITION INFORMATION: Cal: 183 Pro: 5g/11% Carb: 35g/74% Fat: 3g/15% Chol: .4mg Sodium: 45mg Potassium: 699 mg Fiber: 4g C: 35% B1: 12% B3: 18% B6: 23% P: 11% Mg: 10% Cu: 20% Mn: 10% Cr: 17%
EXCHANGE: Bread: 2¹/₄ Fat: ¹/₂

Cornish Hens with Forty Cloves of Garlic
by Ceri Hadda

Since the pan juices in this recipe are ample, you can use part of them to make a flavorful couscous to accompany the hens.

  4 Cornish hens (thawed if frozen), about 1 pound each
      Salt (optional)
      Freshly ground black pepper
40 cloves unpeeled garlic (about 2 heads)
  1 tablespoon olive oil

1 teaspoon dried thyme, crumbled
1/8 teaspoon cayenne (optional)
1 cup dry white wine

PREPARATION TIME: 20 minutes
COOKING TIME: 1 1/2 hours
YIELD: 8 servings

Preheat the oven to 375°F. Rinse the hens inside and out; pat them dry. Sprinkle the cavity of each hen with salt and pepper; stuff each hen with 4 cloves of garlic. Place the hens in a roasting pan, breast-side down. Scatter the remaining garlic around them. Sprinkle the oil over the hens, then season with thyme, cayenne, if used, and salt and pepper. Pour the wine around hens. Cover tightly with aluminum foil.

Bake for 1 hour, basting once or twice. Turn hens on their backs; re-cover tightly. Bake 30 minutes longer, or until juices run clear when legs are pricked with a fork, and garlic is tender.

Remove hens and cut in half with poultry shears. Place hens and garlic cloves on a heated serving platter; keep warm. Skim fat from surface of pan juices (this is easier to do if the sauce is transferred to a glass measuring cup). Serve the pan juices on the side.

NOTE: To eat the garlic, squeeze one end of each clove until the softened garlic comes out. The garlic is particularly good spread on slices of toasted bread.

If a golden skin on the hens is desired, place hen halves, skin-side up, under broiler for about 3 minutes prior to serving.

To use pan juices as a base for couscous, reserve 1 cup of juice for serving with the hens. Measure the remainder and add enough water to equal the liquid required in the couscous package directions.

NUTRITION INFORMATION: Cal: 283 Pro: 29g/41% Carb: 5g/8% Fat: 14g/44% (S:29% M:48% P:23%) Alc: 7% Chol: 87mg Sod: 166mg Pot: 317mg Fiber: 0g Panto: 10% Phos: 22% Iron: 10%

EXCHANGE: Lean Meat: 4 Veg: 1 Fat: 3/4

◇ PEPPERS ◇

Peter Piper's Pick: Peppers

by Eileen Behan, R.D.

America is on fire.

From Cajun cafés to Szechuan eateries, we're rediscovering the fiery chili "peppers" that Columbus misnamed nearly five centuries ago. Chilies, indigenous to the New World, made their way to India by 1611; thereafter, everywhere. Capsaicin, their active ingredient, lights the fire under Mexican food, now the second most popular ethnic fare in this country (after Italian). Without capsaicin, Tabasco would be merely pickle juice, and ginger ale a curiously unrefreshing refresher.

It lets the good times roll in Cajun cuisine, gives Korean food some of its jump, and provides the TNT in the Chinese hot oil that ignites Szechuan cookery. Indian curry powder is laced with chili pepper, and paprika is essentially mild or not so mild chili peppers, dried and ground fine.

In hot climates, eating hot foods stimulates sweating, especially from the face and scalp. Sweat cools as it evaporates, so hot heads get . . . cool. That may help explain the popularity of chilies in southern regions.

But why everywhere else? Our search for a healthy culinary excitement may be one reason. When you're holding back on salt or buttery, creamy sauces, hot spices give simple, healthy foods some zip and character—even a touch of danger.

Whole fresh chili peppers range in size from the tiny, ridiculously hot bird peppers that measure less than an inch to the 9-inch Numex Big Jim chili. The hotter and redder, the more vitamins A and C, though few people eat enough to add significant nutrients to their diet. Chili peppers can be served as a spice, a condiment, or a vegetable. Serve the milder ones as vegetables, and you've got a perfect high-impact diet food: lots of taste and nutrients for only 24 calories a cup.

But that's just the beginning. Recent discoveries suggest that chili peppers may lower the risk of blood clots, loosen bronchial congestion in your next cold, stimulate digestion, help your body burn extra calories, improve mood, and, in moderation, help protect against cancer.

And they probably don't even aggravate ulcers, as was once thought. A study by physician David Y. Graham of the Baylor College of Medicine in Houston finds that even after a highly spiced Mexican meal (made with an ounce of jalopēno peppers), there was no damage to the lining of the stomach.

"There are no data to show that peppers do any harm to the stomach," explains Dr. Arnold Levy, Vice President for Education at the American Digestive Disease Society.

Though some people are sensitive to spicy

foods, Levy explains, the stomach protects itself by secreting mucus that coats the lining and shields it from irritants, like chilies. Contrary to legend, chili peppers don't seem to hurt ulcers. In a *British Medical Journal* study, 50 people with ulcers were divided into two groups. Group 1 ate a normal diet without chilies, plus a prescribed antacid. The 25 participants in Group 2 had the same antacid treatment but consumed red chili powder with every meal. At the end of four weeks, 80 percent—20 people in each group—had healed duodenal ulcers. Red chilies, they concluded, did no harm. (If you want extra protection, Levy suggests eating chili peppers in combination with other foods, which act as buffers.)

Hot peppers may even improve digestion and stimulate appetite. They increase the production of saliva and gastric juices. That increased production not only helps us digest foods but sends a message to the brain that food's coming. So eat a hot chili appetizer like salsa cruda to rev up both your mind and your body for the main dish. It will also help you burn it off: Researchers at Oxford Polytechnic find that hot spices—jalapeño peppers and hot mustard—increase the natural rise in metabolism that follows a meal. Volunteers who ate a meal spiced with three grams of chili and three of mustard burned off an average of 45 calories more than those who ate blander food. (Ginger, though, had no effect.)

Chili Thrills

Eating capsaicin-spiked food gives us a thrill, and may leave a glowing mood. Scientists have isolated five so-called capsaicinoid compounds. Three of them hit fast, the other two provide a long, low-intensity bite on the tongue.

They all hurt a little. Capsaicin, an alkaloid irritant, can cause pain, watery eyes, and a runny nose when ingested. It's bitter, like many poisons. Psychologist Paul Rozin of the University of Pennsylvania believes one reason we love hot peppers is because they signal our bodies that we're in danger—but no assault occurs. The enjoyment may result from the appreciation that the sensation, and the body's reaction to it, is harmless. It's like a roller coaster, says Rozin—a controlled risk.

But it's not just the mind that glows. The body's reaction to the false alarm may stimulate anti-pain chemicals. In pain, our bodies often secrete endogenous opioids, or endorphins—human morphine. Though no one has drawn blood samples of chili eaters, the physiological pain response to capsaicin may actually stimulate these euphoria-producing opioids, speculates Rozin.

Spotlight: Pepper Fantasy in Black, White, Green, and Pink

Botanists know that real pepper, ground from peppercorns, the tiny fruits of the vine *(Piper nigrum)*, is totally unrelated to hot chili "peppers." Piperine, rather than capsaicin, gives it punch. Like chilies, peppercorns are nearly free of calories, fat, and sodium. Pepper comes in black, white, green, and even pink.

White pepper is merely black pepper with the dark outer layer removed; use it in recipes where you don't want black specks. Ground peppercorns lose their punch over time, though, and coarsely ground peppercorns release their zing in the stomach instead of the mouth. Your best bet is to grind peppercorns—the larger the fruit, the more pungent—in a peppermill, fresh.

Green peppercorns, the immature fruits, are sold freeze-dried for grinding, or bottled in brine or vinegar. Avoid brine-bottled if you're watching sodium. Bottled and reconstituted forms can be added to vegetables and stews. They add zest to any sauce. Use before the bottle turns cloudy.

There's also a pink pepper, a fruity berry that's not a *Piper nigrum*. It rose to fame via nouvelle cuisine only to tumble to oblivion when it was blamed for causing severe allergic reactions. Then it rose again when a different spice with the same common name was fingered as the true culprit. Real pink peppercorns are safe, concluded the FDA in 1983, when it lifted its ban.

—Robert Barnett

At the same time, hot peppers may be helping your heart. So finds Dr. Sukon Visudhiphan, a hematologist at Thailand's Siriraj Hospital in Bangkok. The Thai researcher suspected that his compatriots' daily doses of chili peppers might explain why they have a low incidence of life-threatening blood clots. He measured the fibrinolytic—that is, clot-dissolving—activity of blood from 88 Thais and 55 Americans. At the study's start, Americans had a lower average than Thais. Visudhiphan then selected 20 volunteers and fed 16 of them noodles laced with freshly ground chili peppers; four got plain noodles. Within 30 minutes, the hot-noodle eaters all experienced a rise in the clot-dissolving activity. Since Thais eat chilies at nearly every meal, their blood is continually being cleared of potential clots, Visudhiphan believes.

Hot peppers, like other hot spices such as mustard and horseradish and curries, are excellent expectorants. They slightly irritate the passages of your nose, throat, and bronchial passages, thinning mucus, making the tissues "weep," all of which makes it easier for your body to expel excess mucus when you have a cold. Capsaicin has even been reported to reduce the frequency of cluster headaches in humans. Try this folklore remedy: chili tea. Just pour boiling water over an eighth of a teaspoon of cayenne pepper and fresh lemon juice, and sip—carefully. Some researchers believe that a regular diet of hot spices may protect against chronic respiratory diseases such as bronchitis. But only if you don't smoke!

Is there such as thing as too hot? Certainly there is in cooking, where fiery excess can wipe out every taste but pain. It's true in health, too. Try this hot potato: Capsaicin, the active ingredient in hot peppers, may be both carcinogenic and cancer-protective.

It depends on the amount you eat. Normal amounts probably protect, but in animal studies at the University of Nebraska Medical Center, a large dose of capsaicin contributed to colon cancer. On the other hand, once the compound is absorbed into the bloodstream, it could prove to be an anti-cancer agent. In the liver, for example, capsaicin appears to change into a compound that acts as a scavenger for free radicals—those dangerous forms of oxygen that damage tissue and cells. As such, it may help protect people from cancer, aging, and perhaps heart disease. "It's not unknown for something to do one thing at one dose and another thing at another dose," says University of Nebraska biochemist Terry Lawson. By studying the actual metabolism of capsaicin at different doses in mice, he hopes to have some clearer answers soon. In the meantime, "I don't think there's cause for panic," says Lawson, who gets his share of concerned calls from residents of the Southwest who eat lots of hot peppers.

You'll probably know if you're getting too much of a hot thing, anyway. That's what participants in a University of Texas pepper-eating contest found out. Two men and three women ate as many jalapeño peppers as they could swallow in three minutes. Average: 50. Almost everyone complained of a hitherto unnamed problem—a burning sensation upon defecation. New medical name: Jaloproctitis.

Cooking Hot

by Kevin Cobb

A decade ago, fresh hot chili peppers could be found only in a few specialty or ethnic markets. Today they're burning their way into mainstream supermarkets and produce stands across the country.

Capsaicin, the active ingredient, can be found in a multitude of prepared products—pickled jalapeño peppers, hot sauce, paprika, chili spices. But nothing compares to the subtle tastes—and low sodium content—of fresh chilies.

Grow your own chilies or buy them fresh, then dry, can, or freeze them for future use. Fresh peppers should be firm, the skins unblemished. If wrapped in a paper towel and put in a paper bag, they will last up to four weeks in the refrigerator. If you boil or roast them first, you can freeze them.

To roast chilies on a gas burner, hold one on a fork or with tongs over the flame; char all sides until blisters form. In an electric or gas oven put the chilies under a broiler until they char or blacken. Turn to char all sides. However you roast them, the next step is to put the chilies into a paper bag to "sweat" for 20 minutes, and finally, peel and seed them. The peels should slip off after roasting.

When peeling and chopping chilies, always wear rubber gloves and keep your hands away from your eyes. After all, capsaicin, a potent skin irritant, is used in dog and mugger repellent. Should your hands or eyes become irritated, rinse them in milk or water. And always wash your hands thoroughly after handling chilies, even when you wear gloves. Dipping your hands in a solution of one part bleach to five parts water and then rinsing in water is very effective, too.

As the veins and the stem ends are the hottest parts, you can reduce the heat by discarding them and soaking the peppers in salted water or a 5-to-1 water/vinegar solution for 45 minutes. Adding bell pepper to chili sauces also will reduce the heat.

When fresh hot peppers are dried and ground, they become spices. Ancho is a mildly hot, dried form of poblano pepper, maroon to almost black. It's the primary chili in most commercial chili powders, as well as in chili con carne. It's high in potassium and vitamin A. Chipotle is a smoked, dried jalapeño. It's brick red and very hot. Available ground or ready to grind, it's great in soups. Caution: Salt is usually added in canning.

Cayenne is a popular ground spice, very hot. It contains about 750 IU vitamin A per teaspoon. "Cayenne spice" may contain red chili peppers other than cayenne. Cayenne is sometimes called red pepper, though red pepper is usually less pungent. Paprika, the unofficial national spice of Hungary, also popular in Spain, is a mild to mildly hot orange-red spice made from a variety of dried ground chili peppers. A teaspoon has 1,273 IU of vitamin A, about a fourth of the USRDA. Add to dishes at the end of cooking, so it won't turn brown.

If you take a bite of a hot chili dish and feel smoke pouring out of your ears, the solution is simple: Eat something bland. Bread, potatoes, rice, avocados, yogurt, beer, wine, or milk will help; water usually makes things worse.

Mexican Corn Chowder

by Susan Feniger and
Mary Sue Milliken

1 cup diced onion
1 tablespoon olive oil
    Salt (optional)
    Freshly ground black pepper
1/2 cup poblano chilies (about 2), roasted, peeled, and seeded
1 cup diced tomatillos (Mexican green tomatoes)
2 cups fresh (from 4 to 6 ears corn) or frozen corn kernels
3 cups unsalted chicken broth or stock (see page 28), or water
2 cups 1% fat milk
1/2 red bell pepper, diced

PREPARATION TIME: 30 minutes
COOKING TIME: 25 minutes
YIELD: 6 servings

In a 4-quart saucepan, sauté the onion in the olive oil with salt and pepper to taste over medium heat until translucent. Add the poblanos, the tomatillos, the corn, and the chicken stock or water; simmer for 10 to 15 minutes.

Puree in batches in blender; return puree to saucepan. Add the milk, bring just to a boil. Season with salt and pepper to taste. Divide among 6 bowls and garnish with diced red bell pepper in the center of each bowl.

NOTE: If a thinner soup is desired, strain the puree before adding the milk.

NUTRITION INFORMATION: Cal: 144 Pro: 8g/ 20% Carb: 21g/56% Fat: 4g/24% (S:28% M:59% P:13%) Chol: 4mg Sodium: 93mg Potassium: 508mg Fiber: 2g A: 19% C: 85% B2: 15% B3: 15% B6: 10% Ca: 12% P: 17% Mn: 10% Cr: 29%
EXCHANGE: Skim Milk: 1/4 Bread: 1 Veg: 1 Fat: 3/4

MICROWAVE METHOD: In a 4-quart microwave-safe casserole or bowl, cook the onion and the olive oil on High (100% power) until translucent, about 2 to 3 minutes. Add salt and pepper to taste, the poblanos, the tomatillos, the corn, and the chicken stock or water. Cook covered on High 5 minutes. Puree in batches in blender. Strain, if desired. Return to casserole. Stir in the milk. Cook, covered, on Medium (50% power) just to boiling, about 8 to 10 minutes. Season and garnish as above.

Thai Melon Salad

by Susan Feniger and
Mary Sue Milliken

  3 *cloves garlic, crushed*
  2 *tablespoons palm sugar or brown sugar (see Note)*
  2 *tablespoons nam pla (Thai fish sauce; optional, see Note)*
 1/4 *cup fresh lemon juice*
 10 *serrano chilies, thinly sliced*
 1/3 *cup dried shrimp (optional, see Note)*
 1/2 *cup unsalted peanuts*
  6 *cups chilled 1/2-inch melon balls (2 canteloupes or honeydew melons)*
 1/4 *cup coriander leaves for garnish*

PREPARATION TIME: 35 minutes plus standing time
YIELD: 7 appetizer or side-dish servings

In a bowl, mix together the garlic, sugar, nam pla if used, lemon juice, and chilies. Rinse the shrimp and pat them dry. Finely chop the shrimp and peanuts. Add to the garlic mixture; set aside 30 minutes.

Arrange the melon balls in a shallow dish or platter. Pour the dressing over them. Garnish with coriander leaves.

NOTE: Palm sugar, nam pla, and dried shrimp are available at Asian food stores. Nam pla and dried shrimp are quite salty, so leave them out if you want less salt.

NUTRITION INFORMATION (without nam pla or dried shrimp): Cal: 142 Pro: 4g/10% Carb: 23g/

59% Fat: 5g/31% (S:14% M:52% P:34%) Chol: 0mg Sodium: 20mg Potassium: 609mg Fiber: 2g C: 197% B1: 14% B3: 13% B6: 11% Mg: 10% Cu: 12% Cr: 14%

EXCHANGE: Med. Meat: 1/4 Veg: 1/2 Fruit: 1 1/4 Fat: 1

VARIATION: Try 2 cups each of three different kinds of melons—orange or green honeydew, cantaloupe, watermelon, Crenshaw, canary—choosing contrasting colors. Arrange the melon balls in alternating rows before adding the dressing and garnish.

Summer Garden Salad

by Nao Hauser

Arrange this colorful salad on romaine lettuce leaves and sprinkle with a little bit of Parmesan cheese, if desired, for a light first course. Or serve it with grilled chicken or meat for delightful textural contrast.

  2 *green bell peppers, julienne cut*
  1 *red bell pepper, julienne cut*
  1 *white onion, very thinly sliced*
  1 *tablespoon balsamic vinegar*
 1/8 *teaspoon salt*
  1 *cucumber*
  1 *small yellow summer squash*
  1 *large tomato, coarsely chopped*
 1/2 *cup finely chopped fresh parsley*
  4 *leaves fresh basil, snipped (optional)*
  2 *tablespoons olive oil*
     Freshly ground black pepper

PREPARATION TIME: 30 minutes
YIELD: 5 to 6 servings

Combine the peppers and onion in a large salad bowl. Sprinkle with vinegar and salt; toss well, pressing the onion with a fork to separate the rings and release juice. Let stand 10 minutes.

Peel and seed the cucumber. Slice it thin. Quarter the squash lengthwise and slice it thin. To the onion and peppers add the cucumber, squash, tomato, parsley, and basil if used; toss well. Sprinkle with the oil and black pepper to taste; toss again.

NUTRITION INFORMATION: Cal: 77 Pro: 2g/ 8% Carb: 8g/39% Fat: 5g/53% (S:15% M:72% P:13%) Chol: 0mg Sodium: 51mg Potassium: 371mg Fiber: 3g A: 22% C: 149% Cr: 24% EXCHANGE: Veg: 1½ Fat: 1

Grilled Chicken Breasts with Ancho Chili Paste

by Susan Feniger and
Mary Sue Milliken

The paste made from ancho chilies in this recipe both seasons the chicken and keeps it moist during cooking.

> 12 ancho chilies
> ½ cup vinegar
> 2 onions, diced
> 1 tablespoon vegetable oil
> 1 clove garlic, unpeeled and crushed
> 2 tablespoons ground cumin
> 4 cups unsalted chicken broth or stock (see page 28), or water
> ¼ cup brown sugar
> ¼ cup orange juice
> ⅛ cup fresh lemon or lime juice
> ¼ to ½ cup canned tomato puree, no salt added
> Salt (optional)
> Freshly ground black pepper
> 3 whole chicken breasts (about 3 pounds), halved, skin and visible fat removed

PREPARATION TIME: 40 minutes plus refrigerating time
COOKING TIME: 1 to 1½ hours
YIELD: 6 servings

Remove the seeds from the chilies and lightly toast the chilies to develop their full flavor (see Note). Soak the chilies in the vinegar (add enough water to cover) for 15 minutes; then puree the chilies and liquid.

In a large saucepan, brown the onions in oil over medium-high heat; add the garlic and cumin and cook about 1 minute more. Heat to boiling; reduce heat and add the chili puree and the stock or water. Simmer over medium heat about 20 minutes or until the flavors have all merged.

Make a paste of the brown sugar, orange juice, lemon or lime juice and tomato puree. Whisk the paste into the chili mixture and continue simmering for another 15 minutes. Season with salt and pepper to taste. Remove from the heat.

Pour the mixture into a large glass bowl or dish. Add the chicken breasts and refrigerate covered for 2 hours.

Preheat oven to 400°F. Put the chicken breasts in a large ovenproof pan and bake for 20 to 25 minutes on a side, turning once and basting occasionally with the marinade.

Or grill the chicken over charcoal or broil for 10 minutes on a side, turning once and basting occasionally with the marinade.

NOTE: To toast dry chilies, heat a large skillet over high heat. Place chilies in a skillet, 4 to 6 at a time, and cook, turning over once, just until thoroughly hot. The heat releases the flavor.

NUTRITION INFORMATION: Cal: 276 Pro: 32g/ 46% Carb: 22g/31% Fat: 7g/23% (S:25% M:36% P:39%) Chol: 74mg Sodium: 138mg Potassium: 744mg Fiber: 1g A: 12% C: 194% E: 13% B1: 11% B2: 12% B3: 76% B6: 38% Panto: 10% P: 30% Fe: 21% Mg: 14% Cu: 14% Mn: 10% Se: 63% Cr: 27% EXCHANGE: Lean Meat: 3½ Veg: 1½ Fruit: ¾

MICROWAVE METHOD: Prepare and puree the chilies as described above. In a 2-quart microwave-safe casserole or bowl, cook the onions and the oil on High (100 percent power) until translucent, about 5 minutes. Add the garlic, cumin, chili puree, and only 2 cups of stock or water. Cook covered on Medium (50 percent power) for 10 minutes. Stir together the brown sugar, orange juice, lemon or lime juice, and tomato puree; add to the chili mixture. Cook covered on Medium for 10 minutes. Continue as above.

Red Salsa

by Susan Feniger and
Mary Sue Milliken

You can serve this salsa as a dip with tortillas or use it as a sauce with chicken, pork, or seafood.

1 onion, sliced
2 teaspoons olive oil
5 tomatoes
2 cloves garlic, peeled
2 serrano chilies, stems removed
  Salt

PREPARATION TIME: 15 minutes
COOKING TIME: 10 minutes
YIELD: 3 cups

In a skillet over medium heat, cook the onion in the olive oil until translucent, about 5 minutes. Set aside.

Core the tomatoes and cut into quarters. Place the onion, tomatoes, garlic, and serranos in a blender and puree well. (Strain if you prefer a thin sauce.) Pour the puree into a 1-quart saucepan. Heat to boiling, stirring occasionally. Add salt to taste. Chill well before serving.

NUTRITION INFORMATION (per ½-cup serving):
Cal: 46 Pro: 1g/11% Carb: 7g/57% Fat: 2g/
31% (S:16% M:69% P:15%) Chol: 0mg Sodium:
10mg Potassium: 293mg Fiber: 2g A: 26% C:
93% Cr: 22%
  EXCHANGE: Veg: 1¼ Fat: ¼

MICROWAVE METHOD: In a 2-quart microwave-safe casserole, cook the onion and oil on High (100% power) until translucent, about 2 to 3 minutes. Place the tomato, onion, garlic, and serranos in a blender and puree. Return pureed mixture to casserole; cook covered on High to boiling, about 4 to 6 minutes. Add salt to taste. Chill before serving.

Sweet Pepper Relish

by Nao Hauser

Since peppers and barbecues come into season together, this relish makes an apt accompaniment for grilled meat, poultry, or fish. It's also delicious on cold chicken and turkey sandwiches or spooned over black beans and rice. Process a chili pepper with the sweet peppers if you like things fiery.

½ cup parsley leaves or ¼ cup parsley
    and ¼ cup fresh coriander leaves
2 red bell peppers, cut into chunks
1 green bell pepper, cut into chunks
1 small white onion, cut into chunks
½ teaspoon ground cumin
¼ teaspoon chili powder
¼ teaspoon sugar
⅛ to ¼ teaspoon salt
    Pinch ground cloves
1 tablespoon fresh lime juice

PREPARATION TIME: 15 minutes
YIELD: 1½ cups

Process the parsley and coriander if used in a food processor until minced. Add the peppers, onion, cumin, chili powder, sugar, ⅛ teaspoon salt, and the cloves to work bowl; process until peppers are minced. Add the lime juice; process to blend thoroughly. Stir in remaining salt if desired. Makes 5 servings.

NUTRITION INFORMATION (per ⅓ cup serving):
Cal: 24 Pro: .8g/12% Carb: 5g/75% Fat: .4g/
13% Chol: 0mg Sodium: 86mg Potassium:
177mg Fiber: 1g A: 12% C: 153% Cr: 12%
  EXCHANGE: Veg: 1

Roasted Pepper Dressing

by Nao Hauser

If you like Italian-style roasted peppers, you'll love this dressing on romaine, iceberg, and leaf lettuces tossed with such crisp accents as cauliflowerets and thinly sliced carrots. It's also good with pasta, either hot or in a cold salad. And if you omit the chicken broth, you'll have a thick creamy dip for all kinds of crudités.

1 pound green bell peppers
2 tablespoons plus ¹/₂ teaspoon fresh lemon juice
2 tablespoons olive oil
2 cloves garlic, peeled and sliced
¹/₂ teaspoon dried oregano
¹/₄ cup unsalted chicken broth or stock (see page 28) or water

PREPARATION TIME: 15 minutes plus cooling time
COOKING TIME: 15 minutes
YIELD: 1 cup

Place the whole peppers on a broiler pan lined with aluminum foil. Broil, turning as needed, until blackened on all sides. Wrap the peppers in foil; let stand 15 minutes or until cool. Rub off skin from the peppers, remove the cores, and rinse under cold water to remove the seeds. Pat dry; cut into 1-inch pieces.

Place the peppers in a blender container with 2 tablespoons lemon juice, oil, garlic, and oregano; process until smooth. Taste and add additional lemon juice if desired. Add chicken broth; process until smooth.

NUTRITION INFORMATION (per 1-tablespoon serving): Cal: 21   Pro: .3g/5%   Carb: 1g/23%   Fat: 2g/72%   (S:15%   M:74%   P:11%)   Chol: 0mg
Sodium: 5mg   Potassium: 38mg   Fiber: .2g   C: 45%
    EXCHANGE: Veg: ¹/₄   Fat: ¹/₄

◇ FISH ◇

A World of Fish

by Robert Barnett and
Jeanine Barone

A land with a lot of herring needs few doctors.
—Dutch proverb

Dining on poached salmon or having tuna fish for lunch instead of hamburgers or pizza, a few times a week, may seem a modest dietary change. But it could have profound health effects.

One reason is fat. Fish likely has less of it than beef or pork or cheese. Many fish get fewer than 20 percent of their calories from fat (we list dozens on page 219), whereas even a lean cut of beef such as bottom round is 31 percent fat calories. Fish fat is also low in artery-damaging saturated fat. Beef fat is about 41 percent saturated, chicken fat is 25 percent, but fish fat is less than 4 percent saturated. Choose fish, sensibly prepared, for dinner and you will take in less fat, less saturated fat, and fewer calories.

But the scientific excitement these days isn't over the fat that's missing. It's over the fat that's there—Omega-3 fatty acids, an unusual class of polyunsaturated fats found in all fish that can powerfully influence physiological functions as diverse as blood clotting, immune response, and the development of the brain in infancy. The bottom line: Fish is delicious, nutritious, a good source of low-fat protein, and may contribute something extraordinary to your health.

Evolving on Omega 3s

A 3½-ounce serving of bluefin tuna has 6.5 grams of fat, of which 1.2 grams are Omega-3 fatty acids (herein called fats). What are these special fats?

Long-lost friends, some would say. A probably essential nutrient we have unwittingly almost stripped from our diets, anthropologists report. A balance to the potential harm posed by the preponderance of Omega-6 fatty acids that our vegetable oils, seeds, meats, and grains give us, some biologists and cardiologists concur.

What makes these fish fats so special? They serve as building blocks in our bodies for a class of powerful chemical messengers called eicosanoids. Eicosanoids affect processes as diverse as blood clotting, inflammation, insulin secretion, immune response, and brain/eye development, and disorders as distinct as heart disease, rheumatoid arthritis, and cancer. Omega-6 fats are also precursors of eicosanoids, but very different ones. Omega 6–derived eicosanoids, on balance, make it more likely for blood to clot, a risk factor for heart disease, while Omega-3 fats make blood clotting less likely. Eicosanoids play a role in many inflammatory and immune-related diseases as well, notes University of Illinois biochemist William Lands. (Olive oil, high in monounsaturated Omega-9 fatty acid, doesn't affect eicosanoids.)

Since the dawn of agriculture 10,000 years ago, and dramatically in the last century, our diets have shifted away from Omega 3–rich foods to Omega 6–rich foods. We evolved on fish, wild greens, and wild game, all good sources of Omega 3s; the coming of agriculture, by shifting diets toward seeds and grains, started to change the balance a bit.

In this century, the shift has accelerated. Technology now lets us squeeze vegetable oils from corn and safflower, and feed our livestock with grain rather than let them eat Omega 3–rich grasses. So much of the fat we eat is likely to be Omega 6. "For two to four million years, we were getting a balance of Omega-3 and Omega-6 fatty acids," explains cardiologist Alexander Leaf, chairman of the Department of Preventive Medicine at Harvard Medical School, in a 1987 article in *The American Journal of Clinical Nutrition.* "That was a more normal physiological state. Now we have an epidemic of coronary heart disease."

Omega 3s and Heart Disease

Many factors can contribute to heart disease: diet, genetics, lack of exercise, stress, obesity, high blood pressure, cigarette smoking, drinking, drugs. In the dietary realm, too much saturated fat raises the level of cholesterol in the blood, making heart attacks more likely.

Now a number of researchers believe that the tendency of the blood to form damaging clots, or "thrombi," may be equally important. "Almost our entire dietary and pharmaceutical approach to preventing heart disease today is directed to lowering the plasma [blood] cholesterol level," writes Leaf. Yet "as we learn more about the initiation of atherosclerotic disease, cholesterol may turn out to be only a secondary factor."

It's widely thought that coronary artery disease begins with a tiny injury to the wall of the artery. Such injury can be caused by high blood pressure, high cholesterol, cigarette smoking, infection, diabetes, or eicosenoid metabolism. After injury a process of healing begins. The blood vessel wall begins to grow as it attempts to repair itself. White blood cells migrate to the area, chemical changes occur at the site, and blood clot formation begins.

Wound healing is often benign. But if our blood is too likely to clot or the repair process gets out of hand, the blood vessel can become completely blocked off. That causes a heart attack and dam-

ages some of the heart muscle. Some current strategies to ward off this process aim to reduce blood's clotting activity. That's where diet comes in. By consuming fewer highly unsaturated Omega 6–rich vegetable oils, such as corn and safflower oil, and more fatty fish, we provide Omega 3s to our tissues. These fatty acids counteract or slow down the blood clotting activity, which helps to keep our blood vessels open. Shifting from Omega-6 to Omega-3 fats, writes Leaf, is "strongly antiaggregatory [anti-blood-clotting] and vasodilatory [widens blood vessels]—conditions that should help prevent the development of atherosclerosis."

But let's get to cases. In Japan one major study conducted at Chiba University School of Medicine in Chiba compared residents of a fishing village and an inland farming village. Both groups ate fish, but the fishing village residents, not surprising, ate much more: about half a pound per person per day compared with about a fifth of a pound for the farmers. The fishing villagers had blood that was only half as likely to clot as that of the farming villagers; in one good fishing year, the fish eaters' blood was even less likely to clot.

In one well-designed animal study, fish oil directly inhibited atherosclerosis. The subjects were pigs, in whom the atherosclerotic process closely resembles humans. University of Massachusetts Medical Center researchers fed two groups of pigs a high-fat, high-cholesterol diet. One of the groups also got about two tablespoons of cod liver oil, which contains Omega 3. After eight months, both groups had high levels of blood cholesterol, but there was an 80 percent reduction in the extent of the atherosclerosis process in the pigs that received cod liver oil.

Other studies find that Omega-3 fats may calm irregular heartbeats by making our cardiovascular systems less responsive to catecholamines, chemicals we create in response to stress. Some studies suggest they may also lower blood pressure. And some studies also find they help people who suffer from migraines have fewer and less severe attacks, probably through the widening of blood vessels.

But does eating fish actually prevent heart attacks? Yes. In Zutphen, Holland, men who ate as little as two fish meals a week had half the rate of heart attacks as those who didn't eat fish at all. And in Cardiff, Wales, Dr. Michael Borr found that men who had already survived a heart attack reduced their chance of dying if they began eating fish regularly.

Beyond Diet:
Fish Oil Supplements

Such dramatic effects should encourage all of us to try to include more fish in our diets. Whether you should take fish oil supplements, however, is a medical issue, not a nutritional one. If you're considering it, discuss it with your doctor. Large doses of fish oils may increase the need for vitamin E, among other things.

For a while, increased risk of stroke also seemed to be a concern. Early reports suggested that Eskimos, who eat prodigious amounts of marine mammals such as seals, suffer an above average rate of strokes. But many conditions, including fainting and epilepsy, may have been included in these early reports under "stroke." A more recent study finds that in Japan, where strokes are a common problem, inhabitants of fishing villages had lower rates of strokes than inhabitants of inland towns.

Whether or not Omega 3 supplements benefit people with diabetes is also an unsettled question. Eicosanoids can affect insulin secretion, but the process is not well understood. In one recent abstract, researchers at the University of Washington at Seattle report that giving Omega-3 fatty acids to Type II (adult onset) diabetics lowers their triglycerides but makes it harder to control blood sugar. It's an area that diabetologist Sumer P. Pek at the University of Michigan has been studying for years. "Some studies show beneficial effects on glucose tolerance, some deleterious effects," says Pek. "My own view is that it doesn't make much difference." What that means to Pek is that some "diabetics should be allowed to benefit from fish oil supplements—to reduce the risk of cardiovascular disease. We recommend that our patients increase fish intake. For some patients, for whom the risk is more obvious, we recommend capsules."

In the future, Omega 3 supplements may also be called upon to treat auto-immune and inflammatory conditions. Eicosanoids affect immunity and inflammation; those made from Omega-6 fatty acids may worsen certain inflammatory and immune-related diseases, while Omega 3–derived eicosanoids often improve symptoms.

Take rheumatoid arthritis. The tissues around the joints of people with rheumatoid arthritis are chronically inflamed. The disease is characterized by large amounts of Omega 6–derived eicosanoids. One type are leukotrienes; they encourage inflammation. To reduce inflammation, Albany Medical College researcher Joel Kremer tried giving patients fifteen capsules of fish oil, in addition to their regular medication, for fourteen weeks. The result was a significant, though modest, improvement in many symptoms: fewer and less severe complaints of tender and swollen joints, more hours free of fatigue. "It's not a dramatic breakthrough," notes Kremer. "It's statistically significant, but not clinically dramatic."

Some researchers believe that Omega 3s may also benefit people with asthma, another disorder characterized by a preponderance of proinflammatory eicosanoids. But studies such as those conducted at the University of California Medical Center in San Francisco haven't found any clinical benefit.

The case for psoriasis is more hopeful. Researchers find high levels of pro-inflammatory eicosanoids in the psoriasis lesions. At the University of California, Davis, dermatology professor Vincent Ziboh finds, in a preliminary study, that giving patients very large amounts of fish oils (60 to 75 grams) along with a low-fat low-Omega 6 diet for two months can help. Eight of thirteen patients experienced mild to moderate improvement in scaling, redness, and thickness of the lesions. Although these preliminary results are encouraging, Professor Ziboh notes, excessive intake of fish oil may be hazardous.

Whatever the pros and cons of fish oil capsules, one thing is clear: Eating fish two or three times a week instead of fattier fare is a good thing for your cardiovascular system.

A fish-rich diet may even help protect against cancer, preliminary evidence suggests. In animal studies, animals given carcinogens and then fed an Omega 3–rich diet had fewer tumors than those fed an Omega 6–rich diet. One reason may be that Omega-6 fatty acids are building blocks for eicosanoids (prostaglandins) that, in turn, may suppress the immune system's ability to search and destroy incipient tumor cells. Arachidonic acid is one such substance. "We've found exaggerated arachidonic acid production in animal and human tumors," says cancer researcher Rashida Karmali of Rutgers University in New Brunswick, New Jersey. In another study, giving fish oil to animals given carcinogens increased the response of T-cells, a key component of immunity; corn oil didn't.

Profiles of fish-eating populations support the cancer-protective hypothesis. Greenland Eskimos and the Japanese have very low rates of breast cancer. Mediterranean populations, where the diet is also low in Omega 6s but high in Omega 3s from fish and wild greens (as well as Omega 9s from olive oil), also have low cancer rates. Clearly, more research needs to be done to determine whether fish oils can modulate the immune system, says Dr. Karmali. But the work so far does suggest that returning to the Omega 6/ Omega 3 balance we evolved on may give our bodies what they need to function optimally—on many levels.

Brain Food

Many scientists believe that Omega-3 fatty acids are not just good for us—they're absolutely essential. "Fish is part of the natural diet of man," says Oregon Health Sciences University professor William E. Connor, M.D., one of the earliest investigators of Omega-3 fatty acids.

Paleolithic hunter-gatherers may not have always had fish available 30,000 years ago, note nutritional anthropologists Boyd Eaton and Melvin Konner of Emory University in Atlanta, but their diet was rich in Omega-3 fatty acids. About 2.5 percent of the body fat of wild game from Africa's Rift Valley is Omega-3 fat, they note, while domestic livestock has practically none. "Our ancestors got more Omega-3 fatty acids than we get," concludes Eaton, "but probably less than the Eskimos do now. My guess is that Eskimos are getting too much."

Evolving on these fats, we learned to make good use of them. Docosahexanoic acid (DHA),

one kind of Omega-3 fatty acid, is found in great concentration in the eye's retina, in sperm, and in the brain. It's laid down in the retina and brain before birth and in the first few years of life. "The brain is half fat, so we're all fatheads in that respect," says Framingham epidemiologist Peter W.F. Wilson. "And a third of that fat is Omega 3." One benefit of these highly polyunsaturated fats may be to make the membranes of nerve cells more fluid, so that light, for example, can pass through more easily. Maybe our thoughts, too!

Monkeys bred without Omega-3 fatty acids don't develop good eyesight. When neuroscientist Martha Neuringer, who works with Connor, fed rhesus monkeys an Omega 3–deficient diet, their breastfed monkey infants suffered "impairments in vision in deficient infants. Their visual acuity is reduced by half," she says. She's looking for behavioral changes, to see if the lower levels of DHA in the brain causes problems with learning. In Japan, researchers studying rats report that an Omega 3 deficiency directly impairs the ability to remember and learn. Other studies by Sue Carlson of the University of Tennessee find that in premature infants, a little DHA added to formula can bolster the levels of Omega-3 fatty acids available to make brain and neural tissue. Formula does not yet routinely contain DHA.

"Our findings provide evidence that dietary Omega-3 fatty acids are essential for normal and postnatal development of the retina and brain," writes William Connor. "We further suggest that an adequate quantity of Omega-3 fatty acids be included in the diets of pregnant and lactating women and of the infant who is formula fed."

Omega-3 fatty acids including DHA are found in breast milk, "and so far, everything we've ever found in human milk is there for a purpose—it's not there for fun," says nutrition researcher Artemis Simopoulos, Ph.D., former chairman of the National Institutes of Health Nutrition Coordinating Committee. "If a nursing mother is a vegetarian, she should eat green leafy vegetables, soy products such as soybeans and tofu, canola oil and use flax flour to make bread," she advises. These are all good vegetable sources of Omega 3s. "If she's an omnivore, she should make sure she includes fish in her diet—salmon, bluefish, sardines, herring, tuna—two or three meals a week."

How to Get Your Omega 3s

That's not bad advice for everyone, as it turns out. Indeed, including Omega-3 fatty acids may turn out to be important at all stages of the life cycle. In China, mothers feed cod liver oil to infants at three months, fish at four months.

Whether you're a vegetarian or an omnivore, the proper balance of Omega 6 to Omega 3 is probably between 3 to 1 and 10 to 1, says Connors. Simopoulos's estimate is close: between 2 to 1 and 7 to 1.

That is, for every three grams or so of Omega 6 in our diets, we should get one gram of Omega 3 (a 3 to 1 ratio). Most oils contain both types, but in various degrees. Soybean oil, for example, has a ratio of 7 to 1, which is good. Canola oil is about 2 to 1. But safflower is fifty parts Omega 6 to one part Omega 3, and that's not so great. According to Carolyn Crimmins-Hintlian of Massachusetts General Hospital, the key is to "increase Omega-3 fatty acids from selected vegetable oils and from fish, but don't rely on fish oil capsules."

All fish, lean or fatty, fresh or salt water, contains some Omega-3 fat, and it's in a much more effective form than that found in vegetable oils. "Variety is very important," says Wilson. "You can't eat salmon every day. Or sardines. Today, fortunately, the variety of fish available in supermarkets is so much greater than it has been."

Even freshwater fish have some Omega 3. "Rainbow trout is one of the best freshwater sources," says Crimmins.

Nor do you need fresh fish. Canned tuna retains almost all of its Omega 3, find Massachusetts Institute of Technology researchers. That's good news, as the vast majority of Americans get their tuna from a can, not a steak. Try water-packed tuna: Draining the water and rinsing the tuna, which reduces sodium content, won't drain away Omega-3 fatty acids. Oil-packed fish is more of a problem, as the Omega 3 mixes with the oil, so you'd have to eat all that oily vegetable fat to get the Omega 3. All sardines have lots of Omega 3s, but sardines packed in "sild oil," another word for sardine oil, are even richer.

"You don't have to go overboard," says Connor. "Just include one to three fish meals a week in a low-fat, low-cholesterol diet. It's valuable nutrition and may have some role in prevention of disease."

A Dozen Ways to Eat Safer Fish

To be good for us, the fish we eat must be pure. Unfortunately, it often may not be.

Pesticides, heavy metals, and organic chemicals like PCB can find their way into our fish—and onto our plates. Federal authorities often issue restrictions on fish caught in certain areas. Near Santa Monica Bay, for example, the California State Mussel Watch, part of a national program to monitor mussels and other bivalves, found the highest level of twenty-six different pesticides ever recorded in clams.

The bulk of the toxins in fish are found in the fat. Unlike red meat, fish fat is not that easy to trim away—and in any case, we may not want to. Fish fat, after all, is one reason we're eating the fish in the first place.

Contamination stems from a complex interaction of fish, environment, and toxin. Older, larger, inland freshwater bottom-feeding fish that spend considerable time in heavily polluted waters are among the most contaminated. Predator fish can accumulate toxins; bivalves such as oysters and clams in polluted beds may filter the same contaminated water over and over; high-fat fish such as carp can store toxins in their fat. But distant ocean fish are fairly pure. So are younger fish. Alaskan salmon, for example, spawn in fairly clean estuaries, spend their lives in much less polluted northern oceans, and so are fairly pure. "Most fish in the open ocean are not particularly contaminated," notes environmental epidemiologist Harold Humphrey of the Michigan Department of Public Heath. "This isn't the case with fish from bays and harbors."

What actual risks polluted fish pose to humans

isn't known. In one EPA-sponsored study by the Michigan Department of Public Health, healthy men and women who ate more than 26 pounds of sport fish such as lake trout in polluted Lake Michigan had three times the levels of PCBs in their blood as men and women who ate little or no sport fish. At the University of Wisconsin, Madison, scientists estimate that if a 154-pound man or woman eats two 5-ounce polluted fish meals a week for seventy years, his or her chance of getting cancer may be increased by $1/2$ percent to 3 percent. Because we're unlikely to eat very polluted fish every week for life, actual risk is probably much lower.

"Most of the risks are extrapolated from animal toxicology studies, while the benefits are derived from human studies," notes California Department of Health Services staff toxicologist Jerry Pollock. "A lot of the risk is from local fish taken from a contaminated area." To Dr. Jeffrey Foran, assistant associate professor, School of Public Health, University of Michigan, the benefits of eating more fish clearly outweigh the risks, especially if you "try to eat fish that are low in contaminants."

Here's how:

♦ Eat fish from a variety of sources. "Eat a varied diet so that you are not eating the same fish from the same area," says Pollock.

♦ Favor open ocean fish over freshwater fish, unless it's farmed.

♦ Eat small, young fish. "Older fish have more time to accumulate organic chemicals in their body," says Ken Gall of the Cornell Cooperative Extension Sea Grant Program.

♦ Shop in large commercial markets. These are relatively safe as they mostly sell salt-water, open-ocean fish, usually from a variety of sources.

♦ Check your state advisories for specific warnings. The document is given to those who obtain a fishing license. Or try the Department of Environment Conservation, the State Sea Grant program, or the Department of Public Health. This is particularly true for pregnant or nursing women and young children.

♦ Avoid regular consumption of sport fish. Don't fish off docks or piers in areas identified as polluted regions, e.g., Long Island Sound, the Los Angeles shoreline, Puget Sound, San Francisco Bay, Boston Harbor, Chesapeake Bay. "It's the sportfisherman who may get the greatest contamination load," says Pollock. "Indeed, some fishermen eat the same fish from the same lake week after week for years. This is not a good idea."

♦ Avoid fish oil capsules unless your doctor prescribes them. Because they are concentrated fish fat, any contaminants can be concentrated, too.

♦ If you suspect a fish of being at all contaminated with organic chemicals, carefully trim it by removing the skin and fat from along the top center and edges of the fillet. If it's a whole fish, remove the fat from the belly and top as well as the dark flesh from the lateral line, and the skin. Doing this could decrease organic contaminants by 20 to 60 percent. Grill or broil the fish on a rack so the fat can drain away. Of course, you'll drain away Omega-3 fatty acids as well.

♦ Eat some fish from commercial ranches. Most of the catfish in the market are farmed. Ditto for rainbow trout.

♦ Try lean fish, too. Though you'll get greater amounts of Omega-3 fats in fattier fish, the percentage of fish fat that is Omega 3 is actually greater in lower-fat fish.

♦ When eating freshwater fish, try lean, young fish such as perch, bluegill, or crappie.

♦ Select the freshest fish and cook properly; like any food, fish can carry bacteria.

In unison, public health nutritionists advise us to eat fish, both fat and lean, two or three times a week instead of more-saturated, high-fat meat meals. The best way to do that safely is to eat lots of different kinds of fish from the least polluted waters.

—Jeanine Barone

Cooking Fish

by Nao Hauser

In the best of all possible worlds you catch a fish, consume it within hours, and go to bed with a smile on your face, knowing you have eaten food fit for the gods. If you live near a commercial fishing area, you may be able to duplicate the flavor—if not the triumph—of cooking your own catch by purchasing fish when it is very fresh.

Selection and Storage

Almost any sport or commercial species properly dressed and chilled once it is out of water will taste delicious if cooked the same day. But the fish sold "fresh" in markets may have left the water as long as ten days before. And fish deteriorates quickly; it will last a week (for fatty fish) to ten days (for lean ones) only if kept perfectly chilled the whole time—and often it isn't. That's why every fish shopper must be prepared to examine the goods carefully—and turn to frozen fish if necessary. Freshness is especially important in low-fat cookery, because you don't want to have to use butter or oil to mask "fishy" odors or dryness. Freshness is also much more important than species in the flavor of a dish; many types of fish can be substituted in any given recipe.

So apply these standards when you shop for and store fish:

1. No fish should smell "fishy." If it does, don't buy it. You may have to ask the salesperson to hold up whatever fish you choose so that you can get a whiff; don't be shy—ask and sniff! If the fish is sold wrapped in the supermarket case, pick it up and smell through the wrapper; if there's any question, ask someone to unwrap it for you. Even fish that has a strong flavor, such as shad or trout, smells sweet when absolutely fresh.

2. The fish, whether whole, filleted, or cut into steaks, should feel firm, not soft. Some markets may object to letting you touch the fish; if so, ask them to put a piece of plastic wrap or waxed paper over the fish before you touch.

3. Apart from smell, the surest guide to freshness is the appearance of the whole fish. The eyes should be absolutely clear, with no sign of milkiness; the gills should be bright red. When it's practical to do so, buy a whole fish, have it cleaned, and fillet or cut it into steaks at home, if desired, just before cooking. The fish will keep better in your refrigerator if it's left whole, but you may prefer to have the store fillet it for the sake of convenience (don't forget to ask for the head and bones if you want to make fish stock). If a whole fish is more than you can eat, see if the store will sell you half, or ask if another customer will split it with you.

4. Fish fillets and steaks should look moist and firm, with no signs of dryness or discoloring. The flesh should look fresh enough to be eaten uncooked, as in sashimi or seviche, even though you intend to cook it. Beware of excess water in the display case or package; if it drained out of the fish, the fish has been lying around long enough to lose its juiciness.

5. Cook any market catch the same day if possible; put it in the coldest part of the refrigerator until you're ready. If you need to store it overnight, place the wrapped fish in a plastic bag on a bed of ice in a colander in a pan (to catch dripping water) in the coldest part of the refrigerator.

6. If you have to keep fish longer, freeze it. Place the fish on a baking sheet until frozen solid; then wrap it in moisture/vapor-proof wrap or a freezer bag and keep it in the coldest part of the freezer up to one month. An extra precaution against flavor loss: Glaze the frozen fish by dipping it into ice water several times, to form a protective layer of ice, before wrapping.

7. Commercially frozen fish, and especially whole frozen trout, can be of fine quality. The softened texture of frozen fillets and steaks can be of little significance in fish soups or stews. Don't defrost too quickly or too much; partially thaw in the refrigerator in a bowl of very cold water, or in the microwave on the lowest setting. Cook fish while it is still partially frozen; if allowed to thaw completely before cooking, the fish will lose too much moisture.

Preparation

Fish are sold in three basic forms: whole dressed, which means scaled and gutted but head and tail left on; fillets, or the sides of the fish cut away from the frame and skinned or not; and steaks, or crosswise cuts of a whole dressed fish. Some fish are also sold split, meaning that the whole dressed fish has been split open along the backbone, so that it lies flat; the head and tail are left on and the other bones may or may not be removed.

In most fish cookery, the form in which the fish is purchased is less important than the thickness. Thick fillets and steaks usually can be cooked the same way; so can small or split whole fish of the same thickness, although you'll want to remove the bones before or after cooking. If you want to bake a whole fish with stuffing, for example, but fish fillets look better than whole fish in the market, you can sandwich the stuffing between two fillets; conversely, you can substitute a whole fish of roughly the same thickness in a recipe for broiled fish steaks.

As in all low-fat cooking, the key to flavor lies in making the most of the natural juices and fat in the fish. This means preserving the moistness of lean to moderately lean fish by not exposing it to direct heat. In other words, use moist-heat cooking techniques: poaching, steaming, or baking with vegetables, a stuffing, or a sauce that will insulate the flesh. The lean fish are excellent in soups and stews. You can use dry-heat methods, such as dry baking, broiling, and grilling, with these fish if they are small and whole, since the skin will provide enough insulation for short cooking times; you can also baste them with oil as they cook and remove the skin before serving.

Fattier fish present a more ambiguous situation. Generally, they can be cooked dry when whole, because the fat under the skin will melt and baste them; thus, whole whitefish, bluefish, shad, sardines, and mackerel are favorites on the grill. These fish will taste more delicate once the fatty skin (and any dark strips of muscle hemoglobin around the fillets) is removed. Also, very generally speaking, the flesh of fatty fish will not be as firm as that of a lean fish; so if you want to present attractive rolled poached fillets, for example, haddock or sole will hold its shape better than whitefish or Greenland turbot. Another general caveat: Don't use any fish fattier than, say,

sea bass for a fish stock or soup; the oil will overwhelm the smell of the liquid. (See Fish Fumet recipe, The Healthy Kitchen, page 29).

However, fatty fish tend to be caught and marketed within such a wide range of circumstances that it is harder to generalize about them than it is about lean fish. The whole freshwater trout, catfish, and salmon you are likely to encounter in markets, for example, are usually young and small and should be treated like leaner species. Tuna, swordfish, and orange roughy are commonly sold as fillets or steaks, which should be protected from prolonged direct heat because much of the fat has been removed with the skin and frame. Although these fish retain enough fat to be able to stand up to broiling or grilling, they should be marinated beforehand to prevent drying.

Marinating in seasoned citrus juices is a good way to impart flavor and prevent broiled fish from drying out. Dissolve spices and dried herbs in the liquid before adding to the fish and turning to coat; refrigerate at least 30 minutes and up to 2 hours. The juices of an orange and a lemon or a lime add up to enough for two to three pounds of fish. Because the seasonings are diluted by the juice, you can combine all kinds of assertive herbs and spices, such as fresh or dried basil and oregano with garlic and pinches of cinnamon and nutmeg, or fresh or dried mint with garlic, and curry powder. While the fish is cooking, simmer the marinade until it is reduced by one half to two thirds; remove from heat and stir in some prepared mustard and additional chopped fresh herbs, to make a sauce.

All fish cook fast and overcook even faster. Whatever cooking method you use, checking for doneness is the most important part. Fish is cooked when it looks opaque; check for doneness near the bone at the thickest part of a whole fish by inserting the tip of a knife—the flesh should flake under gentle pressure. The common rule for timing is 9 to 10 minutes per inch of thickness, but this will vary according to oven temperature or distance from heat source. Be careful not to place fish too close to a broiler element, as the surface will overcook before the interior is done. For the same reason, use a covered, rather than an open, grill with any fish thicker than about 1 1/2 inches or larger than about two pounds, and don't place the fish too close to the fire. Make a few deep slashes in a whole fish when broiling or grilling to allow the heat to penetrate faster.

Among the following fish recipes, you will find at least one formula to fit any species. Baking is by far the most versatile method, because it allows cooks to hedge their bets: you can add enough moisture to the baking pan—whether in the form of a liquid, a moist stuffing, vegetables, or even blanched lettuce wrapped around the fish—to protect lean fish, and the source of moisture can be acidic enough to complement oily fish. A small bunch of a relatively mild fresh herb, such as tarragon, dill, chervil, lemon balm, or Italian parsley, stuffed into the cavity, will scent a whole fish as it bakes. If you have time to stuff the fish with rice, couscous, or bulgur mixture, you can add stronger herbs and spices to the grain.

Steaming, a good technique for all but the fattiest fish, also keeps fish moist. Chinese cooks count on a fine julienne of ginger root to counter the "fishiness" of steamed whole fish. Chopped fresh parsley or coriander are also refreshing.

Poaching also permits some hedging. The liquid for poaching whole fish or thick steaks can be as plain as water or half water and half wine, but an infusion is even better. Fattier fish should be poached in an acidic liquid—water or fish stock with wine, citrus juice, or vinegar added. The acid will help to firm the flesh and counter oily smells. Therefore, it is also useful to marinate fattier fish in an acidic mixture for 15 minutes or longer before you steam it. For the sake of convenience, you may want to wrap fattier fish in cheesecloth before poaching; the wrapping will make it easier to remove the less firm fish from the pot.

Whatever the poaching liquid, pre-simmer it with sprigs of parsley, a bay leaf, and dill, sorrel, tarragon, chervil, celery, or fennel before adding the fish. A few cloves and peppercorns add a nice spicy note. After the fish has been cooked, strain the liquid and simmer some of it with chopped fresh herbs and a pat of butter, and spoon over the fish at serving time.

If you have definite fish cooking preferences, it is probably worth investing in the appropriate accessories. A wire basket makes it easy to turn fish on the grill. A Chinese-style bamboo or metal steamer that fits into a wok offers not only convenience but also attractive serving, especially if you line the bottom with lettuce. The cost of a fish poacher may make you think twice, since any pan will work if it has a lid and can accommodate a rack; however, the narrowness of the poacher and its fitted rack do simplify the matter of keeping a large whole fish submerged in liquid.

Tuna, Red Cabbage, and Caper Salad
by Marie Simmons

The secret of this salad is to keep all the chopped ingredients uniform in size. The salad can be served as a first course, and it also makes a delicious filling for a pita bread pocket.

> 2　6 1/2-ounce cans tuna packed in water, well drained, or 1 15 1/2-ounce can pink or red salmon, well drained, skin discarded
> 2 1/2　tablespoons olive oil
> 5　teaspoons red wine vinegar
> 1　clove garlic, peeled and crushed
> 1/8　teaspoon coarsely ground black pepper
> 3　cups finely chopped red cabbage, about half a 1 1/4-pound head
> 1　cup chopped sweet white onion
> 1　cup thinly sliced celery
> 1/4　cup tightly packed finely chopped fresh flat-leaf parsley
> 2　tablespoons small capers, rinsed in several changes of water and drained

PREPARATION TIME: 30 minutes
YIELD: 6 servings

Rinse the tuna or salmon under cold water and drain well in a sieve; let stand until ready to use. Whisk together the oil, vinegar, garlic, and pepper in a small bowl. Combine the cabbage, onion, celery, parsley, and capers in a large bowl. Add the dressing and toss to blend. Add the tuna or salmon; toss lightly just to blend. Serve chilled.

NUTRITION INFORMATION: (salad only) Cal: 147 Pro: 17g/44% Carb: 7g/18% Fat: 6g/37% (S:16% M:70% P:14%) Chol: 37mg Sodium: 241mg Potassium: 407mg Fiber: 2g Omega-3: 1.3g C: 64% E: 20% B3: 35% B6: 18% B12: 43% P: 15% Cu: 22% Se: 89%
EXCHANGE: Lean Meat: 2 Veg: 1½

(salad with 1 slice pita bread) Cal: 252 Pro: 21g/33% Carb: 28g/43% Fat: 7g/24% (S:16% M:70% P:14%) Chol: 37mg Sodium: 456mg Potassium: 452mg Fiber: 3g Omega 3: 1.3g C: 64% E: 20% B1: 15% B3: 42% B6: 18% B12: 43% P: 19% Fe: 12% Cu: 22% Se: 89%
EXCHANGE: Lean Meat: 2 Bread: 1½ Veg: 1½

Warm Potato Salad with Sardines and Mustard Dressing

by Marie Simmons

1½ pounds small new potatoes, scrubbed, skins
    left on
2 3.75-ounce cans Norway brisling sardines
    packed in water
2 tablespoons olive oil
2 tablespoons plain nonfat yogurt
1 tablespoon fresh lemon juice
1 tablespoon whole-grain mustard
⅛ teaspoon coarsely ground black pepper
1 green bell pepper
1 small red onion
1 small cucumber
2 tablespoons chopped fresh dill

PREPARATION TIME: 25 minutes
COOKING TIME: 20 minutes
YIELD: 6 servings

Cook the potatoes in boiling water to cover until tender when pierced with a fork, 15 to 20 minutes. Drain. Cool about 5 minutes. While the potatoes are cooking, drain the sardines in a sieve; set aside. In a cup, whisk together the oil, yogurt, lemon juice, mustard, and black pepper. Set aside.

Clean, seed, and then cut the green pepper thinly crosswise. Halve the onion vertically and cut it lengthwise into thin strips. Pare the cucumber, quarter it lengthwise, and remove the seeds. Slice across into ¼-inch pieces. Combine the green pepper, red onion, cucumber, and dill in a large bowl. Slice the warm potatoes into the bowl, add the mustard dressing, and toss to blend. Add the sardines and carefully toss; try not to break up the sardines too much. Serve warm or at room temperature sprinkled with dill.

NUTRITION INFORMATION: Cal: 207 Pro: 11g/22% Carb: 23g/45% Fat: 8g/34% (S:20% M:58% P:22%) Chol: 36mg Sodium: 273mg Potassium: 688mg Fiber: 2g Omega 3: .7g C: 53% B1: 11% B3: 17% B6: 21% B12: 53% Ca: 17% P: 24% Fe: 11% Cr: 19%
EXCHANGE: Lean Meat: 1¼ Bread: 1¼ Veg: ½ Fat: 1

MICROWAVE METHOD: In a 2-quart microwave-safe casserole, cook the potatoes and ¼ cup water covered on High (100% power) until the potatoes are tender, about 7 to 9 minutes. Drain and proceed as directed above.

Baked Cod with Fennel and Tomatoes

by Marie Simmons

Any thick fillets would be enhanced by this technique and flavorful sauce; both lean and oily fish are suitable. Fillets of red snapper, pompano, bluefish, halibut, salmon, tilefish, weakfish, or haddock are all good substitutes for the cod. Serve with plain boiled potatoes.

1 bulb fennel (about 1 pound)
2 tablespoons olive oil
1 cup chopped sweet white onion
12 ounces tomatoes, chopped
1 clove garlic, peeled and crushed
¼ cup chopped fresh basil, including stems
1¾ pounds cod fillets

PREPARATION TIME: 20 minutes
COOKING TIME: 40 minutes
YIELD: 6 servings

Trim the fennel, cut it into fourths, and then cut it across into ¼-inch slices.

Preheat the oven to 400°F. Spread the oil in a heavy, shallow 2-quart (about 9- by 13-inch) baking dish; stir in the onion and fennel. Bake in the preheated oven until the onion and fennel around the edges of the dish begin to turn golden and the fennel is tender-crisp, about 15 minutes. Remove the baking dish from the oven, stir in the tomatoes and garlic, and bake 15 minutes, or until the tomatoes have cooked down. Remove the baking dish from the oven, stir in the basil, tuck the fish fillets into the sauce, and spoon some sauce over the fillets. Bake 10 minutes or until the fish is opaque and flakes with the tip of a knife.

NUTRITIONAL INFORMATION: Cal: 216 Pro: 31g/ 57% Carb: 10g/18% Fat: 6g/26% (S:21% M:53% P:26%) Chol: 68mg Sodium: 155mg Potassium: 973mg Fiber: 2g Omega 3: .2g A: 73% C: 63% E: 13% B3: 13% B6: 27% B12: 38% Ca: 13% P: 35% Fe: 20% Se: 57% Cr: 16%
EXCHANGE: Lean Meat: 3½ Veg: 2

MICROWAVE METHOD: In a 2½-quart, shallow, microwave-safe baking dish, cook only 2 teaspoons of the oil, with the onions, fennel, and garlic covered on High (100% power), until the fennel is tender, about 5 to 6 minutes. Add the tomatoes and basil. Cook uncovered on High to boiling, about 3 to 4 minutes. Stir. Add the fish fillets and spoon the sauce over all. Cook tightly covered on High until the fish is opaque, about 7 to 10 minutes. Let stand 5 minutes.

Whole Fish Stuffed with Couscous

by Marie Simmons

This delicate stuffing is studded with a simple dice of carrots, cucumber, and scallions. The addition of mint and basil gives it a lovely freshness. Use small fish for individual servings or a whole large fish for two to four servings. Any freshwater fish—trout, pike, bass, carp—or lean round sea fish—red snapper, sea trout, sea bass, redfish, or rock fish—can be stuffed and baked.

   1 cup couscous
   ¾ cup boiling water
   2 plus 1½ tablespoons olive oil
   2 tablespoons fresh lemon juice
   1 small clove garlic, peeled and crushed
  ¼ teaspoon salt (optional)
  ⅛ teaspoon freshly ground black pepper
  ½ cup diced peeled tomato
  ¼ cup diced scallions
  ¼ cup diced peeled seedless cucumber
  ¼ cup diced peeled carrot
   1 tablespoon chopped fresh basil
   1 tablespoon chopped fresh mint
   1 sea bass, striped bass, or other whole fish (about 2½ pounds), cleaned, and dressed or boned, with head and tail left on
   4 lemon wedges for garnish
   4 sprigs fresh basil for garnish

PREPARATION TIME: 25 minutes
COOKING TIME: 40 minutes
YIELD: 4 servings

Place the couscous in a bowl, add the boiling water, and let stand until the liquid is absorbed, about 10 minutes. Do not stir. Whisk 2 tablespoons of the olive oil, 1 tablespoon of the lemon juice, and the garlic together until blended. Add the salt and pepper. Toss the couscous with the olive oil mixture and the tomato, scallions, cucumber, carrot, and chopped basil and mint; set aside.

Preheat the oven to 350°F. Rinse the fish; pat dry with a paper towel. Select a baking dish large enough to hold the fish without crowding; grease with ½ teaspoon of the oil. Rub the top of the fish with the remaining 1 teaspoon oil. Sprinkle the insides of the fish with the remaining 1 tablespoon lemon juice. Carefully fill the cavity with the couscous mixture, mounding as it overflows onto the baking dish. If using several smaller fish, distribute the stuffing equally among them. Bake 40 minutes or until the fish flakes easily when the point of a sharp knife is inserted into the fleshy part. Garnish with lemon wedges and basil.

NUTRITION INFORMATION: Cal: 414 Pro: 29g/
31% Carb: 33g/36% Fat: 14g/33% (S:19% M:64%
P:18%) Chol: 83mg Sodium: 82mg Potassium:
477mg Fiber: 2g Omega 3: .8g A: 65% C: 39%
E: 13% B1: 21% B2: 15% B3: 22% B6: 19%
B12: 26% P: 32% Fe: 20% Mg: 18% Se: 57%
Cr: 16%
EXCHANGE: Lean Meat: 3½ Bread: 2 Veg: ½
Fat: 1

MICROWAVE METHOD: Prepare the couscous
as directed. In a 2½-quart shallow microwave-
safe casserole or 13- by 19-inch microwave-safe
baking dish, stuff the fish as directed above. Cook
tightly covered on High (100% power) until the
fish is opaque, about 4 to 5 minutes per pound of
fish, rotating the dish once. Let stand 3 minutes.
Garnish as above.

Flounder Fillets Rolled with Dilled Julienne Vegetables

by Marie Simmons

A delicate fillet from any of the flounder family
(plaice, grey sole, Dover sole, lemon sole) works
best in this recipe. Delicious served with boiled
new potatoes and topped with a sauce of yogurt,
dill, and lemon juice.

2 small carrots, julienne cut
2 small zucchini, julienne cut
2 scallions, white part julienne cut, tops very
    thinly sliced
1 tablespoon light olive or other vegetable oil
4 teaspoons fresh lemon juice
1 tablespoon chopped fresh dill, including stems
4 4-ounce sole or flounder fillets
    Yogurt, Dill, and Lemon Sauce (recipe follows)
4 sprigs fresh dill for garnish

PREPARATION TIME: 20 minutes
COOKING TIME: 22 minutes
YIELD: 4 servings

Place a steaming rack over gently boiling water; add the carrots; cover and steam 3 minutes.
Add the zucchini, cover, and steam 3 minutes. Add

the scallions, cover, and steam 1 minute more.
Combine the vegetables in a bowl with 2 teaspoons each of the oil and lemon juice, and the
chopped dill.

Preheat the oven to 400°F. Coat the fish fillets
with the remaining oil; sprinkle with the remaining lemon juice. Evenly divide the julienned vegetables into four neat bundles and place one
across the center of each fillet. Fold the edges of
the fillets up over the vegetables, overlapping the
tips of the fillets. Arrange the fillets in a shallow
ovenproof dish. Bake until the fish is opaque,
about 12 minutes, depending on the thickness of
the fillets. Serve with Yogurt, Dill, and Lemon
Sauce. Garnish with sprigs of dill.

YOGURT, DILL, AND LEMON SAUCE

½ cup plain low-fat yogurt
1 teaspoon fresh lemon juice
¼ teaspoon grated or finely chopped lemon
    rind
1 tablespoon chopped fresh dill

PREPARATION TIME: 10 minutes, not including
refrigerating time
YIELD: ½ cup

Combine all the ingredients. Chill to blend flavors. Serve with fish and as a topping for boiled
new potatoes.

NUTRITION INFORMATION (sauce only; per 2-
tablespoon serving): Cal: 19 Pro: 2g/32%   Carb:
2g/47% Fat: .4g/21% (S:68% M:29% P:3%)
Chol: 2mg Sodium: 20mg Potassium: 76mg
Fiber: 0g
EXCHANGE: Skim Milk: ¼

(fish and 2 tablespoons sauce) Cal: 210 Pro: 28g/
54% Carb: 12g/22% Fat: 6g/24% (S:24% M:60%
P:16%) Chol: 73mg Sodium: 171mg Potassium:
759mg Fiber: 3g Omega 3: .3g A: 290% C: 15%
B2: 14% B3: 15% B6: 24% B12: 47% P: 39%
Mg: 23% Mn: 16%
EXCHANGE: Lean Meat: 2¾ Skim Milk: ¼ Veg:
1½

MICROWAVE METHOD: In a 1-quart microwave-
safe casserole, cook the carrots and ¼ cup water
covered on High (100% power) until tender-crisp,
about 3 minutes. Drain liquid; add the zucchini
and scallions to casserole. Cook covered on High

until zucchini is tender-crisp, about 3 to 4 minutes. Drain. Pour a mixture of 1 tablespoon each oil, lemon juice, and dill over the vegetables; divide the vegetables evenly into four bundles and roll the fillets as described above. In a 9- to 10-inch round microwave-safe baking dish, place the stuffed fillets, sprinkle with 1 teaspoon lemon juice and cook, covered, on High until the fish is opaque, about 4 to 6 minutes. Let stand 5 minutes. Serve with Yogurt, Dill, and Lemon Sauce and boiled new potatoes.

Pompano en Papillote with Tomato and Cumin
by Marie Simmons

Either cooking parchment or aluminum foil can be used to make the "packages" in which the fish is cooked—the word *papillote* is French for the oiled paper originally used. The edges of the packages are double-folded to seal in the flavor and natural juices. Although these packages are baked in a hot oven, the cooking method technically is steaming. When parchment is used, the packages will fill with steam and puff up as the fish cooks. Here we simplify the procedure by using foil, which is more readily available to the supermarket shopper than cooking parchment. Any firm-fleshed white fish can be cooked in this way; try bass, snapper, tilefish, cod, turbot, sole, and orange roughy, to name just a few, or even salmon or shelled shrimp or scallops.

 1 *pound tomatoes, cut into ¼-inch dice*
¼ *cup diced green bell pepper*
½ *cup fresh or frozen corn kernels*
 1 *scallion, white part minced, green part thinly*
   sliced
 1 *teaspoon minced fresh chili pepper, or to*
   taste
 1 *teaspoon cumin seeds*
   Coarsely ground black pepper
   Pinch cayenne
 4 *6-ounce pompano fillets*
   Sprigs of fresh coriander, or julienne of fresh
   basil leaves (see page 220), for garnish
 4 *lime wedges for garnish*

PREPARATION TIME: 20 minutes
COOKING TIME: 15 minutes
YIELD: 4 servings

Preheat the oven to 400°F. Combine the tomatoes, bell pepper, corn, scallion, and chili pepper in a bowl. In a medium skillet, heat the cumin seeds, shaking the skillet until seeds are fragrant, about 3 minutes. Stir the tomato mixture into the cumin; heat, stirring, over medium heat just until heated through, about 2 minutes. Remove from heat. Add black and cayenne pepper to taste.

Place a baking sheet on the lowest rack of the oven; heat 5 minutes. Cut off four 15-inch lengths of aluminum foil. Fold in half crosswise and then open out flat. Place a pompano fillet on one side of the fold line. Spoon a quarter of the warm tomato mixture over the fillet and tightly fold over the edges of foil to make an airtight packet. Repeat for the other three fillets.

Place the packages on the hot baking sheet; bake 10 minutes for fillets less than ½ inch thick and 15 minutes for thicker fillets. Slash open the packets and transfer fillets, topping, and juices to individual plates. Garnish each with coriander or basil and a lime wedge.

NUTRITION INFORMATION: Cal: 287 Pro: 28g/ 47% Carb: 20g/33% Fat: 5g/20% (S:25% M:36% P:39%) Chol: 88mg Sodium: 89mg Potassium: 626mg Fiber: 4g Omega 3: .8g A: 37% C: 63% B1: 18% B2: 14% B3: 23% B6: 19% B12: 28% Panto: 11% P: 32% Fe: 21% Mg: 18% Se: 69% Cr: 24%
EXCHANGE: Lean Meat: 3 Bread: ½ Veg: 2½

MICROWAVE METHOD: Combine the tomatoes, bell pepper, corn, scallion, and chili pepper in a bowl. In a 1-quart microwave-safe casserole or bowl, cook the cumin seeds on High (100% power) until fragrant, about 1½ to 2 minutes. Add the tomato mixture. Cover and cook on High just to boiling, about 3 to 4 minutes. Add black and cayenne pepper to taste. Cut four 15-inch square pieces of parchment or 15-inch lengths of plastic wrap. Place a fillet in the center of each; top with tomato mixture; fold the edges of package together and crimp to seal. Place in a 12- by 8-inch microwave-safe baking dish and cook on High until the fish is opaque, about 6 to 8 minutes; rotate the dish once. Let stand 3 minutes. Open packages carefully to avoid steam.

Red Snapper Wrapped in Lettuce with Provençal Vegetables

by Marie Simmons

When baking a whole fish the trick is to choose a fish that will fit comfortably into one of the baking dishes you already have. A 2-pound fish is a manageable size and will serve three or four. Wrapping a fish in blanched lettuce leaves makes a dramatic presentation and also helps retain the moisture and flavor. This method works well with bass, carp, rockfish, trout, pompano, red snapper, and salmon. The flavorful vegetables also work well with oily fish such as bluefish, sablefish, swordfish, and mackerel. A side serving of rice rounds out the meal.

    1¹/₂ tablespoons olive oil
       1 large sweet white onion (8 ounces), cut
         into ¹/₂-inch pieces
       1 large green bell pepper (8 ounces), cut
         into ¹/₂-inch pieces
       1 large red bell pepper (8 ounces), cut into
         ¹/₂-inch pieces
       1 clove garlic, peeled and minced
       1 tablespoon chopped, pitted brine-cured
         black olives (Niçoise, Gaeta, or Kalamata)
       1 teaspoon chopped fresh oregano, or ¹/₂
         teaspoon dried
       2 tablespoons fresh lemon juice
       1 red snapper (about 2 pounds), dressed,
         with head and tail left on
  6 to 8 outside leaves of Boston, romaine, or
         curly-leaf lettuce, rinsed
       1 teaspoon freshly grated Parmesan cheese

PREPARATION TIME: 20 minutes
COOKING TIME: 40 minutes
YIELD: 4 servings

Heat 1 tablespoon of the oil in a medium skillet; add the onion and peppers. Sauté over medium heat until the edges begin to turn golden, about 5 minutes. Stir in the garlic; sauté 1 minute. Add the olives, oregano, and 1 tablespoon of the lemon juice; remove from heat.

Preheat the oven to 400°F. Rinse the fish under cold running water and clean the cavity thoroughly; pat dry. Place in a 2-quart baking dish (approximately 9 by 13 inches) and drizzle with the remaining oil and lemon juice. Place a spoonful of the vegetable mixture in the fish cavity. Immerse the lettuce leaves in a saucepan of boiling water and let stand until limp, about 2 minutes. Pat the leaves dry with paper toweling. Carefully wrap the fish with the lettuce leaves, trimming any thick leaf bases if necessary. Spoon the remaining vegetable mixture around the fish; sprinkle with grated cheese. Cover the pan with foil and bake 30 to 35 minutes. Serve with rice.

NUTRITION INFORMATION (without rice): Cal: 228 Pro: 31g/52% Carb: 10g/17% Fat: 8g/ 31% (S:20% M:60% P:20%) Chol: 72mg Sodium: 98mg Potassium: 913mg Fiber: 3g Omega 3: .7g A: 15% C: 228% E: 10% B1: 12% B3: 23% B6: 28% B12: 32% Folic: 14% P: 17% Mg: 15% Cr: 24%
    EXCHANGE: Lean Meat: 3¹/₂ Veg: 2

MICROWAVE METHOD: Wrap damp lettuce leaves in paper towels and cook on High (100% power) until wilted, about 2 to 3 minutes. Let stand. In a 1-quart microwave-safe casserole, cook only 1 teaspoon oil and the onion, peppers, and garlic on High until the peppers are tender, about 4 to 6 minutes. Add the olives, oregano, and 1 tablespoon of the lemon juice. In a 2¹/₂-quart shallow oval microwave-safe casserole or a 9- by 13-inch microwave-safe baking dish, stir 1 tablespoon oil and the remaining lemon juice. Stuff and wrap the fish and arrange in the dish with the vegetables as directed above. Cook covered on High until the fish is opaque, about 4 to 5 minutes per pound of fish, rotating the dish once. Let stand 3 minutes. Serve with rice.

Red Snapper with Rosemary, Lemon, and Caramelized Garlic

by Marie Simmons

The trick here is to place the fish far enough away from the heat of the broiler to ensure thorough, even cooking as well as a nicely crisped surface. Use a broiler-proof platter rather than a perforated broiler pan rack; it is important to spoon the flavorful fish juices back over the fish while it is cooking. For best results when grilling outside, use a hinged wire basket to hold the fish. This recipe is particularly delicious served with sautéed bitter greens (broccoli de rabe, escarole, romaine leaves, or spinach) flavored with a dash of red wine vinegar. Other fish to use in this recipe include: bluefish, scrod, pompano, salmon, rockfish, or whiting. You may use two or more fish to equal the 2 pounds total weight, but be careful not to overcook smaller fish.

1 2-pound red snapper, dressed, with head and
*   tail left on*
1 tablespoon fresh lemon juice
1 tablespoon olive oil
2 tablespoons thinly sliced peeled garlic
3 strips lemon rind (yellow only), cut into thin
*   crosswise slivers*
1 tablespoon fresh rosemary leaves, or 1
*   teaspoon dried*
*   Freshly ground black pepper*

PREPARATION TIME: 10 minutes
COOKING TIME: 25 minutes
YIELD: 4 servings

Rinse the fish under cold running water and clean the cavity thoroughly; pat dry. Make three deep slashes, about 1 inch apart, diagonally across the width of the fish. Turn over and repeat on the other side. Set on a broiler-proof platter and sprinkle the cavity and surface of the fish with the lemon juice.

Heat 2 teaspoons of the oil in a medium skillet. Sauté the garlic over low heat until the edges begin to turn golden, about 5 minutes. Stir in the rind; sauté until fragrant, about 2 minutes. Stir in the rosemary; remove from heat. With a slotted spoon, place the garlic mixture in the fish cavity. Drizzle the remaining 1 teaspoon oil over the surface of the fish. Sprinkle with black pepper. Broil 6 to 8 inches from the source of heat 8 minutes, or until the skin is golden. Carefully turn; spoon the juices over the fish. Broil until skin on second side is crisped and flesh flakes when tested with tip of a knife, about 8 minutes. Serve with rice.

NUTRITION INFORMATION (without rice): Cal: 160 Pro: 27g/67% Carb: 2g/5% Fat: 5g/28% (S:20% M:60% P:20%) Chol: 68mg Sodium: 60mg Potassium: 573mg Fiber: 0g Omega 3: .7g B3: 19% B6: 15% B12: 30% P: 12% Se: 271%
EXCHANGE: Lean Meat: 4

Skewered Swordfish and Orange with Thyme
by Marie Simmons

The fine texture of swordfish is perfect for threading on skewers. Other possible fish are salmon, cod, tuna, or marlin. Try this recipe with other herbs such as basil, chives, or oregano. An especially pretty entrée, this recipe is great for entertaining. Serve it with basmati rice cooked with currants.

* 1/2 cup orange juice*
1 1/2 tablespoons olive oil
*   1 teaspoon grated or finely chopped*
*   orange rind*
*   1 teaspoon fresh thyme leaves, or 1/2*
*   teaspoon dried*
* 1/4 teaspoon freshly ground black pepper*
*   12 ounces (about 8) small yellow or white*
*   onions, peeled*
2 or 3 navel oranges, cut into 12 wedges
* 1 3/4 pounds swordfish (1 1/4 inches thick), cut*
*   into 12 1 1/2-inch squares*

PREPARATION TIME: 15 minutes plus marinating time
COOKING TIME: 10 to 13 minutes
YIELD: 6 servings

In a large bowl, combine the orange juice, olive oil, rind, thyme, and pepper; whisk to blend. Add the onions, orange wedges, and swordfish pieces. Cover and marinate 2 hours in refrigerator or 1 hour at room temperature. Stir often. Thread the onions, orange wedges, and swordfish on six skewers, distributing evenly. Reserve the marinade. Broil the skewers 6 to 8 inches from the source of heat 5 minutes. Then baste with the remaining marinade, turn skewers, and broil until browned and fish is cooked through, 5 to 8 minutes.

NUTRITION INFORMATION: Cal: 240 Pro: 26g/ 45% Carb: 13g/23% Fat: 9g/33% (S:24% M:65% P:11%) Chol: 50mg Sodium: 119mg Potassium: 612mg Fiber: 2g Omega 3: .9g C: 81% B3: 60% B6: 26% B12: 33% P: 36% Cu: 14%
EXCHANGE: Lean Meat: 3¼ Veg: 1 Fruit: ½

Poached Salmon with Cucumber, Yogurt, Mint, and Dill Sauce

by Marie Simmons

The stunning pink flesh of the salmon makes an especially attractive whole poached fish presentation. Other firm-textured whole fish such as red snapper, trout, sole, haddock, bass, or tilefish also poach successfully. This salmon is served either chilled or at room temperature, with a refreshing Cucumber, Yogurt, Mint, and Dill Sauce, which can also be served as a salad.

3 cups water
2 cups dry white wine
¼ cup chopped shallots
1 carrot, chopped
1 rib celery, chopped
1 bay leaf
1 sprig fresh flat-leaf parsley
1 salmon (about 3 pounds), dressed, with head and tail left on
    Sprigs of fresh dill, mint, and/or parsley for garnish
    Lemon slices for garnish
    Cucumber, Yogurt, Mint, and Dill Sauce (recipe follows)

PREPARATION TIME: 20 minutes, excluding sauce
COOKING TIME: 1 hour
YIELD: 6 servings

Simmer the water, wine, shallots, carrot, celery, bay leaf, and parsley in a saucepan for 20 minutes. Pour through a sieve into an oval pan or fish poacher fitted with a wire rack, large enough to hold the salmon comfortably.

Rinse the fish thoroughly under cold running water and clean the cavity. Pat dry with paper towels. Tie the fish around the belly, closing up the belly portion so it will not open up as it cooks. Lower the fish, on the rack, into the poaching liquid. If there is not enough liquid to cover the fish, add more water. Cover the pan and heat the liquid, over medium heat, to a slow simmer (do not boil), then simmer 25 minutes for a 3-pound fish. Test for doneness with a skewer or the point of a knife inserted into the flesh to the bone; the flesh should be opaque.

Carefully lift the rack from the liquid, set on a tray, and let stand 5 minutes. While fish is still hot, carefully peel off the skin from the top side, using a small knife and your fingers. Transfer the fish to a platter. Cover with plastic wrap and refrigerate until cold; or let stand at room temperature. Serve fish either at room temperature or chilled, garnished with dill, parsley, and/or mint sprigs and lemon slices. Pass the Cucumber, Yogurt, Mint, and Dill Sauce.

CUCUMBER, YOGURT, MINT, AND DILL SAUCE

½ large seedless cucumber, washed, trimmed, and thinly sliced
1 cup plain low-fat yogurt
1 scallion, finely chopped
1 tablespoon chopped fresh mint
1 tablespoon chopped fresh dill
1 small clove garlic, peeled and crushed
⅛ teaspoon freshly ground black pepper

PREPARATION TIME: 15 minutes
YIELD: 1½ cups

Combine the cucumber slices, yogurt, scallion, mint, dill, garlic, and pepper in a bowl; stir to blend. Keep cold until ready to serve. Best when eaten the same day as prepared.

NUTRITION INFORMATION (sauce only, per ¼-cup serving): Cal: 28 Pro: 2g/31% Carb: 3g/49% Fat: .6g/20% (S:69% M:28% P:3%) Chol: 2mg Sodium: 27mg Potassium: 126mg Fiber: .3g
EXCHANGE: Skim Milk: ¼

(fish and ¼ cup sauce) Cal: 321 Pro: 36g/
37% Carb: 8g/37% Fat: 10g/26% (S:26% M:41%
P:33%) Alc: 16% Chol: 62mg Sodium: 191mg
Potassium: 973mg Fiber: 1g Omega 3: 1.7g
A: 128% C: 13% B1: 19% B2: 18% B3: 42% B6:
17% B12: 119% Ca: 10% Fe: 11% Mn: 17%
   EXCHANGE: Lean Meat: 4 Skim Milk: ¼ Veg:
¾ Fat: 1

MICROWAVE METHOD: In a 2½- to 3-quart
shallow microwave-safe casserole, cook only 2
cups water, only 1 cup wine, and the shallots,
carrot, celery, bay leaf, and parsley on High
(100% power) 10 minutes. Let stand 5 minutes.
Prepare the fish as directed above (cut in half if
necessary to fit in casserole) and place in the
poaching liquid in the casserole. Cook tightly covered on Medium (50% power) until the fish is
opaque, about 17 to 22 minutes. Carefully lift the
fish from liquid and continue as directed above.

Dover Sole with Shallots and Tarragon

by Marie Simmons

This is a simple method for preparing a tender
fish fillet. It works as well with red snapper or
pompano fillets, trout, salmon, or any of the
larger fillets from round fish as it does with the
more delicate flat fish fillets in the flounder family.

   1 tablespoon vegetable oil
¼ cup finely chopped shallots
   4 4-ounce skinless Dover sole or other sole
      fillets
   1 tablespoon fresh lemon juice
   1 teaspoon chopped fresh tarragon, or ½
      teaspoon dried
      Freshly ground black pepper
      Lemon wedges for garnish

PREPARATION TIME: 10 minutes
COOKING TIME: 20 minutes
YIELD: 4 servings

Preheat the oven to 400°F. Heat the oil in a
small skillet; add the shallots and sauté over low
heat until tender and golden, about 10 minutes.
Scrape into a large, shallow baking dish. Lay the
fillets in the baking dish, turning to coat with the
shallots and oil. Arrange in a single layer. Sprinkle with the lemon juice, tarragon, and black pepper. Bake in the preheated oven until the fish is
opaque and the flesh flakes, about 10 minutes.
Serve with lemon wedges.

   NUTRITION INFORMATION: Cal: 147 Pro: 23g/
64% Carb: 2g/6% Fat: 5g/31% (S:17% M:25%
P:58%) Chol: 40mg Sodium: 60mg Potassium:
484mg Fiber: 0g Omega 3: .1g E: 14% P: 18%
   EXCHANGE: Lean Meat: 3

MICROWAVE METHOD: In a 9- or 10-inch round
microwave-safe baking dish, cook the oil and
shallots on High (100% power) until tender, about
1½ to 2 minutes. Season and arrange the fillets
in the baking dish as directed above, tucking the
thin ends under. Cook, covered with a paper
towel, on High until the fish is opaque, about 4
to 5 minutes. Serve with lemon wedges.

Cold Poached Salmon Steaks with Avocado and Tomato Salsa

by Marie Simmons

One of the simplest and most versatile ways to
prepare fish is poaching steaks or fillets. You can
poach from one to six or even more servings and
feel in complete control of the procedure. If the
fish is to be served chilled, it can be completely
prepared ahead, or if it is to be served warm, the
cooking time is so short it can be accomplished
on the spot with a minimum of energy. Salmon
steaks or fillets, halibut or haddock steaks, scrod
fillets, flounder fillets, or red snapper fillets work
best. A totally different dish can be created just
by serving a different sauce or accompaniment.
The Avocado and Tomato Salsa suggested here
can be varied by omitting the avocado.

4 cups water, or 2 cups water and 2 cups dry
   white wine
1 thick slice sweet white onion
1 bay leaf
1 sprig fresh dill, basil, or flat-leaf parsley
   (include flavorful stem)
1 tablespoon fresh lemon juice
1/4 teaspoon salt (optional)
4 4-ounce salmon steaks, about 1 inch thick
   Lime slices for garnish (optional)
   Sprigs of fresh coriander for garnish
   (optional)
   Avocado and Tomato Salsa (recipe follows)

PREPARATION TIME: 10 minutes plus
refrigerating time
COOKING TIME: 15 minutes
YIELD: 4 servings

Combine the water or water and wine, onion, bay leaf, fresh herb, lemon juice, and salt if used in a large shallow skillet with a tight-fitting lid. Heat to boiling, cover, and simmer gently 5 minutes. Gently lower the fish into the simmering broth. Cover and simmer over low heat (do not boil) 5 minutes. Remove the skillet from heat. Let stand covered off heat 5 minutes. Using a wide spatula, gently turn the fish in the poaching liquid; carefully peel off and discard the skin. Refrigerate in the poaching liquid until chilled. To serve, place a salmon steak on each plate and garnish with a slice of lime and a sprig of coriander. Pass the Avocado and Tomato Salsa.

AVOCADO AND TOMATO SALSA

1 avocado, peeled and coarsely diced
1 cup coarsely diced tomato (1 medium to
   large)
1/2 cup fresh or frozen corn kernels (from 1 ear
   corn)
1/2 cup coarsely diced green bell pepper
1/2 cup coarsely diced red bell pepper
2 tablespoons diced red onion
1/4 cup plain low-fat yogurt
2 tablespoons fresh lime juice
2 tablespoons chopped fresh coriander

PREPARATION TIME: 15 minutes
YIELD: about 2 1/2 cups

Combine all the ingredients in a bowl, toss gently, and refrigerate until ready to serve. Best if served as soon as possible after preparation.

NUTRITION INFORMATION (avocado salsa only, per 2-tablespoon serving): Cal: 26 Pro: .7g/9% Carb: 3g/46% Fat: 1g/45% (S:23% M:59% P:18%) Chol: 1mg Sodium: 4mg Potassium: 132mg Fiber: .6g C: 20%
   EXCHANGE: Veg: 1/2 Fat: 1/4

(salmon and 2 tablespoons avocado salsa) Cal: 200 Pro: 26g/52% Carb: 5g/10% Fat: 8g/38% (S:23% M:45% P:32%) Chol: 45mg Sodium: 59mg Potassium: 654mg Fiber: .8g Omega 3: 2g C: 26% B1: 15% B2: 11% B3: 31% B6: 14% B12: 82%
   EXCHANGE: Lean Meat: 3 1/4 Veg: 1/2 Fat: 1/4

MICROWAVE METHOD: In a 12 by 8 inch microwave-safe baking dish, cook only 2 tablespoons water or wine and water and the onion, bay leaf, fresh herb, lemon juice, and salmon steaks tightly covered on High (100% power) until the fish is opaque, about 4 to 6 minutes. Vent the cover; let fish cool slightly. Peel off and discard the skin. Refrigerate, and continue as directed above.

Steamed Fillets with Black Bean Sauce, Cucumber, and Scallion
by Marie Simmons

Steamed fish served with the flavor combination of this sauce is classically Chinese. This version uses fillets, but often a whole fish is used (see Variation). Any one of the following fillets works well: pompano, grouper, scrod, sea bass, red snapper, monkfish, any of the flounder family (rolled if they are very thin), pike, salmon, or turbot. Traditionally, a Chinese bamboo steamer is used with a plate set inside on which the fish, sauce, and vegetables are arranged. A rather successful improvisation is to use a skillet with a tight-fitting lid large enough to hold the plate, set on a small rack, and still leave about 1/2 inch between the plate's edge and the skillet.

4 6-ounce fish fillets
1 tablespoon Chinese fermented black beans (see Note)
1 tablespoon reduced-sodium soy or tamari sauce
1 tablespoon Chinese rice wine or sherry
1 teaspoon grated or minced fresh ginger
1 teaspoon sesame oil
1 small clove garlic, peeled and crushed
2 tablespoons fresh lemon juice
1/2 seedless cucumber, pared, halved lengthwise, and thinly sliced
1 scallion, julienne cut

PREPARATION TIME: 15 minutes
COOKING TIME: 10 minutes
YIELD: 4 servings

Select a heat-proof plate large enough to set inside a large skillet (see Headnote). Add about 1 inch water to the skillet; set a small rack in the center; place the plate on the rack. Arrange the fish on the plate.

Place the black beans in a small sieve; rinse well under cold running water; drain; pat dry with paper toweling. Finely chop the beans. In a small bowl, combine the beans, soy or tamari, rice wine, ginger, sesame oil, garlic, and 1 tablespoon of the lemon juice. Mix. Sprinkle the remaining lemon juice over the fish. Spoon the black bean sauce over the fish, distributing evenly. Sprinkle the cucumber and scallion over all. Over high heat, bring the water to a boil; cover tightly and steam 10 minutes for fillets 1 1/2 inches thick, 7 minutes for fillets 1 inch thick, and 5 minutes for rolled thin fillets. Serve with brown rice, spooning the juices over fish and rice.

NOTE: Fermented black beans and Chinese rice wine are available in Asian food markets and many supermarkets.

VARIATION: Substitute 1 whole firm-fleshed, mild-flavored fish, about 2 pounds, such as red snapper, sea bass, porgy, or pike for the fillets. Thoroughly rinse the fish under cold running water; pat dry. Make three deep slashes, about 1/2 inch apart, diagonally across the width of the fish. Turn over and repeat on the other side. Continue as directed above. Steam until the flesh at the base of the slash marks is opaque and firm, about 20 to 25 minutes.

NUTRITION INFORMATION: Cal: 189   Pro: 35g/ 77% Carb: 3g/7% Fat: 3g/16% (S:26%   M:34% P:40%) Chol: 96mg Sodium: 300mg Potassium: 575g Fiber: .5g Omega-3: .1g B2: 11% B3: 17% B6: 19% B12: 59% P: 43% Mg: 22%
EXCHANGE: Lean Meat: 4 1/2

MICROWAVE METHOD: In a 9- or 10-inch shallow round microwave-safe casserole or pie plate, arrange the fish, tucking the thin ends under. Prepare the black beans and top the fish as directed above. Cook tightly covered on High (100% power) until the fish is opaque, about 5 to 7 minutes. Serve as above.

◇ SHELLFISH ◇

Another Look at Shellfish

by Robert Barnett and Eileen Behan

If your mind worries as your mouth waters over the thought of a lobster dinner or an oyster stew, fret no more.

Once considered high in cholesterol, we now know shellfish are only low-to-moderate sources of cholesterol, and contain chemicals that may actually inhibit cholesterol absorption (plus some Omega-3 fatty acids that help protect the heart).

What's more, shellfish are low in fat, high in protein, and rich in iron and potassium. Some also contain good amounts of zinc, selenium, and other trace elements whose importance in safeguarding health is increasingly appreciated.

Shellfish are either mollusks or crustaceans. Crustaceans include lobster, crab, and shrimp. Mollusks include clams and oysters. From steamed clams to shrimp marinara, the whole kettle offers a perfect light source of protein—and taste.

The Cholesterol Question

Shellfish do contain sterols, a type of fat which includes cholesterol. But "only 30 to 40 percent of the sterols are actually cholesterol," explains Jacob Exler, a nutritionist at the U.S. Department of Agriculture. In the 1950s, scientists counted all sterols as cholesterol—a mistake only rectified in the early 1970s. "So, instead of a serving of shellfish containing 200 milligrams of cholesterol, much of it really has only 60 to 70 milligrams." Shellfish that moves by itself (shrimp, crab, lobster) has more cholesterol than shellfish that doesn't (clams, oysters, mussels, scallops).

New research makes the heart picture even rosier. Some of the other sterols in shellfish may actually compete with cholesterol absorption, scientists find. These sterols are found primarily in the mollusks, and resemble the plant sterols found in olive oil (which is known to help lower blood cholesterol). In animal studies, oyster sterols reduced cholesterol absorption 25 to 40 percent. In one of the few human studies done with shellfish, University of Washington nutrition professor Marian Childs fed one volunteer group a diet including clams and oysters, another group a similar diet *sans* mollusks. The clam/oyster eaters absorbed 24 percent less cholesterol. Shellfish are also low in total fat and saturated fat—more important considerations than dietary cholesterol—and contain some heart-healthy Omega-3 fatty acids. Conch is particularly Omega 3 rich.

Gems in a Shell

Shellfish are more than just heart-healthy. They're loaded with many minerals the American diet often lacks.

Consider an oyster.

A 3½-ounce serving of Eastern oysters—about 7 oysters—has only 69 calories. For those few calories, you get only about 2 grams of fat, mostly mono- and polyunsaturated. But you also get about 7 grams of protein, more than 10 percent of a 150-pound adult's daily needs. Plus a whopping 6.7 milligrams of iron. That's nearly half a woman's daily needs, more than half a man's. You also get 91 milligrams of zinc (six times the US-RDA), a little calcium, a good amount of potassium, very little sodium (73 milligrams), more than the daily requirement for copper, and some selenium. There's also 25 milligrams of cholesterol (much less than you'll find in a similar serving of chicken or beef), and just under half a gram of Omega 3s.

Zinc, copper, and selenium? Who needs them? Everybody.

Zinc is apparently particularly important for the elderly. In Detroit, 8 of 23 subjects showed mild levels of zinc deficiency, reports Wayne State University School of Medicine researcher Ananda S. Prasad. In a New Jersey survey of 100 elderly people aged sixty to eighty-nine, less than 10 percent took in the zinc RDA of 15 milligrams.

Such "mild" deficiency, finds Prasad, results in low levels of the infection-fighting cell-mediated immune substance interleukin-2. It also causes an abnormality in flavor perception (a metallic taste), and, in elderly males, low testosterone. In the New Jersey survey, those subjects with low zinc levels in their blood also had low immune responses. Nor is it just an academic measure: In a study of over 10,000 Dutch men and women by the Erasmus University Medical School in Rotterdam, high levels of blood zinc were strongly linked to a lower risk of cancer.

Copper may be key for a healthy heart. It's essential for two enzyme systems that clear cholesterol from the body. In one USDA study, researcher Leslie M. Klevay found that a diet with only 0.8 milligrams of copper (an inadequate amount) raised blood cholesterol by 30 milligrams per deciliter in human volunteers. Yet only one American in four gets the recommended 2 to 3 milligrams a day.

Selenium is another rising star. Along with vitamin E, selenium fuels an enzyme system that detoxifies dangerous free oxygen radicals—bad actors implicated in everything from aging to heart disease to cancer. In France, a study of 357 hospital patients found that people with cancer,

alcoholism, chronic infection, diabetes, heart disease, depression, or psychosis (in the elderly) all had lower than normal blood levels of selenium.

Although trace elements may be life-saving, that doesn't mean you should rush out and get mineral supplements. High-dose supplements of individual elements are dangerous: Interactions can backfire badly. Oysters, properly cooked, are a safer not to mention infinitely more delicious choice.

The Contamination Risk

Henry IV would often stimulate his appetite by downing as many as three hundred raw oysters before dinner. Perhaps the waters were cleaner then. In one *New England Journal of Medicine* study, during an eight-month period in New York State over 1000 people became ill from eating raw or undercooked shellfish.

"Twenty years ago the problem was probably uncommon," explains Dr. Herbert L. DuPont of the University of Texas Health Sciences Center at Houston. Now the dangers of hepatitis, gastroenteritis, even salmonella from raw shellfish are rising. Bacterial contamination is also an increasing problem. So is Norwalk virus, which causes flu-like symptoms. According to the federal report *Seafood Safety* (National Academy of Sciences, 1991), "The major risk of acute disease [from fish and shellfish] is associated with the consumption of raw shellfish, particularly bivalve mollusks."

If you have diabetes, cancer, or liver disease, DuPont is clear: Avoid all raw shellfish. And healthy people? "I don't say everyone should stop eating raw shellfish. But people should know there's a risk, and make their own judgment."

To reduce risk, refrigerate or freeze shellfish immediately. This won't kill harmful bacteria, but it will inhibit them from multiplying.

And when you cook shellfish, be sure to cook it long enough. Steaming or boiling clams, oysters, or mussels just until they open—the old rule of thumb—isn't enough. That can happen in as little as one minute. To make sure that internal temperatures reach a safe 100°F, cook these mollusks at least 4 to 6 minutes, advises DuPont.

Other dangers are rarer. Filter feeders—clams, oysters, mussels—can carry a nasty, sometimes fatal disease called paralytic shellfish poisoning (PSP). The cause: poisonous microorganisms picked up during a red tide. Scallops are filter feeders too but are always safe: we only eat the "eye," the muscle part, which doesn't carry PSP. Lobsters, shrimp, and crabs are safe, too.

To be safe from PSP, buy filter feeders only from reputable fish stores, whose suppliers comply with federal programs to prevent PSP. Avoid roadside sellers. If you're a summer clam harvester, make sure the waters you rake are clean. (PSP, incidentally, is one source of the old but practical advice about eating mollusks only during months with an R in them. Red tide is rare in winter.)

Fortunately, shellfish are rarely carriers of significant amounts of environmental toxins such as pesticides or PCBs. These are stored in fat, and shellfish have little fat. (For more on safe fish, see "A Dozen Ways to Eat Safer Fish," page 216).

Cooking With Shellfish

by Marie Simmons

Simplicity is the key to cooking shellfish. Their delicate flavors are best served by steaming, broiling, or braising—with a minimum of light and uncomplicated seasonings. Combinations such as lime and coriander; orange and basil; zucchini, thyme, and lemon; chili peppers, cumin, and tomatoes enhance, rather than mask, the delicate yet rich shellfish flavors.

Technically, shellfish, both mollusks and crustaceans, are cooked when the fragile muscular tissue is subjected to just enough heat that the muscle protein coagulates. If shellfish are overcooked the tissue will dry out and either toughen or disintegrate.

When buying shellfish, trust your nose. Seek a distinctive, fresh aroma; shellfish should never smell "fishy." They should be displayed on plenty of crushed ice. The exception is lobster, which should be resting patiently, alive and well, in a clean lobster tank.

Mollusks

Mollusks—mussels, clams, oysters, and scallops—are at their best during the cool months from September through early spring. In the warmer months they are spawning and are usually not as plump or flavorful.

Many mussels are now farm-raised, although wild mussels are available, especially in shoreline regions. Ask your retailer which type is being sold. Farm-raised are generally less gritty than wild. A classic, delicious, and nutritious way to cook mussels is to steam them in white wine. Just heat 1 to 2 cups of white wine, a parsley sprig, a whole garlic clove, an onion slice, and a pinch of salt to boiling in a large saucepan. Add the mussels, and cook covered until they open, 4 to 6 minutes. Serve hot with crusty bread to mop up the juices or cold with thin slices of red onion and chopped parsley sprinkled over the top.

Oysters and clams are popular raw, which entails risks, and deep-fried, which entails other risks. But clams are also delicious steamed, baked, and cooked in pasta sauce. Oysters are classic in early American stews and pies, and are fine steamed with bay seasonings as well. The scallop, for its part, is so famous for its gracefully designed shell that the noun has become a verb. Americans eat the sweet tender adductor muscle (it holds the top and bottom shells together), but in Europe the orange roe attached to the adducter muscle is also eaten. The scallop is usually cleaned at sea so that we rarely see the beautiful shells in fish stores. If you come upon a good source of fresh snails, you're lucky. Steamed in the shell or broiled with garlic and a touch of olive oil, these often overlooked mollusks make a rich-tasting, low-fat dish.

Crustaceans

Crustaceans include lobster, crab, and shrimp. Here's a fairly foolproof method for cooking shrimp: Heat a saucepan filled with water (and appropriate seasoning such as bay, dill, salt, thyme, red pepper flakes) to a rolling boil. Stir in the shrimp, cover, and cook for 2 minutes for small shrimp and 3 minutes for larger shrimp. Drain immediately and rinse with cool water.

If you are unsure if the shrimp are cooked

enough, pluck one from the boiling water and cut it in half crosswise. The flesh should be milky-white through to the center, not pink. Allow six to eight shrimp per person depending on the dish, the rest of the menu, and, of course, the size of the shrimp.

Of all shellfish, American lobster is the most expensive and the most physically fascinating. Lobsters are usually sold from a holding tank, with the claws either pegged or banded so that they won't attack each other. Or the cook.

If the dish you are cooking requires the lobster to be cut up before it is cooked, try not to be squeamish. We are told by people who should know these things that lobsters do not have any feeling, but then some of us have never really been convinced. Like plunging a lobster into boiling water, plunging a large heavy knife deep into the head section ensures instant death. Once the lobster is dead, split it in half lengthwise; pull the beige intestine from the tail and remove the papery stomach sac located just behind the eyes; discard. Leave the green tomalley and coral intact. Cut the tail portion crosswise where it joins the body. Cut off the claws. Cut lobster into smaller pieces, if desired (a cleaver is good for this task).

Artichoke Bowl with Dilled Shrimp

by Four Seasons Hotels Alternative Cuisine

Leftover Tangy Vinaigrette and Tarragon-Dill Sauce may be refrigerated up to one week and served with salads, meats, fish, or sandwiches. The Tarragon-Dill Sauce has to be made the day before.

2 tablespoons Tangy Vinaigrette (recipe follows)
1/2 cup Tarragon-Dill Sauce (recipe follows)
4 artichokes
1 clove garlic, bruised
1 thick lemon slice

2 cups cooked and shelled shrimp, deveined (about 1 pound)
1 cup diced celery
4 sprigs fresh parsley for garnish
4 red bell pepper stars for garnish (cut with a star-shaped canapé cutter)

PREPARATION TIME: 30 minutes plus refrigerating time
COOKING TIME: 30 minutes
YIELD: 4 appetizer or first-course servings

Make the Tangy Vinaigrette and Tarragon-Dill Sauce. Rinse the artichokes. With a sharp knife, cut off the stems and about 1 inch straight across the tops. With scissors, trim the thorny tips of the leaves. Turn the artichokes upside down and press firmly to open them up as much as possible. In a large saucepot, in 1 inch of boiling water, place artichokes on their stem ends; add the garlic and lemon; cover tightly and simmer about 30 minutes, or until fork-tender.

Remove the artichokes from the water and place upside down to drain until cool enough to handle easily. Pull out and discard the center leaves and spread artichokes open very carefully. With a grapefruit spoon, reach down into the centers and remove and discard the furry choke, pulling out a little at a time, to form a "bowl" in the center of the artichokes. Place right side up and spoon some of the Tangy Vinaigrette into each "bowl." Cover tightly with plastic wrap and refrigerate several hours before serving.

Combine the shrimp, celery, and 1/2 cup Tarragon-Dill Sauce, then divide the mixture evenly among the hollowed-out artichoke bowls. (Chop the shrimp if they're too large.) Garnish each with a parsley sprig and a pepper star. Provide more Tarragon-Dill Sauce in small bowls for dipping the artichoke leaves.

TANGY VINAIGRETTE

1/2 cup chicken or beef consommé, or unsalted broth
1/4 cup red wine vinegar
1 tablespoon fresh lemon juice
1 1/2 teaspoons olive oil

1 1/2 teaspoons Dijon-style mustard
1/2 teaspoon sugar
1 garlic clove, peeled and minced
1 teaspoon Worcestershire sauce
1/8 teaspoon freshly ground black pepper

PREPARATION TIME: 10 minutes
YIELD: about 1 cup

Combine all the ingredients and mix well. Refrigerate until ready to use.

TARRAGON-DILL SAUCE

1 1/2 cups plain nonfat yogurt
1 tablespoon tarragon vinegar
2 teaspoons finely chopped fresh tarragon
1 teaspoon finely chopped fresh dill
1/4 teaspoon salt

PREPARATION TIME: 10 minutes
YIELD: about 1 1/2 cups

Combine all the ingredients and mix well. Prepare a day ahead and store in the refrigerator.

NUTRITION INFORMATION (vinaigrette per 1-tablespoon serving): Cal: 7 Pro: .2g/10% Carb: 1g/31% Fat: 1g/59% (S:16% M:75% P:9%) Chol: 0mg Sodium: 21mg Potassium: 12mg Fiber: 0g
EXCHANGE: Fat: 1/4

(Tarragon Dill Sauce per 1-tablespoon serving) Cal: 8 Pro: .8g/40% Carb: 1g/56% Fat: .03g/4% Chol: 1mg Sodium: 31mg Potassium: 39mg Fiber: 0g
EXCHANGE: Skim Milk: 1/8

(Artichoke Bowl with Vinaigrette and Tarragon Dill Sauce) Cal: 146 Pro: 16g/40% Carb: 21g/52% Fat: 1g/8% Chol: 98mg Sodium: 251mg Potassium: 728mg Fiber: 5g Omega-3: .1g A: 13% C: 55% B1: 12% B2: 11% B3: 15% B6: 16% B12: 15% Folic: 19% Ca: 14% P: 21% Fe: 25% Mg: 21% Zn: 11% Cu: 13% Mn: 14% Cr: 14%
EXCHANGE: Lean Meat: 1 Skim Milk: 1/4 Veg: 3

MICROWAVE METHOD: Prepare the artichokes as directed above. In an 8-inch square or 9-inch round microwave-safe casserole, arrange the ar-tichokes bottoms up around the outer edge, leaving space in the center. Add 1/4 cup water and the garlic and lemon. Cook tightly covered on High (100% power) until fork-tender, about 8 to 10 minutes for small (5- to 6-ounce) artichokes. Drain and continue as above.

Mussel Salad with Tomato and Orange
by Marie Simmons

Be sure to allow enough time for the mussels to stand for 1 to 2 hours as part of the cleaning process.

3 pounds fresh mussels (about 4 dozen; discard any that don't close tightly when tapped)
1/2 cup dry white wine
12 ounces tomatoes, cut into 1/4-inch dice
2 cloves garlic, peeled, bruised with the side of a knife
1 strip (2 by 1/2 inch) orange rind (remove with vegetable peeler)
1 tablespoon olive oil
2 teaspoons fresh lemon juice
1/8 teaspoon freshly ground black pepper
1 small bulb fennel, quartered and sliced thin
1/4 cup finely chopped red onion
1 tablespoon julienne of fresh basil leaves
4 large leaves curly-leaf lettuce (red oak or garden)
1 small orange cut into 1/2-inch-thick wedges for garnish
4 sprigs fresh basil for garnish

PREPARATION TIME: 45 minutes plus standing and refrigerating time
COOKING TIME: 20 minutes
YIELD: 4 servings

Pull the tufts of fiber (called beards) off the mussels. Scrub the mussels thoroughly with a stiff brush; rinse well. Place the mussels in a large bowl; fill with cold water; add a pinch of salt and a handful of cornmeal. Let stand 1 to 2 hours. (If the room is warm, add a few ice cubes to keep the water cold.) Lift the mussels from the water; rinse well.

Heat the wine, half of the diced tomatoes (about ³/₄ cup; cover and refrigerate the remaining ³/₄ cup for later), the garlic, and rind to boiling in a large shallow pan over high heat. Add the mussels, cover tightly, and cook over medium heat until the mussels are opened, about 5 minutes. Remove the pan from the heat; remove the mussels with tongs to a platter to cool. Reserve the rind. Pour the broth into a large measuring cup; let stand 5 minutes so that any grit will settle to the bottom of the cup. Spoon the broth and the solids into a fine sieve set over a bowl, leaving a small amount of the juices and any grit in the bottom of the cup. Press on the solids to extract as much flavor and pulp from the tomatoes and garlic as possible.

Rinse and dry the mussel-cooking pot; return the strained broth to the pot. Heat to boiling; boil until the broth is reduced to ¹/₂ cup, about 10 minutes. Transfer to a bowl and refrigerate until well chilled, about 30 minutes. Meanwhile, carefully remove the mussels from their shells. Reserve six of the prettiest shells for garnish. Cover the mussels and refrigerate until ready to assemble the salad.

When the reduced mussel juices are well chilled, whisk in the olive oil, lemon juice, and black pepper. Cut the reserved rind into very thin (¹/₁₆-inch) julienne strips. In a large bowl, combine the mussels, the reserved ³/₄ cup diced tomato, the fennel, red onion, orange rind julienne, and basil julienne. Add the mussel broth and fold together. Line a platter with the lettuce leaves. Spoon the mussels into the center. Garnish the edges with the shells and the orange wedges. Garnish the mussels with the basil sprigs.

NUTRITION INFORMATION: Cal: 198 Pro: 20g/ 39% Carb: 18g/35% Fat: 6g/26% (S:15% M:70% P:15%) Chol: 200mg Sodium: 346mg Potassium: 921mg Fiber: 4g Omega 3: .5g A: 64% C: 94% B1: 20% B2: 21% Folic: 24% Ca: 20% P: 33% Fe: 34% Mg: 14% Se: 81% Cr: 25% EXCHANGE: Lean Meat: 2 Veg: 3 Fruit: ¹/₄

Thai-Style Squid Salad
by Marie Simmons

1 pound small squid (see Note)
1 teaspoon salt
3 tablespoons fresh lime juice
2 tablespoons nam pla, (Thai fish sauce, optional; see Note)
¹/₂ teaspoon sugar
1 clove garlic, peeled and crushed
1 teaspoon minced hot chili pepper, or ¹/₄ teaspoon hot red pepper flakes (or to taste)
¹/₂ cup julienne-cut red and/or green bell pepper
¹/₂ cup pared, quartered, seeded, thinly sliced cucumber
¹/₂ cup thinly sliced celery
¹/₂ cup thinly sliced scallions, cut on the diagonal
1 tablespoon chopped fresh coriander
1 teaspoon minced fresh mint leaves
Leaves of iceberg, romaine, or curly-leaf lettuce
1 tablespoon whole fresh coriander leaves for garnish (optional)
1 tablespoon whole fresh mint leaves for garnish
Lime wedges for garnish

PREPARATION TIME: 40 minutes
COOKING TIME: 10 minutes
YIELD: 3 servings

Rinse the squid well in a large bowl of water. To clean squid: Under cool running water, grasp the head with one hand and the body sac with the other; pull gently to separate the body from the head. Set the head section aside. Feel for the quill, a long, thin plastic-looking structure in the body sac; pull out and discard. Rinse the body sac well inside and out. Rub the outside speckled skin with your fingertips or the dull side of a knife and pull the skin off. Pull off the fins and set aside. On a board, cut the tentacles from the head; discard the hard "beak" and other matter. Cut the body sac into thin ¹/₈- to ¹/₄-inch rounds, and the fins into ¹/₄-inch strips; separate the tentacles by cutting through at the core. Rinse all the pieces well and drain until ready to cook.

Stir the cut-up squid into a large pot of gently boiling salted water. Reduce the heat to medium and gently simmer the squid 4 minutes. Drain at once in a colander; rinse with cool water; set aside. In a medium bowl, stir the lime juice, nam pla (if used), and sugar together until the sugar is dissolved. Add the squid and all the remaining ingredients except the lettuce, whole coriander and mint leaves, and the lime wedges. Toss gently to blend. Arrange the lettuce leaves on a small platter; spoon the salad onto the lettuce. Garnish with the coriander and mint leaves and the lime wedges. Serve chilled or at room temperature.

NOTE: If squid is purchased already cleaned, cut it into thin strips, rinse, drain, and omit the first step of recipe. Nam pla is available at Asian food stores and many large supermarkets. It is quite salty, so be aware that if you use it, the dish will be high in sodium.

NUTRITION INFORMATION: Cal: 119 Pro: 19g/ 64% Carb: 8g/26% Fat: 1g/10% Chol: 0mg Sodium: 206mg Potassium: 291mg Fiber: 2g Omega 3: .9g A: 17% C: 106% B3: 14% P: 25% EXCHANGE: Lean Meat: 2 Veg: 1½

Cioppino
by Robert Grenner

The name of this dish comes from Genoa, Italy, where it means "fish stew." The dish has become a San Francisco hallmark, and it was probably introduced by Italian immigrants.

> 1 pound clams (discard any that don't close tightly when tapped)
> 1 pound mussels (discard any that don't close tightly when tapped)
> 1½ quarts fish stock (see Fish Fumet, page 29—double the recipe or use half fish fumet and half water, or half clam juice and half water)
> 1½ stalks celery, diced
> 2 tomatoes, peeled, seeded, and coarsely chopped
> 1 carrot, thin sliced
> 1 potato, chopped

> 1 zucchini, sliced
> 1 clove garlic, peeled and finely minced
> ½ bulb fennel, thin sliced
> ¼ pound fresh button mushrooms, sliced
> ½ teaspoon saffron
> ¼ to ½ teaspoon cayenne
> ¼ cup Pernod (see Note)
> ½ pound shrimp (8 to 10), shelled and deveined
> ½ pound scallops, rinsed
> ½ pound boned halibut, cut into small pieces
> Chopped fresh parsley for garnish

PREPARATION TIME: 45 minutes, plus standing time
COOKING TIME: 35 minutes to make stock, plus 20 minutes
YIELD: 5 to 6 servings

Pull the tufts of fiber (called beards) off the mussels. Scrub the mussels and clams thoroughly with a stiff brush; rinse well. Place the mussels and clams in a large bowl; fill with cold water; add a pinch of salt and a handful of cornmeal. Let stand 1 to 2 hours. (If the room is warm, add a few ice cubes to keep the water cold.) Lift the mussels and clams from the water; rinse well.

Place the stock in a soup pot, add all the ingredients except the seafood and parsley, and heat over medium heat to a simmer; simmer 10 minutes. Add the seafood in order of cooking time: First add the clams and the mussels and cook covered 5 minutes. Add the shrimp and scallops; cook covered 3 minutes. Add fish and cook until clams and mussels are open and all the seafood is cooked, 2 to 3 minutes. Serve in individual bowls, sprinkled with parsley.

NOTE: If fennel is not available, increase the celery to 2 stalks. To substitute for Pernod, toast 1 tablespoon fennel seeds in a small saucepan over medium heat; add ½ cup white wine, boil until reduced by half, and strain.

NUTRITION INFORMATION: Cal: 262 Pro: 38g/ 56% Carb: 19g/31% Fat: 4g/13% (S:29% M:38% P:33%) Chol: 140mg Sodium: 672mg Potassium: 1375mg Fiber: 4g Omega 3: .5g A: 165% C: 50% B1: 15% B2: 21% B3: 40% B6: 17% B12:

423% Ca: 17% P: 48% Fe: 31% Mg: 16% Cu:
21% Mn: 21% Se: 93% Cr: 37%
EXCHANGE: Lean Meat: 4 Bread: ¹/₂ Veg: 2

Shellfish Stew with Tomato, Leek, and Saffron

by Marie Simmons

This fresh, chunky sauce provides the perfect base for shellfish stews. Chopped fresh herbs and slivers of orange rind add an exciting flavor contrast to the pungency of the saffron. Choose a single type of shellfish or a combination. Flavor compatibility is rarely a problem among creatures of the sea.

4 dozen mussels or littleneck clams (discard any that don't close tightly when tapped)
¹/₄ cup boiling water
¹/₄ teaspoon saffron threads
2 tablespoons olive oil
1 leek, rinsed and chopped
3 pounds red and/or yellow tomatoes, peeled and chopped
2 cloves garlic, peeled and crushed
2 strips orange rind (¹/₂ by 2 inches)
¹/₄ cup chopped fresh basil
¹/₄ cup chopped fresh flat-leaf parsley
1 teaspoon fresh thyme leaves, or ¹/₂ teaspoon dried
1 teaspoon fresh oregano leaves, or ¹/₂ teaspoon dried
Garlic croutons (see Notes)

PREPARATION TIME: 35 minutes, plus standing time
COOKING TIME: 35 minutes
YIELD: 4 servings

Pull the tufts of fiber (called beards) off the mussels. Scrub the mussels and/or clams thoroughly with a stiff brush; rinse well. Place the mussels and/or clams in a large bowl; fill with cold water; add a pinch of salt and a handful of cornmeal. Let stand 1 to 2 hours. (If the room is warm, add a few ice cubes to keep the water cold.) Lift the mussels and/or clams from the water; rinse well.

Combine the boiling water and saffron in a small cup; let stand 10 minutes. In a large skillet (at least 12 inches in diameter) or Dutch oven with a tight-fitting lid, heat the oil. Add the leek and sauté over low heat until tender and fragrant, about 10 minutes. Stir in the tomatoes; heat to a gentle simmer. Cover and cook over low heat until the tomatoes cook down to a chunky sauce, about 10 minutes. Stir in the garlic, saffron mixture, and orange rind (twist the rind first to release the oils). Cook over low heat, uncovered, 5 minutes. Just before serving, stir in the herbs and shellfish. Cover tightly and cook over medium heat until clams or mussels are opened, from 5 to 8 minutes.

Place the croutons in the bottom of individual soup plates, pile the shellfish on top, and ladle the tomato and leek mixture over all.

NOTES: To vary the seafood substitute, for each dozen mussels or clams, ¹/₄ to ¹/₃ pound shelled shrimp or scallops.

To make garlic croutons, cut a lofa of French bread into twelve ¹/₂-inch-thick slices. Rub the surfaces lightly with the cut side of a halved clove of garlic. Brush very little with a little olive oil (1 teaspoon per twelve slices is adequate). Spread in a single layer on a baking sheet and baske in a 350°F oven until edges are golden, about 15 minutes.

NUTRITION INFORMATION: Cal: 477 Pro: 37g/ 30% Carb: 54g/45% Fat: 14g/25% (S:18% M:65% P:17%) Chol: 73mg Sodium: 448mg Potassium: 1630mg Fiber: 4g Omega 3: 1.4g A: 103% C: 119% E: 16% B1:32% B2: 50% B3: 41% B12: 1781% Folic: 16% Panto: 11% Ca: 24% P: 51% Fe: 196% Mg: 22% Zn: 25% Cu: 57% Mn: 14%
EXCHANGE: Lean Meat: 3 Bread: 2 Veg: 4
Fat: 1¹/₂

Kitchen Clambake For Four

by Eileen Behan

You'll need two 10-quart pots to handle all this shellfish.

1 pound mussels
1 pound clams
3 to 4 quahogs (large hard-shell clams) for the
    steaming base (see Note)
1 head romaine lettuce, torn apart
4 unpeeled medium red potatoes
2 unpeeled medium onions
2 ears of corn, cleaned and shucked
2 lobsters (up to 1¼ pounds each)
Lemon wedges

PREPARATION TIME: 20 minutes, plus standing time
COOKING TIME: 50 minutes
YIELD: 4 servings

Pull the tufts of fiber (called beards) off the mussels. Scrub the mussels and clams thoroughly with a stiff brush; rinse well. Place the mussels and clams in a large bowl; fill with cold water; add a pinch of salt and a handful of cornmeal. Let stand 1 to 2 hours. (If the room is warm, add a few ice cubes to keep the water cold.) Lift the mussels and clams from the water; rinse well.

Place the quahogs in the bottom of one pot to act as the base for steaming. Arrange a layer of lettuce on top (the lettuce acts as a seaweed substitute); layer the potatoes and onions and cover with lettuce. Pour 2 cups of water into the pot, bring to a boil, cover, and steam for 30 minutes, or until the potatoes are almost completely cooked. In the other pot, start boiling enough water to cover the lobsters (but don't add the lobsters yet).

When the potatoes are tender, add the corn to the original pot, followed by another layer of lettuce, a layer of clams, and finally the mussels. Cover and cook for 6 minutes. Before layering the mussels and clams, put the lobsters in the boiling water; boil for 5 to 6 minutes for each pound. (When the shellfish are done, the lobsters will turn bright red and all of the clams and mussel shells will be open.)

With a large slotted spoon, place the clams and mussels in separate bowls. Discard all the cooked lettuce and arrange the potatoes, onions, and corn on a large platter; cut onions and corn in half. Cut the lobsters in half lengthwise with a large, heavy knife and place each lobster half on an individual plate. Serve with lemon wedges, shellfish broth, hot bread, and lots of napkins. You'll need a hammer or claw crackers to remove the lobster from its shell.

NOTE: If quahogs are not available, several 2- to 3-inch clean stones can be used as the base for the steaming.

NUTRITION INFORMATION: Cal: 351   Pro: 33g/ 36%   Carb: 50g/56%   Fat: 3g/7%   Chol: 71mg Sodium: 430mg   Potassium: 1293mg   Fiber: 8g Omega 3: .2g   C: 37%   B1: 25%   B2: 20%   B3: 23%   B6: 30%   B12: 522%   Folic: 21%   Ca: 15%   P: 46%   Fe: 61%   Mg: 24%   Zn: 25%   Cu: 92%   Se: 71% EXCHANGE: Lean Meat: 3   Bread: 2½   Veg: 1¼

Scallops with Spinach

by Four Seasons Hotels Alternative Cuisine

2 large potatoes
1 pound spinach, stems trimmed, well rinsed
½ cup minced shallots
1 teaspoon corn-oil margarine
¼ cup dry white wine
1 pound sea scallops, rinsed
½ cup low-fat milk
1 tablespoon Dijon-style mustard
12 thin black truffle slices for garnish (optional)
2 cooked artichoke hearts, halved, for garnish
    (optional)
4 small scallions, chopped, for garnish

PREPARATION TIME: 30 minutes
COOKING TIME: 25 minutes
YIELD: 4 servings

Cut each potato in half crosswise, then cut each half lengthwise into four equal pieces. Working one at a time, hold a potato piece in one hand; with the tip of a sharp knife, gradually turn the potato, paring off small curving pieces from the ends and along the length to make a smooth, 2- by ¹/₂-inch oval (football) shape. In 1 inch of boiling water, cook the trimmed potatoes, covered, about 5 minutes, or until tender but still firm.

In a covered saucepan, simmer the spinach in just the water that clings to the leaves from rinsing, about 3 minutes or just until wilted. Drain and squeeze dry. Chop coarsely.

In a skillet, sauté the shallots in the margarine until golden, about 5 minutes. Stir in the white wine; continue cooking, uncovered, until reduced slightly, about 3 minutes. Add the scallops and cook, stirring frequently, until tender, about 5 minutes. With a slotted spoon, remove the scallops to a bowl. Add the milk and mustard to the skillet and continue cooking, stirring constantly, until thickened slightly, another 5 minutes.

For each serving, place a bed of spinach in the center of a plate, arrange some scallops on the spinach, and spoon sauce over the scallops. Garnish each plate with four potato "turns," three truffle slices, an artichoke half, and some chopped scallions.

NOTE: You may wish to save time by cutting the potatoes into small wedges or cubes instead of shaping them into ovals.

NUTRITION INFORMATION (including potatoes): Cal: 249 Pro: 31g/49% Carb: 26g/40% Fat: 3g/ 11% Chol: 62mg Sodium: 426mg Potassium: 1078mg Fiber: 2g Omega 3: .2g A: 85% C: 27% E: 11% B6: 15% Folic: 16% Ca: 26% P: 48% Fe: 27% Mg: 14% Cu: 10% Mn: 17% Se: 90% Cr: 22%
EXCHANGE: Lean Meat: 3 Bread: 1 Veg: 1¹/₄

MICROWAVE METHOD: Shape the potatoes as directed above. In a 1-quart microwave-safe casserole, cook the potatoes and 2 tablespoons water covered on High (100% power) until just tender, about 5 to 7 minutes. Let stand. In a 4-

quart microwave-safe casserole, cook the spinach with the water that clings to the leaves, loosely covered, on High until wilted, about 4 minutes. Drain and squeeze dry. Chop coarsely. In a 1-quart shallow heat-proof and microwave-safe casserole, cook the shallots and margarine on High until tender, about 3 to 4 minutes. Add the wine and scallops. Cook covered on High until just tender, about 3 to 4 minutes, stirring every minute. Remove the scallops with a slotted spoon. Cook uncovered on High until the liquid is reduced slightly, about 2 to 3 minutes. Whisk in only ¹/₄ cup milk and the mustard. Cook on High until reduced slightly, about 3 to 4 minutes, stirring every minute. Serve as directed above.

Shellfish Soup

by Eileen Behan

Mussels and clams will need to stand for an hour or two as part of their cleaning; remember to add that time when doing your planning.

> 2 pounds mussels and/or clams (discard any
>   that don't close tightly when tapped)
> 1 cup dry white wine
> ¹/₂ cup chopped onion
> 1 large clove garlic, peeled, bruised with the
>   side of a knife
> ¹/₂ teaspoon dried thyme
> 2 teaspoons unsalted butter or margarine
> 2 teaspoons flour
> 2 potatoes, diced
> 2 carrots, grated
> ¹/₄ pound scallops, rinsed
> ¹/₄ pound shelled shrimp, deveined (about ¹/₂ lb
>   before shelling)
> 1 12-ounce can evaporated skim milk
>   Salt
>   Freshly ground black pepper

PREPARATION TIME: 35 minutes, plus standing time
COOKING TIME: 25 minutes
YIELD: 4 servings

Pull the tufts of fiber (called beards) off the mussels. Scrub the mussels and/or clams thoroughly with a stiff brush; rinse well. Place the mussels and/or clams in a large bowl; fill with cold water; add a pinch of salt and a handful of cornmeal. Let stand 1 to 2 hours. (If the room is warm, add a few ice cubes to keep the water cold.) Lift the mussels and/or clams from the water; rinse well.

Combine the wine, onion, garlic, and thyme in a large pot. Add 2 cups of water; bring to a boil. Add the cleaned mussels or clams, cover, reduce the heat to medium, and cook until the shellfish are open, about 6 minutes (discard any that fail to open). Drain the mussels or clams in a colander lined with paper towel or cheesecloth and collect the strained broth in a bowl. Set the broth aside. Remove the mussels or clams from their shells and set aside.

Melt the butter or margarine in a large pan; add the flour, stir into a paste, and cook at low heat for 1 minute. Add the strained broth, potatoes, and carrots. Simmer until the potatoes are tender, about 8 to 10 minutes. Add the scallops and shrimp; cook for 3 minutes. Add the mussels or clams and milk. Heat for 1 minute but do not boil. Taste and adjust seasoning with salt and pepper. Serve hot with good bread and a salad.

NUTRITION INFORMATION: Cal: 385   Pro: 31g/ 32%   Carb: 36g/37%   Fat: 5g/11%   (S:23%   M: 33%   P:44%)   Alc: 20%   Chol: 73mg   Sodium: 576mg   Potassium: 1217mg   Fiber: 3g   Omega 3: .4g   A: 292%   C: 15%   D: 21%   B1: 18%   B2: 28%   B3: 11%   B6: 23%   Panto: 12%   Ca: 40%   P: 53%   Fe: 31%   Mg: 22%   Zn: 11%   Cu: 13%   Mn: 23%   Se: 74%   Cr: 19%

EXCHANGE: Lean Meat: 2½   Skim Milk: ¾   Bread: 1   Veg: 2   Fat: 1

◇ RED MEAT AND GAME ◇

Thoroughly Modern Meat

by Trish Ratto, R.D.

"Much meat, much malady."
—Thomas Fuller (1608–1661)

Fear of fat and cholesterol has steered us away from red meat. But the 1990s welcomes red meat back to the table in a new, leaner form. Served in small, lean portions with plenty of vegetables and grains, red meat has much to contribute: iron, zinc, trace minerals, B vitamins, and protein with little fat.

Not that we need red meat. We can live healthy lives without ever eating it. Overreliance on red meat gives us more saturated fat, protein, and calories than is good for us; an excess of each of these nutrients is suspected of contributing to certain cancers, for example. Red meat contributes much of our dietary saturated fat and cholesterol, which raises blood cholesterol and increases the risk of coronary heart disease. In studies of Seventh Day Adventists, some meat-eaters and others vegetarians, red meat consumption had a moderately strong positive association with death in men from all causes.

The riskiness of great reliance on land mammals for our protein was dramatically demonstrated in a major study of over 88,000 female nurses published in the *New England Journal of Medicine* on December 13, 1990: Women who ate red meat—beef, lamb, and pork—as a main dish every day were two-and-a-half times more likely to develop colon cancer than women who ate red meat less than once a month. Women who also ate organ meats such as liver and processed meats such as bologna every week had an even higher risk. On the other hand, eating more chicken, fish, and fruit was associated with a lower risk; dairy foods, even those with high fat such as ice cream, didn't appear to increase risk.

Such findings support the central theme of this book, that we should be eating more plant foods, such as whole grains, vegetables, legumes, and fruit. With these foods as the core, servings of low-fat dairy foods and small amounts of animal protein—fish, seafood, and skinless poultry and, less frequently, lean red meat—round out an omnivore's diet.

Some argue that the less red meat we eat, the better, down to zero. Certainly it's possible to replace the iron, zinc, and other minerals that red meat so efficiently provides by consuming more legumes (including tofu, made from soybeans), dark green leafy vegetables, broccoli, shellfish, game birds, and other good sources. Whether it's necessary to do so is another question. Even the study of nurses mentioned above found that it was red meat's saturated fat, not its protein, that's associated with increased risk. Today, a lot of meat is much leaner than it was a decade ago.

Whether beef, lamb, and pork contribute posi-

242

tively to your well-being may depend not only on how lean it is, how frequently you consume it, and how you prepare it, but on who you are, including your gender. Take iron. It's what makes red meat red.Too much iron is as bad as too little. Men with excess body stores of iron, a National Cancer Institute study of 14,000 adults reports, have a 37 percent increased risk of developing cancer, especially of the colon, bladder, esophagus, and lungs. In women, there was no increased risk. We've read a lot about antioxidants—iron, in excess, is an "oxidant." When you consistently take in more than your body can use, it isn't absorbed and, essentially, "rusts." That's bad for a body.

But most women and many children take in less iron than they need. Indeed, iron-deficiency anemia is the nation's most prevalent nutritional deficiency. Primarily because of menstruation, a woman needs half again as much iron every day as a man does: 15 milligrams as opposed to 10 milligrams. Yet red meat is often the first item a woman who's dieting or concerned about health will omit. National surveys show nine out of ten women fall short of their daily iron needs. Ditto for nearly 60 percent of the population, particularly children. Iron-deficiency anemia, which can occur after months of low iron intake, can lead to reduced work capacity, irritability, apathy, and lowered resistance to infection. But you needn't be overtly anemic to suffer from iron deficiency. In children, new studies show too little iron may result in behavioral abnormalities and impaired intellectual performance.

Serving meat in balanced proportions may help bring everyone into balance. Small lean portions of beef or pork or lamb once or twice a week is less than many men are used to, more than many women choose. Using red meat as a condiment or as an occasional feast food, that's a healthy approach.

Even in quite small amounts, red meat provides a bounty of nutrients. A moderate 4-ounce serving of cooked round steak, for example, packs a storeload of nutrients: 8 percent of the USRDA of thiamine, 15 percent of riboflavin, 21 percent of niacin, 13 percent of B-6, 53 percent of B-12, and 8 percent of magnesium. All this for 220 calories. Iron and zinc are even bigger pluses. That same serving delivers 17 percent of the USRDA of iron and 55 percent of zinc. Lean cuts of lamb, pork, and veal are similarly nutrient-dense.

About half that iron is in the form the body can most easily use: heme iron. Vegetable sources of iron, such as beans, are entirely non-heme, but red meat helps the body absorb iron from vegetable proteins that are eaten in the same meal. A 1988 study found that with equal quantities of iron consumed, women who ate red meat had iron stores superior to women who ate chicken and fish or vegetarian diets. (Veal, because it's usually raised anemic to be pale, is not a good source of iron.)

Zinc's story is similar: Its availability is enhanced in meat and somewhat inhibited by numerous compounds, including fiber, in grains and legumes.

For red meat to do us good, though, it's got to be lean. Since saturated fat raises our blood cholesterol levels, health organizations advise us to cut our saturated fat intake by at least a third, from the current 13 percent of calories to under 10 percent. Red meat contributes just under a fifth (18 percent) of the saturated fat we eat. About 39 percent of beef fat is saturated; pork and lamb fat is 35 percent saturated; veal is 24 percent; chicken, 25 percent; fish, 1 percent to 20 percent. Although beef fat does contain some stearic acid, a kind of saturated fatty acid which new studies show may not raise blood cholesterol, it also contains enough cholesterol-raising saturated lauric, mystiric, and palmitic acids to make us want to trim and trim again.

Today's beef and pork is trimmer and leaner than ever. But the antiquated USDA grading system still "encourages the overfattening" of animals, reports the National Research Council (NRC) in their 1988 report *Designing Foods: Animal Product Options in the Marketplace.* "Prime" beef, veal, and lamb, which is marbled with tenderizing fat still gets top dollar. (Pork is not marketed by grades.) The more predominant grade for beef is "Choice," second in amount of marbling and the current goal most ranchers target to achieve. "Good," the less fatty grade that has been considered less desirable, is now making a comeback under the new, more marketable name "Select." The USDA is now encouraging both *more* fat

(Prime) and *less* fat (Select) in its grading system! "The real solution," argues the NRC, "lies in the production of leaner animals."

That's already happening to a degree. The USDA allows any meat cut—beef, lamb, pork or veal—that's 25 percent less fat than the standard to be called "Lite." Cattlemen strive to earn the label by breeding leaner animals. Italian Chianina—now raised domestically—is an example of a skinny steer that stores little fat as it grows. Changes in feeding techniques, less time in the feedlot, and early slaughter are all being used to bring lighter meat from the pasture to the table. Some breeders also manipulate the animals, own natural growth hormones—rather than using steroids, as they have in the past—to produce animals with more lean tissue, less fat.

In addition to the Lite designation, many stores have initiated their own "trim" or "lean" grades (USDA grading is optional). This confusing system is likely to get worse before it gets better. Here's how to interpret:

Lite refers to a breed of poultry or red meat that has 25 percent less fat than what is standard *for that breed.* So a Choice steer that's Lite has 25 percent less fat than a Choice steer that's not. Therefore, meat with the least fat of all would be *Lite Select.* Then comes *Select,* then *Lite Choice, Choice, Lite Prime,* and—still the fattiest—*Prime.*

To compare two commonly available cuts: Select Top Round has 17 percent less fat and saturated fat and 5 percent fewer calories than Choice Top Round. For many trimmed cuts, you can save as much as 30 percent fat in choosing Select over Choice.

And choosing leaner cuts of meat (see Food Profiles, page 368), can save even more fat. For instance, a quarter pound of regular hamburger (27 percent) with 23 grams of fat uses up nearly half a woman's daily total fat allowance of 53 grams (eating a 1600 calorie diet), whereas the same 4 ounces of well-trimmed eye of the round steak adds only 8 grams to the total. Top round, a low-fat cut of beef, is extremely versatile, lending itself to being ground, cubed for stew, or sliced for stir-fry. Likewise, pork tenderloin, at 5 grams per 4 ounces is by far the leanest pork cut, followed by fresh ham and loin chops. Lamb's lean

cuts include cuts from the leg and loin chops. All veal except the breast is low in fat.

Trimming makes an even bigger difference. At the retail level, many butchers now regularly trim fat to ¼ inch. A regular untrimmed 4-ounce serving of Choice T-bone steak, for example, has 28 grams of fat when cooked; trimmed, only 12 grams. Calories plummet from 366 to 222.

Cured Meats

About a third of all meat eaten in America has been processed as luncheon meats. These meats vary considerably in fat content. A ham at 5 percent fat by weight carries 6 grams of fat per 4 ounces. Bologna and pastrami, on the other hand, average 32 grams, plus large amounts of sodium.

Some processed meats are naturally lean at less than 10 percent fat, while an entire array of sausages, hot dogs, and other cured meats claim lite, light, and lean in big bold letters. But read carefully: The USDA allows some meats to be labeled lean simply because they have less fat than a similar product. As always, check labels.

Luncheon meats, bacon, hot dogs, and sausage are also cured with nitrates or nitrites—precursors to cancer-causing nitrosamines. The safety of nitrates is a complex, confusing, and unsettled issue. It is complicated by the fact that our exposure occurs naturally at far greater amounts than we ingest from cured meats. Nitrates prevent botulism, but, in food or the stomach, they can convert to nitrites; stomach acidity further enhances their coupling to amines, forming carcinogenic nitrosamines. Frying bacon at high temperatures creates nitrosamines. Adding antioxidants, such as the vitamins C and E, as some manufacturers do, helps prevent the formation of nitrosamines.

It's up to you if you want to continue eating cured meats. Most studies that show increased cancer risk are based on populations where cured meats are a much larger part of the diet than they are in this country. So the risks involved in eating, say, two slices of bacon once a week is fairly small. At best, avoid cured meat, or at least select those with 10 percent fat maximum and eat them cold or microwaved (cooking cured meat in a microwave produces far fewer nitrosamines than pan-frying).

Organ Meats

If you like sweetbreads, dine on these delicacies infrequently. Organ meats contain anywhere from two to twenty times the cholesterol of lean meat. Brains tops the list with a 2350-milligram cholesterol count for a 4-ounce portion; tripe comes in low at 100 milligrams. (By contrast, steak supplies just 25 milligrams.) Fat content is just as variable. The thymus gland (sweetbreads) and tongue average 24 to 28 grams total fat per serving, much of that saturated fat. Brains are in the middle with about 14 grams. Liver and kidneys are low in fat, high in cholesterol, rich in nutrients, and may contain pesticide residues (see Food Profiles, page 369).

Contamination: Safety in Leanness

Livestock is high on the food chain, and ingests and stores many chemicals: pesticides, hormones, antibiotics, steroids, and other chemical feed additives.

In their search for pure red meat, many consumers are turning to organic, antibiotic and hormone-free "natural" meat. Some veal calves, steer, lamb, and pigs are now being grown on "organic" farms, raised outdoors without drugs or pesticides in their feed. Look for the natural label, but expect to pay about a third more.

If that's too expensive, the good news is that the same leanness you're seeking for the health of your heart may be protecting you from many toxins. Potentially toxic organic chemicals accumulate not in lean tissue but in fat tissue, according to Darrell Wilkes of the National Cattlemen's Association, and particularly in fatty organs. "If anything bad is going to be found," says Wilkes, "it will be found in the liver" (another strike against organ meats). So trimming fat has many benefits.

Besides additives, the biggest concern with red meat, as with any animal product, is bacterial contamination. Here, we're probably our own worst enemies. Buy meat that looks fresh and has no odor and rinse raw cuts thoroughly in cold running water: Thoroughly wash anything that blood drippings touch. Because bacteria grow best at room temperature, keep meat cold. Cook or freeze it soon after buying, and thaw it in the refrigerator, not on the kitchen counter. Cook beef to at least 160°F to kill any Salmonella. Always cook pork thoroughly. (For more safe cooking tips, see Safe, Nutritious Food, page 333.)

Cooking with Meat

by Trish Ratto, R.D., and Nao Hauser

More and more of us are already using meat to complement, not dominate, a meal. We are serving meat more as part of mixtures to balance a high-carbohydrate diet of whole grains, fruits, and vegetables.

Judicious use of lean cuts of beef, pork, lamb, and veal—trimmed of visible fat, served once or twice a week—nutritionally boosts your diet without damaging your heart. A 3- to 4-ounce portion sliced, diced, or ground goes a long way to add taste, texture, nutrition, and satisfaction to your palate.

The marvelous secret you'll discover as you combine red meat with grains and vegetables is that it has such an intense taste that a little goes a long way: It will season whatever it's cooked with. That's one of the secrets of great ethnic cuisines: French, Italian, Thai, Chinese, Mexican. They all combine the aromas of sauces and spices, the colors of myriad vegetables and the complement of breads, pasta, rice, or beans with small amounts of meat for a rich, balanced culinary experience. Grandma, with her stuffed cabbage, spaghetti sauce, and kettles of soups and stews, did too.

Cooks all over the world apply this approach when they make meat stock and use it instead of water to braise vegetables and cook grains. When time allows, make some yourself. A way to shortcut this process is to sauté a tender cut of meat and then add some liquid to the pan to create savory "pan juices." The meat and juices won't have the seasoning magnitude of a pot of stock, but they will be more than ample for a single dish. Cut the meat into small pieces and add it with the juices to vegetables or a grain, and you'll still enjoy the distinctive taste of meat.

Selecting Lean Meats

The food profiles on page 368 can help you select the leanest cuts available. Be on the lookout for Select and Lite grades to save even more on fat. Lean Choice cuts, often more economical, when used as described above, fit the nutrition bill nicely.

Tips for keeping the meal lean when cooking or serving:

♦ Trim all external fat before cooking.

♦ Prepare 4 ounces (raw) of meat or less per person. Combine this with lots of grains and vegetables.

♦ To make large cuts of meat as convenient as they are economical, trim them of all fat and cut the meat into small portions. Freeze the portions in the form you plan to use them, such as sliced for stir-fries or chunks for stews.

Spotlight: The Call of the Wild

Our quest for lean meat has taken us full circle. Wild game, a dietary staple of our paleolithic ancestors, is making a civilized comeback. Like other red meats, game animals provide iron, zinc, protein, and many B vitamins. But, running and foraging in forests and ranges, game animals are free of feedlot additives and their meat is a lot leaner than most red meats. Antelope, anyone?

From venison to bear, game animals are extraordinarily lean, touting body fats of less than 5 percent compared to their modern-age relatives' 25 to 30 percent fat. A 4-ounce serving of cooked venison, for instance, has just 4 grams of fat compared to 17 grams for an equal serving of beef rib roast. Rabbit can have as little as 3.5 grams of fat; bison, 2.5 grams. Bison gets a mere 17 percent of its calories from fat; even very lean red meat gets more than 30 percent from fat.

Wild game's fat may provide unique heart benefits, as well. It's more saturated than other red meats, but the total fat is so low that the actual amount of saturated fat is tiny. What's more significant is that some fat is of the highly unsaturated Omega-3 type, originally thought to be found only in fish. As the creatures munch on the Omega 3–rich greens of the land, their muscles become laced with these heart-healthy fats.

Wild game are typically "raised" on game preserves or farms where the buffalo can roam and the antelope can play. Retail shops, such as Game Exchange in San Francisco, stock truly international fare befitting our Stone Age ancestors. Swedish elk, Scottish deer, and American buffalo are just a few of the 450 different game animals—none on an endangered species list—that can be shipped to your kitchen overnight.

Some game is actually wild. Mike Hughes, of Broken Arrow Ranch in the hill country of central Texas, hunts overpopulated exotics such as Axis deer and Nilgai antelopes. Licensed hunters, under the watchful eye of state and USDA inspectors, bring a veritable Noah's ark to your table.

If you hunt, of course, your supply of truly wild game meat is secure. Experienced woodsmen know to clean and chill their prize as quickly as possible. But you needn't hang the meat, according to Joan Cone, author of *Easy Game Cooking*. The modern-day hunter has one advantage our ancestors didn't: the freezer. Freezing game breaks down the cellular structure of the meat, says Cone, accomplishing the same tenderizing effect as hanging.

—Trish Ratto, R. D.

◆ Cook a large roast and freeze the leftovers in small packets. They can be used interchangeably with raw meat in quick-cooking recipes such as stir-fries.

◆ Use a well-seasoned cast-iron or nonstick skillet to sear or sauté meat without adding fat. Cast iron holds heat extremely well, so that when meat is added to a preheated pan it sears immediately and doesn't stick.

◆ Cook braised or stewed dishes the day before; then skim off any fat hardened at the surface before reheating.

◆ Use a rack when broiling or roasting to allow fat to drip away. Drain fat well when browning ground beef.

◆ Stretch ground beef with ground turkey or extenders such as rice or bulghur.

◆ When a recipe calls for browned meat, microwave the meat in a microwave-safe colander in a baking dish. You'll drain off more fat than you would in a skillet on top of the stove.

◆ For extra-lean ground beef, purchase a piece of top round, trim it well, and grind it in a food processor or ask the butcher to trim and grind it for you.

◆ Barbecue kebabs made with strips of marinated flank steak or cubes of tenderloin woven around vegetables. A serving as small as two ounces will provide a filling portion with the grilled vegetables.

Seasoning Red Meats

The intrinsic richness and complexity of red meats allow for all kinds of seasoning intrigues, especially with large roasts, braises, and stews. To maximize the effects, pierce large cuts all over with the tip of a knife, spread the desired mixture of herbs and spices over the surface, and let stand 1 hour at room temperature, or up to overnight in the refrigerator (longer for lamb). Toss cubes or strips of meat with seasonings and let stand 5 minutes. Spread herb and seasoning mixtures over chops and steaks and let stand 5 to 10 minutes. The point is to allow some of the meat juices to mingle with the seasonings, both to revive the dried ones and to help all of them to adhere. For

the same reasons, you'll get most savory results if you make a paste by mincing dried spices and herbs with four or more cloves of garlic or mixing them with prepared mustard or horseradish before applying them to the surface of large cuts. Almost all red meats take well to mixtures of hot and sweet spices and assertive herbs; thus the origins of French *fines épices*. You can add a bouquet garni to the cooking liquid for any braise or stew.

These are just a few good meat/seasoning matches:

Pork: For roasting, garlic, dried chili, oregano, and black pepper, moistened with orange or lime juice. For braising, apples, onions, garlic, bay leaves, rosemary, cardamom, cinnamon, and nutmeg. For braising or roasting, garlic, ginger, and Chinese 5-spice powder, moistened with sherry.

Lamb: Garlic, rosemary, and finely grated lemon rind are lamb's French allies. Greek cooks use thyme, oregano, and cinnamon. Indians season lamb stew with garam masala. Lamb goes exceptionally well with herbs of the mint family—use them with garlic, mustard, sweet spices, and lemon rind or red wine for a touch of acid to cut the richness of the meat.

Beef: For a pot roast, coat meat with horseradish, oregano, and a pinch each of cinnamon and allspice; then simmer the meat with bay leaves and an onion studded with cloves. For sauerbraten, marinate meat in red wine with onions, cloves, peppercorns, bay leaves, and a generous amount of ginger. For pot roast or stew, add thyme, bay leaves, and nutmeg.

Veal: A little tarragon, basil, parsley, or oregano will stand out against a delicate cutlet or chop. For braised roasts, shanks, and stews, spread meat with mustard, garlic, thyme, savory, or dill, and a touch of sweet spices, such as cinnamon, cloves, cardamom, or allspice.

Spotlight: Thoroughly Modern Meat Loaf

Making meat loaf used to be like pouring whiskey: You served up as much of "the good stuff" as you could afford. If you "extended" the meat with oatmeal or bread, you tried to conceal the fact—just as party hosts would fuss over a garnish for watered-down punch. Things have changed since then, of course. Nowadays, rich folks drink water, and nutrition-wise cooks advertise ways to minimize the meat in meat loaf.

The trick to such healthful cookery is to cut the fat while keeping the flavor meaty. The most important step is to start with very lean meat. Use beef round steak, veal steak or stew meat, pork loin or tenderloin, or fresh (unsmoked) ham. The classic ratio is one third each of beef, veal, and pork, but you can use all beef or half beef and half veal or pork. All beef works best when potatoes are the meat-loaf extender; half veal is good with bulgur, half pork with rice.

If possible, buy the meat unground, trim away all visible fat, and chop the meat in a food processor. The texture of processor-chopped meat seems meatier than ground meat; it's not unlike the sensation of a proper steak tartare, which should always be chopped rather than ground.

To chop the meat in the food processor, cut into uniform one-inch pieces and process no more than a half pound at a time in a standard-size machine (you can do a pound at a time in a model with a larger work bowl; follow the manufacturer's instructions). Chop to a fine texture so that the meat can be mixed thoroughly with the extender.

To add a grain extender, mix up to 2 cups cooked grain, such as bulgur, barley, or rice into 1 pound of meat, or use the equivalent of uncooked grain and liquid, such as $^2/_3$ cup white rice and $1^1/_3$ cups juice or broth. Bulgur wheat works well as an extender because the grains are small enough to blend thoroughly with the meat, but they don't become mushy, as a large quantity of oats will. Grated potatoes complement the beef in a meat loaf no less felicitously than French fries meet a steak on a plate; you just have to cook the loaf long and slowly enough to soften them completely.

To counter the dryness of very lean meat, you need to add some liquid to the loaf; the mixture should be wet when you put it in the oven. Tomato sauce and juice work fine. Vegetable juice adds a spicier note. Unsalted beef stock or broth enhances the meaty flavor. You also need some egg whites to bind the loaf; otherwise the mixture won't hold its shape when sliced.

—Nao Hauser

Meat Sauce for Pasta

by *American Health*

3/4 pound extra-lean ground beef
2 tablespoons chopped fresh parsley
1 medium carrot, shredded
1 small onion, diced
1 medium stalk celery, diced
1 28-ounce can tomatoes, no salt added
1 6-ounce can tomato paste, no salt added
1/2 cup cooking or dry red wine

1 teaspoon sugar
1 teaspoon dried basil
1/4 to 1/2 teaspoon fennel seeds
1/4 teaspoon freshly ground black pepper

PREPARATION TIME: 15 minutes
COOKING TIME: 40 minutes
YIELD: about 5½ cups (enough for a 16-ounce package spaghetti, serving 8 persons)

In a heavy, 4-quart saucepan over high heat, cook the ground beef, parsley, carrot, onion, and celery, stirring frequently, until all pan juices evaporate and the beef is well browned. Add the tomatoes with their liquid and the remaining ingredients; heat to boiling, stirring to break up the tomatoes. Reduce heat to low; cover and simmer 30 minutes, stirring occasionally.

NUTRITION INFORMATION (sauce only, per $^2/_3$-cup serving): Cal: 140 Pro: 15g/40% Carb: 11g/31% Fat: 5g/29% (S:43% M:48% P:9%) Chol: 37mg Sodium: 65mg Potassium: 655mg Fiber: 1g A: 76% C: 44% B3: 16% B6: 19% B12: 18% P: 15% Fe: 16% Zn: 22% Cu: 16%
EXCHANGE: Lean Meat: 1$^3/_4$ Veg: 1$^3/_4$

MICROWAVE METHOD: In a 3- to 4-quart microwave-safe casserole or bowl, cook the beef, parsley, carrot, onion, and celery on High (100% power) until meat loses its pink color, about 5 to 7 minutes; stir once. Add the tomatoes with liquid and the remaining ingredients. Cook covered on High 5 minutes; stir. Reduce power to Medium (50% power) and cook covered 7 minutes. Let stand 5 minutes.

Matambre

by Nao Hauser

This is the classic Argentine steak roll, lightened by the substitution of mushroom caps for hard-cooked eggs in the center. The name means "kill hunger," and refers to the custom of serving the cold sliced roll as an appetizer or snack. Here, it's a main course. Serve it hot with rice. Or, serve it cold and mix a tablespoon of red wine vinegar with a few tablespoons of the pan juices to make a dressing.

    4 ounces spinach or mustard greens, rinsed
    1 small onion, minced
    4 cloves garlic, peeled and minced
    2 tablespoons Dijon-style mustard
    1$^1/_2$ teaspoons dried oregano leaves
    $^1/_2$ teaspoon Worcestershire sauce
    1 flank steak (1$^1/_2$ pounds), all fat removed
    2 large carrots, shredded
       Freshly ground black pepper (optional)

    5 fresh mushrooms, stems removed
    1$^1/_2$ cups unsalted beef broth
    $^1/_2$ cup red wine
    10 sprigs fresh parsley, thick stems removed, minced

PREPARATION TIME: 35 minutes
COOKING TIME: 1 hour 50 minutes
YIELD: 4 servings

Preheat the oven to 350°F. Cook the spinach with the water that clings from washing in a large covered saucepan over medium heat just until wilted, about 2 minutes. Rinse immediately under cold water and drain well. Mix the onion, garlic, mustard, oregano, and Worcestershire sauce in a small bowl or process to a paste in the food processor. Spread the mixture on one side of the steak. Spread the drained spinach over the onion mixture; cover with the carrots. Sprinkle with pepper, if desired. Arrange the mushrooms cap-side down in a row along the length of the center of the steak. Roll the steak lengthwise (beginning with a long edge, with the grain of the meat) and, using a needle and thread, sew closed to make a roll.

Place the steak roll seam-side up in a wide skillet or metal baking dish. Pour in the broth and wine and heat to simmering on top of stove. Cover with aluminum foil. Bake in the preheated oven until tender, about 1 hour and 30 minutes, turning the roll over after 45 minutes. Remove the foil and bake until the meat is lightly browned, 5 to 10 minutes. Remove the meat to a serving platter. Place the pan on top of the stove, stir in the parsley, and simmer until the juices are reduced by about half. To serve, remove the thread, cut the meat into $^1/_2$-inch slices, arrange on a serving platter, and spoon some of the juices over all.

NUTRITION INFORMATION: Cal: 297 Pro: 42g/59% Carb: 10g/15% Fat: 8g/27% (S:43% M:48% P:9%) Chol: 97mg Sodium: 243mg Potassium: 985mg Fiber: 3g A: 236% C: 17% E: 10% B2: 30% B3: 46% B6: 24% B12: 60% Folic: 16% Panto: 13% P: 41% Fe: 33% Mg: 19% Zn: 49% Cu: 18% Mn: 19% Se: 67% Cr: 16%
EXCHANGE: Lean Meat: 4$^3/_4$ Veg: 1$^3/_4$

Meat and Potato Loaf

by Nao Hauser

>   3/4 pound potatoes (about 2 medium),
>   pared
>   1 pound (trimmed weight) beef round
>   steak, all fat removed, chopped or
>   ground
>   1 medium onion, minced
>   2 cloves garlic, peeled and minced
>   2 tablespoons ketchup
>   1 tablespoon Dijon-style mustard
> 1/4 to 1/2 teaspoon chili powder
>   1/4 teaspoon salt (optional)
>   Freshly ground black pepper to taste
>   1/2 cup tomato sauce, no salt added
>   2 egg whites, lightly beaten

PREPARATION TIME: 30 minutes
COOKING TIME: 1 hour 40 minutes
YIELD: 6 servings

Preheat the oven to 350°F. Grate the potatoes over a large bowl to catch the liquid or grate in a food processor. Mix in all the remaining ingredients except the tomato sauce and egg whites; knead with your fingers to mix thoroughly. Stir in 1/4 cup of the tomato sauce and the egg whites. Press the mixture into an ungreased 9 by 5-inch loaf pan and spread the remaining tomato sauce over the top. Bake in the preheated oven 1 1/2 hours. Increase the heat to 450°F; bake until top is lightly browned, about 10 minutes.

NUTRITION INFORMATION: Cal: 185 Pro: 21g/ 46% Carb: 16g/35% Fat: 4g/19% (S:44% M:49% P:7%) Chol: 46mg Sodium: 151mg Potassium: 506mg Fiber: .8g C: 11% B2: 12% B3: 20% B6: 15% B12: 28% P: 19% Fe: 11% Zn: 23% Se: 30%
EXCHANGE: Lean Meat: 2 1/2 Bread: 3/4 Veg: 1/2

Meat/Wheat Loaf

by Nao Hauser

>   3/4 cup bulgur wheat
> 1 1/2 cups vegetable juice cocktail or tomato
>   juice, no salted added
>   2 medium onions, minced
>   1 large clove garlic, peeled and minced
>   1 cup minced parsley sprigs
>   1 teaspoon dried oregano
>   1/4 teaspoon salt (optional)
>   Freshly ground black pepper
>   1 teaspoon teriyaki sauce
>   1 pound (trimmed weight) beef round steak,
>   all fat removed, chopped fine or ground
>   1/2 cup plain nonfat yogurt
>   2 egg whites, lightly beaten

PREPARATION TIME: 25 minutes
COOKING TIME: 2 hours 10 minutes
YIELD: 8 servings

Spread the bulgur in a heavy 10-inch skillet and toast over medium-high heat, stirring often, 3 or 4 minutes. Remove and reserve. Add the vegetable juice, onions, and garlic to the skillet; cook covered over medium-low heat 30 minutes. Add the parsley and oregano; cook uncovered 3 minutes. Stir in the salt, if used, and pepper to taste. Remove 1/2 cup of the sauce, stir the teriyaki sauce into it, and set aside.

Preheat the oven to 350°F. To the sauce remaining in the skillet add the bulgur, beef, yogurt, and egg whites; stir well to combine thoroughly. Pat the mixture into an ungreased 9 by 5-inch loaf pan and spoon the reserved sauce evenly over the top. Bake in the preheated oven 1 hour 30 minutes. Let stand 15 minutes before slicing.

NUTRITION INFORMATION: Cal: 186 Pro: 20g/ 43% Carb: 19g/41% Fat: 3g/16% (S:44% M:49% P:7%) Chol: 41mg Sodium: 255mg Potassium: 500mg Fiber: 3g A: 14% C: 29% B2: 14% B3: 19% B6: 11% B12: 26% P: 23% Fe: 17% Zn: 21%
EXCHANGE: Lean Meat: 2 Bread: 3/4 Veg: 3/4

Veal Medallions in Green Peppercorn Sauce

by Four Seasons Hotels Alternative Cuisine

1 tablespoon plus 1 teaspoon unsalted
    margarine
4 cups coarsely chopped leeks, white part only
³/₄ cup skim milk
¹/₄ teaspoon salt
¹/₄ teaspoon freshly ground black pepper
1 pound veal cutlets, cut into 1-inch strips
¹/₃ cup cognac
¹/₄ cup unsalted chicken broth or stock (see
    page 28)
1 tablespoon fresh tarragon, finely chopped,
    or 1 teaspoon dried tarragon, crushed
2 tablespoons green peppercorns, rinsed and
    drained
3 cups hot cooked rice
1 large tomato, peeled, cored, seeded, and
    diced, for garnish
4 teaspoons snipped fresh chives for garnish
4 sprigs fresh tarragon for garnish

PREPARATION TIME: 30 minutes
COOKING TIME: 30 minutes
YIELD: 4 servings

In a covered heavy saucepan, heat 1 tablespoon of the margarine and cook the leeks for 3 minutes. Add ¹/₄ cup of the milk; continue cooking, uncovered, until the liquids evaporate; keep warm.

Melt the remaining margarine in a large skillet. Lightly salt and pepper the veal, then sauté half of the veal on both sides until brown. Remove, and sauté the remaining veal. Return all the veal to the skillet and continue cooking about 2 minutes longer or until the veal strips are tender. Remove the veal from the skillet. Pour the cognac into the hot skillet; over high heat, cook, stirring constantly, to loosen the brown bits from the bottom of the skillet. Add the chicken broth, tarragon, and green peppercorns and the remaining ¹/₂ cup milk; cook until the mixture is reduced to about ¹/₂ cup. Return the veal to the skillet, turning the strips to coat with sauce.

Serve on individual warm plates. For each serving arrange ³/₄ cup rice in a ring around the outer edge; place about ¹/₂ cup cooked leeks in the center; fan about 5 strips cooked veal over the leeks; and spoon sauce over the top. Sprinkle with tomato and chives for garnish, and top with a tarragon sprig.

NUTRITION INFORMATION: Cal: 485 Pro: 30g/ 25% Carb: 49g/40% Fat: 13g/25% (S:39% M:45% P:17%) Chol: 88mg Sodium: 234mg Potassium: 683mg Fiber: 6g A: 24% C: 32% E: 15% B1: 20% B2: 22% B3: 36% B6: 31% B12: 26% Folic: 13% Panto: 15% Ca: 15% P: 38% Fe: 35% Mg: 13% Zn: 29% Cu: 22% Mn: 45% Se: 40% Cr: 26%

EXCHANGE: Lean Meat: 3¹/₄ Skim Milk: ¹/₄ Bread: 2 Veg: 2¹/₄ Fat: 1

Veal and Vegetable Goulash

by Ceri Hadda

2 cups chopped onions
¹/₂ cup chopped carrot
1 tablespoon corn oil
1 pound lean veal stew meat, all fat
    removed, cut into 1¹/₂-inch cubes
2 cloves garlic, peeled and minced
2 tablespoons paprika
2 tablespoons tomato paste, no salt added
1 cup unsalted beef broth
¹/₂ cup dry white wine
2 carrots, sliced into ¹/₂-inch pieces
4 celery ribs, cut into 1-inch pieces
¹/₂ pound fresh mushrooms, halved
4¹/₂ cups hot cooked egg noodles (8 ounces
    uncooked)

PREPARATION TIME: 30 minutes
COOKING TIME: 1 hour 15 minutes
YIELD: 4 servings

Sauté the onions and chopped carrot in the oil in a medium Dutch oven over moderate heat for 3 minutes, or until tender but not brown. Add the veal; sauté for 3 minutes, or until the veal is white all over. Add the garlic; sauté 1 minute longer. Stir in the paprika and cook, stirring constantly, 1 minute. Add the tomato paste, beef broth, wine, and 1/2 cup of water. Bring to a boil; lower the heat and cover. Simmer 30 minutes, or until veal is almost tender. Add the sliced carrots and celery to the pot. Cover; simmer 20 minutes. Add the mushrooms; cover and simmer 10 minutes longer, or until veal and vegetables are tender. Serve over the cooked noodles.

VARIATION: If you like, the sauce can be flavored with yogurt. Remove the meat and vegetables from the pot with a slotted spoon to a serving dish and keep warm. Stir 1 cup plain non-fat yogurt into the sauce but do not reheat. Pour the sauce over the meat and vegetables and serve immediately.

NUTRITION INFORMATION: Cal: 442 Pro: 32g/ 29% Carb: 44g/39% Fat: 16g/32% (S:88% M:4% P:8%) Chol: 87mg Sodium: 218mg Potassium: 1301mg Fiber: 6g A: 405% C: 36% B1: 28% B2: 43% B3: 60% B6: 26% Folic: 13% Panto: 18% Ca: 12% P: 42% Fe: 36% Mg: 20% Cu: 27% Mn: 25% Se: 43% Cr: 47%
EXCHANGE: Lean Meat: 3 1/2 Bread: 1 1/4 Veg: 4 Fat: 1

MICROWAVE METHOD: In 2- to 2 1/2-quart microwave-safe casserole or bowl, cook the onions, chopped carrot, oil, and garlic on High (100% power) until tender, about 3 to 4 minutes. Add the paprika and cook on High 30 seconds. Add the veal, tomato paste, beef broth, wine, sliced carrot, and celery (omit the water). Cook covered on High 10 minutes; stir. Reduce to Medium (50% power); cook until the veal and vegetables are tender, about 20 to 30 minutes. Add the mushrooms and cook covered on High until wilted, about 3 to 4 minutes. Serve as directed above.

Baked Potatoes with Pork and Greens
by Nao Hauser

This is new-fashioned down-home eating: rich and filling but low in fat. The recipe illustrates a valuable low-fat cooking technique that can be used in other dishes. You don't need to add oil to brown naturally tender red meats such as beef sirloin and pork loin. Preheat a heavy pan (preferably cast-iron) over high heat, add the meat, and cook, stirring or turning as needed, just a few minutes. The high heat will sear the meat in its own fat. Be careful not to overcook; longer cooking will only toughen the meat. Pour broth, juice, or wine into the pan and scrape up the little bits that stick; you'll then have a basis for a savory sauce.

  8 ounces lean pork or beef, with all fat
    removed, cut into small pieces
  1 teaspoon curry powder
1/2 teaspoon ground coriander
1/4 teaspoon chili powder
1/8 teaspoon ground cardamom
1/2 cup orange juice
  1 tablespoon unsalted butter
  2 onions, very thinly sliced
  2 apples, unpared, chopped
  1 10-ounce package frozen chopped collard
    greens or spinach, thawed, thoroughly
    drained
  1 teaspoon cider vinegar
1/4 teaspoon ground cinnamon
    Nutmeg
    Freshly ground black pepper
  2 tablespoons plain low-fat yogurt
  6 baked sweet or white potatoes

PREPARATION TIME: 25 minutes
COOKING TIME: 40 minutes
YIELD: 6 servings

Sprinkle the pork with the curry powder, coriander, chili powder, and cardamom and toss to coat evenly; let stand 5 minutes. Preheat a large, heavy skillet over high heat. Add the pork and cook, stirring constantly, until browned and cooked through, about 4 minutes. Add the orange juice and cook, stirring to scrape up bits of meat, until the juice just coats the pan. Remove the pork and juice and reserve. Reduce heat to medium. Add the butter to the skillet; heat until melted. Add the onions, toss to coat, and cook uncovered, stirring often, 15 minutes. Stir in the apples, collard greens, vinegar, cinnamon, a generous grating of nutmeg, and pepper to taste; cook uncovered 15 minutes. Stir in the yogurt and reserved pork and juice; cook until heated through. To serve, split the potatoes, mash lightly, and top with the meat mixture.

VARIATION: Another, faster way to apply the same concept: Prepare the meat as directed, but substitute beef for the pork and red wine for the orange juice. Cook the onions as directed and combine with the meat to top baked white potatoes. Omit the remaining ingredients. Serve a plain steamed vegetable on the side.

NUTRITION INFORMATION: Cal: 379 Pro: 14g/ 15% Carb: 68g/69% Fat: 7g/16% (S:46% M:42% P:12%) Chol: 33mg Sodium: 98mg Potassium: 1259mg Fiber: 8g A: 60% C: 92% B1: 38% B2: 15% B3: 25% B6: 50% Folic: 20% Panto: 15% Ca: 15% P: 22% Fe: 23% Mg: 22% Zn: 14% Cu: 36% Mn: 25% Se: 21% Cr: 37%
EXCHANGE: Lean Meat: 1 Bread: 3 Veg: 1¼ Fruit: ½ Fat: ½

Lightweight Burritos

by Nao Hauser

These burritos are so easy to make, and so much better than Taco Bell, that you'll never go for the grease again. A real Mexican burrito can be any mixture wrapped in a flour tortilla. This one mingles Mayan and Spanish influences by mating New World tomatoes and chilies with Old World pork, olives, and limes.

    12 ounces boneless pork or beef, all fat
        removed, cut into ¼- by 1½-inch strips
    1½ teaspoons ground cumin
    ½ teaspoon chili powder
    2 small zucchini, diced

    1 large green bell pepper, diced
    1 small onion, quartered and thinly sliced
    2 cloves garlic, peeled and minced
    1 tablespoon dried oregano
    1 tablespoon vegetable oil
    1 cup pitted black olives, chopped
    4 tablespoons fresh lime juice
    8 10-inch flour tortillas (see Note)
    2 tomatoes, cored and chopped (reserve the
        juices)
    1 small bunch fresh parsley or coriander,
        chopped
    2 tablespoons canned chopped chilies,
        drained, or 1 jalapeño pepper, seeded and
        chopped
    6 cups hot cooked kidney beans or rice

PREPARATION TIME: 25 minutes
COOKING TIME: 8 minutes
YIELD: 8 servings

Sprinkle the pork with the cumin and chili powder, toss to coat evenly, and let stand 5 minutes. Preheat a large, heavy skillet over high heat. Add the pork and cook, stirring constantly, 1 minute. Add the zucchini, pepper, onion, garlic, and oregano; sprinkle with the oil. Cook, stirring constantly, 2 minutes. Stir in the olives and 3 tablespoons of the lime juice; cook 2 minutes. Divide the mixture among the tortillas; fold in the ends and roll up. Keep warm in a 300°F oven while preparing the sauce.

Combine the tomatoes with their juice, the remaining 1 tablespoon lime juice, and the parsley and chilies in a medium saucepan. Cook uncovered over medium-low heat just until heated through. Spoon the sauce over the burritos and serve with rice or beans.

NOTE: Try to purchase whole wheat tortillas made with oil rather than lard.

NUTRITION INFORMATION: (with beans and beef) Cal: 398 Pro: 25g/24% Carb: 50g/49% Fat: 12g/ 27% (S:40% M:52% P:8%) Chol: 32mg Sodium: 181mg Potassium: 460mg Fiber: 17g A: 24% C: 73% B2: 14% B3: 17% B12: 20% Ca: 11% P: 13% Fe: 23% Mg: 11% Zn: 23% Cr: 16%
EXCHANGE: Lean Meat: 1½ Bread: 3 Veg: 1¼ Fat: 1½

MICROWAVE METHOD: Prepare the pork or beef as directed above. In a 10-inch round microwave-safe dish or pie plate, cook the pork tightly covered on High (100% power) 2 minutes. Add the zucchini, pepper, onion, garlic, oregano, and only 1 teaspoon oil. Cook, tightly covered, on High 1 minute. Stir in the olives and 3 tablespoons of the lime juice. Cook covered on High 1 minute. Fill the tortillas as directed above; place on a microwave-safe plate. In a 1-quart microwave-safe casserole, cook the remaining ingredients covered on High until heated through, about 3 to 4 minutes. Cook burritos on High until hot, about 3 to 4 minutes. Serve as directed above.

Fresh Pork Sausages
by *American Health*

Most commercial sausages have additives; this one doesn't. Serve it for a hearty breakfast. Or for a flavorful low-fat dish, crumble the cooked sausages and spoon over baked acorn squash or sweet potatoes, or stir into mixed steamed vegetables.

1 1/2 *pounds ground pork (see Note)*
 1/4 *cup minced fresh parsley*
  1 *teaspoon dried sage*
  1 *teaspoon paprika*
 1/2 *teaspoon onion powder*
 1/2 *teaspoon dried thyme*
 1/2 *teaspoon fennel seeds*
 1/2 *teaspoon freshly ground black pepper*

PREPARATION TIME: 10 minutes
COOKING TIME: 20 minutes
YIELD: 1 1/2 pounds of sausage (6 main-course servings)

In a medium bowl, combine all the ingredients with your hands. Shape the mixture into six 1-inch-thick round patties. In a 12-inch skillet over medium heat, cook the patties until they are browned on both sides and cooked throughout, about 20 minutes, turning occasionally. Drain on paper towels.

NOTE: For leaner pork, buy boneless pork loin or shoulder and have the butcher trim and grind

it, or trim it yourself and chop it in the food processor (see page 248). But do not remove all of the fat—you need some for juicy flavor and moist texture.

NUTRITION INFORMATION (sausage only): Cal: 219 Pro: 26g/48% Carb: .9g/2% Fat: 12g/50% (S:38% M:49% P:13%) Chol: 82mg Sodium: 64mg Potassium: 354mg Fiber: .1g B1: 55% B2: 14% B3: 25% B6: 20% P: 20% Zn: 14% Se: 29% EXCHANGE: Lean Meat: 4

(served with 1/2 cup acorn squash) Cal: 276 Pro: 27g/39% Carb: 16g/22% Fat: 12g/39% (S:37% M:49% P:14%) Chol: 82mg Sodium: 69mg Potassium: 802mg Fiber: 2g A: 16% C: 23% B1: 66% B2: 15% B3: 30% B6: 30% Panto: 11% P: 25% Fe: 14% Mg: 17% Zn: 15% EXCHANGE: Lean Meat: 4 Bread: 1

Roasted Fresh Ham with Apple-Red Wine Sauce
by *Nao Hauser*

  1 *fresh ham, shank portion (about 6 1/2 pounds)*
  2 *tablespoons red wine vinegar*
  1 *tablespoon minced fresh ginger*
  4 *cloves garlic, peeled and minced*
  2 *tablespoons hoisin sauce (see Note)*
1 1/2 *cups red wine*
  2 *tablespoons frozen apple juice concentrate*
  1 *tablespoon apple brandy*
  1 *tablespoon fresh lemon juice*
 1/2 *teaspoon Chinese 5-spice powder (see Note)*
 1/4 *teaspoon toasted Szechuan peppercorns (see Note)*

PREPARATION TIME: 15 minutes plus standing time
COOKING TIME: 2 hours 45 minutes
YIELD: 8 servings

Cut slits all over the surface of the ham with the tip of a knife. Combine the vinegar, ginger, and garlic in a small bowl; rub the mixture over the surface of the ham. Spread the hoisin sauce over the ham. Let stand 1 hour or refrigerate up to 24 hours.

Preheat the oven to 350°F. Place the ham in a roasting pan. Pour the wine into the pan; cover with aluminum foil. Roast in the preheated oven 1 hour and 15 minutes. Pour the pan juices into a medium saucepan; reserve. Continue roasting the ham uncovered until cooked through, about 1 hour and 30 minutes longer. Spoon the excess fat from the reserved pan juices. Stir in the apple juice concentrate, brandy, lemon juice, 5-spice powder, and Szechuan peppercorns and heat to boiling; reduce heat and simmer 5 minutes. Strain, if desired. Slice the meat, arrange on a platter, and spoon the sauce over all.

NOTE: Hoisin sauce, Chinese 5-spice powder, and Szechuan peppercorns are available at Asian food stores and many large supermarkets. Toast peppercorns in a small saucepan over medium heat just until they smell fragrant, a minute or two.

NUTRITION INFORMATION: Cal: 217 Pro: 26g/ 49% Carb: 5g/9% Fat: 7g/29% (S:36% M:53% P:11%) Alc: 13% Chol: 64mg Sodium: 524mg Potassium: 434mg Fiber: 0g C: 45% B1: 62% B2: 15% B3: 25% B6: 25% B12: 13% P: 25% Fe: 12% Zn: 24% Se: 82%
EXCHANGE: Lean Meat: 3½

Parsley, Sage, Rosemary, and Lamb

by Nao Hauser

    2 tablespoons Dijon-style mustard
    2 cloves garlic, peeled and minced
    1 teaspoon dried rosemary
  ½ teaspoon dried thyme
  ½ teaspoon dried sage
  ½ teaspoon finely grated lemon rind
     Pinch ground cinnamon
    4 loin lamb chops (1¼ to 1½ pounds), all fat
       removed
  ½ cup dry white wine
    1 small bunch fresh parsley (about 12 sprigs),
       thick stems removed, minced

PREPARATION TIME: 15 minutes
COOKING TIME: 20 minutes
YIELD: 4 servings

Mix the mustard, garlic, rosemary, thyme, sage, lemon rind, and cinnamon in a small bowl. Place the chops in an ovenproof skillet; spread with half of the mustard mixture. Broil until the topping is lightly browned, about 8 minutes. Turn the chops over and spread with the remaining mustard mixture; broil until topping is browned and chops are cooked to desired doneness, about 8 minutes for medium. Remove chops from the skillet and keep warm. Place the skillet on top of the stove over medium heat. Pour in the wine and whisk until smooth; simmer until reduced by half. Stir in the parsley. Spoon the sauce over the chops to serve.

NUTRITION INFORMATION: Cal: 252 Pro: 32g/ 53% Carb: 1g/2% Fat: 12g/45% (S:50% M:43% P: 6%) Chol: 112mg Sodium: 178mg Potassium: 381mg Fiber: .1g B1: 13% B2: 18% B3: 31% B6: 16% B12: 41% P: 25% Fe: 16% Zn: 33% Se: 29% Cr: 13%
EXCHANGE: Lean Meat: 4½

Mustard-Sauced Roast Lamb

by American Health

Leg of lamb tastes much better if you trim all visible fat.

  ½ cup Dijon-style prepared mustard
    1 tablespoon reduced-sodium soy sauce
    1 tablespoon fresh lemon juice
    1 clove garlic, peeled and minced
    1 teaspoon dried rosemary
  ¼ teaspoon ground ginger
    2 teaspoons vegetable oil
    1 6-pound leg of lamb, all visible fat removed

PREPARATION TIME: 15 minutes plus
refrigerating time
COOKING TIME: 2½ hours
YIELD: 12 servings

Whisk the mustard, soy sauce, lemon juice, garlic, rosemary, and ginger in a small bowl until combined. Whisk in the oil until smooth. Place the meat in a shallow pan and brush with the sauce. Cover and refrigerate several hours.

Preheat the oven to 325°F.

Place the meat on a rack in a shallow open baking pan and roast 2 to 2½ hours, or until done as desired, 140°F internal temperature for rare, to 170°F for well done.

VARIATION: To make a light pan gravy for the lamb, pour 1 cup dry red wine into the roasting pan when you place the lamb in the oven. Every 30 minutes add another ½ cup liquid to the pan (veal stock, beef broth, or half stock and half wine work well). When the lamb is done, remove to a serving platter. Pour the pan juices into a saucepan; spoon off the fat. Stir in 2 tablespoons brandy and fresh lemon juice to taste. Boil 5 minutes; stir in chopped fresh parsley if desired. Slice the lamb and spoon the juices over it.

NUTRITION INFORMATION: Cal: 239 Pro: 34g/ 61% Carb: .4g/1% Fat: 9g/38% (S:84% M:5% P:11%) Chol: 113mg Sodium: 265mg Potassium: 407mg Fiber: 0g B1: 14% B2: 21% B3: 37% B6: 17% B12: 43% P: 30% Fe: 15% Zn: 40% Se: 31%

EXCHANGE: Lean Meat: 4¼

Venison Burgundy

by Diane M. Kochilas

Venison is so lean that it tends to dry out during cooking. For this reason, it is important to flour the meat and to cook it over low heat.

    2 pounds venison round, trimmed, fat
      removed, and meat cut into cubes
    1 cup unbleached all-purpose flour
  ¼ cup olive oil
    1 cup chopped onions
2 to 3 cloves garlic, peeled and minced

  ½ cup chopped bell pepper
    1 cup Burgundy wine
  ½ teaspoon dried marjoram
  ½ teaspoon ground nutmeg
  ½ teaspoon dried thyme
2 to 3 bay leaves
    2 pounds fresh or canned, peeled plum
      tomatoes, no salted added if canned
    1 tablespoon dried basil
  ¼ teaspoon salt (or to taste)
      Freshly ground black pepper to taste
    6 cups hot cooked noodles (10 ounces
      uncooked)

PREPARATION TIME: 25 minutes
COOKING TIME: 2 hours 15 minutes
YIELD: 6 servings

Place the venison cubes and flour in a paper bag and shake until the meat is coated with flour. Heat the olive oil in a large heavy saucepan or medium Dutch oven and brown the floured meat, a little at a time, over low heat. When all the meat is browned, put it back in the pot and add the onions, garlic, and pepper and cook until the onions are wilted—not browned—and the garlic is soft, about 10 minutes. Add the wine and enough water to cover the meat completely. Add the marjoram, nutmeg, thyme, and bay leaves. Stir well, scraping the bottom of the pot, and bring to a slow boil. Add the tomatoes, basil, and salt and pepper, breaking up the tomatoes once they are in the pot. Cover and cook slowly, over low heat, for 45 minutes. Remove the lid and cook another 45 minutes, until meat is tender and the sauce has thickened. Remove bay leaves before serving. Serve over noodles.

NUTRITION INFORMATION: Cal 594 Pro: 47g/ 31% Carb: 67%/45% Fat: 13g/20% (S:15% M:74% P:11%) Alc: 4% Chol: n/a Sodium: 215mg Potassium: 1053mg Fiber: 3g A: 42% C: 79% E: 18% B1: 62% B2: 39% B3: 65% B6: 12% P: 48% Fe: 43% Mg: 24% Se: 114% Cr: 40%
EXCHANGE: Lean Meat: 4 Bread: 3½ Veg: 2 Fat: 1

◇ FOWL ◇

Fowl: Poultry and Game Birds

by Robert Barnett and
Lisa Chobanian, R.D.

"Poultry is to the cook what canvas is to the painter," wrote nineteenth-century French food writer Anthelme Brillat-Savarin, To the health-conscious cook, fowl, in all its array from chicken-breast sandwiches to roast turkey dinners, is even more: a mainstay source of low-fat protein. Americans now consume more poultry than either beef or pork. As a matter of taste, game birds, intensely flavored and dark of meat, substitute quite well for red meat.

Nutritionally, fowl is good fare—not a superstar like fish with its heart-protective Omega-3 fatty acids, but not saddled with red meat's burden of saturated fat either. The fat in fowl is mostly monounsaturated, a kind that recent studies suggest lowers blood cholesterol. (Chicken, squab, and guinea hen are highest in monos; turkey, pheasant, quail, and duck have a fairly equal mixture of monos and polys; goose has about as much saturated fat as beef.) Fowl is low in cholesterol as well: 3½ ounces of white-meat chicken, with skin removed has 57 milligrams, a modest amount; the same serving of goose has 90 milligrams.

Most fowl brims with B vitamins. That 3½-ounce serving of chicken gives us more than half the USRDA of niacin and nearly a third of the USRDA of B-6. Turkey light meat gives us just under a third for both nutrients. Game birds, too: Guinea hen, for example, provides 44 percent of niacin and 25 percent of B-6.

Fowl also supplies some iron, zinc, and other minerals—more than fish, though less than red meat and certain shellfish. Poultry dark meat has more iron and zinc than white meat—a serving of dark-meat turkey provides 21 percent of the USRDA for zinc—but the real mineral bounty is in game. Guinea hen, for example, provides 44 percent of the USRDA of iron; quail, 25 percent. (Domestic duck gives us 13 percent of both iron and zinc.)

Fowl can often be very low in fat, depending on how it's prepared. A 3½-ounce serving of light-meat chicken or turkey without skin has less than 2 grams of fat, and dark meat without skin is under 4 grams. Dine on a modest 3½-ounce serving of Peking duck and you'll swallow 29 grams of fat, about half the daily limit for many people. But an unadorned 3½-ounce guinea hen, pheasant, quail, or duck without skin are all under 6 grams, and truly *wild* game birds such as wild duck are often much leaner than that. After all, they have to run around all the time, and that will keep just about anyone lean. Even goose, that epitome of extravagance, can be cut down to 7 grams of fat if you cook it without the skin.

Some poultry breeders, who for years concentrated on faster-growing, fatter chickens—between 1960 and 1979, the average percentage of fat in chickens nearly tripled, from 5 to 15 percent—now breed leaner birds, and cluck about it. That's all to the good. But the average reduction in fat in the "new, leaner" chicken is less than 2 grams in an average serving, or about a half teaspoon of fat.

The real fat servings can occur on your cutting board. That's because the preponderance of the fat in fowl is in the abdominal cavity and in the skin—and you can remove that fat yourself.

Some Tips for Leaner Poultry

♦ Always remove all visible fat. With a whole bird, remove the fat from inside the cavity with your fingers or a sharp paring knife. With parts, remove the visible fat from inside the thigh and rib.

♦ Always remove the skin, but not necessarily before you cook the bird. According to a National Broiler Council study, cooking a chicken with the skin on and then removing the skin results in very little more fat than if you removed the skin first. Skin insulates the meat during cooking, making it more tender and juicy.

♦ If you buy from a butcher you know, ask for male birds. Just as in humans, they tend to be leaner.

♦ Light meat has less fat but also fewer minerals.

Lean . . . and Clean?

In its rush to maximize efficiency with crowded facilities and automated machines, the poultry industry has given the consumer a little something extra: salmonella and campylobacter. Either bacteria can make us sick, usually with flulike symptoms. One in every three chickens is contaminated with salmonella. (Salmonella is a problem with eggs as well—see page 271.) It may be the most serious public health concern in the nation's food supply.

So we've got to be a little careful. Fortunately, that is fairly easy: Neither salmonella nor campylobacter can survive in poultry that's cooked until it reaches an internal temperature of 165°F, or on knives, cutting boards, or dishes that get properly washed. When roasting Thanksgiving turkey, the point to remember is that bacteria

don't like extreme heat or cold, but love moist warmth. So: *Don't* cook the turkey in a warm oven overnight, or let warm stuffing sit in a warm turkey for hours, or stuff a just-cooked bird with warm stuffing and then refrigerate it. Do make the stuffing in advance, if you'd like, and then refrigerate it by itself. (For more tips on safe cooking, see page 21.)

Another problem is the drugs used on chickens. Antibiotics used in humans such as penicillin and streptomycin are not only used to fight infection but are routinely fed to chickens as growth stimulants; when we dine on the meat of chickens raised on medicated feed, we may develop resistance to those drugs. Then when we need those drugs, they don't work. Fortunately, the poultry industry now says it's backing away from using routine low doses of human antibiotics.

For ordinary consumers, there's no way to know exactly what goes into most chicken feed. To be safe, some are turning to organically raised and/or free-range birds. Free-range chickens, ducks, turkeys, and geese, increasingly available today to anyone who can afford the price, are allowed to roam freely outside, and tend to need fewer antibiotics. Some are raised organically; some not.

Free-range birds also taste better. They have better muscle tone and are a little chewier and probably more flavorful from having eaten wild garlic and other wild plants and seeds and also fermented grains. As one poultry scientist puts it, "It's like the difference between catfish from a pond and those from a wild cold stream."

Cooking with Poultry and Game Birds

by Nao Hauser

When cooking poultry or game birds, the key questions are: whole or parts, skinned or skinless. A whole bird, insulated by its skin, can be grilled, broiled, roasted, or baked. You can then remove the skin easily after cooking. To roast a turkey, place the stuffed, trussed bird on a rack, breast up; rub with olive oil; baste every twenty minutes or so with chicken broth. Toward the end of cooking, place aluminum foil as a tent over the bird to keep browned skin from burning. Before you carve, let the bird sit for a half hour to allow the juices to set. Remove the stuffing as soon as the juices have set. (Turkeys are also delicious "oven-steamed"; see The Healthy Kitchen, page 21.)

A delicate chicken or turkey breast without the skin, on the other hand, is so lean that it can easily become dried out if cooked in an oven. For skinless breasts or parts, the best techniques are those that protect lean foods, such as steaming, poaching, or stir-frying, but not braising, which is too slow for the delicate nature of skinless fowl.

Turkey breast meat without skin is an inexpensive substitute for veal scallops; use it in any recipe calling for veal. Ground turkey, which contains a maximum of 15 percent fat by weight, can be substituted for ground beef, which is either about 20 percent (lean) or 30 percent (regular) fat.

Skinless boneless duck breast, broiled, lightly sautéed, or grilled over an open fire until just pink, is a quick meal. And small birds such as quail are nearly fast food: On an open grill or under the broiler, they cook in under 10 minutes.

SEASONINGS

Cooking method largely determines the kinds and amounts of seasonings most appropriate for poultry.

Broiling, Grilling, and Roasting: You can use strong seasonings with chicken parts, split Cornish hens, or quail, but you should take some precaution to prevent the meat from drying out and the spices from burning. One effective technique is to dissolve the seasonings in a marinating liquid; then coat the poultry and refrigerate it at least one hour, turning it over halfway through. Yogurt diluted with citrus juice, sherry diluted with rice wine vinegar, white wine, or tomato juice can be used for the marinade; you need only enough to moisten the poultry thoroughly. Yogurt with lime juice goes well with curry-type spices; yogurt and orange juice with chili powder, cumin, and cinnamon; white wine with crushed rosemary and garlic; sherry with 5-spice powder, ground ginger, garlic, and soy sauce; tomato juice with cumin, ground coriander, and mint, basil, oregano, or fresh coriander.

Another way to season poultry and keep it moist is to stuff seasonings under the skin, cook the meat, and then remove the fatty skin before serving. Run your fingers underneath the skin to loosen it all over. Then spread seasonings between the meat and the skin, using a small rubber spatula or your fingers. Fresh tarragon is a favorite with chicken, with or without a little mustard and nutmeg. Dill, mustard, and garlic is another easy, savory blend. Rosemary and garlic work well with chicken or turkey. Turkey also takes beautifully to curry and chili-type mixtures. Pheasant begs for a little sweetness, which can be accomplished with garam masala, 5-spice powder, or even pumpkin pie spice; these can be combined with strong herbs, such as bay leaf, oregano, or thyme.

Steaming: This method especially honors the delicacy of chicken breast, whole or cut into strips. It also respects spice and herb fragrances that fade fast during dry-heat cooking. Ginger is the classic Oriental accompaniment. You can add to this a julienne of basil, apple mint, lemon balm, or fresh coriander. Or adapt the technique to Western bouquets with chervil and a little cardamom; or a julienne of fennel, tarragon, and red bell pepper; or saffron, a hint of cloves, and chopped seeded tomato. Steam the chicken in a dish placed on the steamer rack to catch all savory juices.

Poaching: This is the best way to cook chicken or turkey for serving cold, either sliced or in a salad. You can apply seasonings lavishly to the poaching broth, strain them out after cooking, reduce the liquid to intensify the flavor, and then thicken it with some yogurt and prepared mustard, if desired, to make a dressing. Virtually any kind of mixture can work well, because the seasonings don't come into direct contact with the delicate meat. Ginger, garlic, and 5-spice powder are wonderful with chicken; add chopped fresh basil or coriander and parsley to the accompanying dressing. Add unground toasted garam masala spices to the poaching liquid for chicken or turkey; season the dressing with chopped fresh mint or coriander and curry powder.

Indian Chicken Kabobs

by *American Health*

4 whole boneless chicken breasts, halved, skin and visible fat removed
$1/2$ teaspoon ground ginger
$1/8$ teaspoon crushed red pepper flakes
$1/8$ teaspoon prepared mustard
$1/8$ teaspoon ground cardamom
$1/8$ teaspoon ground turmeric
1 teaspoon curry powder
2 teaspoons fresh lemon juice
1 tablespoon vegetable oil
1 small onion, quartered and separated into pieces
　Paprika
1 lemon, cut into sixths
2 tablespoons chopped fresh parsley for garnish

PREPARATION TIME: 15 minutes plus marinating time
COOKING TIME: 15 minutes
YIELD: 6 servings

Flatten the halved chicken breasts with the heel of your hand, then cut each crosswise into thirds. In a medium bowl, combine the ginger, pepper, mustard, cardamom, turmeric, curry powder, lemon juice, vegetable oil, and 1 tablespoon of water; add the chicken; mix well. Refrigerate 1 hour.

Preheat the broiler. On six 8-inch skewers, alternate the chicken pieces with a piece or two of onion. Sprinkle lightly with paprika. Place the kabobs in a jelly roll pan; broil 15 minutes, turning once, or until chicken is cooked. Serve garnished with lemon wedges and sprinkled with parsley. Serve with rice.

NUTRITION INFORMATION: Cal: 176　Pro: 27g/63%　Carb: 4g/9%　Fat: 5g/28%　(S:23%　M:35%　P:42%)　Chol: 72mg　Sodium: 67mg　Potassium: 298mg　Fiber: .4g　C: 15%　E: 12%　B3: 59%　B6: 29%　P: 21%　Se: 29%　Cr: 24%
EXCHANGE: Lean Meat: 3　Veg: $1/2$

Baked Marinated Chicken

by *American Health*

Serve with rice and steamed vegetables or a salad for an easy weekday meal.

2 tablespoons fresh lemon juice
2 tablespoons reduced-sodium soy sauce
1 teaspoon dry mustard
2 teaspoons vegetable oil
2 $2^{1}/_{2}$-pound broiler-fryers, cut up, skin and visible fat removed

PREPARATION TIME: 10 minutes plus marinating time
COOKING TIME: 50 minutes
YIELD: 8 servings

In a large bowl, combine the lemon juice, soy sauce, dry mustard, and oil; add the chicken and toss to coat the pieces well. Cover. Refrigerate at least 4 hours, turning occasionally.

Preheat the oven to 400°F. In a $15^{1}/_{2}$- by $10^{1}/_{2}$-inch jelly roll pan, arrange the chicken pieces flesh side down; pour the lemon juice mixture over the chicken. Bake in the preheated oven 20 minutes; turn and bake 25 to 30 minutes longer, until chicken pieces are fork-tender, basting occasionally with the pan juices. Spoon the pan juices over the chicken and serve with rice.

NUTRITION INFORMATION (with 1 cup rice per serving): Cal: 436　Pro: 36g/35%　Carb: 51g/48%　Fat: 8g/17%　(S:29%　M:39%　P:32%)　Chol: 98mg　Sodium: 247mg　Potassium: 354mg　Fiber: 2g　E: 12%　B1: 21%　B2: 13%　B3: 67%　B6: 70%　Panto: 31%　P: 30%　Fe: 18%　Zn: 19%　Mn: 64%　Se: 90%　Cr: 20%
EXCHANGE: Lean Meat: 4　Bread: 3　Fat: $1/4$

Chicken Cacciatore

by Four Seasons Hotels Alternative Cuisine

1 large tomato, peeled, cored, seeded, and
  diced
1 cup finely chopped onion
2 cloves garlic, peeled and minced
1 teaspoon dried rosemary, crushed
1/2 teaspoon dried oregano, crushed
2 whole boneless chicken breasts, halved, skin
  and visible fat removed
  Salt (optional)
  Freshly ground black pepper
1 teaspoon corn-oil margarine
6 tablespoons tomato paste, no salt added
1/2 cup dry white wine
1/2 cup dry Marsala wine

PREPARATION TIME: 20 minutes
COOKING TIME: 45 minutes
YIELD: 4 servings

Preheat the oven to 350°F. In a 10- by 6-inch baking dish, combine the tomato, onion, garlic, rosemary, and oregano. Lightly sprinkle the chicken pieces with salt if desired and pepper.

Heat the margarine in a skillet and brown the chicken evenly on both sides, then arrange on top of the tomato mixture. Bake, covered, in the preheated oven 10 minutes. Combine the tomato paste and wines, pour over the chicken, and continue baking, covered, until the chicken is tender, about 35 minutes. To serve, place each chicken piece on a plate; stir the sauce in the baking dish and spoon over the chicken.

NUTRITION INFORMATION: Cal: 329   Pro: 37g/ 46%   Carb: 13g/16%   Fat: 6g/15%   (S:30% M:39% P:31%)   Alc: 23%   Chol: 96mg   Sodium: 195mg Potassium: 900mg   Fiber: .9g   A: 30%   C: 44%   B1: 13%   B2: 13%   B3: 85%   B6: 45%   Panto: 15% P: 33%   Fe: 16%   Mg: 18%   Cu: 15%   Se: 43% Cr: 44%
EXCHANGE: Lean Meat: 4   Veg: 1¾   Fat: 1½

MICROWAVE METHOD: Season the chicken pieces with salt and pepper to taste. Stir together only 1/4 cup each white wine and Marsala with the tomato paste. In a 12- by 8-inch microwave-safe baking dish, cook the margarine, onion, and garlic on High (100% power) until onion is tender, about 3 to 4 minutes. Stir in the tomato paste-wine mixture and the chopped tomato, rosemary, and oregano. Cook on High to boiling, about 4 to 7 minutes. Add the chicken, thicker portion toward the outside. Cook covered on High until the chicken is tender, about 10 to 12 minutes, stirring and rotating the dish once.

Grilled Chicken with Yogurt Topping

by American Health

1/2 cup dried breadcrumbs
1/4 teaspoon onion powder
1/4 teaspoon garlic powder
1/4 teaspoon salt
1/4 teaspoon cayenne
1/8 teaspoon ground ginger
2 whole medium chicken breasts, halved, skin
  and visible fat removed
1/3 cup plain low-fat yogurt
  Vegetable oil

PREPARATION TIME: 10 minutes
COOKING TIME: 30 minutes
YIELD: 4 servings

Prepare the outdoor grill for barbecuing. Mix the crumbs and seasonings. Dip the chicken into the yogurt, and then into the crumb mixture. Brush oil over the grill rack. Place the chicken on the grill, flesh-side up, over medium heat; grill 15 minutes. Turn and grill 10 to 15 minutes longer, or until fork-tender.

TO BROIL IN STOVE: Brush the top of the broiling pan with oil. Place the chicken flesh-side down on the broiling pan. About 7 to 9 inches from source of heat (or at 450°F), broil the chicken 15 minutes. Turn and broil 10 to 15 minutes longer, or until fork-tender.

NUTRITION INFORMATION: Cal: 202   Pro: 29g/ 60%   Carb: 10g/21%   Fat: 4g/18%   (S:39% M:39% P:22%)   Chol: 74mg   Sodium: 292mg   Potassium: 287mg   Fiber: 0g   B2: 11%   B3: 62%   B6: 26% P: 24%   Se: 36%   Cr: 19%
EXCHANGE: Lean Meat: 3   Bread ½

Roast Chicken Stuffed with Herbed Potatoes

by Nao Hauser

The herb-seasoned potatoes lend some of their fragrance to the chicken and keep it very moist.

1 small bunch fresh parsley (about 12 sprigs), thick stems removed
4 cloves garlic, peeled
1 teaspoon dried rosemary
1 teaspoon dried thyme
1/2 teaspoon dried sage
1 1/2 cups unsalted chicken broth or stock (see page 28)
1 1/2 pounds potatoes (about 4 medium), pared and diced
1 roasting chicken (3 to 3 1/2 pounds), skin on but visible fat removed

PREPARATION TIME: 25 minutes plus cooling time
COOKING TIME: 1 hour 30 minutes
YIELD: 4 servings

Process the parsley, garlic, rosemary, thyme, and sage in the food processor until minced. Reserve 2 tablespoons of the mixture and heat the rest with 1 cup of the chicken broth to simmering in a medium saucepan. Stir in the potatoes; heat to a boil. Reduce the heat and simmer, covered, until the potatoes are completely tender, 15 to 20 minutes. Let stand to cool.

Preheat the oven to 375°F. Spoon about half of the potatoes into the chicken; close the cavity with skewers or a needle and thread. Place the chicken in a baking dish; rub the skin with the reserved herb mixture. Arrange the remaining potatoes around chicken. Spoon a few tablespoons of the remaining broth over the chicken and roast in the preheated oven about 1 hour and 15 minutes, until the juices run clear when the thigh joint is pierced with a fork. Baste with the remaining broth and pan juices every 15 minutes. Let chicken stand 5 to 10 minutes. Remove the skin when carving.

NUTRITION INFORMATION: Cal: 429 Pro: 48g/46% Carb: 36g/34% Fat: 10g/21% (S:32% M:41%

P:27%) Chol: 132mg Sodium: 164mg Potassium: 1088mg Fiber: 4g C: 40% B1: 19% B2: 19% B3: 91% B6: 60% B12: 10% Panto: 25% P: 41% Fe: 18% Mg: 21% Zn: 23% Cu: 24% Se: 49% Cr: 37%
EXCHANGE: Lean Meat: 5 Bread: 2 Veg: 1/4

MICROWAVE METHOD: Prepare the chicken and herb mixture as directed above. In a 2-quart microwave-safe casserole or bowl, stir together 1 cup of the chicken broth, the remaining herb mixture and the potatoes. Cook covered on High (100% power) until the potatoes are tender, 10 to 15 minutes; stir once. Stuff the chicken as directed above, using wooden skewers if using skewers, and arrange in a 9-inch-square microwave-safe baking dish. Cook on High until the juices run clear when the thigh joint is pierced with a fork, about 22 to 27 minutes. Let stand, tented with foil, 10 minutes.

Barbecued Chicken

by Four Seasons Hotels Alternative Cuisine

1 cup unsalted chicken broth or stock (see page 28)
1/2 cup diced onion
1/2 cup reduced-sodium ketchup
1 celery stalk, diced
1 garlic clove, peeled and minced
2 tablespoons packed brown sugar
2 tablespoons cider vinegar
1 tablespoon teriyaki sauce
1 tablespoon Worcestershire sauce
1 teaspoon dry English mustard
1 small bay leaf, crushed
1/8 teaspoon thyme
1/8 teaspoon rosemary
1/8 teaspoon ground cloves
1/8 teaspoon coriander
Dash liquid red pepper seasoning (like Tabasco)
12 chicken drumsticks, skin removed

PREPARATION TIME: 20 minutes
COOKING TIME: 1 hour 50 minutes
YIELD: 6 servings

In a heavy saucepan, simmer all the ingredients except the drumsticks for 1 hour, stirring occasionally.

Preheat the oven to 350°F. In a baking dish, arrange the drumsticks in a single layer. Spoon the sauce over the chicken, cover with foil, and bake in the preheated oven for 30 minutes. Discard the foil; baste the chicken, then bake 20 minutes longer, or until the chicken is fork-tender.

NUTRITION INFORMATION: Cal: 258 Pro: 32g/50% Carb: 10g/16% Fat: 10g/34% (S:31% M:42% P:27%) Chol: 104mg Sodium: 390mg Potassium: 472mg Fiber: .2g C: 15% B2: 17% B3: 40% B6: 22% Panto: 14% P: 24% Fe: 12% Zn: 22% Se: 24%

EXCHANGE: Lean Meat: 4 Veg: 1/4 Fruit: 1/2

MICROWAVE METHOD: In a 4-cup microwave-safe measuring cup, stir only 3/4 cup of the stock and the remaining ingredients except the chicken. Cook covered on High (100% power) 5 minutes. Reduce to Medium (50% power) and cook 10 minutes. In a 12- by 8-inch microwave-safe baking dish, arrange the chicken, thicker portions toward the outside. Pour in the sauce and cook, covered with wax paper, on High until the chicken is tender, about 14 to 17 minutes. Let stand 3 minutes.

Braised Turkey Breast with Cocoa Sauce

by Madelaine Bullwinkel

2 tablespoons unsalted butter
1 1/2 pounds turkey breast half, skin on but visible fat removed
1/2 cup diced white onion
1/2 cup sliced carrots
1/2 cup thinly sliced celery
2 slices fresh ginger (the size of a quarter)
2 tablespoons unsweetened cocoa powder
1 1/2 cups dry white wine
Bouquet garni: 1 bay leaf, 1/2 teaspoon dried thyme, 1/2 teaspoon fennel seed, 1 sprig parsley, tied in cheesecloth
Salt (optional)
Freshly ground black pepper

PREPARATION TIME: 30 minutes
COOKING TIME: 1 hour
YIELD: 4 servings

Melt the butter in a 5-quart casserole and gently brown the turkey breast on all sides. Lift out the turkey, remove all but 1 tablespoon of the fat; then sauté the onion, carrots, celery, and ginger for 5 minutes. Dissolve the cocoa in a few tablespoons of the wine. Return the turkey to the pot, skin-side down; pour in the cocoa solution, the remaining wine, and 1/2 cup water. Bring the liquid to a simmer, add the bouquet garni, and cook at a gentle simmer for 30 minutes, covered, turning the turkey after the first 15 minutes. Test the turkey for an internal temperature of 165°F and continue cooking if necessary.

Lift the turkey to a warm plate and cover. Remove the ginger slices and the bouquet garni from the sauce, skim off the fat, and press the liquid and vegetables through a food mill. Heat the sauce to simmering, and cook to thicken if desired. Season with salt and pepper to taste. Slice the turkey breast, removing skin if desired. Ladle the cocoa sauce onto warm plates and overlap the turkey slices on it. Serve with rice or polenta.

NUTRITION INFORMATION (without rice): Cal: 436 Pro: 44%/41% Carb: 13g/12% Fat: 10g/20% (S:62% M:30% P:8%) Alc: 27% Chol: 138mg Sodium: 216mg Potassium: 861mg Fiber: 1g A: 100% B2: 19% B3: 53% B6: 45% B12: 12% Panto: 13% P: 42% Fe: 20% Mg: 20% Zn: 20% Mn: 29% Cr: 38%

EXCHANGE: Lean Meat: 4 1/2 Veg: 2 Fat: 3

MICROWAVE METHOD: In a 12- by 8-inch microwave-safe baking dish or 2 1/2-quart shallow oval microwave-safe casserole, cook only 1 tablespoon butter and the onion, carrots, celery, and ginger covered on High (100% power) until tender, about 3 to 5 minutes. Stir in the cocoa. Add the turkey, breast side down, only 1 cup wine (omit the water) and the bouquet garni. Cook covered on High until tender and instant-read or microwave thermometer registers 165°F, about 15 to 20 minutes; turn over once and rotate the dish halfway through the cooking. Let stand 5 to 10 minutes, until the temperature reaches 170°F. Continue as directed above.

Salpicon of Turkey Leg with Corn and Peanuts
by Madelaine Bullwinkel

   1 dozen stems and leaves fresh coriander
   3 slices onion
   2 turkey drumsticks (1 1/2 pounds each)
2 1/2 tablespoons fresh lemon juice
   3 tablespoons unsalted peanuts (1 ounce)
  1/2 cup cooked sweet corn kernels
   2 tablespoons minced hot chili peppers
     (jalapeño, serrano, or other fresh chili)
  1/4 teaspoon salt
     Freshly ground black pepper to taste
   3 cups hot cooked white rice
   6 corn tortillas

PREPARATION TIME: 30 minutes
COOKING TIME: 1 hour 45 minutes
YIELD: 6 servings

Preheat the oven to 325°F. Fit a clear plastic cooking bag into a shallow pan large enough to hold the turkey legs. Remove the coriander leaves from the stems, reserving the stems; chop the leaves coarsely and set aside. Lay the onion slices and coriander stems in the bag. Rinse off and dry the turkey legs before placing them on the seasonings. Close the bag tightly and puncture the top with a few small holes. Bake the legs for 1 1/2 hours, or until they register an internal temperature of 170°F.

When the meat is cool enough to touch, take the turkey from the bag and remove the skin, bones, and sinews. Cut or tear the meat into small bite-sized pieces; place in a bowl. Carefully pour the baking juices out of the bag and skim off the fat. Boil the juices in a small saucepan until reduced to 1/4 cup; stir in the lemon juice and set aside.

On a baking sheet, roast the peanuts for 10 minutes in a 325°F oven, coarsely crush, and add to the turkey pieces. Add the corn, reserved corainder leaves, and chili pepper. Sprinkle with salt and the reserved meat juice, and toss well. Serve with rice and warm tortillas.

NOTE: This salpicon can be made a day in advance and refrigerated. Let it return to room temperature or reheat over low heat before serving.

NUTRITION INFORMATION (turkey only): Cal: 254 Pro: 34g/55% Carb: 5g/8% Fat: 10g/37% (S:34% M:32% P:34%) Chol: 96mg Sodium: 175mg Potassium: 407mg Fiber: .8g C: 11% B2: 18% B3: 25% B6: 23% Panto: 16% P: 26% Fe: 16% Mg: 10% Zn: 35% Cu: 12% Cr: 11%
   EXCHANGE: Lean Meat: 4 Bread: 1/4 Fat: 1/2

(turkey with 1 tortilla and 1/2 cup rice) Cal: 434 Pro: 38g/36% Carb: 43g/40% Fat: 12g/ 24% (S:34% M:32% P:34%) Chol: 97mg Sodium: 233mg Potassium: 488mg Fiber: 3g C: 11% B1: 19% B2: 20% B3: 32% B6: 49% Panto: 26% Ca: 10% P: 34% Fe: 24% Mg: 17% Zn: 40% Cu: 22% Mn: 35% Se: 30% Cr: 15%
   EXCHANGE: Lean Meat: 4 Bread: 2 1/2 Fat: 1/2

MICROWAVE METHOD: Prepare a microwave plastic bag as the label directs. Place the bag in a 2 1/2- to 3-quart shallow oval casserole; add the onion slices, coriander, and turkey as directed above. Cook on High (100% power) until an instant-read or microwave thermometer registers 170°F, about 15 to 18 minutes. Continue as directed above. On a paper plate, cook the peanuts on High until roasted, about 2 to 2 1/2 minutes. Add to the turkey and continue as directed above.

Stuffed Turkey Cutlets on a Bed of Onions
by Madelaine Bullwinkel

   1 pound onions, chopped
  1/4 cup wine
   1 crumbled bay leaf
   3 teaspoons olive oil
  1/2 tablespoon capers
   3 salt-cured salad olives (Greek Kalamata) or
     other black olives, pitted and diced
  1/3 cup scallions, white part and 1 inch of the
     green, minced
  1/3 cup green bell pepper, minced
1 1/2 tablespoons hot chili pepper, minced

1 tablespoon peeled and minced garlic (about
   2 cloves)
½ teaspoon dried oregano
¼ teaspoon salt
6 4-ounce turkey cutlets
3 tablespoons freshly grated Parmesan cheese

PREPARATION TIME: 35 minutes
COOKING TIME: 45 minutes
YIELD: 6 servings

Heat the onions, ¾ cup water, wine, bay leaf,
and 2 teaspoons of the olive oil in a deep 9-inch
skillet and gently simmer, covered, for 15 minutes. Uncover and cook slowly until all liquid in
the pan has evaporated. Stir in the capers and
olive pieces.

While the onions are cooking, make the turkey
filling: Sauté the scallion, peppers, and garlic in
the remaining 1 teaspoon olive oil over medium
heat for 2 minutes. Remove from heat and add
the oregano and salt. Let the mixture cool.

Flatten each turkey slice by gently pounding it
between layers of wax paper. Center a tablespoon of the scallion and pepper mixture on each
cutlet. Top with ½ tablespoon of the cheese. Fold
the meat over the stuffing, sealing the edges
closed with gentle finger pressure. Lay the stuffed
cutlets on the bed of onions.

Simmer the cutlets covered for 5 to 8 minutes,
until the edges of the meat turn opaque. Carefully
turn the turkey over and cook 5 minutes more.
Turn off the heat and wait 5 to 10 minutes before
serving.

NUTRITION INFORMATION: Cal: 212   Pro: 29g/
55%   Carb: 5g/11%   Fat: 8g/35%   (S:34% M:43%
P:23%)   Chol: 71mg   Sodium: 263mg   Potassium:
408mg   Fiber: .7g   C: 40%   B2: 11%   B3: 25%
B6: 27%   Panto: 10%   P: 24%   Fe: 12%   Zn: 20%
   EXCHANGE: Lean Meat: 3¼   Veg: 1   Fat: ½

MICROWAVE METHOD: In a 12- by 8-inch baking dish or 2½-quart shallow oval microwave-safe
casserole, cook the onions, 2 tablespoons water
or wine, the bay leaf, and 2 teaspoons olive oil
uncovered on High (100% power) until the onion
is tender and all liquid has evaporated, about 6
to 8 minutes. Stir in the capers and olives; set
aside. In a 1-quart microwave-safe casserole or

bowl, cook the scallion, peppers, garlic, and 1 teaspoon olive oil covered on High until tender,
about 1½ to 2 minutes. Stir in the oregano and
salt. Cool. Flatten the turkey and fill as directed
above. Place on the onions. Cook covered on
High until opaque and tender, about 7 to 9 minutes, turning, rearranging, and rotating the dish
after 4 minutes. Let stand 5 minutes.

Bulgur Stuffing with Fruits, for Roast Turkey
by Marian Burros

¼ cup unsalted butter
¼ cup unsalted chicken broth or stock
   (see page 28)
2 large onions, chopped
1 to 1½ teaspoons ground coriander
1 teaspoon ground cumin
1½ cups slivered, blanched almonds
1½ cups coarsely chopped dried apricots
1 to 1½ cups raisins
4 cups cooked bulgur wheat (1½ cups
   dry)
2 teaspoons ground cinnamon
½ teaspoon ground cloves
½ teaspoon salt
   Freshly ground black pepper to taste

PREPARATION TIME: 20 minutes
COOKING TIME: 20 minutes
YIELD: about 11 cups (enough for a 20-pound
turkey, serving 20 persons)

Heat the butter and chicken broth in a skillet
and sauté the onions, coriander, and cumin until
the onion is translucent, about 10 minutes. Add
the almonds, apricots, and raisins and cook, uncovered, stirring occasionally, until the almonds
are almost golden. Transfer to a large bowl. Add
the bulgur, cinnamon, cloves, salt, and pepper and
toss well. Cool briefly. Use immediately or keep
refrigerated until ready to use.

NUTRITION INFORMATION: (stuffing only) Cal:
185   Pro: 4g/8%   Carb: 31g/62%   Fat: 6g/30%
(S:27% M:56% P:17%)   Chol: 5mg   Sodium:

74mg Potassium: 345mg Fiber: 3g A: 15% E: 11% P: 12% Fe: 11%
 EXCHANGE: Bread: 1 Veg: ¼ Fruit: 1 Fat: 1¼

(stuffing and turkey) Cal: 338 Pro: 38g/45%
Carb: 31g/36% Fat: 7g/19% (S:28% M:53% P:19%)
Chol: 99mg Sodium: 133mg Potassium: 676mg
Fiber: 3g A: 15% E: 11% B1: 10% B2: 15%
B3: 50% B6: 36% P: 38% Fe: 20% Mg: 17%
Zn: 16% Cu: 12%
 EXCHANGE: Lean Meat: 4 Bread: 1 Veg: ¼
Fruit: 1

MICROWAVE METHOD: In a 2-quart microwave-safe casserole, cook the butter, onions, coriander, and cumin on High (100% power) until the onions are tender, about 3 to 4 minutes. Add the broth, apricots, raisins, cinnamon, cloves, salt, and pepper. Cook covered on High to boiling, about 3 to 4 minutes. Let stand. On a paper plate cook the almonds on High until lightly browned, about 3 to 4½ minutes. Stir the bulgur and almonds into the onion-raisin mixture. Cool and continue as directed above.

Fragrant Rice Stuffing, for Roast Turkey

by Marian Burros

 2 cups raw brown rice
 2 tablespoons vegetable oil
 4 large onions, sliced
 2 cloves garlic, minced
24 fresh medium mushrooms, sliced
 1 cup raisins
 4 teaspoons minced fresh ginger
½ teaspoon ground cardamom
½ teaspoon ground cinnamon
½ teaspoon ground cloves
   Freshly ground black pepper to taste
 6 ounces unsalted roasted cashews, coarsely
   chopped (about 1 cup)
 2 cups unsalted chicken broth or stock (see
   page 28)

PREPARATION TIME: 30 minutes
COOKING TIME: 1 hour
YIELD: 12 cups (enough for a 20-pound turkey, serving 20 persons)

Combine 4 cups water and the rice in a saucepan and bring to a boil over high heat. Reduce heat to low, cover, and simmer the rice until tender, about 40 minutes. Heat the oil in a large skillet over medium heat. Add the onions and garlic, cover, and cook, stirring occasionally, until the onion is translucent, about 10 minutes. Add the mushrooms, raisins, ginger, and spices and cook until the mushrooms are tender, about 5 minutes. Remove from heat. Stir in the rice and cashews. Stir in the broth and cool briefly. Refrigerate until ready to use.

NUTRITION INFORMATION (stuffing only): Cal: 174 Pro: 5g/10% Carb: 27g/60% Fat: 6g/30% (S:19% M:52% P:29%) Chol: .1mg Sodium: 42mg Potassium: 310mg Fiber: 4g E: 17% B3: 12% Cu: 18% Se: 43%
 EXCHANGE: Bread 1 Veg: ¾ Fruit: ½ Fat: 1

(turkey and stuffing) Cal: 367 Pro: 38g/41%
Carb: 27g/30% Fat: 12g/29% (S:30% M:39% P:31%)
Chol: 86mg Sodium: 113mg Potassium: 647mg
Fiber: 4g E: 17% B1: 14% B2: 19% B3: 43%
B6: 33% Panto: 17% P: 32% Fe: 15% Mg: 15%
Zn: 28% Cu: 23% Se: 43% Cr: 12%
 EXCHANGE: Lean Meat: 4 Bread: 1 Veg: ¾
Fruit: ½ Fat: ½

MICROWAVE METHOD: Cook the rice as directed above. In a 2-quart microwave-safe casserole, cook the oil, onions, and garlic on High (100% power) until the onions are translucent, about 4 to 5 minutes. Add the mushrooms, raisins, ginger, and spices. Cook covered on High until the mushrooms are tender, about 4 to 5 minutes, stirring once. Stir into the rice with the cashews and continue as directed above.

Duck Breasts with Ginger-Orange Sauce

by Marian Burros

6 tablespoons ginger preserves
2 tablespoons Grand Marnier
6 tablespoons orange juice
2 tablespoons fresh lemon juice
1 tablespoon grated orange rind

2 whole duck breasts, skinned and boned
1 teaspoon vegetable oil for basting
2 cups hot cooked wild rice

PREPARATION TIME: 30 minutes
COOKING TIME: 8 minutes
YIELD: 4 servings

Mix the ginger preserves, orange liqueur, orange juice, lemon juice, and orange rind together in a small saucepan.

Place the duck breasts on the broiler pan; brush with oil and broil close to the heat, about 4 minutes on the first side and 2 to 4 minutes on the second side, brushing occasionally with oil. Large breasts will be medium rare. For rare or for smaller breasts, broil a shorter time. Breasts should be no more done than medium rare. While the breasts broil, heat the sauce. Slice the breasts on the diagonal and serve with warm ginger-orange sauce and wild rice.

NUTRITION INFORMATION (duck with ½ cup wild rice): Cal: 471   Pro: 29g/25%   Carb: 51g/44%
Fat: 14g/28%   (S:42%   M:43%   P:15%)   Alc: 3%
Chol: 102mg   Sodium: 77mg   Potassium: 440mg
Fiber: 3g   C: 28%   B1: 27%   B2: 34%   B3: 36%
B6: 15%   Panto: 18%   P: 24%   Fe: 22%   Zn: 20%
Cu: 19%   Se: 54%
EXCHANGE: Lean Meat: 4   Bread: 1½   Fruit: 1¾
Fat: ¾

Roasted Pheasant with Chanterelles and Asparagus

by Four Seasons Hotels Alternative Cuisine

An elegant dish—time-consuming to make, but worth it for a special dinner. Cut up the pheasants and make the sauce early in the day or even the day before serving, if you wish. If you're making the sauce ahead, cool and refrigerate it covered after straining; then heat to boiling and reduce to 1 cup before serving.

2 pheasants (2¾ pounds each)
1 carrot, cut into 1-inch peices
1 onion, cut into 1-inch pieces
1 celery stalk, cut into 1-inch pieces
3½ tablespoons tomato paste, no salt added
2 sprigs fresh thyme
1 tablespoon black peppercorns
1 quart unsalted chicken broth or stock (see page 28)
2 tablespoons brandy
4 tablespoons dry white wine
Salt to taste (optional)
Crushed green peppercorns (optional)
½ pound chanterelle mushrooms, trimmed
⅓ cup minced shallots
2 teaspoons olive oil
1 pound asparagus, trimmed
4 teaspoons snipped fresh chives for garnish

PREPARATION TIME: 1 hour, 15 minutes
COOKING TIME: 3¼ hours
YIELD: 4 servings

Preheat the oven to 300°F. Remove the breasts (meat with skin) from the pheasants, trimming all visible fat; refrigerate until ready to use.

Discard the skin and any visible fat from the pheasant carcasses and legs; cut up. In a roasting pan, brown the cut-up pheasant in the preheated oven for about 40 minutes; add the carrot, onion, and celery and continue roasting until they are golden brown. Place the roasting pan on top of the stove; add the tomato paste. Over medium heat, cook until the tomato paste darkens slightly, stirring occasionally. Transfer the ingredients to a stockpot; add the thyme, peppercorns, chicken broth, brandy, and 2 tablespoons wine; simmer 1½ hours, removing all scum and fat as necessary. Strain the sauce through a sieve lined with a dampened kitchen towel into a saucepot. Discard all solids. Over medium heat, boil the sauce, uncovered, until reduced to 1 cup. Skim off any fat, and adjust the seasoning with salt and green peppercorns, if desired.

Arrange the pheasant breasts in a nonstick skillet, skin-side down; sauté until tender, turning once. In another nonstick skillet, sauté the mushrooms and shallots in the olive oil until tender;

add 2 tablespoons wine and cook until the wine evaporates. In a saucepan with water to cover, simmer the asparagus covered until tender-crisp.

To serve, remove the skin from the pheasant breasts and cut each breast into eight slices. Arrange the slices on individual plates in a fan pattern. Place the asparagus in the middle of each fan. Spoon some sauce around each plate, and arrange the mushroom mixture around the edges. Sprinkle with chives.

NUTRITION INFORMATION: Cal: 406 Pro: 44g/ 46% Carb: 20g/21% Fat: 14g/33% (S:56% M:27% P:16%) Chol: 66mg Sodium: 200mg Potassium: 1444mg Fiber: 5g A: 177% C: 56% E: 13% B1: 18% B2: 38% B3: 98% B6: 20% Folic: 27% Panto: 14% P: 50% Fe: 33% Mg: 11% Cu: 24% Mn: 25% Cr: 24%

EXCHANGE: Lean Meat: 5 Veg: 3¼ Fat: 1

◇ EGGS ◇

Scrambled Logic

by Cheryl Jennings-Sauer, R.D.

Eggs, their botanical counterparts the seeds, and milk are among the most nutritious foods on earth, and for much the same reason. Unlike meats or vegetables, they are all *designed* to be foods.... Eggs are ... one of the more versatile foods we have....

—Harold McGee, in *On Food and Cooking: The Science and Lore of the Kitchen* (Charles Scribner's Sons, 1984)

Healthy Americans over the age of two should limit whole eggs or egg yolks to no more than four per week, including those used in cooking.

—*1990 American Heart Association Guidelines*

Eggs have an image problem.

"I could *never* eat an egg," confesses one young athlete, who regularly overindulges in high-fat peanut butter. "I guess I've convinced myself that eggs will give me a heart attack."

So she gives up one of nature's most economical and nutritious convenience foods. Eggs are easy to store and prepare, a boon to the busy, and easy to digest, a plus for the elderly. Low-income shoppers couldn't find a better source of protein.

Eggs are a low-to-moderate source of fat. At 80 calories, one egg has about as much fat (6 grams) as an ounce of mozzarella cheese—and egg fat is less saturated. For that amount of fat and calories, an egg provides 6 grams of high-quality protein—more than 10 percent of the daily requirement. Eggs also provide good amounts of vitamins A, D, and B-12 (an elusive nutrient for vegetarians) and iron (anti-anemia insurance for women). Only vitamin C is absent, so keep citrus on the morning menu.

Cholesterol vs. Saturated Fat

But that egg also provides something else: cholesterol. An egg is considered to have about 214 milligrams of cholesterol, close to the 300-milligram limit recommended by the American Heart Association (AHA) for an entire day. Egg farmers in California and Pennsylvania are producing specialty eggs, raised on different feed and under less glaring lights, that are purported to have less cholesterol.

But this still may be too much for the American Heart Association. The AHA is concerned that eating too much cholesterol will raise the level of cholesterol in your blood—a known risk factor for heart disease.

It can. But saturated fat raises blood cholesterol twice as effectively. Add eggs to your diet and you won't necessarily raise your blood cholesterol; subtract them and you may not lower it. If your diet is low-fat to start with, avoiding eggs little effect, if any. "Excluding eggs is the *least* effective way of dealing with a high cholesterol level," argues University of Arizona nutrition researcher Dr. Donald McNamara. Most of the cholesterol in our bodies is manufactured by our bodies, which need it in tissues and for metabolism. Some people respond to an increase in dietary cholesterol by making less in their bodies, he finds. Only about a quarter to a third of healthy people respond to excess dietary cholesterol with increased blood cholesterol levels, says McNamara.

Nutritionist Dr. Margaret Flynn of the University of Missouri at Columbia found that eating three eggs a day—twenty-one per week—does produce a slight average increase in people's blood cholesterol. But more important than the group average is the difference among individuals. According to Flynn, cholesterol levels go up in some people, stay the same in others, and actually decrease in the rest. Only an experimental procedure can now determine who is actually sensitive to dietary cholesterol.

Not everyone agrees that healthy people can consume more than a few eggs a week. The AHA's John LaRosa, a cardiologist, remarks that "average serum [blood] cholesterol *did* increase with egg consumption. *Any* increase in serum cholesterol increases your risk of heart disease." Says pathologist Henry McGill of Texas Health Sciences Center at San Antonio, "If you stay away from eggs you'll have a *slightly* lower risk of heart disease. It's like looking both ways when you cross the street: You'll have less chance of getting run over, but of course there's no guarantee."

Though experts disagree over dietary cholesterol, they speak in one clear voice against saturated fats. "Dietary cholesterol by itself is not the most potent elevator of serum cholesterol," says LaRosa. "Saturated fat is more potent." Dietary recommendations usually lump saturated fat and cholesterol together as equally incriminating, notes the USDA's Gerald Combs, "but it's far more important to restrict saturated fat." Saturated fat not only raises total cholesterol levels but it may interfere with the body's ability to clear artery-damaging LDL cholesterol from the bloodstream.

Saturated fat and cholesterol are often found in the same foods. Beef, pork, lamb, and cheese all have high levels of both saturated fats and cholesterol. Eggs are a notable exception here: They contribute 10 to 30 percent of our dietary choles-

Spotlight: How to Beat Egg Whites

To beat the maximum amount of air into egg whites, start with eggs at room temperature. Be sure that there's no trace of egg yolk in the whites. Use any kind of electric mixer, an egg beater, or a large wire whisk. The bowl and beaters must be clean and free of grease. A little bit of cream of tartar helps egg whites to hold the air beaten in.

When mounds of the beaten whites hold their shape and look shiny, stop beating.

Sugar makes the whites harder to beat, so don't add it until the whites are close to maximum volume, and then, do it very gradually, so that the weight doesn't deflate the egg whites.

—Nao Hauser

terol, but only 2 to 4 percent of our dietary fat.

That makes eggs one of the few high-quality protein foods that are moderately low in fat, and calories. And, if you are careful about what else you eat, those benefits can offset the danger of cholesterol in eggs. If your serum cholesterol level is high, reduce the amount of fat and saturated fat in your diet; add fiber-rich plant foods such as oats, beans, and carrots. Get regular vigorous exercise: it raises the level of "good" HDL cholesterol. Enlist your doctor in your campaign; only he or she can accurately gauge your health risks.

If you do cut down on eggs, be sensible about how you switch. Hearty complex carbohydrates, from oatmeal to whole grain toast, are an altogether more suitable start to the day than protein-heavy egg dishes. But a light omelet is a kinder protein source for dinner than fried chicken. And if you trade in your omelet for sausage and biscuits, or a pastry or doughnut with coffee, you're loading up on saturated fats that are much worse for the heart than cholesterol.

How you cook your eggs also matters. There's a world of difference between a soft- or hard-boiled egg and eggs scrambled with bacon and butter. In studies of Seventh Day Adventists, egg consumption is strongly associated with increased ovarian cancer and, less strongly, colon cancer. But it may be the frying of the eggs that's largely responsible. For ovarian cancer, fried eggs, fried chicken, fried fish, and fried potatoes all showed up as independent risk variables. Shirred eggs, anyone?

In searching for the perfect egg, you may want to consider those from hens raised without drugs or pesticide-laden feed. Eggs can collect pesticide residues. "Nest Eggs," marketed by the Chicago's Food Animal Concerns Trust (FACT), are laid by hens fed roasted whole grains like corn and soybeans rather than by-products from food processing that contain pesticides.

If you're allergic to eggs, avoid protein-rich egg whites in particular; egg replacers, which contain no egg, can pinch-hit in baking.

Cooking with Eggs
by Cheryl Jennings-Sauer, R.D.

One of the most elegant ways to get more egg taste with less cholesterol is to cook with more whites than yolks. It is the yolk that carries the cholesterol, fat, and most of the calories (though it also delivers the iron, thiamin, vitamin A, and half the protein). The whites, though lacking in many of the yolk's vitamins, have the rest of the egg's protein and virtually no fat or cholesterol.

Fortunately, the whites are responsible for just about everything that's special about eggs in the kitchen. The elasticity of the protein in the egg whites yields the airy pleasures of meringues, soufflés, and angel-food cakes. Two whites can be substituted in most recipes that call for one whole egg. The exceptions are foods such as muffins or pancakes that have no other source of fat, and egg-emulsified sauces such as mayonnaise. You can substitute one whole egg for every two yolks called for in custard sauces, soufflés, and omeletes.

On average, we eat the equivalent of about one egg per week in baked goods. But the typical American also eats three a week directly, mainly at breakfast. Don't ruin the nutritional benefits of a breakfast egg by frying it. Try coddling your eggs, poaching them, or boiling them, hard or soft. A heavy, nonstick skillet and a coating of vegetable cooking spray reduce the need for fat in cooking omelets and frittatas.

One word of caution: *Do not eat raw eggs.* It's long been known that the bacteria salmonella, which can cause serious flu-like symptoms, can migrate through the tiny cracks in the shell to the yolk. Now new research finds that salmonella may even be transmitted via the ovum of the mother chicken to the inside of clean, intact eggs. So eating any raw egg, whether in eggnog or Caesar salad or even "well warmed" in hollandaise sauce, is quite risky. Even sunny-side-up eggs, or soft and runny scrambled eggs, can harbor salmonella. So cook your eggs well.

Fresh Fruit Omelet
by Debbie Maugans

Each serving of this omelet is lightly sauced with fruit syrup, making it taste more indulgent than it actually is. It's a great change-of-pace breakfast.

¹/₂ cup fruit juice (apple, orange, or pineapple)
¹/₄ teaspoon plus ¹/₈ teaspoon ground cinnamon
 2 cups thinly sliced pears, nectarines, plums, apples, or peaches, mixed with assorted berries, drained (see Note)
¹/₂ teaspoon vanilla extract
 2 teaspoons powdered sugar
 4 eggs (at room temperature), separated
 2 egg whites (at room temperature)
  Pinch of cream of tartar
  Vegetable cooking spray
 2 teaspoons safflower oil

PREPARATION TIME: 20 minutes
COOKING TIME: 10 minutes
YIELD: 6 servings

Position a rack in the upper third of the oven and preheat to 425°F.

Combine the fruit juice and the ¹/₄ teaspoon cinnamon in a small saucepan; bring to a boil.

Boil until the mixture measures $1/4$ cup. Remove from heat, and stir in the fruit and vanilla. Set aside. Combine the powdered sugar and the $1/8$ teaspoon cinnamon; set aside.

In a small mixing bowl, beat the egg yolks until thick and pale in color (about 5 minutes). Beat the egg whites and cream of tartar until stiff but not dry. Gently fold the yolks into the whites.

Spray a 10-inch nonstick oven-proof skillet with cooking spray. Heat over medium heat. Add the oil; heat until sizzling. (Note: The oil can be omitted if you like. Cooking spray alone will keep the omelet from sticking. However, a little oil keeps the bottom more moist. Without it, the exterior of the omelet is quite dry.) Add the egg mixture and smooth the surface with a spatula. Reduce heat to low and cook 2 minutes for omelet to brown on the bottom and begin to puff. Shake the skillet gently to prevent sticking. Arrange fruit and juices on top to within 1 inch from the edge of the egg mixture. Transfer to the preheated oven and bake 5 minutes, or until puffed and brown. Slide onto a serving platter, and dust the top with reserved powdered sugar mixture. Serve immediately.

NOTE: You can use fresh fruit in season or fruit canned in its own juice or frozen without sugar.

NUTRITION INFORMATION: Cal: 133 Pro: 5g/ 16% Carb: 17g/49% Fat: 5g/35% (S:29% M:36% P:35%) Chol: 142mg Sodium: 63mg Potassium: 218mg Fiber: 2g B2: 10% P: 13% Cr: 12%
EXCHANGE: Med. Meat: $3/4$ Bread: $1/2$ Fruit: 1 Fat: $3/4$

Poached Huevos Rancheros

by Debbie Maugans

Quick Ranchera Sauce (recipe follows)
4 corn tortillas
4 eggs, cold
  Toppings:
    1 tablespoon minced ripe olives (optional)
    1 tablespoon chopped scallion

    1 tablespoon minced fresh coriander
    1 tablespoon sliced jalapeños

PREPARATION TIME: 10 minutes
COOKING TIME: 10 minutes
YIELD: 4 servings

Prepare the Quick Ranchera Sauce the day before and refrigerate. Warm the tortillas in the oven at 350°F, wrapped in foil, while poaching the eggs. Heat the sauce in a large skillet until bubbling. Reduce heat to low; carefully break the eggs directly into the sauce. Simmer, uncovered, until the whites are mostly set. Cover and cook 30 seconds to 1 minute longer, or until eggs are cooked to desired degree of doneness. To serve, place a tortilla on each serving plate; top with an egg, and spoon 4 tablespoons sauce over each egg. Sprinkle with desired toppings.

QUICK RANCHERA SAUCE

1 $14^1/2$-ounce can whole tomatoes, no salt added, drained and chopped
1 $6^1/2$-ounce jar roasted red peppers, drained and chopped
$1/2$ cup canned tomato puree, no salt added
2 fresh green chili peppers, minced
2 cloves garlic, peeled and minced
$1/2$ cup minced red onion
3 tablespoons minced fresh coriander
$1/4$ teaspoon cayenne
1 teaspoon vinegar
$1/4$ teaspoon salt

PREPARATION TIME: 15 minutes
YIELD: $1^3/4$ cups

Combine all the ingredients; mix well. Cover and refrigerate overnight.

NOTE: Reserve leftover sauce for another use; reheat to boiling and try it over broiled chicken or fish.

NUTRITION INFORMATION: (salsa only, per $1/4$-cup serving) Cal: 31 Pro: 1g/15% Carb: 7g/78% Fat: .3g/7% Chol: 0mg, Sodium: 85mg Potassium: 284mg Fiber: 1g A: 17% C: 90%
EXCHANGE: Veg: 1

(Huevos Rancheros with salsa) Cal: 180 Pro: 10g/ 21% Carb: 21g/45% Fat: 7g/34% (S:36% M:47%

P:17%) Chol: 213mg Sodium: 208mg Potassium: 425mg Fiber: 2g A: 28% C: 104% B1: 11% B2: 14% B6: 15% B12: 13% Folic: 12% Panto: 12% P: 18% Fe: 15% Mg: 11% Cu: 16%
EXCHANGE: Med. Meat: 1 Bread: 1 Veg: 1

MICROWAVE METHOD: Prepare the Quick Ranchera Sauce as directed above. In a 9-inch round microwave-safe shallow casserole or pie plate, cook the sauce covered on High (100% power) until bubbling, about 5 to 7 minutes. Stir. Carefully break the eggs into the sauce around the edge of the casserole at least 1 inch apart. Pierce the yolks several times with a toothpick. Cook, covered with waxed paper, on Medium (50% power) until the eggs are cooked almost to the desired degree of doneness, about 9 to 12 minutes. Let stand. Meanwhile, wrap the tortillas in a moist paper towel and cook on High until hot, about 1 minute. Serve as directed above.

Herbed Egg Salad

by Debbie Maugans

4 hard-cooked eggs (use only two yolks), chopped
1 cup acini de pepe or orzo pasta, cooked al dente and drained
1 rib celery, very thinly sliced
1 medium carrot, coarsely grated
3 tablespoons minced fresh dill
3 tablespoons minced fresh basil
3 tablespoons minced scallions
3 tablespoons plain nonfat yogurt
2 tablespoons reduced-calorie mayonnaise
2 cups fresh watercress
 Freshly ground black pepper
 Cherry tomatoes for garnish

PREPARATION TIME: 30 minutes
YIELD: 6 servings

Combine the eggs, pasta, celery, carrot, dill, basil, and scallions. Stir together the yogurt and mayonnaise, add to the egg mixture, and toss lightly to blend. Arrange the watercress on individual serving plates; mound the egg mixture on top. Sprinkle with pepper and garnish with cherry tomatoes.

NUTRITION INFORMATION: Cal: 106 Pro: 6g/ 22% Carb: 18g/47% Fat: 4g/31% (S:36% M:46% P:18%) Chol: 80mg Sodium: 79mg Potassium: 342mg Fiber: 2 A: 177% C: 24% E: 16% B2: 10% Se: 29% Cr: 10%
EXCHANGE: Med. Meat: ½ Bread: ½ Veg: ¾ Fat: ½

Souffléd Tomatoes with Pasta

by Debbie Maugans

This is a variation of the classic French tomato soufflé. Since tomatoes are particularly compatible with pasta, the two are layered in this recipe to make a refreshing entrée. Serve with a green salad.

2 tablespoons fine dry breadcrumbs
2 tablespoons freshly grated Parmesan cheese
 Vegetable cooking spray
1⅔ pounds tomatoes, peeled and coarsely chopped
2 cloves garlic, minced
3 tablespoons tomato paste, no salt added
¼ cup minced scallions
¼ cup minced fresh parsley
2 tablespoons minced fresh tarragon
¼ teaspoon salt
2 tablespoons reduced-calorie margarine
2 tablespoons unbleached all-purpose flour
¾ cup skim milk
4 eggs (at room temperature), separated
8 ounces rotini or corkscrew pasta, cooked al dente and drained

PREPARATION TIME: 45 minutes
COOKING TIME: 1 hour 10 minutes
YIELD: 6 servings

Combine the breadcrumbs and cheese. Spray a shallow 2-quart baking dish with cooking spray; sprinkle 2 tablespoons of the breadcrumb mixture on the bottom and up the sides of the baking dish. Place in the freezer until ready to fill. Combine the tomatoes and garlic in a large nonstick skillet; simmer uncovered 20 to 25 minutes or until thick. Stir in tomato paste, scallions, parsley, tarragon, and salt; simmer 5 minutes. Melt the margarine in a small saucepan; stir in the flour. Cook over medium heat 1 minute, stirring constantly. Stir in the milk; cook, stirring constantly, until thickened. Remove from heat, and stir in the tomato mixture. Cool 10 minutes.

Preheat the oven to 350°F. Beat the egg yolks in a small mixing bowl until thick and pale in color (about 5 minutes). Stir into the tomato mixture. Beat the egg whites in a large mixing bowl until stiff but not dry. Gently stir one fourth of the whites into the yolk mixture; then fold in the remaining whites. Arrange the cooked pasta in the baking dish from the freezer. Spoon the soufflé mixture over the top; smooth gently with a spatula. Sprinkle the top with the remaining 2 tablespoons breadcrumb mixture. Bake in the preheated oven for 35 minutes, or until puffed and brown and a knife inserted in the center comes out clean.

NUTRITION INFORMATION: Cal: 259 Pro: 12g/ 19% Carb: 37g/56% Fat: 7g/25% (S:32% M:43% P:25%) Chol: 143mg Sodium: 261mg Potassium: 595mg Fiber: 4g A: 50% C: 55% D: 12% E: 12% B1: 20% B2: 20% B3: 12% B12: 11% Folic: 12% Panto: 11% Ca: 11% P: 21% Fe: 16% Mg: 12% Se: 71% Cr: 24%

EXCHANGE: Med. Meat: ¾ Bread: 1¾ Veg: 1½ Fat: ¾

Wild Rice and Green Pea Frittata

by Debbie Maugans

Frittatas are flat Italian omelets, traditionally cut in squares and served at room temperature as finger food. This tender version is thick with rice and peas and is delicious served hot as well.

    4 eggs
    2 egg whites
      Vegetable cooking spray
    2 teaspoons olive oil
    ¼ cup minced onion
    ¼ teaspoon curry powder
    1¼ cups cooked wild rice

    ⅔ cup fresh garden peas, blanched and
      drained, or frozen peas, thawed
      Freshly ground black pepper
      Minced fresh parsley for garnish

PREPARATION TIME: 30 minutes
COOKING TIME: 15 minutes
YIELD: 6 servings

Place the broiler rack 4 inches from the heat source. Preheat the broiler on highest setting. Combine the eggs and egg whites in a large bowl; beat with a fork just until combined. Set aside. Spray a 10-inch nonstick oven-proof skillet with cooking spray. Heat over medium heat, add the oil to the skillet, and heat until sizzling. Add the onion and sauté until tender. Stir in the curry powder, mixing well; stir in rice and peas. Remove from heat, and spread the rice mixture evenly over the surface of the skillet. Reduce heat to low.

Gently stir the egg mixture, just to mix; pour evenly over the rice mixture. Cook over low heat 4 to 5 minutes, lifting up an edge of the frittata with a spatula after about 3 minutes to see how quickly the bottom is browning. When the bottom is golden and top is somewhat liquid, immediately slide the skillet under the preheated broiler. Broil about 2 minutes or until the top is puffed and speckled brown.

Loosen the edge of the frittata from the skillet using a spatula, and slide onto a serving platter. Grind pepper over the surface, and sprinkle with parsley. Serve in wedges.

NUTRITION INFORMATION: Cal: 210 Pro: 10g/ 20% Carb: 26g/49% Fat: 7g/31% (S:25% M:62% P:13%) Chol: 142mg Sodium: 81mg Potassium: 172mg Fiber: 3g B1: 14% B2: 20% P: 18% Fe: 12% Mg: 12%

EXCHANGE: Med. Meat: ½ Bread: 1½ Veg: 1 Fat: 1

MICROWAVE METHOD: Beat the eggs as directed above; set aside. In a 10-inch round microwave-safe casserole or pie plate, cook the oil, onion, and curry powder on High (100% power) until the onion is tender, about 2 to 3 minutes. Stir in the rice and peas; spread evenly. Beat the eggs lightly. Gently pour in the eggs. Cook, covered with wax paper, on High 2 minutes. Stir gently, moving the outer edges to the center. Smooth the surface. Cook, covered, on High until the center is set yet moist, about 2½ to 3½ minutes. Let stand 2 minutes. Serve in wedges with pepper and parsley.

Fresh Corn Timbales
by Debbie Maugans

If you are planning to unmold these custards, you may want to arrange crisscrossed blanched scallion tops in the bottoms of the cups before adding the custard mixture. These will provide an attractive garnish after unmolding. Garnish custards served in the cups with chopped unblanched scallion tops.

>   2 cups fresh corn kernels (5 to 6 ears)
>   4 eggs
>   ½ cup plus 2 tablespoons evaporated skim milk
>   ¼ cup packed fresh breadcrumbs
>   ¼ cup minced fresh parsley
>   ¼ cup minced red or green bell pepper
>   ¼ teaspoon cayenne or hot sauce
>   Vegetable cooking spray

PREPARATION TIME: 30 minutes
COOKING TIME: 35 minutes
YIELD: 6 servings

Preheat the oven to 350°F. Combine the corn and 2 tablespoons of water in a small skillet; simmer 2 to 3 minutes or until the corn is just tender. Drain and cool. In a mixing bowl, beat eggs and evaporated milk lightly with a whisk just until blended. Stir in the remaining ingredients except cooking spray. Spoon the corn evenly into six small ramekins or custard cups that have been coated with cooking spray. Spoon the egg mixture over the corn. Place the ramekins in a roasting pan. Pour boiling water into the pan halfway up sides of molds. Bake in the preheated oven 25 to 30 minutes, or until a knife inserted in the centers comes out clean. Unmold if desired.

NUTRITION INFORMATION: Cal: 175 Pro: 9g/20% Carb: 26g/56% Fat: 5g/24% (S:32% M:44% P:24%) Chol: 143mg Sodium: 122mg Potassium: 358mg Fiber: 7g A: 13% C: 30% B1: 15% B2: 15% Folic: 16% Panto: 14% P: 19%
   EXCHANGE: Med. Meat: ½ Skim Milk: ¼ Bread: 1¼ Fat: ½

MICROWAVE METHOD: In a 1-quart microwave-safe casserole, cook the corn and 2 tablespoons water covered on High (100% power) until the corn is just tender, about 2 to 4 minutes. Drain; cool. Divide the corn evenly among six 6-ounce microwave-safe custard cups or ramekins. Prepare the custard mixture as directed above; pour about ¼ cup mixture into each cup. Place the cups 1 inch apart in a circle in the microwave. Cook uncovered on Medium (50% power) until a knife inserted in the centers just comes out clean, about 9 to 11 minutes. Let stand 5 minutes.

Custard in Peppers
by Debbie Maugans

This custard doesn't have to be cooked in a water bath, because the moist peppers insulate the egg mixture and protect it from toughening. Blanching the bell pepper cases tenderizes them, so the baking time is cut and the eggs won't overcook. For best results, choose evenly shaped, sturdy-looking peppers.

>   6 medium red, green, or yellow bell peppers
>   Vegetable cooking spray
>   1 teaspoon olive oil
>   1 medium onion, minced
>   1 clove garlic, peeled and minced
>   3 fresh green chili peppers, seeded and minced
>   1 red potato, finely diced
>   2 tablespoons diced pimiento
>   3 eggs
>   ½ cup evaporated skim milk
>   1 tablespoon minced fresh coriander

PREPARATION TIME: 45 minutes
COOKING TIME: 1 hour
YIELD: 6 servings

Lay the peppers on their most level sides on a cutting board. Slice off the top fourth of each pepper, leaving the stem end intact. Reserve the tops.

Scoop out the inside seeds and membranes with a sharp-edged spoon. Blanch the pepper cases and tops in a large pot of boiling water for 3 minutes. Drain and rinse under cold running water to stop the cooking process. Drain upside down on paper towels. Dry inside and out with paper towel.

Preheat the oven to 350°F. Spray a medium nonstick skillet with cooking spray. Heat over medium-high heat. Add the oil; heat until sizzling. Add the onion, garlic, chili peppers, and potato; sauté until the potato is just tender. Stir in the pimiento; cool. Beat the eggs, evaporated milk, and coriander lightly with a whisk just until blended. Divide the onion mixture evenly among the pepper cases; spoon the egg mixture into the cases. Cover with the pepper tops. Bake in the preheated oven for 35 minutes or until the eggs are set.

NUTRITION INFORMATION: Cal: 114 Pro: 6g/ 21% Carb: 14g/49% Fat: 4g/30% (S:31% M:51% P:18%) Chol: 117mg Sodium: 66mg Potassium: 397mg Fiber: 2g A: 15% C: 250% B2: 11% B6: 14% P: 12% Cr: 16%

EXCHANGE: Med. Meat: 1/2 Skim Milk: 1/4 Bread: 1/4 Veg: 1 1/4 Fat: 1/2

Mocha Angel Food Cake

by Debbie Maugans

1/2 cup plus 2 tablespoons sifted cake flour
1/2 cup sifted powdered sugar
  3 tablespoons unsweetened cocoa powder
  1 tablespoon instant espresso or coffee
    powder
1/4 teaspoon salt
1 1/2 cups egg whites (from about 11 eggs), at
    room temperature
  1 teaspoon vanilla extract
  1 teaspoon cream of tartar
3/4 cup superfine sugar
    Mocha Sauce (recipe follows)

PREPARATION TIME: 45 minutes plus cooling time
COOKING TIME: 45 minutes
YIELD: Makes 12 to 14 servings

Preheat the oven to 350°F. Sift the flour, powdered sugar, cocoa, coffee powder, and salt together three times. Set aside.

Beat the egg whites, 2 tablespoons of water, and vanilla in a large mixing bowl until foamy; add the cream of tartar and beat until stiff but not dry. Beat in the superfine sugar, 1 tablespoon at a time. Sift the flour mixture over the batter, about 1/4 cup at a time, folding in gently and quickly after each addition. Spoon the batter into an ungreased 9-inch tube pan with a removable bottom. Bake in the preheated oven for 45 minutes.

To cool, invert the pan and let the cake hang by resting the pan on its legs for about 1 1/2 hours. When completely cooled, turn it right side up and loosen by running a knife around the outside edge and center tube. Invert onto a serving platter, and slice with a serrated knife. Spoon about 1 tablespoon sauce over each slice, if desired.

MOCHA SAUCE

1/3 cup skim milk
  2 teaspoons cornstarch
  2 ounces bittersweet chocolate, chopped
  1 tablespoon dark brown sugar
  1 teaspoon instant espresso or coffee powder
1/4 teaspoon ground cinnamon

PREPARATION TIME: 10 minutes
COOKING TIME: 10 minutes
YIELD: 1 cup

Combine the milk and cornstarch in a small bowl; mix well. Combine the remaining ingredients and 1/3 cup of water in a small saucepan; cook over low heat, stirring constantly, until smooth. Stir in the cornstarch mixture; cook over low heat, stirring constantly, until thick. Serve warm, or cool to room temperature with a piece of plastic wrap or waxed paper placed on the surface to prevent the formation of a crust.

NUTRITION INFORMATION(cake only): Cal: 90 Pro: 4g/15% Carb: 19g/80% Fat: .6g/6% Chol: 0mg Sodium: 75mg Potassium: 76mg Fiber: .3g Se: 86%

EXCHANGE: Bread: 1

(sauce only, per 1-tablespoon serving) Cal: 28
Pro: .6g/8% Carb: 3g/33% Fat: 2g/59% (S:71%
M:29% P:0) Chol: 0mg Sodium: 3mg Potassium:
47mg Fiber: 0g
   EXCHANGE: Fruit: 1/4 Fat: 1/4

(cake and sauce) Cal: 117 Pro: 4g/13% Carb:
22g/68% Fat: 3g/19% (S:85% M:11% P:4%)
Chol: 0mg Sodium: 78mg Potassium: 123mg Fiber:
.3g Se: 86% Cr: 21%
   EXCHANGE: Bread: 1 Fruit: 1/4 Fat: 1/2

MICROWAVE METHOD (Mocha Sauce only):
In a 2-cup microwave-safe measure or 1-quart
microwave-safe bowl, stir the milk, cornstarch,
water, sugar, and coffee powder. Cook on High
(100% power) until slightly thickened, about 2 to
2 1/2 minutes; stir once. Stir in the chocolate and
cinnamon. Cook on High until thickened and
smooth, about 1 to 1 1/2 minutes; stir once. Serve
as above.

Vanilla Angel Food Cake with Poached Plums

by Debbie Maugans

 1 3-inch piece vanilla bean
 5 tablespoons sifted cake flour
 1/2 cup sifted powdered sugar
 1/8 teaspoon salt
 2/3 cup egg whites (from about 5 large eggs), at
    room temperature
 1/2 teaspoon cream of tartar
 2 tablespoons superfine sugar

   PREPARATION TIME: 40 minutes
   COOKING TIME: 1 hour
   YIELD: 8 servings

Split the vanilla bean lengthwise to expose the
tiny seeds; scrape out the seeds onto a sheet of
waxed paper. Reserve half the seeds for cake and
half for the Poached Plums.
   Preheat the oven to 300°F. Sift together the
flour, powdered sugar, and salt three times. Combine the egg whites and half the vanilla bean
seeds in a large mixing bowl; beat until foamy.

Add the cream of tartar, and beat until stiff but
not dry. Beat in the superfine sugar, one tablespoon at a time. Sift the flour mixture over the
whites, about 1/4 cup at a time, folding in gently
and quickly after each addition. Spoon the batter
into an ungreased 4-cup ring mold. Bake in the
bottom third of the preheated oven for 30 minutes. Turn off oven (do not open oven door), and
leave cake in oven for 10 minutes. Remove from
oven, and invert onto a rack; let cool in pan 40
minutes. Loosen cake from pan using a metal
spatula, and invert onto a platter.
   To serve, cut the cake into thin slices using a
serrated knife. Arrange two or three slices on
each serving plate. Spoon Poached Plums and
juice around the cake slices.

POACHED PLUMS

   *Reserve vanilla bean seed from Vanilla
   Angel Food Cake*
 1/4 cup granulated sugar
 1 1/2 pounds ripe plums, cut into 1/2-inch slices
 2 teaspoons fresh lemon juice

   PREPARATION TIME: 10 minutes
   COOKING TIME: 20 minutes
   YIELD: About 2 cups

Preheat oven to 400°F. Combine the remaining
vanilla bean seeds with the granulated sugar,
mixing well. Arrange the plum slices in a shallow
baking dish, and sprinkle with the sugar mixture
and lemon juice; toss gently. Bake uncovered at
400°F for 20 minutes or until tender, stirring once.

VARIATION: 1 1/2 pounds cored and thinly
sliced ripe pears can be substituted for the plums.

NUTRITION INFORMATION: Cal: 147 Pro: 2g/
6% Carb: 38g/94% Fat: 0g Chol: 0mg Sodium:
58mg Potassium: 179mg Fiber: 2g
   EXCHANGE: Lean Meat: 1/4 Bread: 1/4 Fruit: 2

MICROWAVE METHOD (Poached Plums only):
In a 1 1/2-quart microwave-safe casserole, stir the
vanilla bean seeds, sugar, lemon juice, and 3 tablespoons water. Add the sliced plums. Cook covered on High (100% power) until tender, about 3
to 5 minutes; stir once. Serve as directed above.

◇ Milk and Yogurt ◇

Lean Calcium

by Robert Barnett

MILK

Calcium, soft and silvery-white, is one of the few nutrients in chronic short supply in the American diet. Our bones may be weaker for that: Low calcium intake throughout life may increase the risk of developing osteoporosis, the brittle bone disease, in later years. More calcium and magnesium and less sodium may also help lower high blood pressure. In the West, milk and its cultured cousins yogurt and cheese are our primary calcium sources.

The osteoporosis problem is more complex than just a lack of calcium. Genetics, exercise, age, gender, prescription drugs, and smoking each play a role. Women suffer from osteoporosis much more often than men, whites more often than blacks, thin people more than fat, the pale more than the ruddy, smokers more than non-smokers. Nutrition is only one factor in building and retaining bone strength.

Estrogen plays a role: It helps regulate calcium levels in the blood and bones. After menopause, when estrogen levels plummet, many women lose calcium from their bones; low doses of estrogen along with supplemental calcium are often effective in reducing such losses.

Exercise is central: Weight-bearing exercise—walking, running, tennis, basketball, but not bicycling or swimming—stimulates the process by which bones are built up. It's a remarkable osteoporosis preventive habit: In one study of 100 postmenopausal women, physiologist Roy Talmage of the University of North Carolina School of Medicine found that those who play tennis three times a week had no loss of bone density for ten to fifteen years after menopause.

A varied but balanced diet is crucial. It's more than just calcium: Vitamin D, essential for the body's regulation of calcium, is found not only in foods such as fortified milk but is created in our skins by exposure to sunlight, a missing "nutrient" in many of our indoor lives. The body also needs adequate intake of a number of trace elements to be able to use dietary calcium effectively to build bone: manganese, copper, zinc, fluoride, and boron. Consider some good food sources of those elements—beans for manganese, oysters for copper and zinc, water or tea for fluoride, apples and pears for boron—and it's clear that a varied diet is key.

Dietary balance also affects how our bodies will be able to absorb the calcium we take in. Consume too much protein, as most Americans do, and you'll excrete more calcium. Caffeine stimulates calcium excretion, too. Too much phosphorus interferes with the body's ability to use calcium. Excess alcohol consumption can interfere with calcium absorption. (Smoking also weakens bones, so quitting smoking is a prime way to safeguard health.)

That said, the absolute amount of dietary calcium we take in still counts. You don't need to get it entirely from dairy products, of course. In the Far East, where few adults can digest milk, foods such as bok choy, tofu, and sea vegetables provide substantial amounts of calcium. It's an approach American vegans would do well to emulate. And it's not a new one: Our paleolithic ancestors managed a substantial 1200 milligrams of calcium a day with no dairy foods but plenty of calcium-rich wild plants, report Emory University professors Boyd Eaton, M.D., Melvin Konner, M.D., and Marjorie Shostak.

But it's not so easy today. In the West, dairy foods have a special place in calcium nutrition. One reason is pure calcium density: Two cups of 1%-fat milk provide 600 milligrams of calcium for only 200 calories and 4 grams of fat (18 percent of total calories). Skim milk yields that much calcium with essentially no fat; whole milk has the same calcium as skim with the fat equivalent of two pats of butter in every cup.

Two cups of low-fat milk, with 600 milligrams of calcium, are a good step toward the calcium USRDA of 800 milligrams for adult men and women and a reasonable start toward the USRDA for adolescents (up to age 25) of 1200 milligrams. (Calcium-fortified milk, now available, provides 500 milligrams in a single cup.)

Milk calcium may also be easier to absorb than calcium from certain greens, such as spinach, which is high in calcium-blocking oxalic acid. A number of the nutrients in milk—vitamin D and the milk sugar lactose, in particular—aid calcium absorption.

Calcium from milk may also be better absorbed than calcium from supplements; one comparison of two studies suggests that supplemental calcium is less effective in promoting bone rebuilding than the same amount of calcium from milk. Calcium supplements may also interfere with iron absorption.

Teens in particular have great needs for calcium that often go unmet. In the first twenty-five years of life, bones have an apparently unique ability to incorporate excess dietary calcium. In later years, when we consume more calcium than we need, we absorb less. One recent study of 225 middle-aged women, conducted at the University of Pittsburgh School of Health-Related Profes-

sions, found that those who drank milk at each meal up to the age of thirty-five had more mineralized (read: strong) bones than those who rarely drank it. Highly mineralized bones are good insurance against the bone losses of calcium that accelerate in women after menopause. A 1986 study published in the *American Journal of Clinical Nutrition* found that the more women drink milk throughout early adulthood, the denser their bones will be.

Calcium is also important for women after menopause. Some studies have found no benefit to calcium supplementation in such women. But they may have studied women too soon after menopause, when the dramatic drop in estrogen may overwhelm any effects of diet on bone density, and they may have failed to consider diet carefully. A 1990 study, by USDA/Tufts University nutrition professor Bess Dawson-Hughes, looked at women who had undergone menopause at least five years earlier. She found that 500 milligrams of calcium supplementation strengthened bones, but only in women whose diets were already terribly low in calcium—under 400 milligrams a day. For women whose diets were closer to the 800-milligram goal, extra supplementation did no extra good.

For men, drinking milk every day has been associated with reduced colon cancer risk. Calcium, along with vitamin D, may help prevent colon cancer by binding with toxic bile acids and food carcinogens, reports University of California, San Diego, nutrition professor Cedric Garland. (Women in sunstarved northern cities, whose bodies produce little sunlight-stimulated vitamin D, have higher breast cancer rates, he also finds.)

So low-fat, vitamin-D-fortified dairy drinks and foods—and other nutritious sources of calcium such as bok choy, sardines, salmon with bones, tofu—are important throughout life for men, women, and children.

Fortified low-fat milk is also a fine source of protein, vitamin B-12, riboflavin, and vitamins A and D. Vegetarians who consume some dairy foods will find it easy to get enough B-12; vegans, who consume no milk or eggs, may find it harder. Athletes may benefit from the riboflavin. A team of researchers at Cornell University led by nutrition professor Daphne Roe found that women who begin exercising regularly (in one study, jog-ging daily for twenty to fifty minutes) need more than twice the 1.2-milligram USRDA for riboflavin, which helps release energy from the carbohydrates and fats we eat. Though most Americans get plenty of riboflavin, young women who exercise regularly and also lose weight may be at real risk for deficiency.

Kids need milk too. But until your child is two, don't feed him or her skim or even low-fat milk. Infants up to six months can't drink cow's milk straight—it's too high in protein and low in iron. They need breast milk or infant formula, which closely resembles it. After six months, vitamin D-fortified whole milk is fine. Within two to three months of introducing milk, about half of your child's diet should consist of solid foods, including iron-fortified cereals. After two years, low-fat milk is okay.

For the rest of us, low-fat or skim milk is the ticket. Of course, most of us like ice cream, too. Unfortunately, it's mostly fat. Premium ice cream has as much as twice the fat per cup as regular ice cream. Best low-fat choices: ice milk and frozen yogurt.

Whatever milk you choose, however, *don't drink it raw,* i.e., unpasteurized. Unpasteurized, raw milk, touted in some circles for its health "benefits" (never substantiated), can be a great carrier of disease. Salmonellosis and campylobacteriosis are two main toxins linked with raw milk. "At the turn of the century we were killing babies with filthy milk," explains Dr. Morris Potter of the Centers for Disease Control in Atlanta. "Mortality went down quickly when pasteurization began."

If you've got an ulcer, new studies show that milk, long considered a mainstay in treatment, probably does little good. It may actually make the condition slightly worse. Milk may quiet the stomach initially, reducing pain temporarily, but both the protein and calcium cause the stomach to increase acid. One recent study found that in patients on ulcer medication, those who drank milk actually took longer to heal than milk abstainers. Today, many physicians recommend antacids over milk for symptomatic relief. These buffer the stomach without causing a rebound in acid production. If you like milk, don't avoid it. Just treat it like any other food. The best bet for those with ulcers: Eat a normal diet, including milk, vegetables, fruit, grains, and meat, with plenty of fiber, but avoid coffee (caffeinated *or* decaf) and alcohol, especially on an empty stomach. And don't go too long between meals.

In time, most adults lose some of their ability to digest lactose (milk sugar)—a condition called lactose intolerance. The symptoms of intolerance are clear: Drinking a large glass of milk can bring on diarrhea, gas, bloating. A simple lab test can determine if you suffer from it. If you do, it doesn't have to mean you can't consume *any* dairy products. Many people can't tolerate the 12 grams of lactose in a cup of milk, but do quite nicely on a half-cup. For these folks, four or five half-cups over the course of a day fit the bill. Drinking milk with meals, rather than by itself, helps too. Lactose-reduced milk, cottage cheese, and other dairy products, often low-fat, are also available.

But the best answer for many may lie in a good dose of culture. Milk's younger cultured cousin—yogurt, buttermilk, kefir—help lactose digestion, and many people can handle the older cousin—cheese—as well.

YOGURT, FACT AND FANCY

Yogurt is a marvelous food, about which some people believe extraordinary things. A few of those claims may even have some merit. Yogurt's primary proven benefit is its digestibility, especially for lactose-intolerant people. Nearly three-quarters of the world's population—mainly Hispanics, Asians, and blacks, but also a number of whites of European descent as they age—are lactose-intolerant.

Yogurt finesses lactose three ways. The active cultures added to milk to produce yogurt, primarily *Lactobacillus bulgaricus* and *Streptococcus thermophilus,* digest some of the lactose as they make yogurt. As those bacteria turn milk to yogurt, though, they also produce acids that inhibit their own activity. So yogurt's beneficial bacteria lie dormant—until you eat it. In 1984, researchers at the University of Minnesota reported in the *New England Journal of Medicine* that yogurt cultures return to life as they are digested in the small intestine, and more of the lactose-digesting enzyme lactase is released. Lactase then goes to work on the remaining lactose in the yogurt, digesting it. Yogurt cultures also makes dairy protein easier to digest, animal studies have found. Kefir, a related cultured milk product, presumably has the same benefits, although it hasn't been specifically studied, says Professor Emeritus Marvin L. Speck of North Carolina State University in Raleigh.

But yogurt can only do us good if we give it the chance. Heating yogurt after it's been made to extend its shelf-life (a form of pasteurization) kills the beneficial bacteria. "Heating yogurt is a travesty against the consumer, especially those who are lactose-intolerant," says Speck. "All yogurt should be made from pasteurized milk, but it shouldn't be heated after that." The irony, he notes, is that active live cultures help preserve yogurt from being spoiled by pathogenic (disease-causing) bacteria. Look for the words "contains active cultures" on the label.

Fortunately, freezing yogurt doesn't seem to have the same effect, says Speck. Though a little lactase is lost, what remains is active for weeks—if the manufacturer uses yogurt that hasn't been reheated in making frozen yogurt.

"Labels can be misleading, too," says Speck. "Some yogurt makers will say that their product contains active live cultures. They may add some back after heating, but it's usually not in significant numbers." According to federal regulations, yogurt makers that heat their product after fermentation are required to say so. Homemade yogurt, rarely exposed to very high heat, is likely quite active, too. Don't hesitate to cook with yogurt to replace sour cream, as many recipes here suggest; just be sure to consume some uncooked if you want more advantages than its lower fat content.

To true believers, yogurt does more than digest lactose. It also lets the digestive system work like a song, cures cancer, and prolongs life easily past the century mark, they say. Such high hopes may be misplaced, however; recent studies suggest that *L. bulgaricus* doesn't survive in the intestinal tract. It's hard to see how it can help digestion if it doesn't survive. Nor does yogurt appear to lower blood cholesterol, as some early studies suggested it might.

Ironically, some of the claims made for yogurt are now being proven—but for acidophilus milk. *Lactobacillus acidophilus,* yet another beneficial strain of bacteria that curdles milk, has been proven to survive in the intestinal tract, where it may help prevent colon cancer and might even harmonize the digestive process. In 1978, Stanley Gilliland, M.D., of Oklahoma State University, demonstrated that *Lactobacillus acidophilus,* when eaten in food, will survive and grow in the human intestines. Since then, two Tufts University Medical School researchers in Boston, biochemist Barry R. Goldin and infectious diseases expert Sherwood Gorbach, M.D., have shown that the bacteria may help prevent colon cancer.

"When you feed acidophilus to either humans or animals, it lowers levels of enzymes that have the potential to generate carcinogenic by-products," says Goldin. Those enzymes are associated with a high-fat, low-fiber diet: Vegetarians have low levels, and switching animals from meat to grain diets lowers enzyme levels. In one Tufts study of twenty-one volunteers, simply adding acidophilus culture to two glasses of milk—without any other change in the diet—significantly reduced the levels of these enzymes. "*Lactobacillus acidophilus* makes levels similar to those found on a low-fat high-fiber diet," says Goldin.

Acidophilus may also help digestion. In Scandinavia, it's fed to premature infants to help recolonize the gut with beneficial bacteria and lower the concentration of harmful bacteria, says Goldin. Adds Speck: "It's a beautiful example of microbial ecology. When acidophilus is in the gut in normal amounts, then the general microbial population is in good balance. When it's absent, gas and diarrhea are often a problem."

It may not work with American cultured milk products, however. A particular strain of lactobacilli, dubbed GG, found in Finnish yogurt products, is particularly effective. In a study of Finnish travelers, for example, those who ate yogurt products had about 12 percent lower incidence of travelers' diarrhea. Goldin and Gorbach report similar success in treating colitis patients with lactobacilli GG.

Yogurt with acidophilus culture, available in some local American yogurts, however, may help women avoid yeast infections. In a small study at

Long Island Jewish Medical Center in New Hyde Park, women who ate acidophilus-containing yogurt reported a three-fold decrease in yeast infections.

To get acidophilus into your diet, you can buy yogurt made with it (only a few yogurt makers use it), or buy sweet acidophilus milk in the supermarket and either drink it or use it to make your own yogurt. Sweet acidophilus milk is simply milk, usually low-fat, to which acidophilus culture has been added. In Europe, sour acidophilus milk, a truly cultured product, is available, too. Acidophilus powders or capsules are also available in health food stores.

Cooking with Cultured Milk

by Robert Barnett

Beyond its direct health benefits, cultured milk is often a healthy cook's secret weapon. Yogurt, buttermilk, kefir, and even acidophilus milk each have unique tangy qualities that can easily replace cream or sour cream in many recipes to lower the fat content.

In the summer, try horseradish yogurt dolloped over cold poached fish or chicken; quench your thirst with a fruit yogurt shake, rich in vitamin C and calcium but with no more calories than a regular soda. For a summer fruit salad, mix yogurt and bananas and berries with chopped lemon balm, spearmint, cinnamon, or cardamom.

In the Middle East, they add mint to yogurt; in Scandinavia, dill. Try beets with dilled yogurt. For a sweet potato topping, toss a chopped apple or pear (moistened with lemon juice to prevent discoloring) with caraway or poppy seeds and yogurt. Yogurt is also a perfect marinade base. For chicken, dilute it with citrus juice, white wine, sherry diluted with rice wine vinegar, or tomato juice; you need only enough to moisten the poultry thoroughly.

When cooking with yogurt, stir 1 tablespoon of cornstarch or 2 tablespoons of flour into each cup of yogurt used and use low heat to prevent curdling. To replace sour cream for dips, dressings, and sauces, mix nonfat yogurt with low-fat ricotta or cottage cheese in a food processor with a steel blade; it won't liquefy as it may in a blender.

Kefir behaves much like yogurt and can be used in much the same way.

Buttermilk has a distinct tart richness and thickness much beloved in baking and as a base for low-fat ranch salad dressings and cold creamy soups. In muffins or pancakes, it adds tenderness and moisture. In recipes that call for cream, use buttermilk with a little baking soda added, but don't boil it—it will curdle. Or add some buttermilk to pasta sauce to make it into a cream sauce; stir it in toward the end of cooking.

Sweet acidophilus milk, on the other hand, tastes very much like milk, if a bit tangier, so it can go into any recipe that calls for milk. You'll notice that some of the recipes that follow use yogurt cool or warm, and so should preserve the active cultures; the rest illustrate the culinary possibilities of low-fat or nonfat yogurt when it's cooked or frozen.

Homemade Buttermilk

by the American Dairy Association

Not as thick as commercial buttermilk, but homemade flavor.

1 quart skim milk
1/2 cup commercial buttermilk

PREPARATION TIME: 10 minutes plus standing time
YIELD: 1 quart

Combine the milk and buttermilk in a sterilized glass container until well blended. Cover loosely with a lid or plastic wrap. Let stand at room temperature until thickened, 5 to 10 hours. Stir, then refrigerate. Save 1/2 cup homemade buttermilk to use as a "starter" for the next batch.

NUTRITION INFORMATION: Cal: 98 Pro: 9g/ 39% Carb: 13g/55% Fat: .7g/7% Chol: 5mg Sodium: 157mg Potassium: 451mg Fiber: 0g A: 10% D: 26% B2: 23% B12: 17% Ca: 34% P. 24%

EXCHANGE: Skim Milk: 1

Homemade Yogurt

by the American Dairy Association

To ensure active cultures and great taste, make your own yogurt. Yogurt-makers come with their own instructions. But you don't need an appliance to make good homemade yogurt. A few tablespoons of any still-active yogurt serves as a perfectly good "starter."

    1 quart skim or low-fat milk (see Note)
 ½ cup instant nonfat dry-milk powder
    3 tablespoons lowfat plain yogurt at room
      temperature
      Kitchen thermometer

PREPARATION TIME: 15 minutes plus standing, incubating, and refrigerating time
COOKING TIME: 10 minutes
YIELD: approximately 1 quart or four 1-cup servings

Preheat the oven to 110°F. Combine 1 cup of the milk and the nonfat dry milk in a small bowl; stir until the dry milk is dissolved. Pour the remaining milk into a saucepan; stir in the dry milk mixture.

Heat the milk mixture slowly over low heat to 190° to 210°F on the thermometer. Remove from heat and cool to 110°F. Remove the protein film from the top and discard. In a small bowl stir the yogurt until smooth; stir in about ⅓ cup of the warm milk mixture until well combined. Add the yogurt mixture to the remaining milk in the saucepan; stir well.

Pour into one large container or smaller individual containers, leaving about ½ inch at the top of each container. Cover and incubate 3 to 4 hours (longer for more tartness) at a constant 110°F temperature in the preheated oven. (An insulated jar will also work.) Do not disturb. After three hours, gently shake to see if the yogurt is firm. If not, let stand another hour or longer. Refrigerate at least 6 hours before serving.

NOTE: For a richer and thicker yogurt, use whole milk instead of low-fat or skim and do not add dry milk. (This will add more calories and 9 to 10 grams fat per 1-cup serving.)

NUTRITION INFORMATION: Cal: 123   Pro: 12g/39% Carb: 17g/56% Fat: .7g/5% Chol: 6mg Sodium: 180mg Potassium: 575mg Fiber: 0g A: 14% D: 25% B2: 30% B12: 22% Panto: 11% Ca: 42% P: 34%
EXCHANGE: Skim Milk: 1½

FLAVORED YOGURT FOR INDIVIDUAL 8-OUNCE SERVINGS:
Apple Raisin: Place 3 tablespoons chopped unpeeled apple, 1 tablespoon chopped raisins, and 1 teaspoon sugar in the bottom of an individual 8-ounce yogurt container. Fill with yogurt mixture (prepared as directed above) to ½ inch from the top; stir to distribute. Cover and incubate.
Spicy Tomato: Place 2 tablespoons vegetable juice cocktail (no salt added) in the bottom of an 8-ounce individual yogurt container. Fill with yogurt mixture (prepared as directed above) to ½ inch from the top; stir to distribute. Cover and incubate.
Pineapple-Carrot: Place 1 tablespoon each drained crushed pineapple and shredded raw carrot in the bottom of an individual 8-ounce container. Fill with yogurt mixture (prepared as directed above) to ½ inch from the top; stir to distribute. Cover and incubate.
Maple-Nut: Place ¼ teaspoon maple extract and 1 tablespoon chopped walnuts in the bottom of an individual 8-ounce yogurt container. Fill with yogurt mixture (prepared as directed above) to ½ inch from the top; stir to distribute. Cover and incubate.

Yogurt Cream Cheese

by the American Dairy Association

This spread, a low-fat substitute for cream cheese, is delicious on crackers, with vegetables, on bagels, or where cream cheese is called for in recipes that don't require cooking.

    1 quart plain low-fat yogurt

PREPARATION TIME: 10 minutes, plus refrigerating/draining time
YIELD: about 1 pint

Line a colander with cheesecloth. Place the yogurt in the colander, place the colander over a bowl to catch the drippings, and cover the colander. Refrigerate and drain 8 to 10 hours. Remove the cheese from the cheesecloth; discard the drippings; store in a covered container for up to 3 weeks.

NUTRITION INFORMATION (per 2 tablespoons): Cal: 36   Pro: 3g/33%   Carb: 4g/45%   Fat: 1g/22% (S:66%   M:31%   P:3%)   Chol: 3mg   Sodium: 40mg   Potassium: 133mg
EXCHANGE: Skim Milk: ¹/₂

Cold Tomato, Buttermilk, and Basil Bisque

by Marie Simmons

1¹/₄   pounds ripe tomatoes, cored
  2   whole scallions
  1   clove garlic, peeled and halved
  4   large leaves fresh basil
  2   cups cold buttermilk
  2   tablespoons finely diced green bell pepper
    Salt (optional)
    Freshly ground black pepper
  1   tablespoon julienne of fresh basil (about 3 large leaves) (see Note)

PREPARATION TIME: 25 minutes plus refrigerating time
COOKING TIME: 10 minutes
YIELD: 4 cups

Select one of the smallest tomatoes (or use half of a large tomato); cut in half and squeeze the juice and pulp out into a medium saucepan. Chop the tomato flesh into ¹/₄-inch dice; reserve for later. Cube the remaining tomatoes and place in the saucepan. Chop the white parts of the scallions and add to the saucepan. Cut the green tops into thin slices (there should be about 3 tablespoons); reserve for garnish. Add the garlic and whole basil leaves to the saucepan. Simmer the tomato mixture over low heat, covered, 10 minutes. Cool slightly. Puree in the food processor until very smooth. Transfer to a large bowl. Add the buttermilk, the reserved diced tomato, and the green pepper. Season to taste with salt and

pepper. Refrigerate until well chilled. Ladle into bowls. Garnish each with sliced scallion tops and julienne of basil.

NOTE: To make the julienne of basil, stack two or three large fresh basil leaves and roll up into a tight roll. Cut the roll of basil into thin crosswise slices. You'll have about 1 tablespoon of fresh basil julienne—enough for a fragrant pretty garnish for this soup or any other tomato dish.

NUTRITION INFORMATION: Cal: 89   Pro: 6g/24%   Carb: 15g/61%   Fat: 2g/14%   Chol: 5mg   Sodium: 143mg   Potassium: 584mg   Fiber: 3g   A: 43%   C: 67%   B2: 16%   Ca: 16%   P: 16%   Cr: 24%
EXCHANGE: Skim Milk: ¹/₂   Veg: 2

Buttermilk and Corn Chowder with Fennel

by Marie Simmons

  2   medium potatoes, cut into ¹/₄-inch cubes (2 cups)
  2   carrots, cut into ¹/₈-inch slices (about 1¹/₂ cups)
  1   teaspoon dried fennel seeds
    Salt to taste (optional)
  2   cups fresh or frozen corn kernels (1 large ear fresh corn yields about ²/₃ cup kernels)
¹/₄   cup chopped onion
  1   sprig fresh parsley
  2   cups buttermilk
  4   green leaves from celery tops (optional) for garnish

PREPARATION TIME: 30 minutes plus standing time
COOKING TIME: 20 minutes
YIELD: 6 cups

Combine 2 cups water, potatoes, carrots, and fennel seeds in a medium saucepan. Add salt, if desired. Cook covered over medium heat, until the potatoes and carrots are tender, about 10 minutes. Remove half of the cooked vegetables from the broth with a slotted spoon; reserve for later. Add 1 cup of the corn and the onion and parsley to the broth and vegetables remaining in the saucepan.

Cook covered 5 minutes. Let stand covered 10 minutes to cool slightly. With a slotted spoon, transfer the contents of the saucepan to the food processor (leave some of the broth in the saucepan if the processor bowl is more than half full). Puree the vegetables until very smooth. Return to the saucepan; add the reserved cooked vegetables, the remaining 1 cup corn kernels, and the buttermilk. Heat gently so that there is still a little crunch left in the corn. Do not boil; the buttermilk will curdle. Ladle into bowls and garnish each with a celery leaf, if desired.

NUTRITION INFORMATION: Cal: 130 Pro: 6g/16% Carb: 27g/78% Fat: .9g/6% Chol: 3mg Sodium: 117mg Potassium: 430mg Fiber: 3g A: 195% C: 11% B2: 11% B6: 15% Ca: 12% P: 13% Mn: 13% Cr: 24%
EXCHANGE: Skim Milk: 1/4 Bread: 1 1/4 Veg: 3/4

Chili-Flavored Vegetable Stew with Yogurt

by Marie Simmons

Stirring yogurt into this lean dish gives it a deceptive richness. To turn the vegetable stew into a main dish, serve it with cheddar cheese-flavored cornbread or polenta seasoned with Monterey Jack cheese.

1 tablespoon vegetable oil
1 large Spanish onion, cut into 1/2-inch chunks
1 large green bell pepper, cut into 1/2-inch pieces
2 cloves garlic, peeled, bruised with the side of a knife
1 large tomato, cored and cut into 1/2-inch chunks
  Salt (optional)
1 teaspoon chili powder
1 teaspoon ground cumin
1/2 teaspoon red pepper flakes (or less to taste)
4 teaspoons dried oregano
8 ounces sweet potato, cut into 1/2-inch pieces
8 ounces russet potatoes, cut into 1/2-inch pieces
2 long thin carrots, cut into 1/2-inch lengths
2 small zucchini, cut into 1/2-inch pieces
1/2 cup plain low-fat or nonfat yogurt
  Thin slices of scallion for garnish

PREPARATION TIME: 30 minutes
COOKING TIME: 25 minutes
YIELD: 4 to 6 servings

Mix the oil, onion, pepper, and garlic in a large nonstick skillet. Sauté over high heat, stirring often, until the peppers are blistered and the onion and garlic are browned on the edges, about 5 minutes. Reduce the heat; stir in the tomato, salt if desired, chili powder, cumin, red pepper flakes, and oregano until blended. Add the potatoes and carrots and enough water to cover the bottom of the skillet (about 1/4 to 1/2 cup) and prevent the vegetables from sticking while cooking. Cover and cook over low heat 10 minutes. Stir in the zucchini and add more water to cover the bottom of the skillet if necessary. Cover and cook over low heat 10 minutes, or until the vegetables are all tender. Let stand covered 5 minutes to cool slightly. Stir in the yogurt until blended. Reheat if necessary over very low heat; yogurt will curdle if the heat is too high. Garnish with scallions and serve as a side dish.

NUTRITION INFORMATION (for 4 servings): Cal: 221 Pro: 5g/9% Carb: 42g/72% Fat: 5g/19% (S: 20% M: 24% P:56%) Chol: 2mg Sodium: 87mg Potassium: 773mg Fiber: 6g A: 498% C: 143% E: 29% B1: 13% B2: 14% B6: 31% Ca: 12% P: 14% Fe: 12% Mg: 13% Cu: 18% Mn: 25% Cr: 24%
EXCHANGE: Skim Milk: 1/4 Bread: 2 Veg: 1 Fat: 3/4

MICROWAVE METHOD: In a 3- to 4-quart microwave-safe casserole, cook only 1 teaspoon oil and the onion, pepper, and garlic on High (100% power) until tender, about 5 to 7 minutes. Stir in the tomato, salt, chili powder, cumin, red pepper flakes, and oregano. Cook covered on High 3 minutes. Stir in the potatoes and carrots. Cook covered on High until the potatoes and carrots are almost tender, about 5 to 7 minutes. Stir in the zucchini; cook covered on High until all the vegetables are tender, about 3 to 4 minutes. Let stand 5 minutes. Stir in the yogurt and serve as directed above.

Beet Koshumbir (Beet Salad)

Stonyfield Farm Recipe Contest Winner 7

The word *koshumbir,* in Maharastra, India, refers to a salad dish usually served with rice and lentils. Since beets have their own distinctive flavor, salt and pepper seem unnecessary. The beets may be cooked a day or two ahead of time and kept in the refrigerator with skins on until needed.

3 to 4 medium beets
   16 ounces low-fat plain yogurt
      Chopped fresh dill and/or parsley
      (optional) for garnish

PREPARATION TIME: 10 minutes
COOKING TIME: 30 minutes
YIELD: 6 servings

Boil the beets in water to cover until tender when pierced with a fork, 20 to 30 minutes. Cool; peel. Cut the beets into small dice or strips (size is dependent upon personal choice). Fold gently into the yogurt. Place in a serving bowl, and garnish with dill and/or parsley.

NOTE: This is a very creamy, Indian-style salad—almost like a sauce in texture. If you prefer a more traditional beet side dish, use only 8 ounces of yogurt.

NUTRITION INFORMATION: Cal: 58 Pro: 4g/ 30% Carb: 8g/52% Fat: 1g/18% (S:68% M:29% P:3%) Chol: 5mg Sodium: 69mg Potassium: 284mg Fiber: .7g Ca: 14%
   EXCHANGE: Skim Milk: 1/2 Veg: 1

Honey-Lime Yogurt Dressing (for Fruit)

by the American Dairy Association

1 cup plain low-fat yogurt
2 tablespoons honey
4 teaspoons fresh lime juice

PREPARATION TIME: 10 minutes
YIELD: 1 cup

Combine the yogurt, honey, and lime juice. Chill covered to allow flavors to blend. Spoon over assorted fresh fruits of the season.

NUTRITION INFORMATION (per 1/4-cup serving): Cal: 70 Pro: 3g/17% Carb: 13g/72% Fat: .9g/11% Chol: 4mg Sodium: 40mg Potassium: 143mg Fiber: 0g Ca: 10%
   EXCHANGE: Skim Milk: 1/4 Fruit: 1/2

Blue Cheese Salad Dressing

by the American Dairy Association

1/4 cup crumbled blue cheese
 1 teaspoon vinegar
1/2 teaspoon prepared mustard
1/2 teaspoon sugar
 1 cup plain nonfat yogurt

PREPARATION TIME: 10 minutes
YIELD: 1 cup

In a small bowl, mash the cheese with a fork; add the vinegar, mustard, sugar, and 1/4 cup of the yogurt and combine. Fold in the remaining 3/4 cup yogurt. Cover and chill several hours to blend flavors.

NUTRITION INFORMATION (per 1/4-cup serving): Cal: 64 Pro: 5g/32% Carb: 5g/32% Fat: 3g/36% (S:69% M:28% P:3%) Chol: 7mg Sodium: 169mg Potassium: 167mg Fiber: 0g Ca: 16% P: 12%
   EXCHANGE: Low-fat Milk: 1/2

Espresso-Flavored Frozen Yogurt

by Marie Simmons

1/3 cup sugar
 2 tablespoons freeze-dried espresso coffee
 granules

2 cups plain low-fat yogurt
1/2 teaspoon vanilla extract

PREPARATION TIME: 10 minutes plus freezing time
COOKING TIME: 5 minutes
YIELD: about 1 1/2 pints

Combine 1/2 cup water, sugar, and coffee in a small saucepan. Heat, stirring, over low heat, until the sugar and coffee are dissolved; do not boil hard. Cool. Stir the yogurt and vanilla into the coffee syrup until blended. Transfer to an ice cube tray without the dividers or a metal loaf pan. Freeze until the edges are firm and the center is still soft, about 2 hours. Puree in a food processor until light and creamy. Transfer to plastic container with a tight-fitting lid. Freeze for at least 6 hours or overnight. Texture is best if served within 24 hours of preparation.

NUTRITION INFORMATION (per 1/2-cup serving):
Cal: 87   Pro: 4g/18%   Carb: 16g/71%   Fat: 1g/12%
Chol: 5mg   Sodium: 53mg   Potassium: 177mg
Fiber: 0g   Ca: 14%   P: 11%
   EXCHANGE: Skim Milk: 1/4   Fruit: 1

Strawberry Slush

by *American Health*

8 ounces plain low-fat yogurt
1 pint ripe strawberries, hulled
1/4 cup sugar

PREPARATION TIME: 15 minutes plus freezing time
YIELD: about 2 cups, or 4 1/2-cup servings

In a covered blender at medium speed, blend the yogurt, strawberries, and sugar until smooth. Pour into an 8-inch square baking pan; freeze about 3 hours. Spoon the strawberry mixture back into the blender, cover, and blend at medium speed until smooth but still frozen. Return to pan, cover; freeze until slush consistency, about 30 minutes. If frozen longer, let slush thaw slightly at room temperature before serving.

NUTRITION INFORMATION: Cal: 103   Pro: 3g/13%   Carb: 21g/78%   Fat: 1g/9%   Chol: 4mg
Sodium: 41mg   Potassium: 256mg   Fiber: 2g
C: 71%   Ca: 11%
   EXCHANGE: Skim Milk: 1/4   Fruit: 1 1/4

Peach Tapioca

by Marie Simmons

This comforting pudding is excellent when made with ripe seasonal peaches, but frozen unsweetened peaches can be used out of season.

1/3 cup packed light brown sugar
1/4 cup quick tapioca
1 tablespoon cornstarch
1 cup unpeeled chopped ripe peaches
2 1/2 cups skim or 1%-fat milk
1/2 teaspoon vanilla extract
1/4 teaspoon almond extract
   Ground cinnamon

PREPARATION TIME: 15 minutes plus cooling or chilling time
COOKING TIME: 10 minutes
YIELD: 4 servings

In a saucepan, stir the sugar, tapioca, and cornstarch together until blended. Add the peaches; stir until all the dry ingredients are moistened with the peach juice. Gradually stir in the milk. Cook, stirring constantly, over medium heat until the mixture comes to a full rolling boil. Remove from heat; let stand 10 minutes. Stir in the vanilla and almond extracts. Transfer to dessert dishes or a serving bowl. Let stand at room temperature to cool or chill in the refrigerator. Sprinkle the top lightly with a little cinnamon before serving. Serve at room temperature or cold.

NUTRITION INFORMATION: Cal: 173   Pro: 6g/13%   Carb: 35g/79%   Fat: 2g/8%   Chol: 6mg
Sodium: 83mg   Potassium: 390mg   Fiber: 1g
A: 11%   D: 16%   B2: 16%   Ca: 21%   P: 16%
   EXCHANGE: Skim Milk: 1/2   Bread: 1   Fruit: 1

MICROWAVE METHOD: In a 2-quart microwave-safe casserole or bowl, combine the ingredients as directed above through stirring in the milk.

Cook uncovered on High (100% power) until the mixture is at full rolling boil and thickened, about 5 to 8 minutes; stir every 2 minutes. Let stand 10 minutes. Stir in the vanilla and almond extracts. Continue as directed above.

Chocolati
by *American Health*

This is a surprisingly rich-tasting frozen dessert, considering its low-fat ingredients.

3/4 cup nonfat dry milk powder
1/3 cup unsweetened cocoa powder
1/4 cup sugar
 1 envelope unflavored gelatin
 2 cups skim milk
1/4 cup crème de cacao

PREPARATION TIME: 10 minutes plus freezing time
COOKING TIME: 5 minutes
YIELD: 6 servings

In a heavy 2-quart saucepan, combine the nonfat dry milk powder, cocoa, sugar, and gelatin; stir in the skim milk. Cook over medium-low heat, stirring constantly, until gelatin is completely dissolved, about 5 minutes. Remove the saucepan from the heat; stir in the crème de cacao. Pour the mixture into a large bowl; freeze until partially firm, about 4 hours. With an electric mixer at high speed, beat the mixture until smooth, scraping bowl with rubber spatula. Spoon into six 6-ounce freezer-safe dessert glasses. Freeze until firm. To serve, remove Chocolati from freezer and let stand at room temperature 10 minutes for a creamier texture.

NUTRITION INFORMATION: Cal: 160 Pro: 9g/19% Carb: 26g/57% Fat: 3g/13% (S:59% M:36% P:5) Alc: 11% Chol: 3mg Sodium: 93mg Potassium: 455mg Fiber: .6g B2: 19% B12: 11% Ca: 22% P: 25% Mg: 20% Cu: 24% Se: 350%
EXCHANGE: Skim Milk: 1 Fruit: 1/2 Fat: 1

Strawberry or Raspberry Ice Milk
by Marie Simmons

1 10-ounce package frozen strawberries or raspberries in syrup (in light syrup, if preferred), slightly thawed
1 cup 1%-fat or skim milk
1 tablespoon fresh lemon juice

PREPARATION TIME: 15 minutes plus freezing time
YIELD: about 1 pint

Puree the berries in the food processor. (If using raspberries, press the berries through a sieve into a bowl to remove seeds, if preferred.) With processor running slowly, add the milk and lemon juice through feed tube. (Or if berries have been sieved, whisk together the berry puree, milk, and lemon juice.) Transfer to a metal loaf pan or an ice cube tray without the divider and freeze until the edges are firm and the center is still slushy, 1 to 2 hours. Scrape back into the food processor; process until mixture is soft and creamy. Scrape into a plastic container with a tight-fitting lid and freeze at least 6 hours or overnight. Texture is best when served within 24 hours of preparation.

NUTRITION INFORMATION (per 1/2-cup serving): Cal: 51 Pro: 2g/17% Carb: 10g/71% Fat: .7g/12% Chol: 3mg Sodium: 32mg Potassium: 204mg Fiber: 2g C: 53%
EXCHANGE: Skim Milk: 1/4 Fruit: 1/2

◇ CHEESE ◇

Milk's Leap: Cheese

by Leni Reed, R.D.

Cheese, "milk's leap toward immortality," is one of our most delicious foods. From fresh mozzarella pulled from its crock to aged Parmesan, cheese enlivens our cooking and gives us a bounty of nutrients.

It takes nine to ten pounds of milk to make just one pound of cheese. That's why just one ounce (a bite or two) of most hard cheeses contains about 25 percent of an adult's RDA for calcium. As with milk, the vitamin D and the lactose (milk sugar) help us absorb that calcium.

But many cheeses are very high in fat, calories, and sodium. The trick is to learn how to pick cheese that gives us great taste and a bounty of nutrients, especially calcium, with the least amount of fat and salt.

Natural cheeses contain roughly 175 to 200 milligrams of sodium per ounce; processed cheeses, about twice that amount. To measure that in mouthfuls rather than milligrams, consider a cheese sandwich: two slices of natural Cheddar (about 2 ounces), two slices of whole wheat bread, a tablespoon of mayonnaise, a few leaves of lettuce, and a few slices of tomato. Total sodium: about 800 milligrams, half from the cheese. Make the sandwich with processed American cheese, and it has about a whopping 1,200 milligrams— two thirds from the cheese.

The fat content of cheese varies considerably, accounting for 20 to 90 percent of its calories. While that's also true for meat, the fat in cheese is not nearly as visible. Cheeses like Cheddar and colby have about nine grams of butterfat—most of it saturated—per ounce. That's the equivalent of some two small pats of butter (about 70 calories) in every walnut-size piece: The calories per ounce for these cheeses hovers around 110. Thus, 70 out of the approximately 110 calories are from fat. A lot!

Don't be fooled if a cheese is labeled with a "percent of fat," however. It's not the same as the "percent of calories from fat." It's simply the cheesemaker's designation for the weight of fat, expressed as a percentage of the weight of the cheese solids (moisture-free cheese). It appears on labels as "% FIDM" (percent of fat in dry matter) or "% BF" (percent of butterfat). The % FIDM or % BF is almost invariably less than the percent of calories from fat. For example, a Cheddar labeled "50% FIDM" may actually have 70 percent or more of its calories from fat.

So, beware, buyer, the next time the cheese expert at your favorite cheese shop tells you that a cheese is low in fat. Ask him to tell you the calories and grams of fat per ounce, and then draw your own conclusions. Look for cheeses with four grams per ounce, or less. (A gram of fat has nine calories.)

Here are a few other terms to watch out for: *reduced fat, lower fat,* and *part-skim milk.* Manufacturers would like you to believe that these cheeses are low in fat, but are they? Not necessarily.

"Reduced" or "lower fat" does not automatically mean low-fat. These terms only tell you that the finished product contains less fat than the original one—and that doesn't tell you much. For example, 91 percent of the calories in cream cheese come from fat; in the "lower fat" version called Neufchâtel, that number tumbles to a humble 85 percent. Won't your arteries be relieved to hear that!

Similarly, "part-skim milk" doesn't tell you what part; also cheeses that are "part-skim" could contain cream. The only way to make certain you are buying truly low-fat cheeses is to check the percent of calories from fat for yourself, or the total number of fat grams.

A few more label terms: pasteurized process cheese is made from one or more natural cheeses which have been shredded, mixed with an emulsifier, and heated. Pasteurized process cheese *food* is similar to pasteurized process cheese but it also contains one or more of the following: cream, milk, skim milk, buttermilk, nonfat dry milk, or whey. Pasteurized process cheese *spread* is similar to pasteurized process cheese food except that an edible stabilizer may be added. This product has more moisture and a lower milk-fat content than pasteurized process cheese food. Thus, it's lower in fat.

Calcium Per Calorie

Most cheeses fall into one of three groups according to percentage of calories from fat: under 20 percent, 20 percent to 60 percent, and over 60 percent.

The first category is a singlet: cottage cheese. Unfortunately, low-fat cottage is fairly low in calcium, especially for dairy products (140 milligrams per cup)—less than a milligram per calorie.

In the mid-fat range, you'll find a pretty wide selection, including creamed cottage, gjetost, sapsago, part-skim mozzarella, and part-skim ricotta, as well as reduced-calorie pasteurized process cheese products. A few other selections that are reported to be low in fat but for which nutritional analysis is not available at this time include Nor-wegian gammelost, German hand cheese, and Swiss St. Otho.

For the most calcium per calorie the best cheeses, surprisingly, are the low-calorie pasteurized process cheese products. These have $3^{1}/_{2}$ to $4^{1}/_{2}$ milligrams of calcium per calorie. That's at least one half a milligram more than Parmesan, the natural cheese that has the most calcium per calorie.

Cavity Prevention

Say Cheese! may be more than a photographer's ploy to get shy kids to smile. Cheddar cheese appears to help prevent cavities. So do Monterey Jack and other well-aged cheeses, find researchers at the University of Toronto Medical School. These cheeses reduce the process by which tooth enamel loses calcium and becomes prone to cavities.

Exactly how a few bits of Cheddar "fight cavities" isn't known, but scientists have postulated several different mechanisms. Cheese stimulates salivary flow, which helps rinse sugar from the mouth and prevents the increase of acidity. The salivary flow also bathes teeth in a calcium-rich solution which helps prevent the dissolving of tooth enamel. Another possibility: Cheese proteins adhere to the teeth surfaces and buffer the acids that hurt enamel. Whatever the mechanism, that slice of Cheddar cheese on top of apple pie might be doing your teeth more good than you know. You'll still need to brush and floss, of course.

Digestibility

Cheese doesn't agree with everyone, particularly people who are lactose-intolerant. Though the bacteria that make cheese from milk digest some of the lactose (milk sugar) in the process, some cheeses—those made from lactose-rich whey—may still be too high in lactose. These include ricotta, gjetost, mysost, and sapsago. Also, unripened cheese contains more lactose that ripened cheese.

Safer selections for the lactose-intolerant are well-aged cheeses made from curds. A cheese aged six months or more should be well tolerated by most lactose-intolerant people; younger cheeses may be okay for some.

However, cheeses low in lactose tend to be high in the amino acid tyramine—and that could be a problem for people being treated with MAO-inhibitor antidepressants. These drugs interfere with the tyramine metabolism, and this may lead to headaches, nosebleeds, and even temporary high blood pressure.

People who suffer from migraines may also be affected by tyramine. A recent survey of 550 migraine specialists revealed a widespread belief that many foods, including aged cheeses high in tyramine, can trigger migraines in susceptible individuals, though scientific proof is still lacking.

High tyramine cheeses are aged cheeses. The more a cheese ages, the more tyramine it contains. Examples: Mild Cheddar has only 2.5 milligrams of tyramine per ounce, while extra-sharp (aged much longer) has about 7.7. Edam has about 8.8, Gouda 8.2, Roquefort and blue 10.2, and Swiss 11.6. Soft, unripened cheeses such as cream and cottage contain negligible amounts, if any, of tyramine. The tyramine content of most foods is not entirely predictable, however, so it is best to seek medical advice.

Cooking with Cheese
by Leni Reed, R.D.

Cheese is such a rich food—in taste, fat, calories, and nutrients—that one should make the most of small amounts. The recipes that follow demonstrate how to stretch flavor by using sharp cheese, by grating, by mixing low-fat and high-fat varieties, plus a few other tricks. The flavor of cheese is generally unaffected by freezing, but its texture often becomes more crumbly after thawing.

Let most cheeses come to room temperature for fullest flavor before serving. Two exceptions: ricotta and cottage cheese, best served cold. Leftover cheese can be frozen; the flavor won't be affected much, but the texture may become more crumbly after thawing.

Cheese dishes should be cooked at a low temperature for a short time. Cooking at too high a temperature or for too long results in a stringy, rubbery product. Melting cheese in a double boiler over simmering water works well, especially if the cheese has been diced, shredded, or crumbled so that it will melt quickly.

A few tips on getting the best flavor and nutrition from cheese:

♦ Try part-skim ricotta instead of reduced-fat cream cheese as a spread for your bagel or toast.

♦ Choose extra-sharp cheeses over milder ones. There's no difference in fat between mild and sharp Cheddar, for example, but a smaller amount of sharp has more flavor.

♦ Shred or grate cheese whenever possible. This helps a little go a lot farther.

♦ Instead of sawing off a hunk of cheese with a knife, use a cheese plane to get a thin slice.

♦ Rinse regular cottage cheese by placing it in a strainer under cold running water. This removes a considerable amount of the fat and some of the sodium as well.

♦ Remove the surface salt from feta by crumbling the cheese into chunks and placing these in a strainer that you hold under cold running water for about 10 seconds.

♦ When you use a high-fat cheese, eat it along with low-fat or nonfat foods such as vegetables and bread.

♦ Don't hide the cheese by mixing it in a casserole; put it on top so you can see it. Seeing is an important part of tasting.

Mock Mayonnaise
by *American Health*

1 cup 1%-fat cottage cheese
2 tablespoons vegetable oil
1 tablespoon cider vinegar
2 teaspoons sugar
1/4 teaspoon salt (optional)
1/2 teaspoon dry mustard
1/2 teaspoon paprika
Dash white pepper

PREPARATION TIME: 5 minutes
YIELD: 1 cup

In a covered blender at medium speed, blend all the ingredients until smooth, stopping occasionally to scrape the container down with a rubber spatula (see Note). Transfer to a plastic container, cover, and refrigerate. Serve within 2 weeks.

NOTE: Because the consistency of cottage cheese varies, you may have to add 1 tablespoon or more skim milk to process to smoothness.

NUTRITION INFORMATION (per 2-tablespoon serving): Cal: 56g Pro: 4g/25% Carb: 2g/15% Fat: 4g/60% (S:14% M:14% P:72%) Chol: 1mg Sodium: 119mg Potassium: 30mg Fiber: 0g
EXCHANGE: Lean Meat: ½ Fat: ¾

Breakfast Potato Treat
by Leni Reed

Extra-sharp Cheddar cheese blended with part-skim-milk mozzarella yields great taste with little fat.

   1 medium sweet potato, baked (see Note)
 ½ ounce extra-sharp Cheddar cheese, shredded
 ½ ounce part-skim mozzarella cheese,
       shredded
   1 tablespoon raisins or currants
   1 tablespoon Grape Nuts cereal

PREPARATION TIME: 10 minutes
COOKING TIME: 5 minutes
YIELD: 1 serving

Preheat the oven to 350°F. Cut the sweet potato down the center and mash the potato pulp in the skin with a fork. Sprinkle cheeses and raisins (or currants) over the potato. Bake to just melt cheeses, about 3 to 5 minutes; top with cereal. Serve hot.

NUTRITION INFORMATION: Cal: 264 Pro: 10g/ 15% Carb: 41g/61% Fat: 7g/24% (S:66% M:31% P:3%) Chol: 23mg Sodium: 217mg Potassium: 514mg Fiber: 4g A: 509% C: 47% E: 26% B1: 12% B2: 20% B3: 10% B6: 22% B12: 10% Folic: 13% Ca: 23% P: 22% Cu: 15% Mn: 19%
EXCHANGE: High-Fat Meat: 1 Bread: 2 Fruit: 1

MICROWAVE METHOD: To bake the sweet potato, prick with fork tines in several places; microwave on paper toweling on High (100% power) until tender, about 5 minutes. Let stand 5 minutes. Prepare potato as above. Place on paper towel or plate. Microwave on Medium (50%) just until cheeses melt, about 1 minute.

Fettuccine Gorgonzola
by Leni Reed

The fat in this traditionally rich dish was cut by mixing high- and low-fat cheeses together. The sauce is also nice served over baked potatoes.

 10 ounces spinach fettuccine
 ¾ cup 1%-fat cottage cheese
 ¾ cup part-skim ricotta cheese
 ¼ cup nonfat buttermilk
   3 ounces Gorgonzola cheese, crumbled
       (substitute blue or Roquefort, if desired)
   2 tablespoons shredded Parmesan cheese
   2 Italian plum tomatoes, finely chopped
       Freshly ground black pepper

PREPARATION TIME: 15 minutes
COOKING TIME: 25 minutes
YIELD: 6 servings

Bring a large pot of water to a rapid boil. Gently drop the fettuccine in and allow the water to return to boiling. Cook uncovered for 9 to 12 minutes, or until al dente (slightly chewy), stirring occasionally. When cooked, drain immediately.

While the pasta is cooking, make the sauce. Place the cottage and ricotta cheeses and the buttermilk into the blender or food processor and process until smooth. Pour the mixture into a heavy-bottomed pot (or the top of a double boiler) and heat over low to medium heat (or over simmering water). When heated through, add the Gorgonzola and Parmesan cheeses and stir until nearly melted. Add the tomatoes and stir to mix in. Spoon the sauce over the hot fettuccine and toss. Serve immediately, garnished with freshly ground black pepper as desired.

NUTRITION INFORMATION: Cal: 305 Pro: 18g/ 23% Carb: 40g/52% Fat: 9g/25% (S:66% M:30% P:4%) Chol: 25mg Sodium: 460mg Potassium: 267mg Fiber: 2g A: 15% C: 12% B1: 17% B2: 20% Ca: 25% P: 26% Se: 100%

EXCHANGE: Med. Meat: 1½ Bread: 2½ Veg: ¼

MICROWAVE METHOD: In a 1-quart, microwave-safe casserole, cook the pureed cottage cheese, ricotta, and buttermilk covered on Medium (50% power) until heated through, about 5 minutes. Stir in the remaining cheeses and continue as above.

Stuffed Pizza

by Leni Reed

Part-skim-milk mozzarella cheese, lots of vegetables, and a double-layer crust minimize the fat in this pizza.

> 1 package active dry yeast
> 1 teaspoon sugar
> 1 cup warm water (105° to 115°F)
> 1¾ cups whole wheat flour
> 1 cup whole wheat bread flour
> ½ teaspoon salt
> Vegetable cooking spray

FILLING:

> 5 ounces spinach, stems removed, chopped
> 6 ounces part-skim mozzarella cheese, shredded
> 1 ounce Parmesan cheese, shredded (about ½ cup shredded; not grated)

TOPPING:

> 1 tablespoon extra-virgin olive oil
> 1 small onion, chopped
> 3 cloves garlic, peeled and minced
> 2 14½-ounce cans Italian plum tomatoes, no salt added
> ¼ cup canned tomato puree, no salt added
> ¼ teaspoon Italian herb seasoning, crushed

PREPARATION TIME: 1 hour plus rising time
COOKING TIME: 40 minutes
YIELD: 6 servings

Add the yeast and sugar to the warm water; stir to dissolve the sugar. Let stand until bubbly, about 5 minutes. Mix the flours and salt in a large

bowl. Make a well in the center of the flours; slowly add the yeast mixture, mixing as you pour. Knead dough 6 to 8 minutes, or until smooth yet elastic. If dough is sticky, add more bread flour as you knead. Lightly flour the dough and a 3- to 4-quart bowl. Put the dough in the bowl; cover with plastic wrap and then with a towel. Place in a warm, draft-free place and let rise until double in bulk, 60 to 90 minutes.

To make the filling, chop the spinach in the food processor or with a knife. Mix spinach with cheeses; set aside.

To make the topping, heat the oil in a nonstick skillet over medium heat. Add the onion and garlic; sauté until onion is translucent, about 4 minutes. Drain the tomatoes and squeeze the liquid out of each one. Chop the tomatoes and drain liquid again. (You should have about 1 cup drained, chopped tomatoes.) Stir the tomatoes, tomato puree, and herbs into the onion. Set aside.

Preheat oven to 475°F. When the dough has doubled, punch it down and divide in half. Cover one half with plastic wrap and a towel; keep at room temperature. Place the other half of the dough on a lightly floured work surface; knead 2 minutes. Roll out to an 11-inch circle. Spray the bottom and sides of a 9-inch glass pie plate with cooking spray; place the rolled dough in the pie plate, covering the bottom and sides. Prick the bottom of the crust all over with fork tines. Bake crust 4 minutes. Spread with the filling.

Punch down the remaining dough; roll out to an 11-inch circle; place over the filling. Crimp the edges to seal and make a ridge around the perimeter. Press down on the filling with your hands. Cut a 1-inch slit in the top of the pie. Spread the topping evenly over the top crust. Reduce oven temperature to 450°F and bake the pie on the middle rack 15 minutes. Lower the temperature to 350°F; bake 15 minutes longer.

NUTRITION INFORMATION: Cal: 338 Pro: 18g/ 20% Carb: 49g/56% Fat: 10g/24% (S:48% M:40% P:12%) Chol: 20mg; Sodium: 426mg Potassium: 710g Fiber: 7g A: 55% C: 54% E:13% B1: 28% B2: 21% B3: 21% B6: 19% Folic: 30% Ca: 33% P: 37% Fe: 20% Mg: 23% Zn: 14% Cu: 22% Se: 29%

EXCHANGE: Med. Meat: 1¼ Bread: 2½ Veg: 2 Fat: ½

Mixed Green Salad with Feta Cheese

by Leni Reed

3 ounces feta cheese
1 medium head romaine lettuce, torn into bite-sized pieces
1½ tablespoons extra-virgin olive oil
1½ tablespoons red wine vinegar
1 small carrot, shredded
1 small purple onion, thinly sliced
Coarsely ground black pepper

PREPARATION TIME: 20 minutes
YIELD: 6 servings

Coarsely crumble the cheese into a bowl of cold water; allow the cheese to soak in the water for 15 seconds; drain well.

Place the lettuce in a salad bowl, sprinkle with the olive oil, and toss to distribute the oil evenly. Sprinkle with the vinegar and toss again. Distribute the lettuce over six plates, layer with shredded carrot and sliced onion, sprinkle with black pepper to taste, then top with crumbled feta cheese. Serve cold.

NUTRITION INFORMATION: Cal: 94 Pro: 4g/ 15% Carb: 6g/24% Fat: 7g/61% (S:42% M:50% P:8%) Chol: 13mg Sodium: 172mg Potassium: 320mg Fiber: .6g A: 142% C: 35% Folic: 27%
EXCHANGE: Med. Meat: ½ Veg: 1 Fat: ¾

(with 1 slice bread) Cal: 156 Pro: 6g/15% Carb: 17g/42% Fat: 8g/43% (same fat breakdown) Chol: 13mg Sodium: 331mg Potassium: 364mg Fiber: 4g A: 142% C: 35% B1: 12% Folic: 30% Ca: 12% P: 16% Cr: 20%
EXCHANGE: Med. Meat: ½ Bread: 1 Veg: 1 Fat: ¾

Lemon Cheesecake

by Leni Reed

Drained nonfat yogurt and part-skim-milk ricotta cheese are substituted for the high-fat cream cheese in the traditional recipe. You can drain the yogurt overnight and bake the cake the next day, if you wish. Serve with pureed unsweetened frozen strawberries or blueberries for complementary taste and color.

FILLING:

4 cups plain nonfat yogurt (made without gelatin)
2 cups part-skim ricotta cheese
2 eggs
2 tablespoons unbleached all-purpose flour
Rind of one lemon, minced
1 tablespoon fresh lemon juice
½ cup sugar, or more to taste
Berries for garnish (optional)

CRUST:

3 shredded wheat biscuits
⅓ cup toasted wheat germ
¼ cup old-fashioned rolled oats
¼ teaspoon ground nutmeg
¼ teaspoon ground cinnamon
3 tablespoons corn oil or canola oil
3 tablespoons honey
Vegetable cooking spray
1 tablespoon sugar

PREPARATION TIME: 20 minutes plus refrigerating time
COOKING TIME: 1 hour plus standing time
YIELD: one 8- or 9-inch cheesecake (10 servings)

To drain the yogurt for the filling, place two layers of fine-mesh cotton cheesecloth inside a strainer and place the strainer in a bowl, making sure that there is at least one inch distance between the bowl and the cheesecloth. (You can raise the strainer higher by setting it on a small cup turned upside-down.) Pour the yogurt into the cheesecloth-lined strainer and place in the refrigerator for at least 5 hours, or until there are 2 cups of drained yogurt.

Preheat the oven to 325°F. *To make the crust,* place the shredded wheat into the food processor and crush with the metal blade into a fine consistency; pour the crumbs into a mixing bowl. Add the wheat germ, oats, nutmeg, and cinnamon; mix well. Add the corn oil, 2 tablespoons water, and honey. Mix well to moisten all ingredients. Spray the bottom and sides of an 8- or 9-inch springform pan with cooking spray and dust the bottom with the sugar. Press the crust mixture into the bottom of the pan.

Place the drained yogurt and remaining filling ingredients except berries into a food processor and process about 20 seconds. Pour the filling into the prepared springform pan and bake in the preheated oven for 1 hour. Turn the oven off and allow the cake to sit in the oven for 15 minutes more. Remove from oven and cool to room temperature before removing the side from the pan. Chill at least 2 hours or overnight before serving. Garnish with berries if desired.

NUTRITION INFORMATION: Cal: 284   Pro: 14g/ 20%   Carb: 36g/49%   Fat: 10g/31%   (S:38%   M:30% P:32%)   Chol: 60mg   Sodium: 146mg   Potassium: 379mg   Fiber: 1g   E: 23%   B1: 11%   B2: 23% B12: 14%   Ca: 33%   P: 33%   Mg: 13%   Zn: 17% Mn: 28%

EXCHANGE: Med. Meat: 1¼   Skim Milk: ½ Bread: ¾   Fruit: 1   Fat: 1

◇ FRUIT ◇

Nature's Dessert: Fruit
by Evette Hackman, Ph.D., and Lisa Chobanian, R.D.

Mostly what we want from a piece of fruit is that it taste delicious. That it crack tartly across the tooth like a Granny Smith apple or slide sweetly past the gullet like a ripe Washington State cherry.

Fruits give our bodies a little more than that. They supply a readily available source of carbohydrates, and, except for the avocado, olive, and coconut, are low in fat. They give us vitamins such as C and A, fiber, potassium, and water. And something sweet to eat instead of cheesecake.

Eating more fruits, along with more vegetables, may be the most important cancer-protective dietary change we can make. Numerous studies find that people who eat fresh fruits and vegetables on a daily basis have a lower incidence of cancer than people who do so rarely. Whether that's because of the carotenoids, the vitamin C, the fiber—or maybe even the cheesecake they're *not* eating—no one knows for sure. Too many of us eat fruit but rarely. According to one USDA survey, 41 percent of those surveyed hadn't had a single piece of fruit on the day surveyed. Prove statistics wrong: While you're reading this, take a bite out of some sweet fruit.

Some fruits are extraordinarily rich in the carotenoids that our bodies turn into vitamin A. One lone mango, for example, gives us nearly twice the USRDA for vitamin A equivalent, in the form of beta-carotene. A mango may be the perfect summer food. Ultraviolet rays, as in sunlight, cause blood levels of beta-carotene in human volunteers to fall, Cornell University research reveals. So summer sun-lovers may need more carotene-rich foods.

Many fruits give us fiber. Eat an apple, with a little over 4 grams of dietary fiber, a banana (3 grams), and an orange (3 grams) a day and you're already getting as much fiber as most Americans typically eat in their entire daily diet. The National Cancer Institute recommends we get 20 to 30 grams of dietary fiber a day.

The fiber in many fruits is primarily pectin, which helps us gel jams. It may also lower blood cholesterol levels. In one study, 9 healthy volunteers who consumed 15 grams of pectin a day for three weeks dropped blood cholesterol a significant 13 percent on average. Pectin, which slows stomach emptying, also helps us feel full (ever wonder why an apple is so filling?) and helps stabilize blood sugar, a boon to diabetics and good news for all of us. In one study, a whole apple kept blood sugar in balance much more effectively than did apple juice, which has hardly any pectin. Apples, pears, quince, blackberries, and citrus fruit contain 1 to 3 grams of pectin per serving. In citrus fruits, much of the pectin is in the white layer called the "albedo" surrounding the fruit. An apple peel is 15 percent pectin. So eat whole fruits!

Most fruits give us a good amount of vitamin C. A wonderful nutrient, vitamin C. It helps our wounds heal and collagen form. It reduces the severity of the common cold, studies show. As an antioxidant, it protects our eyes from radiation damage from sunlight, and, along with other antioxidants, may prevent cataracts. Three population studies find that people who eat more fruits and vegetables rich in vitamin C (and other antioxidant vitamins such as beta-carotene and vitamin E) have fewer cataracts. (If your orange juice tastes flat, it's probably lost much of its vitamin C, finds USDA research.)

Vitamin C also helps us make better use of other nutrients. It unlocks the iron in vegetables, grains, and beans, helping our bodies absorb that essential mineral. And it appears to protect vitamin E, according to test-tube research by Etsuo Niki from the Department of Reaction Chemistry at the University of Tokyo. Both are antioxidants, which means they protect cells from the damaging effects of oxygen—damage that's been linked to aging and many diseases. Water-soluble vitamin C seems to regenerate damaged fat-soluble vitamin E, Niki finds, so the two enhance each other's effectiveness. That's good news if you like blueberries. A cup of that purple-blue summer berry supplies 27 percent of the USRDA for vitamin E and 33 percent for vitamin C.

Like vegetables, fruits are at the peak of their nutrient content when fully ripe and fresh. Smaller fruits also have relatively more vitamins, which are concentrated in and around the outer layers of fruits and vegetables. By buying two small fruits instead of one large one, you'll get more "surface to volume" and thus more vitamins.

Of all the nutrients that fruits supply, though, the simplest, and perhaps the most important, is water. It's an essential nutrient, constituting about 50 percent of the weight of an average woman and 60 percent of that of a man. There is three times more water in muscle than in fat; because men are generally leaner and more muscled than women, they contain more body water. A 154-pound man at 60 percent water would contain about 46 quarts.

In hot weather or when doing persistent exercise, you can lose up to 2 quarts of water per hour. Some marathoners have been known to lose 4 to 5 quarts of water per race—a serious loss requiring immediate attention. (For more on water needs, see Beverages, page 314.)

We've all heard the suggestion to take in 2 or more quarts of water per day. Most people can't imagine drinking that much. Fortunately, we don't have to. We get about a quart of water from food and a little over a quart from beverages on average. Fruits and vegetables contain a high proportion of water, whereas fats and dried foods are very low. Fruits are 80 to 90 percent water by weight on average.

Many fruits are also high in potassium; all are low in sodium. That helps us keep our internal ratio of sodium and potassium in balance. Sodium and potassium work together to establish an electrical gradient across the membrane of our cells that keeps the proper amount of fluid inside the cell, the proper amount outside. Sodium and potassium balance also facilitates the sending of nerve impulses, the working of muscles, and the functioning of glands. A high sodium intake can lead to high blood pressure in some; conversely, too little potassium in the diet has been linked with increased risk not only of high blood pressure but of stroke. Eating a few pieces of fruit a day can help keep our intake of sodium and potassium in balance. A cup of cantaloupe, for example, provides 13 percent of the potassium we need.

All in all, fresh fruit may be the perfect food to wake up with. It's sweet, cold, easy to digest, high in the fiber and vitamin C we expect from breakfast, full of the water and potassium our muscles need to get going. It may also help us move our bowels after a long night's sleep: Many fruits have a mild laxative effect, from the water, fiber, and, often, sorbitol sugar. Sorbitol is digested by bacteria in the intestines that produce mild irritants and acts as a mild laxative.

Fruits aren't nutrient powerhouses. If you really want vitamins, you're better off eating a few forkfuls of broccoli or mustard greens. If you're searching for minerals, you're better off with a few oysters or slices of lean beef.

What fruit supplies best is something to eat that's sweet and delicious and low in calories. It's not only an eye-opener for breakfast but a satisfying mid-afternoon snack or a simple dessert after a mid-week meal. A ripe Bartlett pear may not be a vitamin pill, but it sure tastes better than a radish after dinner. Besides, what else makes such a handy snack, tastes so great raw, or packs so easily into a lunch bag?

If you try a new fruit and don't like it the first time, try it again. In one experiment on children that may also apply to adults, Leann Birch, professor of human development at the University of Illinois, offered children unusual fruits they had not seen or tasted before. The more the child tasted or just saw the new food, the more the child accepted the food, she found. It took 10 to 15 exposures to the food to get some children to like it.

If it's concern about the pesticides and fungicides that get sprayed on fruit crops that's keeping you from eating more fruit, you may want to pick fruits that have a rind, such as melons and oranges, or a peel, such as bananas. Domestic produce is probably safer than imported; Western produce is less likely to have fungicides than fruits from the humid East Coast. Wash all produce well. In some supermarkets, organic and guaranteed-no-pesticide-residue fruits and vegetables are available.

Cooking with Fruit

by Nao Hauser

There's not much you can do to improve on the taste of fresh ripe fruit eaten out of hand. But you can use that intensely sweet flavor to season other foods or highlight other fruits, and the fruit seasoning will often minimize the need to add fat, salt, or sugar. Here are a few ways:

♦ Braising. Many foods that are commonly braised, or cooked a long time in a covered pot with some liquid, will taste better if you add 1 or 2 chopped apples to the pot. Try it with pork or veal loin or shoulder roasts, fresh ham, beef pot roast, stews, and cabbage. A good way to begin: Place 2 chopped onions and 2 chopped apples for every 2 or 3 pounds of meat or cabbage in a heavy pot; cook covered over low heat until apples soften completely and onions wilt, about 30 minutes. Season with spices, such as nutmeg, cinnamon, cardamom, or curry powder, if desired. Place the seasoned meat over this braising base and bake in a low oven until completely tender. Spoon off excess fat and serve pan juices with meat. Or place shredded cabbage over base and cook covered on top of the stove over medium-low heat until completely wilted.

♦ Roast poultry. The cranberry sauce traditionally served with turkey and the oranges in duck à l'orange testify to the affinity between fruits and roast poultry. Other delicious combinations: duck with sliced mango, peaches, pears, figs, or blackberries; chicken with apricots, plums, apples, or papaya; turkey with a compote of briefly cooked apples, pears, and grapes, or mango and strawberries. Fruit should be heated through and cooked to tenderness, if necessary, in some of the meat juices on top of the stove before serving; season to taste with sweet spices, grated orange or lemon rind, and, if desired, a splash of rum, Port wine, or fruit liqueur.

To accompany all kinds of roast poultry, pork, or veal: Arrange thinly sliced and cored, but unpared, pears in a single layer in a baking dish. Sprinkle lightly with rosemary, pepper, and freshly ground nutmeg; drizzle very lightly with balsamic or raspberry vinegar. Bake in a moderate oven until fruit is completely tender but not mushy.

♦ Chicken and turkey salads. Add a cup of chopped fruit (apples, peaches, mango, or grapes—just to name a few options) to 3 cups of diced poultry to moisten a salad and minimize the need for a fatty dressing. Or dress the sliced cold poultry with a puree of ripe plums, strawberries, or mango, seasoned to taste with balsamic vinegar or lemon juice. (See recipe for Strawberry Dressing, page 183.)

♦ Grains. Cook 1 cup rice with 2 tablespoons raisins or currants for great flavor and less salt. Try chopped dried apricots or currants with bulghur or couscous, and chopped fresh apples and raisins with kasha or barley.

♦ Beverages. Puree ripe strawberries and substitute for part of the water to make pink lem-

Spotlight: The Fragrant, the Bitter, and the Bony

Some fruits have unique salutary charms. Ellagic acid, found in fragrant fruits (strawberries, raspberries, grapes, cherries, loganberries, plums, apples) may prevent cancer-causing chemicals from damaging DNA, report Medical College of Ohio researchers. Liminoids, bitter substances in citrus fruits and juices, stimulate the production of detoxifying liver enzymes in animal studies, and so may help protect against cancer, USDA researcher Shin Hasegawa reports. Cranberries have an as-yet-unidentified substance that appears to help prevent urinary tract infections by interfering with the ability of bacteria to adhere to cell membranes, according to microbiologist Anthony Sobota of Youngstown State University. Prunes have 12 grams of sorbitol per three ounce serving, a large amount, and they also contain diphenylisatin, a laxative chemical. Boron, a trace element found in a wide variety of fresh fruits and vegetables but especially in pears, apples, and grapes, may help keep bones strong. In USDA studies, adequate boron prevents the excretion of calcium, magnesium, and phosphorus, so it may play a role in preventing osteoporosis. Boron also maintains alpha-brain waves associated with alertness. An apple a day? Of course, but even more: Two to four servings of fruits, including citrus fruits (and juice), melons, and berries, every day. That's what the USDA's Dietary Guidelines for Healthy Americans advise, and it's probably an even smarter habit than we can yet know.

—Robert Barnett

onade with minimal sugar. Puree pineapple to sweeten iced tea without sugar; add chopped fresh mint for great taste.

♦ Dessert sauces. Puree raspberries, strawberries, or blueberries to make a satisfying sauce for ice milk, frozen yogurt, angel food cake, poached pears or peaches, or a summer fruit salad. Sweeten with 2 teaspoons sugar or maple syrup per cup of fruit and add, if you wish, a pinch of cinnamon or cardamom and 2 teaspoons Amaretto to strawberries, raspberry or black currant liqueur to raspberries, and Cointreau or cherry liqueur to blueberries.

If you have a microwave oven, you can poach pears, peaches or figs in a berry puree for elegant flavor. Pour 1 cup puree into a glass pie plate; arrange 6 or 8 pared, cored pear halves, unpared peach halves, or whole ripe figs in the sauce, cut-sides down and thicker parts toward the outside of the dish. Spoon some of the sauce over the fruit. Microwave covered with plastic at High until the fruit is soft, about 30 seconds per piece of fruit. Spoon sauce over fruit to serve warm or chilled.

Seasoning Fruit

Because fruits are high in sugar, they welcome any herb or spice—or none at all. Generally, fruits can be seasoned more liberally when they are cooked than when eaten raw, because the liquid given off dilutes the impact and the heat dissipates it somewhat. Raw apples, for example, would taste terrible if simply sprinkled with the same quantities of cinnamon and other sweet spices that make a cobbler or applesauce wonderful. If you cut up very juicy raw fruits, such as pineapple, oranges, and fully ripe pears, and let them stand long enough to give off liquid to dissolve the herbs and spices, they are quite hospitable to a sprinkling of chopped lemon balm, spearmint, cinnamon, or cardamom. With less juicy fruits, such as bananas and berries, the same seasonings are more aptly applied if mixed into yogurt.

Cooking opens up much broader possibilities, as can be seen in all the recorded recipes for spiced chutneys and herbed fruit jellies. You can try various combinations most easily with poached fruits and applesauce. If you've only known applesauce with cinnamon, cook separate batches with anise, cardamom, and rose geranium leaves—all fine accompaniments for pork or poultry. Poach pears in different wines, with some sugar or a dried fruit for added sweetness, and match the seasonings accordingly; e.g., a spicy zinfandel with star anise and ginger; a flowery gewürztraminer with vanilla seeds, cinnamon, and nutmeg; a light chenin blanc with lemon verbena or apple mint. If you remember how well apples and sage mingle in a stuffing for pork or poultry, you'll recognize that other matings of mint-family herbs and fruits, such as basil with poached peaches and rosemary with oranges, are not really far-fetched—indeed, they're delicious!

Chicken Salad with Fruits and Curry

by Four Seasons Hotels Alternative Cuisine

2 whole chicken breasts
2 sprigs fresh parsley
1 carrot, cut into 1-inch pieces
1 celery rib, cut into 1-inch pieces
1 onion, cut into 1-inch pieces
2 peaches, cut into cubes
3/4 cup Curried Yogurt Dressing (recipe follows)
4 lettuce leaves
1/4 cup blueberries
1/4 cup raspberries
2 peaches, thinly sliced, for garnish

PREPARATION TIME: 30 minutes plus refrigerating time
COOKING TIME: 30 minutes
YIELD: 4 servings

In a covered saucepan, simmer the chicken, parsley, carrot, celery, onion, and 2 cups water until the chicken is fork-tender, about 25 minutes. Remove the chicken. When cool enough to handle, discard the skin and bones, then cut into bite-size pieces. Mix the chicken pieces with the cubed peaches and 3/4 cup Curried Yogurt Dressing.

For each serving, arrange some chicken salad on a lettuce leaf. Spoon 1 tablespoon each blue-

berries and raspberries around salad. Garnish with peach slices arranged in a fan design.

CURRIED YOGURT DRESSING
2 cups plain low-fat yogurt
2 tablespoons strong coffee
1 teaspoon curry powder
1 teaspoon sugar
1/4 teaspoon ground ginger
Salt to taste (optional)

PREPARATION TIME: 5 minutes
YIELD: About 2 cups

In a bowl combine all ingredients and mix well. Store in refrigerator. Serve leftover dressing with fruit salads or cold meats and poultry.

NUTRITION INFORMATION (chicken and dressing): Cal: 255 Pro: 30g/47% Carb: 25g/39% Fat: 4g/14% Chol: 76mg Sodium: 96mg Potassium: 724mg Fiber: 5g A: 24% C: 28% B2: 16% B3: 69% B6: 29% Panto: 14% P: 29% Mg: 12% Se: 29% Cr: 16%
EXCHANGE: Lean Meat: 3 Skim Milk: 1/4 Fruit: 1 1/2

NUTRITION INFORMATION (dressing only per 2-tablespoon serving): Cal: 20 Pro: 2g/31% Carb: 2g/48% Fat: .5g/21% (S:68% M:29% P:3%) Chol: 2mg Sodium: 20mg Potassium: 70mg Fiber: 0g
EXCHANGE: Skim Milk: 1/4

MICROWAVE METHOD: In a 2-quart, microwave-safe casserole, cook the chicken, parsley, carrot, celery, onion, and only 1/2 cup water covered on High (100% power) until chicken is tender, about 10 to 14 minutes. Remove skin and bones and continue as directed above.

Braised Rabbit with Ginger and Prunes

by Elizabeth Schneider

Prunes add lush texture and sweetness to lean, mild rabbit—and many other meats, such as pork or veal, as well. The marinade of prune juice, ginger julienne, and garlic yields a rich, complex sauce. Do not raise the heat to hurry the braising, or the meat toughens. This dish can be gently reheated.

1 rabbit (3½ to 4 pounds), cut into 8 serving
    pieces (see Note)
1 small carrot, thinly sliced
1 tablespoon thinly sliced peeled garlic
2 medium bay leaves, crumbled
2 tablespoons very finely slivered fresh ginger
½ teaspoon freshly ground black pepper
1 cup prune juice
3 tablespoons fresh lemon juice
2 tablespoons cider vinegar
    Vegetable cooking spray
2 tablespoons peanut oil
    All-purpose unbleached flour
¼ teaspoon salt (optional)
1½ cups unsalted chicken, veal, or beef broth
    or stock (see pages 28, 29)
14 moist-packed prunes, preferably unpitted
    (see Note)
    Minced fresh parsley for garnish
    Minced chives for garnish

PREPARATION TIME: 30 minutes plus marinating
time
COOKING TIME: 2½ hours
YIELD: 5 servings

Trim and discard visible fat from the rabbit
pieces. In a large nonmetal bowl, combine the
carrot, garlic, bay leaves, ginger, pepper, prune
juice, lemon juice, and vinegar. Put the rabbit
pieces in the bowl and turn to coat. Cover tightly;
refrigerate 12 to 36 hours, turning occasionally.

Preheat oven to 300°F. Remove the rabbit from
the marinade, reserving the liquid; pat the pieces
dry. Spray a heavy skillet with cooking spray;
heat 1 tablespoon oil over medium-high heat. Add
the rabbit, a few pieces at a time; cook until
brown on all sides; add the remaining oil as
needed. Spoon off all but 1 tablespoon drippings.
Sprinkle the rabbit pieces very lightly with flour;
return them to the skillet and cook the rabbit
pieces until brown on all sides.

Remove the loin pieces. Transfer the remaining
rabbit to a 3- or 4-quart casserole or baking dish;
sprinkle with the salt, if desired. Add the broth
and reserved marinade to the skillet; cook over
medium-high heat, stirring to loosen sticky brown
bits, until heated through; pour over the rabbit in
the casserole.

Cover the casserole tightly; bake in the oven
45 minutes. Add the loin pieces, pressing them
down into the liquid. Cover; bake 45 minutes longer.

Increase the heat to 400°F. Add the prunes,
stirring them gently into the liquid. Bake uncovered about 15 to 20 minutes, until rabbit is very
tender and prunes are puffed and juicy.

Skim the fat from the casserole. Sprinkle with
parsley and chives. Serve hot.

NOTE: Mature rabbits vary in size from 3 to 5
pounds. Some will be packed with hearts, kidneys, and livers. If these are available, remove
and refrigerate. When rabbit is done, sauté them
in ½ tablespoon peanut oil for about 2 minutes,
or until tender. Cut into thin strips. Sprinkle over
the rabbit stew.

Prunes with pits have a more pronounced flavor. The recipe was tested with moist-packed
prunes, which are quite soft and cook quickly. If
you have firm dried fruit, double the cooking
time.

NUTRITION INFORMATION: Cal: 435 Pro: 34g/
30% Carb: 46g/42% Fat: 14g/28% Chol: n/a
Sodium: 82mg Potassium: 1054mg Fiber: 5g A:
173% Vit C: 16% B2: 13% B3: 70% B6: 11% P:
35% Fe: 22% Cu: 17% Mn: 14% Cr: 42%
    EXCHANGE: Lean Meat: 4½ Veg: ¾ Fruit: 2¾
Fat: ½

Poached Pears

by *American Health*

4 ripe, medium pears
¼ cup orange-flavor liqueur
1 teaspoon grated lemon peel
½ teaspoon whole cloves
3 3-inch-long cinnamon sticks
    Fresh mint sprigs for garnish

PREPARATION TIME: 15 minutes
COOKING TIME: 35 minutes
YIELD: 4 servings

Peel the pears. With an apple corer, remove
the cores from the bottom, but do not remove
the stems. In a 10-inch skillet over medium-high

heat, bring the pears, ¹/₂ cup of water, and all remaining ingredients except the mint sprigs to a boil. Reduce the heat to low; cover, and simmer 30 minutes or until tender, turning occasionally.

To serve, discard the cinnamon sticks and cloves. Arrange each pear, stem-side up, in a wine glass or dessert dish; spoon some of the cooking liquid over each pear. Garnish each with a fresh mint sprig.

NUTRITION INFORMATION: Cal: 145 Pro: .7g/2% Carb: 30g/75% Fat: .7g/4% Alc: 19% Chol: 0mg Sodium: 2mg Potassium: 214mg Fiber: 4g C: 12% Cu: 10% Cr: 24%
EXCHANGE: Fruit: 2

MICROWAVE METHOD: In a microwave-safe casserole, cook the pears, placed on their sides with thicker ends toward the outside, only ¹/₄ cup water, and all remaining ingredients covered on High (100% power) 5 minutes. Turn and baste the pears. Cook, covered, on High until tender, about 2 to 6 minutes more (depending on ripeness). Serve as directed above.

Orange Compote

by Elizabeth Schneider

Sweet navel oranges and zesty blood oranges steeped in spicy juices taste both refreshing and exotic. Serve this quickly prepared winter fruit cup as a breakfast or brunch opener or to round out a multicourse dinner.

1 large juice orange (Valencia)
2 tablespoons orange blossom honey
1 medium cinnamon stick, broken in half
6 allspice berries
4 whole cloves
¹/₄ teaspoon anise seeds
¹/₄ cup golden raisins
 About ¹/₂ teaspoon orange flower water
2 medium navel oranges
2 large blood oranges, preferably the dark Moro variety (see Note)
2 tablespoons pistachio nuts, coarsely chopped, for garnish (see Note)

PREPARATION TIME: 20 minutes plus refrigerating time
COOKING TIME: 15 minutes
YIELD: 4 servings

Grate the rind from the Valencia orange. In a small, nonaluminum saucepan, combine the rind with ³/₄ cup water, the honey, cinnamon, allspice, cloves, anise, and raisins. Bring to a boil. Cover and simmer gently 10 minutes.

Remove from heat; uncover, then let cool to room temperature. Discard the cinnamon, allspice, and cloves. Squeeze the juice from the grated orange; pour it into a serving dish with the orange flower water to taste and spiced liquid.

Remove the peel and pith from the navel and blood oranges. Halve each lengthwise, then cut across into slim half-rounds. Add to the serving dish. Chill until serving time. Garnish with pistachio nuts.

NOTE: If blood oranges are not available, substitute navels. Pomegranate makes a bright and unusual alternative to pistachios, if you prefer; or use both.

NUTRITION INFORMATION: Cal: 170 Pro: 3g/6% Carb: 38g/82% Fat: 2g/11% Chol: 0mg Sodium: 4mg Potassium: 451mg Fiber: 5g C: 158% B1: 12% Folic: 14%
EXCHANGE: Fruit: 2¹/₂ Fat: ¹/₂

MICROWAVE METHOD: Grate the rind as above. In a 1-quart microwave-safe casserole or bowl cook the rind, ³/₄ cup water and next six ingredients on High (100% power) to boiling, about 2 to 3 minutes. Reduce power to Medium (50% power); cook 4 minutes more. Let cool to room temperature and continue as directed above.

Cidery Dried Fruit

by Mary Estella

Stewed fruits can top ice cream, be topped with granola or fill a pie. You can also add them to yogurt or puree them and add to a cookie or muffin mix. Or wrap with a bow to give as a gift.

1 pound of the following dried fruits in any
   combination: apricots, raisins, figs, peaches,
   and pears
3 cups apple cider
1/4 teaspoon ground nutmeg
1/4 teaspoon ground ginger
1/4 teaspoon ground allspice
1/4 teaspoon ground mace
   Pinch ground cloves
1 cinnamon stick
   Dash vanilla extract
   Juice of one lemon

PREPARATION TIME: 10 minutes
COOKING TIME: 10 minutes
YIELD: 4 to 5 cups or 8 to 10 servings

Fill a quart jar with the dried fruit, allowing
room for the fruit to swell. In a medium saucepan
bring the cider to a boil and add the remaining
ingredients. Pour the cider mixture over the dried
fruit in the jar. Cool, cover, and label. Keep refrigerated up to 2 weeks.

NUTRITION INFORMATION: Cal: 151   Pro: 2g/4%
Carb: 39g/94%   Fat: .4g/2%   Chol: 0mg   Sodium:
6mg   Potassium: 536mg   Fiber: 4g   A: 21%   C: 12%
Fe: 10%
EXCHANGE: Fruit: 2 1/2

Pears and Berries with Maple Raspberry Sauce

by Elizabeth Schneider

An unusual seasoning pair—maple syrup and
balsamic vinegar—add depth and finish to a simple raspberry puree.

2 cups raspberries
   About 3 tablespoons pure maple syrup
   About 1 1/2 teaspoons balsamic vinegar
1 1/2 tablespoons sweet vermouth
4 medium, very ripe, tender pears, such as
   Bartlett
1 cup blueberries or blackberries

PREPARATION TIME: 30 minutes plus standing
time
YIELD: 4 servings

Combine 1 1/2 cups of the raspberries, the maple
syrup, vinegar, and vermouth in a large nonaluminum dish. Crush together to a coarse mash.
Cover and let stand at least 1/2 hour.

Press the raspberry mixture through a fine
nonaluminum sieve, extracting every last bit of
the berry puree. Discard the seeds. Taste the
sauce and add a few drops of maple syrup and/
or vinegar to achieve a subtle, sweet-tart balance.

Peel and core the pears. Cut them lengthwise
into thin slices and arrange on four large plates.
Top with blueberries and remaining raspberries.
Spoon the sauce over the fruit. Serve at once.

NUTRITION INFORMATION: Cal: 200   Pro: 1g/3%
Carb: 49g/90%   Fat: 1g/5%   Alc: 2%   Chol: 0mg
Sodium: 30mg   Potassium: 336mg   Fiber: 11g
C: 44%   Cu: 16%   Mn: 24%   Cr: 24%
EXCHANGE: Fruit: 3

Pear-Applesauce

by American Health

1 1/2 pounds cooking apples, unpeeled, cored,
   and sliced
2 ripe medium pears, unpeeled, cored, and
   sliced
1/8 teaspoon ground cinnamon
   Dash ground cloves

PREPARATION TIME: 20 minutes
COOKING TIME: 20 minutes
YIELD: About 3 3/4 cups or 8 servings

Heat 1/2 cup water to boiling in a 4-quart saucepan. Add the apples, pears, cinnamon, and cloves
to the saucepan and bring to a boil over medium
heat. Reduce heat to low; cover and simmer 15
minutes or until fruits are tender, stirring occasionally.

In a food processor or a blender, process half
of the mixture until pureed; pour into a medium

bowl. Repeat with the remaining mixture. Serve warm or cover and refrigerate to serve chilled.

NUTRITION INFORMATION: Cal: 74 Pro: .3g/2% Carb: 19g/93% Fat: .5g/5% Chol: 0mg Sodium: 1mg Potassium: 149mg Fiber: 3g C: 11% EXCHANGE: Fruit: 1½

MICROWAVE METHOD: In a 2-quart microwave-safe casserole or bowl, cook only ¼ cup water and remaining ingredients on High (100% power) until fruit is tender, about 8 to 12 minutes; stir once. Puree and serve as directed above.

Cranberry-Applesauce

by Elizabeth Schneider

A stunning garnet color, this medium-smooth sauce is intended as an accompaniment to savory dishes. Its tart fruitiness suits turkey, chicken, roasted pork, lamb, and virtually all game. It is also good on top of baked winter squash or sweet potatoes.

1 large sweet-tart apple, such as Granny Smith
1 cup dry red wine
1 12-ounce package fresh cranberries, rinsed
    and picked over
    About ⅓ cup frozen apple juice concentrate
    (do not dilute)
    About 2 tablespoons brown sugar
⅛ teaspoon ground cardamom
⅛ teaspoon ground cinnamon

PREPARATION TIME: 20 minutes
COOKING TIME: 25 minutes
YIELD: 6 servings

Peel and core the apple, then slice it thin.

Combine the wine, ½ cup water, and the apple slices in a nonaluminum saucepan and bring to a boil. Cover and simmer until the apple slices are very tender, about 15 minutes. Add the cranberries, raise the heat to medium high, and bring to a boil, stirring. Boil gently about 3 minutes, stirring occasionally, until most of the cranberry skins have popped.

Press the mixture through the medium disk of

a food mill. Stir in the apple juice concentrate and brown sugar, adjusting the amounts to taste. Stir in the cardamom and cinnamon. Cool to room temperature, then cover.

Serve the sauce at room temperature or chilled, as desired.

NUTRITION INFORMATION: Cal: 100 Pro: .6g/2% Carb: 25g/93% Fat: .6g/5% Chol: 0mg Sodium: 29mg Potassium: 151mg Fiber: 3g C: 13% EXCHANGE: Fruit: 1¼ Fat: ½

MICROWAVE METHOD: In a 2-quart microwave-safe casserole or bowl, cook the wine, only ¼ cup water, and the apple slices tightly covered on High (100% power) 3 minutes. Add the cranberries. Cook tightly covered on High until cranberries pop, about 5 to 7 minutes. Press the mixture through a food mill and continue as directed above.

Baked Apples Plus

by Nao Hauser

Here is a basic method for baking apples plus two ways to embellish them. Bake as many as you want at a time; the oven time will be the same, and the baked apples will keep refrigerated up to 10 days.

Large sweet apples (Rome, Delicious, or other variety)
Cinnamon (optional)

PREPARATION TIME: 10 minutes for six apples
COOKING TIME: 45 to 60 minutes
YIELD: 1 apple per person

Preheat the oven to 350°F. Core the apples, leaving bottoms intact, and pare a ½-inch strip of skin from the top of each. Sprinkle the tops with cinnamon if desired. Place the apples in a shallow baking pan; add water to the pan to a depth of ½ inch. Bake uncovered until apples are tender when pierced with a knife tip, 45 to 60 minutes.

VARIATIONS:

♦ **Jam-filled apples:** Place 2 teaspoons no-sugar raspberry or apricot jam in the hollow of each apple before baking; proceed with the recipe.

♦ **Currant-filled apples:** For each apple, heat to simmering 1 tablespoon dried currants, 1 tablespoon port wine, and a pinch of cinnamon in a small saucepan; let stand to cool. Spoon the mixture into the apples before baking; proceed with the recipe.

NUTRITION INFORMATION: (per baked apple) Cal: 56 Pro: .3g/2% Carb: 14g/92% Fat: .4/6% Chol: 0mg Sodium: 1mg Potassium: 93mg Fiber: 2g
EXCHANGE: Fruit: 1

Banana Pops
by *American Health*

2 cups mashed bananas (about 3 bananas)
1 cup orange juice
2 tablespoons granulated sugar
1 teaspoon fresh lemon juice

PREPARATION TIME: 10 minutes plus freezing time
YIELD: 6 servings

In a medium bowl, combine ¼ cup water, the bananas, and all remaining ingredients, mixing well. Divide among 6 4-ounce paper cups. Freeze until firm. (If desired, add popsicle sticks or wooden spoons when somewhat firm.)

To serve, let stand at room temperature for a few minutes. To eat, peel the paper cup down from the pop.

NUTRITION INFORMATION: Cal: 102 Pro: 1g/4% Carb: 26g/93% Fat: .4g/3% Chol: 0mg Sodium: 1mg Potassium: 380mg Fiber: 2g C: 46% B6: 22%
EXCHANGE: Fruit: 1¾

Strawberry Frost
by *American Health*

½ cup nonfat dry-milk powder
2 tablespoons fresh lemon juice
¼ cup granulated sugar
1 pint fresh strawberries, hulled

PREPARATION TIME: 30 minutes plus freezing time
YIELD: About 2 cups or 4 servings

In a large bowl, stir together the milk powder, ½ cup cold water, the lemon juice, and sugar. Beat with an electric mixer at high speed about 10 to 15 minutes, until the consistency of whipped cream. Meanwhile, in a blender or food processor, process the strawberries until smooth. Fold the pureed strawberries into the milk mixture.

Freeze in the same bowl until the mixture is solid about 3 inches in from the sides of the bowl. Then beat with a electric mixer until smooth. Refreeze until firm.

NUTRITION INFORMATION: Cal: 100 Pro: 4g/13% Carb: 22g/84% Fat: .3g/3% Chol: 2mg Sodium: 48mg Potassium: 277mg Fiber: 2g C: 77% B2: 11% Ca: 12%
EXCHANGE: Skim Milk: ½ Fruit: 1

Cantaloupe Cooler
by *American Health*

1 medium cantaloupe, halved and seeded
2 tablespoons honey
2 tablespoons fresh lemon juice

PREPARATION TIME: 15 minutes plus freezing and standing time
YIELD: About 3 cups or 6 servings

Scoop out the cantaloupe in small pieces. In a covered blender at medium speed, blend the cantaloupe pieces, honey, and lemon juice until smooth. Pour the cantaloupe mixture into an 8-inch square baking pan. Cover and freeze.

Let stand at room temperature about 15 minutes, occasionally breaking up the mixture with a spoon. In a large bowl with an electric mixer at low speed, beat the mixture until mushy, about 3 to 5 minutes, scraping down the bowl with a rubber spatula. Serve immediately.

NUTRITION INFORMATION: Cal: 51 Pro: .7g/5% Carb: 13g/92% Fat: .2g/3% Chol: 0mg Sodium: 7mg Potassium: 256mg Fiber: .8g A: 52% C: 60%
EXCHANGE: Fruit: 1

◇ SUGARS AND SWEETENERS ◇

Sweet Reason

by Robert Barnett

"Only the dose makes the poison."
—Paracelsus (1493–1541)

Every day in America, millions of cups of sugar are poured into mixing bowls, mixed with flour and eggs and other ingredients, and baked into cookies, cakes, and pies. Millions more go into soda pop, over cereals, into coffee, and are added to a universe of processed foods, from ketchup to hams.

Why are we so sweet on sugar? An inborn evolutionary preference, scientists say. Even a day-old infant prefers sugar water to plain, finds taste researcher Gary K. Beauchamp of the Monell Chemical Senses Center in Philadelphia. Sweet tastes signal a safe source of calories, one that, before modern processing learned to take the sucrose from the beet and the cane, was generally nutritious as well.

So banishing sweetness from your diet probably goes against the grain. The trick, say nutritionists, is to moderate—and substitute. Cooking and baking with fruit and other natural sweeteners satisfies our sweet tooth and nourishes us with some vitamins and minerals. Dates give us iron and calcium, for example.

Nor is sugar itself a demon. It doesn't cause diabetes, heart disease, cancer, or criminal behavior, according to an FDA consensus report, and has "no unique role" in the etiology of obesity. "Sugar ingestion does not cause diabetes," says Dr. Ronald A. Arky, past president of the American Diabetes Association. "Obesity does. If sugar adds excess calories to the diet, and that results in obesity, the obesity increases the odds of becoming a diabetic."

A sweet tooth may actually be characteristic of a thin person's appetite. Thin women, reports Adam Drenowski of the University of Michigan, prefer sweet milkshakes with less fat. Fat women prefer milkshakes with less sugar, more butterfat.

Sugar's not entirely innocent, of course: Too much causes tooth decay, may make children jittery, and has little nutritional value. Sucrose, or table sugar, has no vitamins, no minerals, no fiber, no protein. Just calories. By crowding out more nutritious foods, a sweet may harm you indirectly.

Honey has a few more nutrients, but not in significant amounts. Fructose, a popular commercial sweetener, is less bad for the teeth than honey or sugar, but it actually interferes with our ability to absorb a crucial nutrient: copper. Most Americans don't get enough copper, and low levels of copper in the body can raise cholesterol.

Sugar consumption has been increasing for centuries. "Sugar in it Selfe be opening and cleansing, yet being much used produceth dangerous effects in the body" wrote James Hart in London in 1633, "as namely, the immoderate uses thereof, as also of sweetconfections, and Sugar-plummes . . . rotteth the teeth . . . and therefore let young People especially, beware how they meddle to much with it."

Spotlight: New Sweeteners, New Hungers?

If sugar is relatively benign, what are we doing pouring artificial sweeteners in our coffee? From cyclamates to saccharin to aspartame, every artificial sweetener on the market raises some health concerns. Nor is there any evidence that they (or, for that matter, fake fats such as Simplesse) help people control weight in the long run. Artificial sweeteners may even stimulate appetite, some studies find. Others do find that using them helps dieters consume fewer calories, and they can be helpful to diabetics. Only more research will confirm or deny weight-control claims and safety concerns. In the meantime, we'll sweeten our coffee with a little sugar. One packet: 16 calories.

—Robert Barnett

Today, young people are often shoo'd from sugar for fear of hyperactivity. But Markus Kruesi, a child psychiatrist at the National Institute of Mental Health, reviewed eight studies and found that large amounts of sugar have little or no effect on hyperactivity. But the possibility that children respond differently to sugar remains open. A new small study by Yale University pediatric professor William V. Tamborlane finds that children, but not adults, respond to a sugary morning sweet by producing more adrenaline. That can cause anxiety, crankiness, and a feeling of weakness.

Rather than overstimulating adults, sugar may actually calm. Pure carbohydrates can temporarily relax you, stimulating natural brain opiates, according to animal studies at Johns Hopkins University. Perhaps it's even an addictive taste. Refined sugars have certainly charmed their way into our diets. In Britain, consumption rose from 4 pounds per person in 1700 to 12 pounds in 1780 to 18 pounds in 1800 to 105 pounds in the 1970s, writes anthropologist Sidney W. Mintz of Johns Hopkins University in Baltimore.

In desserts, especially, sugar often keeps bad company: fat. Surely it's the butter in the cake and the palm oil in the candy bar that harm the body more than the sucrose. But perhaps the sucrose and the fat together are what's irresistible.

Americans now consume nearly 130 pounds of caloric sweeteners per person per year, up 3 pounds from 1978. These account for one fifth to one quarter of our calories. For most everyone except endurance athletes who need calories, that's too much.

If you do burn it up on the track, "sweetconfections and Sugar-plummes," as long as they're not made with fat, are a fairly harmless source of extra calories. Don't consume them in the half hour before you exercise, however. That stimulates insulin release, dropping your blood sugar and zapping your energy, explains physiologist Bill Fink of Ball State University in Muncie, Indiana. Once you start to exercise, insulin response is naturally dampened, so sugar during an event—especially glucose polymers that are easy to digest—can help provide energy.

Spotlight: Licorice

Glycyrrhizin, the active component of licorice, is 50 times sweeter than sugar. Structurally, it resembles a steroid. Confectioners mix true licorice with anise oil to make the candy we call licorice.

But licorice is a medicinal spice as well. In the test tube, it inhibits a number of viruses. In one human study, 9 out of 21 patients given glycyrrhizin in an intravenous solution showed an increase in interleukin, an immune substance. It may have anti-inflammatory properties as well. Licorice is often used as a folk remedy to treat colds and flu.

But it's not a good idea to eat much of it if you're concerned with blood pressure. Glycyrrhizin affects the liver much like the hormone aldosterone, stimulating water and sodium retention, causing blood levels of potassium to fall, raising blood pressure. If you have heart disease, avoid it.

—Jim Duke

Cooking with Natural Sweeteners

by Mary Estella

The sweet baking smells that delight children and adults alike don't have to disappear if your sugar bowl stands empty. A world of fruit and grain syrups adds flavor, minerals, texture, and sweetness when used in place of refined white sugar. Dried fruits, fruit-only preserves or jams, rice or barley malt, maple syrup, molasses, or granulated maple sugar can easily be substituted in your favorite recipes.

In the classic oatmeal cookie recipe on the back of the Quaker Oats box, for example, you can replace the half cup of sugar with one cup of dates simmered in ½ cup of orange juice. Mash the softened dates and combine with the remaining ingredients for a chewy, moist cookie. You'll get a bonus of some potassium and a little iron.

Dates make a versatile and easy-to-use sweetener. When they are a little dry from sitting for months in the back of your cupboard, dates can be quickly reconstituted in boiling juice or water flavored with vanilla and cinnamon or nutmeg (liquid should barely cover the dates), pureed and used to fill oat squares, to top cakes or yogurt, or to sweeten muffins and quick breads.

Apricots simmered in fruit juice with spices can be pureed for cake or pie fillings; figs or prunes, for Danish or strudel delight; raisins or currants, for oatmeal cookies. Dried apples soaked in cider overnight makes a sweet fruit pie.

A combination of dried fruits mixed in a jar and covered with boiling juice and spices soaks up flavor to make a chutney-like treat to savor alone, or to spoon over steaming breakfast cereal, cool yogurt, and granola.

Look for unsulfured dried fruits; once opened, store them in zip-lock baggies or jars in your refrigerator. They keep for months, ready to be diced up and added to grain dishes, curries, stuffings, or desserts. For a special treat look for dried cherries or cranberries (which are processed with a little sugar—but not much); they are wonderful stewed with pears or added to corn bread.

When you're looking for a liquid sweetener to replace sugar, use honey sparingly, as its strong flavor can dominate a dessert.

Maple syrup is excellent in cakes and cookies; you can usually cut back on the amount of sweetener when you substitute it for sugar in a recipe, and you may have to reduce the liquid ingredients. Grade A maple syrup is preferred for pouring over pancakes, while slightly thicker and less expensive grade B is fine for baking. Granulated maple sugar, now available in some natural foods and specialty stores, is perfect in fine pastries or delicate desserts or to sweeten meringues.

Spotlight: Vanilla's Charms

Mexican folklore looks to vanilla to help with childbirth; in Haiti, it's considered a treatment for syphilis. In Turkey, traditional texts call it an aphrodisiac, as well as a settler of stomachs. So does Egyptian folklore. Kernels of truth?

More like sweet nonsense. Unlike other herbs and foods, such as peppermint, or onions, there's really no scientific support for any of the widely disparate claims. But vanilla can still be a revelation—in the kitchen.

True vanilla, the seeds of the cured pod of a tropical orchid (or their distilled extract), add a fragrant, heavenly sweetness to custards (see Light Crème Brulée, page 313), puddings, milk drinks, and stewed stone fruits such as apricots, peaches, and plums. Artificial vanilla doesn't have the same richness.

Try dribbling a few drops of vanilla extract on fresh summer berries, or any fruit salad. Grind some vanilla pods with your fresh coffee beans, or let a pod infuse a cup of milk, and use that in your coffee or tea. If you fall in love with this natural sweetener, does that make it a culinary aphrodisiac?

—Robert Barnett

The "grain sweeteners" are great in desserts and breads. Dark, rich, and thick barley malt is similar to molasses in flavor and can be substituted for it in most recipes. While barley malt is a little too thick to sweeten cakes, it's perfect for pumpkin pies, whole grain breads, sweet and sour sauces, marinades, cookies and gooey pecan buns. Or simply drizzle a teaspoon over your oatmeal or toast.

Rice malt or rice syrup is a mildly sweet, golden ingredient in baking or cooking. Unlike maple syrup, rice syrup bakes up crunchy in cookies; and it adds a delicate sweetness to cornbreads, muffins, cakes, or pies. Rice malt is a little less sweet than honey, and has a light, almost lemony flavor. If the malt becomes thick during storage, place the jar in a hot water bath to soften.

Remember, there are no hard and fast rules when substituting sweeteners. All that's needed is an adventurous spirit. In most recipes, excepting those for delicate cakes, using less sweetener will simply result in a less sweet product. Using a sweetener other than sugar will imbue desserts with a new range of flavors. So it's quite likely that adjustments in your favorite recipes will yield sweet success.

Cranberry Bread

by *American Health*

> Vegetable cooking spray
> 2 large oranges
> 2 cups whole wheat flour
> 3/4 cup sugar
> 1 1/2 teaspoons double-acting baking powder
> 1/2 teaspoon baking soda
> 2 tablespoons vegetable oil
> 2 egg whites
> 1 1/2 cups fresh or frozen cranberries, coarsely chopped

PREPARATION TIME: 30 minutes
COOKING TIME: 60 to 70 minutes
YIELD: 1 loaf or 12 servings

Preheat the oven to 350°F. Coat an 8 1/2- by 4 1/2-inch loaf pan with cooking spray. Grate 1 tablespoon of rind and squeeze 3/4 cup juice from the oranges; set aside.

In a large bowl, use a fork to mix together the flour, sugar, baking powder, and baking soda. In a medium bowl, use a fork to beat together the oil, egg whites, and orange juice until blended; stir into the flour mixture just until flour is moistened. Gently stir in the cranberries and orange peel. Spoon the batter evenly into the loaf pan.

Bake until a toothpick inserted into the center of the bread comes out clean, 60 to 70 minutes. Cool the bread in the pan on a wire rack for 10 minutes; with a sharp knife loosen the bread from the sides of the pan, then remove the bread from the pan. Cool bread completely on wire rack before slicing.

NUTRITION INFORMATION: Cal: 142 Pro: 3g/9% Carb: 28g/76% Fat: 3g/15% (S:16% M:25% P:59%) Chol: 0mg Sodium: 82mg Potassium: 117mg Fiber: 3g C: 15% E: 13%
EXCHANGE: Bread: 1 Fruit: 1 Fat: 1/2

No-Sugar Apple Grape Jam

by Madelaine Bullwinkel

Apples and grapes are complementary fruits that hardly ever appear together. Without sugar, their flavors remain naturally tart, and the fresh, hot ginger root slices heighten the fruit tastes.

For best results, cook jams in a heavy pan with a nonreactive surface of coated aluminum, stainless steel, or ceramic. Sterilize empty jars in boiling water for 15 minutes. Vacuum-seal the jam-filled jars by submerging them in simmering water for 10 minutes. After they are sealed airtight, no-sugar jams may be stored safely at room temperature for several months. Refrigerate the jars after opening.

> 3 pounds MacIntosh apples
> 1 12-ounce can frozen unsweetened grape juice concentrate (undiluted)
> 2 slices fresh ginger, the size of a silver dollar

PREPARATION TIME: 30 minutes
COOKING TIME: 50 minutes
YIELD: 3 cups

Peel, core, quarter, and thinly slice the apples.

Combine all the ingredients with 1 cup of water in a heavy, nonaluminum 4-quart saucepan. Bring to a boil and simmer over low heat for 30 minutes or until the apples are soft and the juice is reduced enough to form a jamlike consistency.

Remove from heat. Remove the ginger and pour the jam into hot, sterilized jars to within 1/8 inch of the lips. Tap jars on the counter to force out air pockets in the jam. Wipe the rims clean, attach new lids, and screw the caps on tightly. Process in a boiling water bath, submerged by 1 inch, for 10 minutes.

NUTRITION INFORMATION (per 1 tablespoon): Cal: 21 Pro: .1g/2% Carb: 5g/94% Fat: .1g/4% Chol: 0mg Sodium: 1mg Potassium: 45mg Fiber: .8g
  EXCHANGE: Fruit: 1/4

MICROWAVE METHOD: In a 4-quart microwave-safe casserole or bowl cook only 1/2 cup water and other ingredients on High (100% power) until apples are soft and the juice forms a jamlike consistency, about 15 to 17 minutes; stir several times toward the end to break up the apples. Remove the ginger; fill jars as directed above.

Apricot-Oat Bread

by *American Health*

 Vegetable cooking spray
 1/2 cup raw oats
  1 cup whole wheat flour
 1/2 cup dried apricots, cut into fourths
 1/4 cup wheat germ
  3 tablespoons chopped almonds
  2 teaspoons double-acting baking powder
  1 teaspoon ground cinnamon
 1/2 teaspoon baking soda
 1/2 teaspoon salt
 3/4 cup skim milk
 1/2 cup honey

  3 tablespoons vegetable oil
 3/4 teaspoon vanilla extract
  1 egg, beaten slightly

PREPARATION TIME: 30 minutes
COOKING TIME: 50 minutes
YIELD: 1 loaf or 12 servings

Preheat the oven to 350°F. Coat an 8 1/2- by 4 1/2-inch loaf pan with cooking spray. Lightly flour the pan. In a blender at low speed, blend the oats to a coarse flour, stopping the blender occasionally to stir the oats.

In a large bowl, mix the oats and all the dry ingredients.

In a small bowl, mix the milk and the remaining ingredients. Stir into the flour mixture just until the flour is moistened. Pour the batter into the prepared pan. Bake 45 to 50 minutes, or until a toothpick inserted into the center comes out clean. Cool in pan on a wire rack for 10 minutes; remove from pan and cool completely on rack before slicing.

NUTRITION INFORMATION: Cal: 158 Pro: 4g/10% Carb: 26g/62% Fat: 5g/28% (S:16% M:33% P:51%) Chol: 17mg Sodium: 187mg Potassium: 191mg Fiber: 2g E: 21% P: 13%
  EXCHANGE: Bread: 3/4 Fruit: 1 Fat: 1

Fruit Crisp

by Evette Hackman

 Vegetable cooking spray
 1 very large or 2 medium apples
 1 cup sliced fresh strawberries or other berry
 1 cup diced rhubarb
 1/2 cup packed brown sugar
 2 tablespoons unsalted butter
 1 teaspoon vanilla extract
 1 cup quick rolled oats
 3 tablespoons cornmeal
 1/2 teaspoon ground cardamom
 1/2 teaspoon ground cinnamon

PREPARATION TIME: 30 minutes
COOKING TIME: 25 minutes
YIELD: 6 servings

Preheat the oven to 350°F. Coat a 9-inch square baking pan with cooking spray. Peel, core, quarter, and thinly slice the apples. Combine the fruits in the pan. Sprinkle half the brown sugar over the top.

Melt the butter; stir in the vanilla extract and remaining brown sugar. In a small bowl, combine the oats, cornmeal, and spices; stir in the butter mixture. Sprinkle the mixture evenly over the fruit. Bake 25 minutes.

VARIATION: Use ³/₄ cup quick oats plus ¹/₄ cup ArrowHead Mills pancake mix instead of 1 cup oats and 3 tablespoons cornmeal.

NUTRITION INFORMATION: Cal: 227   Pro: 3g/5%
Carb: 43g/73%   Fat: 6g/21%   (S:63%   M:30%   P:7%)
Chol: 11mg   Sodium: 5mg   Potassium: 250mg
Fiber: 4g   C: 30%
EXCHANGE: Bread: 1   Fruit: 2   Fat: 1

Blackberry Cobbler

by Evette Hackman

Vegetable cooking spray
6 cups blackberries
¹/₂ cup packed brown sugar
2 tablespoons fresh lemon juice
2 tablespoons dry tapioca
¹/₄ cup unsalted butter
1¹/₂ cups quick rolled oats
1 teaspoon ground cinnamon
1 teaspoon vanilla extract

PREPARATION TIME: 15 minutes
COOKING TIME: 25 minutes
YIELD: 10 servings

Preheat the oven to 350°F. Coat an 11³/₄- by 7¹/₂-inch baking pan with cooking spray. Put in the berries and half the sugar. Sprinkle with the lemon juice and tapioca. Let stand 15 minutes.

Melt the butter. Pour the butter into a medium bowl and stir in the remaining sugar, the oats, cinnamon, and vanilla extract. Mix well. Sprinkle evenly over the blackberries. Bake for 25 minutes.

NUTRITION INFORMATION: Cal: 195   Pro: 3g/6%
Carb: 34g/67%   Fat: 6g/27%   (S:64%   M: 31%   P: 5%)
Chol: 13 mg   Sodium: 4mg   Potassium: 266mg
Fiber: 7g   C: 33%   Mg: 10%   Mn: 32%
EXCHANGE: Bread: 1   Fruit: 1   Fat: 1¹/₄

MICROWAVE METHOD: In a deep, 10-inch round microwave-safe pie plate or dish mix together the berries, ¹/₄ cup sugar, lemon juice, and tapioca; let stand 15 minutes. In a small microwave-safe bowl, cook the butter on High (100% power) until melted, about 45 to 60 seconds. Stir in the remaining sugar, oats, cinnamon, and vanilla extract. Sprinkle over the berries. Cook, uncovered, on High until bubbly, about 6 to 8 minutes. Let stand 15 minutes.

Carrot Cake

by Jenny Matthau

Vegetable cooking spray
1¹/₂ cups oat flour
1 cup whole wheat pastry flour
1 teaspoon salt
1 tablespoon baking powder
2 teaspoons ground cinnamon
2 eggs, beaten
1¹/₄ cups maple syrup
¹/₂ cup cold-pressed safflower oil
2 teaspoons vanilla extract
3 cups grated carrots
¹/₂ cup walnuts (optional)

PREPARATION TIME: 30 minutes
COOKING TIME: 50 to 60 minutes
YIELD: 16 servings

Preheat the oven to 350°F. Coat a 9- by 13-inch pan with cooking spray and lightly flour it.

In a large bowl, combine the dry ingredients. Set aside.

In a separate bowl, whisk together the eggs, syrup, oil, and vanilla extract. Combine with the flour mixture, using a wooden spoon. Add the carrots and walnuts if desired.

Pour the batter into the prepared pan and bake 50 to 60 minutes, or until a toothpick comes out clean when inserted into the center of the cake. Allow to cool for 10 minutes before turning cake out of pan.

NUTRITION INFORMATION: Cal: 217   Pro: 3g/6% Carb: 35g/62%   Fat: 8g/32%   (S:12%   M:16% P:72%)   Chol: 26mg   Sodium: 245mg   Potassium: 134mg   Fiber: 2g   A: 117%   E: 16%   P: 10%   Fe: 10%   Cu: 10%
EXCHANGE: Bread: 1   Veg: 1/4   Fruit: 1   Fat: 1 1/4

MICROWAVE METHOD: Prepare the batter as directed above. Pour into a 10- to 12-cup microwave-safe Bundt pan coated with vegetable cooking spray. Place the pan on an inverted saucer or cereal bowl in the microwave oven. Cook on Medium (50% power) 9 minutes. Increase power to High (100% power); cook until cake tests done, about 6 to 8 minutes. Let cake stand on counter 15 minutes. Turn out and cool completely.

Poppy Seed Cake

by Jenny Matthau

Vegetable cooking spray
2 cups whole wheat pastry flour
4 teaspoons baking powder
    Pinch salt
2 tablespoons plus 1 teaspoon poppy seeds
2 eggs
1/4 cup cold-pressed safflower oil
3/4 cup maple syrup
1 6- to 8-ounce package soy milk
2 teaspoons vanilla extract

PREPARATION TIME: 20 minutes
COOKING TIME: 40 to 50 minutes
YIELD: 1 loaf or 12 servings

Preheat oven to 350°F.
Coat a loaf pan with cooking spray and lightly flour.
In a large bowl, combine the flour, baking powder, salt, and poppy seeds. Set aside.
In a small bowl, beat the eggs and whisk in the oil, maple syrup, 6 ounces soy milk, and vanilla

extract. Blend into the flour mixture. Stir in additional soy milk or skim milk if needed for a pourable consistency.
Pour the batter into the prepared loaf pan and bake 40 to 50 minutes or until light brown.

NUTRITION INFORMATION: Cal: 194   Pro: 4g/9% Carb: 30g/61%   Fat: 7g/31%   (S:15%   M:19% P:66%)   Chol: 36mg   Sodium: 207mg   Potassium: 115mg   Fiber: 3g   E: 15%   P: 14%   Fe: 11%
EXCHANGE: Med. Meat: 1/4   Bread: 1   Fruit: 1 Fat: 1

Banana Bread

by Jenny Matthau

Vegetable cooking spray
1/4 cup cold-pressed safflower oil
1/2 cup maple syrup
1 teaspoon vanilla extract
2 eggs, beaten
1 cup mashed bananas
1 cup whole wheat pastry flour
1 cup oat flour
2 1/2 teaspoons baking powder
1/2 teaspoon salt
1/2 cup walnuts, chopped (optional)

PREPARATION TIME: 30 minutes
COOKING TIME: 60 to 70 minutes
YIELD: 1 loaf or 12 servings

Preheat oven to 350°F. Coat a 9- × 5-inch loaf pan with cooking spray.
In a medium bowl, combine the oil, syrup, and vanilla extract and whisk until very well blended. Add the eggs, stirring well. Whisk the bananas into the mixture.
Sift together all the dry ingredients except the walnuts. Pour the egg mixture into the flours and mix thoroughly. Stir in the walnuts if desired.
Pour the batter into the prepared loaf pan and bake for 60 to 70 minutes, or until golden brown and a toothpick inserted into the center of the loaf comes out clean.

NUTRITION INFORMATION: Cal: 173 Pro: 4g/8%
Carb: 28g/62% Fat: 6g/30% (S:15% M:18%
P:67%) Chol: 36mg Sodium: 187mg Potassium:
133mg Fiber: 2g E: 12% P: 10%
  EXCHANGE: Med. Meat: ¼ Bread: 1 Fruit: ¾
Fat: 1

Light Crème Brulée

by *American Health*

Serve with fruit.

  2 tablespoons sugar
  1 tablespoon cornstarch
    Dash salt
1½ cups skim milk
  1 egg yolk
  ½ teaspoon vanilla extract
  1 tablespoon dark brown sugar

PREPARATION TIME: 15 minutes plus
refrigerating time
COOKING TIME: 10 minutes
YIELD: 6 servings

In a heavy 2-quart saucepan, combine the
sugar, cornstarch, and salt; gradually stir in the
milk and egg yolk. Cook over medium-low heat,
stirring, until the mixture boils; continue boiling
1 minute. Stir in the vanilla extract.

Spoon the mixture into a 2-cup serving dish;
sprinkle the top with the brown sugar. Refrigerate until chilled, about 4 hours.

NUTRITION INFORMATION: Cal: 60 Pro: 3g/17%
Carb: 10g/68% Fat: 1g/15% (S:40% M:46%
P:14%) Chol: 36mg Sodium: 98mg Potassium:
112mg Fiber: 0g
  EXCHANGE: Skim milk: ¼ Fruit: ½

MICROWAVE METHOD: In a 2-quart microwave-
safe casserole or bowl, combine the sugar, cornstarch, and salt, then stir in the milk. Cook on
High (100% power) until slightly thickened, about
4 to 6 minutes. In a small bowl beat together the

egg yolk and ½ cup of the hot milk mixture. Stir
back into the remaining milk mixture. Cook on
High until thickened, about 2 to 4 minutes; stir
every minute. Stir in the vanilla extract and continue as directed above.

Chocolate Meringue Drops

by *American Health*

  2 egg whites, at room temperature
  ¼ teaspoon cream of tartar
  ⅛ teaspoon salt
  ⅔ cup sugar
  2 tablespoons unsweetened cocoa powder
  ¾ teaspoon almond extract
  2 tablespoons semisweet chocolate mini-pieces

PREPARATION TIME: 30 minutes
COOKING TIME: 1 hour 15 minutes
YIELD: About 2 dozen cookies

Preheat oven to 200°F. Line 2 large cookie
sheets with foil. In a small bowl and using a mixer
at high speed, beat the egg whites, cream of tartar, and salt until soft peaks form. Beating at high
speed, gradually beat in the sugar, 2 tablespoons
at a time, beating well after each addition. Add
the cocoa and almond extract and continue beating until meringue stands in stiff, glossy peaks.

Drop the mixture by level tablespoonfuls onto
cookie sheets. Sprinkle some chocolate pieces on
top of each cookie.

Bake 1 hour and 15 minutes or until set. Cool
on cookie sheets on wire racks 10 minutes. With
a metal spatula, carefully loosen and remove
cookies from the foil; cool completely on wire
racks. Store in tightly covered container.

NUTRITION INFORMATION (per 2-cookie serving):
Cal: 57 Pro: 1g/6% Carb: 13g/79% Fat: 1g/15%
(S:78% M:20% P:2%) Chol: 0mg Sodium: 27mg
Potassium: 41mg Fiber: .1g Se: 57%
  EXCHANGE: Fruit: 1

◇ BEVERAGES ◇

A Good Drink: Beverages

by Robert Barnett

*I made a snowman and my brother knocked it
down and I knocked my brother down and then
we had tea.*

—Dylan Thomas, in
A Child's Christmas in Wales

Why do human beings drink beverages? To
quench thirst, to be sure, but also to satisfy taste,
to be nourished, to be entertained, to get drunk,
to stay alert, to calm down, to cool off, to get
warm, to soothe a sore throat. Perhaps most important, to share a social moment.

Our bodies are simpler. Our bodies primarily
need one thing from beverages: water. Every cell
in our bodies contains water—an aqueous stock
that needs to be replenished daily. Water is what
we mainly get from beverages, from seltzer to
soda pop.

Even alcoholic and caffeinated beverages are
mostly water, but we don't necessarily drink them
to quench thirst. Nor could we: caffeine has a diuretic effect. So does alcohol; it interferes with
the "antidiuretic hormone," stimulating urination.

What, then, are these beverages? They're legal,
liquid, socially acceptable drugs. That makes their
role in our lives a little more complicated than,
say, that of apples.

Quenchers

If you're thirsty, water is the best quencher. It's
the most dramatically essential of human nutrients. A man or a woman can survive weeks
without food but not more than 10 days without
water. It's the main component of blood that carries oxygen-rich hemoglobin to muscles and organs. It's the medium of urine that carries wastes
from the body.

Take in too little water and blood becomes
thicker and harder to pump—a strain on the heart.
We may get constipated; water is what softens
stools. It also lubricates joints and facilitates perspiration, a major regulator of body temperature.

The average healthy adult requires $2\frac{1}{2}$ to 3
quarts of water per day. The more muscle you
have, the more water you need: Muscle is 72 percent water; body fat only 20 to 25 percent. Men,
being leaner, have more body water than women.
If you're sick with a high fever, or lose a quantity
of blood, or sunbathe for hours on end, you will
lose more.

During prolonged exercise, especially outdoors
in hot weather, you can lose up to 2 quarts of
water per hour. Performance lags and fatigue en-
sues at 5 percent body weight loss, and if dehydration becomes severe enough, heat exhaustion
may occur.

"A hardworking male can easily sweat off eight
eight-ounce glasses of water in a ten-mile race on
a summer day," says Boston sports nutritionist
Nancy Clark, R.D. "Most athletes pay too much

314

attention to the food they eat, when what they really need is liquids."

One good way to tell if you're dehydrated is to weigh yourself before and after workouts. A pint of sweat weighs a pound. So if you've "worked off" a pound, you've lost about two eight-ounce glasses of water. Another good way: Monitor your urine. "In active people, urine should be clear and in significant amounts," says Clark.

Don't rely on thirst: You can lose up to 1 percent of your body weight before the kidneys, sensing dehydration, kick in the thirst mechanism. In the elderly and the young in particular, thirst is an inadequate guide.

To combat dehydration, drink and then drink some more. Be sure you are well hydrated before a competitive exercise event by drinking at least 8 8-ounce glasses of fluid a day in advance. Ten to fifteen minutes before exercising, drink at least 2 to 4 glasses (16 to 32 ounces) of water.

Eight glasses a day of water is a good guide for everyone. It's two quarts. Fruit juice, milk, sodas, even beer gives us water, as do vegetables and, particularly, fruits.

Water itself comes in many varieties: tap, mineral, spring, carbonated, noncarbonated, distilled. In many parts of the country, tap water is a perfectly safe, and certainly inexpensive, way to quench thirst. But water pollution, from groundwater contamination by pesticides or salt or from lead in the pipes themselves, is a problem in many communities.

Lead is a great concern. Newer studies have demonstrated that even fairly low levels of lead can impair the learning ability of children. In 1988, the EPA lowered the acceptable standard for lead in water supplies. But often the lead doesn't come from the source of the water, but from the pipes in the house. It's always a good idea to use cold water for both cold drinks and for cooking, and to let the water run cold from the tap for at least three minutes before using it. In a single-family home, that minimizes any lead, which builds up in water standing in the pipes; it may also be helpful in apartments.

It's also a good idea to have your water tested. A number of labs will do a battery of tests on a home water supply for a reasonable fee. Says Gene Rosov, president of the Watertest Corpora-

tion in Manchester, New Hampshire, "A test for bacteria, nitrates, chloride, fluoride, pH, hardness, iron, manganese, sodium, lead, and copper will cover the essential items."

If you suspect that your water supply is near a hazardous waste dumpsite, advises Rosov, ask the lab to test for volatile chemicals; if pesticide runoff is a problem in your area, get the name of area pesticides from your county agricultural agent and test for those; if you're in a radon area, test for radon. To find a list of labs near you, write to the American Council of Independent Laboratories, Inc., 1725 K Street, N.W., Washington, D.C., 20006. You may also want to call your public health department for their tests on the community water.

On the plus side, your tap water may contain some beneficial elements. In regions where water is naturally hard—rich in minerals such as calcium and magnesium—cardiovascular disease is less common. Calcium, some studies show, can help lower high blood pressure in some people. A magnesium deficiency has also been associated with high blood pressure, both in animals and in humans. Both minerals are essential for strong bones; neither is present in adequate amounts in the American diet. So if your water is hard, you may not want to get it softened. (Most tap water in the U.S. also contains added fluoride, to prevent cavities. There has been some concern that fluoride may add to cancer risk, based on animal studies, but a major review of fifty human population studies by the federal Public Health Service in 1991 found no evidence of any cancer risk in humans.)

If you're concerned about pollution, bottled water offers an alternative. There are many kinds. Spring water rises naturally to the earth's surface from an underground aquifer (reservoir); it can be naturally carbonated or still. To be deemed natural it cannot contain any added minerals or be artificially injected with carbonation, though it may be filtered.

By FDA standards, club soda or soda water is nothing more than carbonated tap water that is unflavored and unsweetened. Like all sodas, including colas, the water used in club soda is carefully filtered to remove any possible unwanted tastes, so it may be safer than some tap waters.

Seltzer is similar to club soda, noncaloric and unsweetened, but it is generally much lower in sodium content, as well as other minerals. Flavored seltzer with hints of lemon, lime, or orange is also unsweetened and low sodium; however, some drinks calling themselves seltzer may be sweetened with high fructose corn syrup. In that case, they're really sodas, with all the calories; check labels.

Then there are the true mineral waters. A mineral water is usually a spring water, but many spring waters are actually low in minerals to speak of. Mineral waters have been popular in Europe for many years, primarily for the purported health benefits of the minerals—such as magnesium or calcium—they contain. In the United States, mineral waters have become popular primarily as a noncaloric substitute for alcohol or soda pop.

But new research indicates that mineral waters can supply one essential class of nutrients: minerals! Some mineral waters yield as much as 200 to 400 milligrams of calcium per quart, for example, plus many other minerals. That's 25 to 50 percent of the adult requirement of 800 milligrams. Check labels. It's well absorbed, too. Research at the University of California at Davis reveals that magnesium and calcium in mineral waters is absorbed very efficiently.

Fruit Juice

We get nutrients from many beverages: fruit juice, milk, some herbal teas, even soda. Fruit juice is one of the best beverage choices. Pure fruit juice is almost entirely water. It is a rich source of potassium. Like potassium-rich broth, fruit juice gives flu sufferers both the fluids and the potassium they need to restore themselves.

According to nutritionist Nancy Clark, the three most nutritious common juices are tomato, orange, and grapefruit. Each is a good source of vitamin C. Some fruit juices, such as apple or grape, have more sugar and fewer nutrients. But any pure fruit juice is preferable to soft drinks, which have little or no potassium, usually more sugar, and few nutrients or none.

Fruit *drinks* are sometimes sweetened with corn syrup, however, which can make them as sugar-laden and caloric as soda pop. So read labels. Unlike whole fruit, fruit juice has little or no fiber, and some can be high enough in natural sugar that diabetics need to restrict excess consumption.

One way to get more water, fewer calories and less sugar is to stretch fruit juice with seltzer or mineral waters. Fruit itself, whether it's an orange or a mango, can quench thirst with less concentrated sugar and more fiber than fruit juice. So eat a peach. Still thirsty? Chase it with water!

Soda Pop and a Girl's Bones

Soda, of course, is the worst nutritional choice, offering little other than calories, sugar, water, and phosphorus. Diet sodas give us water, phosphorus, and artificial sweeteners. Both often are spiked with caffeine, which makes us thirstier. (For more sodas, perhaps?)

Not that one Coke is going to hurt you. A regular soda has 150 calories and about a quarter cup (nearly ten teaspoons) of sugar. "If you're a thirsty athlete who's burned off four thousand calories, that's no big deal," says Clark. "There's nothing wrong with diet soda, either; it's when you drink quarts instead of food. I do get concerned about teenagers who eat hardly anything and just drink regular or diet sodas."

For teenagers, there's increasing evidence that sodas are edging out milk. The timing is terrible: In the late teens and early twenties, a young woman's body has a unique ability to build bone mass from extra dietary calcium. After menopause, women often start to lose bone and draw down the calcium stores built up in early years. (For more on calcium and bone strength, see Milk and Yogurt, p. 00.) In one large USDA survey that included 4,455 teenagers, boys and girls who drank more soda consumed significantly less calcium, riboflavin, vitamin A, and magnesium—all nutrients supplied in abundance by milk. They also consumed more calories, fat, and iron, which may reflect the burgers that often go with the sodas. Teenagers, concludes the researcher, nutrition analyst Patricia M. Guenther, "may be substituting soft drinks for milk at meals."

The Mild Drugs of Daily Life

Wine is the most healthful and most hygienic of beverages.

—French scientist Louis Pasteur

If war claims victims, certainly alcohol claims more.

—French Proverb

Quenching thirst doesn't fully explain why we drink beer or wine or vodka, or coffee, or tea, or herbal teas. Quenching may be part of it, but each of those has a pharmacological action. They're liquid drugs. Caffeinated coffee is our society's primary legal stimulant; alcohol our primary legal depressant. Herbal teas often have proven pharmacologic actions, some therapeutic, some mood enhancing. From gin to ginseng, we drink them to feel better.

There's nothing intrinsically wrong with that, but there's nothing free in this world. Any chemical that affects the body as a drug exacts a price. For most people, a glass or two of wine or beer, a cup or three of coffee, a pot of tea or of most herbal teas does no harm, and may do some good. You just have to know what you're getting.

Alcohol "I have lived temperately, eating little animal food," wrote Thomas Jefferson. "I double, however, the doctor's glass and a half of wine and even treble it with a friend!" Even today, many doctors would give the same prescription.

Alcohol is the ultimate case for moderation. A glass or two a day of wine or beer or a mixed drink may relax, benefit the cardiovascular system, aid conviviality, and prolong life. That kind of information gives new meaning to the international toast: "to your health." Some drinkers, however, become addicts; we call them alcoholics. Some binge. Others drink three or four drinks steadily every day. That does damage; over time, it can kill.

"At three or more drinks a day, you don't see adverse coronary effects, but you do see increases in blood pressure, in cirrhosis of the liver, in throat cancer, in accidents, in hospitalizations, and in mortality," says cardiologist Arthur L. Klatsky, chief of cardiology at Kaiser Permanente Medical Center in Oakland, Califor-

nia. For men with high blood pressure, for example, going from three drinks a day to none for one week may lower pressure. Heavy drinking also blocks good nutrition: It interferes with absorption of the vitamins C, B-1, B-2, and folic acid; impairs vitamin D metabolism and thereby calcium and phosphorus; increases urinary loss of zinc; ups the body's requirement for B vitamins and magnesium.

Or it may kill quickly. Half the car fatalities, half the homicides, a third of the suicides, as many as two thirds the drownings in teenagers and adults and a quarter of the burns, fires, and falls in this country involve alcohol, says epidemiologist Mary Dufour of the National Institute on Alcohol Abuse and Alcoholism. Young people aged 16 to 24 account for over a third of all alcohol-related deaths.

The two-drink limit, for people who can control their drinking, is clear from the evidence. But every rule invites exception. One is pregnancy: The Surgeon General advises that even one drink is too much when you're pregnant or even trying to get pregnant, though some obstetric researchers believe one drink is pretty safe. Alcohol consumption is associated with fetal abnormalities.

If you suffer from migraines, you're another exception. You needn't avoid all alcohol, but steer clear of cheap red wine. It triggers migraine, report researchers at Queen Charlotte's Hospital in London; vodka doesn't. The researchers suspect that certain flavonoids that inhibit an intestinal enzyme needed to break down toxic phenols in alcoholic beverages are the bad guys. Flavonoids are leached out of red wine as it ages. White wine has hardly any flavonoids. If you're sulfite sensitive, you may need to avoid all wines; it's difficult to know how much sulfite a particular wine, red or white, contains.

Other contaminants are less troublesome. Nitrosamines, potentially carcinogenic chemicals, were once a problem in beer, when sprouted barley was dried by direct firing. In recent years, the industry has responded to this health concern by changing to indirect heating of barley, making the nitrosamine problem pretty much a thing of the past. Urethane, which causes cancer in lab animals, is now being somewhat controlled as well, but beware of aged whiskey that was bottled before 1988; imported fruit-flavored brandies have the highest levels.

"Dark" liquor has been linked to increased throat cancer in at least one case-controlled study. Then there's breast cancer. One study at Harvard of more than 87,000 nurses found that more than one drink a day is associated with an increase in the chances of a woman's getting breast cancer. A National Cancer Institute study found this link even at 3 drinks per week. But a Centers for Disease Control Study of 6,655 women between 20 and 54 found no such relationship. A "meta-analysis" of 21 studies conducted by Harvard School of Public Health researcher Matthew P. Longnecker, M.D., reveals that two drinks a day or more is associated with increased breast cancer risk, but at one drink a day, the link is weak.

"If alcohol is a risk factor for breast cancer, it's a relatively modest one," says associate professor David Klurfeld, of the Wistar Institute in Philadelphia. Women at high risk for breast cancer may want to be especially careful, notes Klatsky.

The real story is far from understood: Quercein, a compound found in red wine, is currently being studied for its strong cancer-protective potential. "A woman should look at the role drinking plays in her life and make a decision," says Boston University epidemiologist Lynn Rosenberg. "There's a lot to be said for women not drinking heavily for general health and well-being."

When it comes to the cardiovascular system, the story is more clearly positive. A drink or two a day may protect the heart and even prolong life. In the Harvard nurses study mentioned previously, women who consumed 3 to 9 drinks a week had fewer heart attacks and strokes than women who didn't drink at all; the protection continued up to 15 drinks a week on average. Klatsky's ten-year Kaiser-Permanente study of over 2,000 persons found that those who drank two drinks or fewer had a lower mortality rate from heart disease than either heavy drinkers or nondrinkers. An American Cancer Society study of over 250,000 men found a similar effect. In part, this protective effect may be due to beneficial changes in the concentration of HDL (high-density lipoprotein), the "good" cholesterol, though the case is far from closed. Alcohol may

also affect blood clotting; one small French study found that red wine inhibited the tendency of blood to form artery-damaging clots, and also raised beneficial HDL cholesterol. White wine didn't inhibit blood-clotting tendencies; pure alcohol actually increased the likelihood of clots. Alcoholic beverages may benefit the heart simply by reducing psychological stress, as well. (Drinking more than two servings a day on a regular basis, however, may enlarge and weaken the heart.)

Moderate tippling may even make us nicer. Psychologist Claude Steele, now at the University of Michigan in Ann Arbor, has found that college students who had had a few drinks were more likely to help a friend with a tedious task than teetotalers. The mechanism, he postulates, is that alcohol reduces a person's ability to think about consequences—including those that might flow from helping a person in need. Nor will moderate drinking make us duller. Research professor Oscar Parsons of the University of Oklahoma's Center for Alcohol and Drug-Related Studies, reviewing a decade of studies, concluded that there's "no consistent evidence that two drinks a day causes cognitive deficits."

You'll get a few nutrients in beer and wine, too. Though alcohol itself is nutritionally worthless, these alcoholic beverages are low in sodium, and some are relatively high in potassium. Red wine adds a little iron to the list. Beer may help us better utilize copper, an essential nutrient. Home-made or traditionally processed beer and wine can be quite nutritious, retaining much of the protein, calcium, iron, and other nutrients that get distilled, filtered, and clarified out of commercial versions. In Germany, beer has long been called "liquid bread." Wine, which is nearly as acidic as stomach acid, also has a folk reputation for aiding digestion when drunk with a meal, though this has never been clinically demonstrated.

What alcohol won't do is quench thirst. It dehydrates. Alchemists may know how to turn water into wine, but our bodies, it seems, can't turn wine's alcohol into water. The water in an alcoholic beverage may counteract the dehydrating effect to a degree; that's why wine is more quenching than whiskey, beer more than wine, and our wine spritzers, which combine mineral waters or fruit juices, perhaps best of all.

As a diuretic, alcohol is a bad companion to exercise, especially in the summer, when we need to replace large quantities of water lost as perspiration. "Beer often comes along with sports activities," says Nancy Clark, R.D. "But if you're going to have a beer, have two or three glasses of water before and after your exercise, enjoy the natural high of exercise, and then have a beer with friends."

Friends may be the key word. Alcohol is a social drug. A glass of wine or two with dinner, or a beer after work, is one of life's pleasures. But as a drug, alcohol is easy to abuse. That's especially true for people with a genetic susceptibility to alcoholism; research at the University of California at Los Angeles and at the University of Texas finds that many alcoholics carry a specific gene not found in other people.

Women may also be somewhat more susceptible to the effects of alcohol; because they produce less of the enzyme that breaks alcohol down and because they generally weigh less, a single drink may affect a woman like two do a man. That research has been incorporated into the current USDA Dietary Guidelines for Healthy Americans, which advises an upper limit of one daily drink for women, two for men. For men and women, how one uses alcohol is the telling point. "How a person handles alcohol is important," says Klatsky. "It's unhealthy to use alcohol as a drug, as a sedative, a tranquilizer, or to drown one's troubles."

The Work Drug

Coffee should be black as Hell, strong as death, and sweet as love.

—Turkish proverb

In 1511, coffee was new to Islamic society and so controversial that it went on trial in Mecca. The charge: "Large amounts can cause . . . insomnia and melancholic anxiety." The defense countered that coffee "brings the drinker a sprightliness of spirit and sense of mental well-being." The anti-coffee side prevailed, but it was a Pyrrhic victory: Coffee was banned and burned but never really banished. A few years later, prohibition was lifted.

Both sides, we now know, were partly right. Like alcohol, caffeine is a mild drug. It's the dose that counts. One or two cups a day, a safe dose for nearly any adult who's not pregnant, can lift your mood and increases alertness. Five or six or seven cups may make you jittery and, possibly, be bad for your heart.

Coffee's mental lift has been evident since Kaldi, the Arab goatherder, as the story goes, saw his goats chew some and start dancing on their hind legs. Muslims would drink it to stay alert during long religious ceremonies. But it was only in the late 1980s that scientists, at Johns Hopkins Medical School and Sweden's Karolinska Institute, discovered how it works. Caffeine, it turns out, mimics adenosine, a brain chemical, so well that it binds to adenosine receptors. That is, it prevents adenosine from being effective. Adenosine normally blocks brain chemicals that boost alertness and lift mood, making us sleepy when we're tired. By blocking the blocker, caffeine helps those alertness chemicals stay around. As author Melvin Konner, M.D., notes, "Caffeine's usage as a folk remedy for mild depression is widespread."

Spotlight: Cooking with Alcohol

It's no longer safe to assume that all the brandy in your cherries jubilee goes up in a magnificent blaze. As much as 75 percent may stay in a dish cooked with alcohol, finds assistant food science professor Evelyn Augustin at Washington State University. She measured only 5 percent of the burgundy in a pot roast that simmered for two and a half hours, but scalloped oysters, made with dry sherry and baked in a 375°F oven for 25 minutes, retained 45 percent of its alcohol. Given the small amounts of alcoholic beverages used in most dishes, what's left on the dish isn't likely to make anybody tipsy. But recovering alcoholics, who need to avoid all spirits, may want to stay clear of certain dishes.

—Gillian Weiss

Spotlight: The Gestalt of Tea and Coffee

Like food, our beverages not only affect us, they reflect us. "I have a feeling that tea drinkers are different sorts of people than coffee drinkers," says Kaiser Permanente's Arthur Klatsky. "Tea drinking, for example, is not related to smoking, as coffee is. It's a gestalt."

Heavy coffee drinkers, finds Harvard University epidemiologist Alan Leviton, are more likely to smoke than are people who drink coffee more moderately. They tend to consume more fat and less fiber in their diets and are less likely to take vitamin and mineral supplements. People who drink a lot of coffee also tend to drink more alcohol as well. "Coffee drinkers also perceive their health as better," says Leviton. "They act as if they don't need to be concerned about their health."

A recent study of men in Scotland reveals a similar correlation in alcohol consumption, this time between teetotalers and light drinkers: "Low-intake drinkers . . . eat a healthier diet and smoke less than nondrinkers," was the finding.

Coffee drinkers themselves may vary from culture to culture. "In France, they did a big study of coffee use and blood pressure," recalls psychiatry professor David Shapiro of UCLA. "The study took place in Paris. They found that the more coffee Parisians drank the higher the blood pressure. In Italy, in a similar study, they found the exact opposite effect. The more coffee people drank, the lower blood pressure tended

to be." Shapiro doesn't think it has to do with the coffee at all. In the lab, regular coffee drinkers often experience a mild temporary blood pressure boost; noncoffee drinkers who drink coffee get a much bigger boost. But drinking coffee in a lab is a different experience from drinking it in the Piazza San Marco in Venice. "In Italy," says Shapiro, "there may be something in the social aspects of coffee drinking that's a contributing variable."

For tea, conviviality is the watchword, East and West. In China, tea is a social drink and is served as a token of friendship. The English have built an entire social institution around the serving of afternoon tea. In Japan, one of the "ways" of zen is the tea ceremony.

"In Japan, when you are invited into someone's house, tea is served—sometimes ceremonial tea, sometimes regular, but always tea is served. If I fail to serve you any tea, I feel very bad," says Hisashi Yamada, executive director of the Urasenke Tea Ceremony Society in New York City, where the Japanese tea ceremony is taught.

"Offering tea is social, a friendly peaceful time, and also a kind of meditation," says Mr. Yamada. "You concentrate yourself for the moment on what you are doing. Do not negate the little things, for the little things are not little things."

—Robert Barnett

Coffee may also benefit asthmatics. It opens up the bronchial passages. In Italy, a study of 72,284 men and women found that coffee drinkers had less asthma than nondrinkers. Those who drank three cups a day had less asthma than those who drank two cups or one cup a day; more than three cups a day yielded no further benefits. Three cups have a bronchodilator effect similar to a 200-milligram dose of the anti-asthma medicine theophyline, researchers calculate.

Too much coffee, however, may be bad for the

heart. "Coffee has been linked to many diseases, including pancreatic and breast cancer, but those links haven't been confirmed, nor is there sound evidence for benign (fibrocystic) breast disease," says Boston University's Lynn Rosenberg. The chief concern, she says, is coffee and heart disease: "The evidence is that really heavy coffee drinkers—those who drink five or more cups a day—have an increased risk of heart disease." In one study at Johns Hopkins Medical School in Baltimore, for example, men who drank an average of five cups of coffee a day had more than twice the chance of having a heart attack as non-drinkers.

The reasons are less clear. "The concern now is that coffee raises blood cholesterol," says Rosenberg. "Here again, the concern is for real heavy hitters, those who drink six, eight, ten cups a day." Though coffee can also raise blood pressure, she notes, regular java drinkers quickly become acclimatized, and the effect disappears.

The full story is still far from known. For example, it has widely been assumed that decaffeinated coffee is better for the heart. Without caffeine, it's not a cardiovascular stimulant. But drinking decaffeinated coffee may raise cholesterol, suggests a recent study by Assistant Professor of Medicine H. Robert Superko of the Lipid Research Clinic at Stanford University in Palo Alto, California. The study followed 180 healthy middle-aged male coffee drinkers over four months. Those who drank decaffeinated coffee showed a rise in LDL cholesterol, which raises heart disease risk; those who drank regular coffee had no such rise. A Dutch study found no significant change in blood cholesterol when individuals switched from caffeinated to decaffeinated coffee. One possibility: Decaffeinated coffee is usually made from strong robusta coffee beans rather than the milder arabica used in regular coffee. Robusta beans may contain higher concentrations of compounds that raise cholesterol.

Brewing technique makes a difference as well. Here the news is more reassuring. Boiled, or "campfire," coffee, popular in northern European countries—boiling water is poured over coffee grounds, then the liquid is decanted—raised blood cholesterol by 10 percent in healthy individuals, in one Dutch study. But filtered coffee has no effect on blood cholesterol. And whether it's electric drip or a filter cone, about 75 percent of the coffee Americans drink is filtered. One recent study identified a fat-like substance in coffee that may be partly responsible for raising cholesterol; filter-brew methods may remove it.

To Andrea LaCroix, an epidemiologist at the National Institute on Aging, who directed the Johns Hopkins study, the first step if you're concerned about heart disease isn't to quit drinking coffee. It's to stop smoking if you do, control high

blood pressure if you have it, and make sure your blood cholesterol level is in check. To further reduce risk, "consider drinking two cups a day or less," she says.

Pay attention to your own definition of "a cup," however. Technically, a cup is 5 ounces. If your "cup" is a mug, you could be drinking twice that amount, 10 ounces. The average "cup" of coffee is 6.7 ounces, according to a survey of 3,000 people in 20 cities, conducted by General Foods. The amount of caffeine in a given volume of coffee can vary wildly, too, from 50 to 150 milligrams of caffeine. On the East Coast, for example, coffee is twice as strong on average as it is in the West. Drink 4 weak 5-ounce cups of coffee, and you may only get 220 milligrams of caffeine, but down 4 10-ounce mugs of strong java and you could be pumping 1200 milligrams into your system. "I drink two cups of coffee a day," says LaCroix, "but it's so weak you can see through it."

For pregnant women, coffee is more of a concern. In one study of 3,135 women conducted at Yale University, as little as one cup of very strong coffee a day (three or four cups of weak coffee) can nearly double a pregnant woman's chances of spontaneous abortion. There may be a threshold, the authors speculate, of 150 milligrams of caffeine a day. The breast milk of coffee drinkers also tends to be lower in iron than is optimal. Caffeine itself is expressed into breast milk, yet infants have very little of the enzymes needed to metabolize it, so if you're breastfeeding, it's a good idea to limit coffee to a few sips, or a cup, a day. Your child may sleep better for it.

If you decide to quit drinking caffeinated coffee, be prepared to feel cranky for a few days. A Dutch study of 45 heavy coffee drinkers who quit found that 19 suffered headaches, starting a day or two later, and lasting for up to six days.

Cocoa

Chocolate is a rage, a craving, a soft pleasure center. Aztecs processed bitter cocoa beans into cocoa to make a spicy drink. Columbus introduced the beans to Europeans, who added sugar, making hot cocoa, and, later, added fat and sugar, making chocolate.

In one study of college women published in the *Journal of the American Dietetic Association,* the only food craving during their periods that could be isolated was for chocolate. Nobody is sure why chocolate elicits such passion. Chocolate does contain chemicals similar to brain chemicals associated with euphoria—phenylethylamine, dubbed "the molecules of love"—but careful study reveals a slim likelihood they even enter the bloodstream. In any case, cheese, hardly a love food, has higher levels. One plus for chocolate: Like Cheddar cheese and tea, it retards the plaque that causes cavities—although its high sugar content still makes it a dental risk. Researchers suspect chocolate's protective substance is similar to tannin.

The main nutritional problem with chocolate is that it's nearly pure fat. The fat is mostly saturated, which raises blood cholesterol. Recent research reveals that stearic acid, a saturated fatty acid found in chocolate (as well as in beef) actually lowers blood cholesterol, but chocolate has other saturated fats that do raise cholesterol. So it's not quite a health food, yet.

Cocoa is leaner. To make cocoa, the beans are fermented, dried, roasted, cracked; the germ or nib is then ground and reduced to a liquor. For cocoa, part of the fat, or cocoa butter, is removed. Cocoa powder may contain between 10 and 22 percent fat or more. It's got some nutrition, too: magnesium, phosphorus, and potassium. Cocoa is high in oxalic acid, which binds with calcium, so adding milk may not make it an effective calcium source. Like coffee, cocoa contains caffeine, but only about 5 to 10 milligrams a cup. It also contains small amounts of a weak stimulant similar to caffeine: theobromine.

When making hot chocolate, first put a small amount of cold liquid into the powder. Cocoa blends well with cold liquid and will dissolve better this way. Cocoa contains a fair amount of starch so it will lump if you put it directly into hot milk. Unlike coffee or tea, you should boil cocoa so you can cook the starch.

Healing Teas

Perhaps you're tired of caffeine entirely. Many mild herbal "teas," such as peppermint, camomile, and rose hip, are safe, delicious noncaffein-ated alternatives. Some herbal teas provide minerals and vitamins as well, though few good studies have been done on the amounts that actually get into the brew. Peppermint tea, for example, probably provides us with useful amounts of potassium.

USDA botanist James A. Duke rates herbal teas as either more or less toxic than coffee. Coffee gets a "2," that means two cups a day seems safe. Zero (0) is very toxic. One (1) is more toxic than coffee; Duke would "discourage all but the most cautious experimentation." Three (3) is safest. Three cups a day are reasonable. "Much more than three cups of anything," he writes, "would seem immoderate." We've used Duke's rating system here. Peppermint tea (3) contains menthol recognized by the FDA for colds and coughs and is reported to settle the stomach and sweeten the breath.

Many herbal teas are closer to drugs. Like drugs, many have side effects. Some have many more benefits than side effects, like good drugs.

Mint julep's too southern for me,
Mint jelly too northern, you see;
But it still makes good sense
To reduce flatulence
With a pleasant peppermint tea.

—Jim Duke

Perhaps you'd like a cup of ginseng tea (rating: 3). It contains biologically active compounds, called ginsenosides, that appear to stimulate the efficiency of the pituitary and adrenal glands. That is, it's a stimulant. Human studies suggest that ginseng might help us withstand physical stress. Nurses given ginseng scored higher on ratings of mood, competence, and performance; radio operators transmitted messages twice as accurately, and soldiers ran a three-kilometer race almost a minute faster. Like coffee, another herbal stimulant, too much may lead to nervousness and insomnia. In China, it's a tonic for the old, not the young, who may have enough adrenal hormones circulating already.

Maybe you have a cold. Echinacea (rating: 3), a native American herb extensively studied by German researchers, boosts immunity and fights viruses. It boosts the levels of invader/attacking

T-cells in human beings. It's passed German regulations as a safe over-the-counter herb. Hyssop tea (rating: 3) is another safe herb in the mint family; it contains ingredients that soothe mild throat irritations and loosen phlegm. Tea made from ginger (rating: 3) calms vertigo and motion sickness. Horehound (rating: 3) is also an expectorant (loosens phlegm), with a long folk tradition for that use; it contains marrubiin, which stimulates secretions of mucosa. Slippery elm (rating: 2) also contains ingredients that soothe throats. Tea made with linden flowers (rating: 2) promotes sweating, a useful effect in certain conditions, though frequent use may be bad for the heart. Ma Huang (rating: 1), or Ephedra, contains ephedrine and neopseudoephedrine, an effective decongestant. Indeed, synthetic pseudoephedrine is an ubiquitous active ingredient in over-the-counter decongestants; however, Ma Huang may raise blood pressure and cause nervousness. Lemon balm, also called Melissa (rating: 3), is loaded with antioxidants and makes a delicious tea with antiviral properties. A tea made from raspberry leaves (rating: 2), which contain astringent tannins, is a good gargle for a sore throat. Drunk as a cold tea, it's said to treat diarrhea effectively—another effect one would expect from tannins.

If you're constipated and go to the drug store for a laxative, you might get senna leaves (rating: 1). If you brew them as tea, drink no more than a half cup; it's a potent cathartic laxative, containing sennosides that act chiefly on the lower bowel, and habitual use can cause irritation of the colon.

If you have the opposite problem, diarrhea, plenty of good old tea is probably the best remedy; tannins in regular tea are effective in treating diarrhea. For best effect, brew it strong.

If you suffer from migraines, feverfew (rating: 3) might be your tea. A few leaves of feverfew taken every day for weeks tends to prevent migraine headaches, find researchers at the City of London Migraine Clinic. Migraineurs who had taken feverfew were given either the herb or a placebo; those who got the placebo got many more migraine headaches. The herb also has some anti-inflammatory properties and may help with arthritis, the researchers speculate. The plant contains sesquiterpene lactones, which reduce sensitivity to serotonin, a brain chemical associated with migraines.

Maybe your stomach is acting up, or you've got menstrual cramps. Camomile (rating: 3) might be your brew. A fragrant herbal tea made from the flowers of Roman or German varieties, camomile relaxes, calms the stomach, may protect against ulcers, and may help relieve menstrual cramps. The oil contains many chemicals, notably azulene and alpha-bisabolol, that have among other effects, anti-inflammatory and antispasmodic (anticramping) qualities. Some raise cautions of allergic potential of the pollen, but azulene is actually antiallergenic, which may explain why so few cases of allergic reactions have been reported for this ragweed cousin. One study finds that dandelion leaves and roots (rating: 3) are as safe and as effective a diuretic as the drug furosemide (Lasix).

Perhaps more serious health problems concern you. If you have heart disease or cancer, you need to be under the care of a physician. But a physician whose practice allows herbal approaches might know that hawthorn (rating: 1) has been shown to dilate blood vessels, lowering blood pressure and reducing the tendency to angina attacks. It may take a few weeks to gain its effect as a mild heart tonic; it contains cyanide compounds, so should be used with great discretion.

Your doctor may also know that Pau D'Arco (rating: 1), a Brazilian tree bark brewed into a tea to treat cancer, contains lapachol, a napthoquinone derivative that suppresses certain tumors in animal studies. (In humans, doses high enough to have therapeutic potential caused some nasty side effects.) Or that pepperbark (rating: 1), alias Winter's bark, contains taxifolin, an antitumor compound. The leaves have proven active against leukemia in lab studies. Poisonous Mayapple (rating: 0) stems and root, used by Penobscott Indians against cancer, contains podophyllotoxins and peltatins, effective in lab tests against certain cancers. It's so poisonous it's proven fatal: Amerindians once used the young shoots for suicide. In 1984, Bristol Meyers received FDA approval for a semisynthetic version of these compounds called etoposide to treat testicular cancer; in 1986, it was approved to treat lung cancer.

Maybe you just want to relax after a long,

stressful day. Valerian (rating: 2) tea, which tastes milder than the odiferous herb itself, has been used as a tranquilizing tea and treatment for anxiety for thousands of years. Recent studies have isolated a class of chemicals in the roots, dubbed valepotriates, that depress the central nervous system in animal and human studies with fewer side effects, in one study, than Valium. Catnip (rating: 3), the smell of which excites kitty—doesn't stimulate if eaten. It also acts as a sedative, probably due to the nepetalactones in the volatile oil, which resemble valepotriates. Sweeter tasting camomile is also a mild sedative.

A Nice Cup of Tea

How about a spot of tea? Black tea, green tea, oolong. It's botanical name is *Camellia sinensis.* It's the universal beverage, fairly benign with some unique benefits.

"The totality of evidence for tea is against any association with disease, especially heart disease," says epidemiologist Andrea LaCroix. "Whenever anyone looks at tea," says Kaiser Permanente's Arthur L. Klatsky, "it doesn't share coffee's association with heart attacks. The general perception is that tea is a healthy beverage." One of the few negative results: Tea drinking may worsen PMS symptoms, according to Oregon State University researchers, probably due to tea's caffeine.

Regular tea contains caffeine, but usually much less than coffee. Strong English tea brewed dark may have as much as 100 milligrams of caffeine, more than some cups of coffee, but a six-ounce cup of black tea steeped for three minutes will have only 36 milligrams.

Tea may even tranquilize. "We have some preliminary evidence that tea has a tranquilizing effect in animals," says psychiatry professor James P. Henry of Loma Linda University in California. The key, he believes, are certain flavonoids, compounds found in tea that may exert tranquilizing effects. If true, of course, caffeine and flavonoids will fight each other, and, indeed, Henry finds a stronger tranquilizing effect on animals with decaf tea. Chinese tea, he suggests, may be relaxing. "The Chinese will even throw away first brew

and pour new hot water into the pot," he says. "This may improve the flavonoids-to-caffeine ratio."

There's more evidence that tea may help prevent cavities. Many teas are a rich source of fluoride, which protects teeth; the tannins in tea also protect by binding to the bacteria that cause cavities. Studies of English school kids show that those who drink tea have fewer cavities than those who don't. One or two cups of tea daily cut tooth decay, and the more tea kids drank, the less decay they had. An average cup of tea may have more than three times as much fluoride as a cup of fluoridated water. Of course, if you drink tea all day long, your teeth will stain, so they'll look unhealthy.

Tea has other advantages. In animal studies, green tea inhibits tumors. Its tannins are antibacterial and antiviral; as noted above, they also treat diarrhea. It's easy to understand why a cup of tea is a folk treatment in our culture for stomach upset and flu. The down side, of course, is that tannins in excess can lead to constipation.

Both coffee and tea in excess can rob us of nutrients partly because of their phenolic compounds and caffeine. Coffee interferes with iron absorption and increases urinary excretion of calcium. Timing is important. Coffee is most likely to interfere with iron if you drink it with meals. Drink coffee an hour after dinner, or between meals, and it's less likely to fight with the iron on your plate.

Tea binds both calcium and iron, finds Lauren S. Jackson of the University of Wisconsin. Tea reduces the absorption of iron from foods when drunk before, during, even after a meal, she notes. What kind of tea makes a difference. "Black tea tends to bind more iron, green tea, more calcium," she says.

Milk or Lemon?

A little milk will improve the nutritional profile of coffee and tea. A cup stimulates the excretion of about 6 milligrams of calcium, finds professor of medicine Robert Heaney of Creighton University of Omaha, Nebraska. Population studies find that heavy coffee drinkers are at risk for osteoporosis. We only absorb about a quarter to a third of the calcium from the foods we eat, so to make up that 6 milligrams we need take in about 20 to 24 milligrams of calcium. But that's easy. "A couple of teaspoons of milk offsets it," says Heaney. You can even use your morning coffee as a way to boost calcium intake, he suggests. "Add five heaping teaspoons of nonfat dry milk," he suggests. That would boost absorbed calcium by 78 milligrams. Because it's caffeine that's largely to blame for calcium losses, decaf coffee—now almost universally decaffeinated using safe water processes instead of the mild carcinogen methyl chloride—is an even better choice. Try decaf café au lait made with skim milk.

Milk in coffee or tea also makes them easier on the stomach. In many ulcer patients, coffee and alcohol are irritants. "There's something in coffee that's capable of causing increased gastric secretion," explains physician Gene Grossman, scientific consultant to the National Coffee Association. "It's not caffeine; decaf can be just as bad. Put milk in coffee, though, and you'll counteract the effect." Milk behaves as a base and neutralizes the acids in coffee.

If you like tea with lemon, that's good, too. Put lemon in your tea and "both iron and calcium become more available," Jackson finds. The vitamin C makes the minerals more soluble and easier to absorb, she finds. Eating vitamin C-rich foods with tea may have the same effect.

Spotlight: Lemons and Steam

Perhaps the pleasure we get in sipping *café con leche,* or jasmine tea with lemon, is itself a health boon. If so, it's worth our while to pursue it. Thankfully, in this instance what nourishes the body also pleases the palate.

The very milk that puts calcium in our cup of coffee can also bring a taste of opulence, while the squeeze of lemon in the teapot complements taste as well as minerals.

When it comes to milk in coffee, there's a world of taste difference between a hasty splash from a refrigerated carton and a few ounces specially warmed for the brew. This is the difference tourists savor in Vienna, Paris, Madrid, Florence, and other locales where coffee accompanies leisure.

Americans may wisely adapt the custom to the microwave, which will scald a cup of milk in about two minutes on the high setting, and smaller amounts proportionately faster. Be sure to use an oversized container to microwave the milk (a large glass measuring cup, or heatproof pitcher will facilitate pouring), because the casein (milk protein) will cause it to bubble up. If you like instant coffee, microwave equal parts of lowfat milk and water to boiling in a large mug and then dissolve the coffee in the hot liquid.

But a stove top's slower pace has benefits, too. As skim or lowfat milk simmers, water evaporates and the milk tastes richer. Add another twist to the rite by boiling a whole vanilla bean or cinnamon stick in the milk to flavor it; a batch of flavored milk can be refrigerated and reheated as needed.

For cappuccino lovers, milk frothed with steam is the *ne plus ultra.* Most electric espresso makers have a nozzle designed to steam milk while the coffee brews. Even if you don't have an expresso maker, consider purchasing a nonelectric stove-top milk steamer. The steamed milk floats elegantly on the brew, and takes well to a sprinkling of freshly grated nutmeg, cinnamon, or shaved chocolate.

It's the strength of the coffee, not the brewing method, that matters most when using milk. When the French, for example, serve café au lait by pouring coffee and hot milk simultaneously into bowl-sized cups, the coffee may have been brewed in any of several ways; the drink will taste delicious regardless, because the flavor of the brew will be intense enough to stand up to the milk. To brew the most flavor into your pot, buy beans where you can be sure they are fresh, store them in the freezer, and grind only as much as you need just before brewing. Nonelectric filter pots generally yield better flavor than electric filter systems, because the coffee is infused more slowly.

Of Teas and Herbal Comforts Some aficionados remain devoted to "real" tea (black or green tea) while others are now enthusiastic about pure herbal teas. Both cults may be aghast at the suggestion of mixing the two. But if you treat tea as a comfort rather than a cause, you'll discover that mixing produces a cup of tea with the strong character of real tea, the scented flavors of the herbs, and usually less bitterness.

Half real tea and half herbal is a good ratio to start with, whether the tea is loose or in bags. You can allow the mixture to steep a little longer than you normally would with real tea, because there are, on average, fewer tannins in the pot. Try a scented black tea with an herbal tea of the same flavor, such as Constant Comment with an orange-spice herb tea. A fruity herb blend can enhance the most ordinary black tea.

A mixture of herbal tea and real tea also blends marvelously with citrus and other fruit juices. Because this trio is less bitter and more flowery than straight black tea, it may need no extra sweetness. Orange juice is a wonderful way to add both natural sugar and vitamin C to a tea mixture that features orange or another citric acid note, like lemon. Apple juice goes well with apple-spice blends, pineapple with mint, and apple-raspberry with rose hips or strawberry tea.

Use restraint, however, to avoid overwhelming the tea. Add a little honey with citrus flavors, or sugar with the others, if you wish. In all cases, a squeeze of fresh lemon (or even lime in minty teas) is at least as welcome in a mixture of tea and fruit juice as it is in a cup of straight tea.

—Nao Hauser

Double Apple-Cranberry Brew
by Marie Simmons

1 quart cranberry-apple juice
4 slices dried apple
1 tablespoon raisins
4 pods whole cardamom

PREPARATION TIME: 5 minutes
COOKING TIME: 25 minutes
YIELD: 4 servings

Combine all the ingredients in a medium saucepan. Heat to simmering; cover and simmer 20 minutes. Ladle into 4 mugs, distributing the apple slices and the raisins evenly.

NUTRITION INFORMATION: Cal: 196 Pro: .3g/1% Carb: 50g/98% Fat: .1g/1% Chol: 0mg Sodium: 21mg Potassium: 105mg Fiber: .2g C: 135%
EXCHANGE: Fruit: $3^1/_2$

Ginger Molasses Tea
by Marie Simmons

2 tablespoons chopped fresh ginger
$^1/_2$ to 1 tablespoon dark molasses
1 tablespoon fresh lemon juice

PREPARATION TIME: 10 minutes
COOKING TIME: 10 minutes
YIELD: 1 serving

In a small saucepan, simmer the ginger and 1 cup of water, covered, 10 minutes. Remove from heat. Strain into a mug; press on the solids to extract as much flavor as possible. Stir in molasses and lemon.

NUTRITION INFORMATION: Cal: 46 Pro: .3g/3% Carb: 11g/95% Fat: .1g/2% Chol: 0mg Sodium: 15mg Potassium: 508mg Fiber: .1g C: 13%
EXCHANGE: Veg: $^1/_4$ Fruit: $^1/_2$

Fresh Hot Tomato Juice with Horseradish

by Marie Simmons

2 pounds ripe juicy tomatoes, quartered
1 thick slice onion
1 leafy celery top
1 sprig fresh basil
1 tablespoon horseradish, or to taste
4 whole scallions, trimmed
4 strips orange rind

PREPARATION TIME: 10 minutes
COOKING TIME: 15 minutes
YIELD: 4 servings

Combine the tomatoes, onion, celery, basil, and 2 cups of water in a medium saucepan. Heat to boiling; cover and simmer 10 minutes. Puree the mixture through a food mill; discard the skins and seeds. Stir in the horseradish. Pour evenly into 4 mugs and garnish each with a scallion to use as a swizzle stick and to nibble on while sipping juice. Twist orange rind, to release flavorful oils, into each mug.

NUTRITION INFORMATION: Cal: 44   Pro: 2g/16%
Carb: 10g/77%   Fat: .5g/7%   Chol: 0mg   Sodium:
61mg   Potassium: 464mg   Fiber: 3g   A: 52%   C: 66%
Cr: 40%
EXCHANGE: Veg: 2

Iced Ginger Lemon Tea

by Susan Feniger and Mary Sue Milliken

Serve over ice for a real thirst quencher.

2 quarts water
1/2 cup fresh ginger, finely grated
Juice of 3 lemons
1/2 cup honey

PREPARATION TIME: 15 minutes plus steeping
and chilling time
COOKING TIME: 10 minutes
YIELD: 8 servings

In a medium saucepan, bring 2 quarts of water to a boil; add the ginger and lemon juice. Remove from heat and steep for 20 minutes. Add the honey and stir well. Strain through a cloth and chill thoroughly.

NUTRITION INFORMATION: Cal: 73   Pro: .1g/1%
Carb: 19g/98%   Fat: .1g/1%   Chol: 0mg   Sodium:
2mg   Potassium: 55mg   Fiber: .1g   C: 12%
EXCHANGE: Fruit: 1 1/4

Gazpacho Froth

by Marie Simmons

2 1/2 cups tomato juice, no salt added
4 slices peeled cucumber, about 1/8 inch thick
1 wedge green pepper, about 1 inch wide
1 scallion, trimmed
1 tablespoon fresh lime juice
Dash of hot pepper sauce (like Tabasco)
4 ice cubes
1/2 cup plain low-fat yogurt
Pinch salt (optional)

PREPARATION TIME: 10 minutes
YIELD: 2 servings

Put the tomato juice, cucumber, green pepper, and the white part of the scallion (save green top for garnish) into a blender. Add the lime juice, hot pepper sauce, ice cubes, and yogurt. Blend until the mixture is frothy and pureed. Taste, and add salt if desired. Pour into 2 tall glasses. Cut the scallion top into thin diagonal slices; sprinkle on top.

NUTRITION INFORMATION: Cal: 94   Pro: 5g/21%
Carb: 18g/70%   Fat: 1g/9%   Chol: 4mg   Sodium:
72mg   Potassium: 844mg   Fiber: 4g   A: 38%   C:
116%   E: 11%   B1: 12%   B2: 13%   B3: 11%   B6:
19%   Folic: 17%   Panto: 12%   Ca: 13%   P: 14%
Fe: 11%   Mg: 12%   Cu: 16%
EXCHANGE: Skim Milk: 1/4   Veg: 2 1/2

Spotlight: The Marriage of Wine and Food

Wine is a civilized complement to any meal. While distilled spirits dull the taste buds, wine brings out the flavors in food.

The old adage, "white wine with fish, red wine with meat," however, no longer works with our lighter, more subtle ways of eating. It may have been a good rule of thumb when fish was bland and covered with heavy cream sauces—and meat was steak and potatoes. Back then, wine in America came in two flavors: Chablis and jug red.

In the 1980s, California wine makers, responding to changes in Americans' eating habits, began tailoring their wines to suit the lighter, healthier modern diet, as well as trendy ethnic cuisines. The West Coast "food wines," as they've been dubbed, show more of the elegance and finesse of their European counterparts.

Increasingly, American wineries are focusing on softer-styled, red pinot noir wines, which allow the delicate flavors of fowl and veal dishes to shine through. White chardonnays are showing up leaner, more subtle and restrained.

In addition, new grape varieties are being introduced to expand the range of possibilities. Here are some of the most rewarding wine and food marriages:

Soups Wines should complement the color, density, and flavor-intensity of the soup. Clear broth or chicken soup needs a light white wine like a chenin blanc or a pinot blanc. For fish soup, try a crisp, zesty sauvignon blanc or a French Sancerre; with vegetable purees, a Chablis. With beef stocks, try a medium-to-heavy red wine like merlot; for winter stews, a French Rhone wine.

Hot, Spicy Cuisines Southwest, Cajun, or Thai cooking demands a bold beverage. To fan the fires, try a racy zinfandel wine (a flaming red—not a blush) or a rich, dense, peppery Rhone. Fish dishes can take a grassy sauvignon blanc. Or, to douse the fire, go with champagne.

Mediterranean Olive oil–based dishes require a certain amount of acidity in a wine to cut through the oil. In general, regional wines from this part of the world are quite compatible. Whites: Italian pinot grigio or Vernaccia. Reds:

Fruit Spritzers
by Marie Simmons

For the fruit, you can use ripe, flavorful hulled strawberries, pared and stoned peaches, unpared and stoned nectarines, pared and seeded cantaloupe or honeydew melon, pared and seeded mango, or any combination you wish.

2 cups cut-up fruit
1/2 cup orange juice
1/2 cup crushed ice
   Chilled seltzer, to taste

PREPARATION TIME: 10 minutes
YIELD: 2 to 4 servings

Place cut-up fruit, orange juice, and ice in a blender; blend until fruit is pureed. Pour into 2 to 4 tall glasses. Top off with chilled seltzer.

NUTRITION INFORMATION: (using strawberries and peaches) Cal: 86 Pro: 1g/6% Carb: 21g/89% Fat: .5g/5% Sodium: 10mg Potassium: 415mg Fiber: 3g A: 12% C: 131% Folic: 13% EXCHANGE: Fruit: 1 1/2

Pink-Orange Lemonade
by Elizabeth Schneider

Less sweet than most lemonades, this bright version is tart and fruity. Decrease the quantity of rind and increase the honey for a sweeter drink.

Spanish Riojas, French Provençal, or Italian Brunello di Montalcino.

Fish Salty seafoods make red wine taste bitter and metallic. Go with a snappy acidic white like Italian Vernaccia, pinot grigio, or French Muscadet. Heavier-flavored fish like bluefish and tuna can take a light red wine if the spirit moves you—a Beaujolais, grenache, or Valpolicello.

Shellfish Classic combos include a zesty Muscadet with clams; champagne or dry sherry with oysters; a rich, expensive chardonnay or white Burgundy with lobster. With scallops, try a sauvignon blanc or an Italian Gavi.

Fowl The degree of gaminess generally determines the match. A simple chicken dish calls for chenin blanc or a Loire Valley Vouvray. A gewürztraminer or a dry rosé might carry a roasted hen, but wouldn't stand up to a duck or a goose. These richer fowl need a chardonnay or a red pinot noir, Burgundy, or Chianti.

Meat White wines cringe in the presence of beef and lamb, so stick with big-bodied reds: cabernet sauvignon, Australian Shiraz, French Bordeaux, or Italian Barolo. With veal: Italian Barbera, merlot, Spanish Rioja. Pork goes with either a light fruity red or full-bodied white.

Vegetables Much depends on the preparation. For simple stir-fries, try a crisp Sancerre or a white Rhone wine. Highly seasoned vegetable casseroles can take a light red wine like Beaujolais or grenache.

Cheese Light cheeses, like Gouda, can support a simple white wine; goat cheese wants a dry white such as a sauvignon blanc; but with strongly flavored cheeses such as Roquefort, only a fine, well-aged cabernet sauvignon–based red wine can match the richness and intensity.

Dessert Use late-harvest whites made from Riesling, semillon, or gewürztraminer. Sugar, like salt, makes most red wines taste bitter—only sweet port can overcome this.

Fruit In general, wine doesn't marry well with fresh grapes. For some it's a matter of incest; others object for aesthetic reasons. When offered grapes at dessert, one serious wine drinker politely declined, saying, "Thank you, but I am not in the habit of taking my wine in pill form."

—Deborah Scoblionkov

---

4 or 5 large, tender lemons
1 large lime
1 cup fresh cranberries, rinsed and
    picked over
1/2 to 3/4 cup orange blossom honey
4 or 5 large, juicy oranges
    Lime, lemon, and/or orange slices for
    garnish

PREPARATION TIME: 25 minutes
YIELD: About 2 quarts lemonade

Rinse 1 lemon and 1 lime well and remove the colored rind in strips, avoiding any white pith. Combine the strips of rind, the cranberries, 1/2 cup of honey and 1 cup of water in the container of a food processor fitted with the steel blade. Process to a medium-coarse texture. Strain, discarding any coarse pieces.

Halve and squeeze the remaining lemons to yield about 1 cup of juice. Halve and squeeze the oranges to yield about 2 cups of juice. Combine the juices with the cranberry juice mixture. Taste and add honey if desired. Chill until serving time.

To serve, add an equal quantity of water (or slightly less, for a strong flavor) to the juices. Combine with ice cubes and a colorful array of citrus slices in a glass pitcher or tall glasses.

NOTE: The amount of juice varies with the variety of fruit and time of year—as does the fruit's sweetness. Adjust the amounts of water and honey to taste.

NUTRITION INFORMATION (for 1 cup): Cal: 128 Pro: .6g/2% Carb: 34g/97% Fat: .2g/1% Chol: 0mg Sodium: 2mg Potassium: 187mg Fiber: 1g C: 80% Folic: 10%
    EXCHANGE: Fruit: 2 1/4

Real Cranberry Juice

by Marie Simmons

> 1 12-ounce bag (3 cups) cranberries,
>   rinsed and picked over
> 1/2 to 2/3 cup sugar
>   Ice cubes
> 4 orange rind strips, 1/2 by 1 1/2 inches

PREPARATION TIME: 20 minutes plus cooling time
COOKING TIME: 10 minutes
YIELD: About 1 quart or 4 servings

Combine the cranberries and 1 quart of water in a large saucepan. Heat to a boil; when the berries begin to pop, cover and simmer over low heat for 10 minutes. Strain into a bowl through a fine sieve or a sieve lined with a double thickness of dampened cheesecloth. Press on the pulp with the back of a large spoon.

Stir the sugar to taste into the hot juice until dissolved. Cool at room temperature. When cool, pour into ice-filled tall glasses. Twist a piece of rind to extract the flavorful oils and add to each glass.

NUTRITION INFORMATION: Cal: 141   Pro: .3g/1% Carb: 37g/98%   Fat: .1g/1%   Chol: 0mg   Sodium: 1mg Potassium: 50mg   C: 16%
EXCHANGE: Fruit: 2 1/2

Two-Berry Yogurt Cooler

by Marie Simmons

> 1 cup rinsed, hulled, halved strawberries
> 1 cup Real Cranberry Juice (see page 330) or
>   store-bought
> 1/2 cup plain low-fat yogurt
> 1/2 cup cracked ice

PREPARATION TIME: 15 minutes
YIELD: 2 servings

Combine all the ingredients in a blender. Blend until pureed. Pour evenly into two tall glasses and serve with straws.

NUTRITION INFORMATION: Cal: 132   Pro: 3g/ 10%   Carb: 28g/82%   Fat: 1g/8%   Chol: 4mg Sodium: 46mg   Potassium: 289mg   Fiber: 2g C: 161%   B2: 11%   Ca: 12%   P: 10%   Mn: 11%
EXCHANGE: Skim Milk: 1/2   Fruit: 1 1/2

Banana Health Shake

by Marie Simmons

> 1 cup orange juice
> 1/2 cup plain low-fat yogurt
> 1 banana, peeled and cut up
> 4 dates, dried apricots, or pitted prunes, or
>   2 tablespoons raisins
> 1 tablespoon wheat germ

PREPARATION TIME: 10 minutes
YIELD: 2 servings

Combine all the ingredients in a blender; blend thoroughly, at least 1 minute. Pour into 2 tall glasses.

NUTRITION INFORMATION (with dates):   Cal: 203   Pro: 6g/11%   Carb: 44g/82%   Fat: 2g/8% Chol: 4mg   Sodium: 42mg   Potassium: 748mg Fiber: 4g   C: 113%   B1: 16%   B2: 15%   B6: 24% Folic: 25%   Ca: 13%   P: 16%   Mg: 14%   Mn: 25% Mo: 11%
EXCHANGE Skim Milk: 1/4   Bread: 1/4   Fruit: 2 3/4

The
American Health
Pantry

SAFE, NUTRITIOUS FOOD: SELECTION, STORAGE, ◇ AND PREPARATION TIPS ◇

by Susan S. Lang

Good food is delicious, nutritious, and safe. But how nourishing and how safe a food is depends a great deal on how you select, handle, store, and prepare it. It's possible to lose 75 percent of certain nutrients in fresh foods by the time you eat them. The most fragile nutrients are vitamins, particularly vitamin C and folic acid, but minerals can also be lost en route from the market to your mouth. For many foods, but particularly for fruits and vegetables, whatever you can do that protects the textures, lively colors, and general good looks will also preserve the nutrient content.

Selecting for Vitamins

In the supermarket, go for deep, dark hues. Take sweet potatoes. Deep orange ones are richer in vitamin A (in the form of beta-carotene) than lighter ones. The same goes for carrots: you get several times more vitamin A from mature, bright-orange carrots than from their younger, pale-faced counterparts. Likewise, the darker your green leafy vegetables are, the higher they are in vitamin A, calcium, and iron. Dark green leafy vegetables—such as kale, spinach, and collards, for example—will always be better choices than pale green iceberg lettuce. (You won't want green potatoes, of course, so buy them packaged in opaque bags; if some are green, peel well; if sprouted, core the eyes out.)

Consider the calendar; buy vegetables in season whenever possible. Tomatoes that are vine-ripened in the summer sun, for example, not only have that savory sunny flavor but also have twice as much vitamin C as tomatoes grown in the greenhouse during the winter.

Not that fresh is always better. Foods that are commercially frozen and properly stored often have more nutrients than fresh fruits and vegetables that have been sitting around for even short periods of time. That's because foods are processed immediately after harvesting and modern high-temperature, short-time treatments are used. So don't buy more fresh foods than you'll use in the next few days; time is one of vitamins' worst enemies.

Storing for Freshness

Now that you've bought your groceries, protect them. Bag your food so it's shielded from sunshine when you walk to your car. Sunshine robs milk of riboflavin, and heat depletes a number of vitamins, so don't leave groceries in the car for long.

Once home, keep foods cool, covered, away from light. Vegetables go into moisture-proof plastic bags or in crispers and get refrigerated. Don't wash or trim anything until you're ready to use it. And do so quickly: Vegetables can lose an average of one third their vitamin C content after two days in the fridge.

Underripe fruits such as tomatoes, bananas, and pears should be left to ripen out of the sun (no windowsills, please) at room temperature and then refrigerated. An overripe fruit has less vitamin C. Although onions and potatoes need not be refrigerated, be sure they're stored in a cool, dark place. Don't hang them from pretty baskets in your kitchen (too bright) or keep them under the kitchen sink (too damp). Dried beans and peas should be stored in dark jars or in the fridge to protect the light-sensitive B vitamins. And don't assume that canned foods are impermeable; keep them cool, too (65°F or cooler). Canned veggies stored for a year at 65°F lose about 10 percent of their vitamin C; at 80°F, up to 25 percent.

Frozen foods should be kept cooler than 15°F, ideally, at 0°F or colder. After one year at 0°F, frozen beans, broccoli, cauliflower, and spinach lose 33 percent to 75 percent of their vitamin C. At 15°F, losses are quicker. Foods such as asparagus, peas, and lima beans will lose half their vitamin C in six months. So try to eat frozen foods within three months. If your freezer isn't very cold, buy smaller quantities of frozen foods and replenish more often.

Don't thaw vegetables before cooking, and when you thaw meats, beware that small amounts of protein, B vitamins, and minerals are lost in the juices, especially with chopped, cubed, and organ meats. For best results, cook stored meats when they're still frozen and use cooking juices in gravies and soups. For safety purposes, never thaw meat on the counter but in the fridge or microwave (see safety tips below).

Whole foods, such as whole wheat bread or pasta, should be kept cool and dark to prevent the oil in the germ from becoming rancid.

Cooking to Preserve Nutrients

When you're ready to cook, wash your vegetables. Thoroughly. A strong water stream and a vegetable scrubber will remove dirt and bugs as well as some pesticide residues and microorganisms that may be present. Don't slice, scrape, or peel until just before cooking because as soon as the vegetables are under the knife and their cells are damaged, enzymes are released, which causes some vitamins to deteriorate.

Here's a dilemma: to pare or not. There's concentrated fiber and vitamins in many vegetable skins, but there's also growing alarm about the extent of pesticide residues in fresh produce (see below). In any case, cut vegetables as little as possible to avoid damaging and exposing more cells than necessary and use the outer leaves whenever possible because they're often more laden with nutrients than the inner ones. Outer leaves of lettuce, for example, have more calcium, iron, and vitamin A than the more tender, inner leaves. Leafy parts of vegetables are generally richer in nutrients than stems or ribs: Collard *leaves,* for example, have more vitamin A than the midrib. Similarly, broccoli leaves are much higher in vitamin A than the stalks or flower buds.

During cooking, nutrient enemies include light, heat, air, and water. Light reduces riboflavin, as well as vitamins A and K; heat destroys vitamin C, thiamin, and folic acid; air attacks vitamins C, E, and A; and water sucks valuable water-soluble vitamins and minerals out of vegetables. Preferred cooking methods for maintaining the nutritional punch of vegetables are steaming, stir-frying, microwaving, or pressure cooking.

Braising meats promotes vitamin leaching but common sense tells us that we don't look to chicken breasts for vitamin C. In this country, the fat and salt we overeat is more damaging than the vitamins and minerals we undereat, so a technique like braising, which releases the tenderness and flavor of many lean cuts of meat, can help us eat lean and well. For more on low-fat cooking techniques, see The Healthy Kitchen, page 16.

A few more nutrient-saving tips follow.

IF YOU OWN A MOSS BALL, FOLLOW THESE STEPS

1: Remove any pets from the water and tank.

2: Remove the ball, other plants and any water from the aquarium and put them into a heat-safe pot.

3: Inspect the ball and tank for zebra mussels and if you find any contact your local Game and Fish regional office.

4: Boil the balls, plants and any water it's been in contact with for at least five minutes.

5: Dispose of the ball and other plants in the trash.

6: Pour out the boiled water on a semi-permeable surface. That could be a houseplant or outside — like grass or soil — not located near standing water or a storm drain.

SAVE YOUR PLACE WHILE YOU SAVE THE STATE

Moss balls are a popular plant choice for aquariums and decorative displays. But they also can be carriers of zebra mussels, which if detected in Wyoming's waters, could have catastrophic impacts to the water, the biodiversity of the area, recreation, municipalities and water users.

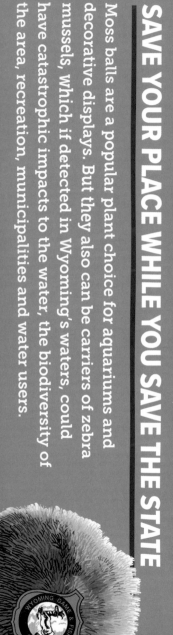

WYOMING GAME & FISH DEPARTMENT

♦ Use as little water as possible. Cover pots with snug lids; when the steam is kept in, foods cook faster with less water.

♦ Be quick: Get the veggies off the heat as soon as they're crisp-tender.

♦ Cook vegetables in their skins whenever possible and pare, if desired, after cooking.

♦ Try microwaving vegetables: Studies at Cornell University have shown that up to 50 percent more vitamin C may be conserved when fruits and vegetables are microwaved rather than boiled or baked. Use just a tablespoon or two of water and keep covered. Use High (100% power) setting for fastest cooking.

♦ Avoid using baking soda to enhance tenderness or color; it destroys much of the thiamin.

♦ Serve vegetables as soon as possible; avoid holding or reheating. Leftover cooked vegetables lose vitamins.

♦ Use liquids from canned foods, especially vegetables—about one third the nutrients are in the liquid!—unless you are particularly concerned about sodium.

♦ Don't wash rice or other grains, and try to avoid presoaking legumes in excess water, which can promote vitamin loss. It's better to boil beans for two minutes, let them sit for an hour, and then cook as usual in the soaking water.

♦ Avoid overbrowning breads and charring meats. Overbrowning breads will destroy thiamin; charring meats will increase the concentration of potential carcinogens.

♦ Leftovers should be covered tightly and cooled immediately. Reheat only what will be eaten. If it won't be used for several days, it's better to freeze and then reheat just prior to eating.

Preventing Food Contamination

You are what you eat, and periodically that means sick. Much of the time, when you're smitten with chills, diarrhea, vomiting, fever, or cramps, it's not the flu, but food poisoning. About one third the diarrhea cases in this country may be caused by contaminated food—that's somewhere between 24 million and 81 million cases every year.

There's much more that the food industry and governmental inspectors could do to prevent, for example, salmonella-contaminated chicken from reaching the market. But they're not doing it. Salmonella is responsible for some 30 percent of bacterial food poisoning, and its incidence is on the rise. More than a third of supermarket chickens are contaminated with salmonella; another third are infected with a microbe called campylobacter, or "campy" for short. According to the Food and Nutrition Board of the National Academy of Sciences, current meat and poultry inspection methods are inadequate for detecting these microbes. Meanwhile, fish and shellfish are hardly inspected at all.

That leaves the consumer—you and me—in the kitchen. When it comes to pesticides, hormones, and other pollutants, the best we can do is eat lean meat (many pollutants concentrate in fat), trim and wash vegetables, and buy organic when we can. But actual food poisoning from bacteria is almost entirely preventable. Heat kills bacteria. Period.

The major culprits are bacteria that contaminate protein foods: beef, poultry, fish, eggs, and dairy products, including cream pies and custards. Bacteria account for two thirds of all food-borne illness outbreaks.

The two main goals here are to prevent contaminating food with your germs and to avoid infecting utensils, sponges, work surfaces, cooked meat and poultry, or other foods with germs from raw meat and poultry.

Here's how:

♦ Start with clean hands, clothes, hair, and nails. Always wash with soap after using the bathroom, blowing your nose, sneezing into your hand, touching your nose or mouth, handling garbage, or smoking.

♦ Always wash with soap after touching any raw meat, poultry, fish, or eggs before touching other foods. Even a faucet handle can be a carrier if you touch it after handling raw meat.

♦ Don't use the same spoon more than once

to taste foods and don't use your fingers to taste.

♦ As soon as you cut raw meat or fish, clean the knife and cutting surface with soapy, hot water. An unwashed knife can easily contaminate the potatoes or onion you're about to slice. Plastic cutting boards are better than wood because bacteria can hide in wood's crevices. Also, plastic boards can be sterilized in the dishwasher.

♦ Don't use sponges or cloths for wiping surfaces that have hosted meat or poultry. Use disposable paper towels instead.

♦ Never put cooked meat or poultry back on the surface or place where it was prepared! This is a common pitfall of barbecuing. Thoroughly clean dishes, utensils, and work surfaces that have been used for raw food before you use them for cooked food.

♦ To avoid pesticide residues on fruits and vegetables, either scrub and then scrub some more (some say with hot water), or peel, or buy pesticide-free produce.

♦ Bacteria, like many living things, thrive in warm, moist places. So, first and foremost, keep hot foods hot and cold foods cold. The danger zone lies between 40° and 140°F. The safety of your food becomes questionable if it has been in this zone for more than two hours.

♦ Microwave ovens sometimes have "cold spots" where heat doesn't penetrate. To avoid this, stir foods, rotate the dish, or buy a carousel that rotates the food. Covering food in a dish creates a moist, steamy atomosphere more successful for killing bacteria. Follow microwave directions carefully; some meat products such as pork require specific internal temperature to ensure harmful organisms have been killed. Check with a thermometer to be sure meat has been properly heated.

♦ Consume fresh roasts, steaks, and chops in three to five days, fresh and cooked poultry, chopped meat, fresh sausage, and variety meats within two days.

♦ Consume cooked meats within four days, processed meats such as bacon, hot dogs, and ham within five to seven days.

♦ In general, use frozen meats within six months.

♦ Fresh meats should be wrapped loosely in plastic for refrigerator storage. Wrap leftovers tightly for refrigerator or freezer storage.

♦ Never use or even taste any food in a can that shows signs of bulging, leaking, odors, or mold, or spurts liquid upon opening.

♦ Canned foods that have frozen in the car or basement should be thoroughly cooked immediately, then eaten or refrozen.

♦ If the seams of a can have rusted or burst, discard it.

♦ Wipe the tops of cans before opening them.

♦ To keep brown bag lunches cold, put a frozen juice or ice pack in it.

♦ Never thaw protein foods, raw or cooked, at room temperature. It's best to defrost them in the refrigerator overnight. If you need to thaw quickly, use a microwave oven or put the package under running cold water.

♦ Rinse raw chicken under cold water to wash away surface bacteria. This won't rid the bird of all the microbes but it'll cut down the numbers. Then wash the sink with hot, soapy water.

♦ When stuffing foods, wait until just before roasting; never put stuffed, uncooked foods back into the refrigerator. Pack the stuffing loosely so the heat can penetrate more fully. Test with a meat theromoter to be sure poultry stuffing reaches at least 165°F during roasting.

♦ Always remove stuffing from leftovers and store separately.

♦ Avoid recipes that call for raw eggs.

♦ Never partially cook meat or poultry and finish cooking on another day.

♦ Be certain that meat and poultry are cooked all the way through. Cut into the meat or bird to look. Use a meat thermometer to be certain that pork has reached at least 160°F, 175°F for poultry. Just because the skin is crisp doesn't mean the bird is cooked through.

♦ Hamburger is particularly vulnerable because it's handled so much and is sometimes eaten raw or rare. Be sure it's brown in the center before eating. Don't eat any that smells when you open the package. Avoid raw meat.

♦ Refrigerate leftovers as soon as possible. Break large quantities into smaller portions so that they'll cool more quickly. *Don't* wait for them to be room temperature.

♦ Cover leftovers to reheat them and be sure they're thoroughly reheated. Make sure gravies come to a rolling boil before serving. Be extra careful during holidays and picnics when food stays out on a table.

♦ Avoid burning food on a barbecue or flame broiler, or by cooking at very high temperatures, close to 500°F. Charred food contains potentially potent carcinogens. During barbecues, avoid fat dripping onto the coals—the smoke contains a chemical called benzopyrene, a known carcinogen. Cover the meat with foil to prevent the fat from dripping.

♦ Finally, avoid burning yourself. Use a pot holder to remove a pan from the stove, turn handles away from the edge of the range, and don't wear loose-hanging garments near an open flame.

The Healthy Utensil

Another potential source of contamination can come from the type of pot you use. Following are ratings of modern pots:

♦ *Glass:* Glass is safe. The exception is lead crystal, which recent research finds can leach lead into alcoholic beverages. Avoid.

♦ *Copper:* Never use unlined copper pots; the copper can leach into foods. Most copper pots are lined with another surface such as stainless steel. Check the lining periodically. If it's damaged, have the pot relined.

♦ *Aluminum:* Although aluminum has been implicated in Alzheimer's disease, its presence in the brain may be a result of Alzheimer's disease rather than a cause of it. Obviously, more re-

search is necessary. Nevertheless, acidic foods, such as tomato sauce, sauerkraut, or fruit juices, can dissolve some aluminum, causing it to leach into the food. Acidic foods stored in aluminum foil can also be affected by leaching. But the amounts we get in such foodstuffs as baking powder and certain antacids is vastly greater.

If you must buy aluminum pots, wash them first with hot sudsy water, rinse, fill with water, boil for 2 or 3 minutes, and discard the water. That greatly minimizes leaching.

♦ *Ceramic or enameled cookware:* American-made pots are safe, but some foreign-made pots in the past had cadmium-containing enamels. Be particularly wary of hobbyists' pots; some potters may be unaware of glazes that could be harmful when in contact with acidic foods. It's best to use "homemade" pots for roses, not roasts.

♦ *Nonstick Pots:* Although considered safe, Teflon and other nonstick surfaces should not be used at extremely high temperatures. There is some evidence that if an empty pot sits on a high burner, harmful and irritating fumes are released. If you accidently allow a nonstick pan to boil dry, open a window until any fumes disperse.

♦ *Iron:* Here's a case where the pot can be good for you. When acidic foods are cooked for a while in a cast-iron pot or skillet, the iron content can increase substantially. When spaghetti sauce is simmered for a few hours, for example, iron content can increase from 3 to 50 milligrams. Fried potatoes or eggs that are cooked in cast iron may end up with nearly twice their normal iron content. A recent study at Texas Tech University in Lubbock reveals that the iron that is taken up by foods cooked in cast-iron cookware is as usable by our bodies as the non-heme food iron.

◇ FOOD PROFILES ◇

Wheat

Nutrient data are based on a half-cup dry serving size, with gram equivalents given, unless otherwise noted. For information on wheat-based pastas, see Pasta food profiles, page 340.

ALL-PURPOSE FLOUR. This is white flour that is a combination of both hard and soft flours. Hard and soft white flours, with the bran removed, are milled separately. Each manufacturer has a different blending proportion.

One-half cup enriched dry (55 g): Cal: 226 Pro: 6g/12% Carb: 47g/86% Fat: .6g/2% Sodium: 1mg Potassium: 66mg Fiber: 2g (lg soluble) B1: 32% B2: 18% B3: 18% Fe: 16% (Note: Calcium fortified all-purpose flour contains 16 percent of the USRDA for calcium per ¹/₂ cup.)

BULGUR WHEAT. Bulgur wheat is made from the wheat berry, partially cooked, then cracked into fine, medium, or coarse grinds.

One-half cup dry (70 g): Cal: 239 Pro: 9g/13% Carb: 53g/83% Fat: .1g/4% Sodium: 12mg Potassium: 287mg Fiber: 12g B1: 11% B2: 18% B6: 12% P: 21% Mg: 28% Mn: 60% Cu: 12%

COUSCOUS. The name refers to the grainlike raw product (granules made from durum wheat) as well as the finished dish, a steamed grain generally served with lamb or beef or chicken in a sauce, variations of which are found in Sicily, France, Senegal, Brazil, and Morocco.

One-half cup dry (92 g): Cal: 346 Pro: 12/14% Carb: 71g/85% Fat: 1g/1% Sodium: 9mg Potassium: 152mg Fiber: n/a B1: 10% B3: 16% Panto: 11% P: 16% Mg: 10% Cu: 11% Mn: 20%

CRACKED WHEAT. Cracked wheat is split from the whole wheat berry and cooks much faster. Add fine cracked wheat to breads and batters; use coarser grinds for salads, pilafs, and breakfast cereals.

One-half cup dry (77g): Cal: 260 Pro: 8g/11% Carb: 55g/83% Fat: 2g/6% Sodium: n/a Potassium: n/a Fiber: 7g B1: 23% B3: 14% P: 31% Fe: 15%

DURUM WHEAT. Durum wheat is high in gluten and used to make semolina, the coarsely ground base for pasta and couscous.

One-half cup dry (96 g): Cal: 325 Pro: 13g/15% Carb: 68g/79% Fat: 2g/6% Sodium: 2mg Potassium: 414mg Fiber: n/a B1: 27% B3: 32% B6: 20% P: 49% Fe: 19% Mg: 35% Zn: 26% Cu: 26% Mn: 83%

WHEAT BERRY. The whole kernel of wheat with only the inedible hull removed, it is nutty and chewy.

Hard red spring, one-half cup dry (96 g): Cal: 315 Pro: 15g/18% Carb: 65g/77% Fat: 2g/5% Sodium: 2mg Potassium: 326 mg Fiber: 12g B1: 32% B3: 27% B6: 16% Folic: 11% P: 32% Fe: 19%

Hard red winter, one-half cup dry (96g): Cal: 314 Pro: 12g/14% Carb: 68g/82% Fat: 1g/4% Sodium: 2mg Potassium: 348mg Fiber: 10–13g B1: 25% B6: 15% P: 28% Fe: 17% Mg: 30% B3: 26%

Soft red winter, one-half cup dry (84 g): Cal: 278 Pro: 9g/12% Carb: 62g/84% Fat: 1g/4% Sodium: 2mg Potassium: 334mg Fiber: 10–13g B1: 22% B3: 20% B6: 11% P: 41% Fe: 15% Mg: 26% Zn: 15% Cu: 19% Mn: 105%

WHEAT BRAN. The fiber-rich outer layer of the wheat berry, it is removed along with the germ when wheat is milled. It's usually purchased ready to eat and adds high fiber to baked goods and cereals, soups, and toppings.

One-quarter cup dry (15g): Cal: 32 Pro: 2g/17% Carb: 10g/72% Fat: .6g/11% Sodium: .3mg Potassium: 177mg Fiber: 6g (.5g soluble) B3: 10% P: 15% Mg: 23% Mn: 49%

WHEAT GERM. This is the "heart" of wheat, very rich in protein and vitamins. Eat it right out of the jar, sprinkled on cereals, or added to muffins and breads and even puddings.

One-quarter cup toasted (28g): Cal: 108 Pro: 8g/28% Carb: 14g/48% Fat: 3g/23% (fat breakdown

n/a) Sodium: 1mg Potassium: 269mg Fiber: 5g (1.3g soluble) E: 20% B1: 22% B2: 14% B6: 14% Folic: 25% P: 33% Fe: 14% Mg: 23% Zn: 32% Mn: 161%

WHITE PASTRY FLOUR. White pastry flour is finely milled and made of soft wheat; it is lower in protein and less granular than all-purpose flour.

One-half cup enriched dry (50 g): Cal: 195 Pro: 4g/9% Carb: 42g/89% Fat: .6g/2% Sodium: 1mg Potassium: 57mg Fiber: 1g (.5g soluble) B1: 32% B2: 14% B3: 18% Fe: 22%

WHOLE WHEAT FLAKES. Cooked wheat berries are rolled into flat flakes, much as rolled oats are made into oatmeal.

One-half cup dry (85 g): Cal: 290 Pro: 8g/5% Carb: 66g/85% Fat: 2g/10% Sodium: 2mg Potassium: 320mg Fiber: 22g B1: 22% P: 30%

WHOLE WHEAT FLOUR. Milled from the entire husked kernel of hard wheat, whole wheat flour includes the bran, germ, and endosperm. Its flavor is richer than that of white flour. The germ can turn rancid at room temperature, so whole wheat flour should be refrigerated or frozen. *Graham* flour is the same as whole wheat flour, but more coarsely ground.

One-half cup dry (60 g): Cal: 200 Pro: 8g/15% Carb: 44g/80% Fat: 1g/5% Sodium: 3mg Potassium: 243mg Fiber: 6g (1g soluble) B1: 18% B6: 10% B3: 19% P: 21% Fe: 13% Mg: 20%

WHOLE WHEAT PASTRY FLOUR. This flour is made from soft and hard red spring wheat but is more finely milled than whole wheat flour.

One-half cup dry (74 g): Cal: 248 Pro: 7g/10% Carb: 55g/83% Fat: 2g/7% Sodium: 2mg Potassium: 112mg Fiber: n/a

One-half cup unenriched dry (55 g): Cal: 226 Pro: 6g/12% Carb: 47g/86% Fat: .6g/2% Sodium: 1mg Potassium: 66mg Fiber: 2g (1g soluble)

Pasta

Storage: All pastas should be stored sealed in a cool, dry place to avoid contamination, dust, moisture, and insects.

ARTICHOKE PASTA. Artichoke pasta is made from the flour of sunchokes (Jerusalem artichokes; see Roots food profiles, page 351) and is light green in color.

Three ounces dry (85 g): Cal: 365   Pro: 11g/12%
Carb: 78g/86%   Fat: 1g/2%   Sodium: 19mg
Potassium: 326mg   Fiber: n/a   B1: 23%   B2: 16%
B3: 22%   Panto: 19%   P: 22%   Fe: 21%   Mg: 20%
Zn: 11%

ASIAN RICE NOODLES. The transparent noodles are made with rice flour and are very fine; they're most commonly sold dried. Also called rice stick, they can be parboiled, steamed, simmered, and stir-fried. They may be stir-fried after soaking without pre-cooking. Broad, fresh rice noodles are available in Oriental markets; keep them refrigerated or frozen. These cook very fast.

Three ounces dry (85 g): Cal: 370   Pro: 7g/8%
Carb: 82g/91%   Fat: 1g/1%   Sodium: 7mg
Potassium: 77mg   Fiber: 3g   Folic: 13%

CELLOPHANE NOODLES. These white noodles, made from mung bean or another vegetable starch, become transparent when cooked, with a mild flavor.

One-half cup dry (2.5 ounces, 71 g): Cal: 246   Pro: .2g/0%   Carb: 60g/100%   Fat: .04g/0%   Sodium: 7mg   Potassium: 7mg   Fiber: .1g

CHINESE EGG NOODLES. Available fresh or dried, prepare Chinese egg noodles as you would other fresh or dried egg and wheat flour pasta.

Three ounces dry (85 g): Cal: 357   Pro: 11g/12%
Carb: 75g/87%   Fat: .4g/1%   Sodium: 674mg
Potassium: n/a   Fiber: 4g   B3: 12%   Fe: 19%

EGG NOODLES, ENRICHED. Egg noodles are more flavorful than semolina pasta, with a more tender texture. They may be sold fresh or dried.

Three ounces dry (85 g): Cal: 325   Pro: 12g/15%
Carb: 61g/75%   Fat: 4g/10%   Sodium: 18mg
Potassium: 199mg   Fiber: 1g   B1: 60%   B2: 24%
B3: 34%   P: 18%   Fe: 21%   Mg: 13%   Zn: 13%   Mn: 17%

ITALIAN-STYLE DRIED SEMOLINA PASTA, ENRICHED. Domestic or imported, dried pasta comes in over 100 shapes.

Three ounces dry (85 g): Cal: 317   Pro: 11g/14%
Carb: 65g/82%   Fat: 2g/4%   Sodium: 6mg
Potassium: 138mg   Fiber: 2g   B1: 58%   B2: 22%
B3: 32%   Fe: 18%   P: 13%   Mg: 10%   Mn: 17%

JAPANESE BUCKWHEAT NOODLES (SOBA). Soba has a nutty flavor with a firm texture. Cook it like spaghetti, being careful not to overcook, or like Japanese wheat noodles (see page 61).

Three ounces dry (85 g): Cal: 300   Pro: 10g/16%
Carb: 61g/82%   Fat: 2g/2%   Fiber: 1.5g
Sodium: 676mg   Potassium: 214mg   B1: 27%
B3: 14%   P: 22%   Fe: 19%   Mg: 20%   Mn: 17%

JAPANESE WHEAT NOODLES. There are three main types: *Udon,* which are thick; *Somen,* which are thin; and *Yaki-Soba,* which are thin egg noodles. These noodles are high in sodium.

Three ounces dry (85 g): Cal: 304   Pro: 10g/13%
Carb: 63g/85%   Fat: 1g/2%   Sodium: 1573mg
Potassium: 151mg   Fiber: 4g

SPINACH PASTA, ENRICHED. This green pasta is available in many shapes. Prepare it as you would semolina pasta; be careful not to overcook it.

Three ounces dry (85 g): Cal: 318   Pro: 11g/16%   Carb: 64g/80%   Fat: 1g/4%   Sodium: 30mg
Potassium: 323mg   Fiber: 9g   B1: 21%   B: 10%   B3: 19%   B6: 14%   Folic: 10%   Panto: 10%   P: 28%   Fe: 10%   Mg: 37%   Zn: 16%   Cu: 21%   Mn: 65%

WHOLE WHEAT PASTA, ENRICHED. This pasta is beige in color, with a nutty flavor and coarse texture; prepare it the same as semolina pasta, though it may require more time to cook.

Three ounces dry (85 g): Cal: 297 Pro: 12g/16% Carb: 64g/81% Fat: 1g/3% Sodium: 8mg Potassium: 184mg Fiber: 8g (1.5g soluble) B1: 27% B3: 21% P: 22% Fe: 17% Mg: 30% Cu: 19% Mn: 74%

Corn

All nutrient data are based on a 3½-ounce (100 gram) serving size, with cup equivalents given, unless otherwise noted.

CORNMEAL. Choose whole over degermed and yellow over white. (Blue cornmeal is also available.) It comes in coarse, medium, and fine grinds. Refrigerate whole cornmeal immediately to avoid spoilage of germ oil.

Two-thirds cup dry whole yellow cornmeal: Cal: 355 Pro: 9g/10% Carb: 74g/80% Fat: 4g/10% Sodium: 1mg Potassium: 284mg Fiber: 6g A: 10% B1: 25% B3: 10% B6: 10% P: 26% Fe: 10%

Two-thirds cup dry enriched white cornmeal: Cal: 364 Pro: 8g/9% Carb: 78g/88% Fat: 1g/3% Sodium: 1mg Potassium: 120mg Fiber: 3g B1: 29% B2: 15% B3: 18% Fe: 24%

Two-thirds cup dry whole ground blue cornmeal: Cal: 395 Pro: 10g/10% Carb: 76g/74% Fat: 8g/16% Sodium: n/a Potassium: n/a Fiber: n/a Fe: 19% Mg: 33% Zn: 19%

CORN ON THE COB. Corn on the cob is available fresh June through September, frozen year-round. Choose corn with husks left on; exposed corn deteriorates quickly. Look for bright green, soft husks with even yellow kernels. It is best if cooked as soon as purchased; otherwise place unwashed, unhusked corn in plastic bags and refrigerate.

One small cob, or two-thirds cup raw kernels (90 g): Cal: 86 Pro: 3g/13% Carb: 19g/76% Fat: 1g/11% Sodium: 15mg Potassium: 270mg Fiber: 6.3g (2.8g soluble) C: 11% B1: 13% Folic: 12%

DRIED CORN. A staple among the Amish in Pennsylvania, it is hard to find elsewhere. It is very sweet and is rehydrated like a cereal to serve as a side dish. Store in a cool, dry place.

Two-thirds cup dry: Cal: 96 Pro: 4g/9% Carb: 22g/83% Fat: 1g/8% Sodium: tr Potassium: 280mg Fiber: n/a C: 12% P: 11%

GRITS. Available year-round in both instant and traditional form, grits are made from hominy, which is dried and ground corn. Store them in a covered, airtight container in a cool, dry place or in the refrigerator.

One-half cup dry: Cal: 371 Pro: 9g/10% Carb: 80g/87% Fat: 1g/3% Sodium: 1mg Potassium: 137mg Fiber: .3g B1: 40% B2: 24% B3: 25% Folic: 13% Fe: 22%

MASA HARINA. Masa harina is corn that has been boiled in a 5 percent lime solution for one hour (which improves its calcium content), then washed, drained, and ground into a flour. It is used to make dough for tortillas and other Mexican dishes.

One cup dry: Cal: 371 Pro: 9g/10% Carb: 76g/86% Fat: 4g/4% Sodium: 4mg Potassium: 344mg Fiber: 11g B1: 93% B2: 46% B3: 47% B6: 20% Ca: 17% P: 26% Mg: 27% Zn: 11%

POPCORN. Store covered in an airtight container, in a cool dry place. Each tablespoon yields two cups popped.

Two tablespoons raw or four cups air-popped, no salt added (24 g): Cal: 125 Pro: 4g/14% Carb: 3g/82% Fat: .3g/4% Sodium: tr Potassium: 85mg Fiber: 8g B1: 8% P: 9%

Rice

BASMATI. Basmati's also known as "aromatic." It can be brown or white, and it has the aroma of popcorn or roasted nuts. Aged basmati has a more exaggerated fragrance but is hard to find. Look for organically grown varieties. Both domestic and imported basmati has been found to contain pesticide residues.

One-half cup dry (112 g): Cal: 310   Pro: 6g/8%
Carb: 70g/92%   Fat: .2g/0%   Sodium: n/a
Potassium: n/a   Fiber: n/a

BROWN. Brown rice, with a chewier texture than white and a nutty flavor, is nutritionally superior to all white varieties. Store it uncooked in the refrigerator to avoid rancidity.

One-half cup dry (95g): Cal: 340   Pro: 7g/9%   Carb: 71g/84%   Fat: 3g/7%   Sodium: 7mg   Potassium: 205mg   Fiber: 7.2g   B1: 25%   B3: 23%   B6: 23%   Panto: 14%   P: 31%   Mg: 33%   Zn: 12%   Cu: 13%   Mn: 98%

PUFFED. Puffed rice is puffed under pressure and expanded by filling the grains with air. It is used to make rice cakes.

One cup dry (14 g): Cal: 56   Pro: 1g/5%   Carb: 13g/95%   Fat: .1g/0%   Sodium: 0mg   Potassium: 16mg   Fiber: .1g

RICE BRAN. Made from the hull, bran, and parts of the germ, it is usually purchased ready to eat. Use it as an extender with ground meats. Refrigerate it to preserve rice oil from rancidity.

One-half cup dry (42 g): Cal: 131   Pro: 6g/12%   Carb: 21g/45%   Fat: 9g/43% (fat breakdown n/a)   Sodium: 2mg   Potassium: 616mg   Fiber: 4g   B1: 76%   B3: 70%   B6: 84%   Panto: 31%   P: 69%   Fe: 43%   Mg: 81%   Zn: 33%   Cu: 15%   Mn: 168%

RICE CREAM. Rice cream is ground rice that cooks in several minutes into a cereal consistency.

One-quarter cup dry (87 g): Cal: 320   Pro: 10g/12%   Carb: 72g/87%   Fat: .4g/1%   Sodium: 2mg   Potassium: 82mg   Fiber: 2.4g

RICE FLOUR. Rice flour is made from milled rice that has been ground into flour. Mix it with wheat or other flours or use it according to a recipe.

One-half cup dry (63 g): Cal: 287   Pro: 6g/8%   Carb: 60g/85%   Fat: 2g/7%   Sodium: 6mg   Potassium: 228mg   Fiber: 1g   B1: 23%   B3: 25%   B6: 29%   Panto: 13%   P: 26%   Mg: 22%   Zn: 13%   Mn: 90%

WHITE. White rice comes in three lengths: long, medium, and short. Longer grains are drier and flakier; shorter grains, moister and stickier.

One-half cup dry white, enriched (48 g): Cal: 336   Pro: 7g/8%   Carb: 74g/90%   Fat: 1g/2%   Sodium: 4mg   Potassium: 106mg   Fiber: 1.3g   B1: 35%   B3: 19%   P: 11%   Fe: 22%   Cu: 10%   Mn: 29%

One-half cup dry white, unenriched (48 g): Cal: 336   Pro: 7g/8%   Carb: 74g/90%   Fat: 1g/2%   Sodium: 4mg   Potassium: 106mg   Fiber: 1.3g   P: 11%   Cu: 10%   Mn: 29%

One-half cup dry white, instant (92 g): Cal: 182   Pro: 4g/8%   Carb: 40g/91%   Fat: .1g/1%   Sodium: 3mg   Potassium: 9mg   Fiber: .8g   B1: 20%   B3: 13%   Fe: 11%

One-half cup dry white, parboiled (92 g): Cal: 341   Pro: 6g/8%   Carb: 75g/90%   Fat: .5g/1%   Sodium: 4mg   Potassium: 110mg   Fiber: 1.8g   B1: 36%   B3: 17%   B6: 16%   Panto: 10%   P: 13%   Fe: 18%

WILD. Wild rice is wild grass, not related botanically to rice. It has a firm, chewy texture with a nutty flavor and comes in long grain, fancy or medium, and select or short grain. Prices vary according to length, the longest being the most expensive.

One-half cup dry (80 g): Cal: 286 Pro: 12g/16%
Carb: 60g/81% Fat: 1g/3% Sodium: 6mg
Potassium: 342mg Fiber: 4g B2: 12% B3: 27%
B6: 16% Folic: 19% P: 35% Mg: 35% Zn: 32%
Cu: 21% Mn: 30%

The "New" Grains

All nutrient data are based on 3½ ounces dry (100 grams), with cup equivalents given, unless otherwise noted.

AMARANTH. Amaranth is nutty and nutritious. It's available in flour, flakes, or whole-grain pearls.

One-half cup whole. Cal. 366 Pro. 14g/15% Carb: 65g/70% Fat: 6g/15% Sodium: 21mg Potassium: 359mg Fiber: 8g B2: 12% B6: 11% Folic: 12% Panto: 10% Ca: 15% P: 45% Fe: 41% Mg: 65% Zn: 21% Cu: 38% Mn: 63%

BARLEY. The flavor is somewhere between that of white and that of brown rice, with a nutty taste and texture. Soaking for a few hours shortens cooking time. Pearled barley has the husk and bran removed, Scotch barley only the husk.

One-half cup pearled: Cal: 326 Pro: 12g/14% Carb: 68g/81% Fat: 2g/5% Sodium: 11mg Potassium: 416mg Fiber: 10g (2.8g soluble) B1: 40% B2: 15% B3: 16% B6: 11% P: 24% Fe: 18% Mg: 30% Zn: 17% Cu: 23% Mn: 51%

One-half cup Scotch: Cal: 348 Pro: 10g/11% Carb: 77g/86% Fat: 1g/3% Sodium: n/a Potassium: 296mg Fiber: n/a B1: 14% B3: 18% P: 29% Fe: 15%

BUCKWHEAT. Related to dock and rhubarb, buckwheat is rich and hearty in flavor. Groats, sold for kasha, are dehulled and lightly milled. Store buckwheat in an airtight container in a cool, dry place, or sealed in the refrigerator.

One-half cup whole: Cal: 292 Pro: 11g/14% Carb: 61g/77% Fat: 3g/9% Sodium: 0mg Potassium: 391mg Fiber: n/a B2: 21% B3: 30% P: 29% Fe: 10% Mg: 49% Zn: 14% Cu: 47%

Three-quarters cup dark buckwheat flour: Cal: 333 Pro: 12g/13% Carb: 72g/80% Fat: 3g/7% Sodium: n/a Potassium: 577mg Fiber: 2.3g B1: 28% B2: 11% B3: 30% B6: 29% Folic: 13% P: 35% Fe: 22% Mg: 62% Zn: 21% Cu: 26% Mn: 58%

Three-quarters cup light buckwheat flour: Cal: 347 Pro: 6g/7% Carb: 80g/90% Fat: 1g/3% Sodium: n/a Potassium: 314mg Fiber: 2.3g

JOB'S TEARS. This is a grass, not a cereal, treat it like barley or rice.

Two ounces (57 grams): Cal: 216 Pro: 8g/15% Carb: 38g/72% Fat: 3g/13% Sodium: 30mg Potassium: 105mg Fiber: n/a B1: 10% P: 20% Fe: 10% Mg: 25% Zn: 10%

MILLET. Millet is a tiny, pale yellow, round cereal with a mild flavor. Look for unbroken kernels free from dust. Buy only as much as you need for a month and store in an airtight container in a cool, dry place. Or keep grains in the freezer where they will last up to a year.

One-half cup whole millet: Cal: 379 Pro: 11g/ 9% Carb: 73g/83% Fat: 4g/8% Sodium: 5mg Potassium: 195mg Fiber: 2.2g B1: 28% B2: 17% B3: 24% B6: 19% P: 28% Fe: 17% Mg: 28% Zn: 11% Cu: 37% Mn: 47%

OATS. The hull is removed after harvesting. Oats have a smooth texture and a creamy taste. Store in an airtight container in a cool, dry place or sealed in the refrigerator.

Two-thirds cup: Cal: 384 Pro: 17g/17% Carb: 66g/ 67% Fat: 7g/16% Sodium: 2mg Potassium: 429mg Fiber: 10g (5g soluble) B1: 49% Folic: 14% Panto: 13% P: 52% Fe: 26% Mg: 44% Zn: 26% Cu: 31% Mn: 140%

QUINOA. This hearty, nutritious seed is often ground to make a flour. Quinoa can be bought in bulk and kept in the freezer. Rinse thoroughly to remove a bitter residue that may be left on the grain.

Two-thirds cup: Cal: 370 Pro: 16g/16% Carb: 64g/68% Fat: 7g/16% Sodium: n/a Potassium: 740mg Fiber: 7g B1: 13% B2: 23% B3: 15% P: 41% Fe: 51% Mg: 52% Zn: 22% Cu: 41%

RYE. A bold and hearty grain, rye flour is sold as dark, medium, or light. Rye berries can be cooked like brown rice, as a cereal or pilaf, after soaking.

Three-quarters cup dark rye flour: Cal: 324 Pro: 14g/16% Carb: 69g/77% Fat: 3g/7% Sodium: 1mg Potassium: 632mg Fiber: 12.7g (2.1g soluble) B1: 21% B2: 15% B3: 21% B6: 22% Folic: 15% Panto: 15% P: 63% Fe: 36% Mg: 62% Zn: 37% Cu: 37% Mn: 192%

One cup light rye flour: Cal: 364 Pro: 8g/10% Carb: 80g/87% Fat: 1g/3% Sodium: 1mg Potassium: 233mg Fiber: 3.2g (1.3 g soluble) B1: 22% B6: 12% P: 19% Fe: 10% Mg: 17% Zn: 12% Cu: 12% Mn: 56%

TEFF. Tiny teff comes in red, white, and brown varieties. Teff flour is also available. Prepare with spring or distilled water to make injera bread; chlorinated tap water may kill the natural symbiotic yeast.

Two ounces (57 grams): Cal: 200 Pro: 7g/14% Carb: 41g/81% Fat: 1g/5% Sodium: 10mg Potassium: 1mg Fiber: 8g B1: 15% Fe: 25%

TRITICALE. Triticale is a cross between wheat and rye. Store it sealed in a cool, dry place, and avoid exposure to moisture, dust, or insects. Cook and prepare whole triticale like wheat berries.

One-half cup whole triticale: Cal: 323 Pro: 12g/15% Carb: 69g/80% Fat: 2g/5% Sodium: 5mg Potassium: 318mg Fiber: 10g B1: 25% Folic: 17% anto: 13% P: 34% Fe: 14% Mg: 31% Zn: 18% Cu: 22%

Legumes

Nutrient data for dry legumes are based on a one-quarter cup dried (50 gram) serving size, unless otherwise noted. Data for fresh beans such as string beans are based on 100 grams, with equivalents in cups given.

Selection and storage: For all dried beans except lentils and split peas (and green beans and okra, which are not legumes): Choose those that are bright in color (for freshness) and uniform in size and shape (for even cooking); avoid beans that are cracked or have pinhole marks. Dried beans may be stored for a year in airtight containers in a cool, dry place. Always wash and pick over, discarding stones or seeds, before cooking. Cook all dried beans like white beans, below. Cooked beans may also be frozen, in sealed containers, up to 6 months, but freezing will soften beans further.

BEAN SPROUTS. Many seeds, from alfalfa to radishes, can be sprouted, but legumes—lentils, soybeans, mung beans, and peas—are among the most popular. Sprouted beans are very nutritious. Research at the University of Idaho College of Agriculture reveals that sprouts have much more vitamin C and beta-carotene than unsprouted seeds. Many types also have more niacin, thiamin, riboflavin, and pantothenic acid. To protect this perishable bounty of nutrients, serve sprouts raw or very briefly cooked. Refrigerate moist in a plastic bag; rinse under cold water before preparing.

One cup mung bean sprouts (104 g): Cal: 32 Pro: 3g/32% Carb: 6g/63% Fat: .2g/5% Sodium: 6mg Potassium: 154mg Fiber: 3g (.6g soluble) C: 23% Folic: 16% E: 10%

BLACK BEANS. A small blackish-blue bean with a soft texture and earthy flavor. Also known as turtle beans.

Cal: 165 Pro: 11g/24% Carb: 30g/73% Fat: 1g/3% Sodium: 3mg Potassium: 719mg Fiber: 8g (3.2g soluble) B1: 29% Folic: 54% P: 17% Fe: 14% Mg: 21% Zn: 12% Cu: 20% Mn: 15%

BLACK-EYED PEAS, a.k.a. Cowpeas. The bean is small- to medium-sized, white with a black oval marking. They have a slightly crunchy texture and a vegetable-like flavor. Yellow-eyed peas are also available. Black-eyed peas in the pods can be kept in a plastic bag in the refrigerator for two or three days.

Cal: 142   Pro: 10g/28%   Carb: 25g/71%   Fat: .5/ 3%   Sodium: 7mg   Potassium: 467mg   Fiber: 11g (4.6 soluble)   B1: 24%   Folic: 66%   P: 18%   Fe: 19%   Mg: 19%   Cu: 18%   Mn: 18%

CHICK-PEAS, a.k.a. Ceci or Garbanzo Beans. Chick-peas are round, medium-sized beans with a firm shape and nutty flavor.

Cal: 183   Pro: 10g/21%   Carb: 30g/66%   Fat: 3g/ 14%   Sodium: 12mg   Potassium: 438mg   Fiber: 7.5g (3.8g soluble)   B1: 16%   B6: 13%   Folic: 70%   P: 18%   Fe: 17%   Mg: 14%   Zn: 11%   Cu: 21%   Mn: 31%

FAVA BEANS. Fava beans are available fresh in the summer and dried and canned. The bean is large and flat with a firm texture and a delicate flavor. Dried favas need a long soak, 24 to 36 hours. Remove the skins after soaking and blanching. Canned favas are already skinned and cooked.

Cal: 128   Pro: 10g/30%   Carb: 22g/69%   Fat: .6g/ 4%   Sodium: 5mg   Potassium: 398mg   Fiber: 6.2g (1.2g soluble)   B1: 14%   Folic: 40%   P: 16%   Fe: 14%   Mg: 18%   Cu: 15%   Mn: 17%

GREEN BEANS. Green beans, both the American variety and the thinner, darker French *haricot verts,* are fairly good sources of beta-carotene; paler wax beans aren't. Wash all green beans under cool water, pick off leaves and stems, and snip off the ends. Cook uncovered in boiling water or steam just until tender. Fresh green beans, bagged and refrigerated, last up to five days; frozen, up to a year.

Cal: 31   Pro: 2g/17%   Carb: 7g/80%   Fat: .1g/3% Sodium: 6mg   Potassium: 209mg   Fiber: 3g (.7g soluble)   A: 13%   C: 27%

KIDNEY BEANS, a.k.a. Cannellini. A medium-sized bean with a soft texture and bland taste, red

and pink varieties are called kidney beans, white ones cannellini.

Cal: 153   Pro: 11g/29%   Carb: 28g/72%   Fat: .4g/ 2%   Sodium: 11mg   Potassium: 647mg   Fiber: 8.8g (3.7g soluble)   B1: 16%   Folic: 41%   P: 19%   Fe: 21%   Mg: 16%   Cu: 22%   Mn: 13%

LENTILS. A small, disk-shaped legume with a firm texture and a mild, distinctive taste, lentils are available in green, yellow, brown, and red varieties. They require no presoaking. Cook in water to cover for 20 to 30 minutes, being careful not to overcook them.

Cal: 162   Pro: 14g/29%   Carb: 27g/69%   Fat: 1g/ 2%   Sodium: 5mg   Potassium: 435mg   Fiber: 8g (1.8g soluble)   B1: 15%   B6: 13%   Folic: 52%   P: 22%   Fe: 24%   Mg: 13%   Zn: 12%   Cu: 20%   Mn: 20%

LIMA BEANS. Limas are available in baby and large varieties. Shell and steam or braise fresh limas; steam frozen limas. Both make delicious salads. Fresh limas can be kept in a plastic bag in the refrigerator for two or three days.

Cal: 150   Pro: 10g/22%   Carb: 28g/76%   Fat: .3g/ 2%   Sodium: 8mg   Potassium: 768mg   Fiber: 5.8g (1.5g soluble)   B1: 14%   B6: 11%   Folic: 44%   P: 17% Fe: 18%   Mg: 25%   Cu: 16%   Mn: 20%

OKRA. The smaller the pod, the more tender it will be; under 2½ inches is best. The pod should be flexible and velvety to the touch. Remove the stems; steam or simmer just until tender. To prevent sliminess, don't overcook. Cooking in iron, tin, copper, or brass utensils will cause okra to turn black—edible but not very attractive.

Cal: 38   Pro: 2g/21%   Carb: 8g/77%   Fat: .1g/2% Sodium: 8mg   Potassium: 303mg   Fiber: 3.2g (1.2g soluble)   A: 13%   C: 35%   B1: 13%   B6: 11%   Ca: 8%   Mg: 14%   Mn: 28%

PEAS. This small green or yellow legume is sold in all forms—fresh, frozen, canned, dried, and split. Sugar or snow peas can be eaten pod and all; mature sweet peas must be shelled. Sugar, snow, or sweet peas may be briefly cooked or eaten raw in salads. Frozen peas need only be thawed under cold water; no further cooking is needed for salads.

Split peas require no presoaking; cook like lentils. Dried whole peas need an overnight soak.

One-quarter cup dry split peas: Cal: 167 Pro: 12g/ 29% Carb: 30g/71% Fat: .6g/3% Sodium: 8mg Potassium: 481mg Fiber: 3.5g (1.1g soluble) B1: 24% B6: 4% Folic: 34% P: 18% Fe: 12% Mg: 14% Zn: 10% Cu: 21% Mn: 19%

Two-thirds cup fresh green garden peas: Cal: 81 Pro: 5g/26% Carb: 15g/71% Fat: .5g/4% Sodium: 5mg Potassium: 244mg Fiber: 5.7g (1.4g soluble) A: 13% C: 67% B1: 18% B3: 10% Folic: 16% P: 11%

PINTO BEANS, a.k.a. Roman Beans. This small, oval bean has a mild flavor and comes in pink or cranberry colors. It is good for chili and Mexican-style bean dishes.

Cal: 163 Pro: 10g/24% Carb: 30g/73% Fat: .5g/ 3% Sodium: 5mg Potassium: 638mg Fiber: 9g (3.4g soluble) B1: 18% B6: 24% Folic: 61% P: 20% Fe: 16% Mg: 20% Cu: 18% Mn: 16%

WHITE BEANS. This category includes great northern, navy, and small white beans. With a firm texture and mild flavor, they are the classics for baked beans and navy bean soup. Wash and pick over the dry beans; combine them with water to cover and bring them to a boil, cooking for 2 minutes; remove them from the heat, cover, and soak for 1 hour. Simmer 1 to 2 hours or until tender.

Navy beans: Cal: 174 Pro: 12g/23% Carb: 32g/ 74% Fat: 1g/3% Sodium: 8mg Potassium: 593mg Fiber: 8.4g (2.4g soluble) B1: 22% B6: 11% Folic: 48% P: 23% Fe: 19% Mg: 22% Cu: 23% Mn: 19%

Soyfoods

MISO. A rich, flavorful fermented soybean paste, miso will keep unrefrigerated, but for long storage it's best to refrigerate it in a container with a tight lid.

One teaspoon (6 g): Cal: 12 Pro: 1g/22% Carb: 2g/ 52% Fat: .4g/26% (S:16% M:23% P:61%) Chol: 0 mg Sodium: 215mg Potassium: 10mg Fiber: 0g

SOYBEANS. Soybeans are round with a bland taste and a firm texture. Do not eat them raw. Fresh soybeans can be cooked in boiling water for 10 to 13 minutes. Dry soybeans must be presoaked: Wash and pick over the beans, place them in a large saucepan with cool water, bring to a boil, remove from heat; let stand for 2 hours. Return to heat, bring to a boil, and simmer 3 to 4 hours until tender.

One-quarter cup dry (47 g): Cal: 194 Pro: 17g/ 33% Carb: 14g/27% Fat: 9g/40% (S:16% P:61% M:23%) Chol: 0mg Sodium: 1mg Potassium: 836mg Fiber: 3g B1: 27% B2: 23% Folic: 44% Ca: 13% P: 33% Fe: 40% Mg: 33% Zn: 15% Cu: 38% Mn: 33%

SOY MILK. Soybeans are soaked, then ground and filtered. Soy milk looks like cow's milk but it is less sweet. Keep it refrigerated. It is also available in aseptic packaging that does not need refrigeration until opened.

Three fluid ounces (100 g): Cal: 33 Pro: 3g/32% Carb: 2g/20% Fat: 2g/48% (S:15% M:62% P:23%) Chol: 0mg Sodium: 12mg Potassium: 141mg Fiber: 0g B1: 11%

TEMPEH. Made from fermented soybeans, tempeh comes in cakes. The texture is sometimes compared to chicken or veal, and it has a nutty flavor. It will stay fresh for about a week from purchase; check the date for freshness.

Three and a half ounces (100 g): Cal: 199 Pro: 19g/ 36% Carb: 17g/32% Fat: 8g/32% (S:15% M:24% P:61%) Chol: 0mg Sodium: 6mg Potassium: 367mg Fiber: n/a A: 14% B3: 23% B6: 15% B12: 14% Folic: 13% P: 21% Fe: 13% Mg: 18% Zn: 12% Cu: 33% Mn: 41%

TOFU. Tofu comes in white bricks (cakes) and has a fresh, milky-sweet flavor. Rinse tofu and place it in a plastic tub with a tight-fitting lid. Fill the tub with water. Fresh tofu keeps for a few days, but the water must be changed daily. Packed (pasteurized) tofu has a 2- to 4-week shelf life, but once opened, use it within a couple of days and change the water daily. It can be kept in the freezer for months; defrost in the refrigerator before use.

One-third of a large brick (100 g): Cal: 145 Pro: 16g/40% Carb: 4g/11% Fat: 9g/49% (S:16% M:23% P:61%) Chol: 0mg Sodium: 14mg Potassium: 237mg Fiber: 2g B1: 11% Ca: 21%

Nuts and Seeds

All nutrient data for nuts are based on a serving size of 1 ounce (28 grams); quantities for seeds are as marked.

NUTS

ALMONDS. Almonds are the seed of a drupe, from a tree closely related to the plum and peach; they are oval, small, and flat, with a tan shell. They are available whole, but nearly all are sold shelled—natural, blanched, sliced, smoked, diced, slivered, or as almond butter.

Dry roasted, unblanched: Cal: 167 Pro: 6g/13% Carb: 6g/13% Fat: 15g/74% (S:10% M:69% P:21%) Sodium: 3mg Potassium: 208mg Fiber: 4g (.5g soluble) E: 34% B2: 13% P: 15% Mg: 21% Cu: 13% Mn: 18%

BRAZIL NUTS. Large, triangular, chalky-white seeds in a very hard, dark brown shell, Brazil nuts are available whole in the shell, roasted, or salted. The shell is quite hard; use a nutcracker or hammer; the nuts are easy to shell after they have been boiled briefly. (Note: Newer selenium data, reported in the Nuts and Seeds chapter, have not yet been incorporated into the USDA's Handbook 8, from which these data come. Actual amounts may be higher.)

Dried, unblanched: Cal: 186 Pro: 4g/7% Carb: 4g/8% Fat: 19g/85% (S:26% M:37% P:37%)

Sodium: 0mg Potassium: 170mg Fiber: 3g (.4g soluble) E: 11% B1: 19% P: 17% Mg: 16% Cu: 25% Se: 41%

CASHEWS. Half moon–shaped nuts with a sweet, rich, buttery flavor, cashews are available raw or roasted, with or without salt. Cashews are only available shelled because the shell contains a toxic, irritating oil.

Dry roasted: Cal: 163 Pro: 4g/9% Carb: 9g/23% Fat: 13g/68% (S:23% M:62% P:15%) Sodium: 4mg Potassium: 160mg Fiber: 2g E: 15% P: 14% Mg: 18% Zn: 11% Cu: 31%

CHESTNUTS. Chestnuts have soft, white, crinkly meat with a sweet, nutty flavor and a brown shell. Fresh chestnuts are quite perishable due to their high moisture content; keep them covered in the refrigerator and use them quickly.

European chestnuts, roasted: Cal: 70 Pro: 1g/5% Carb: 15g/88% Fat: .7g/7% Sodium: 1mg Potassium: 168mg Fiber: 4g (3g soluble) C: 12% Mn: 10%

FILBERTS AND HAZELNUTS. Two names, same nut. Hazelnuts, smaller, sweeter, and more delicate, are prized in Europe; filberts are North American natives. Both have a distinctive, slightly smoky taste and a crunchy texture. They are sold in the shell or shelled, raw or roasted, whole or chopped.

Dry roasted: Cal: 188 Pro: 3g/5% Carb: 5g/11% Fat: 19g/84% (S:7% M:82% P:11%) Sodium: 1mg Potassium: 131mg Fiber: 2g E: 33% Mg: 21% Cu: 22% Mn: 17%

GINKGO NUTS. The nut is the white pit of the ginkgo fruit, with a sweet taste and crisp texture. It is found whole from the trees or canned (ginan) in Oriental shops. Wear gloves if you want to gather wild ginkgo nuts, as the flesh contains a serious skin irritant. Keep gloves on until all the flesh is removed.

Canned: Cal: 32 Pro: .7g/7% Carb: 6g/80% Fat: .5g/12% Sodium: 87mg Potassium: 51mg Fiber: n/a

MACADAMIA NUTS. Small, round, tan nuts with a rich, buttery flavor and crunchy texture, they are usually only found shelled; they're available roasted, and salted or unsalted.

Dried: Cal: 199 Pro: 2g/4% Carb: 4g/8% Fat: 21g/88% (S:15% M:83% P:2%) Sodium: 1mg Potassium: 104mg Fiber: 2g

PEANUTS. Our most common "nut" is actually the seed of an underground legume. Its taste is smooth and rich. It's available roasted in the shell, shelled, raw, dry roasted, salted or unsalted, or roasted in oil. And, of course, as peanut butter.

Dry roasted: Cal: 161 Pro: 7g/16% Carb: 5g/12% Fat: 14g/72% (S:15% M:52% P:33%) Sodium: 5mg Potassium: 204mg Fiber: 2g (.5g soluble) E: 13% B1: 12% B3: 20% P: 11% Mg: 13% Cu: 14%

Two tablespoons chunk-style peanut butter (32 g): Cal: 190 Pro: 8g/15% Carb: 7g/14% Fat: 16g/71% Sodium: 157 Potassium: 241mg Fiber: 1g B3: 22% P: 10% Mg: 13% Mn: 17%

PECANS. This soft, two-lobed nut has a very hard brown shell. The meaty nut has a rich flavor and a firm, crisp texture. Available whole in the shell, halved, or in pieces, pecans are one of the more perishable nuts. Store them sealed in a cool, dry place for up to 2 months. Refrigerate or freeze open containers of shelled nuts.

Dry roasted: Cal: 190 Pro: 2g/4% Carb: 6g/14% Fat: 18g/82% (S:9% M:66% P:26%) Sodium: 0mg Potassium: 111mg Fiber: 2g (.3g soluble) B1: 16% Zn: 10% Cu: 17% Mn: 35%

PIGNOLI, a.k.a. Pignon or Pine Nuts. These soft, white, very oily nuts are found in pine cones and have a pine taste; they vary in size and shape. Most look like orzo and are sold shelled. They're expensive—but a little goes a long way to enliven sauces and stuffings.

Dried: Cal: 146 Pro: 7g/15% Carb: 4g/10% Fat: 14g/75% (S:16% M:39% P:45%) Sodium: 1mg

Potassium: 170mg Fiber: 1g B1: 15% P: 14% Fe: 14% Cu: 14%

PISTACHIO NUTS. The nutmeat is deep green in color with a rich, distinct, buttery flavor and crisp texture. The shells are naturally tan; in the 1930s they were first dyed red when importers attempted to disguise imperfect, blemished shells. They come roasted in red or natural shells, already shelled, salted or unsalted.

Dried: Cal: 164 Pro: 6g/12% Carb: 7g/17% Fat: 14g/71% (S:14% M:72% P:14%) Sodium: 2mg Potassium: 310mg Fiber: 1g B1: 15% P: 14% Fe: 11% Mg: 11% Cu: 17%

WALNUTS. Two-lobed with a tan skin in a bumpy brown shell, walnuts have a rich, full-bodied flavor with a crisp crunchy texture. Black walnuts are the American species; they are smaller in size than their English cousins, with a rounder, harder shell, a smaller and darker edible portion, and a more bitter taste. They are usually sold shelled. English walnuts, the more common variety, originated in Europe and are available in the shell, or as halves, pieces, or chopped.

English walnuts: Cal: 182 Pro: 4g/8% Carb: 5g/12% Fat: 18g/80% (S:9% M:24% P:67%) Sodium: 3mg Potassium: 142mg Fiber: 2g (.2g soluble) C: 20% E: 27% Mg: 12% Mn: 22%

SEEDS

CARAWAY SEEDS. A tiny, dark brown seed of the carrot family known for its distinct and powerful aroma, it is one of the most popular spices in Europe and Scandinavia, used to flavor liqueurs, cheeses, breads, meat, and vegetables.

One tablespoon (6 g): Cal: 22 Pro: 1g/19% Carb: 3g/49% Fat: 1g/32% (S:5% M:85% P:30%) Sodium: 1mg Potassium: 91mg Fiber: n/a

POPPY SEEDS. The tiny, edible seeds of the poppy plant range in color from dark blue-gray to white. White poppy seeds must be stored in the refrigerator as they turn rancid quickly. Usually used whole, they may be ground into a paste, in a special mill, for bread and cake fillings.

One tablespoon (8 g): Cal: 151 Pro: 2g/13% Carb: 2g/17% Fat: 4g/70% (S:12% M:15% P:73%) Sodium: 2mg Potassium: 62mg Fiber: n/a

PUMPKIN/SQUASH SEEDS. The edible seeds of the pumpkin, or of winter squash such as acorn, come enclosed in white shells. Dry them for a few days at room temperature before baking at 325°F for 20 minutes. Shell them before eating.

Two tablespoons dried (17 g): Cal: 154 Pro: 7g/17% Carb: 5g/12% Fat: 13g/71% (S:20% M:32% P:48%) Sodium: 5mg Potassium: 229mg Fiber: 2g P: 33% Fe: 23% Mg: 38% Zn: 14% Cu: 20%

SESAME SEEDS. The tiny seeds from the sesame plant have a crunchy, nutty taste. They are available hulled. Their oil content will cause them to turn rancid unless refrigerated. Ground into a paste they become tahini, a staple of Middle Eastern cooking.

Two tablespoons dried (18 g): Cal: 104 Pro: 3g/12% Carb: 4g/15% Fat: 9g/73% (S:15% M:40% P:45%) Sodium: 3mg Potassium: 84mg Fiber: 2g (.5g soluble) Ca: 18% P: 11% Fe: 14% Mg: 16% Cu: 37% Mn: 13%

SUNFLOWER SEEDS. These have a dry, brittle hull and range from white to gray-black, often with stripes. Sunflower seeds are available whole or hulled; kernels out of their hulls have a very short shelf life as they are high in oxygen-sensitive polyunsaturated fat: refrigerate them immediately.

Two tablespoons dried (18 g) Cal: 102 Pro: 4g/15% Carb: 4g/12% Fat: 9g/73% (S:11% M:20% P:69%) Sodium: .5mg Potassium: 124mg Fiber: 2g (.6g soluble) E: 47% B1: 43% B6: 11% P: 13% Mg: 16% Cu: 16%

Mushrooms

All nutrient data are based on a 3½-ounce (100 gram) serving size, which is 1½ cups of fresh mushrooms. Because fresh mushrooms are about 90 percent water, much of this nutritional information would apply to about 10 grams (about a third of an ounce) of dried mushrooms.

Selection and Storage: Choose fresh mushrooms that are dry and firm. The gills should be completely closed, with no opening between the stem and the cap. Store fresh mushrooms in the refrigerator unwashed in a paper bag, open carton, bowl, or wire basket, or in their original packaging; they'll stay fresh up to 5 days.

Mushrooms lose their flavor if soaked in water. To clean them, wipe with a damp cloth, or rinse quickly in cold water, then blot dry. Never peel a mushroom as both flavor and nutrients are in the skin. Dried mushrooms should be rinsed in cold water and soaked 20 to 30 minutes in warm water in a covered, nonmetal container; use the drained liquid in cooking.

CÈPES, a.k.a. Bolete, Porcini, Steinpilz. Cèpes are available fresh in late spring and fall but in very limited supply; otherwise they are available year-round canned or dried. The heads are somewhat flattened and brown; the stems are light-colored and bulbous. With a deep, distinctive flavor, they're versatile both fresh and dried.

Cal: 34 Pro: 3g/33% Carb: 5g/56% Fat: .4g/11% Sodium: 6mg Potassium: 486mg Fiber: n/a D: 31% B2: 23% B3: 24% P: 12%

CHANTERELLE, a.k.a. Girolle. Chanterelles are available summer through winter, usually canned or dried. Fresh ones are quite fragile; avoid broken, moist caps. They have a delicate flavor that complements poultry or other light meats.

Cal: 23 Pro: 2g/27% Carb: 3g/42% Fat: 1g/31%
(fat breakdown n/a) Sodium: 3mg Potassium:
507mg Fiber: n/a D: 21% B2: 12% B3: 33% Fe:
36%

COMMON BUTTON. Available throughout the
year, they're best and most plentiful during fall
and winter.

Cal: 25 Pro: 2g/27% Carb: 5g/61% Fat: .4g/12%
Sodium: 4mg Potassium: 370mg Fiber: 2.5g
B2: 26% B3: 21% Panto: 22%

ENOKI. A long, thin mushroom with a mild and
slightly fruity flavor, enoki are available year-
round in Oriental markets. Tops and stems should
be creamy white; avoid those with any browning.
Use them as soon as possible after purchase. Trim
the heavy, spongy base from the mushrooms and
separate the strands. They are best eaten raw in
salads or as a garnish.

Cal: 38 Pro: 2g/19% Carb: 7g/76% Fat: .2g/5%
Sodium: 28mg Potassium: 300mg Fiber: n/a
B1: 40% B2: 29% B3: 53%

MOREL, a.k.a. Morille. Available fresh in
early spring through July and dried year-round.
Choose those with a sweet, earthy aroma and
firm, honeycomb-like ridges. Avoid wet or slippery morels; they should be dry and spongy to
the touch. Their magnificent woodsy taste is best
served by quick sautéing, in soups, or with light
meats or starches and grains. Rinse them before
using.

Cal: 31 Pro: 2g/24% Carb: 5g/66% Fat: .3g/10%
Sodium: 2mg Potassium: 390mg Fiber: n/a
D: 31% Ca: 12% P: 16%

OYSTER, a.k.a. Shimeji. Available year-round,
their price fluctuates according to availability. This
fan-shaped, cream-colored mushroom has a tender,
delicate flavor that becomes buttery when cooked.
Choose mushrooms that are cream to pearly gray.
They are very perishable, so be sure to avoid any
that have dark areas or are wet.

Cal: 35 Pro: 3g/32% Carb: 6g/63% Fat: .2g/5%
Sodium: 84mg Potassium: 379mg Fiber: n/a
B1: 33% B2: 29% B3: 54% P: 14%

PINE, a.k.a. Matsutake. Available in the
United States canned or dried, these are the most
popular of the Japanese wild mushrooms, prized
for their subtle pine fragrance. They're best
braised in stews and casseroles.

Cal: 34 Pro: 2g/18% Carb: 7g/75% Fat: .3g/7%
Sodium: 4mg Potassium: 375mg Fiber: n/a
B2: 18% B3: 45%

PUFFBALL. They are usually found dried in
markets, or they can be picked fresh in forests
during the summer. Puffballs have been referred
to as the "eggplant of the mushroom world."
Rather bland in taste, the large, round and white
mushrooms are best cooked with other strongly
flavored ingredients so that, like eggplant, they
can absorb flavors.

Cal: 4 Pro: 1g/44% Carb: .4g/36% Fat: .1g/20%
Sodium: 5mg Potassium: 19mg Fiber: n/a

**SHIITAKE, a.k.a. Black Forest, Golden Oak,
Doubloon.** Available year-round but most plentiful in spring and fall, this brownish, strong-
flavored mushroom has a flattened head that
ranges from 2 to 8 inches across. Look for those
that are firm and dry with a distinct garlicky-pine
aroma. Soak dried ones for 1½ hours to soften
them. Cut the stems of fresh or dried shiittakes
into small pieces before cooking, as they tend to
be tough.

Cal: 39 Pro: 2g/15% Carb: 7g/72% Fat: 1g/13%
Sodium: 6mg Potassium: n/a Fiber: n/a B1: 53%
B2: 29% B3: 27%

STRAW, a.k.a. Padi Straw. Available year-
round canned, they are most commonly used in
Oriental stir-fries. While they are visually appeal-
ing, they offer very little flavor to a dish. Eat them
with cap and stem together.

Cal: 36 Pro: 3g/27% Carb: 6g/57% Fat: 1g/16%
Sodium: 37mg Potassium: 346mg Fiber: n/a
B2: 18% B3: 46%

TRUFFLE. A rare, expensive delicacy, truffles
are available fresh whole, as peelings, or canned.
They come in black or white varieties. White truf-

fles have a stronger flavor and perfume than the black and are a traditional pasta accompaniment. Black ones are wonderful with potatoes, chicken, and other mild foods that will absorb truffle taste. For some, they may be an acquired taste.

Cal: 56   Pro: 6g/39%   Carb: 7g/53%   Fat: 1g/8%
Sodium: 77mg   Potassium: 526mg   Fiber: n/a
Fe: 19%

WOOD EAR, a.k.a. Tree Ear. These are available packaged year-round in Oriental markets. They must be soaked. The dark, translucent mushroom, best used along with other vegetables, will keep its distinctive shape and rubbery texture even after long cooking.

Cal: 37   Pro: 1g/6%   Carb: 8g/83%   Fat: 1g/11%
Sodium: n/a   Potassium: n/a   Fiber: n/a   Fe: 26%

Roots

All nutrient data is based on a 3½-ounce (100 gram) serving size, raw, with equivalent quantity in cups given, unless otherwise noted.

BAMBOO SHOOTS. Bamboo shoots are available year-round, usually canned. They need no preparation. Store them in the refrigerator for up to 10 days after the can has been opened.

Two-thirds cup, sliced: Cal: 27   Pro: 3g/23%
Carb: 5g/68%   Fat: .3g/9%   Sodium: 5mg
Potassium: 533mg   Fiber: 3g   B1: 10%

BEETS. Beets are available most of the year but somewhat less during the summer months. Buy small- or medium-sized beets; those that have stems and greens attached are sure to be fresh. The surface of the beet should be smooth with its tail intact; the greens, bright and fresh. Beets as large as four to a pound can be more flavorful than small ones; larger ones may be woody, even if long boiled. Cut all but 2 inches of the stem and greens off the beets; store greens wrapped in a paper towel in a plastic bag for a day or two.

Refrigerate beets unwashed in a plastic bag and use within 5 days of purchase.

Three-quarters cup, sliced: Cal: 44   Pro: 2g/9%
Carb: 10g/89%   Fat: .1g/2%   Sodium: 72mg
Potassium: 324mg   Fiber: 3g   C: 18%   Folic: 23%
Mn: 10%

CARROTS. Available year-round. Look for slender, firm carrots with a smooth surface and a deep color (the deeper the color orange, the more beta-carotene). If buying carrots with greens attached, make sure the greens are bright and perky. Although flavor is quite unpredictable in carrots, the large ones marketed for juice tend to be sweetest. Use the tops instead of parsley in stocks and soups. Sealed in plastic bags, carrots keep in the vegetable bin for several weeks; reseal the bag carefully after opening to keep remaining carrots from drying out. Carrot juice keeps only a day or two in the refrigerator.

One cup, shredded: Cal: 43   Pro: 1g/6%   Carb: 10g/91%   Fat: .2g/3%   Sodium: 35mg   Potassium: 323mg   Fiber: 3g (1.5g soluble)   A: 562%   C: 15%

CASSAVA, a.k.a. Yucca or Manioc. Available year-round, this roughly 8-inch-long, sweet-potato-shaped tuber is found mostly in ethnic markets specializing in Latin American cuisines. Cassava must be cooked; it is poisonous raw. Select firm cassava free of spots. Its brown skin should be dry and rough. Store whole in a cool, dry, ventilated room for 2 to 3 weeks. Wrapped, a cut cassava can be stored in the refrigerator for two days. Remove the tough skin with a paring knife or peeler.

Two-thirds cup: Cal: 120   Pro: 3g/7%   Carb: 27g/90%   Fat: .4g/3%   Sodium: 8mg   Potassium: 764mg   Fiber: .1g   C: 80%   B1: 15%   Fe: 20%   Mg: 16%

CELERY. Celery is available year-round. Select celery with brittle green stalks; inside should be smooth and firm. Store it unwashed in a plastic bag up to two weeks; to revive wilting stalks, set the bottom end in water in the refrigerator.

Two and a half stalks (four-fifths cup, diced):
Cal: 16   Pro: 1g/11%   Carb: 4g/86%   Fat: .1g/3%
Sodium: 88mg   Potassium: 284mg   Fiber: 2g   C: 11%

CELERY ROOT, a.k.a. Celeriac. Celery root is available October to April. Choose small- to medium-size, firm roots. Be prepared to lose half the weight of each root in parings. Even if you buy small roots—no larger than 4 ounces each—there is the risk that the inside may be too bitter or woody to eat. The stalk end should not be soft. Refrigerate and use within a few days of purchase.

Two-thirds cup: Cal: 39　Pro: 2g/9%　Carb: 9g/85%　Fat: .3g/6%　Sodium: 100mg　Potassium: 300mg　Fiber: 2g　C: 13%　Phos: 11%

FENNEL. Fennel is available late summer through early spring. Once an Italian specialty vegetable, it is now much more readily available. Look for freshly cut edges and a compact bulb. Wash it, trim the bottom and top, remove the outer pieces if bruised. It keeps a week refrigerated in a plastic bag.

One-half cup: Cal: 29　Pro: 3g/34%　Carb: 5g/55%　Fat: .4g/11%　Sodium: n/a　Potassium: 397mg　Fiber: n/a

JERUSALEM ARTICHOKES (SUNCHOKES). Available October to April. Look for smooth-skinned, firm roots, tan to cream in color; avoid any that have sprouted. Keep them in plastic in the refrigerator for up to two weeks. Rinse them under cold water; pare the roots or scrub them well before using. If you peel, slice off the small knobs and remove the skin with a peeler. Grate, shred, or cook them whole. Do not freeze them. (See artichoke pasta, in Pasta food profile, page 340.)

Two-thirds cup, sliced: Cal: 76　Pro: 2g/7%　Carb: 17g/92%　Fat: .01g/1%　Sodium: n/a　Potassium: n/a　Fiber: 2g　B1: 13%　Fe: 19%

JICAMA. Jicama are available November to June, at many Latin, Chinese, and specialty markets. Relatively smooth, taut skin with no sign of shriveling is the key to jicama quality. Store whole jicama as you would potatoes. Wrap unused cut portions in plastic and refrigerate up to a week. For extra crispness, store cut jicama in cold water. The skin is quite tough and should be removed with a paring knife, or pull it away with your fingers. Cut the white flesh into shreds, slices, or cubes.

Four-fifths cup, sliced: Cal: 41　Pro: 1g/13%　Carb: 9g/8%　Fat: .2g/4%　Sodium: 6mg　Potassium: 175mg　Fiber: 1g　C: 33%

PARSNIP. Parsnips are available year-round in bags; fresh ones peak in fall and winter and are best from late fall through early spring. Look for those with a smooth outer skin, well formed, firm, and medium in size. If they're covered in dirt, they may have just been dug. Trim off the greens and store the root unwashed in a plastic bag in the refrigerator for up to 5 days. Scrub with a brush under running water to remove the dirt. Peel with a vegetable peeler or cook with the peels on, removing the skin after cooking. Cut into segments before cooking since the tops are wider and take longer to cook than the tips.

Three-quarters cup, sliced: Cal: 75　Pro: 1g/4%　Carb: 18g/93%　Fat: .3g/3%　Sodium: 10mg　Potassium: 375mg　Fiber: 5g　C: 28%　Folic: 17%　Mn: 16%

POTATO. Available year-round, their quality is better in the winter months. Choose firm, smooth potatoes, avoiding those with wilted, wrinkled, or green skins. Potatoes fare well in commercial cellars, but few homes are suitable for prolonged storage, so don't buy more potatoes than you can use within a couple of weeks. Store them unwashed in a cool, dark place in a bag (such as paper) that allows air circulation. If you refrigerate them, take some out a day or two before using, so the starch that turns to sugar in the refrigerator can return to starch again. Cut away any sprouts, which are harmless, and green spots, which are toxic and caused by exposure to light.

One medium: Cal: 110　Pro: 3g/7%　Carb: 25g/92%　Fat: .2g/1%　Sodium: 11mg　Potassium: 765mg　Fiber: 2g　C: 44%　B6: 19%　Fe: 12%　Cu: 22%

SALSIFY. Look for roots with firm, smooth skins. Salsify is very perishable, so refrigerate it in a sealed plastic bag up to one week. After it is pared it will discolor quickly, so cook it immediately or keep it in water to which lemon juice or vinegar has been added.

Three-quarters cup, sliced: Cal: 82　Pro: 3g/11%　Carb: 19g/87%　Fat: .2g/2%　Sodium: 20mg　Potassium: 380mg　Fiber: n/a　C: 13%　B2: 12%

SWEET POTATO. Sweet potato is available year-round but peaks from October to January. Select rock-hard tubers free from soft or moldy spots. Around Thanksgiving, seek small, newly dug, yellow- or orange-fleshed sweet potatoes for a special treat. Store the potatoes in a cool, dry, dark place, but don't refrigerate them; they'll soften and spoil. Scrub them gently under cold running water with a soft brush and pat them dry. Cook them whole with the skins.

1 medium (130 g): Cal: 136   Pro: 2g/6%   Carb: 32g/93%   Fat: .4g/1%   Sodium: 17mg   Potassium: 265mg   Fiber: 3g   A: 522%   C: 49%   B2: 11%   B6: 17%   Cu: 11%   Mn: 13%

TARO ROOT. Taro is available year-round in the southern United States and Hawaii. Purchase roots that are firm and unblemished, avoiding those with spoils or cut skin. Store them uncut in a cool, dry place for 2 to 3 weeks. They may be refrigerated, but then use them within three or four days. Rinse them under water, pare with a vegetable peeler or paring knife, and cut or slice them fresh as you would a potato. Don't be surprised to see them turn purplish-pink when cooked.

One cup sliced: Cal: 107   Pro: 2g/3%   Carb: 26g/94%   Fat: .2g/2%   Sodium: 11mg   Potassium: 591mg   Fiber: 4g

WATER CHESTNUTS. Available year-round, usually canned, water chestnuts can be found fresh in Chinese markets. If you're lucky enough to find fresh ones, peel, slice, and cook them only briefly. Store them in water in the refrigerator for 7 to 10 days, changing the water daily.

Four-fifths cup, sliced: Cal: 106   Pro: 1g/4%   Carb: 24g/95%   Fat: .1g/1%   Sodium: 14mg   Potassium: 584mg   Fiber: 3g   B2: 11%

YAMS. Available year-round, yams are sold mainly in Latin American, Caribbean, Indian, and African specialty stores. True yams look like very large sweet potatoes but with a rough skin resembling bark. Choose evenly shaped yams with no cracks or soft spots. They are toxic if eaten raw. Wash them under running water, pare away all the outer barklike covering and the inner skin. Keep them in water with lemon juice until ready to cook.

Two-thirds cup, sliced; Cal: 118   Pro: 2g/5%   Carb: 28g/94%   Fat: .2g/1%   Sodium: 9mg   Potassium: 816mg   Fiber: 4g (2.1g soluble)   C: 28%   B6: 15%

Squash

All nutrient data are based on a 3½-ounce (100 gram) serving size, with equivalents given in cup measurements.

Selection and Storage: Summer squashes, harvested when immature, include zucchini, straight or crookneck yellow squash, and pattypan. The soft flesh has a mild taste and can be eaten raw or cooked. One pound yields 3 or 4 servings. Keep summer squash 4 or 5 days in a plastic bag in the refrigerator. You can also freeze it: Wash and slice the squash, steam it for 3 or 4 minutes, and seal it in freezer bags; it will last 6 months or longer.

Winter squashes—acorn, butternut, hubbard, and pumpkin—are harvested fully mature and have a stronger, sweeter flavor. Hubbards and butternuts are the best sources of carotenoids. Select hard, intact rinds without signs of decay, cracks, or watery areas. Spaghetti squash and chayote are somewhere between summer and winter varieties: They have thinner rinds, softer flesh than the winter kinds and are sweeter than the summer ones. (Like summer squash, chayote is harvested immature.) One pound yields 2 to 3 servings. Store at room temperature up to a week or refrigerate for 2 weeks. Cooked winter squash can be frozen, tightly sealed, for up to a year. All varieties are good in breads, soups, and pies.

ACORN. Look for those that are bright and deep green or orange in color. Select hard squash with intact rinds; go for the heavy-weights (1 to 3 pounds). They are available in fall and early winter.

Three-quarters cup, cubed: Cal: 40   Pro: 1g/5%   Carb: 10g/93%   Fat: .1g/2%   Sodium: 3mg   Potassium: 347mg   Fiber: 3.5g   A: 7%   C: 18%

BUTTERNUT. The rind is thin but tough and should be unblemished. Butternut is available in fall and early winter. Pare the rind, remove the seeds, and cut the squash into chunks; the cooked squash makes an unusually smooth puree.

Three-quarters cup, cubed: Cal: 45 Pro: 1g/6%
Carb: 12g/92% Fat: .1g/2% Sodium: 4mg
Potassium: 352mg Fiber: 4g A: 156% C: 35%

CHAYOTE. Chayote are available in fall and early winter. Select those with soft, tender rinds free from cuts or bruises. Tender rinds can be left on; if the rind is hard, peel it off. Steam or boil the pieces; bake halves or whole squash.

Four-fifths cup: Cal: 24 Pro: 1g/9% Carb: 5g/81%
Fat: .3g/10% Sodium: 4mg Potassium: 150mg
Fiber: 3g

CUCUMBER. Cucumber's not very nutritious, but it is low calorie and refreshing. Select firm, medium to dark green cucumbers, available year-round. Wash them well to remove the wax coating or choose the unwaxed Kirby or English varieties. Store them unwrapped in the vegetable crisper.

One cup, sliced: Cal: 13 Pro: 1g/10% Carb: 3g/82%
Fat: .1g/8% Sodium: 2mg Potassium: 149mg
Fiber: 1g

EGGPLANT. Eggplant is not botanically a squash; it's in the nightshade family. Select firm, glossy, purple-black eggplants with clear skin. They should be heavy in relation to their size. Available year-round, they peak in the summer. If the eggplant is small there is no need to remove the peel. They keep 2 or 3 days in a plastic bag in the refrigerator.

One and one-fifth cups, cubed: Cal: 26 Pro: 1g/
14% Carb: 7g/83% Fat: .1g/3% Sodium: 4mg
Potassium: 219mg Fiber: 2.5g

HUBBARD. Hubbards are similar to butternut squash; large ones are sweeter as they're left on the vine longer. They're available in fall and early winter. The puree freezes well.

Seven-eighths cup, cubed: Cal: 40 Pro: 2g/17%
Carb: 9g/74% Fat: 1g/9% Sodium: 7mg
Potassium: 320mg Fiber: 4g A: 108% C: 18%

PATTYPAN. Choose disk-shaped, smooth pattypan that are pale green-yellow with a cream-colored flesh; they are available during the summer months.

Three-quarters cup, cubed: Cal: 20 Pro: 1g/
14% Carb: 4g/77% Fat: .2g/9% Sodium: 2mg
Potassium: 195mg Fiber: 1g C: 25%

PUMPKIN. Select pumpkins with hard, unblemished rinds without punctures, cracks, or soft spots; they're available from October to mid-December. Cut the pumpkin in half, remove its seeds (and toast, if desired), bake, and scoop out the pulp. (For information on Pumpkin Seeds, see Nuts and Seeds food profile, page 347).

Seven-eighths cup, cubed: Cal: 26 Pro: 1g/9%
Carb: 7g/88% Fat: .1g/3% Sodium: 1mg
Potassium: 340mg Fiber: 2g A: 32% C: 15%

SPAGHETTI. Select pale yellow spaghetti squash, available October to mid-December. Pierce and bake the whole spaghetti squash; cut it in half, remove the seeds, and fluff the pulp into spaghetti-like strands.

One cup, cubed: Cal: 33 Pro: 1g/5% Carb: 7g/78%
Fat: 1g/17% Sodium: 17mg Potassium: 108mg
Fiber: 4g Cu: 19%

YELLOW CROOKNECK, a.k.a. Straightneck. Look for small, firm ones, available during the summer months. Serve them like zucchini, raw or cooked; pare them only if the rind is tough.

Three-quarters cup, sliced: Cal: 19 Pro: 1g/12%
Carb: 4g/78% Fat: .2g/10% Sodium: 2mg
Potassium: 212mg Fiber: 1g C: 14%

ZUCCHINI. Choose small but firm, bright-green zucchini; large ones tend to be watery. Zucchini is available mostly in the summer. There is no need to peel zucchini; just wash the skin and cut off the stem end.

Three-quarters cup, sliced: Cal: 14   Pro: 1g/16%
Carb: 3g/76%   Fat: .1g/8%   Sodium: 3mg
Potassium: 248mg   Fiber: 3g   C: 15%

Cruciferous Vegetables

All data are based on a 3½-ounce serving
size (100 gram), raw, with cup equivalents
given, unless otherwise noted.

ARUGULA, a.k.a. Roquett or Rocket Salad.
Available year-round, arugula peaks in spring and
early summer. Purchase it only if it looks very
fresh. Small leaves have the most flavor. Store
them unwashed up to three days in a plastic bag
in the refrigerator.

Two cups, chopped: Cal: 23   Pro: 3g/36%   Carb: 4g/
54%   Fat: .3g/9%   Sodium: n/a   Potassium: n/a
Fiber: 4g   A: 148%   C: 151%   Ca: 31%   Fe: 53%
Mg: 12%

BOK CHOY. Bok choy is available year-round
but is best when harvested in cool weather. Select bunches that are bright and fresh with green
leaves and juicy-looking, firm stems. Smaller
bunches will be more tender and delicate. Wash
and slice the stems at an angle for stir-fried dishes,
or slice them very thin to substitute for celery in
salads. Store them up to four days in a plastic bag
in the refrigerator.

One and a half cups, shredded: Cal: 13   Pro: 2g/36%
Carb: 2g/53%   Fat: .2g/11%   Sodium: 65mg
Potassium: 252mg   Fiber: 2g   A: 60%   C: 75%
Ca: 11%

BROCCOLI. Broccoli peaks in the late spring
and fall. Select tight blue-green flowerets and firm
stalks. Avoid woody stems, open-cored branches,
bunches with a strong smell, or those with yellow
or limp buds. Pare the outer stalks if thick and
fibrous. For fast, even stir-frying, cut off the flowerets in small pieces and thinly slice the stalks.
Cut them into slender stems with the flowerets
for steaming. Store broccoli up to five days in a
plastic bag in the refrigerator. *Broccoli de rabe*, a

nonheading form of broccoli that is also in the
cabbage family, is assertive, pungent, and more
bitter than broccoli; it requires little cooking time;
no nutritional information is available.

One and one-eighth cups, chopped: Cal: 28   Pro: 3g/
33%   Carb: 5g/57%   Fat: .4g/10%   Sodium: 27mg
Potassium: 325mg   Fiber: 3.2g (1.5g soluble)   A: 31%
C: 155%   Folic: 18%

BRUSSELS SPROUTS. Available year-round
except June and July, Brussels sprouts peak from
October to December. Look for small, tight buds
that are crisp and green. Avoid loose or yellow
leaves. Wash, trim the base of the core, remove
bruised outer leaves. Although Brussels sprouts
are usually cooked whole, there's no reason why
you can't slice them into attractive ribbons to
steam or stir-fry. Store them in a plastic bag in
the refrigerator up to five days.

Five sprouts, or one and one-eighth cups: Cal: 43
Pro: 3g/5%   Carb: 9g/69%   Fat: .3g/26%   Sodium:
25mg   Potassium: 389mg   Fiber: 5.8g (2.3 soluble)
A: 18%   C: 142%   B6: 10%   Folic: 15%

CABBAGE. Available year-round, cabbage is
best in the fall. Look for firm, smooth, tight cabbage; it should be heavy in relation to its size.
Remove the core by rotating a large knife around
it; cut the cabbage into wedges. For fast cooking
or cole slaw, slice the wedges into thin ribbons
with a long slicing knife or a food processor. Store
whole heads unwashed in a plastic bag in the refrigerator up to two weeks; shredded cabbage
wilts within a day.

One and one-half cups, shredded: Cal: 24   Pro: 1g/
17%   Carb: 5g/77%   Fat: .2g/6%   Sodium: 18mg
Potassium: 246mg   Fiber: 2g   C: 79%   Folic: 13%

CAULIFLOWER. Cauliflower is at its best in
the fall and winter. Select white or creamy, firm
bunches. The leaves should be fresh, rigid, and
green. The odor should be pleasant, not strong.
Rotate a large knife around the core and remove
it. Break off flowerets, then cut them smaller for
snacking raw, stir-frying, or sautéing. Thinly slice
them for salads. Store, unwashed, covered loosely
in plastic wrap, in the vegetable crisper of your
refrigerator up to four or five days.

One cup, chopped: Cal: 24   Pro: 2g/27%   Carb: 5g/
67%   Fat: .2g/6%   Sodium: 15mg   Potassium:
355mg   Fiber: 3.3g (2.5g soluble)   C: 120%   B6: 10%
Folic: 18%

CHINESE CABBAGE. This is also called celery
cabbage because of its cylindrical shape. It is
available in fall and winter in the southern United
States, in summer and fall in the north. Select
crisp, clean, thick bunches with good density and
heart formation. Stalks should be of medium
length. Slice leaves crosswise without separating
from the core; discard the core. Slice very thin to
serve it raw, thicker for steaming or stir-frying.
Store as cabbage, above.

One and one-third cups, shredded: Cal: 16   Pro: 1g/
25%   Carb: 3g/66%   Fat: .2g/9%   Sodium: 9mg
Potassium: 238mg   Fiber: 6g (3g soluble)   A: 24%
C: 45%   B6: 10%   Folic: 20%

COLLARD GREENS. Collard greens are available year-round. Look for large, smooth, nearly
round leaves with a resilient but coarse texture.
Select those that look fresh—not limp, yellowed,
or with holes. Rinse them; remove and discard
the heavy stalks. Stack the leaves, roll them up,
and slice them into ribbons. Chop the ribbons, if
you wish. If the greens will be simmered a long
time, just tear them into pieces. Store them unwashed in a big plastic bag in the coldest part of
your refrigerator for a day or two.

One-half cup, chopped: Cal: 19   Pro: 2g/28%   Carb:
4g/68%   Fat: .2g/4%   Sodium: 28mg   Potassium:
148mg   Fiber: 3.2g   A: 67%   C: 39%   Ca: 12%   Cu:
13%   Mn: 11%

HORSERADISH. Fresh horseradish is available during the spring months. Choose roots with
one slender, round end and one fatter, gnarled
end. The root should be firm with no soft spots,
wrinkles, or sprouts. Pare the root before grating
it. It will keep, refrigerated, in a plastic bag for
two or three weeks; don't freeze it.
Wasabi, a horseradishlike condiment made
from an Asian plant also in the cruciferous family,
is mixed with soy sauce and served with sushi.
But just dip a little: One medical report details the
case of a 63-year-old man who began sweating
profusely and collapsed after eating the entire
serving at once.

One tablespoon horseradish, chopped: Cal: 1   Pro:
.04g/10%   Carb: .3g/87%   Fat: .0003mg/3%
Sodium: .1mg   Potassium: 7.05mg   Fiber: n/a

KALE. Kale is available year-round except in
the hot summer months. Select resilient, smaller,
bouncy leaves with lacy edges. Tear the raw,
young leaves from small heads for salads and garnishes. For older larger heads, cut or tear the
tender parts of the leaves or chop them into small
pieces; then steam, stir-fry, or simmer like collard
greens. Store in a plastic bag in the refrigerator
for 2 or 3 days.

One and one-half cups, chopped: Cal: 50   Pro: 3g/
22%   Carb: 10g/67%   Fat: 1g/11%   Sodium: 43mg
Potassium: 447mg   Fiber: 6.6g (2.7g soluble)   A: 178%
C: 200%   B6: 14%   Ca: 14%   Cu: 15%   Mn: 22%

KOHLRABI. Kohlrabi is available primarily in
the summer months. Choose small bulbs with the
leaves attached. Remove the leaves and discard
the stems. Pare and thinly slice the bulbs to serve
with dip, or cut them into julienne strips for salad.
They can be blanched to soften their taste and
texture. The leaves can be stir-fried, sautéed,
braised, or simmered in soups. Store them refrigerated in a plastic bag 4 or 5 days.

Three-quarters cup, sliced: Cal: 27   Pro: 2g/21%
Carb: 6g/76%   Fat: .1g/3%   Sodium: 20mg
Potassium: 350mg   Fiber: 1g   C: 103%

MUSTARD GREENS. Available year-round,
they peak in the spring. Choose the smallest,
brightest leaves available. They should be firm
and resilient. Wash the leaves well, remove the
stems, and tear the leaves into small pieces. Prepare them raw (very spicy!) or cooked, like kale.
Store them unwashed in a plastic bag in the
coldest part of the refrigerator for a day or two.

One and three-quarters cups, chopped: Cal: 26   Pro:
3g/34%   Carb: 5g/60%   Fat: .2g/6%   Sodium: 25mg
Potassium: 354mg   Fiber: 2.8g   A: 106%   C: 117%
Ca: 10%

RADISHES. Available year-round, radishes are
best in unwrapped bunches with stems and leaves
intact. Look for firm, plump radishes with unbroken skin. Greens should be bright and resilient.

Radishes should not yield to pressure. Shred or grate them to make a colorful addition to green salads, cole slaw, and cooked green beans or spinach. They are also perfect for garnishing dips and creamy salads. Remove the tops, then store the radishes in a plastic bag in the refrigerator for up to two weeks; before serving, soak them briefly in icy water to revive wilting ones. Don't freeze them.

Five medium (25g): Cal: 4 Pro: .14g/11% Carb: 1g/67% Fat: .1g/22% Sodium: 5mg Potassium: 52mg Fiber: .6g

TURNIP AND RUTABAGA. These roots are available in the fall and winter. Choose turnips that are firm, smooth to the touch, unwrinkled; smaller ones will be sweeter. Choose rutabagas that are heavy, unbruised, globe-shaped with a purple streak on them. Both must be pared. Cut into cubes or strips prior to boiling or steaming. Store the roots unwashed in plastic bags in the refrigerator up to a week.

Three-quarters cup cubed turnips: Cal: 27 Pro: 1g/12% Carb: 6g/85% Fat: .1g/3% Sodium: 67mg Potassium: 191mg Fiber: 2.4g C: 35%

Three-quarters cup cubed rutabagas: Cal: 36 Pro: 1g/12% Carb: 8g/83% Fat: .2g/5% Sodium: 20mg Potassium: 337mg Fiber: 2.4g C: 42%

TURNIP GREENS. Choose relatively small, smooth, resilient leaves that are not limp or wilted. Wash them carefully: immerse them in a bowl of cool water; lift them from the water; repeat until no silt is visible. Remove thick stems; tear or chop the leaves into small pieces.

One and fourth-fifths cup, chopped; Cal: 27 Pro: 2g/19% Carb: 6g/72% Fat: .3g/9% Sodium: 40mg Potassium: 296mg Fiber: 3.9g A: 152% C: 100% B6: 13% Folic: 49% Ca: 19% Cu: 18% Mn: 13%

WATERCRESS. Watercress is available year-round. Select fresh sprigs with firm, crisp stems. The leaves should be bright green and free of bruises. Pick bunches with thinner stems. Remove thick stems before serving, or tear the sprigs into pieces with stems intact. Stand unwashed bunches in a container of water, covered with a plastic bag, in the refrigerator for two or three days; don't freeze.

One and a half cups, chopped (50 g): Cal: 5.5 Pro: 1g/60% Carb: .5g/34% Fat: .05g/6% Sodium: 21mg Potassium: 165mg Fiber: 3.3g A: 47% C: 36%

Salad and Greens

All nutrient data are based on a 3½-ounce (100 gram) serving size, with equivalent amounts given in cups, for example, or by the number of leaves, unless otherwise noted. Note: Dark green leafy vegetables are the best dietary source for vitamin K, yielding from a half to 10 times an adult's needs in a 3½-ounce serving; however, actual data for specific foods are so scant they're not included in this book.

Selection and Storage: Avoid any greens that look wilted or yellowed. Plan to serve greens as soon after purchase as possible. Store greens unwashed in open or perforated plastic bags in the vegetable bin; if lettuces are damp from supermarket misting, wrap them in paper toweling before putting them in plastic bags. In *Keeping Foods Fresh* (Harper & Row, 1989), Janet Bailey suggests storing uncut unwashed lettuce in a sealed plastic bag in the coldest part of the refrigerator. "Stored this way," she writes, "iceberg lettuce lasts one or two weeks, romaine seven to ten days, and butterhead three to four days." Greens are even more evanescent: Spinach lasts two or three days, as do kale, watercress, and dandelion greens.

ARTICHOKE. A member of the sunflower family along with cardoon, chicory, dandelion, sunchoke (jerusalem artichoke), and salsify, artichokes are available year-round. Choose vegetables that are heavy in relation to size, compact, with large, tightly clinging green leaves. Leaves should yield slightly to pressure. Wash and cut 1 inch off the top with kitchen scissors. Remove and discard hard outer leaves and stem. Trim off the thorny tips of remaining leaves. Squeeze lemon juice over the trimmed leaves to prevent browning if desired, before steaming or boiling. (*Cardoon,* a botanical relative, grows in bunches like flat celery; cooked, it tastes a little like artichoke and celery; simmer a half-hour to reduce bitterness before using in recipes.)

One small artichoke: Cal: 51 Pro: 3g/12% Carb: 12g/85% Fat: .2g/3% Sodium: 80mg Potassium: 339mg Fiber: 4g (.5g soluble) C: 18% Folic: 18% Mg: 12%

ARUGULA. See Cruciferous Vegetables.

AVOCADO. The avocado, a fruit, is high in fat, but it's mostly monounsaturated. It is also rich in vitamins, as well as taste, so enjoy it in small amounts. It's available year-round. Buy it when hard, leaving it in a warm place for a few days to ripen. It will yield to slight pressure when it's ready to serve. Never put a firm avocado in the refrigerator.

Once cut, refrigerate it. Use a cut avocado as soon as possible; meanwhile, cover it with plastic and refrigerate. Both peels and pits must be removed. If you cut an avocado in half, don't remove the pit until ready to serve. To avoid a darkening of color, sprinkle with lemon or lime juice.

Half an avocado (86g): Cal: 153 Pro: 2g/5% Carb: 6g/17% Fat: 15g/78% (S:17% M:69% P:14%) Sodium: 10mg Potassium: 548mg Fiber: 3g (1.6g) A: 11% C: 11% B6: 12% Folic: 14% Cu: 12%

BELGIAN ENDIVE, a.k.a. Witloof Chicory. Available year-round, Belgian endive peaks in cooler months. Look for firm, plump, crisp, and unblemished heads with yellow leaf tips.

One and one-eighth cups: Cal: 15 Pro: 1g/25% Carb: 1g/67% Fat: .1g/9% Sodium: 24mg Potassium: 315mg Fiber: 2g (1g soluble) A: 41% C: 11% Folic: 36%

BUTTERHEAD, a.k.a. Boston or Bibb. This lettuce is available year-round. Look for heads that are full and free of brown stem ends.

Two-thirds head, about a dozen leaves: Cal: 13 Pro: 1g/32% Carb: 2g/57% Fat: .2g/11% Sodium: 7mg Potassium: 260mg Fiber: 1.5g (.6g soluble) A: 19% C: 13% Folic: 18%

CELERY. See Roots.

COLLARD GREENS. See Cruciferous Vegetables.

CUCUMBER. See Squash.

CURLY ENDIVE, a.k.a. Curly Chicory. Curly endive is available year-round. Select heads with crisp leaves. Escarole, with its sturdy, slightly bitter leaves, is botanically and nutritionally quite similar.

One-half cup: Cal: 23 Pro: 2g/24% Carb: 5g/66% Fat: 3g/10% Sodium: 45mg Potassium: 420mg Fiber: 2.2g A: 80% C: 40% Panto: 16% Ca: 10%

DANDELION GREENS. Extraordinarily nutritious, dandelion greens are available year-round but are best in the spring. Look for tender greens, picked before the yellow flower develops, as dandelions become bitter with age. Use quickly, in salads or sautéed.

One and four-fifths cups, chopped: Cal: 45 Pro: 3g/ 18% Carb: 9g/66% Fat: 1g/16% Sodium: 76mg Potassium: 397mg Fiber: 4g (1.7g soluble) A: 280% C: 58% B1: 13% B2: 15% Ca: 19% Fe: 17%

ICEBERG, a.k.a. Crisphead. Extraordinarily lacking in nutrients, it could be said to have empty calories except it has hardly any calories. Available year-round with a decline in supply during the winter months. Look for firm, heavy heads with crisp outer leaves that yield slightly when squeezed.

Five whole leaves: Cal: 13 Pro: 1g/29% Carb: 2g/ 59% Fat: .2g/12% Sodium: 9mg Potassium: 158mg Fiber: 1g Folic: 14%

KALE. See Cruciferous Vegetables.

LOOSELEAF LETTUCE. Available year-round, it peaks in spring and fall. Look for soft, tender leaves that are either green or red-tipped.

Ten whole leaves: Cal: 18 Pro: 1g/24% Carb: 4g/ 64% Fat: .3g/12% Sodium: 9mg Potassium: 264mg Fiber: 2.1g (.9g soluble) A: 38% C: 30% Folic: 35%

MACHE, a.k.a. Lamb's Lettuce or Corn Salad. A rare and often expensive treat, the greens are quite delicate; use them immediately after purchase.

One and four-fifths cups: Cal: 21 Pro: 2g/ 31% Carb: 4g/55% Fat: 4g/14% Sodium: n/ a Potassium: n/a Fiber: n/a

MUSTARD GREENS. See Cruciferous Vegetables.

PARSLEY. A nutrient powerhouse—a half cup, twice the serving size analyzed below, provides about 10 percent of the USRDA for iron. Available year-round; the leaves should be green. Common varieties include flat or Italian and curly. Chop or mince it and use it lavishly in salads, grain dishes, soups, and sauces.

One-quarter cup, chopped (16g): Cal: 5 Pro: .4g/24% Carb: 1g/70% Fat: 1g/11% Sodium: 12mg Potassium: 161mg Fiber: 4g (.6g soluble) A: 17% C: 24%

RADICCHIO. Radicchio is available year-round except during the winter months. Look for ruby-colored leaves free of brown spots and wilting. Nutrition information is not available.

ROMAINE, a.k.a. Cos. Romaine is available year-round. Look for firm, unblemished heads with crisp leaves.

Ten inner leaves: Cal: 16 Pro: 2g/36% Carb: 2g/54% Fat: .2g/10% Sodium: 8mg Potassium: 290mg Fiber: 1g A: 52% C: 40% Folic: 34%

SPINACH. Prepackaged spinach is available year-round; loose spinach peaks in late spring and fall. Use small, tender leaves in salads; steam or sauté larger, thicker leaves. Spinach is rich in calcium but also in oxalic acid, which makes that calcium relatively unavailable.

One and four-fifths cups, chopped: Cal: 22 Pro: 3g/ 40% Carb: 4g/49% Fat: .4g/11% Sodium: 79mg Potassium: 558mg Fiber: 2.4g (.6g soluble) A: 134% C: 47% B2: 11% B6: 10% Folic: 48% Ca: 10% Fe: 15% Mg: 20%

SWISS CHARD. Swiss chard is available mostly from farm markets, since it ships badly. Select vegetables with crisp, green leaves; avoid those that are limp, wilted, or yellowing.

One and three-eighths cups, chopped, about one large leaf (50g): Cal: 10 Pro: 1g/30% Carb: 2g/62% Fat: .1g/8% Sodium: 107mg Potassium: 190mg Fiber: 1g A: 33% C: 25% Mg: 10%

TOMATO. Really a fruit, not a vegetable, a good summer tomato is delicious raw or cooked. It's available year-round but the taste and nutritional value fall off after the last local harvest. If you can't find vine-ripened tomatoes, switch to cherry or plum tomatoes, which often taste better than other winter varieties. Never refrigerate a tomato! (See also tomato juice, in Beverages food profiles, page 383.)

One medium tomato (123 g): Cal: 24 Pro: 1g/16% Carb: 5g/76% Fat: .3g/8% Sodium: 10mg Potassium: 255mg Fiber: 1g A: 28% C: 36%

TURNIP GREENS. See Cruciferous Vegetables.

WATERCRESS. See Cruciferous Vegetables.

Sea Vegetables

Sea vegetables are very low in calories and high in minerals, but we tend to eat them in small quantities. To illustrate their nutritional profile, we've calculated the information based on a one-ounce dry weight (28 gram) serving size—about as much as you might eat in a large salad, much more than you'd get wrapped around sushi—and included nutrients that are more than 2 percent of the USRDA.

AGAR. A firm, jellylike substance, agar comes packaged in bars, flakes, or powder. Store dried agar in an airtight container in a cool, dry place. Once made into a gel, it must be refrigerated. It produces a firm jelly and is used in many gourmet ice creams and gelatins. It may be used as a vegetarian substitute for gelatin.

Cal: 7 Pro: .1g/8% Carb: 2g/91% Fat: .01g/1%
Sodium: 2mg Potassium: 64mg Fiber: n/a Fe: 3%
Mg: 5% Mn: 3%

ARAME. Black strands of sea grass, arame is found in dried form. Rinse and soak it in water for 5 to 10 minutes before cooking to remove any sand or tiny shells. After cooking, arame will keep several days refrigerated.

Cal: 14 Pro: 1g/13% Carb: 3g/87% Fat: .01g/0%
Sodium: n/a Potassium: 221mg Fiber: n/a Ca: 7%
Fe: 4%

DULSE. Reddish-purple, feathery, and slightly salty, if bought packaged, it can be eaten right out of the bag. It comes raw or roasted.

Cal: 16 Pro: .1g/1% Carb: 5g/97% Fat: .03g/2%
Sodium: 3mg Potassium: 457mg Fiber: n/a
Ca: 2%

HIJIKI. Rinse these dried, black strands of sea grass and soak them in water for 30 minutes before cooking. Once cooked, hijiki will keep several days refrigerated.

Cal: 8 Pro: .3g/15% Carb: 2g/79% Fat: .1/6%
Sodium: n/a Potassium: 833mg Fiber: n/a
Ca: 8% Fe: 9%

IRISH MOSS. Irish moss is available fresh or dried. Fresh moss needs to be thoroughly washed in cold water; soak dried moss in enough cool water to cover it, let it sit ½ hour, pick out any foreign specks, and cut it into flowerets. Boil it with liquids to produce a gel or thickener.

Cal: 14 Pro: 1g/11% Carb: 3g/86% Fat: .1g/3%
Sodium: 19mg Potassium: 18mg Fiber: 1g B2: 7%
P: 4% Fe: 14% Zn: 4% Mn: 2%

KOMBU, a.k.a. Kelp. Kombu comes dried, usually brown, and cut into 6- to 12-inch lengths. Keep indefinitely in a cool, dry place. After opening, store it in an airtight container for several months. Wipe kombu clean of any dust. It can also be roasted and ground into a powder and used for seasoning.

Cal: 12 Pro: .5/13% Carb: 3g/77% Fat: .2g/10%
Sodium: 66mg Potassium: 25mg Fiber: 1.2g
B2: 3% Folic: 13% Ca: 5% Fe: 4% Mg: 9%
Zn: 2%

NORI. The paper-thin 8- by 10-inch black sheets are sold pretoasted and ready to use. Store unopened packages in an airtight container in a cool, dry place. After opening, store unused sheets in the freezer or with a few grains of rice in an airtight container in a cool, dry place. Use nori quickly since flavor deteriorates.

Cal: 10 Pro: 2g/50% Carb: 1g/44% Fat: .1g/6%
Sodium: 14mg Potassium: 101mg Fiber: 1g
A: 29% C: 18% B2: 7% Fe: 3% Cu: 4% Mn: 8%

WAKAME. Feathery and dark green, wakame is now available in "instant" form in sealed envelopes. Keeps indefinitely when dry; after soaking it must be refrigerated. It will remain fresh if kept in a little salt water in a sealed container. Soak for 10 to 15 minutes to reconstitute it; cut away tough outer rib.

Cal: 13 Pro: 1g/22% Carb: 3g/68% Fat: .2g/11%
Sodium: 248mg Potassium: 14mg Fiber: 1.2g
B2: 4% Ca: 4% Fe: 3% Mg: 8% Cu: 4% Mn: 11%

Ginger

Fresh ginger root should be plump; very young roots may be used skin and all, but most ginger needs to be peeled. Wrap unused portions tightly and refrigerate for two to three weeks. Fresh ginger may also be stored in a glass jar filled with sherry in the refrigerator for six months or more; the infused sherry is delicious in cooking. Fresh ginger can also be frozen in an airtight bag for three or four weeks. (Dried ginger, like any dry spice, should be kept covered in a cool dry place no longer than a year.)

One-quarter cup, sliced (24g): Cal: 17   Pro: .4g/8%
Carb: 4g/83%   Fat: .2g/9%   Sodium: 3mg
Potassium: 100mg

Garlic and Onions

All nutrient data are based on a 3½-ounce (100 gram) serving size, with equivalents in cups or amounts given, unless otherwise noted (as in the case of garlic).

ASPARAGUS. A faint botanic cousin of onions and garlic, asparagus tips should be dry, firm, purplish, and tight and come to a point. Tips that are soft or open signal a past-prime asparagus likely to be tough and woody; wet or slimy signals rotten—something your nose will verify. The greener the stalks the better. Thin varieties tend to be more tender. Store in the coldest part of the refrigerator; flavor deteriorates rapidly at room temperature. Break off each stalk as far down as it will snap easily to get tender portions.

Seven spears, or three-quarters cup (100 g):
Cal: 25   Pro: 3g/33%   Carb: 4g/59%   Fat: .3g/8%
Sodium: 4g   Potassium: 310mg   Fiber: 2g   A: 18%
C: 45%   Folic: 24%

GARLIC. Seek large, firm, unsprouted heads. Store uncovered in a cool place with good air circulation. Do not refrigerate. If sliced, diced, minced, or crushed, store in an airtight container in the refrigerator. Loosen skins by placing a couple of cloves on a cutting board, covering them with the flat side of a knife, and hitting the knife gently with your fist. They can also be peeled like an onion: after cutting off the ends, work the knife tip under the skin and peel back. To peel a quantity: put cloves in boiling water for 30 seconds, rinse under cold water, and drain. The skins will come off easily.

Three cloves (9g): Cal: 13   Pro: 1g/11%   Carb: 3g/
85%   Fat: .1g/4%   Sodium: 2g   Potassium: 36mg
Fiber: .2g

LEEKS. Choose leeks no more than 1½ inches in diameter; large ones can be fibrous. They should be crisp and the tops unwithered and green. Leeks keep up to 3 weeks, wrapped, in the crisper of the refrigerator.

One cup, chopped (100 g): Cal: 61   Pro: 2g/12%
Carb: 14g/84%   Fat: .3g/4%   Sodium: 20g
Potassium: 180mg   Fiber: 3.1g   C: 20%   Folic: 16%
Fe: 12%

RED ONION. Look for tight, dry skins, the absence of blemishes, and no sign of sprouting. A fine onion will have no scent whatsoever. Store onions in a cool, dry, and dark place. When cut, wrap tightly in plastic and use as soon as possible.

Two-thirds cup, chopped (100g): Cal: 42   Pro: 1g/
11%   Carb: 9g/87%   Fat: .1g/2%   Sodium: 4mg
Potassium: 156mg   Fiber: 2g   C: 13%

SCALLION, a.k.a. Green Onion. Choose scallions that are free of soil and unscarred, with long green stems. Wipe them off and refrigerate wrapped in a moist paper towel inside a plastic bag.

One cup, chopped (100 g): Cal: 26   Pro: 2g/24%
Carb: 6g/73%   Fat: .1g/3%   Sodium: 4mg
Potassium: 257mg   Fiber: 3g   A: 100%   C: 75%

SHALLOTS. Select shallots with firm, dry skins; avoid sprouted or shriveled ones. Store them like garlic, or keep them in plastic bag in the crisper of the refrigerator. Wash them before using.

One tablespoon, chopped (10g): Cal: 30   Pro: .25g/
11%   Carb: 2g/88%   Fat: .01g/1%   Sodium: 1mg
Potassium: 33mg   Fiber: 0g

WHITE AND YELLOW ONIONS. Select firm onions and store them in a cool, dark place. If the skin is tight, pierce the onion before dropping it into boiling water for 1 minute; rinse in cool water; trim both ends. The skin will come off easily.

Two-thirds cup white or yellow onions, chopped
(100g): Cal: 38   Pro: 1g/11%   Carb: 7g/81%   Fat:
.3g/8%   Sodium: 10mg   Potassium: 157mg   Fiber:
3.1g (1g soluble)   C: 14%

Peppers

Storage and Preparation for Hot
Peppers: Make sure hot peppers are wrapped so that they do not come in contact with other foods. When cutting and seeding hot peppers, wear rubber gloves and avoid contact with eyes. Much of the heat is in the seeds and veins, so remove these if you want less-hot chili flavor.

The USDA has no nutrition data on specific hot chili peppers, only on sweet green and red peppers and on hot green and red peppers. That information is below, followed by descriptive information on specific chilies.

Sweet green bell peppers. One-half cup, chopped (48g): Cal: 12 Pro: .4g/12% Carb: 3g/73% Fat: .2g/15% Sodium: 2mg Potassium: 98mg Fiber: 1g (.3g soluble) C: 106%

Sweet red bell peppers. One-half cup, chopped (48g): Cal: 12 Pro: .4g/12% Carb: 3g/73% Fat: .2g/15% Sodium: 3mg Potassium: 195mg Fiber: 1g (.4g soluble) A: 57% C: 158%

Green hot chili pepper. One-half pepper (24g): Cal: 9 Pro: .5g/17% Carb: 2g/79% Fat: .1g/4% Sodium: 2mg Potassium: 76mg Fiber: .5g C: 91%

Red hot chili pepper. One-half pepper (24g): Cal: 9 Pro: 1g/17% Carb: 2g/79% Fat: .1g/4% Sodium: 2mg Potassium: 76mg Fiber: .5g A: 48% C: 91%

ANAHEIM. Also called California green, long green/red chili, and chili colorado, this pepper is broad, rough, and triangular, mildly hot, bright green when young, about 7 inches long. As it matures, its color deepens to red.

ANCHO. A dried poblano chili, it is about 5 inches long, deep maroon to almost black in color, and mildly hot. It can be found in Mexican and some Caribbean specialty stores. Soak in warm water for 30 minutes before using.

BELL. Named for its shape, the mild, sweet bell pepper is broad and blocky, and may be colored green, red, yellow, orange, or brown. The redder the pepper, the sweeter the flavor. It's easy to buy peppers: if they look good they will be top quality. Choose peppers that are well shaped, very firm, smooth, and bright, with a colorful uniform gloss. They peak in late summer.

BLACK PEPPER. Black to grayish black in color, the larger the peppercorn, the more pungent the taste. Bottled peppercorns should be used before they turn cloudy.

CAYENNE. Cayenne is often called "red pepper," but cayenne is hotter than other ground red chili peppers. It may be found fresh—young and green—in Indian, Chinese, or Korean specialty stores.

CHIPOLTE. Chipotle is a smoked and dried form of a jalapeño.

GREEN PEPPERCORNS. Green immature peppercorns with a mild to sweet flavor, they can be bought dried or packed in brine or vinegar.

HABEÑERO. These peppers are small, very hot, green or red, and shaped like a lantern. They can be found in Mexican or Caribbean specialty stores.

JALAPEÑO. Jalapeños are medium to dark green, about 2 inches long, of medium width, and very hot; they're usually marketed green, while flavor is at its peak. They are available fresh, canned, or bottled.

PAPRIKA. A colorful powder made from a variety of dried, ground chili peppers, paprika comes in sweet, semi-sweet, or pungent varieties. Top-quality paprika is rich red in color. Add it at the end of cooking; it scorches and loses flavor quickly.

POBLANO. Dark, almost black-green, poblano is about 5 inches long, mild to mildly hot. Don't accept soft, spotted, or cracked peppers. Pale color and soft seeds are signs of immature peppers. Blister spots are a sign of age. It peaks in summer and fall.

SERRANO, a.k.a. Chile Verde. Lighter, smaller, and thinner than jalapeños, serrano peppers are about 2 inches long. Some varieties are short and fat. They're branding-iron hot. They're often available fresh in specialty stores.

WHITE PEPPER. Off-white in color, this is black pepper without the outside skin. It should have a smooth surface and a fine scent. It's ideal for sauces where the color of black pepper would be inappropriate.

Fish

All fish quantities are based on a serving of 3½ ounces (100 grams), raw. For information on selection and storage, see Cooking Fish, page 218.

BASS. Whole fish (½ to 5 pounds) and fillets are available September through March.

Whole sea bass: Cal: 93   Pro: 19g/88%   Carb: 0g/ 0%   Fat: 1g/12%   Chol: n/a   Sodium: 68 mg   Potassium: 256mg   Omega 3: n/a   P: 21%

Striped bass: Cal: 105   Pro: 19g/77%   Carb: 0g/0%   Fat: 3g/23%   (S:26%   M:34%   P:40%)   Chol: 80mg   Sodium: 68mg   Potassium: 256mg   Omega 3: 1g   B12: 64%

White bass: Cal: 98   Pro: 18g/79%   Carb: 0g/0%   Fat: 2g/21%   (fat breakdown n/a)   Chol: 59mg   Sodium: n/a   Potassium: n/a   Omega 3: .3mg

BLUEFISH. Whole fish (3 to 6 pounds) and fillets are available year-round, but bluefish peaks December to April in Florida, August and September in the mid-Atlantic states.

Cal: 124   Pro: 20g/69%   Carb: 0g/0%   Fat: 4g/31%   (S:24%   M:47%   P:29%)   Chol: 59mg   Sodium: 60mg

Potassium: 372mg   Omega 3: 1g   B3: 30%   B6: 20%   B12: 89%   P: 23%

BUTTERFISH. Whole (½ to 3 pounds) and dressed fish and fillets are available year-round, especially in the East.

Cal: 146   Pro: 17g/50%   Carb: 0g/0%   Fat: 8g/50%   (fat breakdown n/a)   Chol: 65mg   Sodium: 89mg   Potassium: 375mg   Omega 3: n/a

CATFISH. Whole (½ to 6 pounds) and dressed fish fillets, steaks, and chunks are available year-round, peaking August to October.

Cal: 116   Pro: 18g/67%   Carb: 0g/0%   Fat: 4g/33%   (S:28%   M:44%   P:28%)   Chol: 58mg   Sodium: 63mg   Potassium: 349mg   Omega 3: .3g   B3: 11%

COD, ATLANTIC AND PACIFIC. Cod is available year-round dressed, as fillets and steaks, or salted; smaller Pacific cod may be sold whole.

Atlantic cod: Cal: 82   Pro: 18g/92%   Carb: 0g/0%   Fat: 1g/8%   Chol: 43mg   Sodium: 54mg   Potassium: 413mg   Omega 3: .3g   B3: 10%   B6: 12%   B12: 15%   P: 20%

Pacific cod: Cal: 82   Pro: 18g/92%   Carb: 0g/0%   Fat: 1g/8%   Chol: 37mg   Sodium: 71mg   Potassium: 403mg   Omega 3: .2mg   B3: 10%   P: 17%

CROAKER. Whole (1 to 4 pounds) and dressed fish and fillets are available year-round with the peak in the spring.

Cal: 105   Pro: 18g/72%   Carb: 0g/0%   Fat: 3g/28%   (S:41%   M:41%   P:18%)   Chol: 61mg   Sodium: 56mg   Potassium: 345mg   Omega 3: .2g   P: 21%

CUSK, a.k.a. Tust. Whole fish (1½ to 5 pounds), fillets, or salted fish are available year-round, but cusk is hard to find.

Cal: 87   Pro: 19g/89%   Carb: 0g/0%   Fat: 1g/11%   Chol: 41mg   Sodium: 31mg   Potassium: 392mg   Omega 3: n/a   B3: 14%   B6: 20%   B12: 17%   P: 20%

FLOUNDER. Whole (2 to 10 pounds) and dressed fish and fillets are available year-round, with a peak in early spring and late fall off the New England coast.

Cal: 91   Pro: 19g/90%   Carb: 0g/0%   Fat: 1g/10% Chol: 48mg   Sodium: 76mg   Potassium: 366mg Omega 3: .2g   B3: 14%   B6: 10%   B12: 25%   P: 18%

GREENLAND TURBOT. Fillets are available year-round.

Cal: 188   Pro: 14g/33%   Carb: 1g/1%   Fat: 14g/ 66%   (S:20%   M:69%   P:11%)   Chol: 46mg   Sodium: 80mg   Potassium: 268mg   Omega 3: n/a   B3: 11% B6: 28%   B12: 37%   P: 16%   Mg: 13%

GROUPER. Whole (3 to 25 pounds) and dressed fish, fillets, and steaks are available year-round, but they are most plentiful in the summer.

Cal: 94   Pro: 20g/91%   Carb: 0g/0%   Fat: 1g/9% Chol: 24mg   Sodium: 53mg   Potassium: 483mg Omega 3: .3g   B12: 10%   P: 16%

HADDOCK. Whole (3 to 17 pounds) and dressed as fillets, steaks, or smoked, haddock is available year-round, peaking in May and June.

Cal: 87   Pro: 19g/93%   Carb: 0g/0%   Fat: 1g/7% Chol: 58mg   Sodium: 68mg   Potassium: 311mg Omega 3: .2g   B3: 19%   B6: 15%   B12: 20% P: 19%

HALIBUT. Whole fish (5 to 20 pounds or more), fillets, and steaks are available year-round. Due to regulations, Pacific halibut is only available from May to mid-July; Atlantic halibut peaks in the spring off Nova Scotia.

Cal: 110   Pro: 21g/81%   Carb: 0g/0%   Fat: 2g/19% (S:17%   M:44%   P:39%)   Chol: 32mg   Sodium: 54mg Potassium: 450mg   Omega 3: 1g   B3: 29%   B6: 17% B12: 20%   Mg: 20%

LING. Whole (3 to 20 pounds) and dressed fish, fillets, and steaks are available year-round.

Cal: 85   Pro: 18g/88%   Carb: 0g/0%   Fat: 1g/12% Chol: 40mg   Sodium: 59mg   Potassium: 437mg

Omega 3: .1g   B2: 11%   B3: 11%   B6: 15% P: 20%   Mg: 16%

MACKEREL. Atlantic varieties peak November through April; Spanish mackerel is in season November through April.

Cal: 205   Pro: 19g/39%   Carb: 0g/0%   Fat: 14g/ 61%   (S:27%   M:34%   P:39%)   Chol: 70mg   Sodium: 90mg   Potassium: 314mg   Omega 3: 3g   B1: 12% B2: 18%   B3: 45%   B6: 20%   B12: 145%   P: 22%

MAHI MAHI. Steaks and fillets are available in late spring and summer.

Cal: 90   Pro: 19g/88%   Carb: 1g/5%   Fat: 1g/7% Chol: 73mg   Sodium: 88mg   Potassium: 416mg Omega 3: .1g

MONKFISH. Tail and fillets are available year-round.

Cal: 76   Pro: 15g/81%   Carb: 0g/0%   Fat: 2g/19% (fat breakdown n/a)   Chol: 25mg   Sodium: 18mg Potassium: n/a   Omega 3: n/a

MULLET. Whole fish (1/2 to 4 pounds) and fillets, smoked and salted, or in boneless blocks: all are available in fall and summer.

Cal: 117   Pro: 19g/71%   Carb: 0g/0%   Fat: 4g/29% (S:38%   M:38%   P:24%)   Chol: 50mg   Sodium: 65mg Potassium: 357mg   Omega 3: 1g   B6: 20%   P: 22%

OCEAN PERCH. Most ocean perch is frozen, but some is available fresh by air freight from Iceland and Canada (1/2 to 2 pounds).

Cal: 94   Pro: 19g/85%   Carb: 0g/0%   Fat: 2g/ 15%   (S:17%   M:50%   P:33%)   Chol: 42mg   Sodium: 75mg   Potassium: 273mg   Omega 3: .2g   B12: 17% P: 22%

ORANGE ROUGHY. Frozen fillets are available year-round.

Cal: 126   Pro: 15g/50%   Carb: 0g/0%   Fat: 7g/50% (S:3%   M:94%   P:3%)   Chol: 20mg   Sodium: 63mg Potassium: n/a   Omega 3: n/a

PIKE. Whole and dressed fish and fillets are available year-round.

Cal: 88 Pro: 19g/93% Carb: 0g/0% Fat: 1g/7%
Chol: 39mg Sodium: 39mg Potassium: 259mg
Omega 3: .1g P: 22%

POLLOCK. Whole (1 to 12 pounds) and dressed fish, fillets, and steaks are available year-round, peaking in late fall.

Cal: 92 Pro: 19g/90% Carb: 0g/0% Fat: 1g/10%
Chol: 71mg Sodium: 86mg Potassium: 356mg
Omega 3: 1g B2: 11% B3: 16% B6: 14%
B12: 53% P: 22%

RED SNAPPER. Whole and dressed fish and fillets are available year-round.

Cal: 103 Pro: 22g/90% Carb: 0g/0% Fat: 1g/10%
Chol: 37mg Sodium: 65mg Potassium: 432mg
Omega 3: .2g P: 20%

ROCKFISH. Whole (1 to 5 pounds) and dressed fish and fillets are available in the fall.

Cal: 95 Pro: 19g/85% Carb: 0g/0% Fat: 2g/15%
(S:31% M:28% P:41%) Chol: 35mg Sodium: 59mg
Potassium: 405mg Omega 3: 1g B3: 17% P: 18%

SABLEFISH. Whole (average 8 pounds) and dressed fish, fillets, and steaks are available year-round.

Cal: 195 Pro: 13g/29% Carb: 0g/0% Fat: 15g/71%
(S:24% M:61% P:15%) Chol: 49mg Sodium: 56mg
Potassium: 358mg Omega 3: 2g

SALMON. Salmon comes whole (3 to 20 pounds) and dressed, as steaks and fillets, smoked or canned; due to the variety of forms, it is available year-round. The fresh fish peaks from early summer to the end of fall.

Cal: 168 Pro: 21g/53% Carb: 0g/0% Fat: 9g/47%
(S:20% M:56% P:24%) Chol: 62mg Sodium: 46mg
Potassium: 391mg Omega 3: 1g B1: 13%
B3: 29% B6: 10% P: 22%

SARDINES. Sardines are ready to eat from the can packed in oil, mustard sauce, or tomato sauce.

Raw Pacific sardines: Cal: 160 Pro: 19g/52% Carb: 0g/0% Fat: 9g/48% (fat breakdown n/a) Chol: 61mg Sodium: n/a Potassium: n/a Omega 3: n/a B2: 14% B3: 21% B12: 150% P: 22%

Atlantic sardines, canned in oil, drained solids with bone: Cal: 208 Pro: 25g/50% Carb: 0g/0% Fat: 12g/50% (S:14% M:37% P:48%) Chol: 142mg Sodium: 505mg Potassium: 397mg Omega 3: 2g B2: 13% B3: 26% B12: 149% Ca: 38%

SEA TROUT, a.k.a. Weakfish. Whole (1 to 6 pounds) and dressed fish and fillets are available year-round, but they peak in spring, summer, and fall. There are extreme highs and lows in the abundance of sea trout.

Cal: 107 Pro: 17g/65% Carb: 0g/0% Fat: 4g/35%
(S:38% M:34% P:28%) Chol: 83mg Sodium: 59mg
Potassium: 341mg Omega 3: .2g P: 25%

SHARK. Steaks, chunks, and fillets are available year-round.

Cal: 130 Pro: 21g/65% Carb: 0g/0% Fat: 5g/35%
(S:24% M:46% P:30%) Chol: 52mg Sodium: 79mg
Potassium: 160mg Omega 3: 1g B3: 15% B12: 17%
P: 21% Mg: 12%

SKATE. The wings, the only part eaten, are available, sometimes skinned, year-round.

Cal: 93 Pro: 20g/87% Carb: 0g/0% Fat: 1g/13%
Chol: 52g Sodium: 90mg Potassium: 250mg
Omega 3: .5g B3: 10%

SMELT. Whole fish (4 to 15 of these small fish per pound) are available September to May. In April, a 10-day smelt run usually leads to a harvest of millions of pounds of smelt.

Cal: 97 Pro: 18g/78% Carb: 0g/0% Fat: 2g/22%
(S:25% M:30% P:45%) Chol: 70mg Sodium: 60mg
Potassium: 290mg Omega 3: 1g B12: 57% P: 23%
Zn: 11%

SOLE. Whole (1/2 to 7 pounds) and dressed fish and fillets are available year-round, peaking from late spring to fall.

Cal: 88   Pro: 18g/88%   Carb: 0g/0%   Fat: 1g/12%
Chol: 48mg   Sodium: 73mg   Potassium: 391mg
Omega 3: .1g   B3: 14%   P: 18%

SQUID. Whole (10 to 12 inches) or cut into rings and pieces, squid is available year-round.

Cal: 94   Pro: 17g/80%   Carb: 2g/10%   Fat: 1g/10%
Chol: n/a   Sodium: 44mg   Potassium: 246mg
Omega 3: .3g   B3: 16%   B12: 22%   P: 22%   Zn: 10%

SWORDFISH. Steaks and chunks from the Atlantic peak from April to September and from the Pacific from September to December.

Cal: 120   Pro: 20g/77%   Carb: 0g/0%   Fat: 4g/19%
(S:31%   M:43%   P:26%)   Chol: 37mg   Sodium: 90mg
Potassium: 288mg   Omega 3: .2g   B3: 37%   B6: 16%   B12: 23%   P: 13%

TILEFISH. Whole (average 20 pounds) and dressed fish, fillets, and steaks are available from late fall to early winter.

Cal: 96   Pro: 18g/78%   Carb: 0g/0%   Fat: 2g/22%
(S:25%   M:38%   P:37%)   Chol: n/a   Sodium: 53mg
Potassium: 433mg   Omega 3: n/a   P: 19%

TROUT. Whole (2 to 8 pounds) and dressed fish, fillets, and steaks, fresh or smoked, are available year-round, peaking in spring, summer, and fall.

Cal: 118   Pro: 21g/75%   Carb: 0g/0%   Fat: 3g/25%
(S:22%   M:37%   P:41%)   Chol: 57mg   Sodium: 27mg
Potassium: 495mg   Omega 3: 1g   B2: 11%   P: 25%
Fe: 11%

TUNA. Dressed, steaks, fillets, and canned are available year-round, in the Atlantic from July to October, in the Pacific from May to December.

Cal: 144   Pro: 23g/69%   Carb: 0g/0%   Fat: 5g/31%
(S:30%   M:37%   P:33%)   Chol: 38mg   Sodium: 39mg
Potassium: 252mg   Omega 3: 2g   A: 44%   B1: 16%
B2: 15%   B3: 43%   B6: 23%   B12: 157%   Panto: 10%

FRESH WATER WHITEFISH, including Grayling, Chub, Lake Herring, Bloater, and Cisco. Whole (1/2 to 6 pounds) and dressed fish, fillets, and steaks, smoked and canned are available year-round.

Cal: 139   Pro: 19g/59%   Carb: 1g/3%   Fat: 6g/38%
(S:18%   M:40%   P:42%)   Chol: 60mg   Sodium: 51mg
Potassium: 317mg   Omega 3: 2g

WHITING. Whole (3/4 to 5 pounds) and dressed fish, fillets, and smoked are available in July and August.

Cal: 96   Pro: 17g/76%   Carb: 0g/0%   Fat: 3g/24%
(S:24%   M:33%   P:43%)   Chol: 31mg   Sodium: 92mg
Potassium: 249mg   Omega 3: .1g   B12: 38%   P: 22%

YELLOW PERCH. Whole (less than 1 pound) and dressed fish and fillets are available year-round.

Cal: 91   Pro: 19g/91%   Carb: 0g/0%   Fat: 1g/9%
Chol: 90mg   Sodium: 62mg   Potassium: 267mg
Omega 3: .3g   P: 20%

Shellfish

All nutrient data is based on a 3 1/2-ounce (100 gram) serving size, raw.

ABALONE. Available year-round, abalone peaks from September to early spring. Fresh abalone, usually caught near California's Catalina Island, is only available in that state; California doesn't permit canning or shipping of fresh abalone due to its limited supply. Frozen Mexican or canned Japanese abalone is sometimes available. Once removed from the shell, it's highly perishable. It requires diligent pounding with a mallet to tenderize it.

One to two medium abalone: Cal: 105   Pro: 17g/69%   Carb: 6g/24%   Fat: 1g/7%   Chol: 85mg
Sodium: 301mg   Potassium: n/a   Fiber: 0g
Omega 3: tr.   Panto: 30%   Fe: 18%   Cu: 10%

CLAMS. *Quahogs* (hardshell clams) are by far the most popular and available. The largest quahogs are *chowder,* then *cherrystone,* and finally tender *littlenecks. Softshell* clams include *steamers* in the East; in the West, similar clams include *littlenecks, butter, razor,* and *geoduck.* Worldwide, there are thousands of varieties. Clams, available year-round, may be sold by weight, volume, or the dozen. Buy only clams that are tightly closed or that close up immediately when the shell is firmly tapped. Do not buy clams with chipped or cracked shells. Clams tend to be quite sandy, so scrub with a stiff brush and rinse in several changes of water.

Five large clams: Cal: 74   Pro: 13g/72%   Carb: 3g/15%   Fat: 1g/13%   Chol: 34mg   Sodium: 56mg
Potassium: 314mg   Fiber: 0g   Omega 3: .1g
B2: 12%   B12: 817%   P: 17%   Fe: 78%   Cu: 15%
Mn: 14%

CRAB. Common varieties are *hardshell* blue crab available year-round; *softshell* blue crab, available May through September; *Dungeness* (West Coast only); *Alaskan king crab* (legs only and sold frozen or thawed), December through the summer. Fresh-picked cooked crabmeat is also readily available. Crabmeat, always sold cooked, should be sweet and fresh smelling.

Meat from a half leg, Alaskan king crab: Cal: 84
Pro: 18g/93%   Carb: 0g/0%   Fat: 1g/7%
Chol: 42mg   Sodium: 836mg   Potassium: 204mg
Fiber: 0g   Omega 3: .3g   P: 22%   Zn: 40%   Cu: 46%

Meat from five blue crabs: Cal: 87   Pro: 18g/88%
Carb: 0g/0%   Fat: 1g/12%   Chol: 78mg   Sodium:
293mg   Potassium: 329mg   Fiber: 0g   Omega 3: .3g
P: 23%   Zn: 23%   Cu: 35%

LOBSTER. A 1¼- to 1½-pound lobster will serve one person. Available year-round, lobster peaks May to December. Buy only live whole lobsters. When tapped or picked up, a lobster's tail should curl under the body; avoid any that seem lifeless. *Spiny lobster,* usually sold frozen as lobster tails, come from southern waters—Australia, New Zealand, South America. Lobsters from California or Florida are really crayfish.

Meat from two-thirds of a 1½-pound lobster: Cal: 90
Pro: 19g/88%   Carb: .6g/2%   Fat: 1g/10%   Chol: 95mg
Sodium: n/a   Potassium: n/a   Fiber: 0g   Omega 3: .2g
B12: 15%   Zn: 20%   Cu: 85%

MUSSELS. Mussels are usually purchased by the pound, which includes about 12 to 15 of the shellfish. Anywhere from 6 to 12 mussels serves one person, depending on the rest of the menu. They peak October through April. Mussels are usually tightly closed when they are fresh and healthy, although they will open partially when subject to fluctuating temperatures; this is called gaping. To test a gaping mussel for freshness, squeeze it closed with your fingers, then press the shell crosswise as if trying to slide the shells across each other. A fresh mussel will remain rigid; a dead mussel will slide. Don't buy mussels with cracked shells or eat any that fail to open when cooked.

Two-thirds of a cup of blue mussels, shelled: Cal: 86   Pro: 12g/56%   Carb: 4g/18%   Fat: 2g/24% (S:27% M:33% P:40%)   Chol: 28mg   Sodium: 286mg   Potassium: 320mg   Fiber: 0g   Omega 3: 1g   P: 20%   Fe: 22%   Zn: 11%

OYSTERS. Oysters are an extraordinary source of zinc and copper. Different varieties include *Blue Point* (Long Island), *Chincoteague* (Maryland), *Wellfleet* (Cape Cod), and *Apalachiola* (Florida). The peak season is fall through spring. Sold in the shell or shucked; freshly shucked oysters should be creamy white, surrounded by liquid.

Seven medium Eastern oysters, shelled: Cal: 69
Pro: 7g/43%   Carb: 4g/23%   Fat: 3g/34% (S:37% M:19% P:44%)   Chol: 55mg   Sodium: 112mg   Potassium: 229mg   Fiber: 0g   Omega 3: 1g   B2: 10%   B12: 318%   Fe: 37%   Zn: 600%   Cu: 223%   Mn: 13%

SCALLOPS. There are two main types: large *sea scallops* and smaller, sweeter *bay scallops.* Sea scallops are off-white, firm, with a nutty flavor. Bay scallops are sweet and delicate. Available year-round, they peak September to April. Rinse well to remove any grit or shell. Pat dry with paper toweling before cooking.

Two large or five small scallops: Cal: 88   Pro: 17g/80%   Carb: 2g/11%   Fat: 1g/9%   Chol: 33mg
Sodium: 161mg   Potassium: 322mg   Fiber: 0g
Omega 3: .2g   B12: 25%   P: 22%   Mg: 14%

SHRIMP. *Jumbo:* fewer than 12 per pound; *extra large:* 12 to 16; *large:* 16 to 20; *medium:* 21 to 25. Available year-round, the peak for average-size shrimps is August through January, for jumbo shrimps March through July. They should be fresh and sweet-smelling with no "off" or ammonia aroma. Most are frozen when harvested; much "fresh" shrimp has been frozen and thawed.

Four large shrimp: Cal: 106 Pro: 20g/81% Carb: 1g/4% Fat: 2g/15% (S:23% M:23% P:54%) Chol: 152mg Sodium: 148mg Potassium: 185mg Fiber: 0g Omega 3: 1g B3: 13% B12: 19% P: 20% Fe: 13% Cu: 15%

SNAILS. The peak season for fresh snails is November to March, but they're available canned year-round. Look for those that are clean and do not protrude. They should smell fresh.

About two-thirds cup, shelled: Cal: 137 Pro: 24g/73% Carb: 8g/24% Fat: 4g/3% Chol: 65mg Sodium: 206mg Potassium: 347mg Fiber: 0g Omega 3: n/a B6: 17% B12: 151% P: 14% Fe: 28% Zn: 11% Cu: 50%

Red Meat and Game

All nutrient data are based on 3½ ounces (100 grams) raw weight, unless otherwise noted.

RED MEAT

Storage: Refrigerator storage time is 2 to 4 days; freezer storage time 6 to 12 months. Meat should be stored in the coldest part of the refrigerator (36° to 40°F). Packaged meat should be stored in its original wrapper and used within four days. If it is not prepackaged, wrap meat in plastic or aluminum foil to keep it from drying out. Do not wash meat before refrigerating, since moisture encourages growth of bacteria.

If you are not going to use the meat within a few days, freeze it below 10°F, and preferably below 0°F, while fresh and in peak condition.

Wrap in portion sizes, if desired, in a moisture-proof wrapping to prevent freezer burn. Overwrap in aluminum foil or freezer storage bags. Seal, date, and label. Frozen meat is best thawed in the refrigerator for 1 to 2 days; room-temperature thawing may promote salmonella growth.

Defrosted meats are more perishable than fresh meats. Cook as soon as possible; 2 days is the storage limit. Leftover cooked meats can be stored 4 to 5 days in the refrigerator or frozen for 2 to 3 months.

BEEF. The leanest cuts are flank steak, round roast, round steak, and sirloin steak:

Flank Steak: Other retail labels are plank steak and London broil. Slice cooked steak at an angle, across the grain, to ensure tenderness. Butterfly uncooked steak and cut into thin strips for excellent stir-fry beef.

Choice. Cal: 169 Pro: 20g/69% Carb: 0g/0% Fat: 9g/31% (S:49% M:46% P:5%) Chol: 50mg Sodium: 73mg Potassium: 365mg Fiber: 0g B3: 24% B6: 20% B12: 52% P: 20% Fe: 11% Zn: 24%

Round Roast: Other retail labels are rump roast, top round roast, bottom round roast, eye round roast, tip roast, and sirloin tip roast. Great for pot roast—it won't fall apart after long, slow simmering. Cook with liquid; otherwise it's likely to be tough.

Select. Cal: 146 Pro: 22g/63% Carb: 0g/0% Fat: 6g/37% (S:41% M:55% P:4%) Chol: 59mg Sodium: 59mg Potassium: 371mg Fiber: 0g B2: 11% B3: 22% B6: 25% B12: 47% P: 21% Fe: 12% Zn: 19%

Choice. Cal: 150 Pro: 22g/61% Carb: 0g/0% Fat: 6g/39% (S:40% M:55% P:5%) Chol: 59mg Sodium: 52mg Potassium: 371mg Fiber: 0g B2: 12% B3: 21% B6: 30% B12: 48% P: 21% Fe: 13% Zn: 20%

Round Steak: Other retail labels are round steak center cut, and round steak full cut. This cut may be quite tough if broiled or pan-fried, but it's an excellent choice to slice thin for stir-frying. It is also good for lean ground or chopped beef.

Select. Cal: 133 Pro: 22g/69% Carb: 0g/0% Fat: 4g/31% (S:42% M:52% P:6%) Chol: 58mg Sodium: 56mg Potassium: 375mg Fiber: 0g B2: 11% B3: 20% B6: 25% B12: 50% P: 21% Fe: 12% Zn: 23%

Choice. Cal: 139 Pro: 22g/67% Carb: 0g/0% Fat: 5g/33% (S: 43% M:52% P:5%) Chol: 58mg Sodium: 56mg Potassium: 375mg Fiber: 0g B2: 11% B3: 20% B6: 25% B12: 50% P: 21% Fe: 12% Zn: 23%

Sirloin Steak: Other retail labels are sirloin steak wedge bone, sirloin steak flat bone, sirloin steak pin bone, New York steak (not New York strip), and top sirloin steak. It is very flavorful but be sure to trim the fat.

Select. Cal: 131 Pro: 21g/68% Carb: 0g/0% Fat: 4g/32% (S: 43% M:52% P:5%) Chol: 61mg Sodium: 58mg Potassium: 361mg Fiber: 0g B2: 12% B3: 18% B6: 20% B12: 53% P: 21% Fe: 15% Zn: 27%

Choice. Cal: 138 Pro: 21g/64% Carb: 0g/0% Fat: 5g/36% (S: 44% M:50% P:6%) Chol: 61mg Sodium: 58mg Potassium: 361mg Fiber: 0g B2: 12% B3: 18% B6: 20% B12: 53% P: 21% Fe: 15% Zn: 27%

LAMB. Two of the leanest cuts are lamb leg shank and loin chops:

Leg Shank: Other retail labels are whole leg of lamb, lamb leg shank half, lamb leg sirloin off, French-style lamb leg, American-style lamb roast, boneless leg of lamb. Remove all surface fat and fell. Roast all bone-in cuts; roast or grill boneless pieces.

Cal: 121 Pro: 21g/71% Carb: 0g/0% Fat: 4g/29% (S:38% M:51% P:11%) Chol: 63mg Sodium: 63mg Potassium: 339mg Fiber: 0g B2: 12% B3: 28% B12: 42% P: 20% Zn: 21%

Loin Chops: Other retail labels are double loin chops, English chops, boneless double loin chops. Trim any excess fat.

Cal: 143 Pro: 21g/60% Carb: 0g/0% Fat: 6g/40% (S:40% M:51% P:10%) Chol: 66mg Sodium: 70mg Potassium: 322mg Fiber: 0g B2: 12% B3: 30% B12: 35% P: 20% Fe: 23% Zn: 21%

ORGAN MEATS. Although *liver* is an extraordinarily nutritious food, rich in many minerals including iron as well as A and many B vitamins—the liver is, after all, where the organism stores many nutrients—it's very high in cholesterol. It also stores toxins such as pesticides from animal feed; so do *kidneys*, also high in cholesterol (387mg of cholesterol per 3½ oz). *Brains* are even higher in cholesterol: a 3½-oz serving has a whopping 2350mg of cholesterol, more than six times the daily maximum the American Heart Association recommends. So it's probably best to eat organ meats only rarely, if at all.

Four ounces of beef liver (113g): Cal: 143 Pro: 23g/57% Carb: 7g/17% Fat: 4g/25% (S:53% M:18% P:30%) Chol: 400mg Sodium: 82mg Potassium: 365mg Fiber: 0g A: 237% B1: 20% B2: 105% B3: 72% B6: 53% B12: 130% Folic: 70% Panto: 86% P: 36% Fe: 42% Zn: 30% Cu: 156%

PORK. Fresh ham is very lean; it's not cured, so it doesn't have the salt and chemicals of smoked ham. Pork loin chops are also quite lean.

Fresh Ham: Other retail labels include pork leg, boneless or rolled fresh ham, or pork leg roast. Slices are occasionally sold as fresh ham steak. Store in the refrigerator whole up to 1 week, slices 3 to 4 days; freeze up to 60 days. Treat whole roast like pork loin; roast with some liquid.

Cal: 136 Pro: 21g/64% Carb: 0g/0% Fat: 5g/36% (S:38% M:50% P:12%) Chol: 68mg Sodium: 55mg Potassium: 369mg Fiber: 0g B1: 59% B2: 12% B3: 27% B12: 12% P: 23% Zn: 15%

Pork Loin Chops: Another retail label is center cut pork chops. Store in the refrigerator no longer than four days; freeze up to 3 to 6 months. Broil, grill, pan-broil, bake, or braise.

Cal: 156 Pro: 21g/57% Carb: 0g/0% Fat: 8g/43% (S:38% M:59% P:12%) Chol: 60mg Sodium: 64mg Potassium: 353mg Fiber: 0g B1: 81% B2: 13% B3: 26% B6: 27% B12: 10% P: 20%

VEAL. Blade steak, chops, and cutlets are three very lean choices:

Blade Steak: Other retail labels are veal arm steak, veal round bone steak, veal shoulder steak, veal shoulder chop, veal sirloin chop. It's best braised.

Select. Cal: 99   Pro: 20g/87%   Carb: 0g/0%   Fat: 2g/13%   Chol: 104mg   Sodium: 109mg   Potassium: 285mg   Fiber: 0g   B2: 18%   B3: 39%   B12: 35%   Panto: 22%   P: 21%   Zn: 30%

Choice. Cal: 116   Pro: 20g/72%   Carb: 0g/0%   Fat: 4g/27%   (S:35%   M:50%   P:14%)   Chol: 88mg   Sodium: 94mg   Potassium: 296mg   Fiber: 0g   B2: 18%   B3: 28%   B12: 30%   Panto: 14%   P: 20%   Zn: 29%

Chops: Other retail labels include veal rib chops, veal loin chops, veal top loin chops.

Select. Cal: 102   Pro: 20g/83%   Carb: 0g/0%   Fat: 2g/17%   (S:39%   M:54%   P:7%)   Chol: 203mg   Sodium: 118mg   Potassium: 292mg   Fiber: 0g   B2: 18%   B3: 50%   B12: 32%   Panto: 18%   P: 20%   Zn: 21%

Choice. Cal: 119   Pro: 20g/73%   Carb: 0g/0%   Fat: 4g/27%   (S:41%   M:57%   P:2%)   Chol: 76mg   Sodium: 86mg   Potassium: 330mg   Fiber: 0g   B2: 12%   B3: 45%   B12: 18%   Panto: 13%   P: 21%   Zn: 16%

Cutlet: Other retail labels include veal leg round steak, scallops or scallopine.

Select. Cal: 103   Pro: 21g/90%   Carb: 0g/0%   Fat: 1g/10%   Chol: 93mg   Sodium: 77mg   Potassium: 360mg   Fiber: 0g   B2: 22%   B3: 63%   B12: 30%   Panto: 20%   P: 22%   Zn: 17%

Choice. Cal: 107   Pro: 21g/85%   Carb: 0g/0%   Fat: 2g/15%   (S:35%   M:44%   P:21%)   Chol: 75mg   Sodium: 62mg   Potassium: 374mg   Fiber: 0g   B2: 15%   B3: 45%   B12: 15%   P: 22%   Zn: 15%

GAME

Game may be frozen in its natural state or after it has been cleaned and is ready for cooking. (For information on wild game birds, see Fowl food profiles, page 371). After thawing, game should be cooked immediately. Ground meats may be frozen for 2 to 3 months; cut, they may be frozen 6 to 12 months. Game keeps somewhat longer than beef.

BUFFALO, a.k.a. Bison. This meat is gaining in popularity in the United States. American bison is found in the Western Plains and from Lake Erie south to Georgia. Available as loin, round flank, brisket, neck, and shoulder, younger animals will be more tender. Don't overcook!

Cal: 146   Pro: 21g/82%   Carb: 0g/0%   Fat: 2g/17%   (S:43%   M:45%   P:12%)   Chol: 46mg   Sodium: 52mg   Potassium: 315mg   Fiber: 0g   P: 18%   Fe: 14%   Zn: 16%

ELK. Elk is one of the largest members of the deer family, commonly weighing between 400 and 700 pounds. Younger elk, 2½ to 5 years old, will be more tender. Usually the cow is more tender than the bull. Elk is hunted in the fall only. Limit fresh elk to 8 months in the freezer; seasoned or cured elk lasts half as long.

Cal: 137   Pro: 23g/75%   Carb: 0g/0%   Fat: 3g/25%   (S:72%   M:26%   P:2%)   Chol: 67mg   Sodium: 58mg   Potassium: 312mg   Fiber: 0g   P: 16%   Fe: 15%   Zn: 16%

RABBIT. Wild rabbits are used for cooking, but a farmed rabbit will be more tender and taste less gamey. Substitute it for chicken in any braising recipe, such as stew; it's good marinated and grilled, too. Rabbit is best when fresh. Young rabbits will be most tender; the flavor will depend on the diet and age of the animal. Refrigerate in a sealed wrapper at 40°F, 1 to 2 days; freeze in a sealed wrapper at 0°F or colder for up to 12 months.

Cal: 124   Pro: 22g/76%   Carb: 0g/0%   Fat: 3g/24%   (S:43%   M:43%   P:14%)   Chol: 65mg   Sodium: 50mg   Potassium: 400mg   Fiber: 0g   B3: 40%   P: 22%   Fe: 13%

VENISON (DEER). Good-quality venison is dark red, finely grained, the fat white and firm. Haunch, loin, and fillets are the best cuts. The male (buck) is said to be more flavorful than the female (doe). The optimum age is 1½ to 2 years, tending to be dry if over 3 years old. Refrigerate in a sealed wrapper for 3 to 5 days, or freeze in a sealed wrapper at 0°F or colder for 6 to 12 months.

Cal: 126 Pro: 21g/72% Carb: 0g/0% Fat: 4g/28%
(S:70% M:24% P:6%) Chol: 77mg Sodium: 61mg
Potassium: 330mg Fiber: 0g B1: 15% B2: 28%
B3: 31% P: 25% Fe: 17%

WILD BOAR. Hunted in France and in certain states in North America, young boar are also known as *marcassin,* a delicacy in Paris. The flavor of wild boar is similar to pork, only leaner, with a distinct "wild" flavor. Young boar are best. Marinate to improve flavor and tenderness.

Cal: 147 Pro: 17g/52% Carb: 0g/0% Fat: 7g/
48% (S:45% M:44% P:11%) Chol: n/a Sodium:
n/a Potassium: n/a Fiber: 0g B1: 26% B3: 20%
P: 12%

Fowl

All nutrient data are based on a 3½-ounce (100 gram) serving size, raw and skinned.

Selection: All poultry moved across state lines is federally inspected. About two-thirds will be graded by the USDA. *Grade A:* choicest, full fleshed. *Grade B:* next best, slightly less meaty but attractive. *Grade C:* used mostly for turkeys. Lower-grade birds tend to be smaller and much less attractive physically but still good for eating. Look for well-fleshed breasts, short but plump legs, a moist, soft, smooth skin free of feathers. Select young birds with a flexible breastbone. Buy solidly frozen birds with no discoloration or signs of freezer burn. Make sure there is not a block of frozen juice at the bottom of the package; this indicates a bird has been thawed and refrozen.

Storage: Fresh, chilled poultry, including wild game birds, can be kept in the coldest part of the refrigerator for 2 days. Repackage birds that are loosely wrapped or in bags. Freeze birds at 0°F or lower. Most whole birds can be frozen up to 1 year; parts from 6 to 9 months. Label and date. Defrost them in the refrigerator: birds under 4 pounds will take 12 to 15 hours; larger birds 24 hours or more, depending on size; parts will thaw in 4 to 9 hours. Poultry may also be thawed successfully in a microwave.

CHICKEN. A *broiler-fryer* is a 2- to 4-pound all-purpose chicken. A *roaster* is a 4- to 8-pound chicken. A *capon* is a young cock that has been castrated while young, with a full breast and tender meat. They usually weigh from 4 to 10 pounds. They're available whole, ready to cook, cleaned and dressed. The chicken's breastbone should be pliable. Grading has more to do with appearance than with flavor. Check the expiration date.

Light meat: Cal: 109 Pro: 22g/86% Carb: 0g/0%
Fat: 2g/14% Chol: 57mg Sodium: 68mg
Potassium: 239mg Fiber: 0g B3: 53% B6: 27%
P: 19%

Dark meat: Cal: 113 Pro: 19g/70% Carb: 0g/0%
Fat: 4g/30% (S:31% M:38% P:31%) Chol: 72mg
Sodium: 95mg Potassium: 227mg Fiber: 0g
B2: 10% B3: 30% B6: 15% Panto: 12% P: 18%
Zn: 11%

DUCK. A *broiler or fryer duckling* is a very young bird weighing about 3 pounds. A *roaster duckling* is an older bird weighing 3 to 5 pounds. Look for those with broad, flat backs with well-padded fat, which must be trimmed. The skin should be white. The peak season is early summer, and November through December. Duck parts are usually marketed frozen, but some specialty stores may carry them fresh. *(Wild duck has a distinct and stronger flavor than domestic duck; it is usually leaner than domestic duck.)*

Cal: 132 Pro: 18g/57% Carb: 0g/0% Fat: 6g/43%
(S:48% M:36% P:16%) Chol: 77mg Sodium: 74mg
Potassium: 271mg Fiber: 0g B1: 24% B2: 18%
B3: 17% B6: 31% Fe: 25%

GOOSE. Geese are fat birds, weighing 4 to 14 pounds. The meat is sweet, tender, juicy, and dark. Geese are available fresh, whole, and ready to cook in November and December or frozen year-round. Look for youthful birds; they'll be more tender. The weight is an indication of age: the heavier the bird, the older and fattier it will be.

Cal: 161 Pro: 23g/59% Carb: 0g/0% Fat: 7g/41%
(S:50% M:34% P:16%) Chol: 84mg Sodium: 87mg
Potassium: 420mg Fiber: 0g B2: 22% B3: 22%
B6: 30% P: 31% Fe: 14%

GUINEA HEN. A 2- to 4-pound bird, it is cousin to the pheasant, with a dry, delicate, gamey white meat. The guinea hen is more tender than the cock, so choose female birds. Wash and dry it thoroughly and prepare it like chicken.

Cal: 110   Carb: 0g/0%   Pro: 21g/79%   Fat: 3g/21% (S:34%   M:36%   P:31%)   Chol: 63mg   Fiber: 0g Sodium: 69mg   Potassium: 220mg   B3: 44%   B6: 25%   P: 17%   Fe: 44%

PHEASANT. Pheasant is a plump 2- to 4-pound bird that's flavorful but very lean, so it can become dry. It's tough when old, so choose young birds. Allow one for 2 to 3 people. To keep it moist, baste often and cover with foil, or fill cavity with cut-up onions, carrots, celery, garlic, and sage. The peak season is October through February. It's available whole, usually frozen; sometimes it is available fresh, whole, and ready to cook at specialty butchers. Female birds have more fat but will be more tender. Males will be drier with a stringy flesh and gamier flavor.

Cal: 133   Pro: 24g/74%   Carb: 0g/0%   Fat: 4g/26% (S:40%   M:40%   P:20%)   Chol: 66mg   Sodium: 37mg Potassium: 262mg   Fiber: 0g   C: 10%   B3: 34% B6: 35%   B12: 13%   P: 23%

QUAIL. Quail are small birds ranging from 5 to 7 ounces, with a less gamey flavor than other birds. Choose young birds. Allow two per person. Make sure the legs and feet are smooth and pliable. A young bird will have pointed feathers and soft feet with rounded spurs.

Cal: 134   Pro: 22g/68%   Carb: 0g/0%   Fat: 5g/32% (S:34%   M:34%   P:32%)   Chol: 70mg   Sodium: 51mg Potassium: 237mg   Fiber: 0g   B1: 19%   B2: 17% B3: 41%   P: 30%   Fe: 25%   Cu: 30%

SQUAB. This is a specially raised, young, domesticated pigeon, which weighs 1 pound or less. It's available whole, fresh, and ready to cook, but is more plentiful frozen. Choose northern squab: they're juicier than their southern counterparts.

Cal: 142   Pro: 18g/51%   Carb: 0g/0%   Fat: 8g/49% (S:32%   M:43%   P:25%)   Chol: 90mg   Sodium: 51mg Potassium: 237mg   Fiber: 0g   B1: 20%   B2: 16% B3: 35%   B6: 25%   Panto: 31%   Zn: 18%

TURKEY. A fryer-roaster turkey will be a small, young bird of either sex weighing 4 to 10 pounds, with tender meat. Turkey is available whole, ready to cook, fresh, or frozen, as quartered or half roasters. Turkey parts are also sold. Young turkeys (4 to 6 pounds) are usually only available in the spring. Turkeys should be plump, rounded over the breastbone with a white, even, faintly blue flesh. The younger the bird, the more tender it will be. The hen (female) will be more tender than the tom. Fresh turkeys are juicier than frozen.

Light meat: Cal: 115   Pro: 24g/87%   Carb: 0g/0% Fat: 2g/13%   Chol: 60mg   Sodium: 63mg Potassium: 305mg   Fiber: 0g   B3: 29%   B6: 30% P: 20%   Zn: 11%

Dark meat: Cal: 125   Pro: 20g/67%   Carb: 0g/0% Fat: 4g/33%   (S:40%   M:26%   P:34%)   Chol: 69mg Sodium: 77mg   Potassium: 286mg   Fiber: 0g B2: 13%   B3: 15%   B6: 18%   Panto: 11%   P: 18% Zn: 21%

Eggs

Selection Choose AA grades for delicate meringues and soufflés. Grade A is okay for nearly any purpose; grade B, with thinner whites and flatter yolks, is fine for baking. Discard cracked eggs. Cloudy whites indicate a super-fresh egg.

Storage Store with the small end down, covered, in an egg carton or keeper for up to 10 days. Store whites up to 1 week in an airtight nonmetal container. Yolks may be covered with cool water and stored in an airtight container for a few days. Hard-boiled eggs may be stored in the shell or in plastic up to 10 days.

NOTE: Vitamin D information is not available from the USDA.

One whole egg (50g): Cal: 79   Pro: 6g/31%   Carb: 1g/3%   Fat: 6g/66%   (S:37%   M:48%   P:15%) Chol: 214mg   Sodium: 69mg   Potassium: 65mg Fiber: 0g   A: 6%   B12: 8%   Fe: 4%

One large egg yolk (17g): Cal: 63 Pro: 3g/18%
Carb: .04g/0% Fat: 6g/82% (S:37% M:48%
P:15%) Chol: 214mg Sodium: 8mg Potassium: 15
mg Fiber: 0g A: 6% B12: 9% Fe: 3%

One egg white (33g): Cal: 16 Pro: 3g/89% Carb:
.4g/11% Fat: tr/0% Chol: 0mg Sodium: 50mg
Potassium: 45mg Fiber: 0g

Milk and Yogurt

All quantities are one cup, with weight in grams listed, unless otherwise noted.

MILK

EVAPORATED WHOLE MILK. Homogenized whole milk from which half the water has been removed, it's heat sterilized in cans and fortified with vitamin D. (Evaporated skim milk, widely available, is much lower in fat and calories.)

252g: Cal: 338 Pro: 17g/22% Carb: 25g/29% Fat:
19g/49% (S:64% M:33% P:3%) Chol: 74mg
Sodium: 266mg Potassium: 764mg Lactose: 24g
D: 50% B2: 47% Ca: 66% P: 51% Mg: 15% Zn:
13%

GOAT MILK. Strong, somewhat sour-tasting milk from goats, it makes good cheese.

244g: Cal: 168 Pro: 9g/20% Carb: 11g/26% Fat:
10g/54% (S:68% M:28% P:4%) Chol: 28mg
Sodium: 122mg Potassium: 499mg Lactose:
12g B2: 18% Ca: 33% P: 27%

MILK (FROM COWS). It is usually fortified with vitamins A and D, pasteurized to destroy microorganisms, and homogenized to keep fat globules from separating out. Avoid raw milk. Milk is available whole, 2 percent, 1 percent, and skim. Because milk is mostly water, small differences in fat percentages by weight translate to large differences in the percentage of calories from fat:

Whole Milk: About 3.5 percent fat by weight, it is nearly 50 percent by calories.

244g: Cal: 150 Pro: 8g/23% Carb: 11g/29% Fat:
8g/48% (S:65% M:31% P:4%) Chol: 33mg
Sodium: 120mg Potassium: 370mg Lactose: 12g
D: 25% B2: 24% B12: 15% Ca: 29% P: 23%

Two Percent Milk: Milk from which much of the fat has been removed; what remains is up to 2 percent fat by weight, 34 percent by calories. Nonfat milk solids may be added.

244g: Cal: 121 Pro: 8g/28% Carb: 12g/37% Fat:
5g/34% (S:65% M:31% P:4%) Chol: 18mg
Sodium: 122mg Potassium: 377mg Lactose: 12g
A: 10% D: 25% B2: 24% B12: 15% Ca: 30% P:
23%

One Percent Milk: Milk from which most of the fat has been removed; what remains is 1 percent by weight, 22 percent by calories. (In California, a new "extra light" 1 percent milk is also available, with added nonfat dry milk solids to give it a richer body as well as slightly more calcium and riboflavin per serving.)

244g: Cal: 102 Pro: 8g/33% Carb: 12g/44% Fat:
3g/22% (S:64% M:32% P:4%) Chol: 10mg
Sodium: 123mg Potassium: 381g Lactose:
12g A: 10% D: 25% B2: 24% B12: 15% Ca:
30% P: 24%

Skim Milk: Also called nonfat milk, nearly all the fat has been removed; what remains is less than .5 percent by weight, 4 percent by calories.

245g: Cal: 86 Pro: 8g/42% Carb: 12g/54% Fat:
.4g/4% Chol: 4mg Sodium: 126mg Potassium:
406mg Lactose: 13g A: 10% D: 25% B2: 18%
B12: 15% Ca: 30% P: 25%

NONFAT DRY MILK. This is whole milk from which both fat and water have been removed. The process involves spraying concentrated skim milk into a hot air chamber, causing water to evaporate. After reconstituting, store it the same as whole milk.

One-quarter cup (30g): Cal: 109 Pro: 11g/40%
Carb: 16g/58% Fat: .2g/2% Chol: 6mg Sodium:
161mg Potassium: 538mg Lactose: 11g B2: 27%
B12: 20% Panto: 11% P: 29% Ca: 37%

CULTURED DAIRY PRODUCTS

Storage: Yogurt is best stored unopened and up-side down in the refrigerator, up to three weeks. Once opened, store it right-side up; level off any spoon indentations to prevent liquid pools of whey from forming. Don't store yogurt in the coldest part of the refrigerator, however; chilling may destroy some active cultures. Plain yogurt doesn't freeze well, but fruited yogurt can be stored in the freezer up to 6 weeks. Defrost in the refrigerator for 2½ hours.

ACIDOPHILUS MILK. Pasteurized whole or skim milk to which bacteria culture has been added, it has a slightly tart flavor. (Note: the nutritional information given here is for acidophilus whole milk, but low-fat milk may be available in stores.)

244g: Cal: 150 Pro: 8g/23% Carb: 11g/29% Fat: 8g/48% (S:65% M:30% P:5%) Chol: 33mg Sodium: 120mg Potassium: 370mg Lactose: 11g D: 25% B2: 24% B12: 15% Ca: 29% P: 23%

BUTTERMILK. Two products are sold under this title. One is the liquid left after churning out butter from milk. The other is a product manufactured from whole or skim milk fermented by bacteria. Either way, it's pleasant, low-fat, sour-tasting milk that's good in soups, salad dressings, and baked goods.

245g: Cal: 99 Pro: 8g/35% Carb: 12g/45% Fat:. 2g/20% (S:65% M:30% P:5%) Chol: 9mg Sodium: 257mg Potassium: 371mg Lactose: 11g B2: 24% Ca: 29% P: 22%

KEFIR. Fermented milk originally made from camels' milk, it is now made from cows' milk. It is similar to yogurt but more custardlike. Both bacteria and yeast are used to convert the sugar to lactic acid, giving it a tart taste.

300g: Cal: 159 Pro: 8g/23% Carb: 11g/29% Fat: 8g/48% (S:65% M:31% P:4%) Chol: 33mg Sodium: 120mg Potassium: 370mg Lactose: 6g D: 25% B2: 24% B12: 15% Ca: 29% P: 23%

SOUR CREAM. Cream is curdled either with the same bacteria that is used to culture buttermilk, or simply by adding vinegar. Very high in fat; use it rarely if at all. Yogurt is often a good substitute. "Light" sour cream, lower in fat, is now available.

230g: Cal: 493 Pro: 7g/6% Carb: 10g/8% Fat: 48g/85% (S: 65% M:30% P:4%) Chol: 102mg Sodium: 123mg Potassium: 331mg Lactose: 8g A: 36% B2: 20% B12: 12% P: 20%

YOGURT. Yogurt is milk to which live cultures have been added; the bacteria produce lactic acid that sours and thickens the milk into a soft curd.

Nonfat (skim milk) yogurt (227g): Cal: 127 Pro: 13g/45% Carb: 174g/52% Fat: .4g/3% Chol: 4mg Sodium: 174mg Potassium: 579mg Lactose: n/a B2: 29% B12: 23% Panto: 15% Ca: 45% P: 36% Mg: 11% Zn: 15%

Low-fat yogurt (227g): Cal: 144 Pro: 12g/32% Carb: 16g/44% Fat: 4g/24% (S:68% M:29% P:3%) Chol: 14mg Sodium: 159mg Potassium: 531mg Lactose: n/a B2: 29% B12: 28% Ca: 42% P: 33% Mg: 10% Zn: 13%

Whole milk yogurt (227g): Cal: 139 Pro: 8g/22% Carb: 11g/30% Fat: 7g/48% (S:69% M:26% P:3%) Chol: 29mg Sodium: 105mg Potassium: 351mg Lactose: 9g B2: 18% B12: 13% Ca: 27% P: 22%

Cheese

All nutrient data is based on a one-ounce (28 gram) serving.

Storage: After you buy cheese, wrap it tightly in plastic and refrigerate it. The flavor of cheese is generally unaffected by freezing, but its texture becomes more crumbly after thawing. If a mold develops on a hard cheese, cut off at least an inch of cheese on all sides and discard. If mold develops on soft cheese, throw it out. Some cheese, such as Roquefort and blue, are supposed to have mold.

AMERICAN PASTEURIZED PROCESS. Usually made from unripe Cheddar, it lasts for weeks wrapped in the refrigerator.

One ounce (28g): Cal: 93 Pro: 6g/24% Carb: 2g/9% Fat: 7g/67% (S:67% M:30% P:3%) Chol: 18mg Sodium: 337mg Potassium: 79mg Lactose: not detectable Ca: 16% P: 13%

BLUE OR BLEU. It keeps a long time in the refrigerator, wrapped in foil. Blue cheese has a distinct aroma, so store it away from food that will pick up the scent.

One ounce (28g): Cal: 100 Pro: 6g/24% Carb: 1g/3% Fat: 8g/73% (S:69% M:29% P:2%) Chol: 21mg Sodium: 396mg Potassium: 73mg Lactose: n/a Ca: 15% P: 11%

BRIE. A ripe brie yields to the touch, should be creamy and pale yellow. You can ripen a whole young cheese by wrapping it in plastic or foil and leaving it at room temperature for a few days. Once it is to your liking, keep it wrapped in the refrigerator.

One ounce (28g): Cal: 95 Pro: 6g/25% Carb: .1g/0% Fat: 8g/75% (fat breakdown n/a) Chol: 28mg Sodium: 178mg Potassium: 43mg Lactose: n/a

CHEDDAR. Cheddar lasts for weeks wrapped in the refrigerator. A whole cheese may be aged in a cool room, in its wax coating. Or it can be slowly aged in the refrigerator. Leave it at room temperature for an hour or so before serving.

One ounce (28g): Cal: 114 Pro: 7g/25% Carb: .4g/1% Fat: 9g/74% (S:55% M:24% P:21%) Chol: 30mg Sodium: 176mg Potassium: 28mg Lactose: not detectable Panto: 15% Ca: 20% P: 14%

COLBY. Colby has a mild, mellow, or sharp flavor, depending on how it was cured.

One ounce (28g): Cal: 112 Pro: 7g/24% Carb: .7g/3% Fat: 9g/73% (S:67% M:30% P:3%) Chol: 27mg Sodium: 171mg Potassium: 36mg Lactose: not detectable Ca: 19% P: 13%

COTTAGE CHEESE, 1 PERCENT. Buy it only from a cold cabinet and store it in the refrigerator. When cottage cheese is made, all of the lactose is initially discarded with the whey; but then various amounts are added back to enhance flavor, so the lactose content varies greatly by brand.

One-quarter cup 1 percent (57g): Cal: 41 Pro: 7g/71% Carb: 2g/16% Fat: 1g/13% Chol: 3mg Sodium: 229mg Potassium: 48mg Lactose: .2g

CREAM CHEESE. Made with skim milk, the curds are later bathed in cream. It is very perishable; store it wrapped in the refrigerator for about 1 week.

One ounce (28g): Cal: 99 Pro: 2g/9% Carb: 1g/3% Fat: 10g/88% (S:67% M:31% P:3%) Chol: 31mg Sodium: 84mg Potassium: 34mg Lactose: 1g

EDAM. Edam should keep for weeks tightly wrapped in the vegetable bin of the refrigerator.

One ounce (28g): Cal: 101 Pro: 7g/28% Carb: .4g/2% Fat: 8g/70% (S:67% M:30% P:3%) Chol: 25mg Sodium: 274mg Potassium: 53mg Lactose: not detectable Ca: 21% P: 15%

FETA. Feta is made from the milk of sheep or cow. Rinse it well and refrigerate it in cold water.

One ounce (28g): Cal: 75 Pro: 4g/22% Carb: 1g/6% Fat: 6g/72% (S:75% M:22% P:2%) Chol: 25mg Sodium: 316mg Potassium: 18mg Lactose: n/a Ca: 14%

GJETOST. This white to dark-beige whey cheese from goat or cow's milk is extremely sweet.

One ounce (28g): Cal: 132 Pro: 3g/8% Carb: 12g/36% Fat: 8g/56% (S:69% M:28% P:3%) Chol: n/a Sodium: 170mg Potassium: n/a Lactose: n/a Ca: 11% P: 13%

GOUDA. Gouda is a pale yellow cheese with a smooth, mild, nutlike taste.

One ounce (28g): Cal: 101 Pro: 7g/28% Carb: 1g/3%
Fat: 8g/69% (S:68% M:30% P:2%) Chol: 32mg
Sodium: 232mg Potassium: 34mg Lactose: n/a
Ca: 20% P: 16%

MOZZARELLA. The original mozzarella was made with buffalo milk; now it's usually cow's milk. Keep it tightly wrapped in the refrigerator.

One ounce part skim (28g): Cal: 79 Pro: 8g/39%
Carb: 1g/5% Fat: 5g/56% (S:67% M:30% P:3%)
Chol: 15mg Sodium: 150mg Potassium: 27mg
Lactose: .1g Ca: 21% P: 15%

MUENSTER. The European variety is pungent and soft; the American version is semisoft, mild, and buttery with an orange exterior.

One ounce (28g): Cal: 104 Pro: 7g/25% Carb: .3g/1%
Fat: 9g/75% (S:68% M:30% P:2%) Chol: 27mg
Sodium: 178mg Potassium: 38mg Lactose: n/a
Ca: 20% P: 13%

NEUFCHATEL. This is similiar to cream cheese but slightly lower in calories.

One ounce (28g): Cal: 74 Pro: 3g/15% Carb: 1g/4%
Fat: 7g/81% (S:67% M:31% P:2%) Chol: 22mg
Sodium: 113mg Potassium: 32mg Lactose: .3g

PARMESAN. The taste of imported aged Parmesan is sharp and piquant—yielding much flavor in very small quantities.

One ounce (28g): Cal: 110 Pro: 10g/37% Carb: 1g/3% Fat: 7g/60% (S:68% M:30% P:2%) Chol: 19mg Sodium: 454mg Potassium: 26mg Ca: 39% Lactose: not detectable

RICOTTA. A soft and moist cheese, bland and a little sweet, it's made from whey.

One-quarter cup part skim (62g): Cal: 86 Pro: 7g/33%
Carb: 3g/15% Fat: 5g/52% (S:66% M:31% P:3%)
Chol: 19mg Sodium: 78mg Potassium: 78mg
Lactose: 1g Ca: 17% P: 11%

SAPSAGO. This is a low-fat grating cheese with a strong taste.

One ounce (28g): Cal: 68 Pro: 12g/73% Carb: n/a
Fat: 2g/27% (fat breakdown n/a) Chol: n/a
Sodium: 510mg Potassium: n/a Lactose: n/a

SWISS. A hard, smooth cheese with a nutty, distinct taste, its distinctive holes are formed by gas during fermentation. Refrigerate it in foil or plastic. Leave at room temperature for a few hours before serving.

One ounce (28g): Cal: 107 Pro: 8g/30% Carb: 1g/4%
Fat: 8g/66% (S:68% M:28% P:4%) Chol: 26mg
Sodium: 74mg Potassium: 31mg Lactose: not detectable Ca: 27% P: 17%

Fruit

All nutrient data are based on an appropriate serving size, such as one banana or three apricots, followed by the weight in grams.

APPLE. "Ate an apfel avore gwain to bed/ Makes the doctor beg his bread," goes the saying recorded in Devonshire, England, three centuries ago. Eat it whole: the peel of an apple contains only 10 percent of the calories but 21 percent of the fiber, 24 percent of the vitamin A, and 35 percent of the vitamin C. Available year-round, apples should be firm, colorful, and unbruised; seek locally grown apples, especially in autumn. There are over 7000 varieties of apples; about 100 of those are grown commercially. (See also apple juice, in Beverages food profiles, p. 383).

One medium apple (138g): Cal: 80 Pro: .3g/1%
Carb: 21g/94% Fat: 1g/5% Sodium: 1mg
Potassium: 159mg Fiber: 2.76g (1g soluble)
C: 13%

APRICOT. The delicious yellow fruit is extraordinarily rich in the cancer-protective vitamin A precursor beta-carotene (but there is no evidence that the cyanide in the pits, dubbed Laetrile, can treat cancer). Dried apricots are usually preserved with sodium sulphite, which adds sodium and can trigger allergies in some people.

Three apricots, pitted (106g): Cal: 51 Pro: 1g/10%
Carb: 12g/83% Fat: .4g/7% Sodium: 1mg
Potassium: 313mg Fiber: 2.65g (1.4 soluble)
A: 55% C: 17%

AVOCADO. See Salad and Greens.

BANANA. Bananas contain potassium, of course, but also vitamins C and B6 and fiber. Bananas are available year-round. Purchase those that are light green or light yellow and free of bruises. The peel must be removed. If exposed to oxygen, bananas will turn brown; dip them in pineapple or lemon juice to prevent browning.

One peeled banana (114g): Cal: 105 Pro: 1g/4%
Carb: 27g/92% Fat: 1g/4% Sodium: 1mg
Potassium: 451mg Fiber: 2.2g (.7g soluble) C: 17%
B6: 33%

BLACKBERRY. Of all fruits, blackberries and raspberries have the most fiber—even more than most cereals. One cup contains over 9 grams of fiber but only 74 calories. Blackberries are available May to October, with the peak in June and July. Never purchase "leaky" berries.

One cup (144g): Cal: 74 Pro: 1g/5% Carb: 18g/89%
Fat: 1g/6% Sodium: 0mg Potassium: 282mg
Fiber: 9g (1.3 soluble) C: 50% Mn: 53% Cu: 10%

BLUEBERRY. Available May to September, blueberries peak from June to August. Never purchase "leaky" berries. Choose those that are powdery light blue, large, plump, and dry. Refrigerate them, and don't wash them until just before use. They keep longer than other berries and can be frozen.

One cup (145g): Cal: 82 Pro: 1g/4% Carb: 21g/91%
Fat: 1g/5% Sodium: 9mg Potassium: 129mg
Fiber: 5g (.6g soluble) C: 33% E: 27% Mn: 29%

BOYSENBERRY. A cross between the blackberry, which it looks like, and the raspberry, which it tastes like, this berry was developed in California. These berries are available fresh or canned.

One cup frozen (132g): Cal: 66 Pro: 2g/8% Carb: 16g/88% Fat: .4g/4% Sodium: 2mg Potassium: 183mg Fiber: 6g (.8g soluble) Folic: 21% Mn: 21%

BREADFRUIT. A starchy staple, it is available year-round, but import restrictions may vary its abundance. For slightly underripe fruit, to be used within a few days, choose breadfruit that are hard, green, and uniform in color. The outer scales will be large and well developed. Choose fruit that are dense and heavy, not spongy. Breadfruit does not store well. Ripen it at room temperature until the desired ripeness is reached, then refrigerate 1 to 2 days. Cook like squash. Peel by cutting in quarters; core and pare off the skin.

One-quarter small breadfruit (96g): Cal: 99 Pro: 1g/3% Carb: 26g/96% Fat: .2g/1% Sodium: 2mg Potassium: 470mg Fiber: n/a C: 46%

CANTALOUPE. Cantaloupes are a great source of vitamins C and A, fiber, and potassium. They are available from June to November. Buy those which are firm and unbruised and have a yellow skin. They yield to pressure when ripe and have a fragrant aroma. Cut into desired pieces and scoop out the seeds with a spoon.

One cup, cubed (160g): Cal: 57 Pro: 1g/9% Carb: 13g/85% Fat: .4g/6% Sodium: 14mg Potassium: 494mg Fiber: 2g (.5g soluble) A: 103% C: 112%

CARAMBOLA, a.k.a. Star Fruit. Carambolas are rich in vitamin C and available from September to January. Choose those deep yellow in color as they will be less tart. Look for firm fruits with juicy, fresh-looking ribs. Allow them to ripen until they are aromatic (when ripe, they will have a fragrant perfume). Rinse and pat them dry; cut carambolas crosswise to obtain star-shaped pieces.

One medium (127g): Cal: 42 Pro: 1g/5% Carb: 10g/86% Fat: .4g/9% Sodium: 2g Potassium: 207mg Fiber: 1.5g A: 12% C: 45%

CASSABA MELON. Available from July to November, they peak in September and October. Look for ripe melons with a golden-yellow rind and a slight softening at the blossom end. Inside, the flesh should be creamy white without aroma. Avoid melons with dark spots.

One cup, cubed (170g): Cal: 45 Pro: 2g/11% Carb: 11g/86% Fat: .2g/3% Sodium: 20mg Potassium: 357mg Fiber: 1g C: 45%

CHERIMOYA. Cherimoyas are available in December, January, and February. Choose those with a fairly uniform, green color, the larger the better. Don't be afraid of scars, but do avoid those with mold, cracks, or dark brown skin. Usually it's too difficult to remove seeds prior to eating, so remove them as you eat. Cut them in halves or quarters and eat with a spoon. Or quarter, cut out the fibrous center, and pare.

One-quarter (137g): Cal: 129   Pro: 2g/5%   Carb: 33g/92%   Fat: 1g/3%   Sodium: n/a   Potassium: n/a   Fiber: n/a   C: 21%

CHERRY. Like blueberries, cherries are rich in vitamins C and E. They peak in June and July. Select large, firm cherries with stems intact. This is one of the few fruits where size is an indication of flavor. Tart cherries, good for cooked desserts and jams, are brighter red than sweet cherries and available earlier in the season.

One cup (145g): Cal: 104   Pro: 2g/7%   Carb: 24g/88%   Fat: 1g/5%   Sodium: 1mg   Potassium: 325mg   Fiber: 3g (.6g soluble)   C: 17%   E: 13%

COCONUT; COCONUT MILK. Coconut fat is among the most saturated fats in nature, more saturated than beef fat, so eat very sparingly. Available year-round, coconuts are most plentiful during fall and winter. Coconut milk is actually made from the pulp and is high in fat; the liquid that gets drained out is mostly water, however, and has very little fat. It's the safest part of this drupe fruit to eat.

One cup, grated (80g): Cal: 283   Pro: 3g/4%   Carb: 12g/16%   Fat: 27g/80%   (S:95%   M:4%   P:1%)   Sodium: 16mg   Potassium: 285mg   Fiber: 7g (.8g soluble)   Fe: 11%   Cu: 17%   Mn: 29%

One-half cup coconut milk (120g): Cal: 276   Pro: 3g/4%   Carb: 7g/9%   Fat: 29g/87%   (S: 94%   M:5%   P:1%)   Fiber: .6g   Sodium: 18mg   Potassium: 316mg   P: 12%   Mn: 31%

CRANBERRY. A good source of vitamin C and fiber, cranberries are available year-round, peaking in October and November. Select firm, dry, dark berries.

One cup (95g): Cal: 46   Pro: .4g/3%   Carb: 12g/94%   Fat: .2g/3%   Sodium: 1mg   Potassium: 67mg   Fiber: 3g (1g soluble)   C: 21%

DATE. Dates are a good source of fiber. Dried dates are available year-round. Fresh dates may be available in late summer. Look for moist, soft dried dates with a golden brown color and smooth skin. They will keep indefinitely. Store them in the refrigerator: the lower the temperature, the better. Don't store them near onions, garlic, or other items that have strong smells as dates absorb odors.

Five dates (41g): Cal: 114   Pro: .8g/3%   Carb: 31g/96%   Fat: .2g/1%   Sodium: 1mg   Potassium: 271mg   Fiber: 2g (.5g soluble)

FIG. Figs, always available dried, may be purchased fresh from June to November. The ripeness is judged by the degree of softness, not by color. They should be soft to the touch and are best when eaten right away.

Two small dried figs (100g): Cal: 74   Pro: 1g/4%   Carb: 19g/93%   Fat: .3g/3%   Sodium: 2mg   Potassium: 232mg   Fiber: 3g (1.7g soluble)   C: 11%

GOOSEBERRY. Gooseberries are available from May to August. Look for ripe, soft berries with a light amber color. Berries also come in red, green, or white. The bigger the tastier.

One cup (150g): Cal: 67   Pro: 1g/7%   Carb: 15g/82%   Fat: 1g/11%   Sodium: 1mg   Potassium: 297mg   Fiber: 6.6g   C: 69%

GRAPEFRUIT. Eat a grapefruit as you would an orange, and you'll boost your intake of fiber and cholesterol-lowering pectin. Grapefruits are also a good source of potassium. Available year-round, they peak December to June. They should be heavy and thin-skinned. The peel cannot be eaten. The *Pummelo,* the largest of all citrus fruits, is the forebear of the grapefruit; its aromatic pithy rind is perfect for marmalade. (See also grapefruit juice, in Beverages food profiles, page 383.)

One-half pink or red grapefruit (123g): Cal: 37   Pro: 1g/6%   Carb: 10g/91%   Fat: .1g/3%   Sodium: 0mg   Potassium: 158mg   Fiber: 2g (.6g soluble)   C: 78%

One-half white grapefruit (118g): Cal: 39   Pro: 1g/7%   Carb: 10g/91%   Fat: .1g/2%   Sodium: 0mg   Potassium: 175mg   Fiber: 2g (.6g soluble)   C: 65%

GRAPES. Peak availability is June to November. Select bunches that are well formed. Color is a good indicator of ripeness: Dark ones should be free of green tints, white ones should have an amber color. Ripe grapes are soft and tender.

Twenty American seedless grapes (48g): Cal: 30 Pro: .3g/3% Carb: 8g/93% Fat: .2g/4% Sodium: 2mg Potassium: 185mg Fiber: .3g C: 18%

GUAVA. Guavas are *extraordinarily* rich in vitamin C. They are available from December to February. Aroma is the key. They should be rich in fragrance with a perfumey, not musky, scent. They are best when yellow and tender. Ripen guavas at room temperature, then place wrapped in refrigerator for a day or so. Never refrigerate unripe guavas.

One guava (90g): Cal: 45 Pro: 1g/6% Carb: 11g/84% Fat: 1g/10% Sodium: 2g Potassium: 256mg Fiber: 5g (.8g soluble) C: 275%

HONEYDEW MELON. Honeydews peak from July to October. Firm honeydews will ripen after purchase. Buy those which are unbruised, have a sweet aroma, feel silky and soft, and are cream or butter colored. Thumping or knocking a melon will give you no indication of its ripeness. Larger *crenshaw melons* are ripe when golden in color and have a velvety feel; nutritionally, they are similar to honeydews.

One-half cup, cubed (85g): Cal: 30 Pro: .4g/5% Carb: 8g/93% Fat: .1g/2% Sodium: 9mg Potassium: 231mg Fiber: 1.5g (.5g soluble) C: 30%

KIWI. Because kiwis are rich in vitamin C, a natural antioxidant, they will not discolor when you use them for garnishes. They are available year-round. Choose kiwis that are fairly firm. Allow about a week to ripen at room temperature. They will yield to pressure when ready to eat. Pare off the skin and cut the fruit into slices, halves, or quarters. They can also be cut in half and the inside scooped out with a spoon.

One kiwi (76g): Cal: 46 Pro: 1g/6% Carb: 11g/88% Fat: .4g/6% Sodium: 4mg Potassium: 252mg Fiber: 2g (.6g soluble) C: 124%

LEMON. Lemons are available year-round. Select those that are heavy for their size. Thin-skinned lemons will have more juice. Roll a hard lemon on a table or hard surface; this will yield more juice.

One lemon without peel (58g): Cal: 17 Pro: 1g/13% Carb: 5g/79% Fat: .2g/8% Sodium: 1mg Potassium: 80mg Fiber: 3g (.6g soluble) C: 51%

LIME. Available year-round, limes peak July to August. As a lime ages, the skin turns brown. The *key lime* is more aromatic.

One lime without peel (67g): Cal: 20 Pro: 1g/8% Carb: 7g/87% Fat: .1g/5% Sodium: 1mg Potassium: 68mg Fiber: 2g C: 32%

LOGANBERRY. Loganberries are found in warmer climates. Select plump, ripe berries with a rich red color. They have a distinct flavor similar to that of a pomegranate.

One cup frozen (149g): Cal: 104 Pro: 2g/10% Carb: 19g/85% Fat: 1g/5% Sodium: 2mg Potassium: 216mg Fiber: 5g (.7g soluble) C: 87%

LYCHEE. Lychee is a fruit, not a nut! Lychees are available during the summer months. Pick the heaviest and fullest ones with stems that are rosy. They will keep for several weeks in the refrigerator. Peel, halve, and seed.

Five raw lychees (48g): Cal: 33 Pro: .4g/5% Carb: 8g/90% Fat: .2g/5% Sodium: 0mg Potassium: 85mg Fiber: .5g C: 59%

MANGO. Mangoes are an excellent source of vitamins A and C. Peak season is during the summer months. Aroma is the key. If there's no scent, there's not likely to be any flavor. Ripe mangos should have a pleasant scent and be firm. Pare and cut sections from the pit.

One mango (201g): Cal: 132 Pro: 1g/3% Carb: 34g/94% Fat: 1g/3% Sodium: 4mg Potassium: 322mg Fiber: 3g (.6g soluble) A: 161% C: 95% B6: 14% Cu: 11%

NECTARINE. Nectarines are available through the summer months. The flavor peaks in June and

July. Buy nectarines that are colorful and un-bruised. Leave them to ripen at room tempera-ture and then chill in the refrigerator.

One nectarine (136g): Cal: 67 Pro: 1g/6% Carb: 16g/86% Fat: 1g/8% Sodium: 0mg Potassium: 288mg Fiber: 3g (1g soluble) C: 12%

ORANGE. Oranges are available year-round. California oranges peak November to June, Flor-ida oranges from October to July. Look for firm, thin-skinned oranges that are heavy for their size. The *Valencia* has a thinner skin and is a little juicier than the *navel*. Color is no indication of a fresh orange. Florida oranges are thin-skinned and have more juice than those grown in Califor-nia, but they are harder to peel and segment. A *tangelo* is a cross between a *mandarin orange* and a grapefruit. The *minneola,* for example, is a dancy tangerine crossed with a duncan grape-fruit. The *ugli* is a similar hybrid. The *kumquat,* though it looks like a miniature orange, is not a citrus fruit. (See also orange juice, in Beverages food profiles, page 383).

One orange (131g): Cal: 62 Pro: 1g/7% Carb: 15g/91% Fat: .2g/2% Sodium: 0mg Potassium: 237mg Fiber: 2g (.5g soluble) C: 116% Folic: 10%

PAPAYA. Rich in vitamins A and C, papayas are available year-round but are in short supply March to May. Fully ripe papayas are yellow and should yield to the touch. Cut vertically from top to bottom and scoop out the black seeds. Remove the skin with a paring knife or a vegetable peeler.

One cup, cubed (140g): Cal: 54 Pro: 1g/6% Carb: 14g/91% Fat: .2g/3% Sodium: 4mg Potassium: 359mg Fiber: 2g (1.4g soluble) A: 56% C: 144%

PASSION FRUIT. Look for dark passion fruit, available in early spring through summer. They are ready to eat when creased. Firm, smooth fruits should be kept at room temperature until completely dimpled. Cut them in half and scoop out the pulp with a spoon.

One fruit (18g): Cal: 18 Pro: .4g/8% Carb: 4g/86% Fat: .1g/6% Sodium: 5g Potassium: 63mg Fiber: .1g

PEACH. Available May to mid-October, peaches are best in the midsummer months. The best are firm, colorful, and unbruised. Hard peaches may never ripen, so be sure they're firm or slightly soft.

One medium peach (87g): Cal: 37 Pro: 1g/6% Carb: 10g/92% Fat: .1g/2% Sodium: 0mg Potassium: 171mg Fiber: 2g (.7g soluble) A: 10%

PEAR, BARTLETT. An excellent source of fi-ber, they are picked from August through Octo-ber; through controlled-atmosphere storage, they are available year-round. In the 1700s, pears were known as "butter fruits" for the soft flesh that seems to melt away in the mouth. Choose those that are light rather than dark green, unbruised, and firm. Rinse them under cool water, pat dry, and let ripen at room temperature a few days until they yield to the touch; then they can be refrigerated. Bartlett pears, once known as Wil-liam pears, are the most popular; other varieties include the sweet, spicy, juicy, light-green *Anjou;* the juicy, golden-brown *Bosc* with its long taper-ing neck; the large, round, greenish-yellow *Com-ice pear,* a dessert favorite; the tiny dark-red or dark yellow-green blushing sweet *Seckel,* some-times pickled.

One pear (166g): Cal: 98 Pro: 1g/2% Carb: 25g/93% Fat: 1g/5% Sodium: 1mg Potassium: 208mg Fiber: 5g (1g soluble) C: 11%

PEAR, PRICKLY. A good source of magne-sium, vitamin C, and potassium, prickly pears are available fall through spring. Choose ones that are tender and deep colored. To avoid invisible hairs, pierce the fruit with a fork, cut off the top and bottom, slit it from end to end, and peel off the skin.

One prickly pear (103g): Cal: 42 Pro: 1g/6% Carb: 10g/84% Fat: 1g/10% Sodium: 6mg Potassium: 226mg Fiber: 2g C: 24% Mag: 22%

PERSIMMON. Persimmons are a great source of vitamin A, peaking in November and Decem-ber. To avoid the astringent taste, select those that are firm and full of color. Ripen them at room temperature for a few days. They will become shriveled and lose their color. This means they are ready to eat. You can wrap them in foil and freeze them overnight to speed the process. Thaw them before eating. They can be eaten with or without the skin.

One persimmon (168g): Cal: 118 Pro: 1g/3% Carb: 31g/95% Fat: .3g/2% Sodium: 3mg Potassium: 270mg Fiber: 3g A: 72% C: 21% Cu: 10% Mn: 17%

PINEAPPLE. Pineapples are available year-round. Choose fruit that is plump and large. Deep green leaves are a sign of a good pineapple, but it is a myth that fruit with easily plucked leaves is the best. Do not store it in the refrigerator, but keep it at room temperature. Once cut, wrap it in plastic and refrigerate.

One cup pineapple chunks (155g): Cal: 77 Pro: 1g/3% Carb: 19g/90% Fat: 1g/7% Sodium: 1mg Potassium: 175mg Fiber: 3g (2g soluble) C: 40% Mn: 73%

PLANTAIN. A nutritious, starchy tropical fruit, it's available year-round. Plantains can be eaten at any stage of development. If the peel is green to yellow, the taste and texture is starchy: use as a potato. (There is some evidence that these unripe plantains may help ulcers heal.) If yellow to black, they are riper and sweeter and more suitable for sweets or desserts. Do not eat plantain raw. Peel darker plantains as you would a banana.

One cup, sliced (148g): Cal: 181 Pro: 2g/4% Carb: 47g/94% Fat: 1g/2% Sodium: 6mg Potassium: 739mg Fiber: 2g (.7g soluble) A: 33% C: 45% B6: 22% Mg: 14%

PLUM. The season is mid-May to October. Select those that have a bright color, yield slightly to the touch, and are medium to large (relative to the variety) and unbruised.

Two medium plums (132g): Cal: 72 Pro: 1g/5% Carb: 17g/86% Fat: 1g/9% Sodium: 0mg Potassium: 288mg Fiber: 3g (1g soluble) A: 11% C: 21% E: 11%

POMEGRANATE. Pomegranates are available in fall and winter. Buy richly colored, large fruits. Heavier ones have more juice. Slit the skin and then gently break the pomegranate into quarters. Bend back the rind and pull out the seeds.

One pomegranate (154g): Cal: 104 Pro: 2g/5% Carb: 26g/91% Fat: 1g/4% Sodium: 5mg Potassium: 399mg Fiber: 1g C: 16%

PRUNE. Yes, they are mild laxatives, in part due to the sorbitol content. Available year-round. Check the date on the package for freshness. Eat them out of the package or stew them in boiling water until soft, 3 to 5 minutes.

Five prunes (42g): Cal: 100 Pro: 1g/4% Carb: 26g/94% Fat: .2g/2% Sodium: 1mg Potassium: 323mg Fiber: 8g (1g soluble) A: 16% E: 12%

QUINCE. A quince left at room temperature for a week or so is so aromatic it will perfume a room. It's a good source of pectin fiber, which may help lower cholesterol. The pectin makes quince great for jelling jams. Unlike most fruits, quince requires cooking to be edible. Peak season is November and December. Look for firm, unbruised yellow skins. Pare and core before cooking or bake whole like apples.

One quince (92g): Cal: 53 Pro: .4g/2% Carb: 14g/97% Fat: .1g/1% Sodium: 4mg Potassium: 181mg Fiber: n/a C: 23%

RAISINS. Raisins are available year-round. They should be soft and plump. If packaged, check the date for freshness.

One-half cup packed seedless raisins (83g): Cal: 247 Pro: 3g/7% Carb: 66g/84% Fat: .4g/9% Sodium: 10mg Potassium: 620mg Fiber: 2g (1g soluble) E: 52% Cu: 13%

RASPBERRY. One cup of fresh raspberries provides more fiber than a serving of many bran cereals (it's those tiny seeds), plus plenty of vitamin C. Available through the summer months, the berries may be red, purple, black, or amber. Choose those that are firm, dry, and colorful. They can be frozen. Rinse but do not soak them.

One cup (123g): Cal: 60 Pro: 1g/7% Carb: 14g/84% Fat:1g/9% Sodium: 0mg Potassium: 187mg Fiber: 3g (.9g soluble) C: 51% Mn: 36%

RHUBARB. Must be cooked; raw, it's toxic. It's high in oxalates, which may interfere with calcium absorption, so it's not a good calcium source. Peak harvest is in spring and early summer. Choose firm rhubarb with good color, unwilted stalks. Peel strings off the stalk like celery. Dice and it's ready to use. It can be frozen in an airtight bag.

One cup, diced (122g): Cal: 26 Pro: 1g/15% Carb: 6g/77% Fat: .3g/8% Sodium: 5mg Potassium: 351mg Fiber: 2g (.7g soluble) C: 16% Ca: 10%

STRAWBERRY. A cup of strawberries has more vitamin C than an orange. The peak harvest is from April to July. Look for firm, dry, and red berries with a fresh green cap. Avoid those that are pale or have white tops. Beware: Size does not mean sweetness. You may pay too much for large gourmet types. They will last up to 1 week in the refrigerator.

One cup (149g): Cal: 45 Pro: 1g/7% Carb: 11g/83% Fat: 1g/10% Sodium: 2mg Potassium: 247mg Fiber: 3g (.9g soluble) C: 141% Mn: 12%

TANGERINE. The tangerine is really a mandarin orange, a group that includes the *clementine,* the *dancy* (the most popular), and the *satsuma.* The dancy is a deep orange-vermilion with a shiny rind; it's low in acid. Tangerines are available October to January, with the peak in December. For selection, see Orange.

One tangerine (84g): Cal: 37 Pro: 1g/5% Carb: 9g/91% Fat: .2g/4% Sodium: 1mg Potassium: 132mg Fiber: 2g (.5g soluble) A: 15% C:43%

WATERMELON. A good source of vitamin C, it peaks June to August. The only way to tell a ripe watermelon is by cutting it open. Flesh should be dark red and firm.

One cup, diced (160g): Cal: 50 Carb: 12g/82% Pro: 1g/7% Fat: 1g/11% Fiber: 1g (.3g soluble) Sodium: 3mg Potassium: 186mg A: 12% C: 26% B6: 12%

Sugars and Sweeteners

All nutrient information in this section is based on one-quarter cup.

BARLEY MALT SYRUP. A dark, thick liquid resembling molasses, it is less sweet than honey. Store it in a cool, dry place, tightly sealed. It contains maltose and glucose.

One-quarter cup (89g): Cal: 260 Pro: 3g/5% Carb: 59g/95% Fat: 0g/0% Sodium: n/a Potassium: n/a

BROWN SUGAR. Brown sugar is soft and light to dark brown in color. The darker the sugar, the stronger the molasses flavor. Keep sugar in plastic to prevent hardening. It consists mostly of sucrose, with small amounts of glucose.

One-quarter cup, not packed (36g): Cal: 135 Pro: 0g/0% Carb: 35g/100% Fat: 0g/0% Sodium: 11mg Potassium: 125mg

GRANULATED WHITE SUGAR. Pure white and smooth flowing, white sugar is available granulated or finely ground as confectioner's or powdered sugar. Store it airtight in a dark spot. It is almost entirely sucrose.

One-quarter cup (48g): Cal: 193 Pro: 0g/0% Carb: 50g/100% Fat: 0g/0% Sodium: 0mg Potassium: 1mg

HONEY. A clear, thick, golden liquid, honey granulates during storage; this can be reversed by heating it in a warm-water bath. Store it in a cool place or refrigerate. It contains both fructose and glucose.

One-quarter cup (84g): Cal: 244 Pro: .4g/1% Carb: 66g/99% Fat: 0g/0% Sodium: 4mg Potassium: 40mg

MAPLE SYRUP. A dark brown syrup that should be kept in a cool spot or in the refrigerator; it can also be frozen. It's mostly sucrose.

One-quarter cup (80g): Cal: 200 Pro: 0g/0% Carb: 51g/100% Fat: 0g/0% Sodium: 12mg Potassium: 20mg

MOLASSES. Molasses is a slow-pouring, thick, dark-colored syrup with a distinct taste. The darker the color, the stronger the taste and the greater the nutrient content. Seal tightly and store in a cool, dark place. It contains mostly sucrose with some glucose and fructose.

One-quarter cup blackstrap molasses (80g): Cal: 170 Pro: 0g/0% Carb: 44g/100% Fat: 0g/0% Sodium: 76mg Potassium: 2342mg Ca: 55% Fe: 71%

One-quarter cup light molasses (80g): Cal: 200 Pro: 0g/0% Carb: 52g/100% Fat: 0g/0% Sodium: 12mg Potassium: 732mg Ca: 13% Fe: 20%

RICE MALT SYRUP. A syrup made from cooked rice with a mild flavor, it pours like honey. Keep it in a pantry in an airtight container. It contains maltose and glucose.

One-quarter cup (80g): Cal: 216 Other nutritional information not available.

SORGHUM SYRUP. This syrup is mild, sweet, and light amber colored, with a slightly sour taste. Store it in an airtight container in a cool, dry place. About half sucrose, it also contains fructose and glucose.

One-quarter cup (84g): Cal: 208 Pro: 0g/0% Carb: 54g/100% Fat: 0g/0% Sodium: 16mg Potassium: 480mg Ca: 14% Fe: 58%

Beverages

NOTE: A 1-ounce serving of 80 proof alcohol contains a little more than 11 grams of pure alcohol. A 12-ounce beer contains 13 grams of pure alcohol; a 5-ounce serving of table wine, about 14 grams. Our data is based on these standard serving sizes; the percentages refer not to alcohol by weight but to the percent of calories from alcohol. The amount of alcohol in the bloodstream depends on other factors as well: If you drink with meals rather than on an empty stomach, your body will absorb alcohol more slowly, and blood alcohol levels will rise less. So if you drink, eat, too.

BEER. Around the world, there are thousands of beers, fermented beverages usually made from barley and hops. Traditional or homemade beers may contain significant amounts of protein, B vitamins, and other nutrients from the base grains, but modern filtered beers contain few nutrients. Store beer in a cool, dark place; refrigerate before serving; don't allow it to warm up after it is chilled.

Twelve ounces of light beer: Cal: 96 Pro: 1g/5% Carb: 5g/18% Fat: 0g/0% Alc: 12g/77% Sodium: 12mg Potassium: 60mg

Twelve ounces of mild ale: Cal: 145 Pro: 2g/4% Carb: 12g/32% Fat: 0g/0% Alc: 13g/63% Sodium: 24mg Potassium: n/a Cu: 14%

Twelve ounces of regular beer: Cal: 144 Pro: 1.2g/ 3% Carb: 13g/36% Fat: 0g/0% Alc: 13g/61% Sodium: 24mg Potassium: 84mg

COCOA. A dry, powdered, unsweetened chocolate from which the cocoa butter has been removed, cocoa is used to make hot chocolate. Products sold as "breakfast cocoa" have more fat than plain cocoa powder. Store cocoa in a tightly lidded container at room temperature up to 18 months.

Six ounces of cocoa mix prepared with water (206g): Cal: 103 Pro: 3g/11% Carb: 23g/81% Fat: 1g/ 8% Chol: n/a Sodium: 149mg Potassium: 203mg Fiber: 0g B2: 10% Ca: 10% Caffeine: 4mg

COFFEE. For best flavor, grind your own beans at home; ground coffee loses its flavor quickly, especially at room temperature. Store roasted whole beans in the freezer in an airtight container for three or four months; grind only what you need for each pot. Ground coffee beans can be refrigerated in an airtight metal or glass container for up to 10 days or frozen for up to three weeks. Unroasted green beans will last on a shelf for a year.

One six-ounce cup of brewed black coffee: Cal: 2 Pro: 0g/0% Carb: .6g/100% Fat: 0g/0% Chol: 0mg Sodium: 6mg Potassium: 96mg Fiber: 0g Caffeine: 104mg

Cafe au Lait: one six-ounce cup of brewed coffee, three ounces of black coffee, and three ounces of

skim milk: Cal: 35 Pro: 3g/38% Carb: 5g/58%
Fat: .2g/4% Chol: 2mg Sodium: 50mg
Potassium: 200mg Fiber: 0g D: 10% Ca: 12%

FRUIT JUICE. Frozen juice will last up to a year at 0°F. Keep refrigerated after reconstituting, and try to use it within two or three days for peak flavor. Unopened paperboard containers can be refrigerated for up to three weeks; opened, up to 10 days. Aseptic containers store at room temperature for up to a year.

To revive stale juice, aerate it by pouring it back and forth between glasses or putting it in a blender. A little fresh-squeezed orange juice enlivens the taste of packaged. Also, see Fruits food profiles, page 376.

A four-ounce serving of orange juice: Cal: 56 Pro: .9g/6% Carb: 13g/90% Fat: .3g/4% Chol: 0mg
Sodium: 1mg Potassium: 248 Fiber: 1g C: 103%
Folic: 17%

A four-ounce serving of grapefruit juice: Cal: 48 Pro: .6g/5% Carb: 11g/93% Fat: .1g/2% Chol: 0mg
Sodium: 1mg Potassium: 200mg Fiber: .3g
C: 78%

A four-ounce serving of tomato juice: Cal: 21 Pro: .9/15% Carb: 5g/83% Fat: .07g/2% Chol: 0mg
Sodium: 441mg Potassium: 268mg Fiber: 1g A: 14% C: 37%

(NOTE: Low-sodium tomato juice has the same nutritional profile but with only 12mg of sodium.)

A four-ounce serving of apple juice: Cal: 58 Pro: .08g/1% Carb: 15g/97% Fat: .1g/2% Chol: 0mg
Sodium: 4mg Potassium: 148 Fiber: .3g

MILK. See Milk and Yogurt.

TEA. Green tea is unfermented, oolong is partially fermented, and black tea is fully fermented. Keep tea in an airtight container in a cool, dry place, away from light, for up to one year. Don't store tea in the refrigerator, where it will absorb moisture. Store herbal teas according to these same instructions but use within 6 to 9 months.

One six-ounce cup of brewed tea: Cal: 2 Pro: 0g/0% Carb: .6g/100% Fat: 0g/0% Chol: 0mg Sodium: 6mg Potassium: 66mg Fiber: 0g Caffeine: 36mg

WINE. Wine is a fermented beverage made from grapes. Dessert wines contain more natural sugar. The proper cellaring of wines is beyond the scope of this book. But a bottle of wine should be stored on its side, so the cork stays wet, and kept from sunlight and heat. An opened bottle, recorked, can be refrigerated for three days, sometimes longer; you may wish to decant to a small bottle to reduce contact with air. Champagne should be cooled in a refrigerator, then iced; if you open unchilled champagne, it may explode rather than pop. But who would?

Four ounces of champagne: Cal: 80 Pro: .2g/1% Carb: 3g/13% Fat: 0g/0% Alc: 10g/86% Sodium: n/a Potassium: n/a

Three ounces of dessert wine: Cal: 138 Pro: .3g/1% Carb: 11g/30% Fat: 0g/0% Alc: 14g/69% Sodium: 9mg Potassium: 84mg

Five ounces of red table wine: Cal: 105 Pro: .5g/2% Carb: 3g/9% Fat: 0g/0% Alc: 14g/89% Sodium: 95mg Potassium: 203mg

Five ounces of white table wine: Cal: 100 Pro: 0g/0% Carb: 1g/4% Fat: 0g/0% Alc: 14g/96% Sodium: 90mg Potassium: 166mg

◇ SELECTED BIBLIOGRAPHY ◇

The first four sections of this bibliography are primarily scientific, with consumer publications included wherever possible. For the general reader, see V: Further Reading.

I. DIET AND DISEASE PREVENTION

National Academy of Sciences. National Research Council. Committee on Diet and Health. Food and Nutrition Board. 1989. *Diet and Health: Implications for Reducing Chronic Disease Risk.* Washington, D.C.: National Academy Press.

Shields, M. E., and V. R. Young. 1988. *Modern Nutrition in Health and Disease.* Philadelphia: Lea and Febiger.

Sullivan, L. W. 1990. Letter. Healthy people 2000. *The New England Journal of Medicine* 323: 1065-67.

United States Department of Health and Human Services. 1991. *Healthy People 2000: National Health Promotion and Disease Prevention Objectives.* Conference ed. Washington, D.C.: United States Department of Health and Human Services.

United States Department of Health and Human Services. Public Health Service. 1988. *The Surgeon General's Report on Nutrition and Health.* Washington, D.C.: HDDS Publication (PHS) #88-50210. United States Department of Health and Human Services.

A. Cancer and Diet

Ames, B. N., R. Magaw, and L. S. Gold. 1987. Ranking possible carcinogenic hazards. *Science* 236: 271-80.

Chen, J., T. C. Campbell, J. Lee, and R. Peto. 1990. *Diet, Lifestyle, and Mortality in China: A Study of the Characteristics of 65 Chinese Counties.* Monograph. Oxford, England: Oxford University Press; Ithaca, New York: Cornell University Press.

Cohen, L. A. 1987. Diet and cancer. *Scientific American* 257: 42-48.

Creasey, W. A. 1985. *Diet and Cancer.* Philadelphia: Lea and Febiger.

Devesa, S. S., D. T. Silverman, J. L. Young Jr., et al. 1987. Cancer incidence and mortality trends among whites in the United States, 1947–1984. *Journal of the National Cancer Institute* 79: 701–70.

Doll, R., P. Payne, and J. A. H. Waterhouse. 1982. *Cancer Incidence in Five Continents: A Technical Report.* Vol. 4. IARC Scientific Publications #42. Lyon, France: International Agency for Research on Cancer.

Doll, R. and R. Peto. 1981. The causes of cancer: Quantitative estimates of avoidable risks of cancer in the United States today. *Journal of the National Cancer Institute* 66: 1191–1308.

Freudenheim, J. L., and S. Graham. 1989. Toward a dietary prevention of cancer. *Epidemiologic Reviews* 11: 229–35.

Goodwin, P. J., and N. F. Boyd. 1987. Critical appraisal of the evidence that dietary fat intake is related to breast cancer risk in humans. *Journal of the National Cancer Institute* 79: 473–85.

Graham, S. 1987. Fats, calories and calorie expenditure in the epidemiology of cancer. *The American Journal of Clinical Nutrition* 45: 342–46.

McKenna, J. and J. Shea. 1988. How to cut the risk of cancer. *FDA Consumer* 22: 22–25.

Miller, A. B., ed. 1989. *Diet and the Aetiology of Cancer.* Berlin: Springer-Verlag.

Moon, T. E. and M. S. Micozzi. 1989. *Nutrition and Cancer Prevention: Investigating the Role of Micronutrients.* New York: Marcel Dekker.

National Academy of Sciences. National Research Council. Committee on Diet, Nutrition and Cancer. 1982. *Diet, Nutrition and Cancer.* Washington, D.C.: National Academy Press.

Poirier, L. A., P. M. Newberne, and M. W. Pariza, eds. 1986. Essential nutrients in carcinogenesis. *Advances in Experimental Biology and Medicine.* Vol. 206. New York: Plenum Press.

Rose, D., A. P. Boyar, and E. L. Wynder. 1986. International comparison of mortality rates for cancer of the breast, ovary, prostate and colon, and per capita food consumption. *Cancer* 58: 2363–71.

Thind, I. S. 1986. Diet and cancer—an international study. *International Journal of Epidemiology* 15: 160–63.

Wardlaw, G. M. 1985. Assessing the cancer risk from foods. *Journal of the American Dietetic Association* 85: 1122–27.

B. Heart Disease and Diet

Allred, J. B., C. R. Gallagher-Allred, and D. F. Bowers. 1990. Elevated blood cholesterol: A risk factor for heart disease that decreases with advanced age. *Journal of the American Dietetic Association* 90: 574–76.

American Heart Association. 1991. *Heart and Stroke Facts.* Dallas: American Heart Association.

Blumenthal, D. 1990. Making sense of the cholesterol controversy. *FDA Consumer* 24: 13–15.

Blumenthal, D. 1989. Do you know your cholesterol level? *FDA Consumer* 23: 24–27.

Farquhar, W. W., S. P. Fotmann, J. A. Flora, et al. 1990. Effects of communitywide education on cardiovascular disease risk factors. The Stanford Five-City Project. *Journal of the American Medical Association* 264: 359–65.

Havel, R. J. 1988. Lowering cholesterol: Rationale, mechanisms, and means. *The Journal of Clinical Investigation* 81: 1653–60.

Kris-Etherton, P. M., ed. 1990. *Cardiovascular Disease: Nutrition for Prevention and Treatment.* Chicago: American Dietetic Association.

Kris-Etherton, P. M., D. Drummel, M. E. Russell, D. Dreon, S. Mackey, J. Borchers, and P. D. Wood. 1988. The effect of diet on plasma lipids, lipoproteins, and coronary heart disease. *Journal of the American Dietetic Association* 88: 1373–400.

Kritchevsky, D. 1978. How aging affects cholesterol metabolism. *Postgraduate Medicine* 63: 133–36.

LaRosa, J. C. et al. 1990. The cholesterol facts: A summary of the evidence relating dietary fats, serum cholesterol, and coronary heart disease. A joint statement by the American Heart Association and the National Heart, Lung and Blood Institute. *Circulation* 81: 1721–33.

O'Keefe, J. H. Jr., C. J. Lavie, and J. O. O'Keefe. 1989. Dietary prevention of coronary artery disease: How to help patients modify eating habits and reduce cholesterol. *Postgraduate Medicine* 85: 243–61.

Pekkanen, J., S. Linn, G. Heiss, et al. 1990. Ten-year mortality from cardiovascular disease in relation to cholesterol level among men with and without preexisting cardiovascular disease. *The New England Journal of Medicine* 322: 1700–07.

Slattery, M. L. and D. E. Randall. 1988. Trends in coronary heart disease mortality and food consumption in the United States between 1909 and 1980. *The American Journal of Clinical Nutrition* 47: 1060–67.

Sempos, C., R. Fulwood, C. Haines, et al. 1989. The prevalence of high blood cholesterol levels among adults in the United States. *Journal of the American Medical Association* 262: 45–52.

Sytkowski, P. A., W. B. Kannel, and R. B. D'Agostino. 1990. Changes in risk factors and the decline in mortality from cardiovascular disease: The Framingham Heart Study. *The New England Journal of Medicine* 322: 1635–41.

United States Department of Health and Human Services. National Institutes of Health. National Heart, Lung and Blood Institute. 1988. Report of the National Cholesterol Education Program Expert Panel on Detection, Evaluation, and Treatment of High Blood Cholesterol in Adults. *Archives of Internal Medicine* 148: 36–69. (See also: Report of the Expert Panel of Population Strategies for Blood Cholesterol Reduction. In Press. Washington, D.C.: United States Government Printing Office.)

Wilson, P. W. F., J. C. Christiansen, K. M. Anderson, and W. B. Kannel. 1989. Impact of national guidelines for cholesterol risk factor screening: The Framingham Offspring Study. *Journal of the American Medical Association* 262: 41–44.

C. Diabetes and Diet

American Diabetes Association. 1987. Nutritional recommendations and principles for individuals with diabetes mellitus. *Diabetes Care* 10: 126–32.

Crapo, P. A. 1985. Simple versus complex carbohydrates in the diabetic diet. *Annual Review of Nutrition* 5: 95–114.

Etzwiler, D. D., M. J. Franz, P. Hollander, and J. Joynes, eds. 1985. *Learning to Live Well with Diabetes.* Minneapolis: International Diabetes Center.

Franz, M. J. 1987. Exercise and the management of diabetes mellitus. *Journal of the American Dietetic Association* 87: 872–80.

Franz, M. J., P. Barr, H. Holler, et al. 1987. Exchange lists: Revised 1986. *Journal of the American Dietetic Association.* 87: 28–34.

Garg., A., A. Bonanome, S. M. Grundy, et al. 1988. Comparison of a high-carbohydrate diet with a high-monounsaturated-fat diet in patients with non-insulin-dependent diabetes mellitus. *The New England Journal of Medicine* 319: 829–39.

Hagan, J., and J. Wylie-Rosett. 1989. Lipids: Impact on dietary prescription in diabetes. *Journal of the American Dietetic Association* 89: 1104–11.

Javanovic, L. and C. Peterson, eds. 1985. *Nutrition and Diabetes.* New York: Alan R. Liss.

O'Dea, K., K. Trianedes, P. Ireland, et al. 1989. The effects of diet differing in fat, carbohydrate, and fiber on carbohydrate and lipid metabolism in Type II diabetes. *Journal of the American Dietetic Association* 89: 1076–86.

Reaven, G. R. 1988. Dietary therapy for non-insulin-dependent diabetes mellitus. *The New England Journal of Medicine* 319: 862–64.

United States Department of Health and Human Services. National Institutes of Health. 1986. *Consensus Development Conference on Diet and Exercise in Noninsulin-dependent Diabetes Mellitus.* Bethesda, Mar.: United States Department of Health and Human Services.

Vinik, A. I. and D. J. Jenkins. 1988. Dietary fiber in management of diabetes. *Diabetes Care* 11: 160–73.

Wood, F. C. Jr. and E. L. Bierman. 1986. Is diet the cornerstone of management of diabetes? *The New England Journal of Medicine* 315: 1224–27.

D. Diet and Dental Health

American Academy of Pediatric Dentistry. 1989. *Dental Health Objectives for the Year 2000: Statement of the American Academy of Pediatric Dentistry.* Chicago: American Academy of Pediatric Dentistry.

Harper, D. S., J. C. Osborn, J. J. Hefferren, and R. Clayton. 1986. Cariostatic evaluation of cheeses with diverse physical and compositional characteristics. *Caries Research* 20: 123–30.

Newbrun, E., ed. 1982. Sugar and dental caries: A review of human studies. *Science* 217: 418–23.

Nizel, A. and A. Papas, eds. 1989. *Nutrition in Clinical Dentistry: Science and Practice.* 3rd ed. Philadelphia: W. B. Saunders.

Shaw, J. H. 1987. Causes and control of dental caries. *The New England Journal of Medicine* 317: 996–1004.

II. FOOD AND NUTRITION

American Dietetic Association/American Diabetes Association. 1986. *Exchange List for Meal Planning.* See also pamphlets on Mexican-American (1989) Food Practices, Customs and Holidays; Jewish (1990); Chinese-American (1990); Navajo (1990). Chicago: American Dietetic Association.

American Heart Association. *The American Heart Association Diet: An Eating Plan for Healthy Americans.* 1989. Product code #51018-B. Dallas: American Heart Association.

Lecos, C. W. 1987. Planning a diet for a healthy heart. *FDA Consumer* 21: 29–36. (Reprint revised 1991. Rockville, Mar.: Consumer Affairs, United States Food and Drug Administration.)

National Academy of Sciences. National Research Council. Food and Nutrition Board. 1989. *Recommended Dietary Allowances.* 10th edition. Washington, D.C.: National Academy Press.

Patterson, B. H., and G. Block. Food choices and cancer guidelines. *American Journal of Public Health* 78: 282–86.

United States Department of Agriculture. Human Nutrition Information Service. 1991. *The USDA's Eating Right Pyramid: How to Eat Right the Dietary Guidelines Way.* Washington, D.C.: House and Garden Bulletin #249. [Note: Publication suspended]

United States Department of Agriculture. Human Nutrition Information Service. 1990. *Dietary Guidelines for Healthy Americans.* House and Garden Bulletin #232. Washington, D.C.: United States Department of Agriculture.

United States Department of Health and Human Services. National Institutes of Health. National Cancer Institute. 1987. *Diet, Nutrition and Cancer Prevention: A Guide to Food Choices.* NIH Publication #87-2878. Bethesda, Mar.: National Institutes of Health.

A. Carbohydrates/Grains

1. Complex Carbohydrates and Fiber

Anderson, J. W., N. J. Gustafson, C. A. Bryant,

and J. Tietyen-Clark. 1987. Dietary fiber and diabetes: A comprehensive review and practical application. *Journal of the American Dietetic Association* 87: 1189–97.

British Nutrition Foundation Task Force. 1990. *Complex Carbohydrates in Foods.* New York: Van Nostrand Reinhold.

Fernstrom, J. D. 1986. Acute and chronic effects of protein and carbohydrate ingestion on brain tryptophan levels and serotonin synthesis. Supplement to *Nutrition Reviews* 44: 25–36.

Greenwald, P., E. Lanza, and G. A. Eddy. 1987. Dietary fiber in the reduction of colon cancer risk. *Journal of the American Dietetic Association* 87: 1178–88.

Klaus, L. and C. Kulp. 1990. *Handbook of Cereal Science and Technology.* Food Science and Technology Series 41. New York: Marcel Dekker.

Kritchevsky, D. 1989. Dietary fiber. *Annual Review of Nutrition* 8: 301–28.

Pilch, S. M. 1987. *Physiological Effects and Health Consequences of Dietary Fiber.* Life Sciences Research Office. Rockville, Mar.: United States Food and Drug Administration.

Spring, B. J., H. R. Lieberman, G. Swope, and G. S. Garfield. 1986. Effects of carbohydrates on mood and behavior. Supplement to *Nutrition Reviews* 44: 51–60.

2. Sugars and Sweeteners

Kruesi, M. J. P. 1986. Carbohydrate intake and children's behavior. *Food Technology* 40: 150–52.

Newsome, R. L., ed. 1986. Sweeteners: Nutritive and non-nutritive. *Food Technology* 40: 195–206.

North American Association for the Study of Obesity. 1988. *Sweeteners, Appetite and Obesity.* Proceedings of Workshop: The Effects of Sweeteners on Food Intake 11: 1–102. Boston: Academic Press.

Rolls, B. 1991. Effects of intense sweeteners on hunger, food intake and body weight: A review. *The American Journal of Clinical Nutrition* 53: 872–78.

United States Department of Health and Human Services. Food and Drug Administration. 1986. *Evaluation of Health Aspects of Sugars Contained in Carbohydrate Sweeteners: Report of Sugar Task Force.* Rockville, Mar.: United States Food and Drug Administration.

Williams, G., ed. 1988. *Sweeteners: Health Effects.* Princeton, N.J.: Princeton Scientific Publishing.

B. Proteins

Forsythe, W. A., M. S. Green, and J. J. B. Anderson. 1986. Dietary protein effects on cholesterol and lipoprotein concentrations: A review. *Journal of the American College of Nutrition* 5: 533–49.

Fox, P. F., and J. J. Condon. 1982. *Food Proteins.* New York: Applied Science Publishers.

Steele, R. D., and A. E. Harper. 1990. Proteins and amino acids. *Present Knowledge in Nutrition.* M. L. Brown, ed. Washington, D.C.: International Life Sciences Institute, Nutrition Foundation.

C. Fats and Oils

Cambie, R. C., ed. 1989. *Fats for the Future.* New York: Van Nostrand Reinhold.

Grundy, S. M., and M. A. Denke. 1990. Dietary influences on serum lipids and lipoproteins. *Journal of Lipid Research* 31: 1149–72.

Hill, M. J. 1987. Dietary fat and human cancer: A review. *Anticancer Research* 7: 281–92.

Ip, C., D. F. Birt, A. E. Rogers, and C. Mettlin, eds. 1986. Dietary Fat and Cancer. *Progress in Clinical and Biological Research.* Vol. 222. New York: Alan R. Liss.

Holman, R. T., W. W. Chistie, H. Sprecher, M. Crawford, B. Lewis, K. K. Carroll, and K. K. Wahle, eds. 1986. *Essential Fatty Acids, Prostaglandins, and Leukotrienes.* Oxford, England: Pergammon Press.

D. Dietary Cholesterol/Eggs

Flynn, M., et al. 1986. Serum lipids and eggs. *Journal of the American Dietetic Association* 86: 1541–48.

Hegsted, D. M. 1986. Serum cholesterol response to dietary cholesterol: A re-evaluation. *The American Journal of Clinical Nutrition* 44: 299–305.

McNamara, D. J., R. Kolb, and T. S. Parker. 1987. Heterogeneity of cholesterol homeostasis in man: Response to changes in dietary fat quality and cholesterol quantity. *The Journal of Clinical Investigation* 79: 1729–39.

Stamler, J., and R. Shekelle. 1988. Dietary cholesterol and human coronary heart disease: The epidemiologic evidence. *Archives of Pathology and Laboratory Medicine* 112: 1032–40.

E. Salt/Sodium

InterSalt Cooperative Research Group. 1988. InterSalt: An international study of electrolyte excretion and blood pressure: *British Medical Journal* 297: 319–28.

Kaplan, N. M. 1990. New evidence on the role of sodium in hypertension: The InterSalt study. *American Journal of Hypertension* 3: 168–69.

Laragh, J. H., and M. S. Pecker. 1983. Dietary sodium and essential hypertension: Some myths, hopes and truths. *Annals of Internal Medicine* 98: 735–43.

National Heart, Lung and Blood Institute Workshop on Salt and Blood Pressure. 1991. Supplement to *Hypertension* 17: 1–221.

F. Fish

Childs, M. T., C. S. Dorsett, A. Failor, et al. 1987. Effect of shellfish consumption on cholesterol absorption in normolipidemic man. *Metabolism* 36: 31–35.

Kinsella, J. E, V. Lokesh, and R. A. Stone. 1990. Dietary omega-3 polyunsaturated fatty acids and amelioration of cardiovascular disease: Possible mechanisms. *The American Journal of Clinical Nutrition* 52: 1–28.

Kinsella, J. E. 1988. Fish and seafoods: Nutritional implications and quality issues. *Food Technology* 42: 146–52.

Kinsella, J. E. 1987. *Seafoods and Fish Oils in Human Health and Disease.* New York: Marcel Dekker

Lands, W. E. M. 1986. *Fish and Human Health.* Orlando, Fla.: Academic Press.

Leaf, A. and P. C. Weber. 1988. Cardiovascular effects of n-3 fatty acids. *The New England Journal of Medicine* 318: 549–57.

Nettleton, J. A. 1987. *Seafood and Health.* Huntington, N.Y.: Van Nostrand Reinhold (formerly, Osprey Books).

Neuringer, M., G. J. Anderson, and W. E. Connor. 1988. The essentiality of n-3 fatty acids for the development and function of the retina and brain. *Annual Review of Nutrition* 8: 517–541.

Simopoulos, A. P., R. R. Kifer, and R. E. Martin, eds. 1986. *Health Effects of Polyunsaturated Fatty Acids in Seafoods.* Orlando, Fla.: Academic Press.

G. Calcium/Dairy Foods

Cumming, R. G. 1990. Calcium intake and bone mass: A quantitative review of the evidence. *Calcified Tissue International* 47: 194–201.

Dawson-Hughes, B. 1990. A controlled trial of the effect of calcium supplementation on bone density in post-menopausal women. *The New England Journal of Medicine* 323: 878–83.

Garland, C. F. and F. C. Garland. 1986. Calcium and colon cancer. *Clinical Nutrition* 5: 161–66.

Kanis, J. A. and R. Passmore. 1989. Calcium supplementation of the diet: Not justified by present evidence. *British Medical Journal* 298: 137–40, 205–08.

Kumar, N. 1986. Effect of milk on patients with duodenal ulcers. *British Medical Journal* 293: 666.

Nordin, B. E. C., and R. P. Heaney. 1990. Calcium supplementation of the diet: Justified by present evidence. *British Medical Journal* 300: 1056–60.

1. Fermented Dairy Products/Yogurt

Fernandes, C. F., K. M. Shahani, and M. A. Amer. 1987. Therapeutic role of dietary lactobacilli and lactobacillic fermented dairy products. *F.E.M.S. Microbiology Review* 46: 343–56.

Friend, B. A. and K. M. Shahani. 1984. Nutritional and therapeutic aspects of lactobacilli. *Journal of Applied Nutrition* 36: 125–53.

Gorbach, S. 1990. Lactic acid bacteria and human health. *Annals of Medicine* 22: 37–41.

H. Plant Foods

Block, G., B. Patterson, and A. Subar. In Press 1991. Fruit, vegetables and cancer prevention: A review of epidemiologic evidence. *The American Journal of Clinical Nutrition.*

Cody, V., E. Middleton, and J. Harborne. 1986. Plant flavonoids in biology and medicine. *Progress in Clinical and Biological Research.* Vol. 213. New York: Alan R. Liss.

Dwyer, J. T. 1983. Nutrition status and alternative life-style diets with special reference to vegetarianism in the U.S.A. *CRC Handbook of Nutritional Supplements: Human Use* 1: 343–410. M. Reichigl. ed. Boca Raton, Fla.: CRC Press.

Knudsen, I., ed. 1985. Genetic toxicology of the diet. *Progress in Clinical and Biological Research.* Vol. 26. New York: Alan R. Liss.

Kroyer, G. 1986. English abstract. The antioxidant activity of citrus fruit peels. *Z. Ernahrungswiss* 25: 63–69.

Messina, M., and S. Barnes. 1991. The role of soy products in reducing risk of cancer. *Journal of the National Cancer Institute* 83: 541–46.

Mutch, P. B. and P. K. Johnston, eds. 1988. First International Congress on Vegetarian Nutrition. Supplement to *The American Journal of Clinical Nutrition* 48: 707–927.

Patterson, B. H., et al. 1990. Fruit and Vegetables in the American Diet: Data from NHANES II Survey. *American Journal of Public Health* 80: 1443–49.

Peto, R., J. D. Buckley, and M. B. Sporn. 1981. Can dietary beta-carotene materially reduce human cancer rates? *Nature* 291: 201–8.

Reiser, S. 1987. Metabolic effects of dietary pectins related to human health. *Food Technology* 41: 91–99.

Tilvis, R. S., and T. A. Miettinen. 1986. Serum plant sterols and their relation to cholesterol absorption. *The American Journal of Clinical Nutrition* 43: 92–97.

Slater, T. F., and G. Block, eds. 1991. Antioxidant vitamins and beta-carotene in disease prevention. *The American Journal of Clinical Nutrition* 53 (1/supp.).

Wiltrout, R. and R. L. Hornung. 1988. Editorial. Natural products as antitumor agents: Direct versus indirect mechanisms of activity of flavonoids. *Journal of the National Cancer Institute* 80: 220–22.

1. Individual Fruits, Vegetables, and Spices.

Best, R., D. A. Lewis, and N. Nassar. 1984. The anti-ulcerogenic activity of the unripe plantain banana (musa species). *British Journal of Pharmacology* 82: 107–16.

Block, E. 1985. The chemistry of garlic and onions. *Scientific American* 252: 114–19.

Buck, S. H., and T. F. Burks. 1986. The neuropharmacology of capsaicin: Review of some recent observations. *Pharmacological Review* 38: 179–226.

Fenwick, G. R., and A. B. Hanley. 1986. *Genus allium. CRC Critical Reviews in Food Science and Nutrition* 23. Boca Raton, Fla.: CRC Press.

First World Congress on the Health Significance of Garlic and Garlic Constituents. In Press. *Garlic in Biology and Medicine.* Irvine, Calif.: Nutrition International Company.

Graham, D. Y., J. L. Smith, and A. R. Opekun. 1988. Spicy food and the stomach: Evaluation by videoendoscopy. *Journal of the American Medical Association* 260: 3473–75.

Grontved, A., and E. Hentzer. 1986. Vertigo-reducing effect of ginger root: A controlled clinical study. *Journal of Otorhinolaryngology and Related Specialties* 48: 282–86.

Holzer, P. 1989. Letter. Peppers, capsaicin, and the gastric mucosa. *Journal of the American Medical Association* 261: 3244–45.

Henry, C. J. K., and B. Emery. 1986. Effect of spiced food on metabolic rate. *Human Nutrition: Clinical Nutrition* 40: 165–68.

Lawson, T., and P. Gannett. 1989. The mutagenicity of capsaicin and dihydrocapsaicin in V79 cells. *Cancer Letters* 48: 109–13.

Makheja, A. N., and J. M. Bailey. 1981. Letter. Identification of the antiplatelet substance in Chinese black tree fungus. *The New England Journal of Medicine* 304: 175.

Mowrey, D. B., and D. E. Clayson. 1982. Motion sickness, ginger and psychophysics. *Lancet* 1: 655–57.

Shoji, N., et al. 1982. Cardiotonic principles of ginger. *Journal of Pharmaceutical Science* 71: 1174–75.

Sobota, A. E. 1984. Inhibition of bacterial adherence by cranberry juice: Potential use for the treatment of urinary tract infections. *Journal of Urology* 131: 1013–16.

Suekawa, M., et al. 1984. Pharmacological studies of ginger. *Journal of Pharmacobio-dynamics* 7: 836–48.

Sugano, N., et al. 1982. Anticarcinogenic actions of water-soluble and alcohol-insoluble fractions from culture medium of lentinus edodes mycelia. *Cancer Letters* 17: 109–14.

Weil, A. T. 1981. Mushrooms as food and medicine: A review. *McIlvainea: Journal of American Amateur Mycology* 5: 11–15.

2. Herbal Medicine

Duke, J. A. 1985. *Handbook of Medicinal Herbs.* Boca Raton, Fla.: CRC Press.

Leung, A. Y. 1980. *Encyclopedia of Common Natural Ingredients Used in Food, Drugs, and Cosmetics.* New York: John Wiley.

Morton, J. F. 1977. *Major Medicinal Plants.* Springfield, Ill.: C. C. Thomas.

I. Caffeine and Alcohol

Garro, A. J., and C. S. Lieber. 1990. Alcohol and cancer. *Annual Review of Pharmacology and Toxicology* 30: 219–49.

Klatsky, A. L., M. A. Armstrong, and C. D. Friedman. 1990. Risk of cardiovascular mortality in alcohol drinkers, ex-drinkers and non-drinkers. *American Journal of Cardiology* 66: 1237–42.

Lieber, C. S. 1988. The influence of alcohol on nutrition status. *Nutrition Reviews* 46: 241–54.

Rosenberg, L., J. R. Palmer, D. R. Miller, E. A. Clark, and S. Shapiro. 1990. A case control study of alcoholic beverage consumption and breast cancer. *American Journal of Epidemiology* 131: 6–14.

Rosenberg, L., J. R. Palmer, J. P. Kelly, et al. 1988.

Coffee drinking and non-fatal myocardial infarction in men under 55 years of age. *American Journal of Epidemiology* 128: 570–78.

Rosenberg, L. 1990. Coffee and tea consumption in relation to the risk of large bowel cancer: A review of epidemiologic studies. *Cancer Letters* 52: 163–71.

Willet, W. C., M. J. Stampfer, G. A. Colditz, B. A. Rosner, C. H. Hennekens, and F. E. Speizer. 1987. Moderate alcohol consumption and the risk of breast cancer. *The New England Journal of Medicine* 316: 1174–80.

III. FOOD SAFETY AND STORAGE

Ahmed, F. E., ed. 1991. *Seafood Safety*. National Academy of Sciences. Institute of Medicine. Food and Nutrition Board. Publication #90–25996. Washington, D.C.: National Academy Press.

Archer, D. L. 1988. The true impact of foodborne infections. *Food Technology* 42: 53–58.

Biehl, M., and W. B. Buck. 1987. Chemical contaminants: Their metabolism and their residues. *Journal of Food Protection* 50: 1058–73.

Catsberg, C. M. E., and G. J. M. Kempen-Van Dommelen. 1990. *Food Handbook*. New York: Van Nostrand Reinhold.

Goldburg, R., J. Rissler, H. Shand, and C. Hassebrook. 1990. *Biotechnology's Bitter Harvest: Herbicide-Tolerant Crops and the Threat to Sustainable Agriculture*. New York: Biotechnology Working Group. Environmental Defense Fund.

Hall, R. L. and S. L. Taylor. 1989. Food toxicology and safety evaluation: Changing perspectives and a challenge for the future. *Food Technology* 43: 270–80.

Levine, A. S., T. P. Labuza, and J. E. Morley. 1985. Food technology: A primer for physicians. *The New England Journal of Medicine* 312: 628–33.

National Academy of Sciences. Institute of Medicine. Food and Nutrition Board. 1990. *Cattle Inspection*. Publication #90–62817. Washington, D.C.: National Academy Press.

National Academy of Sciences. National Research Council. Board of Agriculture. 1989. *Alternative Agriculture*. Publication #88–26997. Washington, D.C.: National Academy Press.

National Academy of Sciences. National Research Council. Board of Agriculture. 1987. *Regulating Pesticides in Food: The Delaney Paradox*. Publication #87–61095. Washington, D.C.: National Academy Press.

National Academy of Sciences. Institute of Medicine. Food and Nutrition Board. 1985. *Meat and Poultry Inspection: The Scientific Basis of the Nation's Program*. Publication #85–71993. Washington, D.C.: National Academy Press.

Ryser, E. T., and E. H. Marth. 1989. "New" food-borne pathogens of public health significance. *Journal of the American Dietetic Association* 89: 948–54.

Segal, M. 1990. Is it worth the worry? Determining risk. *FDA Consumer* 24: 7–11.

United States Department of Agriculture. 1984. *The Safe Food Book: Your Kitchen Guide*. Home and Garden Bulletin #241. Washington, D.C.: United States Department of Agriculture.

United States General Accounting Office. 1990. *Food Safety and Quality: FDA Surveys Not Adequate to Demonstrate Safety of Milk Supply*. Document #RCED-91-26. Washington, D.C.: General Accounting Office.

Young, F. E. 1989. Weighing food safety risks. *FDA Consumer* 23: 8–13

IV. NUTRITIONAL DATA

Block, G., C. M. Dresser, A. M. Hartman, and M. D. Carroll. 1985. Nutrient Sources in the American Diet: Quantitative Data from the NHANES II Survey. *American Journal of Epidemiology* 122: 27–40.

Gebhardt, S. E. and R. H. Matthews. 1981. *Nutritive Value of Foods*. Home and Garden Bulletin #72. Washington, D.C.: United States Department of Agriculture Human Nutrition Information Service.

United States Department of Agriculture. Human Nutrition Information Service. *Composition of Foods. Agriculture Handbooks*: 8–1, *Dairy and Egg Products*, 1976; 8–2, *Spices and Herbs*, 1977; 8–3, *Baby Foods*, 1978; 8–4, *Fats and Oils*, 1979; 8–5, *Poultry Products*, 1979; 8–6, *Soups, Sauces and Gravies*, 1980; 8–7, *Sausages and Luncheon Meats*, 1980; 8–8, Breakfast Cereals, 1982; 8–9, *Fruits and Fruit Juices*, 1982; 8–10, *Pork Products*, 1983; 8–11, *Vegetables and Vegetable Products*, 1984; 8–12, *Nut and Seed Products*, 1984; 8–13, *Beef Products*, 1990; 8–14, *Beverages*, 1986: 8–15, *Finfish and Shellfish Products*, 1987; 8–16, *Legumes and Legume Products*, 1986; 8–17, *Lamb, Veal, and Game Products*, 1989; 8–18, *Baked Products*, in preparation; 8–19, *Snacks and Sweets*, 1991; 8–20, *Cereal Grains and Pasta*, 1989; 8–21, *Fast Foods*, 1988; 8–22, *Mixed Dishes*, in preparation.

Pennington, J. A. T. and H. N. Church. 1989. *Bowes and Church's Food Values of Portions Commonly Used.* Philadelphia: Lippincott.

V. FURTHER READING

A. Books

1. Nutrition

Algert, S., et al. 1990. *The UCSD Healthy Diet for Diabetes: A Comprehensive Guide and Cookbook.* Boston: Houghton Mifflin.

Brody, J. 1981. *Jane Brody's Nutrition Book.* New York: W. W. Norton.

Brody J. 1985. *Jane Brody's Good Food Book.* New York: W. W. Norton.

Boyle, M. A., and E. N. Whitney. 1989. *Personal Nutrition.* St. Paul, Minn.: West Publishing.

Carper, J. 1988. *The Food Pharmacy.* New York: Bantam Books.

Clark, N. 1990. *Nancy Clark's Sports Nutrition Guidebook.* Champagne, Ill.: Leisure Press.

Connor, S. L., and W. E. Connor. 1991. *The New American Diet System.* New York: Simon and Schuster.

Fletcher, A. M. 1989. *Eat Fish, Live Better.* New York: Harper & Row.

Goor, R., and N. Goor. 1987. *Eater's Choice: A Food Lover's Guide to Lower Cholesterol.* Boston: Houghton Mifflin.

Gershoff, S., and C. Whitney. 1990. *The Tufts University Guide to Total Nutrition.* New York: Harper & Row.

Kwiterovich, P. 1989. *Beyond Cholesterol.* Annapolis: The Johns Hopkins University Press.

Heaney, R. and J. Barger-Lux. 1988. *Calcium and Common Sense.* New York: Doubleday Books.

Herbert, V., and G. Subak-Sharpe. 1991. *Mt. Sinai School of Medicine Complete Book of Nutrition.* New York: St. Martin's Press.

Hess, M. A., 1990. *A Healthy Head Start: A Worry-Free Guide to Feeding Young Children.* New York: Henry Holt.

Mayer, J., and J. Goldberg. 1990. *Dr. Jean Mayer's Diet and Nutrition Guide.* New York: Pharos Books/ Scripps Howard.

Satter, E. 1987. *How to Get Your Kids to Eat . . . But Not Too Much.* Palo Alto, Calif.: Bull Publishing.

Satter, E. 1986. *Child of Mine: Feeding with Love and Good Sense.* Palo Alto, Calif.: Bull Publishing.

Saltman, P., J. Gurin, and I. Mothner. 1987. *The California Nutrition Book: A Food Guide for the 90s.* Boston: Little, Brown.

Smith, N., and B. S. Worthington-Roberts. 1989. *Food for Sport.* Palo Alto, Calif.: Bull Publishing.

Tyler, V. E. 1987. *The New Honest Herbal: A Sensible Guide to the Use of Herbs and Related Remedies.* Philadelphia: George F. Stickley Company.

Whitney, E. N., and E. M. N. Hamilton. 1989. *Understanding Nutrition.* St. Paul: West Publishing Company.

2. Food

Bailey, J. 1989. *Keeping Food Fresh: How to Choose and Store Everything You Eat.* New York: Harper & Row.

Blackman, J. F. 1989. *The Working Chef's Cookbook for Natural Whole Foods.* Morrisville, Vt.: Central Vermont Publishers.

Chalmers, I. 1990. *The Food Professional's Guide.* New York: John Wiley.

Cost, B. 1988. *Bruce Cost's Asian Ingredients.* New York: William Morrow.

Creasy, R. 1988. *Cooking from the Garden: Creative Gardening and Contemporary Cuisine.* San Francisco: Sierra Club Books.

Cunningham, M. 1990. *The Fannie Farmer Cookbook.* New York: Knopf.

Dowell, P., and A. Bailey. 1980. *Cooks' Ingredients.* New York: William Morrow.

Goldbeck, N., and D. Goldbeck. 1987. *The Goldbecks' Guide to Good Food.* New York: New American Library.

Hertzberg, R., B. Vaughn, and J. Greene. 1982. *Putting Food By.* Brattleboro, Vt.: S. Greene Press.

Kafka, B. 1989. *Microwave Gourmet Healthstyle Cookbook.* New York: William Morrow.

King, S. 1990. *Fish: The Basics.* New York: Simon and Schuster.

McGee, H. 1990. *The Curious Cook: More Kitchen Science and Lore.* San Francisco: North Point Press.

McGee, H. 1984. *On Food and Cooking: The Science and Lore of the Kitchen.* New York: Charles Scribner's Sons.

Norman, J. 1990. *The Complete Book of Spices: A Practical Guide to Spices and Aromatic Seeds.* New York: Viking Penguin.

Rosengarten, F. 1984. *The Complete Book of Edible Nuts.* New York: Walker and Company.

Schneider, E. 1986. *Uncommon Fruits & Vegetables: A Commonsense Guide.* New York: Harper & Row.

Tourneau, I. 1990. *Cooksource: An Indispensable Guide to the Best Mail-Order Sources.* New York: Doubleday/Bantam.

Ubaldi, J., and E. Grossman. 1987. *Jack Ubaldi's Meat Book: A Butcher's Guide to Buying, Cutting and Cooking Meat.* New York: Macmillan.

Warshaw, H. S. 1990. *The Restaurant Companion: A Guide to Healthier Eating Out.* Chicago: Surrey Books.

Wiegand, L. 1990. *Food Catalog: The Ultimate Guide to Buying Food by Mail.* New York: Clarkson N. Potter.

Wood, R. 1988. *The Whole Foods Encyclopedia.* New York: Prentice Hall.

B. Newsletters

Action Alert. Public Voice for Food and Health Policy. 1001 Connecticut Avenue, NW, Suite 522, Washington, D.C. 20036. Quarterly.

American Institute for Cancer Research Newsletter. 1759 R Street, NW, Washington, D.C. 20009. Quarterly.

Environmental Nutrition. 2112 Broadway, Suite 200, New York, NY 10023. Monthly.

Herbalgram. American Botanical Council. P.O. Box 201660, Austin, TX 78720. Quarterly.

Nutrition Action Healthletter. Center for Science in the Public Interest. 1875 Connecticut Avenue, NW, Suite 300, Washington, D.C. 20009. Monthly.

Tufts University Diet and Nutrition Letter. 203 Harrison Avenue, Boston, MA 02111. Monthly.

University of California, Berkeley Wellness Letter. 632 Broadway, 11th Floor, New York, NY 10012. Subscription: P.O. Box 420148, Palm Coast, FL. 32142. Monthly.

C. Sources of Information

American Diabetes Association. Cookbooks, 28-day menu planners, exchange lists for meal planning. 1660 Duke Street, Alexandria, VA 22314. For publications list, write to Order Fulfillment Dept., General information, same address.

American Dietetic Association. Publications include *Worksite Nutrition* (1986), *Pocket Supermarket Guide* (1989), *Children, Cholesterol and Diet* (1989). Sales Order Department: American Dietetic Association, 216 West Jackson Blvd., Suite 800, Chicago, IL 60606. For general information, or to request "client education booklets," address inquiries to National Center for Nutrition and Dietetics, above address.

American Heart Association. Numerous consumer publications on heart disease prevention and treatment. Contact local office. For local affiliate address, write to: American Heart Association, National Center, 7320 Greenville Avenue, Dallas, TX 75231.

American Health Foundation (no connection to this book.) *Live Well: The Low-Fat, High-Fiber Way* (1990), *Great Meals, Great Snacks, Great Kids* (1989), *Health Letter,* brochures. 1 Dana Road, Valhalla, NY 10595.

American Health Magazine, 28 West 23rd Street, New York, NY 10010; for subscription information, 1-800-365-5005.

FDA Consumer Communications, 5600 Fishers Lane, Parklawn Building, HFE-20, Rockville, MD 20857. Write for publications list.

Food and Nutrition Information Center. For educators and professionals. Free publications and bibliographies; reading lists for consumers; "Agricola" data base. National Agricultural Library, USDA, Room 304, 10301 Baltimore Blvd., Beltsville, MD 20705-2351.

National Cancer Institute. *Diet, Nutrition and Cancer Prevention: The Good News.* NCI #87-2878. *Good News, Better News, Best News . . . Cancer Prevention.* NCI #84-2671. Office of Cancer Communications, National Cancer Institute, Building 31, Room 10A24, Bethesda, MD 20892. Write for publications list. For information by phone, call National Cancer Institute Cancer Information Service: 1-800-4-CANCER; in Alaska, 1-800-638-6070; in Hawaii, 524-1234.

National Osteoporosis Foundation. *Boning Up on Osteoporosis* (1991); publications for consumers and health professionals. 2100 M Street, NW, Suite 602, Washington, D.C. 20037. Write for publications list or with specific request.

United States Department of Agriculture Human Nutrition Information Service. Publications available on dietary guidelines. 6505 Belcrest Road, Hyattsville, MD 20782. (Also, USDA/*HNIS Good Sources of Nutrients.* 17 fact sheets. Consumer Information Center, Pueblo, CO 81009.)

United States Department of Agriculture Extension Service. Pamphlets on canning, freezing, meat preparation, etc. Room 3323, South Building, Washington, D.C. 20250-0900. Write for publications list. Contact local county and state office for location-specific information.

D. Correspondence

American Health Food Book. Send correspondence to Robert Barnett, 2673 Broadway, Suite 105, New York, NY 10025 or c/o Dutton Books, Penguin USA, 375 Hudson Street, New York, NY 10014.

◇ CONTRIBUTORS ◇

Robert Barnett is a writer and editor in New York City. He writes about food, nutrition, health and the environment for national magazines and books, and teaches science journalism at New York University.

Jeanine Barone, M.S., is a nutritionist and exercise physiologist. She writes for national magazines, television and advertising, and lectures at universities and corporations on disease prevention, health, nutrition, and fitness.

Lidia Bastianich is the chef and owner of Felidia's in New York City.

Madonna Behen, former associate editor at *American Health* magazine, is an editor at *Women's Wear Daily* in New York City.

Joanna B. Bergmann is a private chef and cooking teacher in New York City.

Guiliano Bugialli is the author of *The Fine Art of Italian Cooking* (Times Books).

Madelaine Bullwinkel, owner of Chez Madelaine Cooking School, in Hinsdale, Illinois, is the author of *Gourmet Preserves Chez Madelaine* (Contemporary Books) and publishes a newsletter, Madelaine's Kitchen Secrets.

Marian Burros is a food columnist for *The New York Times,* where she writes the weekly "Eating Well" column. She is the author of several cookbooks, including *Twenty Minute Menus* (Simon & Schuster, Inc.).

Lisa Chobanian, M.S., R.D., is a nutrition consultant for corporate wellness programs in New York City.

Kevin Cobb is a journalist in New York City.

Jack Czarnecki is chef-proprietor of Joe's, a restaurant in Reading, Pennsylvania, and author of *Joe's Book of Mushroom Cookery* (Atheneum).

James Duke, Ph.D., one of the leading world experts on the medicinal uses of plants, is a USDA botanist, lecturer, consultant, folklorist and author of over 100 scientific papers and several books, including the *CRC Handbook of Medicinal Plants* (CRC Press, Inc.).

Mary Estella is a food writer for national magazines, a cooking instructor, and author of *Natural Foods Cookbook: Vegetarian Dairy-Free Cuisine* (Japan Publications) and a forthcoming cookbook.

Susan Feniger and **Mary Sue Milliken** are co-chefs and co-proprietors of the Border Grill and City, two restuarants in Los Angeles. They are also co-authors of *City Cuisine* (William Morrow & Company, Inc.).

Marcy Barbour Fiacco, R.D., M.S., does individual and group counseling, and public speaking through her firm, HealthStyles Nutrition Consultants, in Elmsford, New York.

Four Seasons Hotels Alternative Cuisine was developed by **Alfons Konrad** and a group of executive chefs at Four Seasons Hotels and Resorts in Toronto.

Lee Grimsbo is a specialty food buyer in New York City.

Nao Hauser writes about food and travel for national magazines, including *American Health, Food and Wine, Bon Appetit, Travel & Leisure, Cooking Light, New York, Good Food,* and *Chocolatier.* A former managing editor at *Cuisine,* she is the author of books on microwave cooking and popcorn, and has served as editorial consultant on more than two dozen cookbooks.

Evette M. Hackman, Ph.D., R.D., is a magazine writer, nutrition editor of *Shape* magazine, newspaper columnist, public speaker, and founder of Nutrition Works, in Seattle, WA, where she offers individual nutrition counseling, corporate programs, and culinary training.

Ceri E. Hadda is a food writer who contributes regularly to newspapers and national magazines. She is working on a book on coffee cakes.

Cheryl Jennings-Sauer, R.D., in private practice in Dallas, Texas, is the author of the "anti-diet" book, *Living Lean by Choosing More* (Taylor).

Kathy Johnson-Schlichting, M.S., R.D., is an associate editor at *American Health* magazine. In addition to editorial experience, she is also trained as a clinical dietician with an interest in parenteral and enteral nutrition.

Barrie Kavash lives in Bridgewater, CT, and writes on native American cuisine.

Diane M. Kochilas is a food writer and author of *Greek Food* (St. Martin's Press).

Sonoko Kondo, a food writer, contributes to both American and Japanese magazines on Japanese culture and food, and is the co-author of *The Poetical Pursuit of Food: Japanese Recipes for American Cooks* (Clarkson N. Potter, Inc.).

Susan Lang is the author of more than 125 articles for national magazines, including *American Health, Vogue, McCall's, Women's Day, Parade,* and *Family Circle.* She is also the author of three books, the most recent being *Women without Children: Reasons, Rewards, Regrets* (Pharos, 1991).

Gail A. Levey, M.S., R.D., reports on food and nutrition for national magazines and for television, consults for public health agencies and industry, and is a national spokesperson for the American Dietetic Association.

Pino Luongo is the author of *A Tuscan in the Kitchen* (Clarkson N. Potter, Inc.).

Jenny Matthau teaches cooking at the Natural Gourmet Cooking School in New York City.

Debby Maugans, of Birmingham, Alabama, is a food writer and consultant. Formerly food editor for a national women's service magazine, she develops recipes for the Southern Living Cooking School and styles food for television commercials.

John Major is an editor at the Book of the Month Club.

Jane Merrill is a fiction writer who lives in Princeton, New Jersey.

Trish Ratto, R.D., is a nutritionist and health promotion manager at the University of California at Berkeley.

Leni Reed, M.P.H., R.D., is a Reston, Virginia-based dietician, founder of Supermarket Savvy® Tours, and author of two videos— "Supermarket Savvy®" and "Lower Your Cholesterol Now." She is also collaborator on *The American Heart Association Low-Fat, Low-Cholesterol Cookbook* (Times Books/Random House).

Elizabeth Schneider, a food writer and regular contributor to national food magazines, including *Food & Wine, Gourmet, Vogue,* and *Bon Appetit,* is the author of several books, including *Uncommon Fruits and Vegetables: A Commonplace Guide* (Harper & Row).

Deborah Scoblionkov is the wine columnist for *The Philadelphia Inquirer.*

Marie Simmons is a food writer, a regular contributor to national food magazines, co-author of the "Cooking Healthy" column in *Bon Appetit,* newspaper columnist, and author. She is co-author of *The Bartender's Guide to Alcoholic-Free Drinks* (Signet) (former title: *Good Spirits*) and *365 Ways to Cook Pasta* (NAL), and author of *Better By Microwave* (Dutton) and a forthcoming book on rice. She teaches cooking at the New School for Social Research in New York City.

Andrew Weil, M.D., a professor at the University of Arizona, is a holistic physician, and author of several books, including *Health and Healing* (Houghton Mifflin).

◇ RECIPE INDEX ◇

◇ GENERAL INDEX ◇

Recipes are listed in bold face.